MW00794989

HISTORICAL DICTIONARY

The historical dictionaries present essential information on a broad range of subjects, including American and world history, art, business, cities, countries, cultures, customs, film, global conflicts, international relations, literature, music, philosophy, religion, sports, and theater. Written by experts, all contain highly informative introductory essays of the topic and detailed chronologies that, in some cases, cover vast historical time periods but still manage to heavily feature more recent events.

Brief A–Z entries describe the main people, events, politics, social issues, institutions, and policies that make the topic unique, and entries are cross-referenced for ease of browsing. Extensive bibliographies are divided into several general subject areas, providing excellent access points for students, researchers, and anyone wanting to know more. Additionally, maps, photographs, and appendixes of supplemental information aid high school and college students doing term papers or introductory research projects. In short, the historical dictionaries are the perfect starting point for anyone looking to research in these fields.

HISTORICAL DICTIONARIES OF WAR, REVOLUTION, AND CIVIL UNREST

Jon Woronoff, Series Editor

Spanish Civil War, by Francisco J. Romero Salvadó. 2013.

The Crusades, Second Edition, by Corliss K. Slack. 2013.

The Chinese Civil War, Second Edition, by Christopher R. Lew and Edwin Pak-wah Leung. 2013.

World War II: The War against Germany and Italy, by Anne Sharp Wells. 2014.

The French Revolution, Second Edition, by Paul R. Hanson. 2015.

Chechen Conflict, by Ali Askerov. 2015.

Chinese Cultural Revolution, Second Edition, by Guo Jian, Yongyi Song, and Yuan Zhou. 2015.

Russian Civil Wars, 1916–1926, by Jonathan Smele. 2015.

The Arab–Israeli Conflict, Second Edition, by P. R. Kumaraswamy. 2015.

Historical Dictionary of the Chinese Cultural Revolution

Second Edition

Guo Jian
Yongyi Song
Yuan Zhou

ROWMAN & LITTLEFIELD
Lanham • Boulder • New York • London

LIBRARY
NORTHERN VIRGINIA COMMUNITY COLLEGE

Published by Rowman & Littlefield
A wholly owned subsidiary of The Rowman & Littlefield Publishing Group, Inc.
4501 Forbes Boulevard, Suite 200, Lanham, Maryland 20706
www.rowman.com

Unit A, Whitacre Mews, 26-34 Stannary Street, London SE11 4AB

Copyright © 2015 by Guo Jian, Yongyi Song, and Yuan Zhou

All rights reserved. No part of this book may be reproduced in any form or by any
electronic or mechanical means, including information storage and retrieval systems,
without written permission from the publisher, except by a reviewer who may quote
passages in a review.

British Library Cataloguing in Publication Information Available

Library of Congress Cataloging-in-Publication Data

Guo, Jian, 1953–
Historical dictionary of the Chinese Cultural Revolution / Guo Jian, Yongyi Song, Yuan Zhou.
pages cm. — (Historical dictionaries of war, revolution, and civil unrest)
Summary: "The history of the Chinese Cultural Revolution through a chronology, introduction,
glossary, extensive bibliography, and more than 400 cross-referenced dictionary entries"—Provided
by publisher.
Includes bibliographical references.
ISBN 978-1-4422-5171-7 (hardcover : alkaline paper) — ISBN 978-1-4422-5172-4 (ebook)
1. China—History—Cultural Revolution, 1966–1976—Dictionaries. I. Song, Yongyi, 1949–. II.
Zhou, Yuan, 1954–. III. Title.
DS778.7.G86 2015
951.05'6—dc23
2015005941

∞ ™ The paper used in this publication meets the minimum requirements of American
National Standard for Information Sciences Permanence of Paper for Printed Library
Materials, ANSI/NISO Z39.48-1992.

Printed in the United States of America

Contents

Editor's Foreword

Despite the tendency of history to repeat itself, some eras are truly unique, such as the Chinese Cultural Revolution. This was not a revolution or a civil war; it was more like a free-for-all. There were different sides, but alignments constantly changed. New ruling class vs. old ruling class, have-nots vs. haves, young vs. old, uneducated vs. educated, and country vs. city were just some of the dividing lines. It was a revolution of both ideology and power, and the person pulling most of the strings was an aging Mao Zedong, unwilling to tolerate any rivals or trust old comrades. For the greater part of the decade 1966–1976, the Cultural Revolution wreaked havoc throughout the world's largest country, undermining the government and military; weakening the economy, society, and culture; and adversely affecting China's then 800 million people. The greatest hope among most of the survivors was never to live through such a period again.

Given the confusion that reigned at the time and uncertainty about many events that still prevails today, it is essential to have a work like this *Historical Dictionary of the Chinese Cultural Revolution*—now in its second edition. This book does not claim to be the last word, but it brings us another step closer to understanding what remains a convoluted and confusing era. A chronology traces the events, and the introduction places events and people in context and provides a historical background to the period. Countless details on significant people, places, and institutions; momentous events; and political and ideological movements are contained in the dictionary section. A glossary provides Chinese translations, and an extensive bibliography (which now includes titles in Chinese) contains a wealth of information for further research.

This second edition was written by the same authors as the first. All are scholars who lived through the Cultural Revolution and therefore know the reality as well as the theory. Guo Jian, previously on the Chinese faculty at Beijing Normal University, is a professor of English at the University of Wisconsin–Whitewater. Dr. Guo has written and lectured extensively on the Cultural Revolution and the world of the 1960s. Yongyi Song studied at Shanghai Normal University and is on the library faculty at California State University, Los Angeles. He has published *The Cultural Revolution: A Bibliography, 1966–1996* and *The Cultural Revolution and Heterodox Thoughts*. Yuan Zhou was a member of the Department of Library and Information Science at Peking University and is the curator of the East Asian Library at the University of Chicago. Dr. Zhou edited *A New Collection of Red Guard Publication*. All three have contributed to a much-needed reference that is informative and comprehensive.

Jon Woronoff
Series Editor

Acknowledgments

Our gratitude must first go to a number of colleagues and friends in mainland China, whose works on the Cultural Revolution have been invaluable resources to us but whose names we must leave out due to the unwritten regulations regarding Cultural Revolution studies that the current Chinese government has put in place in recent years. We owe special thanks to Mr. Gao Wenqian, to Dr. Wang Youqin of the University of Chicago, and to Dr. Ding Shu of Normandale Community College, whose pioneering studies and conversations benefited us immensely. We are also indebted to Dr. Eric Purchase for his editorial assistance on the first edition of this book and to Ms. Wenxiao Guo on the second edition.

We are especially grateful to Mr. Yang Kelin, compiler and editor of the photo collection *The Cultural Revolution Museum*, and to Mr. Li Zhensheng, author of the photo album *The Red-Color News Soldier*, for their generosity in permitting us to use the historical photographs from their collections.

Guo Jian thanks the City University of Hong Kong for a generous visiting appointment in 2004, which afforded him much-needed precious time to finalize the first edition of this collaborative effort. Yongyi Song is grateful to the School of Information Studies at Syracuse University and to the American Library Association for their financial and moral support in granting him, respectively, the 21st-Century Librarian National Award in 2004 and the Paul Howard Award for Courage in 2005. Yuan Zhou thanks the Center for East Asian Studies at the University of Chicago for funding the editorial work of the project's first edition.

Reader's Notes

The romanization used in this dictionary for Chinese terms is the pinyin system that was developed and has by now become standard in the People's Republic of China. For example, the full name of Mao, the CCP chairman, is spelled Mao Zedong and not Mao Tse-tung or otherwise. However, names of some well-known figures and institutions (e.g., Confucius; Sun Yat-sen; Kuomintang; Tsinghua University), already deeply embedded in English because of earlier transcriptions according to the Wade-Giles or other conventions, are written here as established terms.

The dictionary presents personal names in the same order they assume in Chinese: the family name preceding the given name. Thus the entry on Mao Zedong can be found under M and not Z.

In the case of certain non-idiomatic and already well-known translations of Chinese terms (e.g., "Four Olds" for "*sijiu*"), the dictionary adopts these translations as established. The same applies in the dating convention. For instance, the "May 16 Circular" is treated as an established term, although the consistent dating method used in this dictionary is date followed by month (e.g., 16 May). For the reader's convenience, a glossary with pinyin spellings, Chinese characters, and English translations is included as an appendix to the dictionary.

Since the names of important bodies like the Chinese Communist Party (CCP) and the People's Liberation Army (PLA), as well as the country's name—People's Republic of China (PRC)—appear repeatedly, acronyms are used after the first occurrence of such names in a dictionary entry. Bolding indicates that there are separate entries corresponding to the bolded items, though only the first appearance of such terms in an entry is bolded. Entries appearing in the *See also* are also related to the topic.

Acronyms and Abbreviations

CC	Central Committee
CCP	Chinese Communist Party
CCRSG	Central Cultural Revolution Small Group
CMC	Central Military Commission
GLD	General Logistics Department
GPD	General Political Department
PLA	People's Liberation Army
PRC	People's Republic of China
SC	State Council

Map

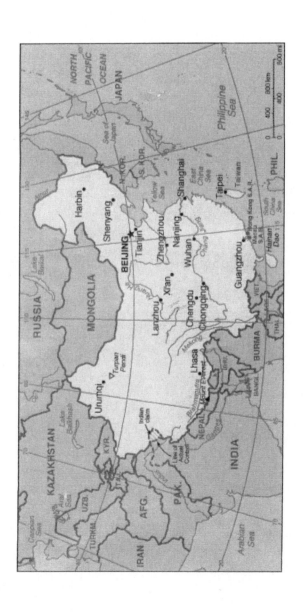

Chronology

1965 10 November: Shanghai's *Wenhui Daily* publishes Yao Wenyuan's "On the New Historical Drama *Hai Rui Dismissed from Office*." The production and publication of the article are arranged by Jiang Qing and Zhang Chunqiao and backed by Mao Zedong. **11 November:** The Chinese Communist Party (CCP) issues a circular to replace Yang Shangkun with Wang Dongxing, Mao's own chief bodyguard, as director of the CCP General Office. **Mid-November:** Mao leaves Beijing for East China. **8–15 December:** Mao chairs an enlarged session of the Politburo in Shanghai, at which Luo Ruiqing is removed as chief of general staff of the People's Liberation Army (PLA) and general secretary of the Central Military Commission (CMC) upon Lin Biao's initiative.

1966 2–20 February: The Symposium on the Works of Literature and the Arts in the Armed Forces, chaired by Jiang Qing with the direct backing of Lin Biao, is held in Shanghai. Later, the summary report of the conference is edited and revised by Chen Boda, Zhang Chunqiao, Jiang Qing, Liu Zhijian, and Mao Zedong. **5 February:** Liu Shaoqi chairs a meeting of members of the CCP Politburo Standing Committee in Beijing, at which the "Outline Report by the Five-Person Cultural Revolution Small Group concerning the Current Academic Discussion" (soon to be known as the February Outline) is adopted—a document that is intended to confine the criticism of Wu Han and others to the academic sphere. **8 February:** Peng Zhen, Lu Dingyi, and Kang Sheng go to Wuhan to report to Mao about the Outline Report. Mao agrees with the document's views. **12 February:** The CCP Central Committee (CC) issues the Outline Report within the party nationwide as a guiding document for the ongoing movement. **28–30 March:** Mao talks with Kang Sheng and others on three occasions: contradicting his earlier view of the February Outline, Mao accuses the CCP Beijing Municipal Committee, the Five-Person Cultural Revolution Small Group, and the CCP Propaganda Department of harboring evildoers and threatens to dissolve all three organs. **2 April:** Zhou Enlai writes Mao a formal report in support of Mao's criticism of the Five-Person Group and the February Outline. **9–12 April:** At a meeting of the CC Secretariat chaired by Deng Xiaoping, Deng and Zhou Enlai criticize Peng Zhen for opposing Mao. They also decide to issue a CC document criticizing the February Outline and form a new group for drafting Cultural Revolution documents. **10 April:** Upon Mao's finalization, the CC issues "Summary of the Symposium Convened by Comrade Jiang Qing at the Behest of Comrade Lin Biao on the Work of Literature and the Arts in the Armed Forces" as an intra-party document, which defines the current academic discussion as a struggle for leadership between the proletariat and the bourgeoisie and calls for a "great socialist revolution on the cultural front" against a long-dominant "anti-party and anti-socialist black line." **16–26 April:** Mao chairs enlarged Politburo Standing Committee sessions in Hangzhou, criticizing Peng Zhen for his alleged anti-party crimes. Decisions are made that the Five-Person Group be dissolved and that a new Cultural Revolution small group be formed. Concurrently, a newly formed document-drafting group is working on the May 16 Circular. **4–26 May:** Under Mao's remote control, Liu Shaoqi chairs the Politburo's enlarged sessions in Beijing to expose and denounce the so-called Peng [Zhen]-Luo [Ruiqing]-Lu [Dingyi]-Yang [Shangkun] Anti-Party Clique. On 16 May, all attendees of the Session (including Peng Zhen) vote to adopt the CC Circular (May 16 Circular) to declare war on the "representatives of the bourgeoisie who have snuck into the party, the government, the army, and the various spheres of culture." The adoption of the Circular marks the official launching of the Cultural Revolution. On 23 May, the Politburo decides to dismiss Peng, Luo, Lu, and Yang from office and fill some of their positions with Ye Jianying as general secretary of the CMC, Tao Zhu as director of the CCP Propaganda Department, and Li Xuefeng as first secretary of the CCP Beijing Municipal Committee. It also decides to reorganize the CCP Beijing Municipal Committee. **7 May:** Mao writes a letter to Lin Biao commenting on a report on "Further Developments of Agricultural and Sideline Production in the Armed Forces" submitted by the PLA General Logistics Department. In the letter, Mao articulates his view of labor in a utopian society. On 15 May, the CC issues the letter nationwide as an intra-party document. The letter later becomes well known as the May 7 Directive. **25 May:** A big-character poster entitled "What Are Song Shuo, Lu Ping, and Peng Peiyun Really Doing in the Cultural Revolution?" written by Nie Yuanzi and others is posted on the campus of Peking University. **28 May:** The CC issues a name list of the newly established Central Cultural Revolution Small Group (CCRSG) members with Chen Boda as head of the group; Jiang Qing, Wang Renzhong, Liu Zhijian, and Zhang Chunqiao as deputy heads; and Kang Sheng as adviser. **29 May:** At a routine meeting of the CC top leadership in Beijing, Liu Shaoqi, Zhou Enlai, and Deng Xiaoping decide to send work groups to *People's Daily* and to Peking University. Zhou reports the decision to Mao by phone and obtains Mao's approval. Some students at Tsinghua University Middle School—mostly children of ranking officials—form in secrecy an organization named "Red Guards." **1 June:** *People's Daily* publishes the editorial "Sweep Away All Cow-Demons and Snake-Spirits," prepared by Chen Boda, who took over the leadership of the newspaper as head of the work group a day before. Following Mao's instructions, the Central People's Radio broadcasts on the same evening the big-character poster written by Nie Yuanzi and others, and *People's Daily* runs the text of the poster on 2 June with a commentary entitled "Hail the Big-Character Poster from Peking University." **3 June:** Liu Shaoqi and Deng Xiaoping hold an enlarged session of the Politburo Standing Committee in Beijing. The meeting approves a proposal made by the new Beijing municipal party committee to dispatch work groups to colleges and middle and high schools in Beijing to lead the movement there. **4 June:** Liu Shaoqi and Deng Xiaoping fly to Hangzhou to report to Mao in person about their decisions concerning the ongoing movement. Mao approves their work group policies and entrusts Liu with the responsibility for leading the movement in Beijing. **Mid-June:** Rebellious students in Beijing begin to have conflicts with the work groups. Following a traditional "class struggle" model, Liu Shaoqi and Deng Xiaoping instruct the work groups to launch an "Anti-Interference" campaign on middle school and college campuses. Those opposing the work groups are persecuted as Rightists and reactionaries. **21 June:** Liu Shaoqi sends his wife, Wang Guangmei, to Tsinghua University as adviser to the work group. Wang leads attacks against those opposing the work group. Kuai Dafu, a representative of student rebels, is persecuted as a reactionary. **16 July:** Mao swims in the Yangzi River, demonstrating his determination to carry out the Cultural Revolution. **18 July:** Mao returns to Beijing, soon to withdraw his support for the work group policy and accuse Liu and Deng of repressing students and misleading the ongoing political movement. **28 July:** The new CCP Beijing Municipal Committee announces its decision to withdraw work groups from college campuses. **29 July:** The Red Guards of the Beijing Institute of Aeronautics Middle School post the couplet "If the father is a hero, the son is a good fellow; if the father is a reactionary, the son is a good-for-nothing—It is basically like this," advocating a theory of blood lineage and making teachers and students from politically disadvantaged families targets of the Revolution. The blood lineage theory causes a heated debate on middle school and college campuses across China and meets strong resistance from a majority of students and teachers. **1 August:** Mao writes a letter to Tsinghua University Middle School Red Guards in support of their "revolutionary rebel spirit," which leads to an explosive development of Red Guard organizations in the country. **1–12 August:** The Eleventh Plenum of the CCP Eighth Central Committee is convened in Beijing. **5 August:** Mao writes "Bombarding the Headquarters—My Big-Character Poster," accusing the Liu-Deng leadership of opposing the Cultural Revolution. Though their names are not mentioned in the poster, Liu and Deng become main targets of criticism at the Plenum. **8 August:** The CC adopts "The Resolution of the CCP Central Committee concerning the Great Proletarian Cultural Revolution" (to be known as the "Sixteen Articles") as a guideline for the unfolding political movement. **12 August:** Major changes in the central leadership are adopted by the CC. Lin

Biao replaces Liu Shaoqi as second in command and becomes Mao's heir apparent. **18 August:** In army uniform and wearing a Red Guard armband, Mao receives a million students (most of them Red Guards) and teachers at Tiananmen Square. A violent Red Guard movement soon spreads across China. **19 August:** Beijing's Red Guards declare war on "old ideas, old culture, old customs, and old habits" on the city's streets. The campaign to destroy the Four Olds soon sweeps the entire country. **23 August:** *People's Daily* carries two editorials applauding the Red Guards' revolutionary rebel spirit and their campaign to destroy the Four Olds in the capital city. The editorials inspire further violence and terror: during the 40 days in late summer known as the "Red August," 1,772 innocent people were killed or committed suicide in the city of Beijing, 33,695 households were ransacked, 85,196 residents were expelled from the city, and 4,922 historic sites were ruined. **5 September:** The CC and the State Council (SC) issue a circular to support the "great revolutionary networking" campaign by granting travelers to Beijing free transportation and accommodation. **6 September:** With the support of the CCRSG, the Capital College Red Guards Revolutionary Rebel Headquarters (commonly known as the Third Command Post) is founded in Beijing. **3 October:** *Red Flag* (Issue No. 13) editorial "March Forward along the Broad Road of Mao Zedong Thought" initiates the nationwide campaign to criticize the Bourgeois Reactionary Line. **6 October:** The Red Third Command Post holds a mass rally of over 100,000 people in Beijing denouncing the Bourgeoisie Reactionary Line of Liu Shaoqi and Deng Xiaoping. Zhou Enlai, Chen Boda, and Jiang Qing appear at the rally to show their support. **9–28 October:** A CC work session is held in Beijing. On 16 October, Chen Boda gives a speech entitled "The Two Lines in the Great Proletarian Cultural Revolution." The script of the speech, with Mao's final touches, is distributed nationwide on 24 October. Liu Shaoqi and Deng Xiaoping criticize themselves at the work session. **13 November:** Zhang Chunqiao, representing the CCRSG, resolves the conflict between the Workers Command Post of Shanghai and the local authorities during the Anting Incident. With Mao's endorsement, Zhang acknowledges the Workers Command Post as the first cross-industry mass organization in the country. **16 November:** The CC and the SC issue a circular to halt the "great revolutionary networking" temporarily. **Mid-November–December:** A number of big-character posters criticizing Lin Biao and the CCRSG appear in Beijing. The CCRSG and rebel Red Guards attack the writers of the posters and name their criticism a "Black Wind in November." **5 December:** Old Red Guards at a number of middle schools in Beijing form the United Action Committee of the Capital Red Guards. The organization opposes the CCRSG's radical policies toward party veterans while upholding the theory of blood lineage. **4–6 December:** Lin Biao convenes an enlarged session of the Politburo Standing Committee to hear reports from Gu Mu on the recently held Industrial and Transportation

Symposium (for national planning). Lin criticizes Gu's *outline report* for diverging the focus from the Cultural Revolution to economic production and vows to push the mass movement further into all sectors of society, including industrial and transportation circles. **15 December:** Directed by Lin Biao, an enlarged session of the Politburo Standing Committee passes "The CC Directive on Implementing the Cultural Revolution in Rural Areas" and authorizes its nationwide dissemination. This is the official beginning of the Cultural Revolution in the countryside. **16 December:** Lin Biao publishes the "Foreword to the Second Edition of the *Quotations from Chairman Mao*." **25 December:** About 5,000 rebels from Tsinghua University demonstrate at Tiananmen Square, shouting the slogan "Down with Liu Shaoqi!" **26 December:** At his 73rd birthday, Mao has a party with the CCRSG members and toasts to the unfolding of a civil war for 1967. **30 December:** The Kangping Avenue Incident, an armed conflict between rebels and conservatives, breaks out in Shanghai. The conflict involves more than 100,000 factory workers.

1967 4–5 January: Rebels begin to seize power at the Shanghai newspapers *Wenhui Daily* and *Liberation Daily*. This is the beginning of the "January Storm." **6 January:** One million Shanghai rebels hold a rally denouncing the CCP Shanghai Municipal Committee and assume its power. **8 January:** At a reception for the CCRSG members, Mao speaks of the Shanghai rebels' power seizure as a great revolution. **11 January:** Following Mao's directives, the CC, State Council (SC), CMC, and CCRSG send a telegram to the rebel organizations in Shanghai, congratulating them for their assumption of municipal power. **13 January:** The CC and SC issue the "Regulations on Strengthening Public Security during the Great Proletarian Cultural Revolution" (also known as the Six Regulations of Public Security). **16 January:** *Red Flag* carries the editorial "Proletarian Revolutionaries Unite" to make power seizure a nationwide campaign. Within a month, the new power structure, the revolutionary committee, is established in several provinces including Shanghai, Shanxi, Heilongjiang, Guizhou, and Shandong. **18 January:** The *Journal of Middle School Cultural Revolution* is premiered in Beijing, carrying Yu Luoke's "On Family Background." **23 January:** Following Mao's instructions, the CC, SC, CMC, and CCRSG issue the "Decision to Provide the Revolutionary Masses of the Left with Firm Support from the PLA." The army's involvement in the Cultural Revolution begins. **5 February:** The Shanghai People's Commune is founded. The name of the new power organ is to be changed to Shanghai Municipal Revolutionary Committee on 24 February at Mao's suggestion. **11 and 16 February:** Zhou Enlai chairs top-level CC briefing sessions in Zhongnanhai. Chen Yi, Ye Jianying, Tan Zhenlin, and other senior PLA and SC leaders criticize the radicals of the CCRSG. Their criticism is soon to be denounced by Mao as a February

Adverse Current. **23 February:** Zhao Yongfu, deputy-commander of the Qinghai Military District, orders the PLA soldiers to retake by force a newspaper office building occupied by rebel civilians. The violent conflict leaves 173 dead and 224 injured. **5 March:** The CC orders military control in Jiangsu Province where widespread chaos caused by factional conflict hindered the establishment of the provincial revolutionary committee. Military control is soon to be applied to other provinces under similar circumstances. **16 March:** Following Mao's directive, the CC authorizes the distribution of materials concerning the release of 61 party veterans, including Bo Yibo, Liu Lantao, An Ziwen, and Yang Xianzhen, from the Kuomintang prison in the 1930s. The group is named a "traitors' clique." The CC document intensifies mass organizations' hunt for "renegades" among party veterans. The CCP Special Case Examination Group on Liu Shaoqi is also set up in March. **18 March:** In response to the February Adverse Current, Mao decides to replace the meetings of the Politburo with the "CCRSG routine meetings" as executive gatherings of the *de facto* CCP top leadership. Zhou Enlai is to chair these meetings. Regular attendees include members of the CCRSG and a number of military and government officials. **19 March:** The CC announces its decision not to resume the "great revolutionary networking" campaign. **30 March:** With Mao's approval, Qi Benyu's article "Patriotism or Betrayal? A Critique of the Reactionary Film *Inside Story of the Qing Court*" is published in *People's Daily*. Without mentioning his name, the article refers to Liu Shaoqi as the "biggest capitalist-roader within the party" and "China's Khrushchev" for the first time, which stirs up a new wave in a nationwide campaign against Liu. **10 April:** A mass rally of 300,000 is held at Tsinghua University to struggle against Liu Shaoqi's wife, Wang Guangmei, and 300 senior party officials. **20 April:** The Beijing Municipal Revolutionary Committee is established. **6 May:** A massive armed conflict between two rebel factions occurs in Chengdu, the capital of Sichuan Province, leaving 40 to 50 people dead and 127 wounded. After the January Storm, factional violence with heavy involvement of the military spreads across China. Armed conflicts, more severe even than that of Chengdu, take place in Yibin (Sichuan Province), Zhengzhou (Henan Province), and Wuhan (Hubei Province) during the summer months of 1967. **6 June:** The CC, SC, CMC, and CCRSG jointly issue a circular order to stop widespread violence and chaos and to reinforce the law. The circular proves ineffective. **14 June:** A number of radical students form the May 16 Capital Red Guard Corps in Beijing and attack Zhou Enlai. With the support of the CCRSG, the Beijing Public Security Bureau disbands the organization and arrests its leaders. **13 July:** Mao departs from Beijing on an inspection tour of North, Central-South, and East China. He arrives in Wuhan, Hubei Province, the following day. **20 July:** Infuriated by some central leaders' unbalanced treatment of the two rival factions and unaware of Mao's presence in Wuhan, members of the mass organization Million-Strong Mighty Army and solders from the PLA Unit 8201 of the Wuhan Military Region storm the hotel where Mao is staying and take Wang Li and Xie Fuzhi by force for questioning. Upon receiving a letter from Lin Biao that depicts the disturbance in Wuhan as a mutiny, Mao quietly leaves for Shanghai on the early morning of 21 July. **25 July:** Upon their safe return to Beijing, Xie Fuzhi and Wang Li receive a heroes' welcome by Lin Biao and other central leaders at a mass rally of a million people at Tiananmen Square. The central leadership is soon to denounce the July 20 Incident as a "counterrevolutionary riot." The leaders of the Wuhan Military Region are removed. The persecution of members of the Million-Strong Mighty Army results in 600 deaths and 66,000 injuries. Following Mao's instructions, Jiang Qing promotes the slogan "verbal attack and armed defense" at a reception for rebels from Henan. **1 August:** *Red Flag* carries an editorial entitled "The Proletariat Must Firmly Grasp the Gun: Commemorating the 40th Anniversary of the PLA." The editorial calls upon the masses to "ferret out a handful of capitalist-roaders inside the army." **7 August:** Wang Li receives rebels at the Ministry of Foreign Affairs and voices support for their effort to seize power at the Ministry. **9 August:** Lin Biao receives new commanders of the PLA Wuhan Military Region and announces his assessment of the Cultural Revolution: "its achievement is greatest, greatest, greatest; its cost is minimal, minimal, minimal." **13 August:** A massacre of the so-called five black categories in Dao County, Hunan Province, begins. In the following 65 days, 4,519 innocent people are killed. **22 August:** About 20,000 students from the Beijing Foreign Language Institute, Tsinghua University, and other schools storm the office of the British Chargé d'affaires in Beijing to protest the arrest of Chinese journalists in Hong Kong. The demonstrators beat the British personnel and set the office building on fire. Under the leadership of CCP underground organizations, ultra-leftists in Hong Kong launch Cultural Revolution–type riots against the British authorities during the summer months of 1967. **30 August:** In response to Zhou Enlai's report about the involvement of Wang Li and some other members of the CCRSG in foreign and military affairs, Mao decides to arrest Wang Li, Guan Feng, and Qi Benyu (Qi's arrest to be implemented in January 1968) to reassure and pacify Zhou Enlai and military leaders. **5 September:** The CC, SC, CMC, and CCRSG jointly issue an order forbidding the seizure of weaponry, equipment, and other kinds of military supplies from the PLA by mass organizations. **8 September:** With Mao's approval, *People's Daily* publishes Yao Wenyuan's article "On Tao Zhu's Two Books." **25 September:** Newspapers report on Mao's inspection tour of North, Central-South, and East China; his return to Beijing; and his call for rival mass organizations to stop factional fighting and form a grand alliance. **7 October:** The CC issues a circular publicizing Mao's talks during his inspection tour, in which Mao offers a positive assessment of the Cultural Revolution: the situation across

China "is not just good but great; it is better than ever." **14 October:** The CC, SC, CMC, and CCRSG issue a notice that classes be resumed at all schools. The decision is implemented with limited success. **7 November:** Drafted by Chen Boda and Yao Wenyuan with Mao's approval, a joint editorial entitled "March Forward along the Road of the October Socialist Revolution: Commemorating the 50th Anniversary of the Great October Socialist Revolution" appears in *People's Daily*, *Red Flag*, and *Liberation Army Daily*, articulating a theory of continuing revolution under the dictatorship of the proletariat. **27 November:** At a forum of Beijing workers, Jiang Qing proposes that a campaign to rectify class ranks be launched nationwide.

1968 22 March: Lin Biao and Jiang Qing accuse generals Yang Chengwu, Yu Lijin, and Fu Chongbi of carrying out anti-party activities. Lin makes false charges against the three at rallies of military officers on 23 March and 27 March. Mao greets the assembly of military officers on 24 March to show his support for Lin. **23 April–26 July:** A "One-Hundred-Day Armed Struggle" takes place at Tsinghua University in Beijing. **25 May:** The CC and the CCRSG issue "The Experience of the Beijing Xinhua Printing Factory Military Control Commission in Mobilizing the Masses to Struggle against the Enemies" with Mao's comments. The document offers guidelines for the Rectify the Class Ranks campaign. **3 July:** The CC, SC, CMC, and CCRSG jointly issue a public notice concerning factional violence in Guangxi Zhuang Autonomous Region. The armed conflict in Guangxi in the summer of 1968 results in casualties numbering in the tens of thousands—perhaps over 100,000—including cases of cannibalism in several counties. **20 July:** The newly established Inner Mongolia Revolutionary Committee moves to hunt for members of the Inner Mongolia People's Revolutionary Party as part of the Rectify the Class Ranks campaign. The operation involves severe physical abuse and continues well into 1969, falsely implicating 346,000 citizens and leaving 16,222 dead. **24 July:** The CC, SC, CMC, and CCRSG jointly issue a public notice concerning factional violence in some areas of Shaanxi Province. Two months after the document is issued, 70,000 pieces of weaponry and four million pieces of ammunition are confiscated. **27 July:** Mao sends a workers propaganda team and the PLA propaganda team to Tsinghua University to end factional violence there. Five workers are killed and 700 are wounded when the armed Red Guards open fire on them. **28 July:** Mao receives the "five Red Guard leaders of Beijing": Nie Yuanzi, Kuai Dafu, Han Aijing, Tan Houlan, and Wang Dabin. At the reception, Mao indicates his resolve to send students away from campus to end the long-standing factional conflict. This meeting marks the beginning of the end of the Red Guard movement. **25 August:** The CC, SC, CMC, and CCRSG jointly issue a circular announcing the decision of the central leadership to dispatch workers propaganda teams to the nation's educational institutions. **7 September:**

People's Daily and *Liberation Army Daily* carry a joint editorial celebrating the establishment of revolutionary committees in all provinces, cities, and autonomous regions in the country and announcing that the Cultural Revolution is entering its "struggle, criticism, reform" stage. A mass rally is held in Beijing to mark the completion of the Cultural Revolution power establishment in the nation as "all red across China." **13–31 October:** The Enlarged Twelfth Plenum of the CCP Eighth Central Committee is held in Beijing. Over 65 percent of the living members and alternate members of the Eighth Central Committee are absent because they had been denounced since 1966. Mao chairs the opening session. A number of senior party veterans are under attack for their involvement in the February Adverse Current of 1967. **5 October:** *People's Daily* publishes a report on the Liuhe "May 7 Cadre School" in praise of its experience in revolutionizing government organizations. The report initiates a nationwide drive to send millions of cadres and government workers to May 7 cadre schools to do manual labor. **31 October:** At its Twelfth Plenum, the Eighth CC approves the "Investigative Report on the Crimes of the Traitor, Spy, and Renegade Liu Shaoqi" by the Central Case Examination Group and moves to expel Liu permanently from the CCP. All delegates, except Chen Shaomin, vote in support of the report and the motion. **22 December:** *People's Daily* publishes Mao's directive calling on urban "educated youths" (middle and high school students) to go to the countryside to receive reeducation from the poor and lower-middle peasants. A nationwide "Up to the Mountains and Down to the Countryside" movement follows. The number of "sent down" urban youths totals 17 million by 1980. The beginning of this movement marks the end of the Red Guard movement.

1969 2–17 March: Sino-Soviet border clashes take place along the Ussuri River. **1–24 April:** The Ninth National Congress of the CCP is held in Beijing. Mao presides over the opening session. He speaks at the Military Region Commander session on 13 April and calls the Ninth Congress a meeting of unity and success. **14 April:** A new CCP Constitution is adopted with the support of all delegates. In the new Constitution, Lin Biao is designated as the successor of Mao. **24 April:** The CCP Ninth Central Committee is elected. Only 27 percent of the Eighth Central Committee members and alternate members retain their seats. **28 April:** The First Plenum of the CCP Ninth Central Committee is convened in Beijing to elect the new Politburo and its standing committee. Nearly half of the new Politburo members are close associates of Lin Biao in the military. **14 October:** In the name of preparations against Soviet military attacks, the CC issues an urgent notice to evacuate senior party leaders from Beijing. Numerous senior leaders leave the capital for the provinces within a week. Most of them do not return until after the downfall of Lin Biao in September 1971. **12 November:** Liu Shaoqi dies in Kaifeng, Henan Province, after three years of abuse in unlawful custody. His family members are not informed of his removal from Beijing to Kaifeng and of his death until years later.

1970 31 January: The CC issues its "Directive concerning the Strike against Counterrevolutionary Destructive Activities." **5 February:** The CC issues its "Directive concerning Anti-Graft and Embezzlement and Anti-Speculation and Profiteering" and "Notice on Anti-Extravagance and Waste." These two documents, along with the 31 January CC Directive, provide guidelines for a nationwide "One Strike and Three Antis" campaign. During a 10-month period (February to November 1970), 1.87 million people are persecuted as traitors, renegades, and counterrevolutionaries, over 284,800 are arrested, and thousands are executed. **5 March:** Yu Luoke, author of "On Family Background," is executed in Beijing. **17–20 March:** Following Mao's instructions, a CC work session is held in Beijing in preparation for the Fourth National People's Congress of the PRC. Mao suggests that the position of the president of state be eliminated in a new PRC constitution. **27 March:** The CC issues its "Notification concerning the Investigation of the 'May 16' Counterrevolutionary Conspiratorial Clique," both to lead the investigation further and to check the excesses of persecution. The hunt for members of the May 16 Counterrevolutionary Clique continues until the end of the Cultural Revolution. An estimated 3.5 million people are falsely implicated in this nine-year-long campaign. **12 April:** In a brief message, Mao rejects Lin Biao's suggestion that Mao serve as president of the PRC. **27 June:** The CC approves the proposal by Peking University and Tsinghua University to resume admissions of students. By the end of 1970, approximately 41,870 "worker-peasant-soldier students" enter colleges nationwide. **22 August:** The Politburo Standing Committee meets in Lushan, Jiangxi Province. At the meeting, all of the committee members, except Mao, favor the restoration of the office of the PRC president. **23 August–6 September:** The Second Plenum of the CCP Ninth Central Committee is held in Lushan. At the opening session, Lin Biao speaks of Mao as a genius and proposes that Mao be the head of the proletarian dictatorship. During the small-group sessions on 24 August, Lin's associates, including Chen Boda, lead the attack on Zhang Chunqiao without mentioning his name and voice support for the restoration of the office of the national president. On 31 August, Mao writes "Some Views of Mine," to be known as his second big-character poster, attacking Chen Boda. A scapegoat of the Mao-Lin conflict, Chen is dismissed from office. **16 November:** The CC issues a document concerning Chen Boda's "anti-party problems." The Criticize Chen and Conduct Rectification campaign is launched within the party. **18 December:** Mao receives U.S. journalist Edgar Snow. During the conversation, Mao indicates his intention to improve Sino-American relations. He also blames Lin Biao for promoting the Mao cult without mentioning Lin's name.

1971 26 January: The CC issues the "Criminal Records of the Anti-Party Element Chen Boda" nationwide. **8 February:** The CC establishes a special investigation group on the "May 16" clique. **18–24 March:** Lin Liguo and his young colleagues in the air force meet in Shanghai to draft an alleged coup plan called the *"571 Project" Summary*. **7 April:** Mao decides to invite the United States ping-pong team to visit China. **29 May:** The Politburo issues a report on China-U.S. talks to prepare the nation for the dramatic change in the PRC government's diplomatic policy toward the United States. **14 August–12 September:** Mao tours South China. During his meetings with local leaders, Mao criticizes Lin Biao and his followers. **12 September:** Lin Liguo's alleged plan to assassinate Mao is aborted. Mao returns to Beijing in the evening. **13 September:** Upon learning of Mao's verbal attack on Lin Biao and Mao's arrival in Beijing, Lin, his wife Ye Qun, and their son Lin Liguo board the aircraft Trident 256 at Shanhaiguan military airfield in the early morning, heading for the Soviet Union. The plane crashes near Undurkhan in Mongolia; all passengers and crew are killed. **18 September:** The CC issues a circular concerning Lin Biao's "renegade escape," charging him with treason. **29 September:** The CC issues a circular announcing its decision to remove Lin Biao's associates Huang Yongsheng, Wu Faxian, Li Zuopeng, and Qiu Huizuo from office. **3 October:** The CC issues the "Circular concerning the Dissolution of the CMC Administrative Group and the Establishment of the CMC Administrative Conference Office." Ye Jianying is appointed head of the Conference Office in charge of the PLA's routine affairs. **25 October:** The United Nations passes a motion to restore the seat of the PRC in the United Nations and its Security Council. **14 November:** At a reception for the participants of the Chengdu Symposium, Mao reverses his early verdict on the February Adverse Current. **11 December:** The CC issues to party committees at the provincial level the first set of materials concerning the "Struggle to Defeat the Counterrevolutionary Coup of the Lin-Chen Anti-Party Clique." The nationwide campaign against the Lin Biao clique is officially launched.

1972 10 January: Mao makes the last-minute decision to attend the memorial service of Chen Yi, one of the senior leaders implicated in the February Adverse Current. **13 January:** The CC issues its second set of materials concerning the "Struggle to Defeat the Counterrevolutionary Coup of the Lin-Chen Anti-Party Clique." The CC also authorizes the distribution of the first set of materials (dated 11 December 1971) at the grassroots level nationwide. **21–28 February:** U.S. president Richard Nixon visits China. Mao meets Nixon on 21 February. A joint communiqué is signed in Shanghai on

27 February, with both sides embracing the prospects of the normalization of relations. **2 July:** The CC issues its third set of materials concerning the "Struggle to Defeat the Counterrevolutionary Coup of the Lin-Chen Anti-Party Clique" and the "Investigation Report on the Past Counterrevolutionary Crimes of the Kuomintang Anti-Communist, Trotskyist, Traitor, Spy, and Revisionist Chen Boda." **3 August:** Deng Xiaoping writes Mao a letter in which he criticizes Lin Biao, vows never to attempt to reverse the verdict of his case, and asks for a second chance to work for the party. **14 August:** Mao comments on Deng Xiaoping's letter, acknowledging his merits and distinguishing him from Liu Shaoqi. **7 September:** Considering Wang Hongwen to be a candidate for the position of his successor, Mao transfers Wang from Shanghai to Beijing.

1973 10 March: With Mao's approval, the CC issues its resolution to reinstate Deng Xiaoping as an active party member and vice-premier of the SC. **20 April:** A decision is made at a CC work session to reinstate a number of the party veterans and to admit Wang Hongwen, Hua Guofeng, Wu De, and a few others into the Politburo. **19 July:** A letter of plea and complaint written by Zhang Tiesheng at the college entrance examination is published in *Liaoning Daily*. With the support of Jiang Qing and the cultural revolutionaries in the central leadership, all major newspapers reprint the letter three weeks later, setting off an anti-intellectual propaganda campaign nationwide. The newly revived attention to examination scores is denounced as a bourgeois counteroffensive against the revolution in education. **20 August:** The CC approves the "Investigation Report on the Counterrevolutionary Crimes of the Lin Biao Anti-Party Clique," permanently expelling Lin Biao, Chen Boda, and other "Clique" members from the party. **24–28 August:** The Tenth National Congress of the CCP is held in Beijing. Wang Hongwen delivers a report on the revision of the CCP Constitution. **30 August:** At the First Plenum of the CCP Tenth Central Committee, Wang Hongwen is elected a vice-chairman of the CCP, Zhang Chunqiao a member of the Politburo Standing Committee, and Jiang Qing and Yao Wenyuan members of the Politburo. **25 November–5 December:** Following Mao's instruction, the Politburo holds an enlarged session to criticize Zhou Enlai's "revisionist line" and "Right capitulationism" because Zhou agreed to negotiate with the United States on military matters. Jiang Qing names the Mao-Zhou conflict the "eleventh line struggle in the party." Deng Xiaoping is also present at the meeting and criticizes Zhou. Jiang Qing, Zhang Chunqiao, Yao Wenyuan, and Wang Hongwen begin to band together as a "gang of four." **12 December:** Mao chairs a Politburo meeting. At this meeting, Mao criticizes the work of the Politburo and the CMC under the leadership of Zhou Enlai and

Ye Jianying. Mao also suggests rotating commanders of the major military regions and appointing Deng Xiaoping to the positions of the PLA chief of general staff and a member of the CMC and the Politburo.

1974 18 January: Following Mao's directive in response to Jiang Qing and Wang Hongwen's request, the CC authorizes the distribution of "Lin Biao and the Way of Confucius and Mencius," a collection of materials prepared by Jiang's supporters at Peking University and Tsinghua University. The "Criticize Lin and Criticize Confucius" campaign is launched nationwide. The campaign implicitly aims at Zhou Enlai. **April:** The PRC delegation, led by Deng Xiaoping, attends the General Assembly of the United Nations for the first time. **17 July:** Mao criticizes the Gang of Four for the first time: at a meeting of the Politburo, Mao calls Jiang Qing, Zhang Chunqiao, Yao Wenyuan, and Wang Hongwen a "little faction of four." **29 September:** The CC issues a circular announcing its decision to redress the case of Marshal He Long. **4 October:** Mao proposes that Deng Xiaoping be first vice-primer of the SC. **18 October:** To gain more government positions at the upcoming Fourth National People's Congress of the PRC, Wang Hongwen, representing the Gang of Four, goes to Changsha to see Mao and lodge complaints about Zhou Enlai and Deng Xiaoping. Mao rebukes him. **7 November:** The big-character poster "On Socialist Democracy and the Socialist Legal System: Dedicated to the Fourth People's Congress" by Li Yizhe (a pen name adopted by three young authors) appears in Guangzhou. The poster suggests that the rule of law be established in a new constitution to protect the rights of ordinary citizens.

1975 5 January: Upon Mao's suggestion, the CC appoints Deng vice-chairman of the CMC and chief of general staff of the PLA and Zhang Chunqiao director of the General Political Department of the PLA. **8–10 January:** The Second Plenum of the CCP Tenth Central Committee is convened in Beijing. Zhou Enlai's agenda for the Fourth National People's Congress and Deng Xiaoping's appointments are approved at the Plenum. **13–17 January:** The Fourth NPC is held in Beijing. Zhu De and Zhou Enlai are reelected as chairman of the National People's Congress and premier of the SC, respectively. Zhou Enlai delivers the government work report, reiterating the blueprint of "four modernizations" for China (modernization in agriculture, industry, national defense, and science and technology), a proposal initially adopted at the first meeting of the Third National People's Congress (December 1964–January 1965). A new constitution is adopted by the Fourth Congress. **25 January:** Deng Xiaoping talks to ranking PLA officers about the rectification of the army. An all-round nationwide campaign aiming to rectify the errors of the Cultural Revolution begins. **1 March:** Zhang Chunqiao speaks against "empiricism" at a meeting of the General Political Department of the PLA, making insinuations against the moderate faction of party veterans headed by Zhou Enlai and Deng Xiaoping. **4 April:** Following instructions from Mao Yuan xin, the authorities of Liaoning Province execute Zhang Zhixin, an outspoken critic of the Cultural Revolution, on a counterrevolutionary charge. **3 May:** At a reception for Politburo members in Beijing, Mao speaks against factionalism in the central leadership, reproaches the Gang of Four led by Jiang Qing, and dismisses Zhang Chunqiao's anti-empiricist remarks concerning veteran leaders. Later, the Politburo holds two meetings to criticize the Jiang Qing group. **24 June–15 July:** Enlarged sessions of the CMC are held in Beijing. Deng Xiaoping and Ye Jianying give speeches calling for a reform and restructuring of the PLA in the overall rectification campaign. **13 August:** Liu Bing, deputy-secretary of the CCP Tsinghua University Committee, and three other committee members write Mao, criticizing Chi Qun and Xie Jingyi, Jiang Qing's trusted leaders at Tsinghua. They write a second letter on 13 October about the same issue. The letters reach Mao via Deng Xiaoping and prompt Mao's angry responses to Liu and Deng. **14 August:** Mao Zedong comments on the classical novel *Water Margin*. A nationwide political campaign to appraise *Water Margin* begins, in which Zhou Enlai is attacked by innuendo as a capitulator within the party. **2 November:** Upon hearing several reports from Mao Yuanxin, his liaison at the Politburo, who is harshly critical of Deng Xiaoping and his rectification program, Mao expresses his concern about the widespread negative attitude toward the Cultural Revolution. **20 November:** Upon Mao's request, the Politburo holds a meeting to evaluate the Cultural Revolution. At the meeting, Deng Xiaoping refuses to take charge of drafting a resolution on the issue. **26 November:** The CC issues Mao's criticism of Liu Bing and others along with their letters to Mao. The "Counterattack Right-Deviationist Reversal-of-Verdicts Trend" campaign begins. Most of Deng Xiaoping's official duties are soon suspended.

1976 8 January: Premier Zhou Enlai dies. **15 January:** Deng Xiaoping delivers a memorial speech at the state funeral for Zhou Enlai. This is Deng's last public appearance until after the Cultural Revolution. **21 and 28 January:** Mao proposes that Hua Guofeng be appointed acting premier of the SC and that Hua take charge of the routine work of the CC. **25 February:** The CC holds a conference of provincial and military region leaders in Beijing to promote the "Criticize Deng, Counterattack the Right-Deviationist Reversal-of-Verdicts Trend" campaign. **Late March and early April:** Millions of Beijing citizens visit Tiananmen Square during the Qingming Festival (4 April in 1976) season to commemorate Zhou Enlai. Numerous posted elegies contain a strong political message against the cultural revolutionary faction of the central leadership. Mourning activities become a mass protest movement in Beijing and a number of large cities around the country. **5 April:** With Mao's approval, Beijing authorities send thousands of soldiers, policemen, and militia members to Tiananmen Square to crack down on the protesters. **7 April:** Following Mao's directives, the Politburo passes resolutions to dismiss Deng Xiaoping from office and appoint Hua Guofeng first vice-chairman of the CC and premier of the SC. **6 July:** Chairman of the National People's Congress Zhu De dies. **9 September:** Chairman Mao Zedong dies. **6 October:** After nearly a month's careful planning with Wang Dongxing and Ye Jianying, Hua Guofeng orders the arrest of the Gang of Four: Jiang Qing, Wang Hongwen, Zhang Chunqiao, and Yao Wenyuan. The Cultural Revolution ends.

Introduction

As a major political event and a crucial turning point in the history of the People's Republic of China (PRC), the Great Proletarian Cultural Revolution (1966–1976) marked the heyday as well as the eventual bankruptcy of Chairman Mao Zedong's ultra-leftist politics. Purportedly to prevent China from departing from its socialist path, Mao mobilized the masses in a battle against what he considered to be the bourgeoisie within the ruling Chinese Communist Party (CCP). This 10-year-long class struggle on a massive scale caused unprecedented damage to traditional culture and to the nation's economy. To a great extent, it was the disaster of the Cultural Revolution that prompted post-Mao Chinese Communist leaders, ahead of their Soviet counterparts, to implement pragmatic economic reforms. Major policies that the post-Mao government has adopted, even today, may still be best understood as a reaction to the radical politics of the Cultural Revolution.

The revolution was *cultural* because Mao conceived of it in Marxist terms as a thoroughgoing revolution in ideological spheres and at superstructural levels. It aimed to eradicate old culture and customs and to educate the masses through a series of political campaigns. Knowledge in general was also under attack because it was permeated by non-proletarian culture. Mao considered a populace with revolutionized consciousness to be the best defense against the country's power takeover by the bourgeoisie. His formulation of cultural determinism against the original Marxist emphasis on an economic base structure as the essential determining factor in social transformation was hailed during the Cultural Revolution as a great contribution to Marxism. Although Mao's program achieved considerable success in destroying much of traditional culture, the Cultural Revolution also brought about a revival of China's feudal and imperial past in the widespread personality cult of Mao and the deification of the leader, so much so that religious fervor often passed as revolutionary enthusiasm, especially in the early stages of the Cultural Revolution.

The Cultural Revolution was *political* as well since the main task of this movement was to purge "those power holders in the party who take the capitalist road" (also known as "capitalist-roaders"). Even though some of the leaders thus named—such as Mao's first chosen successor, President Liu Shaoqi—took an approach less radical than Mao's to China's economic development (in fact, Mao had begun to consider Liu to be his main political rival in the CCP leadership in the early 1960s, largely due to Liu's rather critical assessment of the disastrous Great Leap Forward program and the

1

remedial measures he and other leaders allowed to be implemented in its aftermath), still, all of them were committed communists and had never designed a program, as charged, to "restore capitalism" in China.

The Cultural Revolution had a far greater impact on the lives of ordinary people and on Chinese society in general than any other political movement in the history of the PRC. Citizens classified as being in the "five black categories" were regarded as traditional enemies. They were invariably persecuted and remained downtrodden during the entire 10-year period. A large percentage of school teachers and college professors, as natural targets of a *cultural* revolution, were persecuted as "bourgeois intellectuals" during its early stages and were subject to the orders of factory workers and army soldiers sent by Mao to take control of the nation's schools in the later years of the Cultural Revolution. A vast majority of government officials and party cadres were named capitalist-roaders or followers of a bourgeois revisionist line, and in the late 1960s and early 1970s, most of them were sent to factories or labor camps called "May 7 cadre schools" to reform themselves through manual labor. Enthusiastic urban youths in secondary schools and colleges formed Red Guard organizations and served as Mao's crusading army against the traditional party and state establishment before most of them—17 million in total—were, too, sent to the countryside to receive reeducation from local peasants. Deprived of regular school education in their formative years, most of this "Cultural Revolution generation" were crippled amid the competition for employment in the post-Revolution era of Reform and Opening. During and after a power-seizure campaign in 1967 and 1968, factional violence among mass organizations that included people from all walks of life escalated nationwide into civil war. The armed conflict in this period resulted in substantial military and civilian casualties that still remain uncounted, except for sporadic provincial and local statistics. In the meantime, nationwide campaigns to persecute suspected class enemies continued. According to official estimates, the total number of people affected by these campaigns, including the victims and their family members, amounts to 100 million, which was one-eighth of China's population at the time. Due to its long-lasting, grave impact on China's economy and national life, "ten years of chaos" has become both the official and popular reference to the Cultural Revolution.

PREPARATIONS AND PRELUDES, 1956–1966

Although Mao did not make any concrete plans for the Cultural Revolution until the mid-1960s, some major ideas in what eventually became Mao's Cultural Revolution theory, or his theory of "continuing revolution under the dictatorship of the proletariat," began to form as early as 1956. At the 20th National Congress of the Soviet Communist Party held in 1956, First Secretary Nikita Khrushchev attacked his predecessor, Josef Stalin, accusing him of violating social legality and promoting a personality cult. De-Stalinization in the Soviet Union was soon followed by a popular revolt in Hungary. Apparently associating himself with Stalin and considering Khrushchev's move as a betrayal of the international communist movement, Mao became alert to the danger of a similar power takeover, betrayal, and de-Maoization within the CCP. By 1959, Khrushchev's willingness to negotiate with the United States validated Mao's completely unfavorable assessment of the Soviet situation. In the 1960s, he began to call Soviet leaders "revisionists"—that is, those deviating from the orthodox Marxist-Leninist path—and launched a series of attacks on the Soviet leadership—known as the "Nine Commentaries," to which Mao himself also contributed. In his judgment, revisionist leaders, corrupted officials, and a newly emerging bureaucratic class within a country's ruling communist party, rather than hostile forces from the outside, posed the greatest danger to the legacy of communism. Therefore, Mao writes in a passage in the ninth commentary, entitled "On Khrushchev's Phony Communism and Its Historical Lessons for the World," that Chinese communists must watch out for "careerists and conspirators" like Khrushchev and prevent them from taking over party and state leadership. At the same time, he urged his comrades in the CCP to attend constantly to the training of successors to the revolutionary cause from the highest levels down to the grassroots. Eventually, Mao came to the conclusion that a nationwide cultural revolution was necessary for the purposes of purging revisionist leaders, on the one hand, and offering political education and training for the masses, on the other. In the actual Cultural Revolution, "China's Khrushchev" was adopted as a criminal label for President Liu Shaoqi, who Mao suspected was the leading "revisionist" within the CCP.

On the domestic front, the Cultural Revolution was in some ways Mao's response to the ideological differences and power conflicts between him and other veteran CCP leaders that surfaced in the aftermath of the Great Leap Forward. Encouraged by the completion of collectivization in the PRC in 1956 but unhappy about the cautious economic policies that Zhou Enlai, Chen Yun, and other central leaders put in place to stop the "rash advance" (*maojin*) of an unrealistic production drive, Mao decided to abandon the Soviet model of economic development and began to contemplate more radical measures for the transformation of the Chinese countryside. These measures, which materialized in the 1958 Great Leap Forward program, turned out to be disastrous: they caused the Great Famine of 1958 through 1962, claiming 20 to 30 million lives.

By then, Mao had already retired to the "second front" of the central leadership while maintaining his chairmanship of the CCP. Meanwhile, President Liu Shaoqi, as leader of the "first front," implemented a series of pragmatic and liberal policies, especially in the countryside, to deal with the economic crisis. However, just as the remedial measures were beginning to yield positive results, Mao, in August 1962, criticized the "first front" leaders for reversing the party's socialist agricultural policies and warned his colleagues "never to forget class struggle." In early 1963, Mao launched a nationwide Socialist Education Movement and, in January 1965, designated as the major task of this movement to "purge those power holders in the party who take the capitalist road." The middle stage of this movement—the fourth year of the projected seven years—merged with the beginning of the Cultural Revolution. Its focus on the struggle against capitalist-roaders became the focus of the Cultural Revolution as well, though the main site of the struggle shifted in 1966 from rural areas and local governments to cities and higher levels of the CCP leadership.

In the cultural sphere, Mao began to send out signals of dissatisfaction in late 1963, and again in mid-1964, harshly criticizing the CCP leaders in literature and art circles for allegedly deviating from socialist principles and promoting feudalist and bourgeois art. Based on Mao's criticism and at Mao's proposal, the CCP Central Committee (CC) decided to conduct rectification in literature and art circles and set up a Five-Person Small Group to lead the movement. Peng Zhen, mayor of Beijing, was appointed head of the group. In the meantime, Mao began to assign his wife, Jiang Qing, an increasingly significant role in Chinese politics. In 1965, Jiang Qing and Zhang Chunqiao—both die-hard cultural revolutionaries—made well-calculated moves in Shanghai to have Yao Wenyuan write a critique of *Hai Rui Dismissed from Office*, a play by Wu Han who was a renowned historian and a deputy-mayor of Beijing. Mao read the draft version of this article three times and came to see Wu Han's play as an implicit plea for redressing the case of Marshal Peng Dehuai, who had been dismissed from office in 1959 for criticizing the Great Leap Forward policies. Yao's article, initially carried in the 10 November 1965 issue of Shanghai's *Wenhui Daily* and soon reprinted in a number of provincial newspapers, sparked a nationwide propaganda campaign against "academic authorities." The publication of this article came to be known as the "blasting fuse" of the Cultural Revolution.

The seven-month period from November 1965, when Yao Wenyuan's article was published and when Mao left Beijing for unknown reasons, to May 1966, when the CC document "May 16 Circular" was adopted at an enlarged session of the Politburo, is generally considered the prelude to the Cultural Revolution, during which Mao launched a major offensive against the Peng Zhen–led CCP Beijing Municipal Committee. Both Peng's initial refusal to reprint the Yao article in Beijing newspapers and his later attempt as head of the Five-Person Small Group to draft a party document—to be known as the "February Outline"—to lead the campaign against Wu Han and others in the direction of an "academic discussion" were perceived by Mao as deliberate resistance to the revolution that he was launching. To clear the path for the Cultural Revolution, Mao ordered a group of cultural revolutionary theorists and writers to gather in Shanghai and draft an item-by-item rebuttal of the February Outline. And, for the same purpose, he managed to remove from power three veteran leaders: General Luo Ruiqing, chief of general staff of the People's Liberation Army (PLA); Lu Dingyi, director of the CCP propaganda department; and Yang Shangkun, director of the general office of the CC. By spring 1966, the criticism of "academic authorities" in Beijing had evolved into a militant mass movement against the so-called Three-Family Village Anti-Party Clique consisting of three veteran leaders of the Beijing Municipal Committee. By the time Mayor Peng Zhen decided to give in, it was already too late. In May 1966, enlarged Politburo sessions were convened in Beijing at Mao's proposal. At these meetings, Peng, Luo, Lu, and Yang were denounced together as an "anti-party clique," and the Beijing Municipal Committee was dissolved. Also at these meetings, with the passage of the May 16 Circular abrogating the February Outline, the Cultural Revolution was officially launched.

FROM CHAOS TO ORDER, 1966–1969

The three-year period from May 1966, when enlarged Politburo sessions were held in Beijing to purge the so-called Peng-Luo-Lu-Yang Anti-Party Clique, to April 1969, when the Ninth National Congress of the CCP convened in Beijing upon the establishment of the new power organ—the "revolutionary committee"—at local and provincial levels, may be considered the first, and major, phase of the Cultural Revolution. The date 16 May 1966 marked the official beginning of the Cultural Revolution—the date on which the Politburo adopted a document that repudiates the notion of "academic discussion" as denying the class identity of truth and pivotally defines the current political movement as a nationwide class struggle against the representatives of the bourgeoisie in the party and state leadership. This document, known as the May 16 Circular, was officially designated as the first "programmatic document of the Cultural Revolution." In late May 1966, the CC implemented the decision of the Politburo and formed a Central Cultural Revolution Small Group (CCRSG), with Chen Boda, a leading CCP theorist, as head of the group, Zhang Chunqiao and Jiang Qing as deputy-heads, and

Kang Sheng as adviser. This group, consisting mostly of ultra-leftist theorists and writers, was to serve as the chief advocate of Mao's radical policies and virtually replaced the Politburo in mid-1967.

On the evening of 1 June 1966, the Central Radio followed Mao's directive to broadcast nationwide a big-character poster by Nie Yuanzi and six other people at Peking University attacking leaders of the university and Beijing Municipal Committee. The broadcast of the poster, along with the publication that same day of a militant editorial entitled "Sweep Away All Cow-Demons and Snake-Spirits" in the CCP official organ *People's Daily*, ignited an explosion of public energy, especially on Beijing's secondary school and college campuses, where students began to form Red Guard organizations, and hundreds of thousands of big-character posters appeared in just a few days, charging school authorities and teachers with carrying out a revisionist and counterrevolutionary line in education. Since the May 16 Circular was still an internal document, 1 June 1966, then, became the actual beginning of the Cultural Revolution for the public.

To provide guidance for the explosive mass movement and to restrain rebellious youths, the CCP central leadership, headed by Liu Shaoqi during Mao's absence, made a decision to dispatch work groups to schools and government institutions, a decision then acknowledged by Mao. But only a few days after returning to Beijing in mid-July, Mao began to criticize the work groups for carrying out a fire-containing mission and for repressing the mass movement. In early August, Mao convened the Eleventh Plenum of the Eighth CCP Central Committee in Beijing. At the Plenum, Mao wrote a big-character poster entitled "Bombarding the Headquarters," calling Liu and his supporters' work group policy a measure of "bourgeois dictatorship." Liu's name was not mentioned, but the intent was obvious. Also at the Plenum, Defense Minister Lin Biao, the chief promoter of the personality cult of Mao, was elevated to the second-highest leadership position, and a radical guideline, commonly known as the "Sixteen Articles," designating the purging of capitalist-roaders as the focus of the Cultural Revolution, was adopted.

In the meantime, Mao made a decisive move to mobilize student Red Guards in his effort to topple Liu and to shake up the entire party and state apparatus, of which he had been the chief architect. With Mao's approval, his letter of support for the Red Guards, dated 1 August 1966, in which he reiterates his own words, "To rebel is justified," was circulated at the Eleventh Plenum. After the Plenum, Mao appeared in public eight times between 18 August and 26 November to review a total of 11 million Red Guards from all over China. Mao's beckoning initially inspired Red Guards to enact a war of eradicating vestiges of traditional culture, which led to the destruction of numerous cultural monuments and historical sites and the debasing of knowledge, education, and traditional values. In this general offensive against the so-called Old World, Red Guards assumed authority of the law in the name of "mass dictatorship" and persecuted millions of innocent people of non-proletarian background. In a 40-day period following Mao's first inspection of Red Guard troops, 1,772 people were killed or committed suicide in the city of Beijing alone. In October 1966, when Mao launched a campaign to criticize the "Bourgeois Reactionary Line," aimed more specifically at Liu Shaoqi, student Red Guards became Mao's crusading army against Liu and the old party establishment. After that, Liu lost his freedom and was subject to brutal treatment under "mass dictatorship" until his death in 1969.

The campaign to criticize the Bourgeois Reactionary Line soon merged into a nationwide power-seizure movement, in which mass organizations assumed authority in local and provincial government. Inaugurated by Shanghai's "January Storm" of 1967, the power-seizure operation became a violent competition among mass organizations, and the army's involvement following Mao's late-January order to support the left failed to ease the tension and conflict. Although the new power organ—the revolutionary committee, consisting of representatives of the masses, the army, and veteran party officials—was beginning to be established at various levels in early 1967, factional violence nevertheless escalated and became an armed conflict in many parts of China. By late 1967 and early 1968, an estimated one million guns were in the hands of civilians, causing heavy casualties, and the country, in Mao's words, was in a state of "all-round civil war." In the midst of chaos, elementary and secondary schools, though in session since early 1968, were out of control and without a curriculum, while colleges had not been admitting students at all. And the nation's economy was on the verge of collapse. In July 1968, Mao and the central leadership were finally determined to put an end to the widespread armed conflict and nationwide chaos. In that month, the CC issued two public notices nationwide concerning violence in the provinces. Also in that month, Mao dispatched teams made up of workers and military personnel to school campuses to stop the violence and also to assume leadership there. At a meeting with the five most influential Red Guard leaders in Beijing, Mao informed them of his plan to end violence by sending students off campus. In late 1968, an unprecedented urban youth relocation movement began. Students from the cities went to the countryside to work and to receive reeducation from local peasants; this relocation of urban youths effectively ended the turbulent Red Guard movement. In the meantime, armed conflict in the provinces also gradually came to an end.

As the power-seizure campaign and the subsequent factional violence took place at local and provincial levels in 1967 and 1968, the ideological as well as power conflict at the top between veteran revolutionaries of the old government, led by Premier Zhou Enlai, and newly risen cultural revolutionaries, especially those of the CCRSG, intensified and surfaced from time to time. In February 1967, the CCRSG's attempt to carry out Mao's plan of shaking up the military leadership provoked the indignation of a number of old marshals in the Central Military Commission and vice-premiers of the State Council. The veteran leaders vented their anti–Cultural Revolution sentiment at a high-level meeting, accusing the cultural revolutionaries of persecuting party officials, eliminating party leadership, and instigating disturbances in the army. Mao sided with the cultural revolutionaries and harshly condemned the veteran leaders for creating a "February Adverse Current" against the Cultural Revolution. But, in August 1967, when aggressive intrusions and interferences by the CCRSG in military and foreign affairs met strong resistance from veteran leaders, including Zhou Enlai, Mao decided to make a concession in spite of his ideological sympathy for the cultural revolutionaries: he removed three active members of the CCRSG (Wang Li, Guan Feng, and Qi Benyu) from power and pronounced them an anti-party clique. In March 1968, however, when Jiang Qing and Lin Biao conspired against three generals (Yang Chengwu, Yu Lijin, and Fu Chongbi) of the veteran camp, Mao again sided with the cultural revolutionaries and allowed the generals to be purged.

While all three instances of power conflict were officially named "line struggles within the party," the denunciation of President Liu Shaoqi remained the major, fore-grounded, and longest campaign during this period. The Liu case was closed in October 1968 when a scandalous investigative report on Liu's personal history was approved by the CC at the Twelfth Plenum of the Eighth CCP Central Committee. In the report, Liu was named a traitor, a spy, and a renegade; the evidence, however, was completely fabricated. By this time, in late 1968, though the campaign to "rectify the class ranks" was still under way—a political program focusing on personal histories of ordinary citizens that resulted in more wrongful verdicts and more deaths than any other campaign in the Cultural Revolution—Mao's major political battle against "China's Khrushchev" was won. And, with nationwide factional violence coming to an end and the new power organ, the revolutionary committee, established in all provinces, Mao's plan to move from revolutionary chaos to order and stability seemed to have been accomplished. The stage was set for the Ninth National Congress of the CCP.

In April 1969, the Ninth National Congress was held in Beijing. The meeting produced a new party constitution. In a move unprecedented in the history of the CCP, the new constitution specified Mao Zedong as the leader of the CCP and Lin Biao as Mao's "close comrade-in-arms and successor." The National Congress was in Mao's view one of unity and success, promising closure to an era.

THE FALL OF LIN BIAO, 1969–1971

Mao's handpicked successor had thus been ordained in the new party constitution, and a large number of new members had been elected to the Ninth CC, constituting 70 percent of its total seats, under the newly consolidated "proletarian headquarters." The Ninth National Congress of the CCP could have indeed been the closure of the Cultural Revolution that Mao had hoped for, but two newly emerging issues caused Mao concern. First, the initial alliance in the central leadership between the military generals loyal to Lin Biao and the cultural revolutionaries led by Jiang Qing was breaking down. Second, because of Lin Biao's painstaking political maneuvers in the early years of the Cultural Revolution of replacing leaders of other factions within the Chinese military with his close associates, his power in the PLA and in the CCP central leadership had apparently become too strong in Mao's view.

The power conflict between the Lin Biao camp and the Jiang Qing faction seemed also to have an ideological dimension. In preparation for the Ninth Congress, Mao asked head of the CCRSG Chen Boda, who was by then already alienated from Jiang Qing and her close allies, to lead the drafting of the party's political report. During the writing process, Chen discussed the report with Lin Biao, and apparently both were considering the Ninth Congress to be a turning point for China's economic development. Mao, however, criticized Chen's first draft for its "productionist" tendencies and entrusted Zhang Chunqiao and Yao Wenyuan instead with the task of redrafting and revision. Mao's decision virtually ended Chen's cooperation with his colleagues in the CCRSG and pushed him further toward an alliance with the Lin Biao group.

The first and only open engagement between the Lin Biao group and the Jiang Qing group took place in late August to early September 1970 at the Second Plenum of the Ninth CCP Central Committee, also known as the Lushan Conference. The battle took the form of a noisy dispute over two questions: whether Mao Zedong was a genius and whether the Chinese leadership should, as Mao proposed, eliminate the position of the president of state. In his opening speech, Lin Biao spoke of Mao as head of China's proletarian dictatorship and hence tacitly made known his disagreement with Mao on the issue of national presidency; Lin also spoke of Mao as a genius. Following Lin's steps, Chen Boda compiled a pamphlet entitled "Engels, Lenin, and Chairman Mao on Genius" and distributed it among delegates. Knowing that Jiang Qing's close ally Zhang Chunqiao had opposed the inclusion of "genius" along with two other modifiers praising Mao in the revised PRC constitution, Chen, along with other associates of Lin Biao, stirred up a storm in discussion groups: without mentioning Zhang's name, they called for the denunciation of those who denied Mao's genius. Mao lent full support for the Jiang Qing group in this bizarre power intrigue. He condemned Chen's theory of genius as "fabrication" and "sophistry" and ordered Lin Biao's associates to go through self-examination at the Plenum and in the "Criticize Chen and Conduct Rectification Campaign" after the Plenum. The fall of the Lin faction had thus begun.

In anticipation of Mao's move against Lin Biao, Lin Liguo, the son of Lin Biao, allegedly formed a secret group with a few of his colleagues in the air force and drafted a plan for an armed coup in March 1971. Code-named the *"571 Project" Summary*, this plan contained both details concerning military operations and diagnoses of the current political situation of China, in which Mao was referred to as the "biggest feudal tyrant in Chinese history." In the meantime, Mao made a strategic tour of the south in the summer of 1971, during which he communicated to party and government officials and military generals his critical view of Lin Biao and his associates. This tour allegedly both triggered and foiled Lin Liguo's plot against Mao's life (the extent of Lin Biao's knowledge of the Summary and its execution still remains a mystery). On the early morning of 13 September, within hours of Mao's unexpected early return to Beijing, Lin Biao, his wife Ye Qun, and their son Lin Liguo reportedly fled in panic and died in a plane crash in Mongolia. All of Lin's supporters in the military were subsequently arrested.

The downfall of Mao's handpicked successor and the treason charge against him shocked the nation. Some readers of the Summary, which was distributed nationwide as evidence of Lin's crimes, were surprised by unexpected echoes of their own unformulated judgment in some of its diagnoses of the ills of the Cultural Revolution. The "September 13 Incident" marked not only the end of a stage in the Cultural Revolution but also the beginning of many people's disillusionment with and critical reflection upon the Cultural Revolution.

AGAINST THE REVERSAL OF VERDICTS, 1971–1976

With the downfall of Lin Biao, what had been celebrated as a major achievement of the Cultural Revolution turned out to be Mao's inadvertent making of "China's Khrushchev." The September 1971 incident was a heavy blow to Mao, leaving Premier Zhou Enlai, now the second-ranked leader, with more responsibilities in the daily affairs of the party and the state. His personal view of Lin Biao aside, which he kept to himself exclusively, Zhou made a strategic move in his effort to restore a certain normality to Chinese national life: In the name of rectifying the "ultra-leftist" line of Lin Biao, Zhou began to speak against widespread "anarchism" and called for quality control in industrial production and advanced research in basic sciences. In October

1972, two years after colleges began to admit "worker-peasant-soldier students" with a requirement of a minimum two years of pre-college work experience, Zhou suggested that some outstanding high school students be allowed to enter college directly upon graduation. In the meantime, he devoted much energy to reinstating veteran officials who had been removed from office and persecuted in the early years of the Cultural Revolution. He was instrumental in bringing Deng Xiaoping back to Beijing from exile in 1973.

In the aftermath of the Lin Biao incident, Mao initially acquiesced to Zhou's cautious moves. He also made a series of concessions to the veteran leaders he had formerly denounced; in particular, he acknowledged the "Retaliation against the February Adverse Current" campaign of 1967 to be a mistake, though he blamed Lin Biao for it. Also during this period, a major foreign policy change Mao had been contemplating since the 1969 China-Soviet border clash materialized: in February 1972, U.S. president Richard Nixon visited Beijing, and Zhou Enlai played a major role in executing Mao's plan to normalize China-U.S. relations. However, Mao soon began to regard Zhou's criticism of ultra-leftism as an attempt to reverse the radical course of the Cultural Revolution and therefore supported Jiang Qing and Zhang Chunqiao's suggestion of denouncing Lin Biao's "Right extremism" in the nationwide "Criticize Lin and Conduct Rectification" campaign. The mild de-radicalizing trend that Zhou cautiously set in motion, especially in education, was now dismissed as a "Rightist resurgence," and a number of youths challenging the educational establishment were hailed by cultural revolutionaries as heroes "going against the tide." In 1973 and 1974, the widely supported restorative effort in education suffered a severe setback.

In fact, in the five-year period after the downfall of Lin Biao, Mao remained preoccupied with the potential threat that the course of his Cultural Revolution would be negated, and so preventing a "reversal of verdicts" became the major theme of most of the campaigns during this period. Despite his loyalty to Mao, Zhou Enlai was perceived by the cultural revolutionaries, and by Mao himself, to be potentially the most formidable force behind all such "reversal" efforts and became the implicit and yet real target of attack in a series of propaganda campaigns, including the "Criticize Confucianism and Appraise Legalism" movement and the "Criticize Lin [Biao] and Criticize Confucius" campaign of 1974 and the "*Water Margin* Appraisal" campaign of 1975. The attack on Zhou in all these campaigns took the form of "allusory historiography" in which Zhou was referred to as a Confucius of today, devoted to a reactionary cause of restoring the order of bygone days and a capitulator betraying a revolutionary cause. Despite his perfect execution of Mao's new foreign policy, or perhaps because of it, which had much elevated Zhou's stature, a 10-day enlarged Politburo session was convened in late November and early December 1973, at Mao's suggestion, to criticize Zhou for carrying out a "capitulationist line" in foreign policy in his negotiations with the United States on the sensitive issue of military exchange. It was at this meeting, and in alliance against Zhou, that four die-hard cultural revolutionaries in the Politburo—Jiang Qing, Zhang Chunqiao, Yao Wenyuan, and Wang Hongwen—began to band together and form what was soon to be known as the "Gang of Four."

To ensure the continuation of his Cultural Revolution legacy, Mao had also been searching for a successor after the fall of Lin Biao. Zhang Chunqiao, Mao's true ideological heir, might have been a candidate but for his unpopularity, of which Mao became fully aware at the Lushan Conference of 1970. Wang Hongwen, a rebel leader turned official in Shanghai and a close associate of Zhang Chunqiao and Yao Wenyuan, seemed to be the first candidate whom Mao seriously considered. Mao transferred Wang to Beijing in September 1972, put him in charge of the CCP constitution revision, made him third-ranked leader at the Tenth National Congress of the CCP (August 1973), but eventually gave him up, apparently due to his lack of political skills and his increasing unpopularity as a member of the Jiang Qing group. Mao's next choice was Deng Xiaoping, a choice that Zhou Enlai strongly supported. In January 1975, Deng was given several top official titles and was entrusted with the power to preside over daily affairs of the party, the army, and the state while Zhou Enlai was hospitalized for cancer treatment.

Despite his promise to Mao that he would never reverse the verdicts of the Cultural Revolution, Deng, sharing Zhou's unvoiced critical view of the Cultural Revolution, took a much more aggressive approach in his effort to combat ultra-leftism and to energize the nation's economy. In late February 1975, Deng launched a nationwide "overall rectification" program, and swift reforms were carried out during the rest of the year in the areas of national defense, transportation, industrial production, education, and scientific research. In the most sensitive area of culture, literature, and the arts, Deng used Mao's slogan "let a hundred flowers bloom" and pushed for the release of certain new and classic works that had been condemned by the Jiang Qing group. On the party organization and personnel front, major tasks of the rectification included the enforcement of tough measures against lingering factionalism and the demotion or dismissal of incompetent officials who had enjoyed a meteoric rise for political reasons during the Cultural Revolution. Largely due to this overall rectification program, the China of 1975 was an economic success: the national gross output of industry and agriculture increased by 11.9 percent in 1975, compared to 1.4 percent in 1974. With this program, Deng won broad support across the country.

As Deng was driving his reform program forward with full force, the conflict between him and the Jiang Qing group intensified. Later in the year, via Mao Yuanxin, Mao's nephew and his designated liaison at the Politburo, the Jiang group managed to bring Deng's apparent anti–Cultural Revolution stand to the attention of the increasingly isolated Mao. In the meantime, Deng declined a request from Mao that he be in charge of drafting a resolution concerning the Cultural Revolution at the Politburo. In November 1975, Mao Zedong finally decided to halt Deng's rectification program and launch a nationwide political campaign called "Counterattack the Trend of Right-Deviationist Reversal of Verdicts." Most of Deng's official duties were soon suspended. In late January 1976, within a month of Premier Zhou Enlai's death, Hua Guofeng, Mao's final choice for successor, was named acting premier of the State Council at Mao's proposal, replacing Deng as the man in charge.

In late March and early April 1976, millions of Beijing citizens visited Tiananmen Square during the traditional Qingming Festival season to commemorate the late Premier Zhou Enlai. Similar events took place in a number of provinces as well. Numerous posted elegies contained a strong political message against the cultural revolutionary faction of the CCP central leadership. The mourners' outpouring of grief turned out to be simultaneously a mass protest. Although the authorities cracked down on the protest movement, it became evident that Mao's Cultural Revolution legacy was completely rejected by the populace. On 6 October 1976, within a month of the death of Chairman Mao Zedong, Hua Guofeng, with full support of CC security chief Wang Dongxing and Marshal Ye Jianying, ordered the arrest of Jiang Qing, Zhang Chunqiao, Yao Wenyuan, and Wang Hongwen. Celebrated nationwide, the downfall of the Gang of Four marked the official closure of the Cultural Revolution.

OFFICIAL ASSESSMENT OF THE CULTURAL REVOLUTION

The post-Mao CCP leadership began in late 1976 to implement concrete measures to reverse Mao's Cultural Revolution policies in all areas. The pace of policy change accelerated after the reinstatement of Deng Xiaoping in July 1977. In regard to an overall judgment of the Cultural Revolution, the central leadership took a major step in December 1978 at the Third Plenum of the Eleventh CCP Central Committee. At this meeting, the leadership rejected Hua Guofeng's dogmatic principle of "two whatever's" (uphold whatever decisions Mao had made and adhere to whatever instructions Mao had given) and decided to abandon Mao's theory of class struggle and of continuing revolution under the dictatorship of the proletariat, deciding rather to carry out a thoroughgoing review of all persecution cases of the past, nationwide and at all levels. Hu Yaobang, in the capacity of head of the CCP organization department and then as CCP general secretary, led the review and redress effort. By the end of 1980, virtually all of the cases brought during the

Cultural Revolution—including the case against President Liu Shaoqi, more than three million cases against government officials, and many more against ordinary citizens—had been proven "wrongful, false, and mistaken." By 1984, over 20 million victims persecuted by the CCP since Land Reform (which began as early as 1946) were rehabilitated. In June 1981, at the Sixth Plenum of the Eleventh CCP Central Committee, the central leadership finally adopted the "Resolution on Certain Questions in the History of Our Party since the Founding of the People's Republic of China," a landmark document that contains a comprehensive assessment of the Cultural Revolution.

The stated purpose of the Resolution is to review Mao's legacy and conclude a highly problematic chapter in the CCP history—"preferably in broad strokes rather than in detail," as Deng Xiaoping suggested—so that both the party and the nation may be united, leave the past behind, and look ahead. Of all the issues he discussed on several occasions between March 1980 and June 1981 concerning the drafting of the Resolution, Deng considered the assessment of Chairman Mao Zedong to be the most important. On the one hand, Deng said, the Resolution should be critical of Mao's mistakes, truthfully and unequivocally; on the other hand, however, the legitimacy of the CCP leadership in the Cultural Revolution must be acknowledged, and the banner of Mao Zedong Thought should not be abandoned; for to abandon this banner means to deny the "glorious history of our party." Embracing Deng's concern for both the truth of the Cultural Revolution and the legitimacy of the party leadership under Mao as the principal guideline, the Resolution deals with two conflicting issues: On the one hand, it names the Cultural Revolution as the cause of "the most severe setback and the heaviest losses the party, the state, and the people had suffered since the founding of the PRC," criticizes Chairman Mao Zedong's ultra-leftism as an erroneous ideology informing the Cultural Revolution, and recognizes the partial responsibility of the CCP central leadership for the Revolution. On the other hand, the Resolution blames Lin Biao, Jiang Qing, and their followers for taking advantage of Mao's errors and committing crimes behind his back, and it charges them as the chief culprits responsible for the national disaster. The Resolution upholds Mao Zedong Thought as the guiding principle of the CCP while at the same time excluding Mao's theory of continuing revolution under the dictatorship of the proletariat from Mao Zedong Thought proper in spite of Mao's own judgment. Apparently, the Resolution reflects a dilemma the post-Mao CCP leadership faced: the leadership gained its legitimacy by consenting to the will of an overwhelming majority of the people and abandoning Mao's Cultural Revolution program, and yet, at the same time, the leadership was concerned that a thoroughgoing critique of the Cultural Revolution might again put its legitimacy in question.

The apparent self-contradictions in the Resolution have since been reflected in self-contradictory government policies, especially after the PRC leaders condemned the mass protest of 1989 as a return of the Cultural Revolution (actually a false analogy ignoring the striking contrast between the spontaneity of the one and the supreme leader being the prime mover of the other): though the Cultural Revolution is dismissed as "ten years of chaos" in official media, important Cultural Revolution documents remain classified in Beijing's Central Archives, and serious independent studies of the Cultural Revolution are invariably censored in mainland China. The goal of the Resolution, that of helping the nation leave the past behind and look ahead, has been more than fulfilled with the aid of the invisible hand of the market: the China of the 1990s produced "*xiang-qian-kan*" (turn to the money) as a pun for "look ahead"—preoccupation with material prospects trumped non-profitable memory and retrospection, and economically focused Reform and Opening delivered widespread historical amnesia as a by-product no less important for the ruling party than its immediate aim of economic success. Ironically, officially enforced forgetfulness could backfire at the enforcer, as evidenced in an image of the Cultural Revolution as an era of egalitarianism, popular contentment, and clean government—an image conjured up rather than remembered that has been gaining popularity in recent years in reaction to the increasing economic disparity and official corruption in mainland China.

THE LEGACY OF THE CULTURAL REVOLUTION

Seen from the vantage point of China's reform era and beyond, the legacy of the Cultural Revolution is essentially one of irony and self-negation, because it helped bring about a great many changes that Mao had especially intended to prevent—indeed, to prevent by launching the Cultural Revolution itself. The severe impact of a prolonged stagnant economy on national life, for instance, forced the post-Mao CCP leadership not only to abandon once and for all Mao's policy of "politics in command" in favor of a moderate and pragmatic approach to economic matters but also to embrace the market economy and borrow from capitalism in its effort to rejuvenate China's economy and modernize the nation. Mao's ultra-leftism reached its limits during the Cultural Revolution and began to negate itself: Mao's campaign to purge capitalist-roaders turned out to be the catalyst for the making of Deng Xiaoping's "socialism with Chinese characteristics," which is perhaps more accurately termed "capitalism with Chinese characteristics."

Along with economic hardships, the enormous human suffering caused by, and the widespread weariness and discontent about, incessant class struggle as part of daily life over a 10-year period also contributed to the legitimacy crisis of the CCP that Deng Xiaoping apparently felt when he was giving instructions on assessing the Cultural Revolution. Consequently, to go along with its economic reform policy, the CCP leadership decided to end the practice of class struggle and to abandon the politically discriminating "class line" (biased against people of non-proletarian background) as well; it began to appeal to the entire population for support in the name of the Chinese nation. These historic moves in reaction to the Cultural Revolution constituted no less than a paradigm shift in the party rule: modernization and nationalism took over class struggle and revolution as the dominant ideology in post-Mao China.

In the spheres of culture proper, the Cultural Revolution left China with much desolation and confusion. After a devastating sweeping-away of long-established traditional values—including humaneness, personal loyalty, civility, children's filial duty to parents, and students' respect for teachers—the revolution failed to establish a new set of values upon the ruins of the old. In the meantime, revelations of top-level power conflicts, especially those that led to Lin Biao's downfall, began to have a profound disillusioning impact on the populace regarding revolution. Traditional culture was in shambles, while faith in communism no longer held. This kind of spiritual vacancy created by the Cultural Revolution soon led to a conviction crisis (*xinyang weiji*) among the nation's youths, the emergence of cynicism and moral nihilism, and eventually, in a time of unprecedented economic boom, widespread corruption and abuse of power.

As people's trust in the ruling CCP drastically declined because of the Cultural Revolution, widely shared disillusionment about revolution also turned out to be the beginning of China's new democratic consciousness, which manifested itself forcefully in the spontaneous mass protest of 1989. In fact, without the shock of the totalitarian extremes of the Cultural Revolution, democracy as a defense against such extremes would have been a much more distant vision. Yet it remains to be seen whether this vision can materialize in the near future and whether the current generation of Chinese leaders, who experienced the "ten years of chaos" in their youth or middle age, are willing to extend reform to political spheres to complete the break with the Cultural Revolution.

The Cultural Revolution also aroused considerable interest abroad in the late 1960s and early 1970s when waves of counterculture, student revolt, anti–Vietnam War protest, and feminist and gay rights movements swept much of the world. Many sympathizers from the outside, enthusiastic youths and liberal intellectuals alike, saw China as they wanted to see it: a utopian revolutionary model that they did not find in their own world. The high-flown rhetoric of China's official propaganda, the genuine lack of information in the outside world especially due to China's increasing isolation during the first few years of the Cultural Revolution, and favorable reports by some China observers that were more representative of the reporters' own political stance than of China's reality, also helped create this myth of the Cultural Revolution. For instance, a rather vague but fantastic image of Chairman Mao Zedong commanding an army of rebellious Red Guards in a war against the old world as well as the new party and state apparatuses of his own creation was embraced by Parisian students as an inspiration for their epoch-making May 1968 revolt. The *Quotations from Chairman Mao*, popularly known outside China as the "little red book," became a worldwide best-seller in the late 1960s and early 1970s. Organizations modeled after the Red Guards emerged to challenge the establishment in many countries—communist and non-communist, Western and non-Western. Considering the genuine opposition to, and critique of, the authorities and traditional culture as seen in many of the mass movements outside China, the "cultural revolution" was, in fact, a more appropriate name for what was happening in the world during the 1960s than within China, although Beijing was at the time upheld by many as the world's Yan'an—the holy land of revolution.

In the middle and late 1970s, when the bleak and brutal reality of China's Cultural Revolution became better known abroad, most of its foreign supporters, like their historical counterparts in the 1930s concerning Stalin's Soviet Union, were profoundly disillusioned and began to detach themselves from their earlier position. In the meantime, however, there were those who adhered to their earlier vision of China as a revolutionary model and held on to their faith in Mao's cultural revolution theory as an authentic revolutionary ideology against the bourgeois legacy of Enlightenment. Their ideas contributed considerably to various postmodern critical theories that were formulated in the West in the late 1970s and 1980s. Then, an awkward encounter took place in the late 1980s when these theories, some of them closely associated with China's recent past but lacking a critical perspective, traveled to China and were received as intellectual haute fashion. This highly intellectualized, elitist legacy of the Cultural Revolution as theoretical discourse from abroad re-presented Maoism in a drastically simplified and yet sanitized version. In spite of its disregard for historical reality, such a legacy remains an unignorable challenge to historians of modern China, especially considering the prevalence of historical amnesia on the mainland, the Chinese government's restrictive policy concerning Cultural Revolution studies, and the fact that history is never a faithful recording of what has happened but is always a representation of it.

A

ALL FORCES CULTURAL REVOLUTION SMALL GROUP. (*Quan-jun wenhua geming xiaozu.*) Established in June 1966, this group was responsible for directing the Cultural Revolution in the armed forces and military institutes. Liu Zhijian, deputy head of the General Political Department of the **People's Liberation Army** (PLA) and one of the deputy heads of the **Central Cultural Revolution Small Group** (CCRSG), was appointed head of the All Forces Cultural Revolution Small Group. As the Cultural Revolution unfolded throughout the country, serious differences developed between several marshals in the Central Military Commission and the radical members of the CCRSG led by **Jiang Qing** concerning how the revolution should be carried out in PLA units and military schools. Because Liu and his group sided with the marshals on the issue, Jiang spoke against Liu as she met with **rebels** from military schools on 4 January 1967, accusing Liu of carrying out the **Bourgeois Reactionary Line** of **Liu Shaoqi** and **Deng Xiaoping** in the military. With the approval of Chairman **Mao Zedong**, Liu was replaced by Marshal **Xu Xiangqian** as head of the All Forces Cultural Revolution Small Group on 11 January 1967. Jiang was appointed advisor of the reformed group. Xiao Hua, **Yang Chengwu**, Xie Tangzhong, Wang Xinting, **Guan Feng**, Xu Liqing, and Li Mancun were named deputy heads. Other members of the group included **Yu Lijin**, Liu Huaqing, Wang Hongkun, Tang Pingzhu, **Ye Qun**, Hu Chi, Gu Yan, Wang Feng, and Zhang Tao. In late March 1967, after Mao ordered Xu Xiangqian to go on leave for self-criticism for his role in the **February Adverse Current**, Xiao Hua, head of the PLA General Political Department, became acting leader of the All Forces Cultural Revolution Small Group in Xu's place. However, after a violent incident at the theater of the Beijing Exhibition Hall between two rival mass organizations in the PLA art and literary circles during a performance on 13 May 1967, **Lin Biao** voiced support for one side, whereas Xiao Hua and the PLA General Political Department were accused of having been on the wrong side. Xiao was soon dismissed from office, and the All Forces Cultural Revolution Small Group ceased to function.

ALLUSORY HISTORIOGRAPHY. (*Yingshe shixue.*) This term, coined during the mid-1970s and becoming widely known after the Cultural Revolution, refers to the practice of some high-powered writing teams in the service of the **Jiang Qing** group attacking Premier **Zhou Enlai** and praising Jiang in numerous articles and books that took the form of historical studies. This kind of writing first appeared in late 1973 and continued to appear until early 1976. The topic was invariably "**Confucianism versus Legalism.**" Reflecting on an observation that Chairman **Mao Zedong** had made in mid-1973, these publications projected an image of a conservative or reactionary Confucius and Confucians in contrast to that of progressive or reformist Legalists in Chinese history. The present-day parallel, as suggested by allusions and innuendoes, to this highly innovative account of history was the opposition between the "backward-looking" Zhou and his supporters—ready to reverse the course of the Cultural Revolution at their first chance—and the radical cultural revolutionaries led by Mao who were determined to carry Mao's program through to completion.

See also CRITICIZE LIN AND CRITICIZE CONFUCIUS; PEKING UNIVERSITY AND TSINGHUA UNIVERSITY GREAT CRITICISM GROUP; SHANGHAI MUNICIPAL PARTY COMMITTEE WRITING GROUP.

ANTI-INTERFERENCE CAMPAIGN (1966). This was a campaign launched in late June through early July 1966 by the **work groups** in response to students challenging their authority in leading the Cultural Revolution movement on the campuses of Beijing secondary schools and colleges. These students had accused the work groups of repressing their rebellion against teachers and school authorities, and they attempted to drive the work groups off campus. With the support of the central leadership, then led by **Liu Shaoqi**, the work groups accused the students of interfering with the implementation of the Cultural Revolution movement in their institutions. Some of these students were named rightists and reactionaries and were **struggled against** at mass meetings. The Anti-Interference Campaign ended in late July/early August when **Mao Zedong**, upon returning to Beijing, decided to reverse the policies of the work groups and withdraw all work groups from the campuses.

ANTING INCIDENT (1966). This railway blockade, organized by the mass organization the **Workers Command Post** of Shanghai at the Anting station near Shanghai on 10 and 11 November 1966, marked the beginning of workers' massive engagement in the Cultural Revolution. **Mao Zedong** welcomed such engagement as consistent with his efforts to push the Cultural Revolution beyond government agencies and cultural and educational circles.

On 9 November, a mass rally of about 10,000 people was held in Shanghai's Culture Square to announce the establishment of the Workers Command Post and to denounce the **Bourgeois Reactionary Line** that was allegedly being carried out by the Shanghai municipal party committee. After the Shanghai party committee refused to recognize the Workers Command Post in accordance with the stipulation of the central leadership that disallowed trans-industry organizations, about 2,000 members of the Workers Command Post, led by **Wang Hongwen**, a member of the five-person presidium of the newly established organization, rushed into the Shanghai railway station on 10 November and boarded three trains. They declared that they would go to Beijing to present a petition for their organization. On orders by the Shanghai railway bureau, Wang's train was halted at Anting where some members subsequently got off the train and laid down on the rails to protest. As a result, transportation between Shanghai and Nanjing was paralyzed for more than 30 hours. In response to the report from Shanghai, **Chen Boda**, head of the **Central Cultural Revolution Small Group** (CCRSG), sent telegrams to Shanghai and Anting supporting the municipal party committee's position and asking the workers to go back. On 12 November, the CCRSG sent **Zhang Chunqiao** to Shanghai to work with the East China Bureau and Shanghai party committees to resolve the conflict at Anting. Zhang, however, negotiated directly with Wang Hongwen and other leaders of the mass organization at Anting as soon as he arrived.

On 13 November, Zhang attended a rally held by the Workers Command Post and, probably having already cleared the idea with Mao Zedong, agreed to the organization's demands for recognition and power. The Shanghai party committee pleaded the case with the central leadership but to no avail. The legitimation of the Workers Command Post pushed Shanghai a step closer to the 1967 movement to seize power, known as the **January Storm**. It also helped make Shanghai a base for the ultra-leftist forces in the central leadership, especially the **Gang of Four**, which would form after **Lin Biao**'s downfall and of which both Wang Hongwen and Zhang Chunqiao would become part.

ANTONIONI'S *CHINA* (1974). With Premier **Zhou Enlai**'s special permission, the Italian filmmaker Michelangelo Antonioni visited China in spring 1972. His tour of the cities of Beijing, Shanghai, and Nanjing and the rural areas of Lin Xian County, Henan Province, resulted in a three-and-a-half-hour documentary film entitled *China*. Antonioni's unflattering, realistic representation of various aspects of Chinese social life was seen by the **Chinese Communist Party** (CCP) leadership as a deliberate distortion of reality "with a particular intention to vilify the great achievements of the Cultural Revolution." The film was termed "anti-China" and "reactionary" and became the target of a propaganda campaign in early 1974. Considering Antonioni's political affiliation with the Italian Communist Party, **Yao Wenyuan** saw him as associated with both Italian and Soviet "revisionists." Attacking Zhou Enlai by insinuation, **Chi Qun** said that films like this were actually made by spies and traitors.

APRIL 5 MOVEMENT (1976). Taking place simultaneously in major cities across the nation around the Qingming Festival—traditionally a time to "sweep the graves" (*saomu*) and pay homage to the dead—this political event was at once a public mourning for the late Premier **Zhou Enlai** and a mass protest against the ultra-leftist faction of the **Chinese Communist Party** (CCP) leadership headed by **Jiang Qing**. Commemoration as a form of protest was the invention of the April 5 Movement. The widely shared discontent with **Mao Zedong**'s radical policies erupted for the first time, and this public outburst of grief and rage anticipated the swift ending of the Cultural Revolution soon after the death of Mao and the downfall of the Jiang Qing group, the **Gang of Four**.

See also NANJING INCIDENT (1976); TIANANMEN INCIDENT (1976).

ARMED CONFLICT. (*Wudou.*) Factional fighting among mass organizations became widespread in 1967 when those organizations began to take over provincial and local governments during the **power seizure** movement. In some places, especially where **People's Liberation Army** (PLA) troops took sides while on a "left-supporting" mission, military weapons were used in the fighting. In July and September 1967, **Jiang Qing** twice voiced support for the slogan "Verbal attack but armed defense," which further intensified nationwide violence. Between summer 1967 and summer 1968, factional fighting escalated into large-scale armed conflicts in many provinces. In some provinces, army troops were split and fought among themselves. According to official estimate, a million guns were in the hands of civilians at the time. This was a time that Chairman **Mao Zedong** referred to as a period of "all-round civil war" that eventually claimed hundreds of thousands of lives.

To end factional violence and nationwide chaos, Mao made several decisive moves in July 1968. He authorized nationwide issuance of two party documents (**July 3 Public Notice** and **July 24 Public Notice**) concerning armed conflicts in Guangxi Zhuang Autonomous Region and Shaanxi Province and indicated the broader applications of these documents. He dispatched a **workers propaganda team** of over 30,000 members led by PLA

Escorting captives after a violent factional battle at the Shanghai Diesel Engine Factory, 4 August 1967.

officers to end a prolonged factional battle known as the **One-Hundred-Day Armed Conflict on the Tsinghua Campus** in Beijing. And he sent all college students away from campuses and thus dissolved a major force of factional violence. Later in 1968, armed conflict gradually receded in the nation.

ARMED CONFLICT IN GUANGXI (1967–1968). One of the longest and deadliest factional battles in the country, the escalating armed conflict in Guangxi Zhuang Autonomous Region caused the central leadership, with **Mao Zedong**'s endorsement, to issue a harshly worded **July 3 Public Notice** in 1968 to stop the violence. The nationwide issuance of this document was the first of a series of decisive steps that Mao took in summer 1968 to end what he called an "all-round civil war" in the country.

Beginning in April 1967, mass organizations in Guangxi split into two camps: the **conservative** Joint Headquarters, on the one hand, and the 4-22 **rebel** faction with its allies, on the other. Factional violence started in late 1967 and escalated in 1968. With the support of the former first party secretary of the autonomous region, **Wei Guoqing**, as well as the army troops of the Guangxi military district and the local militia, the Joint Headquarters gained the upper hand in armed fighting. The 4-22 faction and its allies won support from the 141st Division of the **People's Liberation Army** (PLA) field army and initially had much sympathy from central leaders in Beijing until mid-1968 when they began to storm military warehouses, clash with army soldiers, and stop cargo trains to seize military supplies that were being transported to Vietnam. This effectively halted the major railway transportation system in Guangxi for more than a month.

Although the July 3 Public Notice from Beijing did not mention any mass organization by name, the document apparently was aimed more at the 4-22 faction in denouncing its weapon seizures, the clashes with the military, and the railway blockade as "counterrevolutionary crimes" committed by "a small handful of class enemies." This harsh condemnation was then used by the Joint Headquarters and its supporters to justify another wave of persecution and killings of members of its political rivals before the final end of violence and establishment of the Guangxi **Revolutionary Committee** in late August 1968. The persecution in some cases also involved **cannibalism**. Throughout the armed conflict and persecution, tens of thousands—perhaps as many as a hundred thousand—people were killed in Guangxi. Most of the dead were members of the 4-22 rebel faction and those of the so-called **five black categories**.

ARMY PROPAGANDA TEAM. (*Junxuandui.*) This term was a short form for the "**People's Liberation Army Mao Zedong Thought** Propaganda Team" (*jiefangjun Mao Zedong sixiang xuanchuan dui*). As part of **Mao Zedong**'s effort to restore order to the nation—and, in some cases, to end factional violence immediately—teams consisting of army officers and soldiers were dispatched starting in summer 1968 to schools, research institutions, and some government agencies plagued with factional conflicts. The first army propaganda team was sent to Tsinghua University in Beijing on 27 July, together with a **workers propaganda team**, to stop a prolonged bloody clash between two rival **Red Guard** organizations there. As in the case of Tsinghua, an army propaganda team was often joined by a workers propaganda team when it was dispatched to a certain institution, and army officers usually held leading positions within the combined group.

The propaganda teams were instrumental in taking control of widespread anarchy and helping to establish new authorities. But they were much less effective in governing the institutions not only due to their characteristic adherence to a line of political propaganda but also due to their lack of necessary knowledge and experience in managing cultural, educational, academic, and government affairs. In August 1972, about a year after the downfall of Marshal **Lin Biao**, the Central Committee (CC) of the **Chinese Communist Party** (CCP) issued an order to pull out army propaganda teams from the institutions where party authorities had been reestablished. Before long, all army propaganda teams withdrew, while workers propaganda teams, already diminished and still diminishing, stayed on until a year after the Cultural Revolution was over.

AUGUST 4 INCIDENT (1967). Also known as the Shanghai Diesel [Engine Factory] United Headquarters Incident, the bloodshed of 4 August 1967 was the gravest case of factional violence in Shanghai. There were two mass organizations in the Shanghai Diesel Engine Factory that had been in intense conflict with each other for the first half of 1967: the East-Is-Red (*dongfang hong*) Rebels Headquarters who had joined the citywide organization **Workers Command Post** led by **Wang Hongwen**, and the Workers United Rebels Headquarters who had been accusing Wang and the Workers Command Post of jeopardizing production, blockading transportation, and provoking violence. On 18 July 1967, a dispute among workers belonging to different factions turned violent and resulted in the death of a workshop party secretary.

In the capacity of vice-chairman of the Shanghai **Revolutionary Committee**—the current municipal power organ—Wang sided with the Workers Command Post and ordered the Workers United Headquarters to submit a list of murderers for interrogation. On 4 August, Wang mobilized 100,000 workers to carry out a battle plan against the Workers United Headquarters. Heavy fighting lasted more than 10 hours, leaving 18 people dead and 983 wounded. The factory was so badly damaged that production closed down for two months. Members of the Workers United Headquarters who were not in the factory on 4 August were forced to "make up" the beatings they missed. The incident of factional violence ended with a total victory of Wang's **rebel** faction and won the praise of **Zhang Chunqiao** as a "beautiful battle."

AZALEA MOUNTAIN. (*Dujuanshan.*) One of the few modern Peking operas performed during the Cultural Revolution besides the **eight model dramas**, *Azalea Mountain* is about the transformation of a greenwood gang of uprising peasants into an orderly unit of **Mao Zedong**'s army in the Jinggang Mountain revolutionary base area during the early stages of the Chinese Communist revolution. Originally a stage play, *Azalea Mountain* was adapted for the Peking Opera by the Peking Opera Troupe of Ningxia Hui Autonomous Region in 1963 and by the Peking Opera Troupe of Beijing in 1964. During 1968 and 1969, **Jiang Qing** became interested in making over the play according to her idea of model drama, especially the so-called **three prominences** principle. The new version, finally produced by the Peking Opera Troupe of Beijing in 1973 following Jiang's instructions, was vastly different from the 1963 and 1964 versions: the role of the male protagonist, the peasant leader, in earlier versions was modified in the later version to the extent that the heroine Ke Xiang (He Xiang in earlier versions), the female representative of the **Chinese Communist Party** (CCP) who wins the trust and respect of the peasant troops and leads them through struggles against both the armed local tyrants from without and a hidden class enemy—a traitor—from within, became the sole center of the play. She was elevated to such heights as to become a flawless, perfect, superhuman revolutionary stereotype.

B

BADGES OF CHAIRMAN MAO. Although badges carrying the image of **Mao Zedong** first appeared in the 1940s during the Rectification Campaign in Yan'an, it was not until late 1966 and early 1967 that wearing Mao badges became en vogue and a rage for the whole nation, marking the height of the **personality cult** of Mao during the Cultural Revolution. In the early years of the Cultural Revolution, more than 90 percent of the Chinese population wore Mao badges. According to Premier **Zhou Enlai** by the time of his speech on economic planning in March 1969, in which he deplored the wasteful use of aluminum in producing larger and larger badges, some 2.2 billion Mao badges had been produced since summer 1966. In all, some 2.5 to 5 billion badges in more than 20,000 variations were manufactured during the 10 years of the Cultural Revolution.

Most badges show a left profile of Mao's head, some a frontal view, and still others his whole figure. The predominant background color of the badges is red. A common representation of Mao as the "red sun in the heart of the people" shows red or golden rays radiating from Mao's portrait at the center. The badges often have as background a historical theme of Chinese revolution, which is sometimes labeled with a name or highlighted with a slogan. While the badges were considered a display of the wearer's loyalty to Mao and enthusiasm for the revolution, wearing badges also served the purpose of protecting the wearer from suspicion of disloyalty, although in some places and at some times, those who were said to have a bad family background were forbidden to wear them.

Noting the waste of industrial material in badge production, Mao protested in 1969, "Give our airplanes back to us!" After that, the Central Committee (CC) of the **Chinese Communist Party** (CCP) issued the circular "Certain Issues Worthy of Attention concerning the Promotion of Chairman Mao's Image" (dated 12 June 1969) to stop mass production of Mao badges. After the downfall of **Lin Biao**, who was the nation's loudest advocate for Mao's personality cult, in September 1971, the number of people wearing Mao badges declined rapidly. By the mid-1970s, only a handful of government officials and some farmers in the countryside still wore them.

In the initial stages of the Cultural Revolution, Mao badges were primarily obtained through one's work unit or could be purchased at certain stores in urban areas. But production fell so short of the nation's demand in both quantity and variety that in mid-1967 a black market for Mao badges sprang up in cities throughout China. These illegal markets were speedily banned by the government. After the Cultural Revolution, however, Mao badges were traded again on the market and became profitable items for collectors.

BAIYANGDIAN POET GROUP. The Baiyangdian Poet Group was a reading and poetry-writing group of **educated youths** in the Baiyangdian Lake District, Hebei Province. In January 1969, Meng Ke, Genzi, and Duoduo went with their classmates at the Beijing No. 3 Middle School to Baiyangdian to settle down and be reeducated by the farmers there. Soon they organized a reading group. Their readings included some of the "**grey books and yellow books**" (foreign books translated into Chinese for ranking officials). Many of these books were part of the personal collection of Genzi's parents. Others, especially books of foreign literature, were obtained from underground literary salons in Beijing. Sharing the same interest in literature and rejecting the Communist party's propagandistic doctrine of art, the three young men wrote poetry and became readers and critics of each other's work. Meng Ke and Duoduo agreed to exchange "yearbooks" of their poetry every New Year's Eve. Close contact and frequent exchanges among these poets resulted in some remarkable similarities in the early examples of their poetic composition, such as their embrace of free verse, the richness of often personified natural imagery, the occasional use of highly private symbolism, and their shared fondness for a grandiloquent and humorous tone. These affinities showed the distinct features of what scholars later called "experimental poetry." Bei Dao and Jiang He, two prominent voices of the "obscure poetry" of the late 1970s and the early 1980s, visited the Baiyangdian district frequently to exchange materials and views on poetry with Meng Ke, Duoduo, and Genzi while enjoying the beauty of the lake district. These travels also stimulated the writing of experimental poetry.

Despite political repression, young poets of the Baiyangdian group entered a golden era of artistic creation in the early 1970s while in the countryside. Most of their major poems were completed during this period, including some critically acclaimed works of modern Chinese poetry, such as Genzi's "The Month of March and the End" (1971), Meng Ke's "Sky" (1973), and Duoduo's "When People Stand Up for Their Snoring" (1972). Meng Ke completed his three collections of poems in 1972, and Duoduo put together his first collection in the same year. Since no works of literature other than those of propaganda were produced during the Cultural Revolution, underground poetry such as the works of the Baiyangdian group shocked readers with its freshness when it began to surface in the late 1970s and created a new direction for Chinese poetry.

See also UNDERGROUND READING MOVEMENT.

BAREFOOT DOCTOR. (*Chijiao yisheng.*) Barefoot doctors were part farmer and part doctor with minimal training in both Chinese and Western medicine. The idea of a farmer as a doctor originated in rural parts of Shanghai where peasants were usually barefoot (hence the term) while working in the wet rice fields. Although the first group of barefoot doctors was trained in 1958, they did not become popular until a report relating the "revolution in medical education" to barefoot doctors was published in the **Chinese Communist Party**'s official organ *Red Flag* in March 1968. Along with the development of various kinds of collective health care in the countryside, troops of barefoot doctors expanded rapidly nationwide from 1968 on to become a million strong by 1973. Although they lacked professional skills, barefoot doctors helped alleviate the drastic shortage of professionally trained doctors in rural areas and helped improve health and hygiene conditions to a certain extent.

However, the success of barefoot doctors was often blown out of proportion by official media. Additionally, **Mao Zedong**'s dismissal of the central government's Ministry of Hygiene as an agency of "urban masters" led to the invention of a "medical revolution" policy called "post exchange" during the Cultural Revolution. Under this policy, a large number of urban medical professionals were sent to the countryside to be reeducated and reformed, many of them working in the fields, while some barefoot doctors were assigned to work in urban hospitals, which was well beyond their capability. The system of employing barefoot doctors began to phase out after the Cultural Revolution. In January 1985, the Ministry of Hygiene delegitimized the use of the term "barefoot doctors"; in its place were the terms "rural doctors" and "health workers," depending on qualifications.

BEIJING PARTY COMMITTEE REORGANIZATION. The Beijing Party Committee Reorganization was one of the landmark decisions made by the central leadership at the **enlarged Politburo sessions, 4–26 May 1966,** at which the Cultural Revolution was officially launched. The reshuffling of the **Chinese Communist Party** (CCP) Beijing Municipal Committee was a major step **Mao Zedong** took to remove what he considered to be an obstacle to his Cultural Revolution program.

On 10 November 1965, **Yao Wenyuan**'s article "On the New Historical Drama *Hai Rui Dismissed from Office,*" which was soon to be known as the "blasting fuse" of the Cultural Revolution, appeared in the Shanghai news-

paper *Wenhui Daily*. The article accuses **Wu Han**—the author of the historical play who was also a renowned historian and a deputy mayor of Beijing—
of using a story of the past to criticize China's Communist policies. **Peng
Zhen**, mayor and first party secretary of Beijing, called the municipal committee to a meeting that same day to discuss Yao's article. Almost all of the
committee members disagreed with Yao's charge. Without knowing Mao's
full support for Yao, Peng ordered Beijing newspapers not to reprint Yao's
article. A few days later, when the article was printed as a pamphlet by
Shanghai People's Press for nationwide distribution, Peng responded to an
inquiry by the Beijing Xinhua Bookstore with the instruction that bookstores
were not to order any copies. In early 1966, as the criticism of Wu Han and a
few other "academic authorities" continued, the Peng-led **Five-Person Cultural Revolution Small Group** prepared a document that, despite its leftist-
sounding rhetoric, stressed the importance of keeping criticism within the
realm of academia. With approval from the Politburo, the document, known
as the **February Outline**, was disseminated nationwide as a policy guide to
the ongoing academic criticism and debate.

Peng's series of actions appeared to Mao to be a conscious resistance to
his developing Cultural Revolution program. In March 1966, Mao criticized
the CCP Beijing Municipal Committee and the Five-Person Group on several
occasions, calling the Beijing party committee an "impenetrable and watertight independent kingdom." Mao also threatened to dismiss the Beijing
committee should it continue to "protect bad people." In April, Mao chaired
an enlarged meeting of the Politburo Standing Committee at which decisions
were made to abrogate the February Outline and dismiss the Five-Person
Cultural Revolution Small Group. At the enlarged Politburo sessions held in
Beijing in May 1966, Peng was denounced as a member of the **Peng-Luo-
Lu-Yang Anti-Party Clique**, and a motion was adopted that the Beijing
party committee be reorganized. On 4 June, *People's Daily* announced the
central leadership's appointment of **Li Xuefeng**, first secretary of the CCP
North China Bureau, and **Wu De**, first party secretary of Jilin Province, as
first and second secretaries of Beijing's new municipal party committee. In
the meantime, many officials of the old municipal committee and municipal
government were condemned as members of Peng's **"black gang"** and were
subjected to brutal physical abuse by the masses at **struggle meetings**.

Before long, however, the reorganized Beijing Municipal Committee ran
into trouble, too. Because of its decision to dispatch **work groups**, first to
Peking University and then to many other schools in Beijing, the committee
was criticized in autumn 1966 for carrying out a **Bourgeois Reactionary
Line** of **Liu Shaoqi** and **Deng Xiaoping**. It was sidelined from power until
April 1967 when it was finally replaced by the new power organ Beijing
Revolutionary Committee.

BIAN ZHONGYUN (1916–1966). A native of Wuwei, Anhui Province, Bian joined the **Chinese Communist Party** (CCP) in 1941 and graduated from Qilu University in 1945. When the Cultural Revolution began in 1966, Bian was deputy principal of the prestigious Beijing Normal University Female Middle School, where she had worked since 1949. On groundless charges, she was denounced and **struggled against** by students in late June 1966. On 5 August 1966, five days after the **Red Guards** organization was formed at the school, she, along with four other school officials, was attacked by the Red Guards. Bian died after several hours of humiliation and brutal beating. This was Beijing's first case of the killing of education workers by the Red Guards. Many cases followed, and violence and brutality escalated, especially after the **mass rally of 18 August 1966.** At this rally, **Mao Zedong** received a Red Guard armband from **Song Binbin**, a Red Guard leader from Beijing Normal University Female Middle School, whereupon he recommended that her name be changed from genteel "Binbin" to the overtly militant "Yaowu," which means in Chinese "be valiant."

In 1978, Bian's name was officially cleared at a memorial service organized by the CCP committee of Beijing's Xicheng District, but the legal proceedings that Bian's widower, Wang Jingyao, brought against the killers in 1979 were rejected by the district People's Procuratorate on the grounds that the actionable period had already expired. A school photo album entitled *The Glorious Ninety Years* was published for the anniversary celebration of Beijing Normal University Female Middle School (by then renamed Beijing Normal University Experimental Middle School) on 9 September 2007. The inclusion of the picture of Mao receiving a Red Guard armband from Song with Bian's portrait printed on the opposite page prompted protest from Wang and much criticism by the public.

BIG-CHARACTER POSTER. (*Dazibao.*) Written in black ink with penbrushes on large sheets of paper and pasted on walls or specially made poster boards for a standing crowd to read, big-character posters were the major form of mass communication during the Cultural Revolution. While the government controlled major media channels such as newspapers and radio broadcasting, the masses used big-character posters as effective vehicles with which to express their views. The designated areas for posting and reading posters on school campuses and in factories and government agencies became centers of activity and information gathering as well as networking places for visitors.

Chairman **Mao Zedong** used the big-character posters of the masses as a weapon against his political enemies in the party leadership. The nationwide broadcasting and publication of what Mao called the "**first Marxist-Leninist big-character poster**" by **Nie Yuanzi** and her colleagues at Peking University on 1 June 1966 marked the beginning of the Cultural Revolution for the

Big-character posters on the campus of Peking University, summer 1966.

public. To mobilize the masses against **Liu Shaoqi** and **Deng Xiaoping**, Mao attempted to identify himself with the masses by calling his militant piece, "**Bombarding the Headquarters**," "my big-character poster."

After the Cultural Revolution, big-character posters remained popular as a method of expressing dissent, especially during the Democracy Wall Movement in the late 1970s. In September 1980, the National People's Congress outlawed big-character posters in a revised constitution.

BIGGEST CAPITALIST-ROADER WITHIN THE PARTY. Along with "**China's Khrushchev**," this term was a reference to President **Liu Shaoqi** in official media during 1967 and 1968. Liu's name was not mentioned until after the **Twelfth Plenum of the Eighth Central Committee of the Chinese Communist Party** (13–31 October 1968).

See also CAPITALIST-ROADERS.

BLACK GANG. (*Heibang.*) This pejorative term was initially used in summer 1966 to refer to the so-called **Three-Family Village Anti-Party Clique** of **Deng Tuo**, **Wu Han**, and **Liao Mosha**. The reference soon extended to the old Beijing Municipal Committee of the **Chinese Communist Party** (CCP) led by **Peng Zhen**. Anyone who was then associated with the municipal committee was called a member or an element of the "black gang." As the Cultural Revolution evolved, "black gang element" became a label for any denounced "academic authority" or party official. The term continued to be used in this way until 1968 when the central leadership began to distinguish between "unrepentant" and "corrigible" **capitalist-roaders**, associating "black gang" only with the former.

BLACK WIND IN NOVEMBER. (*Shiyiyue heifeng.*) Also known as the "Black Wind in December," this officially sanctioned pejorative refers to a series of **big-character posters** that appeared in Beijing in the last two months of 1966 criticizing the Cultural Revolution faction of the **Chinese Communist Party** (CCP) central leadership—the **Central Cultural Revolution Small Group** (CCRSG) in particular. Although most of the student authors acted independently, they were part of a general reaction of **conservatives**—usually those with a "red" family background—against the campaign to criticize the so-called **Bourgeois Reactionary Line** of **Liu Shaoqi** and **Deng Xiaoping**. In the early stages of the Cultural Revolution, they had either supported or tolerated the **blood lineage theory** and abused students from politically disadvantaged families. Politically, they sympathized with the old party establishment represented by Liu and Deng. The CCRSG became their main target due to its sweeping denunciation of party veterans, its support for the emerging **rebel** faction, and its encouragement of politically disadvantaged students in criticizing their abusers in the Criticize the Bourgeois Reactionary Line campaign.

The better-known posters representing this conservative reaction included "Kick Aside the CCRSG and Closely Follow Chairman Mao in the Revolution" (2 December) by a number of student organizations at Beijing Institute of Forestry and the four installments of "Question the CCRSG" (late November and early December) by the August 1 Column of the Beijing Institute of Aeronautics **Red Guards**. The former questions the legitimacy of the CCRSG by evoking the **Sixteen Articles**, which demanded that power organs for leading the Cultural Revolution be established through a democratic process of broad election under the CCP leadership.

Also prominent among the posters labeled "reactionary" was the voice of students of the rebel faction, such as the "Open Letter to Comrade Lin Biao" (15 November) by two high school students assuming the unified pen name **Yilin Dixi**, which criticized **Lin Biao** for his formulation of a "**peak theory**" and for his promotion of the **personality cult** of **Mao Zedong**. By the end of December 1966, the massive protest by the rebel faction in defense of the CCRSG and the arrest of most of the student authors by the authorities put to an end the so-called Black Wind.

BLOOD LINEAGE THEORY. (*Xuetonglun.*) This popular variation of the long-standing organizational policy of the **Chinese Communist Party** (CCP) known as "**class line**" or "class status" was embraced by some **Red Guards**, especially those who came to be known as the **Old Red Guards**, in the initial stage of the Cultural Revolution. According to the blood lineage theory, one's family background determines and defines who one is. People who belong to the "**five red categories**," especially children of ranking officials, are "**born-reds**" (*zilaihong*). They are trusted as successors to the revolutionary cause and enjoy political privileges. By contrast, people who belong to the "**seven black categories**" are deemed politically untrustworthy. Already deprived of equal opportunity for college education, employment, and promotion in the regular practice of the official CCP class policy, they were dismissed as "sons of dogs" (*gouzaizi*) by many Old Red Guards on the grounds of the "bad blood" in them. The CCP organizational policy required authorities to "consider family class status, but not just family class status, and stress the importance of political behavior." Although more moderate than its popular version, this policy was never seriously implemented.

In June and July 1966, a couplet (*duilian*) that would become the most popular expression of the blood lineage theory was circulating among students at Peking University Middle School. The parallel lines read, "If the father is a hero, the son is a real man," and "If the father is a reactionary, the son is a bastard." The **work group** on a mission to direct the Cultural Revolution at the school was critical of the couplet. But after **Mao Zedong** dismissed the work groups as a repressive force in late July, the couplet circulated rapidly and widely on middle school campuses all over Beijing. On 29 July 1966, some students posted the couplet at the Beijing Institute of Aeronautics Middle School, with the original two parallel lines running vertically in the form of traditional Chinese calligraphy scrolls and an added "It is basically like this, making demons anxious" placed horizontally on top. The couplet, along with its several variations, became a subject of heated debate among students in Beijing. Those who embraced the idea represented by the couplet, including a majority of ranking officials' children, made the family background a primary criterion for admitting fellow students into their own Red Guard organizations, keeping out whoever was not "born-red." The couplet served as both a prompt and a justification for the humiliation, torture, and killing of innocent people of the "seven black categories" and their children during Beijing's **Red August**—a brutal act perpetrated mostly by Old Red Guards whom Chairman Mao Zedong received for the first time at the **mass rally of 18 August 1966**. At a debate on 20 August 1966, **Tan Lifu**, a leader of the Red Guards at Beijing Industrial University and the son of a ranking official, gave a long speech in support of the couplet. Tan's speech, printed and widely distributed, helped make the blood lineage theory and its controversy well known across China.

The blood lineage theory became a political issue in the central leadership in late 1966 during the campaign against the so-called **Bourgeois Reactionary Line** allegedly carried out by **Liu Shaoqi** and **Deng Xiaoping**. To win support of the students from non-proletarian families, **Chen Boda**, head of the **Central Cultural Revolution Small Group** (CCRSG), dismissed "born-redism" as reactionary at the CCP **Central Committee Work Sessions on 9–28 October 1966** and linked it to the Bourgeois Reactionary Line. Chen's speech outlawed the controversial couplet and made the blood lineage theory officially a target of criticism.

A majority of students who had opposed the theory at the outset now became much more vocal with their views. The best known critic was the young worker **Yu Luoke**, who was to present a point-by-point refutation of the blood lineage theory in his article "**On Family Background**." However, since Yu's criticism went so far as to repudiate the system of political discrimination underlying the CCP class policy and to embrace the idea of equality and human rights, he was eventually named a counterrevolutionary and executed by the authorities.

BO XILAI (1949–). First party secretary of Chongqing, China's most populous city, from 2007 to 2012, and a Politburo member, Bo Xilai was brought down on charges of graft; however, the more important cause of his downfall, as widely perceived though officially unacknowledged, was his ambition for power in the form of a challenge to the central leadership of the **Chinese Communist Party** (CCP) by reviving certain Cultural Revolution–style policies in a populist "Chongqing Model."

A native of Beijing and a son of veteran Communist **Bo Yibo**, Bo Xilai was a **Red Guard** at Beijing's elite No. 4 Middle School in the early stages of the Cultural Revolution. An advocate of the **blood lineage theory**, he engaged in brutal activities denouncing and physically abusing his fellow students of the so-called **five black categories**—that is, before he himself was labeled as such when his own father was purged and imprisoned as a leading member of the so-called **Sixty-One Traitors Clique** in 1967. For more than four years, Bo was disciplined for juvenile delinquency and forced to perform manual labor. Then, he became a factory worker in 1972, a student of history at Peking University in 1978, and a graduate student at the Chinese Academy of Social Sciences in 1979.

Bo started his official career in 1982 with both a master's degree and a CCP membership (since 1980) in hand. In late 2007, after serving at various government posts at local, provincial, and central levels, including mayor of Dalian, governor of Liaoning, and minister of commerce, Bo Xilai was elected to the Politburo of the CCP Central Committee and named party secretary of Chongqing. The combination of his trade, public housing, and infrastructure-building policies and a series of popular political campaigns known as "Sing Red and Combat the Black" (*changhong dahei*, requiring citizens to sing Mao-era revolutionary songs and cracking down on alleged organized crimes and widespread corruption) was said to constitute a "Chongqing Model" of reform. Bo's political campaigns, however, were riddled with irony: despite his earlier denunciation of Mao, Bo reportedly acknowledged that reviving "red" culture and Mao cult and embracing Mao-style populism was the only option for him—that is, the only way for him, a disbeliever rather than a faithful, to gather the masses around him and build his political capital for further advancement in the CCP power structure. He was popularly known for cracking down on corruption and organized crimes, but it was his right-hand man and chief executioner of his Mao-style "Combat the Black" campaign who exposed Bo's own involvement in graft and crime cover-up and his wife's implication in a mafia-style murder case. Eventually, charges of bribery, embezzlement, and abuse of power were brought against Bo Xilai. He was dismissed from office and expelled from the CCP in late 2012. From July to September 2013, Bo was tried, convicted, and sentenced to life imprisonment.

BO YIBO (1908–2007). Deputy premier of the State Council (SC) since 1956, Bo was denounced during the Cultural Revolution as a member of the so-called **Sixty-One Traitors Clique**, a major case fabricated by the ultra-leftist faction of the **Chinese Communist Party** (CCP) leadership to incriminate President **Liu Shaoqi**.

A native of Dingxiang, Shanxi Province, Bo Yibo joined the CCP in 1925 and soon became a leader in the CCP's underground work in northern China. In 1931, Bo was arrested in Beijing by the Nationalist government. In 1936, the North China Bureau of the CCP—with the support of Liu Shaoqi, who was then in charge of the work of the bureau, and with the approval of the central party leadership—instructed Bo to sign an anti-Communist declaration prepared by the Nationalists to earn his release. After the founding of the People's Republic of China (PRC), Bo became one of the most influential leaders on economic matters: first as minister of finance (1949–1953) and then director of the State Economic Commission (since 1956).

In autumn 1966, as **Mao Zedong**'s intention to bring down Liu became clear, **Kang Sheng** began to gather material from newspapers from 1936 as incriminating evidence against Bo and others as members of a "traitors clique" allegedly formed by Liu. Soon after Mao approved Kang's work in February 1967, Bo was arrested and imprisoned. The 20,000-word appeal that Bo wrote in prison in summer 1967 was of no avail. Bo's name was not cleared until late 1978 when the CCP Organization Department finally issued an investigative report on the "Case of the Sixty-One," dismissing the charges against Bo and 60 others as groundless.

In 1979, Bo was reinstated as deputy premier of the SC and a member of the CCP Central Committee. In 1982, he was elected deputy director of the Central Advisory Committee, a newly established body of retired ranking leaders. In his retirement, Bo still exerted considerable, mostly conservative, influence on the CCP decision-making process. He was also one of the few ranking CCP leaders to produce substantive, and often revealing, memoirs.

Bo's second son, **Bo Xilai**, a **Red Guard** at Beijing's No. 4 Middle School during the early stages of the Cultural Revolution, was on his way to power after the revolution. In late 2007, after serving various government posts at local, provincial, and central levels, Bo Xilai was elected to the Politburo of the CCP Central Committee and named party secretary of China's most populous city, Chongqing. The combination of his trade, public housing, and infrastructure-building policies and a series of political campaigns known as "Sing Red and Strike Black" (*changhong dahei*, requiring citizens to sing Mao-era revolutionary songs and cracking down on organized crimes and corruption) was said to constitute a "Chongqing Model" of reform. From July to September 2013, Bo Xilai was tried and convicted on charges of bribery, embezzlement, and abuse of power and sentenced to life imprisonment.

BOMBARDING THE HEADQUARTERS. (*Paoda silingbu.*) This was a **big-character poster** that Chairman **Mao Zedong** wrote on 5 August 1966 during the **Eleventh Plenum of the Eighth Central Committee of the Chinese Communist Party** (CCP) attacking President **Liu Shaoqi**. The poster was originally a long note Mao put down in the margins of the 2 June 1966 issue of *Beijing Daily*. Mao's secretary proofread the note and made a verbatim transcription of the original. Mao then added the title "Bombarding the Headquarters—My Own Big-Character Poster." The final version of the poster contains 205 Chinese characters.

In the poster, Mao denounces the leadership of Liu and Deng Xiaoping, without naming either, as "bourgeois headquarters" that had been hostile and repressive toward the Cultural Revolution since early June. In strong terms, he accuses them of persecuting the dissenters and imposing a "white terror" of the bourgeois dictatorship. Mao also connects the current situation with what he calls a right deviation of 1962 and a wrong tendency of 1964 that was "'Left' in form but Right in essence," both implicating Liu. The former points to the critical measures taken by the CCP leadership—especially at an enlarged Politburo meeting chaired by Liu in late February 1962—to adjust the radical policies of the late 1950s that caused the great famine of 1958–1962. The latter refers to the earlier guidelines for the Socialist Education Movement based on Liu's ideas.

On 7 August, copies of Mao's big-character poster were printed and distributed to all participants of the plenum. Liu and Deng immediately became targets of attack. On the following day, the Central Committee (CC) passed the Resolution of the CCP Central Committee concerning the Great Proletarian Cultural Revolution, commonly known as the Sixteen Articles. On 17 August, Mao's big-character poster was issued across China by the CC as a central party document. From then on, the title of the big-character poster, "Bombarding the Headquarters," became a popular slogan for rebels attacking party officials at various levels.

One year after Mao wrote his big-character poster, *People's Daily* published the entire text in its 5 August 1967 issue with an editorial entitled "Bombarding the Bourgeois Headquarters." Another editorial, "Completely Destroy the Bourgeois Headquarters—Commemorating the First Anniversary of the Eleventh Plenum of the Ninth CCP Central Committee," came out in *Red Flag* on 17 August. Both editorials consider Mao's big-character poster to be his bugle call to the campaign to overthrow Liu.

BOMBARDING ZHANG CHUNQIAO. This phrase refers to the efforts of some rebel organizations in Shanghai in bringing down **Zhang Chunqiao**, first in January 1967 and again in April 1968. During the **January Storm** of 1967, four attempts to seize power in Shanghai by different mass organizations—none of them Zhang's choice—were dismissed by Zhang as illegitimate. The College Red Guards **Revolutionary Committee** of Shanghai in particular, which had supported Zhang, felt betrayed when its own attempts to take over the municipal power met Zhang's opposition. On 28 January, some college **Red Guards** challenged Zhang and **Yao Wenyuan** in a six-hour debate. In the meantime, in reaction to Zhang's order to send army troops to Fudan University where his close associate **Xu Jingxian** was detained by two rebel organizations, thousands of students went into the streets with **big-character posters**, leaflets, and banners condemning Zhang for his double dealings with mass organizations and for his attack on the revered modern Chinese writer Lu Xun in the 1930s. The protest came to be known as the "28 January bombardment."

Preparations for another anti-Zhang rally and demonstration were under way in the early morning of 30 January when the **Central Cultural Revolution Small Group** (CCRSG), following instructions from Chairman **Mao Zedong**, sent an emergency missive that identified Zhang as part of Mao's "proletarian headquarters" and forbade demonstrations against him. With the full support of the powerful CCRSG and the largest local mass organization the **Workers Command Post**, Zhang, Yao, and their close associates in

Shanghai were now able to eliminate opposition and further consolidate their power in China's most populous city. Since the bombarding was denounced as "counterrevolutionary action" in the "Urgent Telegram," thousands of participants of the "bombardment" were mistreated, and at least 2,500 people were persecuted. Interrogation and torture left five people dead.

On 12 April 1968, big-character posters and handwritten slogans with the same charges against Zhang appeared again on the main streets of Shanghai. The action was planned by Hu Shoujun and some other students at Fudan University. Also involved were rebels at the Second Army Medical College who had been supported by **Lin Biao**. The protest was again put down. These two protests were said to have involved rebel organizations with some 100,000 to 200,000 members altogether, most of them students. After the events, they were mistreated and persecuted. The best-known case is that of the **Hu Shoujun Clique** in 1970; the number of deaths resulting from its persecution was said to amount to several hundred.

BORN-REDS. (*Zilaihong.*) This term started as a proud self-reference of the **Old Red Guards** embracing the **blood lineage theory**. It first appeared in August 1966 in "The Born-Reds Have Risen," a **big-character poster** by the Peking University Middle School Red Flag Combat Team, one of the earliest **Red Guard** organizations. "Born-reds" later became a popular term referring to anyone from any of the **"five red categories"** of families in the early stages of the Cultural Revolution. Red Guards who invented and first used the term were mostly children of ranking officials of the **Chinese Communist Party** (CCP) and the **People's Liberation Army** (PLA). Already of a privileged class above those of workers, peasants, and soldiers, which were also "red," they regarded themselves as natural successors to China's revolutionary cause—that is, natural successors to the power acquired by their parents' generation. They humiliated and abused students from politically disadvantaged families, especially those of the **"seven black categories,"** provoking much protest and creating much antagonism among students. This abuse took various forms, including the use of the pejorative "born-blacks," "born-yellows," and "sons-of-dogs" in contrast to "born-reds."

BOURGEOIS REACTIONARY LINE. This is a pejorative phrase that Chairman **Mao Zedong** adopted in autumn 1966 to designate the party policies that had been implemented in summer 1966 and, in Mao's view, deviated the thrust of the ongoing mass movement away from what he had intended to be the main target of the Cultural Revolution—the **capitalist-roaders** in the party leadership. Consequently, a Criticize the Bourgeois Reactionary Line campaign was launched in late 1966 against the alleged framers of these policies, President **Liu Shaoqi** and General Secretary **Deng Xiaoping**.

In early summer 1966, when student revolts erupted on college campuses and in middle schools in Beijing, Liu and Deng were in charge of the day-to-day affairs of the **Chinese Communist Party** (CCP). With the approval of Mao, who was away from Beijing, the Liu-Deng leadership adopted an old party policy for leading a political campaign and for dealing with extraordinary situations: it dispatched **work groups** to the most chaotic places to lead the mass movement and keep it under the control of the party. When disputes took place on a college campus, the work group there would typically protect party officials and denounce their challengers. In the meantime, the work groups allowed the persecution of the so-called **seven black categories**, which included those associated with the already fallen "**black gang**" of the old CCP Municipal Committee of Beijing.

Upon returning to Beijing, however, Mao began to criticize the work group policy. He wrote a short piece entitled "**Bombarding the Headquarters**—My Own Big-Character Poster" on 5 August, accusing some unnamed central and regional leaders of taking a "reactionary bourgeois stand" against the proletarian Cultural Revolution. However, in August and September, Mao's idea of getting at "those in power" (*dangquanpai*) and shaking up the party leadership from bottom to top was still not carried out, while student **Red Guards** began to focus their attention on a campaign called **Destroy the Four Olds**, targeting alleged class enemies mostly outside the party. Mao was contemplating a new move, and finally he settled on a Criticize the Bourgeois Reactionary Line campaign.

The term "Bourgeois Reactionary Line" appeared for the first time in an editorial of the party organ *Red Flag* published on 2 October 1966 (issue number 13). On 6 October 1966, the **Third Command Post** of college Red Guards in Beijing held a **mass rally** at the Workers' Stadium to declare war against the Bourgeois Reactionary Line. With the attendance of Premier **Zhou Enlai** and members of the **Central Cultural Revolution Small Group** (CCRSG) along with 100,000 people, this was arguably the most celebrated event of the campaign. In a speech delivered on 16 October at a work session of the CCP Central Committee, **Chen Boda**, head of the CCRSG, defined Mao's proletarian revolutionary line against the Bourgeois Reactionary Line on the basis of their attitudes toward the masses: Mao's line encouraged the masses to educate themselves and liberate themselves, Chen said, while the reactionary line carried out by the work groups was self-righteous and repressive. Chen also attempted to clarify Mao's **class line** while associating the Bourgeois Reactionary Line with the controversial **blood lineage theory** that was in fact more akin to Mao's own ultra-leftism.

Chen's interpretation of Mao's mass and class policies generated much enthusiasm among students from families other than those of the "**five red categories**." These students had been discriminated against in the early stages of the Cultural Revolution. Now that the Red Guard was no longer a patent for those from the so-called red families, these students, as part of the **rebel** faction of Red Guards that had been more tolerant of their family backgrounds than the **Old Red Guards**, were able to join Mao's crusading army against the party establishment from Liu and Deng down to grassroots levels. The Criticize the Bourgeois Reactionary Line campaign continued well into 1967 and prepared the way for the turbulent nationwide **power seizure** movement. This campaign also led to rehabilitations of some ordinary citizens who had been denounced under the work groups and of a still greater number of people who had been condemned and tortured under the "**mass dictatorship**" after the withdrawal of the work groups.

See also CENTRAL COMMITTEE WORK SESSIONS, 9–28 OCTOBER 1966.

BREAKING. (*Juelie.*) Directed by Li Wenhua and produced by the Beijing Film Studio in 1975, this film is based on a story about the forming of the Communist Labor University of Jiangxi Province in 1958. Its intention, however, is to attack the so-called revisionist line in education of both the late 1950s and the mid-1970s. The protagonist—Long Guozheng, president of the university—is a hero going against the tide of the "revisionist line." Long bases college admission decisions not on test scores but on the number of calluses on the palms of the candidate. He regards college professors as bourgeois intellectuals. In a comic episode, a professor with a foreign academic degree is ridiculed for specializing in "the function of a horse's tail." In short, the film epitomizes the Cultural Revolution's belittling of knowledge and politicizing of education. When the film was almost completed in October 1975, the conflict between the **Gang of Four** and **Deng Xiaoping** intensified. Following orders from Gang of Four supporters at the Beijing Film Studio, the crew added episodes to meet the needs of current politics. The veteran revolutionary and Long's political rival Cao Zhonghe, for instance, was labeled an "unrepentant **capitalist-roader**" in the party, a term soon to be associated with Deng in the **Counterattack the Right-Deviationist Reversal-of-Verdicts Trend** campaign.

Shortly after its release, the film became a popular tool for political education across China. With theater tickets distributed by party branches, people were obligated to watch it. The film was also praised by official media as an excellent work taking after the **eight model dramas** and reflecting a complete break with the "revisionist line in education." In the post-Mao era, critics dismissed the film as a notorious piece of "conspiratorial literature."

BRITISH CHARGÉ INCIDENT (1967). In a mass protest against the arrest of Chinese journalists by British colonial authorities in Hong Kong, some **Red Guards** set fire to the office building of the British chargé d'affaires in Beijing on 22 August 1967. Tensions in Hong Kong started in early May 1967 when a labor dispute took place and strikers and demonstrators clashed with the police. Partly due to the interference by members of the **Central Cultural Revolution Small Group** (CCRSG) **Wang Li** and **Guan Feng**, China's reaction to the Hong Kong crisis was so highly confrontational that about a million Beijing citizens, inspired by the official reaction, demonstrated in front of the British chargé office on 15 June 1967. Chaos in foreign affairs escalated after Wang told rebels in the Ministry of Foreign Affairs on 7 August that it was all right to "collar" Minister **Chen Yi** (here Wang was actually rephrasing **Mao Zedong**'s instructions) and to seize power at the Foreign Ministry.

The subsequent arrest of journalists in Hong Kong triggered another angry response from the masses in Beijing: on 22 August, Red Guards from the Beijing Foreign Language Institute, Beijing Normal University, Tsinghua University, and other schools, as well as many factory workers, held a "Mass Meeting of the Capital Proletarian Revolutionary Rebels Denouncing British Imperialist Crimes against China" in front of the British chargé office. Despite Premier **Zhou Enlai**'s specific directive forbidding violence against diplomatic establishments in China, the participants of the rally crashed into the offices of the British chargé that night, beating, smashing, confiscating, and burning automobiles and documents. They also burned the office building and **struggled against** the chargé d'affaires. In late August, Zhou reported to Mao on the chaotic state of foreign affairs. The British chargé incident and Zhou's report prompted Mao to take drastic measures for the first time against his trusted cultural revolutionaries: he named Wang's 7 August speech a "**poisonous weed**" and ordered the detention of Wang and Guan.

BYSTANDERS. (*Xiaoyaopai.*) This term refers to a large number of people who were neither **rebels** nor **conservatives** and who were not engaged in factional fighting during the Cultural Revolution. Bystanders usually did not have their own organizations. In the early stages of the Cultural Revolution, they were mostly students with undesirable family backgrounds who were either lacking revolutionary zeal or shunning dangerous Chinese politics. The setback for the conservative faction during the campaign to criticize the **Bourgeois Reactionary Line** and in the process of the **power seizure** movement turned some of its members into bystanders. As violent sectional fighting escalated nationwide in 1967 and 1968, more and more people, including a large number of rebels, became disillusioned with the revolution; they began to withdraw from their organizations and avoid **armed conflicts**. The mass of bystanders grew larger and faster as the Cultural Revolution continued to unfold.

C

CANNIBALISM IN GUANGXI. In spring and summer 1968, factional violence in Guangxi Zhuang Autonomous Region became so fierce that hatred of the rival faction led to cannibalism in several counties. The victims of this horrific crime also included those classified as the **"five black categories"** (landlords, rich peasants, counterrevolutionaries, bad elements, and rightists). The perpetration of cannibalism against this group was often seen as evidence of one's rightful indignation at class enemies and of one's acute proletarian class sentiment. According to a number of unofficial investigative reports, several hundred people were cannibalized in a six-month period from March to August 1968 in the autonomous region.

CAPITAL RED GUARD PICKETS. (*Shoudu hongweibing jiuchadui.*) Established by some **Red Guard** organizations in Beijing in summer 1966, the Pickets were meant to prescribe rules for Red Guards and to exercise control over the chaotic situation created by the Red Guards themselves. Except for a brief period immediately after the establishment of the Pickets, however, some picket members acted even more self-righteously and more violently than other Red Guards against innocent people in the second half of 1966.

During the campaigns to **destroy the Four Olds** and to sweep away **"cow-demons and snake-spirits"** in summer 1966, especially during the terrifying **Red August**, lawlessness and violence escalated. Humiliation and physical abuse were commonplace on the streets of Beijing. Red Guards **struggled against** and tortured schoolteachers, so-called **black gang** members from academic institutions, art and literary circles, and party and government organs, and people of the **"five black categories."** They searched and ransacked private homes and confiscated personal belongings in the name of Revolution. In the face of widespread chaos, 31 Red Guard organizations of Beijing secondary schools formed the Xicheng District Branch of the Capital Red Guard Pickets on 25 August 1966. In support of what appeared to be the Red Guards' self-regulating effort, leaders of the Beijing party committee and the State Council acknowledged the organization and maintained frequent contact with this organization for some time. Before long, Red Guards in Dongcheng District and Haidian District also formed Pickets. During its brief existence, the Xicheng District Pickets issued 13 decrees forbidding the searching of government offices and the abuse of ranking officials. According to these decrees, Red Guards were to notify the local authorities before searching a residence of anyone labeled under the "five black categories" or a capitalist, and make every effort to avoid violence. These decrees were largely in line with the stated policies of the central leadership at the time and helped contain violence and lawlessness to some extent, but not for long. As the war on the Four Olds raged and reached its height, physical abuse, including whipping, torturing, even downright killing, surged again.

As **Mao Zedong** launched the battle against those in power and moved to shake up the party and state apparatus, parents of many Picket members came under attack. Some members of the Pickets and **Old Red Guard** organizations became increasingly resistant to the new move; they willingly went back to attacking traditional "class enemies," mostly outside the party. To the Cultural Revolution faction of the central leadership, the Pickets now represented roadblocks to the revolution. On 16 December 1966, at a mass rally of Beijing middle school students and teachers to criticize the **Bourgeois Reactionary Line**, the **Central Cultural Revolution Small Group** (CCRSG) announced a decision by the central leadership to disband the Red Guard Pickets; the Pickets were accused of serving as the "military police of the bourgeois reactionary line." After the rally, various picket offices were ransacked and closed. A number of picket members were arrested. Despite several attempts to regenerate, the Pickets and the Old Red Guards they represented were never able to come back again as an effective political force.

CAPITAL RED GUARDS. (*Shoudu hongweibing.*) A major **Red Guard** newspaper, *Capital Red Guards* made its debut on 13 September 1966 as a publication of the Capital Revolutionary Rebel Headquarters of College Red Guards (popularly known as the **Third Command Post**). This was a prominent mass organization supported by **Mao Zedong** and the **Central Cultural Revolution Small Group** (CCRSG) during the Criticize the **Bourgeois Reactionary Line** campaign. As the headquarters sent its members throughout the country to promote **rebel** activities, the paper was distributed across China and had great influence on mass movements far beyond the capital. In February 1967, when college Red Guards in Beijing came together to form a grand alliance known as the Capital Congress of College Red Guards, *Capital Red Guards* became the official newspaper of the new organization after its 32nd issue. As the publication continued—totaling nearly 70 issues from March 1967 to September 1968—it carried policy announcements of the **Chinese Communist Party** (CCP) and speeches by central leaders, publicized stories of Red Guards, and reported on major events on college campuses both in Beijing and in the provinces. In July 1968, Mao Zedong and the CCP Central Committee began to dispatch **workers propaganda teams** and **army propaganda teams** to all college campuses in Beijing. This decisive move of the central leadership soon put to an end the college Red Guard movement as well as the publication of *Capital Red Guards*.

CAPITALIST-ROADERS. (*Zouzipai.*) When first used by **Mao Zedong** in January 1965 in a party policy guideline for the **Socialist Education Movement**, "capitalist-roaders"—literally "those in power within the party who take the capitalist road"—apparently referred to party officials who implemented certain pragmatic economic policies in the countryside in response to the disaster of Mao's Great Leap Forward policies and hence, in Mao's view, betrayed socialism. In the **Sixteen Articles**, a party resolution adopted at the **Eleventh Plenum of the Eighth Central Committee of the Chinese Communist Party** (CCP) in August 1966, the term "capitalist-roaders" refers to party officials who opposed the Cultural Revolution. According to Mao's theory of **continuing revolution under the dictatorship of the proletariat**, capitalist-roaders were representatives of the bourgeoisie within the ruling Communist party; they had either "wormed their way into the party" or had become corrupted while in power; they were China's Khrushchevs aiming to restore capitalism in China. And yet, since the term was never clearly defined and since virtually no party leader advocated capitalism, "capitalist-roader" became a catch-phrase in political witch-hunting.

Mao used this criminal title effectively to mobilize the masses and shake up the party establishment, especially in the early stages of the Cultural Revolution. In the central leadership, those whom Mao considered to be his political rivals or their followers were almost invariably dismissed as capitalist-roaders, as in the case of President **Liu Shaoqi**, a dedicated Communist who was named "the number one capitalist-roader in the party." Elsewhere, it was used to label any party official who was not completely in line with Mao's ultra-leftist politics. In spring 1968, after some formerly denounced party officials were admitted into varying levels of the new power organ, the **revolutionary committee**, the modifier "unrepentant" was prefixed to "capitalist-roaders" in official media to distinguish them from the "majority of corrigible capitalist-roaders." In 1976, when **Deng Xiaoping**, who had earlier been named "the number two capitalist-roader," fell from power the second time, he was dismissed as "unrepentant" and was named a "capitalist-roader who is still on the road." After the Cultural Revolution, the CCP leadership abandoned the term "capitalist-roader."

CENTRAL COMMITTEE WORK SESSIONS, 11 JANUARY–7 FEB-RUARY 1962. Also known as the **Seven Thousand Cadres Conference,** these were a series of enlarged Central Committee work sessions held in Beijing and attended by an unprecedented 7,118 **Chinese Communist Party** (CCP) officials at the county level and above. Originally intended to "oppose decentralism and bolster centralization" in the face of difficulties in grain procurement, the conference changed course when many participants began to vent frustrations and reflect critically upon the radical policies of the party in the 1950s, especially those of the 1958 Great Leap Forward, that led to the Great Famine of 1959–1962 (commonly known by the euphemism of the "three years of natural disasters" or "three difficult years," though the famine years, as later studies show, were longer: from 1958 to 1962) in which 20 to 30 million peasants starved to death. In his work report, President **Liu Shao-qi** offered an assessment of the famine in the words of peasants in Hunan Province: "three-part natural disaster, seven-part man-made calamity in some areas." The adoption of certain remedial policies by the Liu-led "front line" government leadership following the self-reflection and self-criticism at these work sessions was cited as a serious case of "Right deviation" in **Mao Zedong**'s August 1966 **big-character poster "Bombarding the Headquarters."**

CENTRAL COMMITTEE WORK SESSIONS, 9–28 OCTOBER 1966. This work meeting was held in Beijing at **Mao Zedong**'s suggestion to "sum up our experience and perform political-ideological work [on party leaders]." Mao's words, from a speech he gave at the meeting, indicated that there was still much resistance among central and provincial party officials to the Cultural Revolution that had begun a few months before. The purpose of the meeting, then, was to criticize a so-called **Bourgeois Reactionary Line** represented by **Liu Shaoqi** and **Deng Xiaoping** and to educate those party officials who allegedly followed this line and did not support the mass movement. In his speech "Two Lines in the Great Proletarian Cultural Revolution," **Chen Boda** distinguished between the proletarian revolutionary line of Mao and the bourgeois anti-revolutionary line of Liu and Deng in terms of their attitudes toward the masses and criticized Liu and Deng for repressing the mass movement with a **work group** policy. **Lin Biao**, who also spoke at the meeting, pointed out that the Liu-Deng line dominated the nation until Mao's timely reversal of the trend at the **Eleventh Plenum of the Eighth Central Committee of the Chinese Communist Party** (CCP). In Lin's view, the ongoing and widespread violations of legality and human rights were a small element of chaos within a mass movement and were necessary for preventing China from changing its revolutionary color.

Having approved Chen's and Lin's views, Mao instructed that the two speeches be distributed to every party branch and to every **Red Guard** organization in order to push forward the campaign to criticize the Bourgeois Reactionary Line. Chen Boda's speech proved to be influential largely due to its reproach of ranking officials' children for their self-righteousness, its criticism of the controversial **blood lineage theory**, and its call for redressing the wrongs done to ordinary people during the early stages of the Cultural Revolution. These points were made in the name of criticizing the Bourgeois Reactionary Line.

CENTRAL CULTURAL REVOLUTION SMALL GROUP. (*Zhongyang wenhua geming xiaozu*; also known as *zhongyang wenge.*) The Central Cultural Revolution Small Group (CCRSG) was established on 28 May 1966 to replace the **Five-Person Cultural Revolution Small Group** as an organ under the Politburo Standing Committee to direct the Cultural Revolution. The replacement was suggested by **Mao Zedong**, approved by the Politburo at the **enlarged Politburo sessions, 4–26 May 1966**, and documented in the **May 16 Circular. Chen Boda** was made head of the CCRSG. **Kang Sheng** was appointed advisor. **Jiang Qing, Wang Renzhong**, Liu Zhijian, and **Zhang Chunqiao** were named deputy heads. Other members of the group include **Yao Wenyuan, Wang Li, Guan Feng, Qi Benyu**, Xie Tangzhong, Mu Xin, and Yin Da. According to the May 16 Circular, the CCRSG would have an additional member from each of the North-Central, Northeast, Northwest, and Southwest Regions, but these turned out to be members in name at best and only for a short period before they were dismissed from office locally. On 2 August 1966, **Tao Zhu** was added to the CCRSG as another advisor.

As the Cultural Revolution continued to unfold, the CCRSG began to act as a top decision-making office of the party, directly answerable to Mao; it virtually ruled over the Politburo, the Secretariat of the Central Committee, and, to a large extent, the Central Military Commission (CMC), especially after Mao launched an offensive against the so-called **February Adverse Current** and made powerless the old marshals in the CMC and the vice-premiers in the **Zhou Enlai**–led State Council. In the first three years of the Cultural Revolution, Mao used the CCRSG to mobilize the country for the movement, guide the Cultural Revolution in the direction he desired, and exercise his control of the country largely independent of the traditional party apparatus, which made the CCRSG the most powerful and influential organization of the country for the period.

At the same time, a number of politically moderate members, including Wang Renzhong, Liu Zhijian, Xie Tangzhong, Yin Da, Mu Xin, and Tao Zhu, were purged from the group. Some radical members of the group were also expelled: Wang Li and Guan Feng in August 1967 and Qi Benyu in

Key members of the Central Cultural Revolution Small Group (from left): Jiang Qing, Chen Boda, Kang Sheng, Zhang Chunqiao, and Yao Wenyuan.

January 1968. These three were generally considered to be scapegoats—that is, they, rather than the CCRSG as a whole, were made to bear the blame for creating chaos in the armed forces, in the area of foreign affairs, and in the nation in general. After the **Ninth National Congress of the Chinese Communist Party** in April 1969 when the new party apparatus was established and power redistributed, the CCRSG ceased to function.

See also EXTENDED CENTRAL CULTURAL REVOLUTION SMALL GROUP ROUTINE MEETINGS.

CENTRAL MILITARY COMMISSION ADMINISTRATIVE CONFERENCE OFFICE. (*Junwei bangong huiyi.*) Established on 3 October 1971 to replace the **Central Military Commission Administrative Group**, the Central Military Commission Administrative Conference Office was in charge of the daily business of the Central Military Commission (CMC). The Administrative Group was dissolved because its members were mostly **Lin Biao**'s close associates, who were all removed from power after the death of Lin in the **September 13 Incident** in 1971. The newly formed Administrative Conference Office consisted of **Ye Jianying, Xie Fuzhi, Ji Dengkui, Li Xiannian, Zhang Chunqiao, Li Desheng, Wang Dongxing**, Zhang Caiqian, Chen Shiju, and Liu Xianquan. Ye Jianying was named head of the Conference Office. On 5 February 1975, exactly one month after **Deng**

Xiaoping was appointed a vice-chairman of the CMC and chief of general staff of the PLA, the Central Committee of the **Chinese Communist Party** decided to dissolve the CMC Administrative Conference Office and resume the function of the Standing Committee of the CMC. The standing committee, with both old and new members, included Ye Jianying, Deng Xiaoping, Li Xiannian, Liu Bocheng, **Xu Xiangqian**, **Nie Rongzhen**, Zhang Chunqiao, Su Yu, **Chen Xilian**, and **Wang Hongwen**, with Ye as chairman.

CENTRAL MILITARY COMMISSION ADMINISTRATIVE GROUP. (*Junwei banshizu.*) In 1967, when most of the vice-chairmen of the Central Military Commission (CMC) were openly criticized by mass organizations and virtually forced out of power largely due to their involvement in the **February Adverse Current**, the executive office of the CMC—that is, its standing committee—stopped functioning. With **Lin Biao**'s support, the Central Military Commission Administrative Group was formed in August 1967. General **Wu Faxian**, commander of the air force, was appointed head of the group. Other members of the group included **Qiu Huizuo**, **Ye Qun**, and Zhang Xiuchuan. Ye was Lin Biao's wife. Both Wu and Qiu were Lin's close associates. In September 1967, Wu became deputy head when General **Yang Chengwu**, chief of general staff of the **People's Liberation Army**, was appointed head of the Administrative Group at the recommendation of Premier **Zhou Enlai** and with the approval of the **Central Cultural Revolution Small Group**. At the same time, **Li Zuopeng**, another supporter of Lin Biao, replaced Zhang Xiuchuan as a member of the group. In March 1968, Yang Chengwu was dismissed from all his positions because of his involvement in the so-called **Yang-Yu-Fu Affair**. General **Huang Yongsheng**, again a close associate of Lin Biao, soon took Yang's place as head of the Administrative Group. Now the Group was made up of Lin's wife and his "four guardian warriors."

Soon after Huang's appointment, Chairman **Mao Zedong** suspended the already-irregular meetings of the Standing Committee of the CMC. Thus, the CMC Administrative Group virtually replaced the CMC Standing Committee as the leading body in charge of military affairs—a significant victory for Lin Biao and his supporters. In April 1969, the First Plenum of the Ninth Central Committee of the **Chinese Communist Party** approved a move to add five more members to the CMC Administrative Group: Liu Xianquan, Li Tianyou, **Li Desheng**, Wen Yucheng, and **Xie Fuzhi**. After the **Lushan Conference** of 1970 (23 August–6 September), at which the conflict between the Lin Biao group and the **Jiang Qing** group surfaced, Mao no longer trusted Lin Biao and, in April 1971, recommended **Ji Dengkui** and Zhang Caiqian as additional members of the CMC Administrative Group to weaken Lin's influence and control. Finally, after Lin Biao's death in the **September 13**

Incident (1971), the CMC Administrative Group was dissolved, and a new **Central Military Commission Administrative Conference Office** was formed to take its place.

CENTRAL ORGANIZATION AND PROPAGANDA GROUP. The forming of this office was an outcome of the power reshuffle after the **Second Plenum of the Ninth Central Committee of the Chinese Communist Party** (23 August–6 September 1970, also known as the Lushan Conference) when **Chen Boda**, one of the most influential figures in the area of theory and propaganda and an ally of **Lin Biao**, was purged. With **Mao Zedong**'s approval, the Central Committee (CC) of the **Chinese Communist Party** (CCP) announced on 6 November 1970 the dissolution of its Department of Propaganda, an alleged stronghold of Chen Boda, and the establishment of the Central Organization and Propaganda Group so that, according to the announcement, the leadership of the CCP's organization and propaganda work would be more unified. Directly answerable to the Politburo, the Group was charged with overseeing the operation of the CC's Department of Organization, the Xinhua News Agency, the Bureau of Broadcasting Affairs, the All-China Labor Union, the All-China Women's Federation, and a host of official propaganda agencies and organs including *People's Daily* and *Red Flag*. Members of the Group included **Kang Sheng, Jiang Qing, Zhang Chunqiao, Yao Wenyuan, Ji Dengkui**, and **Li Desheng**. Mao made the move to ensure the control of these key party apparatuses by those he trusted and to contain the power of Lin Biao and his group after their differences with Mao surfaced during the Second Plenum of the Ninth CCP Central Committee. Kang Sheng was appointed head of the Group though he did not really assume the responsibility due to poor health. Li Desheng did not become substantially involved in the Group mainly because of his other official duties. The Central Organization and Propaganda Group, therefore, was essentially controlled by Jiang Qing and her close associates.

CHAIRMAN MAO GOES TO ANYUAN **(1967).** Highly praised by **Jiang Qing**, this well-known oil painting by Liu Chunhua and his fellow students and teachers at the Central College of Arts and Crafts promoted the image of **Mao Zedong** at the expense of historical reality. The historical setting of the painting is an Anyuan miners' strike in the early 1920s. Although Mao had been to the Anyuan Coal Mine, it was **Liu Shaoqi**, and Li Lisan as well, who played the leading role in organizing the Anyuan miners' union, the first major union led exclusively by the **Chinese Communist Party**. However, a popular 1961 painting entitled *Liu Shaoqi and the Anyuan Coal Miners*, which portrays Liu as the leader of the strike, was labeled a "**poisonous weed**" in the Cultural Revolution. In the meantime, in 1967, the Museum of

Chinese Revolution planned an exhibition (entitled "**Mao Zedong Thought** Lit up the Anyuan Miners' Movement") with a clear political purpose. Following the instructions of the exhibition organizers, Liu Chunhua and his comrades produced the oil painting portraying Mao in a long blue gown carrying a red umbrella on his way to Anyuan as the organizer of the miners' strike. On 1 October 1967, the painting was displayed at the exhibition and enthusiastically received by the audience. Jiang Qing then called it a model painting. On 1 July 1968, the piece was printed as a large single page attached to both *People's Daily* and *Liberation Army Daily*. The painting was also made into posters, stamps, and badges and became the most reproduced icon of Mao during the Cultural Revolution, with copies of various kinds totaling 900 million.

CHANGPING COUNTY MASSACRE (27 August–early September 1966). Under the influence of the **blood lineage theory**, prompted by public security minister **Xie Fuzhi**'s words on official non-interference regarding the killing of "bad people" by **Red Guards**, and supported, and even organized in some places, by local officials, a slaughter of 327 citizens of the so-called **five black categories** (landlords, rich peasants, counterrevolutionaries, bad elements, and rightists) was carried out by middle school Red Guards, security personnel, and peasants in a 10-day period in late August and early September 1966 in Changping County of suburban Beijing. Fourteen of the county's 24 communes participated in the massacre.

In late August, as Red Guard brutality against alleged class enemies ran rampant at the height of the **Destroy the Four Olds** campaign, a story was rapidly spreading that a 52-year-old Beijing resident named **Li Wenbo** threatened—and even wounded, according to some accounts—Red Guards with a kitchen knife in reaction to their house ransacking and physical abuse. Immediately following the Li Wenbo incident, an enlarged session of the Beijing Public Security Bureau was held on 26 August, at which Xie spoke of cracking down on the counterrevolutionaries who attacked Red Guards. He also responded to the questions from a number of provincial-level public security chiefs by saying, "Should the Red Guards who have beaten people to death be put in prison? There is no need to go further in my view. It is not our business. . . . If you detain or arrest those who beat people, you are committing an error."

On 27 August, Changping public security agencies not only acted upon the instructions Xie gave the previous day of briefing Red Guards on local residents of the "five black categories"; they went further to organize school Red Guards and local peasants for targeted killings that very evening. The massacre was the worst in the China-Vietnam Friendship People's Commune and the Heishanzhai People's Commune. In the former, the commune leadership held teleconferences two days in a row to gather death figures from each production brigade, praising those that executed killing plans forcefully and reproaching those that were slow in doing so. By 6 September, a total of 144 people were killed. Following the example of the China-Vietnam Friendship Commune, public security personnel of the Heishanzhai Commune went to two production brigades and Heishanzhai Middle School to instigate killings. A slogan rooted in the blood lineage theory emerged in the process: "Uproot the weeds; spare females, but not males." By 4 September, the death toll of this commune reached 67, of which 18 were children and adolescents, including a boy only a few months old.

The brutal killings finally stopped a few days after the Beijing municipal party committee issued an emergency decree on 2 September. The Changping County massacre, along with the **Daxing County massacre** and widespread killings in downtown Beijing, made these few days in late August and early September one of the bloodiest periods during the Cultural Revolution, claiming more than 1,000 innocent lives.

CHEN BODA (1904–1989). Head of the **Central Cultural Revolution Small Group** (CCRSG) and a top aide to Chairman **Mao Zedong** in theoretical and ideological matters, Chen was elected to the Standing Committee of the **Chinese Communist Party** (CCP) Central Committee (CC) Politburo in August 1966 and became one of the few veteran cadres entrusted with the new task of leading an unprecedented mass movement. However, his gradual alienation from **Jiang Qing** and her close associates in the CCRSG and his developing alliance with the **Lin Biao** group eventually led to his dismissal in September 1970 at the **Second Plenum of the Ninth CCP Central Committee**.

A native of Hui'an, Fujian Province, Chen was born on 29 July 1904 and worked as an elementary school teacher before he joined the CCP in 1927. Upon finishing his political training at Sun Yat-sen University in Moscow, Chen returned to China and went to Yan'an in 1937. Serving as Mao's political secretary and drafting speeches and theoretical essays for Mao, Chen rose to prominence as a leading theorist of the CCP and was elected to the Central Committee in 1945. After the founding of the People's Republic of China (PRC), Chen served as deputy director of the CCP Propaganda Department, director of the Political Research Institute of the CCP Central Committee, editor-in-chief of the CCP theoretical organ *Red Flag*, and vicepresident of the Chinese Academy of Science. He became an alternate member of the CCP Politburo in 1956.

Appointed head of the CCRSG in May 1966 upon the recommendation of Premier **Zhou Enlai**, Chen began to play an important role in articulating Mao's radical policies and directing the student movement in the early stages of the Cultural Revolution. During the campaign to criticize the **Bourgeois Reactionary Line**, he attempted to explain CCP class policies against a politically discriminatory **blood lineage theory** and became a leading supporter of the emerging **rebel** faction that included many students from politically disadvantaged families. As the Cultural Revolution further unfolded, however, personal and political conflicts began to develop in the CCRSG, especially between Chen and Jiang Qing, deputy head of the CCRSG, and her close associates **Zhang Chunqiao** and **Yao Wenyuan**. The conflicts intensified when Chen began to work on the party's political report in preparation for the **Ninth National Congress of the CCP**, discussing the content of the report with Lin Biao. Mao criticized Chen's first draft for its "productionist" tendencies and entrusted Zhang Chunqiao and Yao Wenyuan instead with the task of redrafting and revision, which virtually ended Chen's cooperation with his colleagues in the CCRSG and pushed him further toward an alliance with the Lin Biao group. Later, Chen made an ironic comment on the Zhang-Yao version of the political report: "all movement and no goal."

In August 1970, at the Second Plenum of the Ninth CCP Central Committee, Chen joined Lin Biao and the majority of CCP leaders in proposing that the PRC state presidency be restored. He was also involved in a strategic move, with the full support of veteran leaders attending the plenum, against Zhang Chunqiao. Opposing both moves, Mao wrote a short piece entitled "Some Views of Mine" in which he singled out Chen as the leader creating chaos. Chen was dismissed from office and was imprisoned. After Lin Biao's downfall, the CCP leadership denounced Chen Boda as a leader in the so-called Lin-Chen Anti-Party Clique. The CCP's investigation report dated 2 July 1972 named Chen a "Kuomintang anti-Communist, Trotskyite, renegade, spy, and revisionist," most of which turned out to be baseless charges. In 1980, Chen was tried as one of the leading members of the "Lin Biao, Jiang Qing Counterrevolutionary Clique" and was sentenced to 18 years in prison. Chen was released in October 1988 for health reasons and died on 20 September 1989.

CHEN ERJIN (1945–). A worker in Xuanwei, Yunnan Province, Chen Erjin, also known as Chen Yangchao, read a great deal of political literature, particularly works by Marx, Engels, Lenin, and Stalin, and wrote between 1975 and 1976 a long treatise entitled *On Proletarian Democratic Revolution,* with an alternative title *On Privileges*, advocating democratic reform of the socialist system. Adhering to what he believed to be true Marxist principles and borrowing much from what he understood as the American political system, Chen argued for a Communist two-party system with a separation of legislative, executive, and judicial powers. Although he quotes **Mao Zedong** frequently, his essay seems to imply strong criticism of **personality cult**, persecution, and the authorities' abuse of power during the Cultural Revolution: "No criticism of a president should constitute a crime," Chen wrote, "much less for anyone to be brutally executed for saying no to a president."

According to his proposal, an elected president should serve for only four years, and there should be no prayer of "Long live" for any president. Chen also proposed that systems of legal counsel, people's jury, and public trial be implemented and that secret trials be abolished. He called for recognition of personal liberty and human rights under a proletarian dictatorship.

Chen's treatise was widely circulated among **underground reading groups** toward the end of the Cultural Revolution. After the Cultural Revolution, it was carried in the underground democratic journal *Forum of April 5* in June 1979 and was published in English translation as *China: Crossroads Socialism* in 1984. Chen was detained by the authorities from April 1978 to March 1979 and imprisoned from April 1981 to April 1991. He has resided in Thailand since 2000.

CHEN LINING (1933–). A low-level party functionary at the Xiangtan city government, Hunan Province, and a mental patient with political paranoia about President **Liu Shaoqi**, Chen emerged in the early stages of the Cultural Revolution as a new star known as "a madman in a new era," a name echoing Lu Xun's well-known story "A Madman's Diary."

While still a young clerk in 1957, Chen began to worry about Liu Shaoqi's opposition to Chairman **Mao Zedong** although he did not have any evidence. The ultra-leftist theory of class struggle that Mao put forth in the 1960s, however, intensified Chen's suspicion of Liu. From 1962 to 1964, Chen sent about 30 letters to Mao Zedong, **Lin Biao**, **Zhou Enlai**, **Chen Boda**, **Kang Sheng**, and party newspapers in which he raved against Liu's speeches and works, including his well-known *Cultivation of a Communist*. At first, the local government treated Chen as a lunatic and sent him to a psychiatric hospital three times. As soon as he was out of the hospital, however, Chen began to send letters to other leaders of the **Chinese Communist Party** Central Committee. In 1965, he was finally arrested by the authorities on a counterrevolutionary charge.

When the Cultural Revolution broke out, Chen was in Beijing's Anding Psychiatric Hospital for a final check of his mental state. During this period, he wrote several letters to the **Central Cultural Revolution Small Group** (CCRSG) to appeal his case. Some of these letters were totally illogical, while others were lucid. When Liu Shaoqi clearly became the main target of the Cultural Revolution, some psychiatrists of the rebel faction in the hospital began to see Chen not as a madman but as a political prisoner. With much help from their allies at Tsinghua University, they sent the CCRSG a proposal for rehabilitating Chen. On 7 January 1967, **Wang Li** and **Qi Benyu**, both members of the CCRSG, went to the hospital to meet Chen, his psychiatrists, and the **Red Guards** from a number of colleges working on his rehabilitation. Wang and Qi regarded Chen as a victim of persecution by Liu Shaoqi and **Deng Xiaoping**; they redressed his case and called him "a new madman in the socialist revolution era." On 17 January, the major Red Guard news-paper *Capital Red Guards* published a four-page report on Chen's heroic deeds. The report claims that Mao also spoke well of Chen's act upon reading a note from **Jiang Qing**. Chen thus burst onto the political stage of the Cultural Revolution and began to give speeches in many places about his battles against Liu Shaoqi, and two stage adaptations of his story, *Dairy of a Madman* and *A Madman in the New Era*, were soon produced.

After Mao decided to remove Wang Li in August 1967, however, the debate about Chen's case resumed in Anding Hospital, and Chen became a pawn of the two rival mass organizations there and a hindrance to a grand alliance that Mao had been calling for. One faction of psychiatrists somehow managed to present enough evidence—contrary to the earlier diagnosis of their rivals—to show that Chen was indeed a mental patient and that he even criticized Mao's works. On 21 October 1967, **Xie Fuzhi**, minister of public security, finally pronounced Chen a madman, but Xie also said that further investigation was still needed because Chen was right to attack Liu Shaoqi but wrong to oppose Chairman Mao. On the same day, Chen was arrested again by security forces and disappeared from China's political scene.

CHEN SHAOMIN (1902–1977). A veteran Communist, Chen was the only member of the **Chinese Communist Party** (CCP) Central Committee (CC) who refused to support the party's resolution to denounce and expel President **Liu Shaoqi** in 1968.

Formerly named Sun Zhaoxiu, Chen was a native of Shouguang County, Shandong Province. She joined the CCP in 1928 and soon distinguished herself as a leader of women's and labor movements and was later a high-level political commissioner in the Communist army. In 1945, she became an alternate member of the CC. Chen led the Textile Workers' Union after 1949 and became deputy chair of the All-China Federation of Trade Unions in 1957. She gained full membership of the CC in 1956 and became a member of the Standing Committee of the National People's Congress in 1965.

When a discussion session was held concerning the "Investigative Report on the Crimes of the Traitor, Spy, and Renegade Liu Shaoqi" during the **Twelfth Plenum of the Eighth CCP Central Committee** (13–30 October 1968), Chen resorted to silence as a way of expressing her disagreement with the fabricated charges against Liu and was therefore criticized by other attendants. An official briefing of the 23 October meeting accused Chen of not drawing a clear line between herself and Liu Shaoqi and of opposing the party's decision. When votes were taken concerning the adoption of the anti-Liu report and the resolution to expel Liu permanently from the CCP, Chen alone did not raise her hand. Later, in response to the reproach by **Kang Sheng** who had also tried to force her to go along with the majority before the voting session, Chen answered, "That was my right [to vote in favor of

Liu]." Chen was soon sent to the Henan countryside for **reeducation**, where the harsh living conditions and lack of proper medical care made her already-poor health deteriorate rapidly. Chen died on 14 December 1977. Ironically, however, the official obituary honored her as "a proletarian revolutionary who firmly opposed Liu Shaoqi and his Bourgeois Reactionary Line."

CHEN XILIAN (1915–1999). A native of Huang'an, Hubei Province, and a member of the **Chinese Communist Party** (CCP) from 1930, Chen was a veteran Red Army soldier and a well-known military general. He served as commander of the Shenyang Military Region from 1959 to 1973, became chairman of the **revolutionary committee** of Liaoning Province in 1968, and was elected to the Politburo of the 9th, 10th, and 11th CCP Central Committees (CC). Chen was transferred to Beijing in late 1973 and became commander of the Beijing Military Region. He was also made vice-premier of the State Council in January 1975 and an executive member of the Central Military Commission (CMC) in February 1975. Politically, Chen stayed rather close to the ultra-leftist faction of the CCP leadership, which led to his appointment in February 1976 as the person in charge of the day-to-day work of the CMC, replacing Marshal **Ye Jianying**. In February 1980, Chen resigned from all his responsible positions. In the remainder of his life, Chen was given a number of honorary titles, including executive member of the CCP Central Advisory Commission.

CHEN YI (1901–1972). A senior leader of the **Chinese Communist Party** (CCP), Chen Yi played a significant role in both the CCP's internal politics as well as in its battle against the Kuomintang before 1949 and in the foreign affairs of the People's Republic of China (PRC) after 1958. During the Cultural Revolution, Chen was one of the veteran officials involved in the 1967 **February Adverse Current**.

Born in Lezhi County, Sichuan Province, Chen initially became engaged in the Communist movement while studying in France from 1919 to 1921, and after he returned to China, he joined the CCP in 1923. A veteran of the Northern Expedition and a leader of the 1927 Nanchang Uprising, he served in such prominent military posts as party secretary of the front committee of the Fourth Red Army (1930s), commander of the New Fourth Army in the war of resistance against Japan, and commander of the Third Field Army of the **People's Liberation Army** (1947–1948). After the founding of the PRC, Chen served as mayor of Shanghai (1949–1958), minister of foreign affairs and vice-premier of the State Council (1958–1972), and vice-chairman of the Central Military Commission (1961–1972). In 1955, he was named one of 10 marshals of the PRC. Chen was elected to the Seventh Central Committee (CC) of the CCP in 1945 and became a member of the Politburo in 1956.

At the **enlarged Politburo sessions, 4–26 May 1966**, Chen supported Mao's decision to purge the so-called **Peng-Luo-Lu-Yang Anti-Party Clique**. He also joined a number of ranking officials in attacking Marshal Zhu De for his alleged ambition to surpass Mao and attempt a coup. As the Cultural Revolution continued to unfold, Chen himself became a major target of the mass movement supported by members of the **Central Cultural Revolution Small Group** (CCRSG) who wanted to take over foreign affairs. In February 1967, Chen, along with **Tan Zhenlin, Xu Xiangqian**, and a few other senior party and military leaders, sharply criticized the radicals of the CCRSG at a top-level meeting in Zhongnanhai. The outburst of their anti–Cultural Revolution sentiment was denounced by Mao as a February Adverse Current. Mao approved **struggles against** Chen by the masses but protected him from further humiliation and removal. Chen retained his seat in the CC at the **Ninth National Congress of the CCP** (1–24 April 1969) because Mao, apparently in an attempt to balance factional power in the central leadership, called for all delegates to vote for him as a representative of the "Right side" of the party. But Chen was nevertheless removed from actual power and sent to a factory for reeducation. At Mao's request, he held a symposium with **Ye Jianying** and other marshals in 1969 on the international situation and made a suggestion that China establish diplomatic relations with the United States.

After **Lin Biao**'s demise in 1971, Mao began to seek support from the "old government" faction of the central leadership and sent friendly signals to Chen and other senior party and military leaders. However, Chen was already gravely ill; he died on 6 January 1972. Two days later, Mao, to everyone's surprise, made a last-minute decision to attend Chen's memorial service, at which he spoke of Chen as "a good man and a good comrade."

CHEN YONGGUI (1914–1986). Born in Xiyang County, Shanxi Province, Chen joined the **Chinese Communist Party** (CCP) in 1948. A hardworking farmer and party secretary of Xiyang's Dazhai village and later Dazhai production brigade, Chen contributed much to the transformation of his poor home village into a highly productive farming community. While Chen earned numerous medals as a model worker, it was **Mao Zedong**'s words, "In agriculture, learn from Dazhai," that made Dazhai the nation's best-known village. Chen also became a positive example in Mao's belittlement of intellectuals in favor of the "uncouth" (*dalaocu*) in the mid-1960s. During the Cultural Revolution, Chen was promoted as an "uncouth" leader and the peasant element in the leadership: he became chairman of the **revolutionary committee** of Xiyang County in 1967, vice-chairman of the revolutionary committee of Shanxi Province in 1969, secretary of the CCP Shanxi provincial committee in 1971, and vice-premier of the State Council in 1975. He was elected to the 9th, 10th, and 11th CCP Central Committees and the 10th and 11th CCP Central Committee Politburos. After the Cultural Revolution, Chen's essentially ceremonial position in the central leadership declined: his vice-premiership ended in 1980, and in 1983, he was appointed advisor of the Dongjiao State Farm east of the city of Beijing. He died on 26 March 1986.

CHEN ZAIDAO (1909–1993). A native of Macheng, Hubei Province, a member of the **Chinese Communist Party** (CCP) from 1928, and commander of the Wuhan Military Region from 1955 to 1967, General Chen was accused by **Lin Biao** and **Jiang Qing** of mutiny because of his support for the mass organization Million-Strong Mighty Army when factional battles started in Hubei in spring and summer 1967. Dismissed from office on 27 July 1967, he was seen as the most prominent of "that small handful (of **capitalist-roaders**) within the armed forces." After the downfall of Lin Biao, Chen was appointed to various positions including deputy commander of the Fuzhou Military Region, advisor of the Central Military Commission, and member of the CCP Advisory Committee. He was also a member of the Executive Committee of the Fifth People's National Congress and a member of the Eleventh Central Committee of the CCP.

See also JULY 20 INCIDENT (1967).

CHI QUN (1932–2001). A native of Rushan, Shandong Province, Chi was deputy chief of the propaganda section of the security troop unit 8341 guarding the Zhongnanhai compound—the headquarters of the **Chinese Communist Party** (CCP) and residential complex of Chairman **Mao Zedong** and a few other top leaders. In July 1968, Chi left Zhongnanhai for the prestigious Tsinghua University as a member of the **army propaganda team**. By the time he became party secretary and **revolutionary committee** head of Tsinghua University, a close alliance had been formed between him and **Xie Jingyi**, a member of the **workers propaganda team** and deputy head of the Tsinghua Revolutionary Committee. Chi and Xie, both closely associated with the **Jiang Qing** group, became the two most powerful officials at Tsinghua and remained as such—the two were almost always mentioned together—until their arrest after Mao Zedong's death in 1976.

Together, they turned both Tsinghua University and Peking University into models of repression and strongholds of ultra-leftism. During the **Rectify the Class Ranks** campaign, 1,228 of Tsinghua's 6,000 staff members were persecuted as class enemies. In autumn 1973, Chi and Xie started a campaign at Tsinghua against what they considered the right-wing resurgence in education; hundreds of people were implicated. In January 1974, Chi and Xie led the effort at the two universities to compile the material for a nationwide **Criticize Lin and Criticize Confucius** campaign. Also in January 1974, they followed Jiang Qing's orders and investigated a student suicide case at Mazhenfu Middle School, Henan Province. Their bulletin, the fruit of their investigation, led to widespread persecution of schoolteachers and school officials across the country. In March 1974, they put together a writing team called the **Peking University and Tsinghua University Great Criticism Group**, better known by its pen name **Liang Xiao** (a homophonic reference to "two schools").

Following directions from Jiang Qing and her faction via Chi and Xie, this writing group published dozens of articles between 1974 and 1976 making insinuations against **Zhou Enlai** and **Deng Xiaoping**. In late 1975, Mao spoke in favor of Chi and Xie in his comments on a letter from **Liu Bing** and three other veteran cadres at Tsinghua that criticized Chi and Xie. Following Mao's comments, Chi and Xie led a "great debate on the **revolution in education**" on the Tsinghua campus, directly attacking Minister of Education **Zhou Rongxin** and implicitly aiming at Deng Xiaoping. This "debate" turned out to be the prelude to a nationwide anti-Deng campaign known as **Counterattack the Right-Deviationist Reversal-of-Verdicts Trend**. After Mao's death in September 1976, Chi and Xie urged staff and students at Tsinghua University and Peking University to pledge loyalty to Jiang Qing in writing. In October, within a month of Mao's death, they were arrested with the **Gang of Four**. The verdict was announced officially in November 1983 that Chi Qun was sentenced to 18 years in prison.

CHINA'S KHRUSHCHEV. Along with the "**biggest capitalist-roader within the party**," this term was a reference to President **Liu Shaoqi** during the Cultural Revolution. He was labeled as such in official media in 1967 and 1968, but his name was not mentioned until after the **Twelfth Plenum of the Eighth CCP Central Committee** (13–31 October 1968).

CHINA-SOVIET DEBATE. A significant prelude to the Cultural Revolution, the heated ideological battle between the world's two largest Communist parties broke out in 1963. Although the conflict between the People's Republic of China (PRC) and the Soviet Union began in 1956 when First Secretary Nikita Khrushchev delivered a speech criticizing Joseph Stalin at the 20th Congress of the Communist Party of the Soviet Union, the differences between the two parties were not publicized until 4 April 1963 when *People's Daily*, following directions from Chairman **Mao Zedong** and the Standing Committee of the **Chinese Communist Party** (CCP) Central Committee (CC) Politburo, published the letter of 30 March from the Central Committee of the Communist Party of the Soviet Union to the Central Committee of the CCP. Then the CCP sent out a carefully composed letter of dispute in mid-June, while the Soviet leadership issued "An Open Letter to

Soviet Party Organizations at All Levels and to All Party Members" on 14 July criticizing China. The CCP's response to this letter and to the subsequent Soviet propaganda campaign took the form of a series of polemics, commonly known as the "Nine Commentaries" (*jiuping*), published between September 1963 and July 1964, in the name of the editorial departments of the CCP official organs *People's Daily* and *Red Flag*. The authors of these articles included **Chen Boda**, **Peng Zhen**, and **Wang Li**. Mao Zedong also contributed to the second and ninth commentaries. **Deng Xiaoping** was in charge of the entire project.

These articles criticized the Soviet leadership for creating a split in the international Communist movement and promoting revisionism, a deviation from the "basic principles of Marxism and its universal truths." Major ideological differences between these two Communist parties, as laid out in the nine commentaries, included the following points: The post-Stalin Soviet leadership had imposed upon the international Communist movement a policy of "peaceful coexistence" of socialist and capitalist states, which was based on the belief that socialism would eventually win the battle against capitalism worldwide due to its higher productivity in a "peaceful competition" in the economy; China, on the other hand, supported a more radical, and supposedly Marxist, "united front" and a violent proletarian revolution against colonialism and imperialism. The Soviets proposed an "all-people party" and "all-people state" against Stalin's proletarian state, whereas the Chinese charged Khrushchev and his comrades with not only abandoning the Leninist proletarian dictatorship but also denying and covering up the class conflicts in the Soviet Union between the working people and a new breed of bourgeoisie consisting of privileged bureaucrats and technocrats. And finally, the Soviets and the Chinese were sharply divided over the assessment of Joseph Stalin: Khrushchev called Stalin a dictator and a tyrant and accused him of promoting a **personality cult** and violating socialist legality, while the CCP leadership considered Stalin to be a great proletarian revolutionary on the world stage who made some mistakes but nevertheless upheld the revolutionary course of Marxism developed and defended by Vladimir Ilyich Lenin; therefore, de-Stalinization in the home of the October Revolution meant betraying the Marxist-Leninist legacy in the Soviet Union as well as reversing the rightful course of the international Communist movement at large.

The political thaw in the post-Stalin Soviet Union alerted the CCP leaders, especially Mao, to the danger of a capitalist restoration after the Communists took power. The last of the nine commentaries, which includes Mao's own writing, concludes on a note about the historical lesson of the proletarian dictatorship: not hostile forces from the outside but political deterioration and moral corruption of the party and state leadership itself pose the greatest threat to a socialist state. As Stalin should have done but failed to do, the

Chinese Communists must "watch out for careerists and conspirators like Khrushchev and prevent such bad elements from usurping the leadership of the party and the state at any level." In order to prevent Khrushchev's revisionism from being reenacted in China and to dash the "hopes of the imperialist prophets for China's 'peaceful evolution'" into capitalism, Mao writes, "we must everywhere give constant attention to the training and upbringing of successors to the revolutionary cause from our highest organizations down to the grassroots."

Mao's contribution to the ninth commentary was to be chosen as the longest passage in the *Quotations from Chairman Mao* and studied as a keynote of his theory of **continuing revolution under the dictatorship of the proletariat**. Its vocabulary was to become standard during the Cultural Revolution, a political movement to mobilize and educate the masses on the grassroots level in the course of **class struggle** against "**China's Khrushchevs**," the "**capitalist-roaders**," and the "bourgeoisie within the party," so that socialist China, unlike the Soviet Union, would never change its color.

CHINESE COMMUNIST PARTY. Both the founding and the ruling party of the People's Republic of China (PRC), the Chinese Communist Party (CCP) was formed in 1921 as a branch of the Soviet-led Comintern (Communist International). Prominent among the intellectual founders of the CCP were Chen Duxiu and Li Dazhao. In 1927, when the Nationalist party Kuomintang broke its alliance with the CCP and cracked down on Communists, the CCP began to build its own armed forces, the Red Army led by **Mao Zedong** and Zhu De, and formed its first revolutionary base in the Jinggang Mountain area of Jiangxi Province. Ten years of civil war ensued, in which the Red Army and the CCP central leadership were forced out of Jiangxi on a Long March toward Shaanxi in the north and eventually resettled in the hills of Yan'an. The alliance re-formed between the CCP and the Kuomintang during the war of resistance against Japan (1937–1945), giving the Communists an opportunity to preserve and develop their military forces and build and enlarge their bases in rural areas. This was also the period in which Mao rose to the top of party leadership. His ingenious sinification of Marxism-Leninism based on his understanding of essentially agrarian Chinese society and his strategies of guerrilla warfare—that of encircling and encroaching cities with a gradual expansion of Communist bases in the countryside—won the respect of his comrades in the CCP and the endorsement of Soviet leaders. Having consolidated his power with a rectification campaign in the early 1940s, Mao was elected chairman of the CCP at the party's Seventh National Congress in 1945 and remained in that position until his death in 1976. Also at the Seventh Congress, **Liu Shaoqi** was at the forefront of a party initiative promoting **Mao Zedong Thought**, which was, for the first time, written into the revised CCP Constitution as "the guideline for all the works" of the party.

After defeating the Nationalist (Kuomintang) military forces in another civil war (1946–1949), the CCP pronounced the founding of the PRC in 1949. Instead of forming a coalition government with other political parties as it had promised in the 1940s, however, the CCP declared itself the only ruling party and imposed a "proletarian dictatorship." In the first 27 years of the PRC, the CCP forcefully transformed the nation into a Communist state: the party largely abolished private property, nationalized industry, collectivized agriculture, and put all civilian institutions (judicial, cultural, educational, etc.) under strict party control. Its characteristic way of achieving this was conducting political campaigns continuously; there was virtually no pause until the end of the Cultural Revolution. Prominent among these campaigns were Land Reform (1946–1952), the Campaign to Suppress Counterrevolutionaries (1950–1951), the "Three Antis" and "Five Antis" Campaigns (1951–1952), Intellectuals' Thought Reform (1951–1952), Cooperation of Agriculture (1949–1956), Socialist Transformation of Capitalist Industry and Commerce (1953–1956), the Anti-Rightist Campaign (1957–1958), the Great Leap Forward (1958–1960), the Campaign against Right Deviation (1959–1961), **Socialist Education** (also known as the "Four Cleans" campaign, 1962–1966), and eventually, the Cultural Revolution (1966–1976).

The two decades following 1956 witnessed an increasing radicalization of CCP ideology and policies. Its repressive Anti-Rightist Campaign persecuted 550,000 intellectuals. Its utopian Great Leap Forward program caused an artificial famine that cost 20 to 30 million lives. And its Anti-Right Deviation Campaign in defense of the Great Leap Forward purged over three million party officials. On the international front, Nikita Khrushchev's anti-Stalin speech at the 20th National Congress of the Soviet Communist Party and the subsequent de-Stalinization in the Soviet Union were perceived by the CCP as a clear departure from genuine Marxism-Leninism and a betrayal of the international Communist movement. Such a perception eventually led to the CCP's break with the Soviet Bloc and to the **China-Soviet Debate** over ideology in the early 1960s. In the course of these events, Mao became increasingly concerned with **class struggle** existing beyond the years of war and revolution, with the deradicalization and degeneration of a revolutionary party when it became a ruling party, and with the rise of the bureaucratic elite as a new class. While calling on his comrades and the populace never to forget class struggle, he gradually developed what was to be known as the theory of **continuing revolution under the dictatorship of the proletariat** and eventually launched the Cultural Revolution to carry out this theory in practice.

For all the similarities among ruling Communist parties the world over in their ways of running a country (in so many ways emulating or simply paralleling the Soviet Union), the CCP under Mao deviated significantly from the Soviet orthodoxy of the international Communist movement with its

Cultural Revolution experiment. To ensure long and total control of the CCP in the hands of his trusted revolutionaries and to resist the almost inevitable deradicalization, bureaucratization, and influence from the democratic West, Mao mobilized the masses to strike out against the party apparatuses of his own creation and against most of his former comrades-in-arms, hoping that the party would emerge from this purgatory regenerated, its totalitarian rule strengthened, and the masses educated and revolutionized. The experiment failed, though. The masses, especially those who called themselves **Red Guards**, did pledge their loyalty to the Chairman, take over power from party officials at various levels, and insert themselves as the new blood of the party co-presiding with military officers and old party cadres in a new power organ called the **revolutionary committee**. But the **Ninth National Congress of the CCP** (April 1969), which passed a new party constitution designating Mao as the leader of the CCP and the Mao-cult engineer **Lin Biao** as Mao's successor, did not bring about a revitalized and unified CCP nor a closure of the Cultural Revolution as Mao had hoped. Intra-party conflicts did not stop, as reflected in the subsequent campaign against the Lin Biao faction, the organized attacks on **Zhou Enlai**, and the rise and fall of **Deng Xiaoping**, and purges at all levels, including purges of the party's new blood, continued through endless political campaigns until after Mao's death in late 1976 when the group of die-hard Maoists that Mao himself nicknamed the **Gang of Four** were arrested. By then, China's national economy was on the verge of collapse, the entire population emerged from 10 years of chaos with both a great relief and a profound disillusionment about Communism, and the CCP leadership was faced with a legitimacy crisis because of the calamities it had brought upon the Chinese nation.

It took post-Mao CCP leadership almost five years to come up with an official assessment of party policies and activities of the Mao era in a landmark document entitled **Resolution on Certain Questions in the History of Our Party since the Founding of the People's Republic of China**. The resolution names the Cultural Revolution as the cause for "the most severe setback and the heaviest losses the party, the state, and the people had suffered since the founding of the PRC," rejects Mao's ultra-leftist theory of continuing revolution under the dictatorship of the proletariat as an erroneous ideology, but still upholds Mao Zedong Thought as the guiding principle of the CCP. Meanwhile, during an eight-year period from 1977 to 1984, **Hu Yaobang**, in the capacity of head of the CCP organization department and then CCP general secretary, led the effort to rehabilitate over 20 million victims persecuted by the CCP since Land Reform. In the late 1970s, Deng Xiaoping came back to power as the supreme leader of the CCP and, with the assistance of Hu Yaobang and Premier **Zhao Ziyang**, advocated "socialism with Chinese characteristics" and engineered market-oriented economic reform in a new era officially named "Reform and Opening." The reform, especially as it abolished the People's Commune, overhauled state enterprises and encouraged private business initiatives, reversed the Mao-era party control and state monopoly of all economic matters, and paved the way for a real great leap forward in national economy in the years to come.

Yet, the reform Deng launched focused mostly on the economic front. Though it was accompanied with waves of political thaw as well, the CCP was not ready to open up for a political liberalization that would eventually end one-party rule and transform China into a democratic society. So, in the late 1980s, Hu was ousted for being reluctant to crack down on the liberal dissent of intellectuals and students, and Zhao was purged for his sympathies for the hunger-striking students during the 1989 Tiananmen democracy movement, which the CCP leadership was determined to suppress with military force. The CCP also censored independent scholars studying CCP history and punished lawyers advocating individual rights. Much of the CCP archives remain classified today: the regime devotes an enormous budget to "maintaining stability" (*weiwen*), and effective state information control and propaganda have resulted in widespread amnesia. Without a democratic system with checks and balances supporting an independent judiciary and freedom of press, official corruption plagues the country on an unprecedented scale. Though the CCP can hardly be considered "Communist" ideologically and policy-wise today, the party still calls itself as such. Boasting over 85 million members and priding itself in the economic miracle achieved under its rule in the past two decades, the CCP as the world's largest political party holds on to one-party rule and yet remains insecure in the face of its perpetual legitimacy crisis as an authoritarian ruling body in an increasingly democratic global environment.

See also CAPITALIST-ROADERS; CENTRAL COMMITTEE WORK SESSIONS, 11 JANUARY–7 FEBRUARY 1962; CENTRAL COMMITTEE WORK SESSIONS, 9–28 OCTOBER 1966; CENTRAL CULTURAL REVOLUTION SMALL GROUP; CLASS LINE; ELEVENTH PLENUM OF THE EIGHTH CENTRAL COMMITTEE OF THE CHINESE COMMUNIST PARTY (1–12 August 1966); ENLARGED POLITBURO SESSIONS, 4–26 MAY 1966; ENLARGED POLITBURO SESSIONS, 25 NOVEMBER–5 DECEMBER 1973; EXTENDED CENTRAL CULTURAL REVOLUTION SMALL GROUP ROUTINE MEETINGS; SECOND PLENUM OF THE NINTH CENTRAL COMMITTEE OF THE CHINESE COMMUNIST PARTY (23 August–6 September 1970); TENTH NATIONAL CONGRESS OF THE CHINESE COMMUNIST PARTY (24–28 August 1973); TENTH PLENUM OF THE EIGHTH CENTRAL COMMITTEE OF THE CHINESE COMMUNIST PARTY (24–27 September 1962); TWELFTH PLENUM OF THE EIGHTH CENTRAL COMMITTEE OF THE CHINESE COMMUNIST PARTY (13–31 October 1968).

CHINESE COMMUNIST PARTY, MARXIST-LENINIST. This was a fabricated case against dozens of ranking leaders of the **Chinese Communist Party** (CCP). In December 1968, four public security officers, following the instructions of **Xie Fuzhi**, extorted from Zhou Ci'ao—an assistant research fellow at the Economics Institute of the Chinese Academy of Science and a suspect of the **May 16 Counterrevolutionary Clique**—a wild tale about a Soviet-backed and coup-minded party within the CCP. According to the confession Zhou gave under torture, Zhu De was general secretary of this so-called Chinese Communist Party (Marxist-Leninist), and **Chen Yi** was deputy general secretary and minister of defense. The party's nine-member standing committee included, among others, **Li Fuchun, Xu Xiangqian, Ye Jianying**, and **He Long**. A congress was said to have been held secretly in July 1967. As planned by an "uprising operation committee," General **Chen Zaidao** was to lead his troops to capture the city of Wuhan, while a telegraph was said to have been prepared by military marshals to seek cooperation with Chiang Kai-shek. Apparently with the backing of the ultra-leftist faction of the CCP leadership, Xie Fuzhi was still able to press aggressively for further investigation of the veteran leaders even after they were elected to the **Ninth National Congress of the CCP** in April 1969. Because no trace of evidence was found to support Zhou Ci'ao's forced confession, the case of the Chinese Communist Party (Marxist-Leninist) finally came to an end around August 1969 without an official conclusion.

CHINESE COMMUNIST PARTY CENTRAL SPECIAL COMMITTEE HANDBILL. On 8 October 1967, copies of a handbill in the form of an open letter to all members of the **Chinese Communist Party** (CCP) appeared on the streets of Beijing. Assuming the authorship of a CCP Central Special Committee, the handbill was critical of the Cultural Revolution. The **Central Cultural Revolution Small Group** (CCRSG) listed this incident as a major counterrevolutionary case. On 20 November 1967, Shen Jianyun, a worker at a briquette factory in Tianjin, and 14 others involved in the handbill case were arrested. Both their confessions and all of the evidence indicated that they had made the handbill on their own and that the "CCP Central Special Committee" was fake. However, apparently for the purpose of attacking their political rivals within the CCP leadership, the CCRSG did not want the case to be closed. **Chen Boda** insisted that there must be a connection between the handbill and the **February Adverse Current**. **Xie Fuzhi**, minister of public security, attempted to link the incident with a long list of ranking leaders including **Deng Xiaoping**. A special investigation group was formed to search for "black backstage bosses," which led to the notorious fabrication of the **Chinese Communist Party (Marxist-Leninist)** case implicating dozens of top-ranking veteran leaders including Zhu De, **Chen Yi**, and **Li Fuchun**.

CIRCULAR OF THE CENTRAL COMMITTEE CONCERNING THE QUESTION OF "FERRETING OUT TRAITORS". A party central document (*zhongfa* [1967] 200) issued on 28 June 1967, this circular contains guidelines and regulations regarding the widespread activities taken by mass organizations to "ferret out traitors." Three months before, on 16 March 1967, the **Chinese Communist Party** (CCP) Central Committee (CC) had issued the "Instructions on Materials concerning Such Self-Confessing Traitors as **Bo Yibo**, Liu Lantao, An Ziwen, and **Yang Xianzhen**" to publicize the falsified case of the so-called **Sixty-One Traitors Clique**, which was a major step **Mao Zedong** authorized to bring down **Liu Shaoqi**. The document inspired mass organizations to launch a political campaign to "ferret out hidden traitors." The movement quickly turned chaotic: many veteran revolutionaries were denounced as traitors without a trace of evidence, and in some places, the campaign became a fierce factional battle.

In order to keep these activities in check, the CC issued the 28 June circular that specified five rules: solid evidence is required for any conclusion on a "traitor"; investigation of betrayal should be focused on **capitalist-roaders** within the party; distinction must be made between a cadre with some ordinary problems in the past and a real traitor or a spy; mass organizations are not to engage in factional battles in the name of "ferreting out traitors"; and no mass organization should attack another because the latter is investigating traitors or spies from within. But, due to the influence of the earlier document, the circular had a limited effect in regulating mass organizations' actions, and numerous falsified cases resulted in an environment of political witch-hunting.

CLASS LINE. The phrase refers to the **Chinese Communist Party**'s class policy: in judging a person, consider the person's family background but not family background alone; give more attention to the person's political performance. This class policy gave rise to widespread political discrimination against and persecution of people from the families of the so-called **seven black categories** during the Cultural Revolution, especially in its early stages. Based on this policy, early **Red Guard** organizations admitted only those from the families of the "**five red categories**."

See also BLOOD LINEAGE THEORY; "ON FAMILY BACKGROUND".

CLASS STRUGGLE. The classical Marxian concept of class struggle—the economically based conflict between a ruling, exploiting class of those who own the means of production and an exploited class of laborers—was much revised by **Mao Zedong** in his theory of **continuing revolution under the dictatorship of the proletariat** to mean the alleged antagonism in political,

COLLAR LIU BATTLEFRONT • 67

cultural, and ideological spheres between the revolutionary proletariat and those who represented the reactionary bourgeoisie both within the ruling **Chinese Communist Party** (CCP) and in Chinese society at large. In 1956, after the completion of the socialist transformation of the nation's economic structure, which eliminated private ownership, Mao temporarily entertained the idea that the "conflict among people" was beginning to outweigh the conflict between mutually antagonistic classes in socialist China. But, under much pressure from within the party leadership after the failure of his radical policies of the Great Leap Forward and concerned with the receding of his authority and power, Mao, in the early 1960s, warned "never to forget class struggle," which turned out to be an early signal of the Cultural Revolution.

During the **China-Soviet Debate** and the **Socialist Education Movement** in the first half of the 1960s, Mao came to the conclusion that class struggle existed and would continue to exist for a long time to come after the proletarian class took power, and that the gravest danger of a capitalist restoration lay within the ruling Communist party in which a new bureaucratic class representing the bourgeoisie was formed and was ready to direct the socialist country to capitalism by way of peaceful evolution. Based on such judgments, Mao decided that carrying out class struggle against **capitalist-roaders** within the party (literally, "those in power within the party who take the capitalist road") in nationwide political campaigns, such as the Socialist Education Movement and the Cultural Revolution, was necessary to ensure that China's political power remained in the hands of proletarian revolutionaries. In addition, Mao believed in carrying out class struggle in cultural and ideological spheres—that is, waging wars against what he considered to be nonproletarian culture and habits of mind—so as to revolutionize the consciousness of the masses; hence the revolution of 1966–1976 was called a *cultural* revolution.

During the Cultural Revolution, Mao's reformulation of class struggle served to justify the persecution of the majority of party leaders and tens of millions of ordinary citizens, especially those of the so-called **seven black categories** and their children, who were, in many cases, also treated as class enemies. According to an estimate by the post-Mao leadership, persecution in the name of class struggle during the Cultural Revolution affected one-eighth of China's entire population.

COLLAR LIU BATTLEFRONT. (*Jiu Liu huoxian.*) This term was a short form for "The Liaison Station of the Battlefront for the Capital Proletarian Revolutionaries to Collar, Struggle, and Criticize **Liu Shaoqi**." The "Battlefront" was a coalition of college **Red Guard** organizations formed in July 1967 for the sole purpose of removing President Liu Shaoqi from Zhongnanhai—the resident compound for top leaders of the **Chinese Communist Party** (CCP) in the heart of Beijing—to face criticism from the masses.

In August 1966, to experience the mass movement firsthand, Liu, accompanied by the newly appointed first secretary of the Beijing municipal party committee, **Li Xuefeng**, went to the Beijing Institute of Architectural Engineering and met with students from two rival Red Guard organizations at the Institute. As the Cultural Revolution continued to unfold following the instructions (sometimes clear and sometimes suggestive) from Chairman **Mao Zedong**'s close associates, the public came to believe that Liu was on the wrong side of the movement. The **rebels** of the Institute, then, began to denounce Liu's visit as an attempt to obstruct the mass movement. They wrote Liu several times, demanding that he talk to the masses at the Institute and openly acknowledge his guilt. This was a prelude to the later organized effort to "collar" Liu.

On 5 January 1967, Liu wrote Mao for instructions on how to respond to the rebels' demands. Mao forwarded Liu's letter to Premier **Zhou Enlai** the next day with a note suggesting not going. The rebels' demands were then put off after Zhou talked to them on 7 January. As a new round of criticism of Liu surged in April 1967, however, the demand from the rebels resurfaced. On 9 July, Liu, following orders from the central leadership, submitted a self-criticism report to the rebels at the Beijing Institute of Architectural Engineering. Dismissing the report as Liu's "manifesto of retaliation" and "a big poisonous arrow" aimed at Mao's revolutionary line, the rebels began to camp around the west gate of Zhongnanhai and set up their "Collar Liu Frontline Command Post" there, demanding from Liu not only a guilty plea but also that he remove himself from Zhongnanhai. On 18 July, some campers declared that they were starting a hunger strike. With support from student organizations at other schools and from members of the **Central Cultural Revolution Small Group** (CCRSG), a "Collar Liu" mass rally was held at the west gate that evening, drawing a crowd of several hundred thousand representing more than a hundred mass organizations. A large coalition of "Collar Liu Battlefront" was then formed.

When the word of the mass rally, the hunger strike, and the Battlefront spread, many mass organizations outside Beijing sent their representatives to join the effort. Hundreds of camps were set up outside Zhongnanhai. More than 100 loudspeakers were blasting the demands of the Battlefront and slogans against Liu from dawn till after midnight, and time and again the campers attempted to storm in from each of the five gates of Zhongnanhai to haul Liu out. The CCRSG lent its support by having medical teams dispatched to tend the campers. In the meantime, the attack on Liu and his family escalated within the compound. Several **struggle meetings** against Liu and his wife were held by the rebels within Zhongnanhai. Physical abuse intensified at these meetings, and Liu's residence was ransacked. Finally, Liu, his wife, and their children were separated and put under surveillance. The Collar Liu Battlefront lasted for more than a month while Mao Zedong was on an **inspection tour of three regions**. It was only by Mao's directive that the crowd outside of Zhongnanhai withdrew in August. Liu, however, never regained his freedom or had a chance to see his family. The humiliation and brutal abuse of Liu continued until his death on 12 November 1969.

COMRADE CHIANG CH'ING. *Comrade Chiang Ch'ing* is a biography of **Jiang Qing**, written by Roxane Witke and published by Little, Brown and Company in 1977 in the United States. This book was the outcome of a series of interviews Witke conducted with Jiang Qing in 1972 when the former, an assistant professor of history at the State University of New York at Binghamton, was visiting China as a member of a delegation of American women.

The original goal of the delegation's visit was to gather information and conduct interviews on Chinese women's liberation. After Witke expressed her desire to meet Jiang Qing, Zhou Enlai instructed that if Jiang agreed to meet with Witke, "they could talk for an hour or two. . . . But it's all right also if Jiang does not want to meet her." Jiang, on the other hand, not only met Witke in Beijing on 12 August 1972 but also managed to have a long series of interviews with Witke in Guangzhou from 25 to 31 August. During the weeklong private interviews—some 60 hours in all—Jiang told Witke about her personal life and expressed her wish for a biography to be published overseas that was comparable to *Red Star over China*, a story of Mao Zedong by Edgar Snow. The result was Witke's five-part story of Jiang Qing, detailing Jiang's impoverished, violence-filled childhood, her acting career in the cosmopolitan city of Shanghai, her first meeting with and later marriage to Mao in Yan'an, her increasingly active engagement in culture and arts, and her emergence as a nationally recognized leader during the Cultural Revolution.

In 1975, when the conflict between the Jiang Qing group and the more moderate and more pragmatic faction of the party central leadership intensified and when the Jiang group became increasingly unpopular among ordinary Chinese citizens, the leak of the Jiang-Witke interview caused a scandal. A popular political rumor spread across China that Witke's *Comrade Chiang Ch'ing* was translated into Chinese with the title **Queen of the Red Capital**, and the book caused an angry response from Mao: "[Jiang Qing is so] ignorant and ill informed. Drive her out of the Politburo immediately. We shall separate and go our different ways." Premier Zhou Enlai ordered a delegation of the People's Republic of China to the United Nations to purchase the copyright of *Comrade Chiang Ch'ing* to prevent it from further distribution. In fact, *Comrade Chiang Ch'ing* was neither published in 1975 nor translated into Chinese. The Chinese *Queen of the Red Capital* came out of Hong Kong and had nothing to do with Witke's yet-to-be-completed book.

After the downfall of the **Gang of Four**, Jiang Qing's self-exposure was listed as a crime. On 23 September 1977, the Central Committee of the **Chinese Communist Party** issued part three of the collected material denouncing the Gang of Four. In this document, Jiang Qing's 1972 interviews with Witke, Witke's newly published book on Jiang, and the historical military maps that Jiang had given Witke were mentioned together as evidence of Jiang Qing's "betrayal of the state in pursuit of personal fame."

CONFUCIANISM VERSUS LEGALISM. (*Ru fa douzheng.*) An observation by Chairman **Mao Zedong** on political conflicts in the early stages of Chinese history, the idea of the "struggle between Confucianism and Legalism" became in late 1973 and early 1974 the focus of a propaganda campaign criticizing the allegedly Confucius-worshipping **Lin Biao**. The real, though unnamed, target of the campaign was **Zhou Enlai**, whose moderate and pragmatic approach to state affairs was perceived by Mao and the ultra-leftist **Jiang Qing** group to be a main obstacle to a full realization of Mao's radical Cultural Revolution program.

Confucianism and Legalism were two of many competing schools of thought in pre-Qin China. Mao's view of the conflict between the two as *the* major political conflict of the ruling class in feudalist China, however, accorded Legalism an unprecedented high status. Concerned with the politics of his own day rather than that of the remote past, Mao seemed to be reacting to the report that quotations of Confucius were found in Lin Biao's residence and that in the *"571 Project" Summary*, allegedly a blueprint for Lin's armed coup, Mao was called the present-day Qin Shihuang (the First Emperor of Qin, or the First Emperor of China, known as a tyrant embracing Legalism and persecuting Confucian scholars to consolidate his power). Mao's high opinion of the Qin emperor and the Legalists and his dislike of Confucius became known from a poem he wrote to Guo Moruo, which was widely circulated at the time. On 4 July 1973, during a conversation with **Zhang Chunqiao** and **Wang Hongwen**, Mao made harsh comments on the work of foreign affairs directed by Premier Zhou Enlai and mentioned "criticizing Confucius" as well.

With Mao's approval, an article entitled "Confucius: A Thinker Who Stubbornly Defended the Slave-Owning System," by Professor Yang Rongguo of Zhongshan University, appeared in *People's Daily* on 7 August 1973. On 4 September, *Beijing Daily* carried the article "Confucius and Reactionary Confucianism" by the **Peking University and Tsinghua University Great Criticism Group**, a major writing team in the service of Jiang Qing and her faction. The *Beijing Daily* article inaugurated a series of publications, both in essay and in book form, examining cases of the Confucian-Legalist conflict in Chinese history but implicitly attacking Zhou Enlai. The tactic of launching an attack by innuendo and insinuation was known later as "**alluso-**

ry historiography." In addition to this high-powered media offensive, the discussion of Confucianism and Legalism also took the form of lectures and study sessions among grassroots units, though the masses were largely unaware of the loaded present-day references of the historical subject.

See also CRITICIZE LIN AND CRITICIZE CONFUCIUS.

CONSERVATIVES. (*Baoshoupai.*) A counter-reference to **rebels** (*zaofanpai*), this term was used to identify negatively the mass faction that stood by party officials (the so-called **capitalist-roaders**) and was supported by the **work groups** in the beginning stages of the Cultural Revolution. Originally, the official label for this faction, as it was referred to in the 5 June 1966 *People's Daily* editorial "Becoming Proletarian Revolutionaries or Bourgeois Loyalists," was the blatantly pejorative "**loyalists**" (*baohuangpai*). After Premier **Zhou Enlai** dismissed the term as inappropriate in a public speech on 10 September 1966, "conservatives" became its replacement but still retained its negative tone and negative connotations. Compared to the rebel faction, the conservative camp had a significantly larger number of people who were closely associated with the **Chinese Communist Party** (CCP) and with a vested interest in the current social and political system—members of the CCP and the Communist Youth League, members of the armed militia, students from families of the "**five red categories**," and so on—although they never called themselves "conservatives."

Because of Mao's support of the rebels, the conservative faction tumbled during the campaign to criticize the **Bourgeois Reactionary Line** (1966), so much so that during the nationwide **power seizure** campaign (1967), competing rebel factions all dismissed their rivals as "conservatives." By then a large number of conservatives had already joined moderate rebel organizations, and it was in the name of rebellion that their conflict with radical rebels continued during the nationwide **armed conflict** in 1967 and 1968. These moderate rebels were sometimes referred to as "new conservatives."

See also BYSTANDERS.

CONTINUING REVOLUTION UNDER THE DICTATORSHIP OF THE PROLETARIAT. Also known as the theory of **uninterrupted revolution**, this is a major theory **Mao Zedong** developed in his later years concerning the course of revolution under socialism. The Cultural Revolution could be considered as an experiment or implementation of this theory. Hailed as Mao's greatest contribution to Marxism-Leninism during the Cultural Revolution, the theory was written into the party constitution twice (1969 and 1973) and the state constitution once (1975) as the "third great landmark in the development of Marxism" and the key to "resolving all conflicts and contradictions under socialism," especially to preventing a "capitalist restoration."

Important elements of this theory began to appear in Mao's political thinking after 1956, the year of the 20th Soviet Congress at which First Secretary Nikita Khrushchev criticized Joseph Stalin. Considering the Soviet de-Stalinization to be a clear signal of departure from socialism and regression to capitalism, Mao began to study the cause of this backward turn under socialism and to search for ways of preventing such a regression from happening in China. During the Anti-Rightist Campaign of 1957, he considered people's political attitudes (rather than just their socioeconomic status) to be one of the defining features of their class identity. In the early 1960s, he called his colleagues' attention to the ongoing **class struggle** in a socialist society. He developed the concept of an emerging bureaucratic class in 1964 and coined the term "**capitalist-roaders** within the party" in 1965. In the early stages of the Cultural Revolution, more ideas relevant to the theory—such as Mao's increasing attention to class struggle in ideological and cultural spheres and the education of the masses through such struggle—appeared in the party documents the **May 16 Circular** and the **Sixteen Articles**. However, the systematic formulation of these ideas into a coherent theory did not take place until 1967.

On 18 May 1967, *People's Daily* and *Red Flag* carried the joint editorial "A Great Historical Document" written by **Wang Li** with Mao's revisions, marking the first anniversary of the passage of the May 16 Circular. This article publishes the phrase "revolution under the dictatorship of the proletariat" for the first time and calls Mao's theory represented by this phrase as "the third great landmark in the development of Marxism." The term is further developed in a joint National Day (1 October) editorial of *People's Daily, Red Flag*, and *Liberation Army Daily* as a theory of "continuously conducting revolution under the dictatorship of the proletariat." And, finally, the complete formulation of the theory appears in "March Forward along the Road of the October Socialist Revolution: Commemorating the 50th Anniversary of the Great October Socialist Revolution." This important theoretical piece was drafted by **Chen Boda** and **Yao Wenyuan**, reviewed and approved by Mao, and published on 6 November 1967 as a joint editorial of *People's Daily*, *Red Flag*, and *Liberation Army Daily*. This article sums up the theory with six major points:

1. The Marxist-Leninist law of the unity of opposites must be employed in observing a socialist society.
2. During the long historical period of socialism, classes, class contradictions, and class struggle still exist; so do the struggle between the socialist and capitalist roads and the danger of a capitalist restoration.

In order to prevent such a "peaceful evolution" into capitalism, a socialist revolution on political and ideological fronts must be carried out to the end.

3. Class struggle under the dictatorship of the proletariat is, in essence, still a battle for power. To prevent a bourgeois takeover, the proletariat must exercise an all-round dictatorship over the bourgeoisie in the superstructure, including all cultural spheres.

4. The struggle between the two classes and the two roads in society will necessarily find expression in the party as well. The handful of those in power within the party who take the capitalist road are simply the bourgeois representatives in the party. To strengthen the dictatorship of the proletariat, we must watch out for the Khrushchevs among us, expose them, and take back the power they have seized.

5. The most important form of continuing revolution under the dictatorship of the proletariat is the great proletarian cultural revolution, in which the masses liberate themselves and educate themselves.

6. The fundamental program of the great proletarian cultural revolution in the ideological sphere is "fight selfishness, repudiate revisionism." This is a great revolution that touches the depths of human consciousness and aims to establish in the people's mind the world outlook of the proletariat.

The same day that the article appeared, **Lin Biao**, at a mass rally, spoke of the Cultural Revolution as Mao's continuing revolution theory in practice, an "indication of enormous significance that Marxism-Leninism, in its developing process, has reached the stage of **Mao Zedong Thought**."

At the Sixth Plenum of the Eleventh Central Committee of the **Chinese Communist Party**, held in June 1981, the central leadership repudiated Mao's continuing revolution theory. According to the **Resolution on Certain Questions in the History of Our Party since the Founding of the People's Republic of China**, adopted at the plenum, Mao's theory of continuing revolution under the dictatorship of the proletariat consists of "erroneous leftist notions" divorced from both Marxist-Leninist theory and Chinese reality. The resolution embraces Mao Zedong Thought as an "integration of the universal principles of Marxism-Leninism with concrete practice of the Chinese revolution" but insists that Mao's continuing revolution theory is inconsistent with, and therefore must be thoroughly distinguished from, the system of Mao Zedong Thought.

COUNTERATTACK. (*Fanji.*) Directed by Li Wenhua and produced by the Beijing Film Studio in 1976 following orders from **Jiang Qing** and **Zhang Chunqiao**, this film was intended to be a propaganda piece against **Deng Xiaoping** during the **Counterattack the Right-Deviationist Reversal-of-**

Verdicts Trend campaign. Portrayed with striking resemblance to Deng in terms of his political views and political experience, a villainous provincial party chief, after his reinstatement, sets in motion a trend against the Cultural Revolution. There is also direct mention of Deng's name and his policies of **overall rectification** in the film. The piece was hastily put together in six months, and by September 1976, it was ready for internal preview. However, before the film was publicly released, Jiang Qing and her supporters were arrested. The post–Cultural Revolution Chinese government named the film a standard piece of conspiratorial literature.

COUNTERATTACK THE RIGHT-DEVIATIONIST REVERSAL-OF-VERDICTS TREND (1975–1977). (*Fanji youqing fan'anfeng.*) Launched in November 1975, this campaign against the so-called reversal of verdicts was **Mao Zedong**'s response to **Deng Xiaoping**'s tactically anti–Cultural Revolution **overall rectification** program. The political campaign became more specifically identified as a "Criticize Deng, Counterattack the Right-Deviationist Reversal-of-Verdicts Trend" movement in February 1976, continued briefly under **Hua Guofeng** after Mao's death, and officially ended with the full reinstatement of Deng in July 1977.

Mao started the campaign initially in educational circles by writing harsh comments on one of two letters **Liu Bing** and three other veteran officials at Tsinghua University had written him in August and October 1975 criticizing **Chi Qun** and **Xie Jingyi**, Mao's trusted **army propaganda team** and **workers propaganda team** leaders at Tsinghua University. Mao considered the two letters to have represented a widespread anti–Cultural Revolution sentiment, and Deng Xiaoping, who took the letters to Mao, was partial to the authors in Mao's view. On 20 November, the Politburo met upon Mao's request to evaluate the Cultural Revolution. Deng disappointed Mao by refusing to take charge of drafting a resolution on the issue. Later that month, Mao's comments on the letters by Liu Bing and his colleagues were presented to ranking officials in the form of a briefing at a meeting organized by the Politburo, and the phrase "a trend of right-deviationist reversal of verdicts" was mentioned for the first time. Implicated in this trend if not yet identified with it, Deng's rectification program was forced to end.

On 1 December, the party organ *Red Flag* carried an article entitled "The Direction of the Revolution in Education Cannot Be Altered" by the **Peking University and Tsinghua University Great Criticism Group**. The publication of this article marked the beginning of a massive propaganda campaign against Deng Xiaoping and, implicitly, Deng's strongest supporter, Premier **Zhou Enlai**. On 25 February 1976, a provincial leaders' meeting was called by the central leadership at which Hua Guofeng, who was made acting premier after Zhou Enlai's death, said that Deng could be criticized by name. Also at this meeting, Mao's order "Criticize Deng, Counterattack the Right-

Deviationist Reversal-of-Verdicts Trend" was presented. Mao's words were said to be gathered by **Mao Yuanxin**, the Chairman's liaison at the Politburo. Mao allegedly said that the bourgeoisie was within the party, that **capitalist-roaders** were still on the road, that some veteran cadres were discontent and would settle scores with the Cultural Revolution, and that Deng Xiaoping did not care for **class struggle**. In the ongoing media campaign, Deng was referred to as "the biggest unrepentant capitalist-roader within the party." On 7 April, the Politburo passed a resolution at Mao's request dismissing Deng from office and implicating him with the **Tiananmen Incident** of 5 April—a historical event at the time of the Qingming Festival, in which millions of people came to Tiananmen Square to commemorate the late Premier Zhou Enlai and protest against the **Jiang Qing** group.

After the downfall of the **Gang of Four** in October 1976, Hua Guofeng, Mao's handpicked successor, insisted on a policy called "two whatever's" (supporting whatever decisions Mao had made and following whatever instructions Mao had given) and decided to continue with the campaign against Deng and against the right-deviationist reversal of verdicts and to defend the Cultural Revolution. Ranking cadres Chen Yun and Wang Zhen, among others, objected to Hua's decisions on Deng, while Deng himself challenged the idea of "two whatever's." Eventually, with broad support from members of the Central Committee of the **Chinese Communist Party**, Deng was reinstated in all his party, government, and military positions at the Third Plenum of the Tenth CCP Central Committee in July 1977.

COUNTERREVOLUTIONARY ARMED REBELLION IN SHANG-HAI (1976). This is the official reference to an ambitious and long-planned armed resistance in Shanghai in anticipation of the political struggle and leadership change in Beijing after the death of **Mao Zedong**. Considering Shanghai to be the base of the cultural revolutionaries, members of the **Jiang Qing** group, **Wang Hongwen** in particular, paid much attention to building up a strong militia and even "the second army" (second to the **People's Liberation Army**), as Wang put it, in Shanghai. In 1975, Wang demanded that the militia be prepared for a guerrilla war. In August 1976, as Mao was dying, 74,000 guns, 300 cannons, and much ammunition were given to the militia troops in Shanghai. However, due to lack of leadership and lack of popular support, the ultra-leftists' battle plan to defend their cause was easily foiled by the central leadership of the party after the arrest of the **Gang of Four** in Beijing on 6 October 1976.

COW-DEMONS AND SNAKE-SPIRITS. (*Niuguisheshen.*) This is a generic term referring to all citizens denounced as class enemies, including landlords, rich peasants, counterrevolutionaries, "bad elements," rightists, capitalists, "**black gang**" members, "reactionary academic authorities," traitors, spies, **capitalist-roaders**, and even the children of the denounced. The term was adopted by the **Chinese Communist Party**'s official organ *People's Daily* in its editorial "**Sweep Away All Cow-Demons and Snake-Spirits**" (1 June 1966). **Mao Zedong** also used the term in his writing and speeches. The official endorsement helped make "cow-demons and snake-spirits" one of the most popular dehumanizing terms during the Cultural Revolution.

COW SHED. (*Niupeng.*) This is a common reference to illegal prisons for those denounced as class enemies, or "**cow-demons and snake-spirits**" (hence the name "cow shed"), during the Cultural Revolution.
　　See also MASS DICTATORSHIP.

CRITICIZE CHEN AND CONDUCT RECTIFICATION (1970–1971).
(*Pi Chen zhengfeng.*) Initiated by **Mao Zedong** at the **Second Plenum of the Ninth Central Committee of the Chinese Communist Party** (23 August–6 September 1970, also known as the Lushan Conference), this political campaign against **Chen Boda** for his support of **Lin Biao** in a power intrigue against the **Jiang Qing** faction at the plenum was also Mao's strategic move against Lin Biao and his associates. After the downfall of Lin in September 1971, the campaign against Chen became the movement to **Criticize Lin and Conduct Rectification** in which the political target, the so-called Lin Biao Anti-Party Clique, was also referred to as the "Lin-Chen Anti-Party Clique," though in official media both campaigns were known as the **Criticize Revisionism and Conduct Rectification** movement until late August 1973 when Lin's downfall was officially publicized.
　　At the plenum, Chen Boda, with Lin Biao's approval, compiled a brief collection of quotations called "Engels, Lenin, and Chairman Mao on Genius" and distributed it in the form of a pamphlet to the delegates. The unstated aim of this move was to make insinuations against the radical faction of the central leadership, especially **Zhang Chunqiao** who had insisted on excluding from the revised constitution (on the agenda to be discussed at the plenum) the word "genius" and two other modifiers praising Mao's contribution to Marxism. After hearing the complaint from Jiang Qing, Zhang Chunqiao, and **Yao Wenyuan**, Mao wrote "Some Views of Mine," accusing Chen Boda of trickery and deceit with a fake Marxist theory on genius, and called on **Chinese Communist Party** (CCP) officials to study classic works of Marxism so as not to be deceived by the likes of Chen. In the meantime, Chen was under investigation.

The CCP Central Committee (CC) officially launched the campaign against Chen internally on 16 November 1970 with a document called "Directives regarding the Anti-Party Question of Chen Boda." Mao's "Some Views of Mine" was attached, and a series of quotations on genius that Chen compiled was included in the document as an appendix. This was the beginning of the campaign to criticize Chen and conduct rectification. The campaign continued and deepened as Mao guided it with a series of directives, mostly in the form of comments on relevant briefings, reports, and self-criticisms of Lin Biao's associates. The targets of the campaign, theoretically, were Chen's "productionism" allegedly in opposition to the revolutionary line of the **Ninth National Congress of the CCP** (the charges were based on his conflict with Zhang Chunqiao and Yao Wenyuan over the drafting of the party's political report for the congress), his revisionism or "fake Marxism," and his divisionism. But the real political aim of the campaign appeared to be, as the process of the campaign itself showed, to implicate Lin Biao's associates and force them to fall into step with Mao's ideological and political line. This effort culminated in a two-week "report session" (15–29 April 1971) in Beijing at which central and local cadres gathered to talk about their experience in exposing and criticizing Chen, discuss written self-criticisms submitted by Lin Biao's cohorts **Huang Yongsheng**, **Wu Faxian**, **Ye Qun**, **Li Zuopeng**, and **Qiu Huizuo**, and study Mao's critical comments on their self-criticisms. On the last day of this meeting, the CC issued a circular to communicate the Chen Boda issue to all party members, and the campaign reached the grassroots level nationwide.

As Mao summarized after Lin Biao's downfall, issuing directives, which he called "throwing rocks," was an approach he adopted to guide the Criticize Chen and Conduct Rectification movement and to undermine Lin Biao's power. The fall of Chen Boda the "scholar," as he was often called, turned out to be a prelude to the fall of Lin Biao the commander and his generals. Both, in Mao's view, were part of the 10th major line struggle in the history of the CCP, which was also a struggle between two headquarters, like the one between Mao and President **Liu Shaoqi** in the early part of the Cultural Revolution.

See also ELIMINATING THE OFFICE OF THE NATIONAL PRESIDENT.

CRITICIZE LIN AND CONDUCT RECTIFICATION (September 1971–August 1973). (*Pi Lin zhengfeng.*) Referred to in official media as the "Criticize Revisionism and Conduct Rectification" until August 1973, when the **Tenth National Congress of the Chinese Communist Party** (CCP) convened to close the case of the **Lin Biao** Anti-Party Clique, the phrase "Criticize Lin and Conduct Rectification" was the name of a political campaign against Lin Biao and his supporters after the **September 13 Incident**.

Also known as part of the 10th line struggle in the history of the CCP, this campaign was a continuation of the **Criticize Chen and Conduct Rectification** movement that began in August 1970 at the **Lushan Conference**.

The campaign proceeded first with a series of emergency notices and measures. On 18 September 1971, five days after the fatal crash of the aircraft Trident 256 at Undurkhan, Mongolia, that killed Lin Biao, **Ye Qun**, their son **Lin Liguo**, and six others aboard the plane, the CCP Central Committee (CC) issued a circular to ranking cadres concerning Lin Biao's flight and death, charging Lin with treason and calling on party members to **"make a clean break"** with him. On 24 September, the CC ordered generals **Huang Yongsheng, Wu Faxian, Li Zuopeng**, and **Qiu Huizuo**—all implicated in the Lin Biao case—to leave office and conduct self-examination. On 3 October, the CC disbanded the Lin Biao–controlled **Central Military Commission Administrative Group** and formed the **Central Military Commission Administrative Conference Office** in its place, with Marshal **Ye Jianying** as chair. On the same day, the CC also formed a special case group with **Zhou Enlai** as director to investigate the problems of the Lin [Biao]-Chen [Boda] Anti-Party Clique. On 6 October, the CC issued another circular concerning the alleged coup d'état by Lin Biao and his associates. This document, to be circulated at the county level of party leadership first, also outlined a schedule for gradually releasing the information to grassroots party organizations and the general public. On 24 October, the CC ruled that the information of the Lin Biao affair be communicated to the masses but not be published in newspapers or on the radio or in the form of **big-character posters** or slogans.

On 11 December 1971, 13 January 1972, and 2 July 1972, respectively, the CC authorized the issuance of part one, two, and three of "The Crushing of the Counterrevolutionary Coup of the Lin-Chen Anti-Party Clique," all of which had been prepared by the special case group. Part one focused on the activities of Lin and company around the time of the 1970 Lushan Conference; part two centered on the *"571 Project" Summary*, said to be Lin's "program of armed coup"; and part three dealt with evidence of the coup attempt itself. On 20 August 1973, four days before the Tenth National Congress of the CCP, the CC approved the special case group's "Investigative Report on the Counterrevolutionary Crimes of the Lin Biao Anti-Party Clique" and expelled Lin Biao, **Chen Boda**, Ye Qun, Huang Yongsheng, Wu Faxian, Li Zuopeng, and Qiu Huizuo from the party. The words about Lin Biao as the greatest defender of Mao's revolutionary line and the statement about Lin as Mao's successor were deleted in the revised CCP Constitution. The deletion was approved by the Tenth CCP National Congress.

The guideline of the Criticize Lin and Conduct Rectification campaign underwent a considerable revision as the movement proceeded. At first, Zhou Enlai characterized Lin Biao's tendencies and policies as "ultra-leftist." In so doing, Zhou, who was in charge of the daily affairs of the central government and had full power for some time when **Mao Zedong** was gravely ill immediately after Lin's fall, attempted to take advantage of the political situation to reverse the kind of extremism that had dominated Chinese politics, sabotaged the national economy, and caused chaos nationwide since the beginning of the Cultural Revolution. Zhou began to be vocal, as he had not before, about the importance of the nation's economy, of the skills and expertise of the workforce, of education, and of diplomatic relations. He also advocated "liberating cadres" and "implementing the party's policies for intellectuals." In the meantime, Mao reflected upon the Lin Biao affair and began to acknowledge some missteps in the past. He suggested the redressing of such unjust cases as the **February Adverse Current** and the **Yang-Yu-Fu Affair** and allowed the practical-minded **Deng Xiaoping** to return from a virtual exile to Beijing to serve as deputy premier—a move that Zhou supported.

However, Zhou's measures and ideas against "ultra-leftism" met with strong resistance from cultural revolutionaries of the **Jiang Qing** group. They labeled Lin Biao and company as "ultra-rightist" and saw Zhou's slogans and policies as symptoms of a resurgence of right-leaning tendencies. Well aware that Zhou's attack on ultra-leftism might lead to a complete reversal of the course of the Cultural Revolution, Mao supported Jiang Qing and her associates. In his conversation with **Zhang Chunqiao** and **Yao Wenyuan** on 17 December 1972, Mao concurred with their judgment of Lin Biao. In September 1972, Mao transferred 38-year-old **Wang Hongwen**, Zhang and Yao's close associate in Shanghai, to Beijing and allowed him to attend top-level meetings of the Politburo, the State Council, and the Central Military Commission. The rapid rise of Wang, who was given the honor of delivering the report on the revision of the CCP Constitution at the Tenth CCP National Congress, entered the Politburo, and became vice-chairman of the CCP, signaled that Mao was choosing another successor after his first choice turned out to be disastrous. As the Criticize Lin and Conduct Rectification movement drew to a close around the Tenth CCP Congress, another campaign, **Criticize Lin and Criticize Confucius**, was about to begin. This movement, supposedly with Lin Biao as the main target, was implicitly a general offensive against Zhou Enlai for his criticism of ultra-leftism and his tactic of revising some of Mao's radical policies.

CRITICIZE LIN AND CRITICIZE CONFUCIUS. (*Pi Lin pi Kong.*) This was a political and ideological campaign that **Mao Zedong** launched in 1974 supposedly for a dual purpose: first, to link **Lin Biao**'s ideology to what Mao saw as China's moralistic, backward-looking, and reactionary legacy (namely, Confucianism); second, to defend the Cultural Revolution against the kind of criticism that in Mao's view paralleled the Confucian resistance to essentially Legalist social transformations in the early "feudal" period of Chinese history. However, with a strong aversion to **Zhou Enlai**'s "Confucian" inclination to moderation and realism and also in reaction to Zhou's well-received critique of Lin Biao's ideology as ultra-leftism, Mao was also directing from behind the scenes a general offensive against Zhou in the name of an anti-Lin campaign. Zhou was never named as a target; rather, by innuendo and insinuation he was referred to as, among other names, "the major Confucian within the party" and "the Duke of Zhou (Dynasty)."

Mao began to connect Lin with Confucius in early 1973 after he learned that notes on Confucius and Mencius and hand-copied quotations from the Analects of Confucius had been found in Lin's residence. Mao also knew that in the *"571 Project" Summary*, allegedly a blueprint for Lin's armed coup, he himself was called the present-day Qin Shihuang (the First Emperor of China). In May 1973, at a work session of the Central Committee (CC) of the **Chinese Communist Party** (CCP), Mao proposed to "criticize Confucius" as he was talking about Lin. On 4 July 1973, Mao told **Wang Hongwen** and **Zhang Chunqiao** that, like the Kuomintang, Lin Biao followed the dictates of Confucius and opposed the Legalists. In Mao's view, the Legalists, who helped the Qin Shihuang build an empire, favored the present over the past, while Confucians, politically short of accomplishments, tended to turn the course of history backward. On 1 January 1974, three official organs, *People's Daily*, *Red Flag*, and *Liberation Army Daily*, carried a joint New Year's Day message that called upon the nation to criticize the tradition of revering Confucianism and debasing Legalism and designated the criticism of Confucius to be a component of the criticism of Lin Biao. On 18 January, Mao authorized the dissemination of the collection entitled *Lin Biao and the Way of Confucius and Mencius*, which was put together by **Jiang Qing**'s followers at Peking University and Tsinghua University. The issuance of this document nationwide marked the beginning of the Criticize Lin and Criticize Confucius movement.

Despite its name, however, the actual content of the campaign had little to do with Lin Biao. Jiang Qing and her associates in the central leadership were prompted by Mao as to the real purpose of the campaign. They directed the campaign with several loyal writing teams, especially the **Peking University and Tsinghua University Great Criticism Group** and the **Shanghai Municipal Party Committee Writing Group**. The writing teams published a series of supposedly historical commentaries with Zhou Enlai as an implicit target. In these articles, Confucius was said to have represented the old order of a slave-owning aristocratic society and to have devoted his life to the reactionary cause of "restoring the perished kingdoms, reviving the doomed dynasty, and recalling those retired from the world." The intended but unsaid parallel was Zhou's painstaking effort, especially after the downfall of Lin Biao, to deradicalize the party's policies, to rehabilitate veteran cadres and intellectuals, and to restore order and normality to the economy, education, and national life in general. In the meantime, some of these articles applauded Qin Shihuang for burning books and burying alive Confucian scholars and, with unmistakable references to Jiang Qing, praised "outstanding stateswomen" of the past, such as Queen Dowager Lü of the Han Dynasty and Empress Wu Zetian of the Tang Dynasty, for upholding the so-called Legalist line of social progress against reactionary Confucianism. Referring to this campaign, Jiang suggested that the 11th line struggle within the party had begun, while Wang Hongwen, who was now closely associated with Jiang, called it the "Second Cultural Revolution," both alluding to Zhou Enlai as the target of the political movement.

This propaganda campaign in the manner of **allusory historiography** did not gain much support from within the party and without, so much so that Mao eventually detached himself from Jiang and said at the Politburo meeting of 17 July 1974, "She does not represent me; she represents herself." Articles of vicious insinuations against Zhou, however, continued to appear in major newspapers in the second half of 1974. But the campaign had lost steam and eventually ended without an official closure when **Deng Xiaoping** as first vice-premier assumed Zhou Enlai's responsibilities in January 1975 and pursued Zhou's course much more aggressively in a nationwide **overall rectification** program.

See also CONFUCIANISM VERSUS LEGALISM.

CRITICIZE REVISIONISM AND CONDUCT RECTIFICATION. (*Pixiu zhengfeng.*) This was the publicized name for both the political campaign against **Chen Boda** (August 1970–September 1971) and the one against **Lin Biao** and his supporters (September 1971–August 1973). In the course of these campaigns, the names of Chen and Lin were not mentioned in official media; Chen was often referred to as a "fake Marxist swindler" and Lin as a "swindler of the **Liu Shaoqi** kind."

See also CRITICIZE CHEN AND CONDUCT RECTIFICATION (1970–1971); CRITICIZE LIN AND CONDUCT RECTIFICATION (September 1971–August 1973).

CULTIVATION OF A COMMUNIST. (*Lun gongchandangyuan de xiuyang.*) Based on a series of lectures that **Liu Shaoqi** had delivered at the Institute of Marxism-Leninism in Yan'an in July 1939, this well-known work appeared in book form for the first time in 1943 and was subsequently widely regarded as an essential textbook and classical literature for **Chinese Communist Party** (CCP) members' ideological education. Its first revised edition came out in 1949 and the second in 1962. On several occasions, **Mao Zedong** offered favorable comments on the book as well. In mid-February

1967, however, Mao spoke of Liu's book as a "deceitful work" that only talks about personal cultivation without addressing the reality of **class struggle** and of the struggle of the proletariat for power, a book that represents "a form of idealism totally opposed to Marxism-Leninism." "Even Chiang Kai-shek," Mao said, "and even the bourgeoisie of the world, could accept the kind of personal cultivation discussed in the book. What individual? What personal cultivation? Everyone is a class person; there is no such a thing as a person standing alone, a person in the abstract. What he talks about is the way of Confucius and Mencius, acceptable to both feudal landlords and capitalists."

On 8 May 1967, *People's Daily* and *Red Flag* carried a joint editorial entitled "The Critical Point of Cultivation Is Betrayal of the Dictatorship of the Proletariat." The publication of this article was authorized by the Politburo with the approval of Mao. On 11 May, the CCP Central Committee (CC) issued a circular concerning Liu Shaoqi's *Cultivation*, in which Liu is referred to as the **"biggest capitalist-roader within the party."** A nationwide campaign criticizing *Cultivation of a Communist* was thus launched. The book that had enjoyed so much prestige in the CCP was now labeled "black cultivation" and a "big anti-Marxist-Leninist and anti–**Mao Zedong Thought poisonous weed**." On 29 February 1980, the CC rehabilitated Liu Shaoqi. *Cultivation of a Communist* was reprinted in the same year.

CULTURAL REVOLUTION COMMITTEE. (*Wenhua geming weiyuanhui.*) This was the name of the temporary power organ in a given institution formed in the beginning stage of the Cultural Revolution for the purpose of directing the ongoing political movement. In some institutions, it was called the Cultural Revolution Preparation Committee (meaning a preparatory committee for setting up the cultural revolution committee). It should be distinguished from the organ of power **revolutionary committee** established at various levels as a result of the **power seizure** movement in 1967. Cultural revolution committees were first created in educational and governmental institutions in early summer 1966 and often consisted of party officials and representatives of the masses. When the party authority in an institution fell, the committee often became the *ad hoc* authority of the institution. In Beijing, where **work groups** were sent to educational institutions in June and July, many such committees were established under the auspices of the work groups.

When Chairman **Mao Zedong** ordered in late July that work groups be withdrawn, the cultural revolution committees of these institutions, then, took over. The **Sixteen Articles**, a programmatic document for the Cultural Revolution adopted at the **Eleventh Plenum of the Eighth Central Committee of the Chinese Communist Party** (1–12 August 1966), endorsed the cultural revolution committee as a temporary organ of power not only suitable for educational and governmental institutions but also adaptable for factories, enterprises, and urban and rural communities. Soon, cultural revolution committees were established in all kinds of institutions at the local level across China. Before long, however, many such committees were accused of having followed the **Bourgeois Reactionary Line** of **Liu Shaoqi** and **Deng Xiaoping** in supporting traditional party authorities and suppressing the rebellion of the revolutionary masses. As a result, most of these committees were either forced to stay on the sidelines or were replaced by various newly established mass organizations in late 1966.

CULTURAL REVOLUTION SMALL GROUP. *See* ALL FORCES CULTURAL REVOLUTION SMALL GROUP.

D

DAILY READING. (*Tiantiandu.*) The phrase refers to a government-endorsed practice of studying **Mao Zedong**'s writing for an hour every day, which contributed much to the popularization of **Mao Zedong Thought** and the **personality cult** of Mao during the Cultural Revolution. The practice originated with the **People's Liberation Army** (PLA), and with **Lin Biao**'s enthusiastic endorsement, the daily reading hour was so firmly set as to become "thunder-proof," as army soldiers put it. With much urging and support from the central leadership, the civilian authorities at the grass-roots—in schools, in factories, and in government institutions—also implemented the daily reading program as a routine (such as the first class hour in school and the first work hour in a government agency) in the first few years of the Cultural Revolution. Mass meetings were often held at which activists would talk about ways they studied Mao's works and applied Mao's ideas in their daily lives. The practice of daily reading discontinued gradually after the downfall of Lin Biao in September 1971.

DAO COUNTY MASSACRE (1967). This was a brutal slaughter of thousands of innocent people under the irrational, chaotic, and lawless mass dictatorship involving not only mass organizations but also local **Chinese Communist Party** officials and militia personnel. From mid-August to late October 1967, 9,093 people were killed or committed suicide in Lingling Prefecture, Hunan Province. The death toll was the heaviest in Dao County where 4,519 innocent lives perished in a period of 66 days between 13 August and 17 October.

During summer 1967, a rumor was circulating in Dao County, Hunan Province, that Chiang Kai-shek's Nationalist troops were going to attack mainland China and that class enemies on the mainland, especially people of the **"five black categories"** (landlords, rich peasants, counterrevolutionaries, bad elements, and rightists), would rise in rebellion in cooperation with Chiang's battle plan and kill all party members, cadres, and poor and lower-middle-class peasant leaders. In a meeting on 5 August 1967, the county leadership, known as the Grasp Revolution Promote Production Leading

Group, confirmed the story and resolved to launch campaigns against class enemies. In the meantime, factional violence escalated in the county: on 8 August, the "Revolutionary Alliance," a rebel organization that dominated the downtown area, stormed the county militia headquarters, confiscated all of its weapons, and forced the rival "Red Alliance," a politically more conservative mass organization, to retreat to its base in the countryside; on 13 August, a violent confrontation occurred in the downtown area ending with the defeat of the Red Alliance, with two people dead and many wounded.

To demonstrate their acute "class consciousness" and perhaps also to vent their frustrations, members of the Red Alliance (many of them local officials) and their supporters in the local militia began to slaughter those of the "five black categories" and their children in the countryside. Over a hundred "poor and lower-middle-class peasants supreme people's courts" were set up to justify the killing. Execution was swift, and the methods used were among the cruelest. Executioners were rewarded with money or grain by head count. Eventually, 4,193 people were killed, 326 committed suicide, and 117 entire households were wiped out. Among those killed were old people in their seventies, babies (the youngest being 10 days old), and pregnant women. The total number of deaths amounted to 1.17 percent of the county's population; 66.5 percent of grassroots cadres and 36.9 percent of Chinese Communist Party members in the county were directly involved in the planning and execution of the massacre. The brutality of the Dao County massacre also spread to other counties in Lingling Prefecture, causing the death toll of the massacre to more than double. Though the **People's Liberation Army** troop unit 6950 under the command of the Hunan Provincial Military District was sent to Dao County to stop the massacre and factional violence as early as 29 August, the situation there was so out of control, largely due to factional conflict, that killings did not end until 17 October in Dao County and 25 October in Lingling Prefecture at large.

DAXING COUNTY MASSACRE (29–31 August 1966). Also known as the Daxing August 31 Incident because more people were killed on 31 August than on other days, this term refers to a local government-sanctioned slaughter of 324 citizens in Daxing County of suburban Beijing during the height of the mass terror that **Red Guards** proudly named **Red August**. The victims were those of the so-called **five black categories** (landlords, rich peasants, counterrevolutionaries, bad elements, and rightists) of class enemies, and their children, too, whose fate was sealed by their **blood lineage**.

A spillover of Red Guard brutality from urban Beijing, the Daxing massacre, very much like the killing rampage in **Changping County** during the same period, was a local response to Public Security Minister **Xie Fuzhi**'s instructions in the wake of the **Li Wenbo** incident in which a 52-year-old man was said to have resisted Red Guard abuse with a kitchen knife. Following a directive by the Beijing municipal public security bureau based on Xie's speech on defending and supporting Red Guards, the Daxing County public security branch convened in its county seat of Huangcun a meeting of college and secondary school Red Guard leaders and Huangcun township officials and police officers on 26 August, briefed them on 27 families of the "five black categories," and planned actions in the name of "**destroying the Four Olds**." Local militia was also involved in these actions. The killings started at Huangcun and quickly spread to other communes in the county. The worst massacre took place in the Daxinzhuang Commune where 110 people were killed on the night of 31 August, and the most brutal killer was praised for slaughtering 56 people from 11 families. In the midst of the Daxing County killing rampage, county party secretary Wang Zhenyuan intervened without success until officials from the Beijing municipal party committee and the Beijing garrison command arrived with task force work teams. On 2 September, the municipal committee issued an emergent decree to stop the killing. By then, 324 people from 171 families were murdered, including a man of 80 and an infant of only 38 days. Twenty-two households were completely wiped out.

The Daxing County massacre, along with the Changping County massacre and the widespread killings in downtown Beijing, made these few days in late August and early September one of the bloodiest periods during the Cultural Revolution, claiming more than 1,000 innocent lives.

DENG TUO (1912–1966). Writer, journalist, veteran revolutionary on the **Chinese Communist Party** (CCP) Beijing Municipal Committee, and author of the popular newspaper column *Evening Chats at Yanshan* under the pen name of Ma Nancun, Deng was an early victim of the campaign **Mao Zedong** launched in the Beijing cultural circles at the preparation stage of the Cultural Revolution.

Born in Minhou, Fujian Province, as Deng Zijian, Deng Tuo joined the CCP in 1930. During the war of resistance against Japan (1937–1945), Deng served, among other important positions related to the party's propaganda work, as head of the Jin-Cha-Ji branch of the Xinhua News Agency. In 1944, he was put in charge of the initial compilation and publication of the *Selected Works of Mao Zedong*. After the Communists took over Beijing in 1949, Deng was appointed director of the Propaganda Department of the CCP Beijing Municipal Committee as well as editor-in-chief of *People's Daily*, the official newspaper of the CCP. In 1956, he led a reform to make *People's Daily* "not only the party's paper but also people's paper." Mao Zedong was not pleased and criticized the newspaper as "being run by bookworms and dead people" after he noticed the rather cautious response of the *People's Daily* to his call for criticism of the CCP preceding the 1957 Anti-Rightist

Campaign. Deng was consequently removed from the position of editor-in-chief but remained as director of the newspaper, from which he later resigned.

In 1958, Deng was appointed culture and education secretary of the CCP Beijing Municipal Committee and editor-in-chief of *Frontline*, the official journal of the Beijing party committee. In 1960, he became an alternate secretary of the CCP North-Central China Bureau. In 1961, Deng, upon invitation, started the column *Evening Chats at Yanshan* (*Yanshan yehua*) for the popular newspaper *Beijing Evening*. A few months later, he also began to coauthor with **Wu Han** and **Liao Mosha** the column *Notes from a Three-Family Village* (*Sanjiacun zhaji*) in *Frontline*. An erudite and brilliant essayist, Deng wove history, philosophy, and popular culture into his entertaining and yet politically sensitive pieces, which were often subtly evocative and satirical, reminiscent of a long Chinese tradition of history writing and criticism in carefully guarded language of allusions and understatement. Between 1961 and 1964, Deng wrote more than 170 essays for the two columns. They were immensely popular among readers of all tastes.

In late 1965 and early 1966, following **Yao Wenyuan**'s attack on Wu Han, the author of the historical play *Hai Rui Dismissed from Office* and a coauthor of *Notes from a Three-Family Village*, a political campaign was spreading across China criticizing the so-called bourgeois counterrevolutionary academic authorities. In April and early May 1966, Deng was openly criticized for his essays published in *Beijing Evening* and *Frontline*. Named the head of a **Three-Family Village Anti-Party Clique**, Deng was accused of conspiring with Wu Han and Liao Mosha in attacking the party and its policies with historical allusions and by innuendo. On 16 May, an article by **Qi Benyu** further humiliated Deng by calling him a traitor. On 17 May, he spent the entire night completing a long letter to the CCP Beijing Municipal Committee refuting all the accusations. He then wrote a short and final note to his wife before taking an overdose of sleeping pills and ending his life in the early hours of 18 May. Deng was the first ranking official to die in the Cultural Revolution. He was officially rehabilitated in 1979.

DENG XIAOPING (1904–1997). General secretary of the **Chinese Communist Party** (CCP) since 1956, Deng was denounced as China's number two **capitalist-roader** in the early stages of the Cultural Revolution. He came back to the central leadership in 1973 to succeed **Zhou Enlai** as the nation's chief administrator, only to be criticized and dismissed again in late 1975 and early 1976 for his opposition to the ultra-leftist faction of the CCP leadership. Eventually, Deng returned a second time in July 1977 to lead the CCP's critical evaluation of the Cultural Revolution and China's economic reform.

A native of Guang'an, Sichuan Province, Deng studied both in France (1921–1925) and in the Soviet Union (1926). He joined the CCP while in France, returned to China in 1927, and soon became an important political leader in the Jiangxi Soviet established by **Mao Zedong**. Deng participated in the Long March (1934–1935). During the war of resistance against Japan, he served as deputy director of the Eighth Route Army's political department. He was appointed a secretary of the CCP Central Committee in 1945 and served as chief political commissar of the Second Field Army of the **People's Liberation Army** (PLA) during the civil war of the late 1940s. After the Communist takeover of China in 1949, Deng became first secretary of the CCP Southwest Bureau. He was transferred to Beijing in 1952 and entered the ruling Politburo in 1955.

In 1956, at the First Plenum of the Eighth CCP Central Committee, Deng was elected to the Standing Committee of the Politburo and became general secretary of the CCP. As a member of the CCP core leadership, Deng was a close assistant of Mao, politically and ideologically, in leading the Anti-Rightist Campaign of 1957 against intellectuals and in taking a tough line against the chauvinistic leadership of the Soviet Union, especially during his several official visits to Moscow. On the other hand, Deng was known for his pragmatism in domestic economic policies, which was to be characterized during the Cultural Revolution as a "cat theory" based on his own words: "Black or white, a cat that catches mice is a good cat." In this aspect, espe-

Deng Xiaoping at the Special Session of the United Nations General Assembly, 10 April 1974.

cially considering his critical assessment of the radical and irrational policies of the Great Leap Forward of 1958, Deng was seen by Mao as a close ally of **Liu Shaoqi**.

In June 1966, when the Cultural Revolution had just broken out while Mao kept himself away from Beijing, Deng Xiaoping joined President Liu Shaoqi, Premier Zhou Enlai, and other members of the Politburo Standing Committee in deciding, with Mao's approval, to dispatch **work groups** to schools to provide instruction and guidance for the masses participating in the revolution. Mao, however, withdrew his support for the decision on work groups after he came back from the south in July. When Mao attacked the work group policy as a **Bourgeois Reactionary Line** and Liu Shaoqi as the commander of the bourgeois headquarters, Deng fell from power along with Liu. Deng was denounced as the second leading capitalist-roader within the CCP. As Liu was dying of abuse and illness in Kaifeng, Henan, in October 1969, Deng was exiled to a factory of tractor parts in a suburb of Nanchang, Jiangxi Province, to work and reform himself.

In early 1973, at Mao's suggestion and with strong support from Zhou Enlai, Deng came back to Beijing and was reinstated as vice-premier. At the enlarged sessions of the Politburo, held in Beijing in November and December 1973 concerning what Mao saw as Zhou Enlai's "capitulationism" and "revisionism" in dealing with the United States, Deng followed Mao's line and criticized Zhou, apparently a necessary step for his winning Mao's trust and coming back to power. In April 1974, Deng, rather than Zhou, represented the People's Republic of China (PRC) for the first time at the General Assembly of the United Nations. In January 1975, at Mao's suggestion, Deng became vice-chairman of the CCP, vice-chairman of the Central Military Commission, chief of the general staff of the PLA, and first vice-premier of the State Council. He was thus entrusted with the power to preside over the daily affairs of the party, the army, and the state while Zhou Enlai was hospitalized for cancer treatment. In late February 1975, Deng launched his **overall rectification** program, which virtually reversed the course of the Cultural Revolution. Late that year, Mao interfered and began a nationwide campaign to criticize Deng: **Counterattack the Right-Deviationist Reversal-of-Verdicts Trend**. When the **April 5 Movement** broke out in 1976 commemorating the late Premier Zhou Enlai and attacking the ultra-leftist **Jiang Qing** group, Deng was stripped of all his official duties for allegedly being both the backer and the hope of all the "counterrevolutionaries" gathering in Beijing's Tiananmen Square and elsewhere in the country.

In July 1977, within a year of the death of Mao and the fall of the ultra-leftist **Gang of Four**, Deng was reinstated again. By the time of the Third Plenum of the Eleventh CCP Central Committee (December 1978), he had already become the virtual center of the CCP leadership. He challenged the dogmatism of Mao's successor, **Hua Guofeng**, who insisted on continuing with "whatever" decisions Mao had made, and Deng won broad support for replacing Hua with the more reform-minded **Hu Yaobang** and **Zhao Ziyang**. Deng played a decisive role in the CCP's critical assessment of the Cultural Revolution, which culminated in the passage of the **Resolution on Certain Questions in the History of Our Party since the Founding of the People's Republic of China** in 1981 at the Sixth Plenum of the Eleventh CCP Central Committee. Deng also put himself behind the "liberation of thinking" movement and made his own words the slogan of the nation: "Facts are the only test for truth." In the meantime, Deng advocated "socialism with Chinese characteristics" and engineered economic reforms creating special economic zones, adopting certain aspects of a market economy, and freeing enterprises from state control, which eventually ended China's centralized economy based largely on a Soviet model. The political aspect of Deng's liberalization program was not so radical, though; it reached its limit during the 4 June democracy movement of 1989 when, with Deng's approval, the army was brought in to crack down on unarmed civilians protesting in Tiananmen Square.

In 1987, Deng began to retire from various high positions he had been holding in the party, the military, and the state, setting an example for other CCP veteran leaders, including those skeptical of Deng's reform. On 19 February 1997, Deng Xiaoping died in Beijing.

See also POLITBURO SESSIONS, 4–7 APRIL 1976; SS *FENGQING* INCIDENT (1974).

DESTROY THE FOUR OLDS. (*Po sijiu.*) This campaign was initiated by **Red Guards** in August 1966, aiming to sweep away all "old ideas, old culture, old customs, and old habits" (hence "Four Olds") in Chinese society. Endorsed by the Cultural Revolution faction of the central leadership, the campaign resulted in unprecedented damage to the nation's historical landmarks, valuable artifacts, and other material witnesses of culture and civilization and claimed thousands of innocent lives nationwide—1,772 in the city of Beijing alone.

The phrase "old ideas, old culture, old customs, and old habits" as a pejorative reference to all traditions—Chinese or foreign—that were deemed non-proletarian from the viewpoint of the Cultural Revolution ideology first appeared in a 1 June 1966 *People's Daily* editorial entitled "**Sweep Away All Cow-Demons and Snake-Spirits.**" **Lin Biao** used the phrase in his speech at the **mass rally of 18 August 1966** and called on Red Guards to wage war against the Four Olds. As a prelude to Lin's battle cry, an ultimatum had already been drafted by Red Guards at Beijing No. 2 Middle School on the night of 17 August, declaring war on barbershops, tailor shops, photography studios, and used bookstores. On the day after the mass rally, Beijing's Red Guards took to the streets and started to smash street signs and name boards of shops, restaurants, schools, factories, and hospitals and re-placed them with new labels. Chang'an (meaning "eternal peace") Avenue in the center of the city, for instance, was renamed East-Is-Red Avenue, and Beijing Union Hospital, which was established by the Rockefeller Founda-tion in 1921, now became Anti-Imperialism Hospital. Red Guards made speeches, distributed pamphlets, and put out posters on the streets that dis-missed various fashions in hair and dress, stylized photos, pointed boots, and high-heeled shoes as evidence of bourgeois lifestyle. They would stop pas-sersby for what they considered unacceptable appearances and humiliate them by shaving their hair, cutting open their trousers, or knocking off their shoe heels. The official endorsement of such actions in two *People's Daily* editorials on 23 August helped spread the fire of the anti–Four Olds cam-paign across the country and prompted Red Guards to move further to raid churches, temples, theaters, libraries, and historic sites, causing irreparable damage. During the raid upon the historic Confucian Homestead, Confucian Temple, and Confucian Cemetery, for instance, more than 1,000 tombs and stone tablets were destroyed or damaged, and over 2,700 volumes of ancient books and 900 scrolls of calligraphy and paintings were set afire. Across the country, countless books that were deemed "old" were burned, especially those in school libraries.

During the campaign to destroy the Four Olds, violence against innocent people escalated. On 23 August, a group of Beijing Red Guards shepherded several dozen writers, artists, and government officials from the Municipal Cultural Bureau to what used to be the National Academy of Imperial China, where a huge pile of theater props and costumes, all deemed "old," was burning. The Red Guards ordered their victims to kneel down around the fire and beat them so hard with belts and theatrical props that several victims lost consciousness. **Lao She**, a well-known writer and one of the victims of this notorious event, took his own life the next day. Such brutality was wide-spread during the campaign, especially at **struggle meetings** that Red Guards held against their teachers, **"black gang"** members, and people of the **"five black categories."** It had become commonplace for Red Guards during the months of August and September to ransack private homes and confiscate personal belongings of alleged class enemies. Some homes were raided sev-eral times by different groups of Red Guards. In Shanghai alone, an estimat-ed 150,000 homes were illegally searched. In the name of sweeping away the Four Olds, the raiders took away not only cultural artifacts that were consid-ered "old," but also currency, banknotes, gold and silver bars, jewelry, and other valuables. At the height of the Destroy the Four Olds campaign, Chair-man **Mao Zedong** continued to hold inspections of millions of Red Guards in Beijing, while Lin Biao, standing by Mao's side at these inspections, continued to praise the Red Guards' attack on the old ways. In late 1966 and

Red Guards toppling the tallest Buddhist statue in Beijing's Summer Palace, 23 August 1966. The poster on the face of the statue reads "Sentence it to death!"

early 1967, when Red Guard organizations became more deeply involved in factional conflicts and **power seizure** struggles, the anti–Four Olds campaign finally lost its impetus and came to an end.

See also RED AUGUST.

DING XUELEI. This pen name was used by the **Shanghai Municipal Party Committee Writing Group**, a writing team headed by **Xu Jingxian** and remotely controlled by **Zhang Chunqiao** and **Yao Wenyuan**. "Xuelei" suggests "following the example of Lei Feng," a **People's Liberation Army** soldier and the most admired Communist hero in the early 1960s for his determination to be a "rust-free screw on the revolution machine." During the Cultural Revolution, the writing group produced numerous articles—many under this pen name—to promote the interest of the ultra-leftist faction of the CCP central leadership and attack its opponents.

DING ZUXIAO (1946–1970) AND LI QISHUN (1947–1970). Labeled counterrevolutionaries, these two women were executed in 1970 for criticizing the **personality cult** of Chairman **Mao Zedong**. Ding, of the Tujia ethnic minority, was an **educated youth** in the countryside of Dayong County,

Hunan Province, since 1965. In a letter, dated 17 March 1969 to the Dayong County **Revolutionary Committee**, Ding is sharply critical of the vogue of the "**three loyalties** (loyal to Mao, Mao Zedong Thought, and Mao's proletarian revolutionary line)." "Our loyalty is," she writes, "to the people, to the motherland, and to truth; it should not go to a particular person. The loyalty promoted today is actually the cult of the personality, a slavish mentality." Ding associates this kind of loyalty to the legacy of feudalism in which "Chairman Mao," she writes, "is treated as an emperor, an object of daily worship." On 21 April 1969, having received no response from the authorities regarding her request that her letter be published in a local newspaper, Ding distributed in downtown Dayong more than a dozen leaflets in which she, again, criticizes the Mao cult: "an unprecedented personality cult in the nation's history" is her way of characterizing the "three loyalties." Ding was arrested on 5 July 1969 on charges of attacking the proletarian headquarters and slandering the mass movement to study **Mao Zedong Thought**. Also arrested was her sister Zuxia who had been involved in both the writing and the distributing of the letter.

On 27 September 1969, Li Qishun distributed in downtown Dayong more than 20 copies of the letter "To the Revolutionary People," which she had written in support of her former classmate and friend Ding Zuxiao. In the letter, she calls Ding a hero deserving the name of a revolutionary vanguard. Li also sent a copy of the letter to the *Red Flag* editorial department in Beijing. She was soon arrested along with her sister Qicai, who had helped distribute Qishun's letter. Some of her former classmates were also arrested as members of the so-called Ding Zuxiao and Li Qishun Counterrevolutionary Clique. On 8 May 1970, Ding Zuxiao, age 24, and Li Qishun, age 23, were executed. In 1980, the Dayong County party committee redressed this case and named Ding Zuxiao and Li Qishun "heroes of the people."

E

ECONOMISM. (*Jingji zhuyi.*) Also known as the "evil wind of economism," this is an official reference to both the demands made by organized contract and temporary workers for job security and job benefits and the way government officials responded to such demands in late 1966 and early 1967. On 8 November 1966, during the campaign to criticize the **Bourgeois Reactionary Line**, contract and temporary workers formed their own organization, the **National Red Workers Rebel Corps**. Soon they envisioned the possibilities of economic gains as a result of their political activities: as they were denouncing the unfair double-tiered class system within the working class, they demanded promotions, raises, and changes of status to regular state employees.

Jiang Qing and some other members of the **Central Cultural Revolution Small Group** (CCRSG) expressed sympathy and support on several occasions. At a reception the CCRSG held for the representatives of the Rebel Corps on 26 December 1966, Jiang analogized the way temporary and contract workers were treated to the way workers in general were treated by capitalists. She reproached the officials from the Ministry of Labor and the All China Workers Union and called upon temporary and contract workers to rebel against these two government agencies. The Rebel Corps distributed Jiang's speech (with comments from other members of the CCRSG as well) across China and forced the Ministry of Labor and the All China Workers Union to accede to their demands. Jiang's speech and the Rebel Corps's success also inspired regular state employees to seek economic benefits by political means. Under pressure from below and above and under attack during the Criticize the Bourgeois Reactionary Line campaign, government officials began to give in to workers' demands for pay raises, bonuses, traveling expenses, and so on, which led to a sudden depletion of operational budget and a financial crisis in a number of big cities in January 1967.

In the meantime, some mass organizations in Shanghai launched an offensive against this kind of materialistically motivated political activity. They wrote and distributed two articles: "Grasp Revolution, Promote Production, and Defeat the Counteroffensive of the Bourgeois Reactionary Line: To the

People of Shanghai" (4 January 1967) and **"Urgent Announcement"** (9 January 1967); both were also carried in Shanghai's newspapers *Wenhui Daily* and *Liberation Daily* and later broadcast nationwide. Upon **Mao Zedong**'s endorsement of the first article as "another Marxist-Leninist **big-character poster**," the CCRSG began to accuse government officials, or alleged **capitalist-roaders**, of bribing and corrupting the masses with economism—a charge detailed in an article that appeared on 12 January 1967 in *People's Daily* as well as *Red Flag*. An official announcement was issued on 24 February 1967 to ban the National Red Workers Rebel Corps as a mass organization. Its leaders were arrested.

EDUCATED YOUTHS. (*Zhishi qingnian* or *zhiqing.*) Although college graduates were also included in its original definition, this term, as commonly understood today, refers mainly to urban and suburban middle school and high school graduates during the Cultural Revolution who went to the countryside to work, to settle down, and to be **"reeducated"** by peasants.

See also UP TO THE MOUNTAINS AND DOWN TO THE COUNTRYSIDE.

EIGHT BLACK THEORIES. (*Heibalun.*) This is a common reference to **Jiang Qing**'s summary of the "anti-party" and "anti-socialist," and therefore "black," literary theories that she considered to have been dictating the production of literature and arts in the People's Republic of China from 1949 to 1966. The eight theories are "theory of depicting things as they are" ("black" because truthfulness means focusing on the dark side of socialism), "theory of the broad path of realism" (broadness implies that it is too narrow for literature just to be a servant to proletarian politics), "theory of deepening realism" (deepening implies that socialist realism lacks depths of real life), "theory of antithesis to thematic determination" (it betrays an aversion to contemporary proletarian themes), "theory of middle characters" (the "middle" implies a focus on problematic characters rather than revolutionary heroes), "theory of aversion to gunpowder smell" (it prefers humor and light-heartedness to the revolutionary spirit of war), "theory of converging elements as the spirit of the times" (it denies the revolutionary spirit as the defining spirit of the times), and "theory of departure from the scripture and rebellion against orthodoxy" (it shows discontent with revolutionary literature).

See also SUMMARY OF THE SYMPOSIUM CONVENED BY COMRADE JIANG QING AT THE BEHEST OF COMRADE LIN BIAO ON THE WORK OF LITERATURE AND THE ARTS IN THE ARMED FORCES.

8-18. *See* MASS RALLY OF 18 AUGUST 1966.

EIGHT MODEL DRAMAS. The term refers to the eight pieces of performing art and music promoted by **Jiang Qing** and her supporters as revolutionary models for all art and literary works during the Cultural Revolution. The eight models include five Peking operas: *Shajia Creek (Shajiabang), Taking Tiger Mountain by Stratagem (Zhiqu weihushan), Raid on the White Tiger Regiment (Qixi baihutuan), The Red Lantern (Hongdeng ji),* and *On the Dock (Haigang)*; two ballets: *The White-Haired Girl (Baimaonü)* and *The Red Detachment of Women (Hongse niangzijun)*; and one symphony: *Shajia Creek (Jiaoxiang yinyue Shajiabang)*. The term "model opera" (*yangban xi*) appeared in the 6 March 1965 issue of the Shanghai newspaper *Liberation Daily* as a reference to *The Red Lantern*. The entire repertoire was listed for the first time as "eight model dramas" in a well-known editorial entitled "Excellent Models for Revolutionary Art and Literature" in the 31 May 1967 issue of *People's Daily*.

Despite Jiang's claims of originality and guidance in producing the entire repertoire, most of the model dramas originated from theatrical pieces that had been created in the early 1960s during the Peking opera reform, in which other local forms of drama participated as well. *Shajia Creek* was originally a Shanghai local opera (*huju*) entitled *Sparks in the Reeds (Ludang huozhong)*. *On the Dock* was based on a local opera of Jiangsu Province called *Morning at the Harbor (Haigang de zaochen)* and was adapted to Peking opera in spring 1965 by the Shanghai Peking Opera Troupe. *Taking Tiger Mountain by Stratagem, Raid on the White Tiger Regiment,* and *The Red Lantern* were first produced at a national modern Peking opera festival—a joint performance by a number of troupes for the purpose of discussion and emulation—in 1964. *The White-Haired Girl* was adapted by the Shanghai Dance Academy from a popular revolutionary story with the same title.

Taking advantage of considerable success already achieved in drama reform, Jiang tempered these pieces with what she considered to be elements of revolutionary art, such as the concept of **"three prominences"** and the idea of **class struggle**. Also under her direction, the China Ballet Troupe adapted the film *The Red Detachment of Women* to a ballet, and the Central Philharmonic Orchestra composed the symphony *Shajia Creek*. Then, the eight revolutionary model dramas became her personal achievements and, for quite some time during the Cultural Revolution, the only works deemed completely revolutionary and allowed onstage; as a popular Chinese saying had it: "Only eight plays for 800 million people." During the Cultural Revolution, some of the artists initially involved in the making of these plays were persecuted, and even imprisoned, because their aesthetic judgments were different from Jiang's. In fact, these model dramas eventually became icons so sacred that any criticism or any attempt to adapt them to other forms might be considered evidence of a crime called "damaging the model dramas." The iconic status of these pieces, as well as the dictatorial and repressive policies imposed by Jiang and her supporters in artistic circles, was largely responsible for the paleness of Chinese art during the Cultural Revolution.

ELEVENTH PLENUM OF THE EIGHTH CENTRAL COMMITTEE OF THE CHINESE COMMUNIST PARTY (1–12 August 1966). A landmark in the course of the Cultural Revolution, this was a meeting organized and presided over by Chairman **Mao Zedong** to rally support within the top leadership, to wage war against what he considered to be the "bourgeois headquarters," and to launch the Cultural Revolution nationwide for the second time. The reorganization of the Politburo at the plenum strengthened Mao's power, while the passage of the "Decision of the Central Committee of the **Chinese Communist Party** (CCP) concerning the Great Proletarian Cultural Revolution," commonly known as the **Sixteen Articles**, provided another "programmatic document" defining the objectives and the party policies for the Cultural Revolution after the adoption of the **May 16 Circular** at an earlier meeting.

Mao's decision to call the meeting in Beijing in late July 1966, shortly after his eight-month tour in the provinces, was based on his perception that the Cultural Revolution had encountered much resistance from above since it was first launched at the **enlarged Politburo sessions, 4–26 May 1966**. The resistance took the peculiar form of **work groups** that the central leadership dispatched to colleges and middle and high schools to cope with turmoil and violence and to guide the course of the revolution under party leadership. Mao's call was urgent. On 27 July, three days after the announcement and with little preparation, the preliminary session began. The plenum officially started on 1 August. Among those attending the meeting were non-voting delegates from the **Central Cultural Revolution Small Group** (CCRSG) and student and teacher representatives from college campuses. At the opening session, President **Liu Shaoqi** delivered a speech, reporting to the Central Committee (CC) on the state of the party since the last plenum and also assuming responsibility for what Mao saw as the problems of the work groups. Mao interrupted the speech and accused the work groups of taking the bourgeois stand against the proletarian revolution. On the same day, Mao's reply to letters from the Tsinghua University Middle School Red Guards in support of their rebellion was distributed among delegates.

Originally on the plenum agenda were the meeting of all delegates to discuss the Sixteen Articles on 4 August and the adjournment of the plenum on 5 August. But this schedule was changed due to the resistance of many delegates to Mao's radical vision of the Cultural Revolution: in discussion sessions on 2–3 August, they acknowledged their "lack of comprehension" and criticized themselves for "not having been able to keep in step with

Chairman Mao." At an enlarged session of the Politburo Standing Committee on 4 August, Mao accused the work groups of repressing the student movement and pointed to the CC as the source of a "white terror." His speech included the alarming words, "**Cow-demons and snake-spirits** are among those present." On 5 August, Mao wrote a 205-word **big-character poster** entitled "**Bombarding the Headquarters**," accusing "certain central and regional leader-comrades" (implicitly Liu Shaoqi and those under his leadership) of exercising a bourgeois dictatorship, practicing white terror, and suppressing the Proletarian Cultural Revolution. Two days later, Mao's poster was circulated among the delegates. On 8 August, after the Sixteen Articles was passed, **Lin Biao** made a long speech during his meeting with the CCRSG, highlighting the significance of Mao's attack on what was soon to be known as the "bourgeois headquarters headed by Liu Shaoqi": "Chairman Mao is the supreme commander of this Cultural Revolution. Chairman Mao has turned the situation around; otherwise, the Cultural Revolution would have been stillborn or interrupted. The bourgeoisie would have gained the upper hand, and we would have been defeated."

On 12 August, at Mao's suggestion, the Central Committee voted to reshuffle the Politburo and its standing committee. The members of the reorganized standing committee were listed in the following order: Mao Zedong, Lin Biao, **Zhou Enlai**, **Tao Zhu**, **Chen Boda**, **Deng Xiaoping**, **Kang Sheng**, Liu Shaoqi, Zhu De, **Li Fuchun**, and Chen Yun. Liu Shaoqi dropped from the original number two position to number eight. Chen Boda and Kang Sheng, both key members of the CCRSG, were promoted to the standing committee and given prominent positions. The plenum did not reelect a chairman and vice-chairmen, but from this point on, Lin Biao alone was referred to as vice-chairman of the CCP, while Liu Shaoqi, Zhou Enlai, Zhu De, and Chen Yun were never mentioned again in association with that title. With these readjustments, the comparatively more pragmatic and moderate "first line" of leadership established in the early 1960s to take charge of daily affairs of the party and the state was virtually eliminated, and Mao's power in the CC consolidated. And, partially repeating the words of Lin Biao's speech at the **Tenth Plenum of the CCP Eighth Central Committee** (24–27 September 1962), the "Communiqué of the Eleventh Plenum" included a statement about the supreme status of Mao and his ideas. This quotation signals the official sanction of the **personality cult** and the hegemony of **Mao Zedong Thought**.

ELIMINATING THE OFFICE OF THE NATIONAL PRESIDENT. (*Bushe guojia zhuxi.*) On several occasions between March and August 1970, **Mao Zedong** proposed that the office of president of state be eliminated. Mao also made it clear that he himself did not want to be president. The majority of the Politburo and of the **Chinese Communist Party** (CCP) Central Committee (CC), including **Lin Biao**, on the other hand, considered it appropriate for a state to have a president and insisted that Mao serve in that position. After the **September 13 Incident** of 1971, however, the proposal to install a national president was attributed to Lin Biao alone, and Mao called the proposal the "political program" in Lin's plan to seize power.

Mao expressed for the first time his wish to eliminate the position of the state president on 7 March 1970 after the issue was raised by **Zhou Enlai** concerning the revision of the Constitution of the People's Republic of China. "Don't write the chapter on president of state in the Constitution," Mao said to his security chief, **Wang Dongxing**. "And I'm not to serve as president, either." Most members of the Politburo and of the CC took Mao's words as a directive and did not differ until 12 April when the Politburo met to discuss Lin Biao's suggestion that Mao be president of state as people desired, that the office of vice-president was not significant, and that Lin himself was not fit even for the position of vice-president. At the meeting, the majority of the Politburo, including Zhou Enlai, supported Lin's view. In late April, and again in mid-June, Mao repeated his negative stand on the issue and pointed out that having a president of state was a formality. Mao had the support of the majority for the second time on 18 July at a constitution revision meeting.

On 22 August 1970, the Standing Committee of the Politburo met at **Lushan** to discuss the agenda of the **Second Plenum of the Ninth CCP Central Committee**. Except Mao, who adhered to his earlier views, all other members were of the opinion that there should be a national president and that Mao should serve. Considering the possibility of Mao's indifference to the ceremonial routine of foreign affairs, Zhou Enlai suggested that a president could authorize others to represent him or her on these occasions. On 23 August, at the opening session of the plenum, Lin Biao made a concession in his opening speech by using the term "head of the proletarian dictatorship" in place of "president of state." **Kang Sheng**, who spoke after Lin, still insisted that all support Mao as president. Two days later, however, Mao's angry words, "Never mention again the question of state presidency. If you want me to die soon, then make me president," finally silenced all the voices in support of installing a national president.

In official history, the opposition to Mao's proposal to eliminate the state presidency was mainly due to Lin Biao's desire to be president. This conclusion is now broadly challenged by historians. The only "evidence" of Lin's wish has been **Wu Faxian**'s confession that **Ye Qun** wanted Lin Biao to be president, but there was no other witness to Ye Qun's saying these words. On the other hand, there was much circumstantial evidence from Lin's subordinates that Lin, for a variety of reasons, might *not* want to serve as president at all. It is also significant, as some historians noted, that Lin Biao fled the country and was killed in a plane crash two to three weeks after Mao commented on the proposal to install the office of the national president as a "political program" for usurpation and made the following judgment: "Someone wanted to be president," Mao said, "and to split the party and couldn't wait to take power." Much of the dispute in the beginning of the 1970s over the national presidency, like many other issues concerning Lin Biao's alleged conspiracy to seize power, remains to be explained.

ENLARGED POLITBURO SESSIONS, 4–26 MAY 1966. Presided over by **Liu Shaoqi** but dictated by the absentee **Mao Zedong** with **Kang Sheng** as a mediating agent, this meeting signaled the official launching of the Cultural Revolution. At the second session on 16 May, the Politburo approved "The Circular of the **Chinese Communist Party** (CCP) Central Committee," also known as the **May 16 Circular**, which was drafted by **Chen Boda**, Kang Sheng, **Wang Li**, and a few others, and meticulously revised by Mao before the meeting. The circular, along with the **Sixteen Articles** adopted in August 1966 at the **Eleventh Plenum of the Eighth CCP Central Committee**, was designated as a "programmatic document" that laid out guidelines for the Cultural Revolution.

Also on the agenda was the criticism of **Peng Zhen, Luo Ruiqing, Lu Dingyi**, and **Yang Shangkun** for their alleged anti-party activities and their "revisionist line." The accusations led to the Politburo's decision to suspend these four of their official duties and to investigate the apparently isolated cases as evidence of a **Peng-Luo-Lu-Yang Anti-Party Clique**. The denunciation and dismissal of Peng, Luo, Lu, and Yang was interpreted at the time as the first major victory of Mao's proletarian revolutionary line over a bourgeois revisionist line during the Cultural Revolution.

The meeting marked a quick ascent of ultra-leftist forces in the party leadership. Most key members of the soon-to-be-formed **Central Cultural Revolution Small Group**—Chen Boda, Kang Sheng, **Jiang Qing, Zhang Chunqiao**, Wang Li, **Guan Feng**, and **Qi Benyu**—had the privilege of attending this high-level meeting. The group was established to replace the **Five-Person Cultural Revolution Small Group** led by Peng Zhen. The decision was announced two days after the meeting. At the initial "forum" session, Kang Sheng gave a lengthy report on Mao's recent directives. Zhang Chunqiao and Chen Boda closely followed Kang to lead the attack on Peng, Luo, Lu, and Yang, setting the tone for the rest of the meeting. Liu Shaoqi, **Zhou Enlai**, and **Deng Xiaoping** expressed support for Mao's move against Peng, Luo, Lu, and Yang and conducted self-criticism of their own political insensitivity. In a long and militant speech delivered at the third enlarged session on 18 May, **Lin Biao** accused Peng, Luo, Lu, and Yang of conspiring to usurp the Communist power and restore capitalism. Lin's aggressiveness apparently inspired so much fear that all participants began to attack Peng, Luo, Lu, and Yang relentlessly while criticizing themselves. On 21 May,

Zhou Enlai gave a speech in support of Mao's criticism of Peng, Luo, Lu, and Yang in which Zhou expressed his wish to maintain his revolutionary integrity in his later years by following Mao closely. At an earlier group session as well as the 23 May meeting, Marshal Zhu De was attacked by a number of ranking leaders, including Lin Biao, Zhou Enlai, **Chen Yi**, and Kang Sheng, because he, having been in semi-retirement for years and out of touch with politics, was rather slow in responding both to the campaign against Peng, Luo, Lu, and Yang and to Lin Biao's promotion of **Mao Zedong Thought** at the expense of Marxism-Leninism.

Some executive and personnel decisions were also made at the meeting: that the Beijing municipal party committee be reorganized with **Li Xuefeng** replacing Peng Zhen as first secretary, that **Tao Zhu** be transferred to Beijing and serve as executive secretary of the Secretariat of the CCP Central Committee, and that **Ye Jianying** replace Luo Ruiqing as secretary-general of the Central Military Commission.

ENLARGED POLITBURO SESSIONS, 25 NOVEMBER–5 DECEMBER 1973. Presided over by **Wang Hongwen** and remote-controlled by **Mao Zedong** through his liaisons with **Tang Wensheng** and **Wang Hairong**, these Politburo sessions were held to criticize Premier **Zhou Enlai** for carrying out a "right-wing capitulationist line" in foreign affairs. **Ye Jianying**, who was involved in negotiations with the United States on military exchange and cooperation, was also implicated. An alternative label for them both was **"Zhou-Ye revisionist line."** Preceded by the high-level meetings in May and June in which Zhou, following Mao's order, criticized himself for committing "grave mistakes" in the early days of the **Chinese Communist Party**, and followed by a series of public political campaigns—including the **Criticize Lin and Criticize Confucius** and *Water Margin* **Appraisal** campaigns, in which Zhou was the unnamed target—the Politburo sessions in late 1973 were Mao's most aggressive effort to humiliate and subdue the premier for his moderate and pragmatic approach to state affairs that Mao found inconsistent with his own radical policies.

The event that directly led to the Politburo sessions was Zhou's meeting on the evening of 13 November 1973 with Henry Kissinger, the visiting U.S. secretary of state, whom Mao had received the previous day. After the farewell banquet on the evening of 13 November, Kissinger proposed another round of talks with Zhou alone on the question of Sino-U.S. military cooperation. Having no time to consult with Mao, Zhou accepted the proposal, talked with Kissinger (Tang Wensheng the interpreter on the Chinese side and Winston Lord on the U.S. side were the only other people present) and promised to give him a response on the unresolved issues next morning—that is, after Zhou had a chance to consult with the central leadership. Having tried but failed to get in touch with Mao during the night, Zhou proposed to

Kissinger the following morning that each side appoint an official to continue the dialogues on military cooperation. After Kissinger's departure, Tang Wensheng, following Mao's instruction, asked Zhou to approve the notes she took of Zhou's talks with Kissinger. Then, on November 17, Mao talked to a number of officials at the Ministry of Foreign Affairs, calling for a criticism of "revisionism" in foreign affairs.

A series of meetings followed that eventually led to the enlarged Politburo sessions in late November and early December. These sessions began with Tang's eight-hour report on foreign affairs and on Mao's critical comments. In Mao's view, Zhou was so afraid of the Soviet Union that once the Soviets invaded he would be their "puppet emperor." Therefore, Mao speculated, Zhou opted for protection under the American nuclear umbrella. Mao's view set the tone for the meeting. The Politburo members and others attending the meeting had to speak against the premier, though most of them, as they later confessed, did so against their own will. **Jiang Qing** proposed, with Mao's approval, to form a "help group" to criticize Zhou. She also said that Zhou "couldn't wait to replace the Chairman" and that the conflict between Mao and Zhou was the "eleventh line struggle within the party," which put Zhou in parallel with **Liu Shaoqi** (enemy of the ninth line struggle) and **Lin Biao** (the tenth). **Deng Xiaoping**, attending the meeting at Mao's request as a non-member of the Politburo and, being obliged to speak, warned Zhou not to go too far because he was so close to Mao that Mao's power was not beyond reach for him. Zhou Enlai listened, took notes, and wrote a self-denouncement.

Eventually, Mao dismissed Jiang Qing's notion of the "eleventh line struggle" and claimed that Tang Wensheng and Wang Hairong's report on the Zhou-Kissinger talks was misleading. After the downfall of the **Gang of Four** in 1976, the records of these sessions were destroyed upon request by Zhou Enlai's widow Deng Yingchao and Marshal Ye Jianying. The existing official version of the event mentions Mao's having been misled by the Tang-Wang report in criticizing the premier but covers up the enlarged Politburo sessions of late 1973 altogether.

EVENING CHATS AT YANSHAN. (Yanshan yehua.) A major target of criticism at the beginning stage of the Cultural Revolution, *Evening Chats at Yanshan* was originally a newspaper column by Ma Nancun, which appeared in *Beijing Evening* from March 1961 to September 1962. Ma Nancun was the pen name of **Deng Tuo**, writer and culture and education secretary of the Beijing municipal party committee. "Yanshan," or Mount Yan, is a reference to Beijing's western hills. The column pieces were also published in book form by Beijing Press with the original column title—first as a five-volume series (1961–1962) and then in one volume (1963).

As Deng writes in one of his essays, in "chatting" with his readers at evening hours, he intended to entertain them with some useful knowledge of the past and the present after their day of labor so that they may find their spare time both interesting and meaningful. Rich in history and wit, his essays address contemporary issues and criticize ills of the times. They were so popular at the time that every 30 pieces were reprinted in book form immediately after they appeared in the newspaper column, and altogether, five volumes were published in less than two years. But the popularity of his writing only made him more vulnerable when the Beijing municipal party committee, headed by Mayor **Peng Zhen**, became the first political target of the Cultural Revolution in 1966. Not long after the historical play *Hai Rui Dismissed from Office* by **Wu Han**, deputy mayor of Beijing, was harshly criticized in official media, *Evening Chats at Yanshan* and *Notes from a Three-Family Village*, coauthored by Deng Tuo and two others associated with the municipal leadership of Beijing, also came under attack, especially for these authors' critical, and sometimes satirical, comments on current politics rendered in carefully guarded language of allusions and understatement.

Since Peng Zhen was denounced at the **enlarged Politburo sessions, 4–26 May 1966**, *Evening Chats at Yanshan* and *Notes from a Three-Family Village* were publicly criticized by **Jiang Qing**'s writing group (under the pseudonym Gao Ju) in the article "Opening Fire at the Anti-Party and Anti-Socialist Black Line" published in *Liberation Army Daily* on 8 May 1966. On the following day, *Guangming Daily* carried He Ming's "Open Your Eyes Wide and Tell Truth from Falsehood." On 10 May, Shanghai's *Wenhui Daily* and *Liberation Daily* published **Yao Wenyuan**'s article "Criticizing the 'Three-Family Village': The Reactionary Nature of *Evening Chats at Yanshan* and *Notes from a Three-Family Village*." All these articles denounced *Evening Chats at Yanshan* as "anti-party and anti-socialist talks of the night." On 18 May 1966, Deng Tuo took his own life.

On 2 March 1979, the Beijing municipal party committee, with the approval of the **Chinese Communist Party** Central Committee, rehabilitated Deng Tuo. Beijing Press reprinted the book *Evening Chats at Yanshan* in the same year with a foreword by Deng's widow, Ding Yilan.

EXTENDED CENTRAL CULTURAL REVOLUTION SMALL GROUP ROUTINE MEETINGS. (*Zhongyang wenge pengtouhui.*) Rather than meetings of the **Central Cultural Revolution Small Group** (CCRSG) members as the name may suggest, these were actually executive gatherings of the *de facto* top leadership of the **Chinese Communist Party** (CCP) after Chairman **Mao Zedong**, reacting furiously to the anti–Cultural Revolution **February Adverse Current** (1967), sidelined veteran vice-premiers in **Zhou Enlai**'s State Council (SC) and old marshals in the Central Military

Commission (CMC). With the traditional, constitution-sanctioned top-level party, army, and state apparatuses—namely, the Politburo, the CMC, and the SC—already disabled after the downfall of **Liu Shaoqi, Deng Xiaoping, Tao Zhu,** and Marshal **He Long,** Mao's decision was a further step in reshuffling the central leadership to make it serve his radical cause.

The first of the CCRSG routine meetings took place in spring 1967. Fifteen members served in this extended group—at least for some time—including eight of the CCRSG members **Chen Boda, Kang Sheng, Jiang Qing, Zhang Chunqiao, Yao Wenyuan, Wang Li, Guan Feng, Qi Benyu,** plus Zhou Enlai, **Xie Fuzhi, Huang Yongsheng, Wu Faxian, Wang Dongxing, Ye Qun,** and Wen Yucheng. Premier Zhou Enlai acted as head of the group. Mao's move to establish this group as the *de facto* leading body of the CCP was a landmark victory of the ultra-leftist faction led by Jiang Qing; it virtually canceled the operation of the *ad hoc* "Politburo Standing Committee routine meetings" and put the "CCRSG routine meetings," dominated by the cultural revolutionaries, in their place. The move also helped strengthen **Lin Biao**'s power in the central leadership since three of his close followers—generals Huang Yongsheng and Wu Faxian and Lin's wife, Ye Qun—were included in the group. But it was a major setback for Zhou Enlai's effort to prevent the CCRSG from interfering with the state and military affairs of the SC and CMC. As the only one left of the "old government," Zhou had to renegotiate his position in this new power circle dominated by cultural revolutionaries and manage state affairs with more caution and more compromise in one of the most difficult periods in his political career.

From then on, the CCRSG routine meetings were virtually the highest "cabinet" meetings at which the most important party and state affairs were discussed. These meetings continued to be held from time to time until the dissolution of the CCRSG itself and the establishment of the new party apparatus in April 1969 at the **Ninth National Congress of the CCP,** at which all CCRSG members (except Wang Li, Guan Feng, and Qi Benyu, who had been ousted in August 1967 and January 1968) and all of the three Lin associates in the group became members of the new Politburo.

F

FEBRUARY ADVERSE CURRENT (1967). This phrase refers to the eruption of anti–Cultural Revolution sentiment by a number of marshals and vice-premiers at two top-level meetings in January and February 1967. The veteran leaders' protest concerned what they perceived as three major problems of the Cultural Revolution: the persecution of veteran cadres, the elimination of party leadership, and the evolving chaos in the army. The subsequent campaign, known as the "Retaliation against the February Adverse Current," which took place from late February to the end of April 1967, virtually disabled the highest decision-making body of the **Chinese Communist Party** (CCP), the Politburo, without due process and put the **Central Cultural Revolution Small Group** (CCRSG) in its place.

The old government officials and military leaders let their opposition be felt on two occasions, known as the "two great disturbances": the Central Military Commission (CMC) meeting on 19–20 January 1967 and the CCP Central Committee (CC) briefing sessions on 11 and 16 February. On the first occasion, members of the CMC and the leaders of all military regions met at Jingxi Guesthouse in Beijing to discuss how the Cultural Revolution should be carried out in the army. **Chen Boda** and **Jiang Qing**, of the CCRSG, who were invited to the meeting, insisted that the "great democracy" be enforced in the armed forces, as it was everywhere else, while marshals **Ye Jianying**, **Xu Xiangqian**, and **Nie Rongzhen** strongly opposed the idea on the grounds of national security and stability. At the meeting, Chen and Jiang also attacked Xiao Hua, director of the General Political Department of the **People's Liberation Army** (PLA), accusing him of belittling the CCRSG in matters of the Cultural Revolution. They demanded that Xiao appear at a mass rally of 100,000 to conduct self-criticism. Upon Ye Jianying's timely report after the meeting, Mao's office advised Xiao Hua to ignore Chen and Jiang. The marshals and generals were encouraged by Mao's support for Xiao. As the meeting reconvened the next day, they vented their rage, excoriating the CCRSG for persecuting army officers and inciting the **rebels** against the armed forces. Ye Jianying pounded the table so hard as he spoke that he fractured a bone in his right hand.

The second "great disturbance" took place at Huairen Hall in the Zhongnanhai compound where veteran leaders in charge of the daily affairs of the CCP, the government, and the army met members of the CCRSG at briefing sessions chaired by Premier **Zhou Enlai**. At the meeting on the afternoon of 11 February, Marshal Ye Jianying reproached **Kang Sheng**, Chen Boda, and **Zhang Chunqiao** for turning the party, the government, factories, and farms upside down and for wanting now to stir up the military. He also asked them what they really had in mind when they seized power in Shanghai and adopted the name "**Shanghai People's Commune**" without putting such important affairs of state through proper procedures of discussion at the Politburo. Marshal Xu Xiangqian slapped the table in anger and asked if their uprooting the army was aimed to take away the army's proper role as the main support of the proletarian dictatorship. On 16 February, as the briefing session reconvened, Vice-Premier **Tan Zhenlin** confronted Zhang Chunqiao at the door, asking him why Chen Pixian, the former first secretary of the Shanghai party committee, was not in Beijing, since Chen, at Zhou Enlai's suggestion and with **Mao Zedong**'s approval, was supposed to come to Beijing and be shielded from the abuses of the **Red Guards**.

At the meeting, Tan once again raised the Chen Pixian question. Joined by other vice-premiers, including **Chen Yi**, Yu Qiuli, and **Li Xiannian**, Tan reproached Zhang Chunqiao and other members of the CCRSG for aiming to get rid of all veteran cadres and to eliminate party leadership. Tan called the Cultural Revolution the cruelest instance of struggle in party history, while Chen Yi named it the biggest *bi-gong-xin* (conviction by forced confession) in all of Chinese history. Recalling the CCP rectification movement in Yan'an in the 1940s to make his criticism of China's current situation suggestive and prophetic, Chen Yi pointed out that the top-ranking leaders who were being denounced, including **Liu Shaoqi** and **Deng Xiaoping**, had previously been among Mao's closest supporters. As Li Xiannian blamed an editorial in the party organ the *Red Flag* for initiating attacks on veteran cadres, Zhou Enlai showed his alliance with the veterans with a question to Kang Sheng: "Such an important matter, why didn't you let us read about it first?" **Xie Fuzhi**, vice-premier and minister of public security, on the other hand, time and again sided with members of the CCRSG.

Immediately after the meeting, on the night of 16 February, Zhang Chunqiao, Yao Wenyuan, and Wang Li prepared the minutes of the briefing sessions. Jiang Qing arranged to have the sessions reported to Mao on 17 February before Zhou Enlai had a chance to see Mao. In the meantime, Chen Yi continued to criticize certain measures of the Cultural Revolution in a long speech addressed to students on the evening of 16 February, while Tan Zhenlin wrote **Lin Biao** a letter on 17 February, denouncing the ultra-leftists of the CCRSG in the strongest possible language: "They are completely ruthless; one word and a person's political life is done. . . . Our party is smeared beyond recognition." Without mentioning her name, Tan spoke of Jiang Qing as "more of a terror than Wu Zetian" (empress of the Tang Dynasty, who reigned 685–705). Lin Biao passed the letter to Mao with a comment that Tan's thinking had unexpectedly deteriorated into confusion.

Mao's immediate reaction to the news of the briefing sessions was fury. On the night of 18 February, Mao convened part of the Politburo to a meeting, during which he sharply criticized the marshals and vice-premiers. He considered the target of their protest to be himself and accused them of siding with the "black headquarters" of Liu Shaoqi and Deng Xiaoping and attempting to reverse the verdicts. Mao also ordered Tan Zhenlin, Chen Yi, and Xu Xiangqian to be on leave to conduct self-criticism. From 25 February to 18 March, seven party cell meetings were held in Huairen Hall to criticize Tan, Chen, and others. At these meetings, members of the CCRSG accused the veteran leaders of creating a "February Adverse Current" to oppose Mao's Cultural Revolution policies and protect a handful of **capitalist-roaders**. Kang Sheng called the Huairen Hall "disturbance" "a rehearsal for a kind of coup d'état, a rehearsal for a capitalist revival." In the meantime, the CCRSG began to leak the news out of the Zhongnanhai compound and initiate a nationwide mass movement to criticize the February Adverse Current and to bring down the marshals and vice-premiers.

Mao, on the other hand, did not want the condemnation of the veterans to go that far. On 30 April, Mao invited the veterans to his home for a "gathering for unity" and allowed them to watch fireworks from Tiananmen on 1 May, International Labor Day. As these old cadres' names were listed in all the newspapers on May Day indicating Mao's judgment, Jiang Qing and her supporters in the CCRSG had to halt for the moment their retaliation against the February Adverse Current campaign. They raised the issue again in October 1968 at the **Twelfth Plenum of the CCP Eighth Central Committee** and in April 1969 at the **Ninth National Congress of the CCP**, but, without much encouragement from Mao, they could not carry the issue further. After Lin Biao's downfall in September 1971, Mao essentially reversed his critical attitude and spoke of the "great disturbance at Huairen Hall" as an act against Lin Biao, Chen Boda, and **Wang-Guan-Qi** (an alleged anti-party clique). He suggested that the February Adverse Current not be mentioned again.

In early 1979, the CCP Central Committee redressed the February Adverse Current case. Since then the reactionary-sounding referent has often been rephrased in official media as a "February resistance" to indicate the righteousness in the veteran leaders' clashes with the ultra-leftist forces within the CCP during the Cultural Revolution.

FEBRUARY MUTINY. This was a rumor used by **Kang Sheng** in the early stages of the Cultural Revolution to persecute **Peng Zhen** and **He Long**. In February 1966, as directed by the Central Military Commission, the Beijing

Military Region began organizing a regiment in its Garrison Command to train militia and maintain security, but a suitable barracks was not immediately available. Since some college students were in the countryside participating in the **Socialist Education Movement** at the time, the Garrison Command at first negotiated with Peking University and Renmin University about the possibility of quartering the troops temporarily in student dormitories but then decided to give up the idea and seek shelter elsewhere. By July 1966, Peng Zhen, mayor of Beijing, was already denounced as a **"black gang"** member and an "anti-party element." Some students at Peking University, in an information-exchange and brainstorming session, recalled the negotiation and began to speculate on a possible connection between the housing issue raised in February and the **February Outline** that Peng Zhen had helped to produce. Pure speculation soon led to the writing of a **big-character poster** entitled "The Mind-Boggling February Mutiny," in which the dormitory negotiation was assumed to be preparation for a coup by Peng Zhen and Deputy Mayor **Liu Ren**.

Speaking at a mass rally at Beijing Normal University on 27 July, Kang Sheng charged Peng Zhen and other leaders of the Beijing party committee with plotting a coup. In September 1966, Kang began to incriminate Marshal He Long with sensational details about the so-called February Mutiny: that He Long mustered troops and built fortresses in Beijing suburbs, that people at the National Sports Commission led by He Long were equipped with guns, and that cannons were set in Shichahai Park and were aimed at the Zhongnanhai compound. In the capacity of advisor to the **Central Cultural Revolution Small Group**, Kang Sheng's charges were widely believed to have been based on credible evidence. On 29 June 1974, the Central Committee (CC) of the **Chinese Communist Party** issued a formal notice rehabilitating He Long, which dismissed the February Mutiny as pure rumor. But Kang Sheng's role in this notorious persecution case was not mentioned until 1980 when the CC formally concluded the investigation of the February Mutiny case, denouncing Kang Sheng for his use of rumor to bring down Peng Zhen and He Long.

FEBRUARY OUTLINE (1966). Officially entitled "**Five-Person Cultural Revolution Small Group**'s Outline Report concerning the Current Academic Discussion," this **Chinese Communist Party** (CCP) document was issued to party organizations nationwide on 12 February 1966 as a guideline for the ongoing political criticism of literary and academic writing. The Politburo's condemnation of this document three months later marked the official beginning of the Cultural Revolution.

Since **Yao Wenyuan**'s critique of **Wu Han**'s historical play *Hai Rui Dismissed from Office* was first carried in Shanghai's *Wenhui Daily* on 10 November 1965, the fire of political criticism had been spreading rapidly across China. Criticism was becoming more militant and threatened to implicate more well-known authors. In the meantime, **Mao Zedong**'s comment that the "vital area" of Wu's play is dismissal and that **Peng Dehuai** (a minister of defense dismissed in 1959) is also Hai Rui oriented the movement toward current politics. To provide guidance for the ongoing political movement, **Peng Zhen**, mayor of Beijing and head of the Five-Person Group, convened an enlarged meeting of the group on 3 February 1966. The ideas discussed at the meeting were summarized by deputy directors of the CCP Propaganda Department Xu Liqun and Yao Zhen in the form of an outline report.

The outline was approved by the Politburo Standing Committee on 5 February and by Mao on 8 February. It was issued as an official document on 12 February. The outline affirms the criticism of Wu Han and the discussion and debate such criticism inspired. It defines the current debate as a great struggle of the proletariat against bourgeois ideas in ideological and academic spheres. On the other hand, it seems also to try to retain as much liberal attitude as circumstances permit. It demands that academic discussions "follow the principles of seeking the truth and of everyone being equal in front of the truth, convince others with reason, and not intimidate others with the arbitrariness and the authority of a scholar-tyrant." The outline also advises caution in criticizing a person by name in a newspaper or magazine.

In late March, Mao, contradicting his initial support for the February Outline, called it erroneous and criticized the Five-Person Group, the CCP Propaganda Department, and the CCP Beijing Municipal Committee. At the **enlarged Politburo sessions, 4–26 May 1966**, Peng Zhen was branded head of the **Peng-Luo-Lu-Yang Anti-Party Clique** largely due to his attempt to limit the issues of a cultural revolution to literary and academic matters. The **May 16 Circular**, approved at the meeting and considered to be one of the programmatic documents of the Cultural Revolution, was essentially an item-by-item refutation of the February Outline.

FEBRUARY SUPPRESSION OF COUNTERREVOLUTIONARIES (1967). (*Eryue zhenfan.*) This term refers to crackdowns on **rebel** organizations by army troops beginning in February 1967 in many places throughout the country. Though these events were considered part of the much-publicized **February Adverse Current** and had a strong impact on the conflicts among mass organizations, the referent was not adopted in the official narrative of the Cultural Revolution.

Following a directive by Chairman **Mao Zedong**, the **Chinese Communist Party** Central Committee, the State Council, the Central Military Commission (CMC), and the **Central Cultural Revolution Small Group** jointly issued on 23 January the "Decision to Provide the Revolutionary Masses of the Left with Firm Support from the **People's Liberation Army** (PLA)."

This document marked the beginning of PLA troops' involvement in the Cultural Revolution mass movement and prepared the stage for the February crackdown.

Mao's original intention was to involve the PLA in his battle against the party establishment in the form of supporting the rebels he had mobilized. But there was no clear indication in his directive or the party document as to which of the competing factions among mass organizations were on the left. Meanwhile, largely because of their close associations with local party and government leadership, many PLA commanders at provincial and regional levels supported **conservative** mass organizations (which were usually on the side of the local party establishment) in opposition to the rebel faction; they even considered the rebel leaders challenging their military control mission to be counterrevolutionary. This position also won support from a number of marshals such as **Ye Jianying** and **Xu Xiangqian**, who were in charge of the daily affairs of the CMC. As a result, massive persecutions and atrocities committed by army troops against civilian populations occurred in many places at the largest scale since the beginning of the Cultural Revolution. In Hunan and Sichuan Provinces, for instance, an estimated 100,000 to 150,000 people were arrested, and thousands of rebel leaders were **struggled against** at mass rallies. In Qinghai Province, 165 civilians were killed by PLA soldiers during the bloody **February 23 Incident**.

In late February to April 1967, as Mao launched a campaign against the February Adverse Current in which Ye Jianying and Xu Xiangqian, among a few other ranking leaders, were implicated, the rebel organizations under attack during the February crackdown were rehabilitated and their leaders released. The tension between rebels and army leaders as a result of the crackdown, however, was never completely resolved; it even lingered beyond the Cultural Revolution.

FEBRUARY 12 PUBLIC NOTICE CONCERNING NATIONAL MASS ORGANIZATIONS (1967). Coded *zhongfa* [67] 47, this is a public announcement jointly issued by the Central Committee (CC) of the **Chinese Communist Party** and the State Council (SC) to delegitimize and disband all national mass organizations. The document begins with the assertion of the CC and the SC that all mass organizations at the national level (not necessarily in schools or work units or at the city or provincial level) are nondemocratic and that some were even put together by reactionary elements of the **"five black categories."** The CC and the SC therefore ordered that no national mass organization be recognized, that all existing ones be disbanded, that all public funds in the possession of these organizations be returned, and that members of these organizations report to agencies of public security in case of counterrevolutionary activities. On 15 February, the Military Control Commission at the Beijing Bureau of Public Security pronounced three national organizations, including the **National Red Workers Rebel Corps**, as reactionary and six others as illegal. Leaders of the first three organizations were arrested. From this point on until the end of the Cultural Revolution, no national mass organization appeared again anywhere in China.

FEBRUARY 23 INCIDENT (1967). Also known as the **Zhao Yongfu** Incident, this term refers to the violent clash between a mass organization and armed troops on 23 February 1967 in Xining, the capital city of Qinghai Province. Zhao Yongfu was deputy commander of the Qinghai provincial military district of the **People's Liberation Army** (PLA). He also served as deputy director of the coordination office set up at the order of Beijing to lead the troops in supporting the left. Following a directive from Beijing authorizing military control of newspapers and radio stations, the coordination office sent troops to take over the provincial newspaper *Qinghai Daily* from the hands of a mass organization called the Xining August 18 Red Guard Battalion. After the **Red Guards** forced the PLA men out, the coordination office decided to take the newspaper office building by force. Zhao was entrusted with the organization and command of the operation. On 23 February, as the armed troops moved in, a violent encounter took place between them and the civilians, who were not armed. The fighting ended with 169 civilians and four soldiers dead, and 178 civilians and 46 military men injured.

The role of the central leadership in this operation is still shrouded in mystery. According to Zhao, he telephoned the office of **Lin Biao** for instructions ahead of the military operation, and Lin's office expressed support. According to **Wang Li**'s recollection, Lin congratulated Zhao on a successful military action but later blamed Marshal **Ye Jianying**, who was then in charge of daily affairs of the Central Military Commission (CMC), for the bloody incident. It is at least clear that sometime after the event, **Ye Qun** spoke for Lin's office and denied any knowledge of Operation February 23, while Lin and **Jiang Qing** began to talk about the bloody event as a local reflection of Beijing's **February Adverse Current**. On 23 March, **Zhou Enlai** announced the decision of the central leadership that Zhao Yongfu had conducted a military coup and suppressed the masses and that he was to be taken into custody and under investigation. Two other ranking officials were also implicated. In the Ten Commands of the CMC dictated by Lin Biao and approved by Mao on 6 April, Zhao Yongfu was mentioned as a "counterrevolutionary."

After the Cultural Revolution, the Central Committee of the **Chinese Communist Party** and the CMC reinvestigated the Zhao Yongfu case and concluded that Zhao had made a mistake in an early stage of the Cultural Revolution in the midst of the chaos caused by Lin Biao, Jiang Qing, and their followers and that Zhao's mistake did not go beyond the "contradictions among the people." For punishment, Zhao was dismissed from his posts in both the party and the government, but his administrative rank was to remain intact.

FIRST MARXIST-LENINIST BIG-CHARACTER POSTER. This was a common reference to the **big-character poster** "What Are **Song Shuo, Lu Ping**, and **Peng Peiyun** Really Doing during the Cultural Revolution?" by seven faculty members of the Department of Philosophy at Peking University: **Nie Yuanzi**, Song Yixiu, Xia Jianzhi, Yang Keming, Zhao Zhengyi, Gao Yunpeng, and Li Xingchen. Most of the coauthors participated in the discussion and revision of the first, second, and third draft versions of the poster, which were written, respectively, by Zhao, Song, and Yang, but because of Nie's position as party secretary of the department and a senior faculty member, her signature tops the others' on the final version that was mounted on the wall of a school dining hall on 25 May 1966. Having this particular poster broadcast nationwide on 1 June was one of the most decisive moves Chairman **Mao Zedong** made to mobilize the masses and stir up the nation for the Cultural Revolution. The poster became known as the "first Marxist-Leninist big-character poster" when Mao called it such in early August in his "**Bombarding the Headquarters**—My Own Big-Character Poster."

The poster accuses Song Shuo, deputy director of the university department of the Beijing municipal party committee, Lu Ping, president of Peking University, and Peng Peiyun, deputy-party secretary of the university, of conspiring with the Beijing Municipal Committee in an attempt to suppress the revolutionary activities of the faculty, staff, and students in the name of "strengthening the leadership" and to contain the ongoing Cultural Revolution on campus in a theoretical and academic discussion. Their actions were, according to the authors, revisionist and counterrevolutionary.

Despite its high-flown political rhetoric, the poster had much to do with an internal political conflict during the Socialist Education Movement between Nie and her colleagues, on the one hand, and Lu Ping and the university party committee, on the other: in 1964, Nie and her colleagues had accused Lu and his party committee of carrying out a bourgeois line but eventually lost the political battle after the Beijing municipal party committee led by Peng Zhen stepped in to support Lu, discounting the accusations by Nie and her colleagues. To assist Lu, the municipal committee appointed Song Shuo a leading member of the Peking University Socialist Education Movement work team and made Peng Peiyun a deputy party secretary of the university. The new political movement now provided an opportunity for the comeback of Nie and her colleagues. They wrote the poster also with the knowledge of the downfall of Peng Zhen, along with the entire Beijing Municipal Committee, at the enlarged Politburo sessions, 4–26 May 1966. Furthermore, according to Nie, as they were drafting the poster, they gained moral support from Cao Yi'ou, wife of Kang Sheng and head of an investigation group sent to Peking University by Kang on 14 May 1966.

Since more than 100,000 big-character posters appearing on campus shortly after the poster of the Nie group demonstrated more opposition than support, Yang Keming sought help from Cao Yi'ou. Eventually, on 1 June, a copy of the poster reached Mao via Kang Sheng, and Mao's reaction was swift and positive. Closely following Mao's directive, the Central People's Radio broadcast the poster at 8:30 p.m., and, on the following day, *People's Daily* published the entire text of the poster under the banner headline "Seven Comrades at Peking University Uncover Secret Plot." The paper also carried a commentary entitled "Hail the Big-Character Poster at Peking University." The unprecedented publicity for a short big-character poster ignited the fire of a mass movement, especially on school campuses, across China that challenged the Chinese Communist Party leadership at various levels. At the Eleventh Plenum of the Eighth CCP Central Committee (1–12 August 1966), Mao called the poster the "declaration of the Paris Commune of the 1960s—Beijing Commune" and the "first Marxist-Leninist big-character poster in China," which sent another shock wave across the country, and this time the challenge was aimed squarely at what Mao called the "bourgeois headquarters"—soon to be revealed as President Liu Shaoqi and his supporters in the party leadership.

FIVE BLACK CATEGORIES. (*Heiwulei.*) A pejorative label commonly used in the Cultural Revolution, the "five black categories" refers to people who were classified as landlords and rich peasants during the Communist-led Land Reform in the late 1940s and the early 1950s and to those labeled as counterrevolutionaries, bad elements, and rightists in a series of political campaigns after the founding of the People's Republic of China. Already seen as "targets of the proletarian dictatorship" before the Cultural Revolution, people in these categories were invariably persecuted and repressed during the entire 10-year period of the revolution. They were subject to public humiliation, physical abuse, forced labor, confiscation of personal property, exile from the cities, and, in a number of isolated cases, even massacre. Their children and even grandchildren—especially in the countryside, where the party's class identification criteria were often applied to the third generation—were discriminated against and were often forced to **"make a clean break"** with their parents. Many of them, like their parents, were also subject to humiliation and abuse, especially at the hands of the **Red Guards** from families of the **"five red categories"** in the beginning months of the Cultural Revolution.

"571 PROJECT" SUMMARY. (*Wuqiyi gongcheng jiyao.*) With "571" (pronounced "wu-qi-yi" in Chinese) homonymically suggestive of "armed uprising" (*wuzhuang qiyi*), *"571 Project" Summary* was allegedly a plan for an armed coup devised in March 1971 in Shanghai by **Lin Liguo**, son of **Lin Biao**, and some young **People's Liberation Army** (PLA) officers close to him, including Yu Xinye (who was said to have drafted the Summary), Zhou Yuchi, and Li Weixin. The document was reportedly discovered after the **September 13 Incident** in a red notebook left by Lin Liguo and his associates at a secret depot at an air force academy in Beijing. On 14 November 1971, the Central Committee of the **Chinese Communist Party** issued nationwide a document that included the *"571 Project" Summary* as evidence of the alleged armed coup by Lin Biao and his supporters, though no evidence was given concerning Lin Biao's involvement in the making of the Summary.

The nine-part Summary claims that a power struggle is going on and that the other side (the **Jiang Qing** group) is planning to replace Lin Biao with someone else as **Mao Zedong**'s successor. Mao, referred to by the code name "B-52" in the Summary, is perceived as no longer trusting Lin Biao and his supporters in the army; as a result, the power struggle is "going in a direction that will benefit those working with pens but not those holding guns." Therefore, rather than waiting to be eliminated, "we"—that is, Lin Biao and his associates—shall launch a "violent revolution," starting with a military action followed by political control, to stop the current "counterrevolution in the manner of peaceful evolution." For this purpose, the alleged designers of the Summary prefer to "round up all the high-ranking cadres while they are at a meeting" and force Mao to give up power, but "poison gas, bacterial weapons, bombing, 543 [a missile], car accident, assassination, kidnapping, and urban guerrilla troops" may also be employed if necessary.

Aside from details concerning the armed coup, the Summary contains a series of diagnoses of China's current political situation that actually articulated the widespread, and yet very much self-censored, discontents of the nation. Among such diagnoses are "the core ruling clique is very unstable in their infighting among themselves for power and profits," "peasants lack food and clothing," "**educated youths** going **up to the mountains and down to the countryside** is virtually forced labor in disguise," "**Red Guards** were deceived and used as cannon fodder at the outset (of the Cultural Revolution) and were later put down as scapegoats," "cadres going to **May 7 cadre schools** is virtually job loss in disguise," and "the freezing of workers' wages is nothing but exploitation."

The Summary was also known for its sharp criticism of Mao. According to the Summary, Mao is not a real Marxist-Leninist; rather, he has abused the trust of the Chinese people and become the "Qinshihuang [First Emperor of

Qin, known for his despotism] of modern China." The Summary dismisses Chinese socialism as fascism and Mao as paranoid, a sadistic persecutor, and the "biggest feudal tyrant in Chinese history."

Ironically, when the Summary was distributed nationwide in late 1971 as evidence of Lin Biao's crimes, many readers, though horrified and disgusted by the alleged coup, nevertheless found its criticism of Mao and the Cultural Revolution to be an echo of their own judgment. Many considered the downfall of Lin Biao and the release of the *"571 Project" Summary* to be the beginning of their disillusionment about Chinese politics and of their consciously critical judgment of the Cultural Revolution.

FIVE OLD PIECES. This term was a common reference to the five most popular works of **Mao Zedong** endorsed by the central leadership as core material for political studies during the Cultural Revolution. As an expansion of the **"three old pieces"** ("The Foolish Old Man Who Removed the Mountains," "In Memory of Norman Bethune," and "Serve the People"), already popular before the Cultural Revolution, the "five old pieces" included two more essays: "On Rectifying Wrong Ideas in the Party" (1929) and "Oppose Liberalism" (1939).

FIVE RED CATEGORIES. (*Hongwulei.*) A political term widely used during the Cultural Revolution, the "five red categories" refers to people from the families of workers, poor and lower-middle-class peasants, revolutionary cadres, revolutionary military personnel, and revolutionary martyrs. Early **Red Guard** organizations adopted a membership policy admitting only those from families of the "five red categories." Of the "revolutionary cadre" category, according to popular definitions made by some Red Guards, those who joined the **Chinese Communist Party** before 1938 (before the war of resistance against Japan) or, in some cases, before 1945 (before the civil war of 1946–1949) were more authentic or more legitimate revolutionary cadres than latecomers. With their family background as inherited political capital, people of the "five red categories" enjoyed considerable political privilege during the Cultural Revolution. Some of them, proud and self-righteous, considered their family background to be evidence of their political identity and therefore saw themselves as natural successors to the revolutionary cause and to the Communist regime.

FIVE-PERSON CULTURAL REVOLUTION SMALL GROUP. (*Wenhua geming wuren xiaozu.*) This group was formed in early July 1964 to lead a rectification movement in literature and art circles, which turned out to be an immediate prelude of the Cultural Revolution. On 12 December 1963 and again on 27 June 1964, **Mao Zedong** harshly criticized party leaders in literature and art circles for deviating from socialist principles and promoting what he considered to be feudalist and bourgeois art. In his judgment, the leadership of the **Chinese Communist Party** (CCP) in this area had been off course from correct party policies since 1949. Based on Mao's criticism and at Mao's proposal, the CCP Central Committee (CC) decided to conduct rectification in literature and art circles and set up a five-person group to lead the movement. The group consisted of **Peng Zhen**, **Lu Dingyi**, **Kang Sheng**, **Zhou Yang**, and Wu Lengxi. Peng, mayor and first party secretary of Beijing, was appointed head of the group, while Lu, director of the Propaganda Department of the CC and a vice-premier of the State Council, served as deputy head. After **Yao Wenyuan** published "On the New Historical Drama *Hai Rui Dismissed from Office*" in Shanghai's *Wenhui Daily* in November 1965 attacking **Wu Han**, author of *Hai Rui* and a renowned historian and a deputy mayor of Beijing, Peng ordered Beijing's newspapers not to reprint Yao's article, without knowing Mao's full support for Yao.

In February 1966, as the criticism of Wu Han continued, the five-person group submitted to the CC a policy guideline entitled "Outline Report concerning the Current Academic Discussion," also known as the **February Outline**. Initiated largely by Peng Zhen, the document attempted to confine the criticism of Wu and a few other writers and scholars to the realm of academia and prevent it from becoming a high-pitched political condemnation campaign. With Mao's approval, the CC quickly distributed the document nationwide. In late March, however, Mao began to criticize the February Outline and accused the Five-Person Cultural Revolution Small Group of suppressing the left and protecting the right. At the **enlarged Politburo sessions, 4–26 May 1966**, the central leadership announced decisions to revoke the February Outline, to dissolve the Five-Person Cultural Revolution Small Group, and to form a new **Central Cultural Revolution Small Group** under the Politburo. And with the passage of the **May 16 Circular** as a critique of the February Outline, the Cultural Revolution was officially launched.

FOUR CLEANS (1962–1966). *See* SOCIALIST EDUCATION MOVEMENT (1962–1966).

FOUR FELLOWS. (*Sitiao hanzi.*) The modern Chinese writer Lu Xun coined this pejorative term to refer to **Tian Han**, **Zhou Yang**, Xia Yan, and Yang Hansheng in one of his polemics written in 1936. "Four Fellows" was used again during the Cultural Revolution and publicized much more broadly by the critics of these four people—all of them were, by then, holding important positions in literary and artistic circles: Zhou was a deputy minister of culture and a deputy head of the Communist party's propaganda department;

Tian, president of the China Federation of Literature and Art Circles and president and party secretary of the Association of Chinese Dramatists; Xia, a deputy minister of culture (until 1965) and president of the Association of Chinese Film Artists; and Yang, party secretary of the China Federation of Literature and Art Circles. With Lu Xun's harsh remark already a liability, the four writers and officials were accused of having carried out a "black line" in the area of literature and art against **Mao Zedong**'s revolutionary policies since 1949, and they were among the first to fall from power during the Cultural Revolution.

FOUR GREATS. (*Sige weida.*) This is a reference to Chairman **Mao Zedong**'s honorific title "great teacher, great leader, great commander, and great helmsman." In a speech delivered at the **mass rally of 18 August 1966, Chen Boda** called Mao "the great leader, the great teacher, and the great helmsman." At the same event, **Lin Biao** spoke of Mao as the "great commander" of the Cultural Revolution. Lin used the four phrases together for the first time in a public speech on 31 August 1966. Lin's handwritten slogan "Long live great teacher, great leader, great commander, and great helmsman Chairman Mao" turned out to be one of the most widely printed pieces of calligraphy during the Cultural Revolution.

FOUR NEVER-FORGETS. (*Sige niannianbuwang.*) This phrase is a common reference to "Never forget **class struggle**, never forget proletarian dictatorship, never forget stressing politics, and never forget holding high the great red banner of **Mao Zedong Thought**," one of the most popular political slogans used at mass rallies and **struggle meetings** during the Cultural Revolution.

See also LIN BIAO: MAY 18 SPEECH (1966).

FOUR OLDS. (*Sijiu.*) This term is a short form for "old ideas, old culture, old customs, and old habits." *See* DESTROY THE FOUR OLDS.

FOURTH INTERNATIONAL COUNTERREVOLUTIONARY CLIQUE. Labeled by the government as counterrevolutionary, this was a reading group active in the first half of the 1970s. The leader of the group was Xu Xiao, an **educated youth** from Beijing. Xu was inspired by her older friend Zhao Yifan's book-reading salon and organized a correspondent group of some 20 young workers and army soldiers in Beijing, Shanghai, and Shanxi Province in the early 1970s. The members of the group shared volumes from two internally published book series known as "**grey books and yellow books.**" They wrote to one another describing what they learned from the books and discussed current politics in their letters without knowing that their correspondence was being monitored by government censors. All members of the group were arrested and imprisoned in late 1975 on the charges of circulating items of counterrevolutionary literature, exchanging ideas against party leaders, and opposing the campaign to **Criticize Lin and Criticize Confucius**. The label "Fourth International" by which the government named the group was based on an accusation that Xu Xiao and Zhao Yifan attempted to organize a group to initiate a new stage of the international Communist movement. The members of the Fourth International Counterrevolutionary Clique were rehabilitated in 1978.

FOURTH NATIONAL PEOPLE'S CONGRESS (13–17 January 1975).
The only National People's Congress held during the Cultural Revolution, the meeting opened in Beijing shortly after the Second Plenum of the Tenth Central Committee (CC) of the **Chinese Communist Party** (CCP); it was presided over by Premier **Zhou Enlai**, and **Deng Xiaoping** was elected vice-chairman of the Central Committee and member of the Politburo Standing Committee. Three days before the plenum, Deng was also appointed vice-chairman of the Central Military Commission and chief of the general staff of the **People's Liberation Army**. In his "Report on Government Work" delivered at the Fourth National People's Congress, Zhou reaffirmed the economic blueprint approved by the pre–Cultural Revolution Third National People's Congress (21 December 1964–4 January 1965) for accomplishing "four modernizations" (the modernization of agriculture, industry, national defense, and science and technology) to make China a strong socialist country by the end of the 20th century. With strong support from Zhou (who was then suffering from cancer and ready to transfer his responsibilities to Deng) and the approval of Chairman **Mao Zedong**, the fourth congress appointed Deng Xiaoping first premier of the State Council. The stage was set for Deng's 1975 **overall rectification**.

On the political and ideological front, however, the fourth congress upheld Mao's radical policies. Both Zhou Enlai's speech and **Zhang Chunqiao**'s "Report on Revising the Constitution" affirmed the party's "basic line (of class existence and **class struggle**) for the entire socialist period" and Mao's theory of **continuing revolution under the dictatorship of the proletariat**. In defining the **revolutionary committee** at a local level as both the permanent organ of the local People's Congress and the local government body, the revised constitution sanctified the power structure established during the Cultural Revolution and granted it both legislative and administrative authority. The 1975 constitution also became the first to rule officially that the power of a political party was superior to that of the state: following Mao's suggestion, it abolished the office of the president of the nation; it stipulated that the National People's Congress was the highest institution of power under the leadership of the CCP and that the chairman of the CCP was also commander-in-chief of all the armed forces. With non-party members constituting only 23.2 percent of all delegates attending the fourth congress, the lowest non-party representation of any congress in the history of the People's Republic, and with the so-called democratic consultation rather than grassroots election as the way of selecting congressional delegates, the *people's* congress became a euphemism for party dominance.

FU CHONGBI (1916–2003). Named commanding officer of the Beijing Garrison Command in 1966, General Fu was persecuted by **Lin Biao** and **Jiang Qing** in 1968 as a member of the so-called Yang-Yu-Fu Anti-Party Clique. Born in Tongjiang, Sichuan Province, Fu joined the Red Army in 1932 and became a member of the **Chinese Communist Party** (CCP) in the following year. Due to his outstanding military service, Fu was named major general in 1955 and became commander of the 10th Brigade of the North-China Military Region and then commander of the **People's Liberation Army** 19th Division. In addition to the position of deputy commander of the Beijing Military Region that he had held since 1965, Fu was made commanding officer of the Beijing Garrison Command in 1966. In the early stages of the Cultural Revolution when cultural revolutionaries in the central leadership, supported by **Mao Zedong**, called upon mass organizations to attack a great number of senior party and military officials, Fu Chongbi, in the capacity of the Beijing Garrison Commander, followed instructions from Premier **Zhou Enlai** and provided certain protection for some senior officials to the displeasure of Jiang Qing and her followers in the **Central Cultural Revolution Small Group** (CCRSG).

In March 1968, when Lin Biao sought support from the Jiang Qing group for the removal of generals **Yang Chengwu** and **Yu Lijin**, Jiang asked Lin to dismiss Fu as well. As a result of this political bargain, Lin, with the approval of Mao Zedong, named the three generals a Yang-Yu-Fu Anti-Party Clique in March 1968. The charge against Fu was that he led soldiers to storm the office of the CCRSG, while the truth was that Fu and three military officers were there for official business with the permission of the CCRSG. Nevertheless, Fu was arrested on this blatantly false charge and was imprisoned for more than six years. After the downfall of Lin Biao and his associates in the army in September 1971, Mao began to seek support from other military factions. He acknowledged some of his mistakes in December 1973, and the CCP Central Committee (CC) rehabilitated the case of the **Yang-Yu-Fu Affair** in July 1974. Fu was reappointed deputy commander of the Beijing Military Region in 1975 and commanding officer of the Beijing Garrison Command in 1977. In March 1979, the CC officially rehabilitated the case of the Yang-Yu-Fu Affair by publicizing its 1974 decision for the first time. Fu died on 17 January 2003.

FU LEI (1908–1966). A native of Shanghai, Fu Lei read Chinese classics at an early age and was trained in literature and the arts in Paris in his early 20s. Starting his career as a translator of foreign—mostly French—literature in the 1930s, Fu put into Chinese major novels by Honoré de Balzac and Romain Rolland and tales of Voltaire. His translated works totaling five million words, Fu Lei was one of the few prolific, refined, and truly great translators in China. He was also a highly respected literary and art critic and a fine letter-writer in his own right. In 1957, Fu was denounced as a rightist during the Anti-Rightist Campaign. In summer 1966 when the Cultural Revolution broke out, Fu's house was ransacked by the **Red Guards**. He and his wife, Zhu Meifu, became targets of the revolution, subject to public humiliation and physical abuse. In the early hours of 3 September 1966, Fu Lei and Zhu Meifu hanged themselves at home to protest the humiliation and torture they suffered at **struggle meetings**. On 26 April 1979, the Shanghai literature and art circles held a memorial service for Fu and Zhu. At the memorial service, an official announcement was made that naming Fu Lei as a rightist in 1957 was a mistake and that all accusations against him in 1966 were groundless.

G

GANG OF FOUR. (*Sirenbang*.) A popular name for the group of die-hard cultural revolutionaries in the party leadership consisting of **Jiang Qing, Zhang Chunqiao, Yao Wenyuan**, and **Wang Hongwen**, the phrase "Gang of Four" was first used by Chairman **Mao Zedong** in 1974 to criticize the factionalism of the four and was later adopted by the Central Committee (CC) of the **Chinese Communist Party** (CCP) in October 1976 as an alternative reference to the "Wang Hongwen, Zhang Chunqiao, Jiang Qing, and Yao Wenyuan Anti-Party Clique." The ordering of the names was in accordance with the rankings of the four within the CCP leadership at the time of their arrest. Later, the official reference to the group was changed to the "Jiang Qing Counterrevolutionary Clique" since Jiang was the real leader of the group.

The Gang of Four was an alliance of Mao's wife, Jiang Qing, with three ultra-leftists originally based in Shanghai. In 1964 and 1965, Jiang, who had no official position in the government, followed Mao's instructions and began to be active in the area of literature and the arts. As her push for a revolution in art and literature met resistance in Beijing, she went to Shanghai and received much support from Zhang Chunqiao, a secretary of the CCP Shanghai Municipal Committee. The two entrusted Yao Wenyuan, director of the art and literature department of the newspaper *Liberation Daily*, with the writing of a critique of **Wu Han**'s historical play *Hai Rui Dismissed from Office*. The publication of Yao's article in *Wenhui Daily* on 10 November 1965 was generally considered to be the "blasting fuse" of the Cultural Revolution. In May 1966, when the **Central Cultural Revolution Small Group** (CCRSG) was formed, Jiang became first deputy head, Zhang deputy head, and Yao a member of the group. In November 1966, Wang Hongwen, a cadre in the security section of Shanghai No. 17 Textile Factory and commander of the mass organization Shanghai **Workers Command Post**, became known for his involvement in a railway blockade at **Anting**. In February 1967, when the Shanghai **Revolutionary Committee** was formed, replacing the old municipal government agencies, Zhang became chairman and Yao and Wang vice-chairmen, though Zhang and Yao stayed most of the time in Beijing for their duties in the CCRSG.

The four became more closely associated after Wang was assigned work in Beijing in September 1972 at Mao's suggestion, and especially after the **Tenth National Congress of the CCP** in August 1973 at which Wang delivered the report on revising the party constitution and was made vice-chairman of the CC and a member of the Politburo Standing Committee. Wang's meteoric rise to the third highest position (after Mao and **Zhou Enlai**) in the central leadership indicated that Mao was making Wang his successor after the downfall of **Lin Biao**. Also at the Tenth CCP National Congress, Zhang entered the Politburo Standing Committee, while both Jiang and Yao continued to be members of the Politburo. At the **enlarged Politburo sessions of 25 November–5 December 1973**, Jiang Qing, with Mao's approval, formed a "help group" to criticize Zhou Enlai. The group included Jiang Qing, Zhang Chunqiao, Yao Wenyuan, Wang Hongwen, **Wang Dongxing**, and **Hua Guofeng**. After a few meetings, Wang Dongxing and Hua Guofeng withdrew, and Jiang, Zhang, Yao, and Wang Hongwen remained close as a group after the Politburo sessions. Frequently meeting at Diaoyutai, an official residential complex in Beijing, they formed an alliance to undermine the efforts of the State Council led by Zhou Enlai and **Deng Xiaoping** to deradicalize government policies and to carry out a modernization program. Following Mao's instructions, Jiang, Zhang, Yao, and Wang led such political campaigns as **Criticize Lin and Criticize Confucius**, Criticize Confucianism and Evaluate Legalism (*piru pingfa*; *see* CONFUCIANISM VERSUS LEGALISM), and *Water Margin* **Appraisal**, all aimed at attacking Zhou and Deng by insinuation.

In the last two years of his life, however, Mao criticized the four on several occasions. The criticism did not concern their ideology, which was closest to Mao's; rather, Mao was warning them against "factionalism"—the "little faction of four" was the phrase Mao used first, and then the "Gang of Four"—because, apparently, he was concerned that his most trusted cultural revolutionaries, sticking together and lacking political tactics, were isolated from the rest of the central leadership. Eventually, the four had become so unpopular that Mao made Hua Guofeng his successor.

On 6 October 1976, within the month of Mao's death, Jiang, Zhang, Yao, and Wang were arrested in Beijing on orders of Hua Guofeng, Wang Dongxing, and **Ye Jianying** in the name of the central leadership. The arrest of the Gang of Four marked the official end of the Cultural Revolution. When the news was made public on 14 October, spontaneous celebrations took place across the nation. Between December 1976 and September 1977, the CC issued three collections of the criminal evidence against the Gang of Four, holding them responsible for virtually all of the excesses of the Cultural

Revolution. At the Third Plenum of the Tenth CCP Central Committee, held in Beijing on 16–21 July 1977, a resolution was passed that Wang, Zhang, Jiang, and Yao (names listed in this order) be dismissed from their official posts and expelled from the party.

GAO, DA, QUAN. Literally, "high, large, and whole (or perfect)," this was a criterion for writers and artists to follow to produce flawless revolutionary heroes as protagonists in their works. In fact, Hao Ran, one of the few literary writers still productive during the Cultural Revolution, named the principal character in his 1972 novel *Golden Road* Gao Daquan (*quan* meaning "spring" punning on whole/perfect). The jargon "gao, da, quan" derived from the **"three prominences"** formula—a formula promoted by **Jiang Qing** for shaping and measuring creative works—especially the third prominence: "give prominence to the central character among main heroes." It specifies ways to achieve the third prominence: portray the principal hero with the highest political consciousness on the highest moral ground; make him/her larger than life (e.g., elegant, dignified, and venerated); and characterize him/her perfect in every aspect. After the Cultural Revolution, the criterion was criticized for being ridiculously formulaic and dogmatic: an imposition on artists as propaganda tools creating God-like revolutionaries that had made artistic creation impossible.

GOLDEN ROAD. (*Jinguang dadao.*) *Golden Road* is a multivolume novel written by Hao Ran (pen name of Liang Jinguang) and published by Beijing People's Literature Press in 1972 (volume 1), 1975 (volume 2), and 1994 (volumes 1 to 4). Focusing on the theme of **class struggle** and the conflict between two "roads" (the capitalist and the socialist roads), in its first two volumes, the novel traces the collectivization of agriculture that peasants at Fangcaodi Village undertook in the 1950s. Writing the novel during the Cultural Revolution, Hao Ran took the **eight model dramas** as his model and adopted artistic formulas promoted by **Jiang Qing**, such as **"three prominences"** and "thematic priority"; he used these formulas so closely as to make the name of his protagonist, Gao Daquan, echo Jiang's creative principle for a positive heroic figure: "high" (*gao*), "large" (*da*), and "perfect" (*quan*; literally "spring" but punning on "perfect"). As a result, Hao Ran's work was well received by Jiang and her followers in artistic circles, and Hao Ran himself was accorded considerable political privilege. In fact, for quite some time during the Cultural Revolution, he and Lu Xun were the only fiction writers of note with works still in print, so much so that Hao Ran was the "one author" in novelist Mao Dun's dismissal of the artistically barren Cultural Revolution as the age of "eight model dramas and one author." After the Cultural Revolution, Hao Ran remained productive, but his *Golden Road* was criticized for embracing ultra-leftist dogma and misrepresenting the life of Chinese peasants.

GRAND FESTIVAL. (*Shengda de jieri.*) This film was under production at Shanghai Film Studio in October 1976 when the **Gang of Four**, its political supporters in Beijing, were arrested. The film, therefore, was never finished. The story of *Grand Festival* is based on the **Anting Incident** (1966), in which **Wang Hongwen** and **Zhang Chunqiao** played leading roles challenging the authority of the Shanghai municipal party committee. Similar roles are given to the two high-minded heroes in the story—Tiegen, a rebel leader at the Railway Bureau, and Jingfeng, deputy party secretary of the bureau—while two ranking officials representing the status quo are referred to as diehard **capitalist-roaders**. The historical **January Storm** is also in the background of the story. *Grand Festival* was first produced as a stage drama in Shanghai on 16 May 1976 to mark the 10th anniversary of the adoption of the **May 16 Circular**. It was adapted to a screenplay by order of the current municipal leadership of Shanghai within the week of its stage production. The shooting of the film started in mid-August but was stopped in mid-October after the fall of the Gang of Four. The film was immediately denounced as a key work of "conspiratorial literature" that served a blatantly political purpose.

GREAT NETWORKING. (*Da chuanlian.*) Participated in by tens of millions of students and teachers, the "Great Networking" was a nationwide traveling activity initiated by students and encouraged by **Mao Zedong** as a way to mobilize the masses and spread the fire of the Cultural Revolution from Beijing to other parts of the country. The **big-character poster** by **Nie Yuanzi** and six others attacking the party leadership of Peking University shook the country after it was broadcast nationwide on 1 June 1966. Students and teachers began to stream into Peking University and other college campuses in Beijing to experience the revolution firsthand in order to wage battles against the authorities of their own institutions—in Beijing and elsewhere. Mutual exchanges of ideas and experiences took place as well. Many students in other parts of the country who felt that the local authorities were trying to put down their rebellion came to these Beijing campuses and to the reception office established by the **Central Cultural Revolution Small Group** to seek sympathy and support. This was the beginning of the Great Networking.

By early August 1966, hundreds of thousands of visitors—many now called themselves **Red Guards**—were in Beijing, and tens of thousands continued to flood in every day. At the **mass rally of 18 August 1966**, Mao came out to receive and inspect an army of one million Red Guards and revolutionary masses in Tiananmen Square. Many of them were visitors. In order to have a glimpse of the chairman in person, many more came to Beijing from all over the country. In the meantime, Beijing students began to travel to other parts of the country to support their comrades in their battles against local authorities and help them keep up with the development in Beijing. Some established provincial and city liaison offices for their organizations, while mass organizations from other parts of the country also established their own liaison offices in Beijing. On 31 August 1966, when Mao received Red Guards for the second time in Tiananmen Square, Premier **Zhou Enlai**, representing the central leadership, spoke in support of the Great Networking.

On 5 September, the Central Committee (CC) of the **Chinese Communist Party** and the State Council (SC) issued a circular, approving travel for networking purposes by students and teachers of colleges and middle schools and granting free transportation and full accommodation to visitors in Beijing. Though the grand fee waiver was supposed to be applicable in the nation's capital alone, this policy was actually carried out in other places as well. Following orders from the central leadership, municipal authorities of Beijing converted tens of thousands of warehouses, auditoriums, and classrooms into reception centers to host "Chairman Mao's guests," as the visitors were called at the time. The municipal authorities also demanded that Beijing citizens donate blankets, comforters, and pillows for the networkers to use. Similar situations occurred in other big cities and in such "revolutionary holy lands" (*geming shengdi*) as Shaoshan (Mao's hometown), Jinggangshan (where Mao established the first Communist base), Zunyi (the site of a party meeting at which Mao's leadership was beginning to be established), and Yan'an. Mao received Red Guards six more times between September and November 1966, each time drawing at least a million people to Beijing. Some students also formed **Long March Teams** and traveled on foot for hundreds or even thousands of miles to Beijing and other places.

This Great Networking that helped Mao mobilize the masses and build an army of rebels against old party authorities across China also threw the country into chaos. During a four-month period, shipments of millions of tons of goods were delayed so that trains carrying networkers might run, which was a heavy blow to the country's economy that had already slowed down considerably since the Cultural Revolution began in mid-1966. Many people took advantage of free travel, roaming the country sightseeing or to visit friends and relatives, while the Cultural Revolution movement in their own institutions halted. The country's transportation system was so overburdened that crowded buses, boats, and trains ran far beyond their capacity for months and were utterly unable to keep to their regular schedules.

By the end of October, it had become clear to central leaders that the Great Networking must stop. Since winter was approaching, the matter became more urgent because hundreds of thousands of reception centers in the country were not equipped for cold weather. In November and December, the CC and the SC issued a number of notices to halt the Great Networking temporarily until spring. However, many networkers ignored orders and continued with their travels. On 19 March 1967, the CC announced that the Great Networking would not resume. In the following months, orders were issued to close all of the networker reception centers that had been set up by the government and the numerous liaison offices that had been established by mass organizations. With these concrete measures, the Great Networking eventually came to an end.

GREY BOOKS AND YELLOW BOOKS. (*Huipishu he huangpishu.*) Printed in the early and mid-1960s for restricted circulation among ranking officials, these translated foreign books were passed around in private among many unintended readers, especially students, during the Cultural Revolution and contributed much to their questioning of official ideology. Some 1,041 titles by well-known modern and contemporary writers of Western countries and of the Soviet-dominated Eastern Bloc were translated and published "internally" (*neibu faxing*) before the Cultural Revolution. These books can be divided into two groups: one group with gray covers includes titles in a broad area of politics, law, and culture; the other group with yellow covers consists mostly of literary works. Among the most popular of the first group were William Lawrence Shirer's *The Rise and Fall of the Third Reich: A History of Nazi Germany*, Theja Gunawardhana's *Khrushchevism*, Anna Louise Strong's *The Stalin Era*, Leon Trotsky's *The Revolution Betrayed: What Is the Soviet Union and Where Is It Going?* and *Stalin, An Appraisal of the Man and His Influence*, Milovan Djilas's *The New Class: An Analysis of the Communist System*, Friedrich A. Hayek's *The Road to Serfdom*, Adam Schaff's *Structuralism and Marxism*, Jules Michelet's *History of the French Revolution*, Nikita S. Khrushchev's *Conquest without War*, and Edward Crankshaw's *Khrushchev: A Career*. The most popular "yellow books" included I. G. Erenburg's *People and Life: Memoirs of 1891–1917* and *The Thaw*, Konstantin Mikhailovich Simonov's trilogy *The Living and the Dead*, Alexander Solzhenitsyn's *One Day in the Life of Ivan Denisovich*, Jean Paul Sartre's *Nausea*, Albert Camus's *The Outsider*, John Osborne's *Look Back in Anger*, Samuel Beckett's *Waiting for Godot*, and J. D. Salinger's *The Catcher in the Rye*.

Of particular and consistent interest to Chinese readers of the time was what seemed to them distant echoes of their experience, such as critical views of revolution by dissenting Communists, the disillusionment of former revolutionaries, the "revisionist" (Khrushchevist) critique of Stalinism, and the sense of alienation and absurdity of modern humanity. Perhaps, the most notable perception that had begun to form during the Cultural Revolution and has since caught the attention of more and more readers is the astonishing parallels of the Chinese Cultural Revolution with both Stalin's Purge in the Soviet Union and the Nazi movement in Germany in the 1930s.

See also UNDERGROUND READING MOVEMENT.

GU ZHUN (1915–1974). Senior revolutionary, economist, and victim of both the Anti-Rightist Campaign and the Cultural Revolution, Gu Zhun was known for finding his own way out of Marxist dogma and formulating a comprehensive Chinese liberalism during the years of strict ideological control and intellectual famine. He was original with the idea of market economy under a socialist system, which predated **Deng Xiaoping**'s post–Cultural Revolution economic reform by 20 years.

Already a published specialist in accounting and finance when he joined the **Chinese Communist Party** (CCP) in 1935, Gu worked in Shanghai and also Communist-controlled areas in eastern China in the 1930s and 1940s. He served in various leading positions managing financial affairs in Shanghai after the CCP took power in 1949. Gu was demoted in 1952 because his views on taxation were in conflict with mainstream party policies. Later, while a researcher at the Chinese Academy of Science in Beijing, he was labeled "rightist" twice: in 1957 and again in 1965. He was attacked and physically abused at numerous **struggle meetings** during the Cultural Revolution. Under pressure, his wife of 30 years divorced him and later committed suicide, and all his five children **made a clean break** with him and even refused to see him upon his deathbed in spite of his pleading.

During the many years of harsh persecution and deep suffering, however, Gu persevered on a journey of intellectual exploration. He read widely, kept a journal that recorded his critical views of Chinese politics, and wrote on a variety of subjects, including history, philosophy, government, and economics. He gradually moved away from Communism and toward liberalism; he described this deeply personal conversion as a turning to "empiricism, pluralism, and democracy" when idealism was turned into dogma in the name of revolution in China. He challenged the predominant theory and practice of central planning in managing the national economy and insisted that socialism should incorporate market economics and that the market, rather than a five-year plan, should be the basis of productive decisions. Based on his close observations of post–Great Depression developments in Western countries, he saw the potential of capitalism for self-critique, self-adjustment, and self-improvement; he questioned Karl Marx and Vladimir Lenin's predictions of rapid demise of the capitalist system through ever-worsening vicious cycles of economic crises; and he rejected their theory of violent revolution. Gu was among the first Chinese intellectuals to embrace the rule of law and constitutionalism against one-party rule and **personality cult**. The posthumous publication of his writing—beginning with *The City-State Constitution of Greece* in 1982 and followed by his collected works in 1994 and his journal in 1997—created a sensation in China's intellectual circles and won him the high praise of contemporary historians for being a lone figure to "use [his] rib as a torch, lit from the fire of thunder" (a line from the Indian poet Rabindranath Tagore) during the dark night of the Cultural Revolution.

GUAN FENG (1918–2005). Mao's radical theorist, deputy editor-in-chief of the Communist party's official organ *Red Flag*, and a member of the **Central Cultural Revolution Small Group** (CCRSG), Guan was dismissed from office in August 1967 as a member of the Wang-Guan-Qi Anti-Party Clique.

Born in Qingyun County, Shandong Province, and originally named Zhou Yufeng, Guan joined the **Chinese Communist Party** (CCP) in 1933. He was appointed president of the Shandong Political Academy in 1952 and vice-president of the Fourth Mid-Level Party School in 1955. When the CCP established its official organ *Red Flag* in 1958, Guan was named head of the journal's philosophy group and a member of the editorial board and, later, deputy editor-in-chief. Guan emerged as one of the CCP's leftist intellectuals around 1962 when he published several radical pieces in Chinese philosophy under the pen name He Ming, which caught the attention of **Mao Zedong**.

In April and May 1966, at the preparation stage of the Cultural Revolution, Guan wrote several pieces attacking the so-called **Three-Family Village Anti-Party Clique** and the CCP Beijing Municipal Committee headed by **Peng Zhen**. An article he coauthored with Lin Jie criticizing **Wu Han** (*Red Flag*, 5 April 1966) and his own piece attacking two official publications of the Beijing party committee (*Guangming Daily*, 9 May 1966), both reprinted in *People's Daily*, were quite influential. Guan was also involved in the drafting of the **May 16 Circular**. With Mao's approval, Guan became a member of the newly formed CCRSG in May 1966. In the early stages of the Cultural Revolution, Guan played a significant role in bringing down **Liu Shaoqi** and **Deng Xiaoping**. During the campaign to criticize the **Bourgeois Reactionary Line** in late 1966 and early 1967, Guan and other CCRSG members pushed the **rebel** movement forward against the old party establishment. With the support of **Lin Biao** and **Jiang Qing** (and with the approval of Mao), Guan Feng, **Wang Li**, **Qi Benyu**, and some other members of the CCRSG began to press the military to adopt Mao's Cultural Revolution policies in 1967: in their public speeches and in several articles they wrote for official media, they called on the masses to "ferret out a small handful [of **capitalist-roaders**] inside the army," which met with strong resistance from the rank and file of the **People's Liberation Army** (PLA). They also began to make similar radical moves in the area of foreign affairs.

Weighing revolutionary chaos against stability and order, Mao decided to remove Guan and his close comrades to maintain order and to pacify the protesting PLA officials and senior party leaders soon after he received an accusatory report from Premier **Zhou Enlai**. Guan Feng was detained on 30 August 1967, and his long imprisonment began on 26 January 1968. He was released in 1982 and expelled from the CCP. Guan devoted the remaining years of his life to the study of Chinese philosophy and classical Chinese language.

See also WANG-GUAN-QI AFFAIR (1967–1968).

H

HAI RUI DISMISSED FROM OFFICE (1961). This is the title of a historical play by **Wu Han**. The publication of **Yao Wenyuan**'s critique "On the New Historical Drama *Hai Rui Dismissed from Office*" in Shanghai's *Wenhui Daily* on 10 November 1965 was generally considered to be the "blasting fuse" of the Cultural Revolution.

At the Seventh Plenum of the Eighth Central Committee (CC) of the **Chinese Communist Party** (CCP) (2–5 April 1959), **Mao Zedong** spoke favorably of Hai Rui (1514–1587), a legendary upright official of the Ming Dynasty (1368–1644). Aware of and concerned with the widespread fear of speaking the truth about the disastrous Great Leap Forward and the People's Commune movements, Mao advised that one should learn from Hai Rui's unbending character and forthright courage to speak his mind. Mao's openness to truth and criticism, however, was qualified by his own comment that, although Hai Rui criticized the emperor, he was after all loyal to him. Three months later, as the truth-speaking Marshal **Peng Dehuai** was criticized and denounced at the **Lushan Conference** (enlarged sessions of the Politburo, 2 July–1 August 1959, and the Eighth Plenum of the Eighth CC, 2–16 August) as the leader of an anti-party clique, Mao spoke of the "leftist" Hai Rui as the true Hai Rui and the "rightist" Hai Rui as the false one.

Between these two meetings, Hu Qiaomu, of the CCP Propaganda Department, suggested to Wu Han, a famed Ming historian and deputy mayor of Beijing, that he write about Hai Rui in support of Mao's call for honesty and truthfulness. Wu soon published two articles on Hai Rui. And, at the invitation by the Peking Opera Company of Beijing, he labored on a play script for a year, went through seven revisions while the company was rehearsing it, and finally, at the end of 1960, completed it as *Hai Rui Dismissed from Office*. The play was first performed in Beijing in January 1961.

In 1962, **Jiang Qing** began to talk to Mao and those in cultural circles about *Hai Rui Dismissed from Office* as a play with serious problems. In 1964, **Kang Sheng** suggested to Mao that the play was related to the Lushan Conference and to the Peng Dehuai question. Jiang and Kang's demand that the play be criticized was largely ignored in Beijing. In early 1965, with the support of Ke Qingshi, first secretary of the CCP Shanghai Municipal Committee, Jiang Qing planned an attack with **Zhang Chunqiao**, an alternate secretary of the Shanghai Municipal Committee and head of its propaganda department. They entrusted Yao Wenyuan with the task of writing a critical piece. For about eight months while Yao was working on the article, the writing was kept secret from top party leaders in Beijing except Mao, who read the article three times before it was published in *Wenhui Daily* on 10 November 1965. The article calls Wu Han's play a **"poisonous weed"** and accuses the author of disparaging the present with a story of the past. In Yao's view, the story of Hai Rui forcing local despots to give the seized land back to the peasants was used in the play as a historical echo of the "rightist" anti-collectivization policies such as "returning the land" (*tuitian*) and "going it alone" (*dan'gan*), which temporarily reversed the radical policies of the Great Leap Forward and the People's Commune. Likewise, the story of an upright official who is wronged echoed the cries of the early 1960s for a reversal of verdicts for the suppressed "class enemies."

Yao's far-fetched accusations and militant style shocked the academic world and inspired speculations on the background of the attack. There was much resistance in Beijing to reprinting the article after quite a few provincial newspapers did. Mayor **Peng Zhen**, away from Beijing at the time, specifically instructed that the article not be reprinted until he came back. Upon hearing Jiang Qing's report about the resistance from Beijing, Mao was convinced that the CCP Beijing Municipal Committee was an "impenetrable and watertight independent kingdom." He suggested to Yao Wenyuan that the article be distributed nationwide in pamphlet form. The Beijing Municipal Committee finally gave in: Yao's article was reprinted in *Beijing Daily* on 29 November with an editor's note stressing the importance of telling truth from falsehood and of allowing dissenting views in the discussion. On 30 November, *People's Daily* carried the article in its academic research section. The same editorial comment was added following instructions from Premier **Zhou Enlai** and Mayor Peng Zhen. It insists that the discussion follow the principles of "letting a hundred flowers bloom and a hundred schools of thought contend" (*baihuaqifang, baijiazhengming*, as Mao famously put it), that there should be freedom both to criticize and to rebut, and that one needs to seek truth from facts and convince people with reasoned argument.

Mao, on the other hand, did not take such a liberal and academic approach. In late December, he made a devastating comment concerning Wu Han's play that further politicized the issue. He said that Yao Wenyuan's article was good but did not quite hit the vital part: "The vital point is dismissal. Emperor Jiaqing dismissed Hai Rui. We, in 1959, dismissed Peng Dehuai. Peng Dehuai is also Hai Rui."

In the face of the heated debate over *Hai Rui Dismissed from Office*, Peng Zhen, as head of the **Five-Person Cultural Revolution Small Group**, convened an enlarged group meeting on 3 February 1966 to discuss the Wu Han question. The meeting produced the "Outline Report concerning the Current Academic Discussion" (commonly known as the **February Outline**), which was approved by the Standing Committee of the Politburo on 12 February as guidelines for the ongoing debate. Despite its leftist-sounding rhetoric, the February Outline was meant to limit discussion and debate within the academic sphere.

In his conversations with Kang Sheng, Jiang Qing, and Zhang Chunqiao in late March, however, Mao began to accuse the Five-Person Group and its Outline of obscuring **class lines** and confusing right and wrong and to blame the CCP Propaganda Department for suppressing the voice of the left. As a result of Mao's new directives, the next two months saw the publication of major attacks on Wu Han by **Guan Feng** and **Qi Benyu** (both soon to be made members of the **Central Cultural Revolution Small Group**) and a host of militant essays attacking the magazine column *Notes from a Three-Family Village* to which Wu Han had been a principal contributor. In April, Peng Zhen was charged with "anti-party crimes" at a top-level meeting. On 16 May, an **enlarged Politburo session** passed the "Circular of the CCP Central Committee" (which came to be known as the **May 16 Circular**) that delegitimized the February Outline and officially launched the Cultural Revolution. What originally appeared to be a critique of a historical play had now evolved into a full-scale nationwide political movement.

HAN AIJING (1945–). One of the well-known "five **Red Guard** leaders" in Beijing, Han was head of the Red Flag Battalion at the Beijing Institute of Aeronautics and a prominent leader of the Capital College **Red Guards' Representative Assembly** during the Cultural Revolution.

A native of Lianshui, Jiangsu Province, Han organized the nationally influential Red Flag Battalion at the Beijing Institute of Aeronautics, a rebel student organization that the **Central Cultural Revolution Small Group** (CCRSG) strongly supported for its battle against the **work group** at the outset of the Cultural Revolution. During the campaign to criticize the **Bourgeois Reactionary Line** of **Liu Shaoqi** and **Deng Xiaoping**, Chairman **Mao Zedong** and his radical supporters relied heavily on the Han-led battalion as one of the ablest and most reliable mass organizations for attacking their political opponents. Following instructions from **Qi Benyu**, a member of the CCRSG, Han sent a team to Sichuan to kidnap Marshal **Peng Dehuai** to Beijing in December 1966 and then subjected him to brutal physical abuse in 1967 at two **struggle meetings**. Han was named head of the **revolutionary** committee at the Beijing Institute of Aeronautics as well as a member of the Standing Committee of the Beijing Municipal Revolutionary Committee in 1967.

During their short political careers as Mao's soldiers, Han and other rebel student leaders developed their own ambitions, and their organizations engaged in violent factional battles and sometimes became such an intractable mass force for the central leadership that, in summer 1968, Mao finally decided to end the Red Guard movement. During **Mao's meeting with the five Red Guard leaders** on the early morning of 28 July 1968, he sent a strong signal to Han and others that they should exit China's political stage. Soon a **workers propaganda team** and an **army propaganda team** were sent to the Beijing Institute of Aeronautics to take over power from Han and his fellow rebel students. Han was detained by the army propaganda team at the institute in 1971 and remained in custody until 1975.

After the downfall of the **Gang of Four**, the authorities formally arrested Han in 1978. He was convicted as a counterrevolutionary and was sentenced to 15 years in prison in March 1983. He was also convicted of a variety of crimes including instigating attacks on party and state officials and framing and persecuting innocent people.

HAO LIANG. *See* QIAN HAOLIANG (1934–).

HE LONG (1896–1969). A top-ranking official of the **People's Liberation Army** (PLA) and one of 10 marshals of the People's Republic of China (PRC), He Long was a vice-chairman of the Central Military Commission (CMC), a vice-premier of the State Council, and a member of the Politburo. He was a victim of **Lin Biao**'s power takeover in the army during the Cultural Revolution.

A native of Hunan Province, He Long was a well-known left-leaning general of the Northern Expedition. At the 1927 Nanchang Uprising, he served as commander-in-chief in response to the call of the Chinese Communist Party (CCP) for military insurrection. One year later, He joined the CCP. He participated in the Long March as commander of the Red Army's Second Front Army. He was commander of the 120th Division of the Communist-led Eighth Route Army during the war of resistance against Japan and a leader of the First Field Army of the PLA during the civil war in the second half of the 1940s. He continued to play an important role in both military and civil affairs after the founding of the PRC. He was in charge of the nation's sports affairs as chairman of the State Physical Culture and Sports Commission beginning in 1952 and a vice-premier from 1954. He became a vice-chairman of the CMC in 1954 and began to take charge of the daily affairs of the CMC in 1964. He was elected to the Politburo in 1956.

Leading a different faction of the army and having conflicts with He Long that resulted from a long history of army politics, Lin Biao began to plot against He Long at the beginning of the Cultural Revolution in order to gain full control of the CMC. With the support of the cultural revolutionaries, including **Jiang Qing** and **Kang Sheng**, Lin and his close associates in the military lodged a false charge against He, accusing him of having ambitions for military power and of plotting a **February mutiny** in 1966. **Mao Zedong** resisted Lin's move at first, but, as the support of Lin and the Jiang Qing group for his Cultural Revolution program became increasingly indispensable, Mao finally approved their proposal to investigate He's past in September 1967. **Zhou Enlai**, too, protected He Long initially and even sheltered him in his own residence from the rebelling masses. But Zhou eventually followed Mao's decision and went along with the radicals' accusations against He.

Consequently, He Long was placed under house arrest and began what was to be a hard life as a political prisoner; sometimes he was not even given enough food and water. He faced ruthless interrogations conducted by a special case group controlled by Lin Biao's associates, which forced him to confess his past "crimes" of "turning a traitor" and "killing Communists." In the meantime, he was deprived of proper medical treatment for the diabetes from which he had been suffering for years. Mistreatment and grave illness eventually led to his death on 9 June 1969.

After the fall of Lin Biao in 1971, Mao began to blame Lin for the persecution of He Long and other ranking leaders. In 1974, Mao acknowledged that He was wronged. On 29 September 1974, the CCP Central Committee issued a circular to redress He Long's case.

HU SHOUJUN CLIQUE. The Hu Shoujun Clique was an underground reading group deemed counterrevolutionary by the government during the **One Strike and Three Antis** campaign in 1970. Hu Shoujun, the best-known member of the group, was the leader of a student rebel organization involved in two well-known protests—one in January 1967 and the other in April 1968—against **Zhang Chunqiao**. In the late 1960s, after Hu and his friends at Shanghai's Fudan University were sent to the countryside, they organized a large underground reading group. They read works of Marxism and Western philosophy as well as a number of internally published "**grey books and yellow books**," including William Lawrence Shirer's *The Rise and Fall of the Third Reich: A History of Nazi Germany*, in whose descriptions of Nazi Germany many readers found a mirror image of the China of the Cultural Revolution. They also recorded some of their reading notes in an underground journal entitled *Correspondences of Comrades-in-Arms from*

Afar. Some of the writing reflected the contributors' questioning of the legitimacy of the proletarian dictatorship and their longings for social legality and democracy in China's political system.

On 3 February 1970, following instructions from Zhang Chunqiao, deputy director of the Shanghai Revolutionary Committee **Xu Jingxian** ordered the **workers propaganda team** and the **army propaganda team** at Fudan University to bring Hu Shoujun and 10 others back to campus for detainment. Hu and his friends were accused of forming a counterrevolutionary clique and attacking leaders of Mao's proletarian headquarters. More than a hundred people were detained as members of the alleged Hu Shoujun Clique, including a number of college professors as instigators and backstage supporters. The Hu Clique became Shanghai's number one counterrevolutionary case in the One Strike and Three Antis campaign. The authorities printed and distributed 500,000 copies of falsified material for mass criticism and organized four mass rallies to **struggle against** Hu and his comrades. In the meantime, the hunt for hidden clique members continued, falsely implicating over 1,000 people. In May 1975, the Shanghai Supreme Court sentenced Hu to 10 years in prison. Ten others were labeled counterrevolutionaries and put under surveillance.

In 1978, the Shanghai municipal party committee rehabilitated Hu and his comrades and pronounced the charges against them wrongful.

See also BOMBARDING ZHANG CHUNQIAO.

HU YAOBANG (1915–1989). The most liberal-minded member of the central leadership of the **Chinese Communist Party** (CCP), Hu Yaobang, in the capacity of head of the CCP organization department (1977–1978) and propaganda department (1978–1980) and the general secretary (1980–1987), introduced and implemented policies for a complete rehabilitation of millions of people persecuted during the Cultural Revolution, orchestrated ideological debates for a liberation of thinking (*sixiang jiefang*) from the shackles of Maoist dogma, and cooperated with Premier **Zhao Ziyang** under the paramount leader **Deng Xiaoping** to institute a free-market-oriented economic reform in the wake of the Cultural Revolution. His ouster in 1987 and subsequent mistreatment by the party elders angered the nation's educated population. His death on 15 April 1989 prompted student demonstrations that would evolve into a nationwide democracy movement (April–June 1989).

Native of Liuyang, Hunan Province, from a poor peasant family, Hu joined the CCP in 1933 and became one of the youngest veterans of the Long March. After Communists took power, Hu's main responsibility was that of first secretary of the Chinese Communist Youth League (since 1952 when the organization was still called the New Democracy Youth League) except for a brief appointment as first party secretary of Shaanxi Province (1964–1965). During the Cultural Revolution, he was denounced, paraded through the streets of Beijing, and forced to do heavy manual labor in exile. In 1975, Hu was recalled to Beijing and appointed deputy party chief at the Chinese Academy of Sciences to carry out Deng Xiaoping's **overall rectification** program. When Chairman **Mao Zedong** launched the **Counterattack the Right-Deviationist Reversal-of-Verdicts Trend** campaign against Deng at the end of the year, however, Hu was implicated and exiled again.

After Mao's death, Hu was recalled to Beijing to lead the party's organization department. In the position appropriate for dealing with personnel issues, Hu immediately began to reassess cases of persecution during and before the Cultural Revolution and reverse the wrongful verdicts. His continued rehabilitation efforts over eight years (1977–1984) were sweeping and monumental: he personally responded to, or commented on, about 900 letters of appeal, and he was chiefly responsible for exonerating, among others, three million people persecuted during the Cultural Revolution, over 99 percent of the 550,000 intellectuals labeled as rightists from 1957 to 1958, 127,000 cadres denounced as Right-leaning opportunists in the wake of the persecution of Marshal **Peng Dehuai** in 1959, and 450,000 former Kuomintang (Nationalist) army personnel persecuted despite their revolt against Kuomintang during the civil war in the late 1940s. He also succeeded in removing the class enemy label of "four black categories" (landlords, rich peasants, counterrevolutionaries, and bad elements, which extended to "**five black categories**" in the late 1950s and "**seven black categories**" during the Cultural Revolution) for 20 million people. A small number of wrongful cases still fell short of full rectification, though, including the overall assessment of the Anti-Rightist Campaign, because Deng Xiaoping, who had led the campaign following Mao's instructions, insisted that the campaign itself was "necessary and correct" except for its problem of "mistaken extension."

The second step Hu took to break away from Mao's legacy was to set in motion a liberal trend on theoretical and ideological fronts by means of the media at his disposal. An editorial article entitled "Practice Is the Only Criterion for Testing Truth" that he supported and revised was published in the 11 May 1978 issue of *Guangming Daily*, the leading newspaper in educational and intellectual circles, and reprinted in the CCP organ *People's Daily* and *Liberation Army Daily* the next day. The publication of this article was a landmark challenge to the authority of Maoist dogma as the absolute truth, and with Deng Xiaoping's support, the title of the article became the slogan of the nation at the beginning stage of Deng's reform and opening program. This program took a zigzagging path due to fierce resistance from the conservative faction of the party leadership; smoother was the economic reform, which Hu, along with Premier Zhao Ziyang, helped engineer. But it was harder on the political front, with a "thawing" periodically interrupted by "cold currents of spring," a contemporary reference to various campaigns against the so-called bourgeois liberalization or spiritual pollution. During these conflicts, Hu was usually on the liberal side. Take the Xidan democracy wall (spring 1978–spring 1979), for instance: Hu saw a good public platform in the 200-meter-long wall along the sidewalk of Beijing's Chang'an Avenue near Xidan on which people pasted **big-character posters** expressing their political views. Initially, party seniors like Deng Xiaoping and **Ye Jianying** welcomed the wall as well. In late March 1979, however, Deng ordered the arrest of Wei Jingsheng, a poster author calling for democratic reforms of China's political system, while Hu favored leniency. Eventually, Hu's liberal sympathies became unbearable to hardliners, and even to Deng himself, when he was reluctant to crack down on demonstrating students as well as their democratic-minded intellectual leaders Liu Binyan, Fang Lizhi, and Wang Ruowang in late 1986 and early 1987. Deng gathered a number of veteran leaders at a private meeting with Hu and Zhao Ziyang to denounce Hu and force him to resign as general secretary and from his other major positions as well. Zhao, whether being candid or making a tactic move under pressure, also criticized Hu harshly at the meeting. Zhao officially succeeded Hu as general secretary at an enlarged Politburo session in January 1987.

Hu Yaobang's death in April 1989 had much to do with the pain he suffered from his forced resignation and subsequent mistreatment. It was a pent-up emotion shared by many in educational, cultural, and intellectual circles along with their grievances over official corruption and currency inflation. Such emotion finally erupted upon Hu's death in the form of mourning and soon turned into an outcry for democratic reforms. Though the event was best known as the Tiananmen democracy movement or "June Fourth" (named after the day military troops massacred protesting civilians in Beijing), demonstrations took place in many cities across China. This was the second time in the history of the People's Republic that popular protest took the form of commemoration, the first time being the **April 5 Movement** or **Tiananmen Incident** of 1976, when the mistreatment and death of Premier **Zhou Enlai** inspired public sorrow and rage during the traditional Qingming Festival; commemoration and massive protest in Beijing's Tiananmen Square and many other cities virtually pronounced the demise of the Cultural Revolution ahead of its actual end upon the death of Chairman Mao Zedong.

HUA GUOFENG (1921–2008). Mao Zedong's successor, Hua played a decisive role in bringing down the **Gang of Four** and putting an end to the 10-year-old Cultural Revolution. But due to his refusal to reverse any decision reached by the ruling Communist party under Mao and to allow reassessments of the Cultural Revolution as a whole, he was forced to resign in the early 1980s from all of the top positions he had held since 1976.

Born in Jiaocheng, Shanxi Province, and originally named Su Zhu, Hua Guofeng joined the **Chinese Communist Party** (CCP) in 1938. From 1949 to 1971, he held various positions in Hunan Province, including party secretary of Mao's hometown, Xiangtan, deputy governor of Hunan, acting chairman of the Hunan **Revolutionary Committee**, and first secretary of the CCP Hunan Provincial Committee. In the early stages of the Cultural Revolution, he supported the **rebel** faction in Hunan. In 1969, Hua was elected to the Ninth CCP Central Committee (CC). In 1971, he was transferred to Beijing and began to work at the State Council (SC). He entered the Politburo in August 1973 and became vice-premier and minister of public security in January 1975.

In late 1975, as Mao was disappointed by **Wang Hongwen**, on the one hand, and wary of **Deng Xiaoping**'s critical stand toward the Cultural Revolution, on the other—both having been candidates to become Mao's successor—more attention was given to Hua Guofeng. In early February 1976, within a month of Premier **Zhou Enlai**'s death, Hua became acting premier of the SC. After the popular anti–Cultural Revolution **April 5 Movement** was put down, Hua was appointed premier and first vice-chairman of the CCP at Mao's suggestion, while Deng Xiaoping was ousted and denounced. In the last days of his life, Mao communicated to Hua his trust: "**I feel at ease with you in charge**," Mao wrote. On 6 October, within the month of Mao's death, Hua, along with **Wang Dongxing** and **Ye Jianying**, ordered the arrest of **Jiang Qing, Zhang Chunqiao, Yao Wenyuan**, and Wang Hongwen. On 7 October, the Politburo made Hua chairman of the CCP and chairman of the Central Military Commission (CMC). Thus, the ultimate power of the party, of the state, and of the military was all in Hua's hands.

In the few years after the downfall of the Gang of Four, however, Hua insisted on being literally faithful to whatever directives and decisions Mao had made. He opposed any attempt to reassess the Cultural Revolution. While leading a campaign against the Gang of Four, Hua insisted on continuing the "Criticize Deng, **Counterattack the Right-Deviationist Reversal-of-Verdicts Trend**" campaign as well. Hua also ignored the repeated calls from both the grassroots and the central leadership to redress the **Tiananmen Incident** of 1976 and to rehabilitate its victims. Under pressure from the central leadership, Hua resigned from the position of the premier in September 1980 and gave up his title as chairman of the CCP and chairman of the CMC in June 1981. Remaining a member of the CC, Hua was assigned an advisory position at the State Agriculture Commission, which marked the end of his political career.

HUANG SHUAI INCIDENT (1973). Initially a not-so-uncommon incident of disagreements between a student and a teacher, the case of Huang Shuai, a fifth grader at Zhongguancun No. 1 Elementary School in Beijing's Haidian District, eventually became, in official propaganda, a story of a student's rightful rebellion against an authoritarian teacher. The official endorsement of Huang Shuai's challenge to her classroom teacher touched off a campaign in elementary and secondary schools against the "resurgence of the revisionist line in education" and against "teacher's authority" (*shi dao zunyan*) and brought further disruption and chaos to schools nationwide.

In some of her journal entries written between April and November 1973, which her teacher also read and commented on, Huang Shuai noted her discontent about her teacher's criticisms. Huang also acknowledged as her inspiration the story of middle school **Red Guards** in Lanzhou correcting their teachers. Apparently, the conflict intensified when Huang's parents interfered: they investigated the teacher in private and wrote the teacher and the school authorities a long letter, criticizing the teacher and celebrating the "revolutionary spirit of going against the tide" that they identified as the inspiration for their daughter's rebellion against her teacher. A few days later, a letter signed by Huang Shuai but containing some passages of her parents' earlier letter was sent to a number of newspapers in Beijing and Shanghai.

Upon reading the letter carried in the internal publications of *Beijing Daily*, **Chi Qun** and **Xie Jingyi**, both close associates of **Jiang Qing** at Tsinghua University, met with Huang Shuai. Following their instruction, *Beijing Daily* published the letter, a selection of Huang Shuai's journal entries, and an editor's note on 12 December 1973. The already highly selective journal entries were also edited in favor of the author as a model of "going against the tide," while the editor's note identified the "revisionist line in education" as the tide. Toward the end of the month, *People's Daily* and other newspapers in the country also carried the letter and journal entries. The 12-year-old Huang was invited to give speeches and to contribute to newspapers. Similar stories of "going against the tide" were then reported from various parts of the country. Meanwhile, dissenting views were invariably suppressed. Identifying themselves with the joint pen name "Wang Ya-Zhuo," three authors wrote Huang from Inner Mongolia criticizing her views. With the approval of Jiang Qing and company, these authors were persecuted as elements of the "bourgeois restoration." Along with the **Zhang Tiesheng** Incident, a case of a "blank examination paper" that also occurred in the second half of 1973, the much-publicized Huang Shuai story contributed to the worsening of the situation in schools in the final three years of the Cultural Revolution.

HUANG YONGSHENG (1910–1983). A close associate of **Lin Biao** and popularly known as one of Lin's "four guardian warriors," Huang Yongsheng was chairman of the Guangdong **Revolutionary Committee** (1968) and, after he was transferred to Beijing, chief of the general staff of the **People's Liberation Army** (PLA) and head of the **Central Military Commission Administrative Group** (1968–1971).

A native of Xianning, Hubei Province, Huang was a veteran revolutionary who participated in the Autumn Harvest Uprising against the Kuomintang in 1927 and joined the **Chinese Communist Party** (CCP) in the same year. He was a division commander in the Red Army during the anti-encirclement struggle in the early 1930s before the Long March. During both the war of resistance against Japan and the civil war of the late 1940s, Huang was a ranking commander under Lin Biao. In 1955, Huang was made full general and commander of the Guangzhou Military Region.

During the first two years of the Cultural Revolution, Huang remained in a top leadership position in Guangdong Province and was responsible for cases of injustice such as the "Guangdong underground party" and the Guangzhou troops "counterrevolutionary clique," the former case implicating more than 7,000 innocent people and causing 85 deaths. In February 1968 when the Guangdong Revolutionary Committee was formally established, Huang became chairman of the committee.

In March 1968, after the **Yang-Yu-Fu Affair**, Huang was appointed chief of general staff of the PLA upon Lin Biao's nomination. At the **Ninth National Congress of the CCP** (1969), Huang was elected to the Central Committee (CC) and the Politburo. In the same year, Huang was appointed president of the PLA's Military and Political University and member of the Central Military Commission. After the **Lushan Conference** of 1970, at which **Mao Zedong** dismissed Lin Biao's ally **Chen Boda** from office and told Lin's other supporters, including Huang, to criticize themselves, Huang was slow and reluctant to carry out the subsequent **Criticize Chen and Conduct Rectification** campaign and was thus reproached by Mao in early 1971. In April 1971, the CC held a meeting reviewing the ongoing campaign. Huang's written self-criticism, along with those of **Ye Qun**, **Wu Faxian**, **Li Zuopeng**, and **Qiu Huizuo**, was discussed at the meeting. In his summary report representing the view of the CC, Premier **Zhou Enlai** chided Huang, Wu, Ye, Li, and Qiu for following a wrong political line and practicing factionalism. In the meantime, Mao continued to make harsh comments on Lin Biao and his supporters. On 6 September, Huang passed to Ye Qun Mao's critical remarks on Lin Biao. Huang's communication allegedly helped Lin Biao and Ye Qun decide on a plan to assassinate Mao (although Lin Biao's role in the alleged conspiracy, even his knowledge of it, remains a question).

After the **September 13 Incident**, Huang Yongsheng was taken into custody, and his involvement in Lin's alleged coup attempt was under investigation. On 20 August 1973, the CC issued a resolution concerning the Lin Biao Anti-Party Clique. As a member of the Lin group, Huang Yongsheng was dismissed from all his official positions and expelled from the CCP. On 25 January 1981, Huang was sentenced to 18 years in prison on the charges of organizing and leading a counterrevolutionary clique, plotting to subvert the government, and bringing false charges against innocent people. On 26 April 1983, Huang Yongsheng died of illness in Qingdao, Shandong Province.

I

"I FEEL AT EASE WITH YOU IN CHARGE". (*Ni banshi, wo fangxin.*) Chairman **Mao Zedong** wrote down this message for **Hua Guofeng** in a private meeting on 30 April 1976, which the post-Mao central leadership quoted as evidence that Mao had designated Hua as his successor. Since Mao's verbal expressions were becoming increasingly difficult to understand as his health deteriorated, he often wrote down key phrases or key sentences with an infirm hand for his listeners as he spoke. The two other messages Mao also put down for Hua on the same occasion read "Take your time and don't worry," and "Act according to previous policy." Hua soon related these two messages to the Politburo but did not mention the other message. These messages became important in the power struggle in the Central Committee (CC) of the ruling Communist party after Mao's death. When **Jiang Qing** and company launched a propaganda campaign to push for their own political agenda in the name of what they called Mao's "deathbed wish" of "Follow the set plan," Hua made a correction with the original "Act according to previous policy" and produced the note "I feel at ease with you in charge," which gave Hua legitimacy as Mao's heir apparent and lent much force to Hua and his senior colleagues in the CC in their rebuttal of the claim of the **Gang of Four** of being the true successors of Mao's political legacy. Qiao Guanhua was then minister of foreign affairs with whom Hua shared Mao's handwritten notes immediately after his meeting with Mao. Years later, Qiao offered a different interpretation of the message "I feel at ease with you in charge." According to Qiao's recollection of what he learned from Hua, Mao's comment was not so much on Hua's trustworthiness as Mao's successor as on a concrete plan that Hua had just proposed to resolve factionalism in Guizhou and Sichuan Provinces.

INNER MONGOLIA PEOPLE'S REVOLUTIONARY PARTY. Commonly known by its abbreviated name the "Inner People's Party" (*Nei ren dang*), this political organization, formed in 1925, was initially affiliated with the Communist International (Comintern). It was essentially a Communist-led united front consisting mostly of Mongolian farmers and herdsmen. In the 1930s, some of its members withdrew, and some others continued their revolutionary activities under the leadership of the **Chinese Communist Party** (CCP). By then, the original Inner People's Party had stopped functioning as an independent organization. A new Inner People's Party formed in 1946 lasted only for a very short period of time and never became a real political force.

Soon after the Cultural Revolution began, the CCP North China Bureau held a long meeting (from 22 May to 25 July 1966) with 146 party officials from the Inner Mongolia Autonomous Region to criticize **Ulanfu**, first party secretary of Inner Mongolia since 1952. At the 2 July session of this meeting, **Liu Shaoqi** and **Deng Xiaoping** denounced Ulanfu in harsh terms for his refusal to carry out the party's **class struggle** policies in Inner Mongolia and accused him of being an "ethnic splittist" promoting "regional nationalism." At the remaining sessions of the meeting, Liu and Deng's criticism served as a guideline for the participants to expose and condemn Ulanfu's alleged mistakes, including Ulanfu's reluctance to punish former members of the new Inner People's Party, now seen as a reactionary organization. In late 1967, with strong support from radical leaders in Beijing, especially **Kang Sheng**, **Jiang Qing**, and **Xie Fuzhi**, cultural revolutionaries in Inner Mongolia began to invent and publicize a notorious story about the Inner Mongolia People's Revolutionary Party's current underground anti-CCP, anti-China activities and used the story against Ulanfu.

In early 1968, as the campaign to **rectify the class ranks** was well under way nationwide, the Inner Mongolian **Revolutionary Committee** headed by Teng Haiqing set up a **work group** to investigate the Inner People's Party case and issued an order that all Inner People's Party members must report and register within three days. Soon, special-case personnel, torture chambers, and illegal courts and prisons appeared throughout Inner Mongolia. Having been a member of the Inner People's Party at any time in the past was automatically a crime, while fabrication and forced confessions led to the persecution of a vast number of people as new members of the Inner People's Party. The cruelty of persecution—with more than a hundred methods of torture—matched the cruelest in Chinese history. And persecution was massive: some 346,220 people were framed and denounced, 75 percent of them Mongols. Widespread humiliation and torture led to 16,222 deaths and 87,188 cases of severe injury, making the Inner People's Party case one of the gravest instances of injustice perpetrated during the Cultural Revolution.

On 9 March 1979, the CCP Inner Mongolia Autonomous Region Committee finally pronounced the Inner People's Party verdict wrongful.

INSIDE STORY OF THE QING COURT. (*Qinggong mishi.*) A dramatization of the fated love between the Guangxu emperor and his concubine Zhen against a background of political conflict between the reform-minded emperor and the conservative, dictatorial Dowager Cixi, *Inside Story of the Qing Court* was a Hong Kong film first shown in mainland China in March 1950 and criticized during the Cultural Revolution as a "big **poisonous weed**." However, the real target of its most notorious critique, "Patriotism or Betrayal: On the Reactionary Film *Inside Story of the Qing Court*," written by **Qi Benyu** with **Mao Zedong**'s approval and published on 1 April 1967 in *People's Daily*, was not the film itself; a classic example of the Cultural Revolution–style political insinuation and slander, the article really aimed at President **Liu Shaoqi** and called him for the first time in official media the "**biggest capitalist-roader within the party**" without ever mentioning his name. The title of the article derived from a remark Mao made in the 1950s: "*Inside Story of the Qing Court* is a traitorous film and ought to be criticized. . . . Some say *Inside Story of the Qing Court* is patriotic, but I say it is traitorous, thoroughly traitorous."

Qi Benyu quoted Mao and then identified Liu Shaoqi as one of those talking about the film as patriotic, which Liu indignantly denied. Other than this groundless accusation, Qi's attack on Liu in the article, such as calling him a "spokesman for imperialism, feudalism, and reactionary bourgeoisie," an "imperialist comprador," and an advocate of "national and class capitulationism," had little to do with the film. Toward the end, Qi listed eight "crimes" in the form of eight rhetorical questions about Liu's life from the 1930s to the beginning of the Cultural Revolution. "There is only one answer," Qi concluded. "You are not an 'old revolutionary'; you are a fake revolutionary, an opponent to revolution. You are simply a Khrushchev sleeping right next to us." Liu was so enraged that he wrote a response to the eight questions and had it copied and posted as a **big-character poster** in the Zhongnanhai compound, but in just a few hours the "revolutionary **rebels**" in Zhongnanhai tore the poster to pieces. Qi's eight questions and his final condemnation soon became a program of the Liu criticism and drastically escalated the campaign against Liu nationwide.

As the Liu Shaoqi case was redressed in late 1979 and early 1980, articles refuting Qi Benyu appeared in newspapers and magazines. *Inside Story of the Qing Court* was rehabilitated as well as a "patriotic film."

J

JANUARY STORM (1967). Also known as the January Revolution, the phrase refers to a series of activities carried out by the self-claimed revolutionary **rebels** in Shanghai, especially the **Workers Command Post** that was supported, and virtually controlled, by **Zhang Chunqiao** and **Yao Wenyuan**, to take over power from Shanghai's party committee and city government in January 1967. Mass organizations in some provinces seized power earlier than those in Shanghai, where the new apparatus of power was not established until early February. But, largely due to **Mao Zedong**'s enthusiastic support for rebels' taking over the Shanghai newspapers *Wenhui Daily* and *Liberation Daily* in early January, Shanghai became a revolutionary model in a nationwide **power seizure** campaign.

On 1 January 1967, the official organs of the **Chinese Communist Party** (CCP), *People's Daily* and *Red Flag*, jointly carried a Mao-authorized editorial that envisioned 1967 to be a year of nationwide all-round **class struggle** in which "the proletariat united with other revolutionary masses shall launch a general offensive against **capitalist-roaders** within the party and **cow-demons and snake-spirits** without." The content as well as the tone of the editorial gave a sufficiently strong signal for Zhang Chunqiao to proceed with his plans. He had focused his attention on the Shanghai party leadership and built his power base there by putting himself firmly behind the Workers Command Post, the largest local mass organization, during such events as the late 1966 railway blockade at **Anting** and the bloody factional fighting on Shanghai's **Kangping Avenue**. On 4 January, one day after rebel organizations took over the two leading Shanghai newspapers *Wenhui Daily* and *Liberation Daily*, Mao Zedong sent Zhang Chunqiao and Yao Wenyuan to Shanghai to investigate and lead the mass movement there. In their capacity as envoys of Beijing, Zhang and Yao summoned **Xu Jingxian**, their close ally in the Shanghai party committee's writing group, and the leaders of the Workers Command Post and told them not to have any illusions about the Shanghai party committee.

On 6 January, Xu Jingxian, **Wang Hongwen**, and their supporters organized a mass rally of a million people at People's Square. First Secretary of the CCP Shanghai Municipal Committee Chen Pixian, Mayor Cao Diqiu, and hundreds of ranking officials were forced to appear at the rally as targets of criticism and denunciation. A circular order was issued at the rally that Cao no longer be recognized as mayor, that Chen confess his "counterrevolutionary crimes," and that the Shanghai party committee be reorganized. As a result, the entire municipal leadership was paralyzed, and power was partially transferred to a number of newly established, Zhang- and Yao-controlled organizations. On 8 January, Mao commented on the upheaval in Shanghai as a great revolution that gave hope to the entire nation. Mao's words were widely read as a call for a nationwide power seizure campaign.

On 5 February, after Zhang Chunqiao put down opposition mainly from student organizations, the new unified power organ **Shanghai People's Commune** was officially established, with Zhang Chunqiao, Yao Wenyuan, Xu Jingxian, and Wang Hongwen holding the top positions. The name of the organ came from Zhang who, upon hearing Mao's speculation on naming the municipal leadership in the capital "Beijing People's Commune," suggested that "People's Commune" be the name for Shanghai's new government. But Mao eventually favored the example of the constitution in Shandong Province with the "three-in-one presence of cadre, military, and masses" in a **"revolutionary committee."** Following Mao's directive, the new power structure of Shanghai changed its name from the Shanghai People's Commune to the Shanghai Revolutionary Committee on 24 February.

The "January Storm" that in official records marked the beginning of the power seizure phase of the Cultural Revolution had boasted at the time a comparison to the Russian October Revolution of 1917 and the French Paris Commune of 1871. Twelve years later, on 4 January 1979, the CCP Central Committee approved a report by the Shanghai municipal party committee concerning the "question of the 'January Revolution,'" denouncing the event as a "carefully plotted scheme by **Lin Biao**, **Chen Boda**, and the **Gang of Four**."

See also BOMBARDING ZHANG CHUNQIAO.

JET PLANE STYLE. (*Penqishi.*) This phrase refers to a most common form of physical abuse and humiliation used by **Red Guards** at **struggle meetings** during the Cultural Revolution. The person being denounced at the meeting was forced to stand or kneel down in front of the crowd, usually on a raised platform. Two guards standing behind the person would press his or her head down while holding his or her arms and raising them up high, like the two wings of a jet plane. The guards might hold their victim in this position for hours while speeches of accusation were read and slogans shouted. Usually, the victim was forced to hang a big sign board from his or her neck with a criminal label written on it and with his or her name crossed in red ink. And usually, a crowd of so-called class enemies were **struggled against** at such rallies, and they would be forced to line up on the platform, all jet plane style.

JI DENGKUI (1923–1988). A native of Wuxiang, Shanxi Province, Ji was a member of the **Chinese Communist Party** (CCP) from 1938 and a prefectural-level party secretary in Henan Province when the Cultural Revolution began. He became vice-chairman of the Henan **Revolutionary Committee** in 1968 and a member of the Ninth CCP Central Committee and an alternate member of the Politburo in 1969. Remembering his past meetings with Ji during his trips to Henan, **Mao Zedong** was said to have inquired about Ji in summer 1967 and received him as "my old friend," which accounted, at least partially, for Ji's meteoric rise during the Cultural Revolution. In June 1969, two months after the **Ninth National Congress of the CCP**, Ji was transferred to Beijing at Mao's suggestion. In 1970, as he was entrusted with responsibilities for the nation's agricultural production, Ji drafted and advocated a radical political program of building "Dazhai counties" to implement Mao's instruction, "in agriculture, learn from the Dazhai (production brigade)." After the **Lushan Conference** of 1970, Mao, enforcing what he called the strategy of "adding sand to the mix," placed Ji in the **Central Military Commission Administrative Group** to undermine **Lin Biao**'s control in the military. Ji was also assigned the important position of political commissioner of the Beijing Military Region, replacing **Li Xuefeng**, whom Mao suspected of being associated with Lin Biao. Ji was elected to the Politburo of both the Tenth and Eleventh CCP Central Committees. In January 1975, he was made vice-premier of the State Council at the **Fourth National People's Congress**.

At the Third Plenum of the Eleventh CCP Central Committee (December 1978), however, Ji was criticized for his ultra-leftist tendencies and for his association with the **Jiang Qing** group. In 1980, Ji resigned, under pressure, from all of his ranking positions. In 1983, he was assigned a researcher's position at the State Council's Research Center for Rural Area Development. Ji died of heart failure in June 1988.

JIAN BOZAN (1898–1968). A well-known historian and professor at Peking University, Jian Bozan, along with **Wu Han**, was denounced during the Cultural Revolution as a chief "bourgeois reactionary academic authority."

Born in Taoyuan, Hunan Province, of an ethnic Uygur family, Jian Bozan was trained in law and economics in his early years, including two years in the United States, before he turned to Marxism as a guide in his historical studies. A veteran of the Northern Expedition and briefly associated with the

Kuomintang, Jian joined the **Chinese Communist Party** (CCP) in 1937, published *A Course in the Philosophy of History* in 1938, and began to work on the long *Outline of Chinese History* in 1942. After 1949, Jian continued with his teaching and research in history while holding a number of political and administrative positions including vice-president of Peking University. He became the champion of the new Marxist historiography in China.

In late 1965, Jian Bozan came to the defense of writer and historian Wu Han by expressing reservations about **Yao Wenyuan**'s critique on Wu's play *Hai Rui Dismissed from Office*, an article that would turn out to be the "blasting fuse" of the Cultural Revolution. In the meantime, **Qi Benyu** published the article "Studying History for the Revolution" in the CCP theoretical organ *Red Flag* in December 1965, attacking Jian Bozan without mentioning his name. On 21 December 1965, **Mao Zedong** had a conversation with **Chen Boda** in Hangzhou, in which Mao singled out Wu and Jian as "those intellectuals going from bad to worse," dismissed Jian's view on the "concession policies" of the landlord class toward peasants as groundless, and praised Qi Benyu's piece—"all but one defect that the target is not named." On 20 March 1966, speaking at an enlarged session of the CCP Politburo, Mao named Wu and Jian as "Communist Party members opposing the Communist Party." Following Mao's condemnation, an article coauthored by Qi Benyu and two others attacking Jian came out in *People's Daily* on 25 March, and when the mass movements were launched during the Cultural Revolution, Jian was not only verbally denounced as an anti-Communist but also physically abused—so brutally and continuously that on the night of 18 December 1968, Jian Bozan and his wife, Dai Shuwan, committed suicide. Jian's name was cleared by the authorities of Peking University in September 1978.

JIANG QING (1914–1991). Mao Zedong's wife, first deputy head of the **Central Cultural Revolution Small Group** (CCRSG), and a member of the Politburo from 1969 to 1976, Jiang was named by the post–Mao Central Committee (CC) of the **Chinese Communist Party** (CCP) as the leader of the Jiang Qing Counterrevolutionary Clique, also known as the **Gang of Four**.

Born as Li Yunhe, Jiang was a native of Zhucheng, Shandong Province. She joined the CCP in 1933. In the following year, she became a film actress in Shanghai, with Lan Ping as her stage name. There she also worked underground for the CCP. Jiang was arrested by the Kuomintang government in 1934 but was soon released. After divorcing her first husband, Tang Na, Jiang went to Yan'an where she met Mao Zedong. Despite the strong reservations of the members of the CC because of Jiang's obscure personal history, Mao married her in 1938 after assuring the CC that Jiang would not be involved in any work of the CCP leadership in the future. Jiang served as

Mao's personal secretary in the 1940s and was head of the film section in the CCP Propaganda Department in the 1950s. During this period, her role in the party's political and cultural affairs was minor, and her poor health kept her at home much of the time.

In the first half of the 1960s, when conflicts between Mao and President **Liu Shaoqi** gradually intensified, Mao began to assign Jiang an increasingly important role in what turned out to be a preparation for the Cultural Revolution. As part of Mao's initial move against the CCP's cultural and literary establishments allegedly controlled by Liu's supporters, Jiang turned the ongoing reform in Peking opera, in which she had been an active participant, into a political movement called the **revolution in Peking opera**. With this movement, Jiang expanded her influence in cultural circles and established herself as a "standard-bearer of the revolution in art and literature." In 1965, Mao sent Jiang to Shanghai to organize an attack on **Wu Han**, deputy mayor of Beijing and the author of the play *Hai Rui Dismissed from Office*, which would pave the way for Mao's major offensive against the CCP Beijing Municipal Committee.

In Shanghai, Jiang met her two loyal allies, **Zhang Chunqiao** and **Yao Wenyuan**. They worked together to ignite the "blasting fuse" of the Cultural Revolution by publishing Yao's article "On the New Historical Drama *Hai Rui Dismissed from Office*." **Lin Biao** also supported Jiang's activities by

Jiang Qing at a mass rally. On her left are Zhou Enlai and Chen Boda.

granting her the title of consultant to the **People's Liberation Army** (PLA) in the area of arts and literature. With the approval of Lin Biao, Jiang Qing invited several ranking PLA officers in charge of literature and art works to a symposium in February 1966. The outline of the meeting was entitled the **"Summary of the Symposium Convened by Comrade Jiang Qing at the Behest of Comrade Lin Biao on the Work of Literature and the Arts in the Armed Forces**," which was partially edited by Mao himself and issued as a CC circular nationwide. It turned out to be another important document in preparation for the Cultural Revolution.

When the Cultural Revolution was launched in May 1966, Jiang assumed a key position as first deputy head of the CCRSG and became the mouth-piece of Mao to lead the radical group. In the early years of the Cultural Revolution, Jiang, as the most powerful woman in China, manipulated the **rebel** movement closely following Mao's strategic steps, instigated the masses to attack veteran revolutionaries in the leadership of the party and the army, and played the most active role in implementing Mao's decision to purge Liu Shaoqi and his alleged followers. She also directed artists in creating a repertoire of revolutionary operas, ballets, films, and plays and was largely responsible for restricting all arts to the rigid molds of the so-called **eight model dramas**. In 1970, Jiang began to be involved in, and even exert certain influence on, Mao's strategic move against Lin Biao and his faction. Jiang attained her seat in the powerful Politburo in April 1969 at the **Ninth National Congress of the CCP** and remained in that position until her downfall in 1976.

In 1973, Jiang, with Mao's consent, began to lead her associates in waging a dubious battle against the moderate and pragmatic party veterans **Zhou Enlai** and **Deng Xiaoping** in a series of political campaigns, including the movements **Criticize Lin and Criticize Confucius**, *Water Margin* **Apprai-sal**, and **Counterattack the Right-Deviationist Reversal-of-Verdicts Trend**. In the meantime, Jiang formed a clique of radical Maoists with **Wang Hongwen**, Zhang Chunqiao, and Yao Wenyuan. Though Jiang's ag-gressiveness, unpopularity, and lack of tact prompted Mao's reference to her group as a Gang of Four, Mao essentially endorsed Jiang and her comrades as the most loyal adherents to his own radicalism, while regarding Zhou and Deng as ideologically unreliable and yet administratively indispensable.

On 6 October 1976, four weeks after the death of Mao, **Hua Guofeng** and **Ye Jianying** ordered the arrest of Jiang and her associates. Jiang was charged with a variety of crimes and was held responsible for virtually all of the excesses of the Cultural Revolution. The term "Gang of Four" eventually turned into the official "Jiang Qing Counterrevolutionary Clique." On 23 January 1981, a special court of the Supreme People's Court sentenced Jiang Qing to death with a two-year reprieve on charges of leading a counterrevo-lutionary clique, plotting to overturn the government, engaging in counterrevolutionary propaganda and instigation, and framing and persecuting innocent people. Jiang was unrepentant, however, and she challenged the court during the trial with what she believed to be Mao's ideas. In 1983, her sentence was commuted to life imprisonment. On 14 May 1991, Jiang committed suicide in Beijing.

See also COMRADE CHIANG CH'ING; WOMEN DURING THE CULTURAL REVOLUTION.

JINGGANG MOUNTAIN. (*Jinggangshan*.) A major **Red Guard** newspaper, *Jinggang Mountain* was the publication of the Tsinghua University Jinggang Mountain Regiment from 1 December 1966 to 19 August 1968, totaling about 190 issues (including special issues). Since the Jinggang Mountain Regiment was a major **rebel** mass organization, the paper initially focused on the campaign to criticize the **Bourgeois Reactionary Line**, carrying a number of articles and reports about the organization's successfully executed plots against President **Liu Shaoqi** and his wife, **Wang Guangmei**, who was deeply involved in the activities of the **work group** at Tsinghua University in the early stages of the Cultural Revolution. From late 1966 on, the Jinggang Mountain Regiment sent its members to many parts of the country, first to stir up the masses for revolution in the provinces and then to engage in provincial factional fighting. Its provincial liaison offices sometimes published joint issues with local mass organizations. In 1967, the Jinggang Mountain Regiment was split into two factions: the general headquarters and the 4-14 headquarters. The latter began to publish its own newspaper, *Jinggang Mountain News* (*Jinggangshan bao*), on 18 June 1967 and continued until April 1968. During this period, both papers mainly focused on factional battles at Tsinghua. On 27 July 1968, the **workers propaganda team** and the **army propaganda team** were dispatched to Tsinghua University at the instruction of Chairman **Mao Zedong** to halt factional violence and take control of the university. Within a month, *Jinggang Mountain* stopped publication.

JOURNAL OF MIDDLE SCHOOL CULTURAL REVOLUTION. (*Zhongxue wenge bao*.) This was a mass-organization publication that carried **Yu Luoke**'s critiques of the **blood lineage theory**. The journal was founded in early 1967 when Mou Zhijing and Wang Jianfu, both students at Beijing No. 4 Middle School and both inspired by Yu Luoke's pamphlet "**On Family Background**," decided to create an outlet for this kind of writing. They named the publication *Journal of Middle School Cultural Revolution* and registered it in the name of a "Revolutionary Rebelling Headquarters of Capital Middle School Students" with Mou as editor-in-chief. They also had the support of Yu Luowen, a student at Beijing No. 65 Middle School and brother of Yu Luoke, as a cofounder and of Yu Luoke himself as the journal's main contributor.

The inaugural issue of the journal came out on 18 January 1967 carrying a revised version of "On Family Background." Yu Luoke wrote for each of the remaining five issues of this journal. The well-known pieces include "On 'Purity'" (second issue, 2 February 1967), "What Does the Disturbance of the '**United Action Committee**' Reveal?—Also a Critique of the Criticism of 'On Family Background' by the Tsinghua University Middle School Red Guards" (third issue, 10 February), and "A New Counter-Offensive of the Reactionary Theory of Blood Lineage: A Rebuttal of 'The Big **Poisonous Weed** "On Family Background" Must Be Torn Up by the Roots'" (fifth issue, 6 March). The contributions from Yu Luoke, who upheld "equal rights"—a taboo at the time—against the bigotry of a new privileged class, take up three-fourths of the journal's published pages. Aside from Yu Luoke's writing, the journal also carries critical commentaries on, and debates about, the blood lineage theory.

The journal became quite popular, with a circulation of 30,000 to 60,000 copies per issue. According to a number of Cultural Revolution memoirs, the editorial board of the journal received thousands of letters from readers per day, most of them supporting the journal's position against the theory of blood lineage. For the same reason, the office of the journal was attacked several times by some **Old Red Guards** and members of the United Action Committee that consisted mostly of the children of ranking officials. Despite the effort of the journal's editorial board to seek support from the **Central Cultural Revolution Small Group** (CCRSG), **Qi Benyu** denounced the article "On Family Background" in a speech on 13 April 1967. With such pressure from the CCRSG, the journal, already facing much hostility from Old Red Guards, was forced to close.

JULY 3 PUBLIC NOTICE (1968). Coded *zhongfa* [68] 103, this is a public announcement issued by the **Chinese Communist Party** (CCP) Central Committee, the State Council, the Central Military Commission, and the **Central Cultural Revolution Small Group** (CCRSG) with the approval of Chairman **Mao Zedong** regarding the escalating violence and chaos in Guangxi Zhuang Autonomous Region. The nationwide issuance of this document, along with that of the **July 24 Public Notice** (1968) regarding the large-scale violence in Shàanxi, is generally considered to be the first clear indication that Mao and the central leadership had finally decided to put to an end nationwide violence and chaos and restore order, which makes summer 1968 an important turning point of the Cultural Revolution.

The chaos resulted from fierce factional fighting between two mass organizations: the Joint Headquarters was supported by the Guangxi Military District and **Wei Guoqing**, first party secretary of the autonomous region, while the 4-22 **rebel** faction initially enjoyed much sympathy from the CCRSG. In May 1968, members of the 4-22 faction began to break into **People's Liberation Army** (PLA) warehouses for military weapons and clash with PLA soldiers. They also stopped cargo trains and seized military and other supplies that were being transported to Vietnam. As a result, the large-scale **armed conflict** between the two organizations turned more violent.

Without mentioning either organization by name but aiming apparently more at the 4-22 faction, the July 3 Public Notice denounces the violent and destructive activities as "counterrevolutionary crimes" committed by "a small handful of class enemies." To resolve the chaotic situation, the author of the notice demands that armed struggle end immediately, that railway transportation be back to normal soon, that the looted army supplies and goods for Vietnam be returned without condition, and that those proven guilty of murder and arson, of jeopardizing transportation and communication, storming prisons, stealing state secrets, and setting up unauthorized radio stations be severely punished by law.

The repeated mention of the July 3 Public Notice by top CCP leaders, including Mao himself (who told **Red Guard** leaders at a reception that the document applies as well to other places than Guangxi), called the public's attention to it. Its effect on the national scene was beginning to be visible in late July. In the case of Guangxi, however, the issuance of the July 3 Public Notice was followed by another wave of brutal factional fighting to the disadvantage of the 4-22 rebels before violence finally began to subside in August 1968.

JULY 20 INCIDENT (1967). In reaction to the instigation of factionalism by the delegates of the **Chinese Communist Party** (CCP) Central Committee (CC), the mass organization Million-Strong Mighty Army of Wuhan, Hubei Province, took **Wang Li**, a chief delegate and a member of the **Central Cultural Revolution Small Group** (CCRSG), by force and interrogated him at a mass rally on 20 July 1967. From 20 to 23 July, this organization also held a massive demonstration and protest, with the military and the civilian population of Wuhan participating, against Wang Li and **Xie Fuzhi**, another leading member of the CC delegation. **Lin Biao**, **Jiang Qing**, and their associates called the event a "counterrevolutionary rebellion," a "mutiny" conducted by **Chen Zaidao**, commander of the Wuhan Military Region. Such charges led to the interrogation and persecution of more than a million people and to the downfall of one of China's most decorated veteran soldiers from the Red Army days; Chen Zaidao's name came to represent "that small handful (of **capitalist-roaders**) within the armed forces," and he became known internationally as a general who dared to "remonstrate with force" against the Cultural Revolution.

During the early stages of factional conflicts in Wuhan and the surrounding areas, the left-supporting troops from the Wuhan Military Region sided with the Million-Strong Mighty Army and opposed its rival, a **rebel** faction called the Workers Headquarters. In March 1967, the troops and the public security authorities arrested several rebel leaders and ordered the dissolution of the Workers Headquarters and its affiliates. This move was not well received in Beijing. On 2 April 1967, *People's Daily* carried an editorial entitled "Treating Properly the Little Revolutionary Soldiers," which alluded to the Wuhan situation as one of repression. On 6 April, the "Ten Commands of the Central Military Commission," dictated by Lin Biao, was issued, forbidding troops on a mission of supporting the left to dissolve any mass organization. On 16 April, Jiang Qing spoke of Wuhan as one of the country's serious problem areas. These signals from Beijing triggered a drastic change in Wuhan. Violent battles between the two mass factions intensified. The city was thrown into chaos.

In the meantime, **Mao Zedong** started an inspection tour of the south on 9 July and arrived in Wuhan on 15 July. **Zhou Enlai** was there with him. Wang Li and Xie Fuzhi came up from Chongqing, Sichuan Province, leading the delegation sent by the CC to inspect and resolve local conflicts. On 15 and 16 July, Mao called meetings to hear reports on several provinces and to resolve the conflict in Wuhan. He instructed that the case of the Workers Headquarters be reversed and its leaders released. He also asked the Wuhan Military Command to support both factions, since both were mass organizations after all. On 18 July, just before he left for Beijing, Zhou Enlai accompanied Commander Chen Zaidao and Political Commissioner Zhong Hanhua to see Mao. Upon Mao's admonition, Chen acknowledged his "directional mistake" of siding with one faction, while Mao assured Chen of his trust and support.

Wang Li and Xie Fuzhi, on the other hand, ignored Mao's apparently broadminded approach to factionalism and Zhou's specific demands that they not make public appearances for the moment and not express any biased views. They talked to the students of the rebel faction and made themselves known. Upon Zhou's departure, Xie and Wang went to the Wuhan Hydroelectric Institute Rebels Headquarters, received the organization's armbands, and expressed their support for the rebel faction. The next day, the Workers Headquarters broadcast Wang and Xie's comments, especially Wang's "four directives": the Wuhan Military Command's left-supporting direction was wrong; the case against the Workers Headquarters must be reversed; the rebels were the revolutionary left; and the Million-Strong Mighty Army was a **conservative** organization. The members of the Million-Strong Mighty Army, on the other hand, began to vent their indignation and rage with anti-Wang posters and slogans.

On 20 July, more than 2,000 Million-Strong Mighty Army members and **People's Liberation Army** soldiers demonstrated in front of the Donghu Guesthouse where Wang and Xie were staying. The demonstrators demanded a debate with Wang Li without knowing that Mao was also in Wuhan and that he was actually staying at Donghu. Wang was taken by force to a mass rally on the premises of the Wuhan Military Command for questioning. At Mao's order, officers of the Wuhan Military Command reasoned with the crowd at the rally and managed to have Wang Li released. In the meantime, four days of mass demonstration began. Slogans posted on the streets were not only against Wang Li and Xie Fuzhi, but also against Jiang Qing and **Zhang Chunqiao**.

Lin Biao saw the opportunity of replacing Chen Zaidao with his ally at Wuhan. On the morning of 20 July, Lin drafted a letter to Mao depicting the crisis in Wuhan as a mutiny and urging Mao to leave. The letter was revised by **Chen Boda**, **Guan Feng**, and **Qi Benyu**, signed by both Lin Biao and Jiang Qing, and secretly carried to Mao by General **Qiu Huizuo**. On the early morning of 21 July, at two o'clock, Mao left Wuhan for Shanghai, though unsure of the story as told by Lin and Jiang. On the night of Wang Li and Xie Fuzhi's return to Beijing, a briefing session was called by Lin Biao at which a decision was made to designate the July 20 Incident as a "counter-revolutionary riot." On 23 July, the CCRSG issued nationwide an emergency notice requiring the civilian population and army troops all over the country to hold armed marches and denounce the July 20 Incident. On 25 July, Lin and Jiang appeared at a rally of over a million people at Tiananmen Square to welcome home Xie and Wang and to support the rebel faction in Wuhan. The meeting ended with cries of "Down with Chen Zaidao!" and "Down with that small handful within the armed forces!" On 27 July, Lin Biao dismissed Chen Zaidao and Zhong Hanhua from their military posts. These "Chen Zaidao types" were hunted everywhere within the military establishment. In Wuhan and surrounding areas, persecution of both civilians and troops who opposed the Workers Headquarters began. In the city of Wuhan alone, more than 600 were beaten to death and about 66,000 were injured.

On 26 November 1978, the CCP Central Committee issued a notice to redress the July 20 Incident. The document accused Lin Biao and the **Gang of Four** of creating an incident for the purpose of usurping power within the party. It also announced the rehabilitation of all the victims of the event.

JULY 21 UNIVERSITY. This term refers to a type of school that was established following the comments **Mao Zedong** wrote on 21 July 1968, upon reading a case study entitled "Shanghai Machine Tool Factory's Way of Training Technicians and Engineers." The study, made by correspondents of *Wenhui Daily* and the Xinhua News Agency, reports on the experience of the training school of Shanghai Machine Tool Factory in recruiting students from young workers of their own factory and training them into technicians and engineers. The study compares the factory-trained technicians and engineers with those trained in universities and comes to the conclusion that the factory-trained ones are far more diligent, creative, and productive in conducting work-related research and innovations than those who are university trained. Mao wrote after reading the case study, "We still need to have universities; I mean science and engineering universities. But we must shorten the period of schooling, make education reforms, put proletarian politics in command, and take the path of [the] Shanghai Machine Tool Factory to turn factory workers into technicians and engineers. [Universities] should select their students from workers and peasants. After a few years of study, students should return to their fields of practice." Mao's comments as well as the case study were made public by *People's Daily* on 22 July.

Mao's comments led to the establishment of more than 10,000 July 21 universities in the later years of the Cultural Revolution. They also had considerable impact on education reforms in traditional colleges and universities. In 1970, when China's universities finally began admitting new students after a long halt of four years, they abandoned the tradition of selecting students via national examinations but took new students from **workers, peasants, and soldiers** recommended by local authorities. In the later years of the Cultural Revolution, the growth of July 21 universities was phenomenal. In 1972, there were 68 such schools in the country with a total of 4,000 students. By July 1976, the number of July 21 universities had jumped to 15,000, with 780,000 registered students. Some of these schools were converted from various "spare time schools" affiliated with factories and other enterprises. Most were newly established in response to Mao's call. Some of these schools had full-day classes; others offered only half-day or evening classes. Yet many provided merely short training programs. Students were often young workers with work experience but with limited—even just elementary school—education. Most students at July 21 universities learned some practical knowledge and skills for their jobs but rarely received a balanced college education. The July 21 universities generally lacked qualified faculty, necessary equipment, and systematic curricula. Their graduates did not meet the basic standards of traditional higher education. After the Cultural Revolution ended, and after China's college system returned to normal, July 21 universities became history.

JULY 24 PUBLIC NOTICE (1968). Coded *zhongfa* [68] 113, this was a public announcement issued by the **Chinese Communist Party** Central Committee, the State Council, the Central Military Commission, and the

Central Cultural Revolution Small Group regarding violence and chaos in some areas of Shaanxi Province. According to the public notice, some professional teams of **armed struggle** had been organized in Shaanxi to loot state banks; set fire to and use explosives on stores, warehouses, public buildings, and private residences; disrupt public transportation, communication, and postal services; and even storm military facilities and clash with military personnel. To stop the escalating mass violence in Shaanxi, the public notice issued six rules, repeating much of the **July 3 Public Notice** (concerning the problem of violence in Guangxi Zhuang Autonomous Region) and commanding the masses to follow obediently the measures prescribed in the earlier document. Both documents were region specific but were distributed nationally; their issuance was generally considered to be a decisive step by **Mao Zedong** to end the situation of a civil war across China.

JUNE 6 CIRCULAR ORDER (1967). A central document (*zhongfa* [67] 178) issued on 6 June 1967 by the **Chinese Communist Party** Central Committee, the State Council, the Central Military Commission, and the **Central Cultural Revolution Small Group** (CCRSG) and posted across China, the circular order was an attempt by **Mao Zedong** and the central leadership to get under control the nationwide violence and chaos that had been escalating since summer 1966. Against what it specifies as a widespread "evil wind of beating, smashing, robbing, confiscating, and arresting" (*da za qiang chao zhua*), the circular order prescribes rules forbidding such common practices of mass organizations as detaining and interrogating citizens without court procedure; seizing and abusing official files, records, and seals; seizing and abusing state and collective property; engaging in **armed struggle** and physically abusing people; and searching private homes and confiscating personal belongings. The circular order gives the **People's Liberation Army** the authority to implement the rules and urged all mass organizations to comply. The effect of the circular order turned out to be very limited, which may have to do with the fact that all of the activities that the circular order forbade had been encouraged or tacitly consented to by Mao and the cultural revolutionaries in the central leadership, especially members of the CCRSG, since the beginning of the Cultural Revolution.

K

KANG SHENG (1898–1975). Close associate of Chairman **Mao Zedong** since the Yan'an period and overseer of the security and intelligence apparatus of the **Chinese Communist Party** (CCP), Kang was a senior ultra-leftist with tremendous, if not always visible, power during the Cultural Revolution as advisor to the **Central Cultural Revolution Small Group** (CCRSG), a key member of the Central Special Case Examination Group, and a member of the Politburo Standing Committee. In 1980, five years after his death, however, he was expelled from the CCP because of his collaborations with the **Gang of Four** in their power intrigues and persecutions during the Cultural Revolution.

Kang was born Zhang Zongke in a rich and well-educated landlord family in Zhucheng County, Shandong Province. While a college student in Shanghai, he joined the CCP in 1925 and worked for the labor union led by the CCP. In the late 1920s and 1930s, he became involved in the work of the Comintern, the international Communist organization under Soviet control, and became an associate of Wang Ming, the Comintern's favorite in the CCP, and a group of Soviet-trained CCP members known as "28 and a half Bolsheviks." In his last two years in Shanghai, he was also put in charge of the CCP intelligence and espionage apparatus. In 1933, he was dispatched to the Soviet Union as deputy representative of the CCP to the Comintern. While in Moscow, Kang was elected a member of the CCP Politburo and, collaborating with Wang Ming, the chief CCP representative, carried out Stalin's Purge among CCP members in the Soviet Union.

Kang Sheng left Moscow for the Chinese Communist base Yan'an in 1937. Soon he shifted political alliance from Wang Ming to Mao Zedong and was put in charge of the party's intelligence and security operations. His support for Mao's marriage to **Jiang Qing**, his old acquaintance from Shandong, against the opposition of many party officials also won Mao's personal trust. With the experience of Stalin's Purge gained during his years in the Soviet Union and as head of the CCP Central Committee's Social Affairs Department, Intelligence Department, and Confidential Work Bureau, Kang was deeply involved in the Rectification Campaign (1942–1945) as Mao's effective tool for consolidating power against alleged inner-party factions supposedly led by Wang Ming and **Zhou Enlai** and persecuting innocent party cadres and intellectuals. In the name of "rescue" (*qiangjiu*), the movement that started as an ideological education was soon turned by Kang, following Mao's instructions, into a widespread political witch-hunt, labeling people as spies, traitors, and counterrevolutionaries. Most cases were fabricated or based on forced confessions. Many were arrested, and some were executed. Though most charges were dismissed eventually, intra-elite conflicts and grievances from this period would come out into the open during the Cultural Revolution.

From 1945, when he was removed as the head of personnel and intelligence departments, to the early 1960s, including the time of his ill health in the mid-1950s, Kang served on various positions of lesser influence. When the ideological battle between the CCP and the post-Stalin Soviet leadership started in the early 1960s, however, Kang, having had firsthand experience of Stalin's Russia and sharing Mao's concern about the current Soviet leader Nikita Khrushchev's de-Stalinization efforts, was promoted to the Central Committee (CC) Secretariat at the **Tenth Plenum of the Eighth Central Committee** of the CCP and began to play a leading role in the theoretical campaign of the CCP against Soviet revisionism. Closely related to his promotion was also his assistance in Mao's move of raising the issue of **class struggle** by calling Mao's attention to a novel based on the life of Liu Zhidan, a Communist leader based in Shaanxi who died in battle in 1936. Kang's speculation that the novel was intended to reverse the verdict on the fallen Communist official Gao Gang led to Mao's remark, "Using a novel to carry out anti-party activities is a great invention," and to a widespread persecution of innocent people, including the author Li Jiantong and Vice-Premier **Xi Zhongxun** (former comrade-in-arms of Liu Zhidan and father of the current CCP general secretary **Xi Jinping**).

In July 1964, Kang was appointed a member of the **Five-Person Cultural Revolution Small Group** to lead a rectification movement in literature and arts circles. When the **enlarged Politburo sessions, 4–26 May 1966**, were held in Beijing, officially launching the Cultural Revolution, Kang served as a mediating agent between the absentee Mao Zedong and central leaders attending the sessions and was named advisor to the newly formed CCRSG. Also in May, Kang sent his wife Cao Yiou to Peking University as head of an investigation group. According to **Nie Yuanzi**, Cao supported her and six other colleagues in posting a **big-character poster** denouncing leaders of Peking University and the Beijing municipal party committee. To mobilize the masses and stir up the nation for the Cultural Revolution, Mao soon made a decisive move to have the poster broadcast nationwide on 1 June and later called this militant piece the "**first Marxist-Leninist big-character poster.**" In the capacity of a member of the Politburo Standing Committee (since

August 1966) and head of the CC Organization and Propaganda Leading Group (since November 1970) and in collaboration with the cultural revolutionaries in the central leadership closely following Mao's voiced or unvoiced intentions, Kang was deeply involved in many activities of persecution, publicly or behind the scenes, including the cases against the **Inner Mongolia People's Revolutionary Party** (*neirendang*), the (Hunan) **Provincial Proletarian Alliance** (*shengwulian*), and ranking leaders like **Liu Shaoqi** and **He Long**. Kang also exerted his influence on foreign policies on ideological grounds during the Cultural Revolution: he advocated support for the Khmer Rouge regime in Cambodia replacing China's longtime ally Prince Sihanouk.

By the time of his death on 16 December 1975, Kang was ranked number four in the CCP leadership. In 1980, CC named him a main culprit of the **Lin Biao** and Jiang Qing counterrevolutionary cliques. Today historians often compare his role to those of the Soviet Union's security chiefs Feliks Dzerzhinsky (under Vladimir Lenin) and Lavrenti Beria (under Joseph Stalin).

KANGPING AVENUE INCIDENT (1966). A brutal attack of one worker organization on another on Shanghai's Kangping Avenue on 30 December 1966, this event was generally considered to be the beginning of the massive factional violence that subsequently occurred throughout China.

In November and December 1966, Mayor Cao Diqiu and the Shanghai municipal party committee were under much pressure from the **Central Cultural Revolution Small Group** (CCRSG) to give in to the demands of the **Workers Command Post** of Shanghai and to give themselves up as targets of criticism. The Red Defenders Battalion, another city-wide worker organization opposed to the Workers Command Post, had supported the Shanghai party committee in the *Liberation Daily* **Incident** and then felt subsequently betrayed when Mayor Cao was forced to endorse the Workers Command Post. Confused and angry, the Red Defenders Battalion decided to go to the secretariat of the Shanghai party committee on Kangping Avenue to reason with Mayor Cao Diqiu and First Secretary Chen Pixian. Upon hearing the report on the Kangping Avenue situation, **Zhang Chunqiao**, deputy head of the CCRSG from Shanghai, telephoned from Beijing and instructed **Wang Hongwen** and other leaders of the Workers Command Post to "wage a blow-for-blow struggle" against their rivals. By the evening of 29 December, about 100,000 members of the Workers Command Post and fewer than 30,000 members of the Red Defenders Battalion converged on Kangping Avenue. At 2 a.m. on 30 December, Wang Hongwen led the charge against the other organization. The violent clash left 91 people injured. Taking the law into their own hands, the Workers Command Post issued an urgent order of arrest the next day and illegally detained more than 240 members of the Red Defenders Battalion. The violence left the city in chaos, and the Shanghai party committee and city government were powerless. With its newly gained dominance among mass organizations, the Workers Command Post was ready to engage in the struggle for power in the 1967 **January Storm**.

KUAI DAFU (1946–). One of the well-known "five **Red Guard** leaders" in Beijing, Kuai was head of the mass organization Jinggang Mountain Regiment at Tsinghua University and a prominent leader of the Capital College **Red Guards' Representative Assembly**.

A native of Binhai, Jiangsu Province, Kuai was a third-year student in chemical engineering at Tsinghua University when the Cultural Revolution began. At the outset of the Cultural Revolution, Kuai was **struggled against** at several mass meetings because of his strong opposition to the Tsinghua **work group** to which **Wang Guangmei**, wife of President **Liu Shaoqi**, was advisor; Kuai was denounced and detained as a "reactionary student." After **Mao Zedong** made a decision to withdraw work groups from college campuses, a number of ranking leaders, including **Zhou Enlai**, **Deng Xiaoping**, **Tao Zhu**, **Li Xuefeng**, and some members of the **Central Cultural Revolution Small Group** (CCRSG), went to Tsinghua on 5 August 1966 to meet students and to redress wrongful cases there, including Kuai's.

On 23 September 1966, the Jinggang Mountain Regiment of Tsinghua University, a rebel student organization that was to become nationally influential, was formed with Kuai as its leader. As one of the founders of the "Capital College Red Guards Revolutionary Rebel Headquarters," popularly known as the **Third Command Post**, Kuai organized the **mass rally of 6 October 1966**, at which more than 100,000 people representing colleges across China gathered to launch the campaign against the **Bourgeois Reactionary Line**. During this campaign, Kuai emerged as a popular hero as well as Mao's foot soldier. Answering Mao's call for rebellion and acting on instructions from the CCRSG, Kuai played a significant role in bringing down Liu Shaoqi and other ranking leaders of the old party establishment; the Jinggang Mountain Regiment was the first mass organization in the country to denounce Liu Shaoqi in name in December 1966. For his achievements as a student leader, Kuai was appointed a member of the Standing Committee of the Beijing Municipal **Revolutionary Committee** in 1967.

In the chaotic years of 1967 and 1968, Kuai and his organization, like other **rebels** nationwide, were deeply involved in factional conflicts. During the well-known **One-Hundred-Day Armed Conflict on the Tsinghua Campus**, for instance, Kuai led the Jinggang Mountain Regiment in a notoriously bloody fight against their rival organization, the 4-14 group. Such widespread and seemingly endless factional violence finally led to Mao's decision, in summer 1968, to end the Red Guard movement altogether. On 27 July 1968, Mao sent a **workers propaganda team** and an **army propaganda team** to Tsinghua University to stop the violence and take control of the campus. On the early morning of 28 July 1968, Mao held a meeting with the five Red Guard leaders, including Kuai Dafu. At the meeting, Mao sent a clear signal to Kuai and others that they should exit China's political stage. Kuai was soon criticized at mass meetings organized by the propaganda teams. He was taken into custody several times in the remaining years of the Cultural Revolution.

Shortly after the downfall of the **Gang of Four**, the authorities formally arrested Kuai on a counterrevolutionary charge. On 10 March 1983, the Beijing Intermediate People's Court sentenced him to 17 years in prison, holding him responsible for the deaths and the injuries caused by both the factional violence on campus and an **armed conflict** with the propaganda teams and charging him with the crimes of instigating attacks on party and state officials and framing and persecuting innocent people during the Cultural Revolution.

See also MAO ZEDONG: MEETING WITH THE FIVE RED GUARD LEADERS (28 July 1968).

L

LAO SHE (1899–1966). A well-known and much-loved modern Chinese writer, Lao She was an early victim of the Cultural Revolution and died in the month of 1966 known as **Red August**. Born in Beijing and originally named Shu Qingchun, Lao She was a son of a Manchurian soldier. While a lecturer in Chinese at the University of London's School of Oriental Studies from 1924 to 1930, he adopted the pen name Lao She and began to write novels and short stories in Chinese. Continuing to teach and write after he returned to China, Lao She established himself as a major writer known for his realistic portrayal of the life of city residents in an authentic Beijing dialect. In 1949, he gave up a teaching position in the United States and returned to Beijing filled with much enthusiasm for the newly established People's Republic. In 1951, he was named "People's Artist" by the city government of Beijing. Many of his works, including the novels *Rickshaw Boy* and *Four Generations under One Roof* and the play *Teahouse*, became immensely popular. Some of them were adapted as films, and five of his novels were translated into English. Although Lao She was given a number of official titles, including member of the Standing Committee of the Chinese People's Political Consultative Conference, vice-chairman of the Chinese Writers Association, vice-chairman of the China Federation of Literary and Art Circles, and chairman of the Beijing Federation of Literary and Art Circles, he was never admitted into the **Chinese Communist Party** despite having applied for party membership numerous times.

In summer 1966 when the Cultural Revolution was just beginning, Lao She became ill and was hospitalized. However, anxious to participate in a revolution that he had been struggling to understand, he left the hospital as soon as he could, despite **Zhou Enlai**'s advice not to hurry. On 23 August 1966, the day after he was released from the hospital, Lao She went to work, only to find himself and his fellow writers and artists in the hands of a group of **Red Guards**. They took Lao She and his colleagues to the large courtyard of what used to be a Confucius Temple in the Imperial Academy, where a huge pile of costumes and props of the traditional theater—confiscated by the Red Guards as material evidence of the **Four Olds**—was burning. The

Red Guards shaved the heads of their captives in a humiliating **yin-yang** style, poured black ink on them, hung big signs on their necks that read "**black gang** element," "reactionary academic authority," and "**cow-demons and snake-spirits**," and forced them to kneel around the burning fire for a "fire baptism." One of the criminal charges against Lao She was that he had been an American spy. The Red Guards beat their victims with stage props and broad leather belts with bronze buckles. Lao She fainted and fell to the ground. Yet another round of beating followed in the evening in another location, continuing into the night. Lao She's refusal to hold the placard with criminal titles only prompted further abuse from the Red Guards. He was then taken to a nearby police station as an "active counterrevolutionary" and was eventually sent home with an order from his captors that he report to his workplace the next day carrying a "counterrevolutionary" label. When Lao She reached home, covered with blood, he found no sign that his family members had full confidence in his complete innocence. On the morning of 24 August, Lao She went alone to the edge of Taiping Lake in the northwestern part of Beijing carrying **Mao Zedong**'s poems that he had copied. He sat there for the whole day and drowned himself in the lake that evening.

LI DESHENG (1916–2011). A native of Xinxian, Henan Province, a member of the **Chinese Communist Party** (CCP) from 1932, and an army veteran from the Long March to the Korean War, Li was made major general in 1955. In 1967, Li, then commander of the Twelfth Army of the **People's Liberation Army** (PLA), led his troops from Jiangsu to Anhui to stop the violent factional fighting among mass organizations. In April 1968, he became chairman of the newly established Anhui **Revolutionary Committee** as well as deputy commander of the Nanjing Military Region. Li's successful handling of factional violence in Anhui caught the attention of **Mao Zedong**, who introduced Li to those present at the First Plenum of the Ninth CCP Central Committee (April 1969) at which Li was elected an alternate member of the Politburo. In July 1969, Li was transferred to Beijing at Mao's suggestion. Li's various military appointments in Beijing, including director of the General Political Department (GPD) of the PLA and commander of the Beijing Military Region, were part of Mao's strategic moves—"dig corners and add sand to the mix," as Mao put it—to weaken **Lin Biao**'s influence in the army. At the time of the **September 13 Incident** of 1971, Li followed Premier **Zhou Enlai**'s orders to take over the command of the air force and reportedly directed the operations of the air force for five days without pausing for a break. In 1973, Li became vice-chairman of the CCP and a member of the Politburo Standing Committee.

In the meantime, however, **Jiang Qing** began reporting to Mao about Li's lack of enthusiasm for the radical cause and significantly weakened Mao's confidence in him, so much so that in January 1975, Li was forced to resign from his position as vice-chairman of the CCP while remaining as commander of the Shenyang Military Region. In 1980, the central leadership approved a GDP report dismissing the slanders that the Jiang Qing group had brought against Li in 1973–1974. Li was appointed political commissioner of the University of National Defense in 1985 and retired from all his military and political duties in 1990.

LI FUCHUN (1900–1975). One of the chief architects of China's socialist economy and a close associate of Premier **Zhou Enlai**, Li Fuchun was vice-premier of the State Council (SC) (1954–1975) and member of the Standing Committee of the Politburo (1966–1969). Born in Changsha, Hunan Province, Li joined the **Chinese Communist Party** (CCP) while a student in France in 1922. He was a leader of the CCP European general branch. A veteran of both the Northern Expedition and the Long March, over the years Li held various high positions in the CCP, including secretary-general of the Central Committee (CC), director of the CC General Office, and minister of finance and economy. In the early 1950s, Li and Chen Yun were in charge of the design and implementation of the new republic's first five-year plan. In 1954, Li was appointed vice-premier of the SC and director of the National Planning Commission. In the early 1960s, Li played a major role in moderating the radical economic policies of the Great Leap Forward to restore the badly damaged national economy.

After the Cultural Revolution began, Li, as head of the SC business group, assisted Premier Zhou Enlai in running the daily affairs of the state during a chaotic time. He was called by **Kang Sheng** "the head of the black club" because of the frequent business gatherings of vice-premiers at Li's residence. At the **Twelfth Plenum of the Eighth CCP Central Committee**, Li was criticized for his involvement in the **February Adverse Current**. Although Li was elected to the CC again at the **Ninth National Congress of the CCP** in 1969, he no longer held any significant leadership position by then. Li Fuchun died of illness in Beijing on 9 January 1975.

LI JIULIAN (1946–1977). In the early stages of the Cultural Revolution, Li was an enthusiastic **Red Guard** leader at Ganzhou No. 3 Middle School in Jiangxi Province. But her revolutionary fervor soon gave way to skepticism and critical reflection. On 29 February 1969, while a factory apprentice, Li wrote to her boyfriend about her questions and critical views concerning the Cultural Revolution. She suspected that the revolution might be a power struggle among different factions within the central leadership, and she sympathized with President **Liu Shaoqi** whose views, in her opinion, were mostly right for China at present. In her private journal, she also criticized **Lin Biao**'s promotion of the **personality cult** of Chairman **Mao Zedong** and expressed her contempt for such popular ideas as the "red sea" (that is, covering all street walls with red paint with Mao's quotations written on them) and **"three loyalties and four limitlessnesses."** In her view, Lin Biao, rather than Liu Shaoqi, might be **China's Khrushchev**. Unfortunately, her boyfriend turned her letter over to the authorities, which led to her arrest by police on 3 April 1969.

In July 1972, 10 months after the downfall of Lin Biao, Li was released, though the authorities still considered her case to be one of "contradictions between ourselves and the enemy but treated as contradictions among the people." Li appealed to all levels of government to clear her name but received no response. In spring 1974, during the **Criticize Lin and Criticize Confucius** campaign, Li put out a number of **big-character posters**, including one entitled "It Is No Crime Criticizing Lin Biao," in downtown Ganzhou, calling on the public to support her rehabilitation. Her sympathizers then organized an "Investigation Committee on the Li Jiulian Case" and won the support of tens of thousands of Ganzhou citizens. In April 1974, the provincial authorities arrested Li again and cracked down on the movement. Later, **Wang Hongwen** and **Zhang Chunqiao** voiced support for the crackdown and named Li a counterrevolutionary. On 30 May 1975, the Xingguo County People's Court sentenced Li to 15 years in prison. After the downfall of the **Gang of Four**, Li went on a hunger strike to protest her persecution. She also criticized the new personality cult of **Hua Guofeng**. With her criticism of Hua as a new charge, Li was executed on 14 December 1977. During the period of 1974–1977, a large number of people in Ganzhou were accused of supporting Li and were persecuted; some of them were imprisoned.

The officials involved in persecuting Li and her supporters tried to dismiss the public call to redress the Li Jiulian case until January 1980 when **Hu Yaobang**, head of the Communist party's organization department, intervened. In April 1981, Jiangxi Provincial Supreme Court finally pronounced Li's verdict unjust.

LI QINGLIN (1928–2004). Li was the author of a well-known letter to **Mao Zedong**, dated 20 December 1972, that prompted an adjustment in the government's policy toward **educated youths** in the countryside and contributed considerably to the improvement of their working and living conditions. An elementary school teacher in Fujian Province and the father of a middle school graduate who had left home to settle in the countryside, Li wrote candidly about the hunger and poverty in which his son had been living, and he also wrote about the common corruption problem called "walking through the back door": families with political power or with connections had been bringing their children out of the countryside by arranging work for them in state institutions and factories or sending them to colleges, while children of ordinary people like himself, without power and without connections, were doomed to remain in the countryside.

Somehow Li's letter reached Mao. On 25 April 1973, Mao mailed Li 300 *yuan* (Chinese currency) and wrote him a brief letter, promising a comprehensive solution to this national problem. Soon the central leadership issued Li's letter nationwide as a **Chinese Communist Party** (CCP) Central Committee (CC) document. In June, the State Council (SC) held a long work session on educated youths in the countryside at which proposals were made that a government agency concerning educated youths be established at the county level, that one child per family be allowed to stay in the city, and that various forms of state aid to educated youths in the countryside be instituted. On 4 August, the CC authorized the SC work session report for nationwide issuance, and an editorial in the 7 August issue of *People's Daily* took up the question of educated youths and demanded that cadres be resolute in "resisting the unhealthy social trends" (referring to the problem of "back-door" dealings) and that those abusing urban youths in the countryside be severely punished.

In the meantime, Mao Zedong's reply made Li Qinglin instantly famous. The ultra-leftists associated with the **Jiang Qing** group characterized him as a hero of "going against the tide" (*fan chaoliu*)—a fashionable substitution for the "spirit of rebellion" of the **Red Guards**. Li then began to identify himself with the ultra-leftists and published an article simply entitled "On Going against the Tide" (*fan chaoliu*) in the November issue of the CCP organ *Red Flag*. In 1974, he was elected a delegate to the **Fourth National People's Congress**. In January 1975, he was made a member of the National People's Congress's Standing Committee. Li Qinglin's deepening implication in ultra-leftist politics at both national and provincial levels eventually led to his arrest after the downfall of the **Gang of Four**.

LI WENBO (1914–1966). A Beijing resident and an early victim of **Red Guard** violence, Li was rumored to have resisted brutal abuse from Red Guards with a kitchen knife and was subsequently beaten to death. This incident drastically escalated violence during the period of Red Guard terror known as **Red August**: in each day of the week immediately following Li Wenbo's death, between 100 and 300 innocent people were slaughtered in Beijing.

Because Li's class status was small proprietor, a group of Red Guards from Beijing's No. 15 Girls Middle School searched and ransacked his apartment on 24 August 1966, at the height of the **Destroy the Four Olds** campaign. They came back the next day to hold a **struggle meeting** denouncing and torturing Li and his wife, Liu Wenxiu. From this point on, there are two versions of what happened. According to the version the Red Guards broadcast at the time, Li was in such a rage over the ransacking and beating that he picked up a kitchen knife and injured several Red Guards. Then he jumped out of the window to kill himself. Though the suicide attempt was not successful, he was beaten to death by the crowd on the spot. According to a witness account published in 1998, the author being one of the Red Guards in Li's apartment on 25 August 1966, "We shut the couple up upstairs in the heat of the summer and didn't allow them to eat, drink, and go to the bathroom. The old woman couldn't hold back anymore and forced a bathroom-run down the stairs. We pushed her down and kicked her. The old man was mad. He came downstairs to argue with us. We beat him up with sticks, and blood came out. So he picked up a kitchen knife and scared us away. Actually, he didn't strike with the knife. We just said that he was vengeful, but somehow the story was changed when it came out that said that he killed people and was sentenced to death."

After Li Wenbo's death at the hands of the Red Guards, the latter demanded that they be allowed to hold a mass rally denouncing his wife, Liu Wenxiu, and to beat her to death at the rally. Their demand was dismissed by Premier **Zhou Enlai**. On 12 September, the Beijing Intermediate People's Court sentenced both Liu and her already dead husband to death. Liu was executed the next day. Meanwhile, with the first version of the story—the only version at the time—widespread, the Red Guards shouted, "Blood for blood," and launched a killing rampage that spread out of downtown Beijing into suburban **Changping County** and **Daxing County**. As a result, over 1,000 people were killed in Beijing during the seven days between 26 August and 1 September, the Red August's bloodiest week.

LI XIANNIAN (1909–1992). Vice-premier of the State Council (SC) from 1954 and a member of the Politburo from 1956, Li was one of the veteran leaders involved in the **February Adverse Current** of 1967. A native of Huang'an, Hubei Province, Li joined the **Chinese Communist Party** (CCP) in 1927, participated in the Long March, and led the military and guerrilla activities in central China during the war of resistance against Japan and the civil war of the late 1940s. In 1954, Li was appointed minister of finance and became known as a moderate economic policy maker under **Zhou Enlai** and Chen Yun. In February 1967, as the Cultural Revolution was evolving toward a turbulent **power seizure** struggle, Li joined the veteran leaders of the SC and of the armed forces at a briefing session in voicing opposition to the Cultural Revolution and in criticizing the members of the **Central Cultural Revolution Small Group** (CCRSG). Li particularly blamed an editorial in the CCRSG-controlled party organ *Red Flag* for initiating attacks on veteran cadres. In 1968, Li was sent to a lumber mill north of the city of Beijing to do manual labor.

After the downfall of **Lin Biao** in 1971, Li resumed his work as vice-premier and became a member of the newly established **Central Military Commission Administrative Conference Office**. He assisted both Zhou Enlai and **Deng Xiaoping** in conducting the daily affairs of the state in the last years of the Cultural Revolution. In 1976, Li played an important role in bringing down the **Gang of Four**. In 1977, at the First Plenum of the Eleventh CCP Central Committee, Li was elected to the Politburo Standing Committee and became vice-chairman of the CCP. He was also entrusted with the daily affairs of the SC. From 1983 to 1988, Li served in a still higher but more or less ceremonial position as president of the People's Republic. He died on 21 June 1992.

LI XUEFENG (1907–2003). Born in Yongji, Shanxi Province, Li joined the **Chinese Communist Party** (CCP) in 1933. In the 1930s, he worked underground as a CCP leader in Shanxi Province and in Beijing. From the early 1940s to the early 1950s, Li was the top CCP official first in the Taihang Mountain area and then in Henan Province. In 1948, he was appointed deputy secretary of the Central China Bureau of the CCP. In 1954, Li was named deputy secretary-general of the CCP Central Committee (CC), and in 1956, he became head of the Department of Industry and Transportation of the CC and a member of the CCP Central Secretariat. In 1960, Li was appointed first secretary of the CCP's North China Bureau and first political commissar of Beijing Military Region.

After **Peng Zhen** was removed from power at the **enlarged Politburo sessions** in May 1966, Li Xuefeng replaced Peng as first party secretary of Beijing and was entrusted with the responsibility of reorganizing the CCP Beijing Municipal Committee. Li's tenure in his new position, however, was rather brief because of his close association with President **Liu Shaoqi** in carrying out a **work group** policy, which Mao dismissed as a repressive **Bourgeois Reactionary Line** against the mass movement. Though Li was promoted to the Politburo as an alternate member at the **Eleventh Plenum of the Eighth CCP Central Committee** (August 1966), he and the Beijing party committee under him were pushed to the sidelines when the Criticize the Bourgeois Reactionary Line campaign started in October 1966. In January 1967, Li was reassigned as chairman of the newly established **revolutionary committee** of Hebei Province. However, because of his alleged conspiracy with **Chen Boda** to attack the **Jiang Qing** group at the **Second Plenum of the Ninth CCP Central Committee** (23 August–6 September 1970), Li was dismissed from office in April 1971 during the **Criticize Chen and Conduct Rectification** campaign. After **Lin Biao**'s downfall in September 1971, the investigation of Li's connection with Chen extended to his alleged involvement with the Lin Biao Anti-Party Clique. As a result, Li was permanently expelled from the CCP in August 1973.

Li's case was reviewed and rehabilitated after the downfall of the **Gang of Four**. In 1982, Li Xuefeng was reinstated as a CCP member. In 1985, he was elected to the Advisory Committee of the CCP Central Committee.

LI YIZHE BIG-CHARACTER POSTER. This was the phrase by which the poster "On Socialist Democracy and the Socialist Legal System: Dedicated to the Fourth People's Congress" was popularly known. This poster was written originally as a petition to the **Fourth National People's Congress** (13–17 January 1975) that the rule of law be established in a new constitution to protect the rights of ordinary citizens, including those "open and honest with their opposing views." Li Yizhe represented an independent reading group in Guangdong Province. As a pseudonym, it was based on the names of the three major members of the group: Li Zhengtian, Chen Yiyang, and Wang Xizhe. Guo Hongzhi, a senior Communist theorist, offered help as an advisor to the group. When the petition was posted on 10 November 1974 at a busy junction of Beijing Avenue in Guangzhou, it attracted large crowds. Subsequently, it was copied, mimeographed, reprinted, and circulated in many Chinese cities.

In the poster, Li Yizhe observes that there has emerged in China a privileged stratum similar to the one in the Soviet Union and that this stratum is a new bourgeois class of party officials represented by **Liu Shaoqi** and his colleagues before the Cultural Revolution and by **Lin Biao** and his cronies during the Cultural Revolution. Though echoing **Mao Zedong**'s theory of **continuous revolution** against the rise of the new bourgeoisie within the party, the Li Yizhe poster touches upon two issues that potentially challenge Mao's authority. First, its condemnation of Lin Biao's "feudalist social fascism" goes beyond the political rhetoric of the times: in the name of social legality it challenges Lin's **personality cult** of Mao and his suppression of dissent. Second, taking "feudal fascism" as the most dangerous threat to China's proletarian dictatorship, the poster calls for the passage of a new constitution representing the "will of the proletariat and the masses of China," a constitution under which those who have persecuted innocent people would be punished; those with dissenting political views, however wrong they may be, would be protected; and those who are in power but have abused their power and hence lost people's trust would be replaced. The author's attempt merely to bring up the forbidden topic of social legality and the rights of the masses made the poster a milestone in the development of political dissent during the Cultural Revolution and inspired further reflections on both the nature of ultra-leftist politics and the possibilities of democracy in a Chinese context.

LI ZAIHAN (1919–1975). One of the few provincial military leaders who supported the rebels in the early stages of the Cultural Revolution, Li became chairman of the Guizhou Provincial **Revolutionary Committee** in 1967 and an alternate member of the Central Committee (CC) at the **Ninth National Congress of the Chinese Communist Party** (CCP) in 1969 but was eventually dismissed from office for his involvement in the violent factional battle in Guizhou.

A native of Fushun, Sichuan Province, Li joined the CCP in 1938. He began his military career as an infantry soldier and eventually became deputy political commissioner of the Guizhou Provincial Military District in 1960. When the Cultural Revolution broke out in 1966, Li was named a member of the Cultural Revolution leading group under the CCP Guizhou Provincial Committee. When a group of students came from Beijing to the provincial capital Guiyang and incited local residents to criticize the provincial authorities, Li sympathized with the masses that rose against the allegedly manipulative and repressive provincial leaders. He wrote several letters critical of the provincial authorities and reported to the **Central Cultural Revolution Small Group** (CCRSG) on the Guizhou situation. **Wang Li**, of the CCRSG, then recommended Li to **Mao Zedong**, referring to him as a "Cultural Revolution activist in the army."

In January 1967, Li traveled to Beijing to receive **Jiang Qing**'s instructions concerning **power seizure** in Guizhou. Upon returning, Li formed a rebel organization called the "General Headquarters of Guizhou Proletarian Revolutionary Rebels" and took over the power of the Guizhou party committee on 25 January 1967. The organization's power seizure announcement and related documents were soon published in *People's Daily* and *Red Flag*, which indicated the approval of Mao and the central leadership in Beijing. However, since the successful power seizure put Li in the most prominent position in the province as chairman of the Guizhou Revolutionary Committee and first political commissioner of the Guizhou Military District, factional violence broke out in the province. Li supported one mass faction against the other in a series of bloody battles, including a large-scale **armed conflict** in Guiyang on 29 July 1969. He also intervened in the mass movement in the neighboring province of Yunnan. Li's deep involvement in factional conflict and his unsettling overreach provoked strong opposition both provincially and nationally. In March 1971, the CC stripped Li of all his official positions and publicly criticized him. Li Zaihan died of illness in 1975.

LI ZUOPENG (1914–2009). A close associate of **Lin Biao** and popularly known as one of Lin's "four guardian warriors," Li was deputy chief of the general staff of the **People's Liberation Army** (PLA), commissar of the navy, and a member of the **Central Military Commission Administrative Group** (1968–1971). Born in Ji'an, Jiangxi Province, Li joined the Red

Army in 1930 and participated in the Long March. During the civil war in the late 1940s, Li was a corps commander in Lin Biao's Fourth Field Army. He was made lieutenant general in 1955 and deputy commander of the PLA navy in 1962. In late 1965, Li, along with Wang Hongkun and Zhang Xiuchuan, both officers in the navy, forged material for Lin Biao to use in bringing down Chief of General Staff **Luo Ruiqing**.

Li Zuopeng was attacked by the rank and file within the navy during the early stages of the Cultural Revolution. Lin Biao intervened and protected him. Lin named him, along with **Wu Faxian** and **Qiu Huizuo**, a leader of the "proletarian revolutionaries of the armed forces." As such a leader, Li authorized the persecution of 120 navy officers (according to a special court verdict) and consolidated the pro-Lin forces in the navy. In 1968, Li was appointed deputy chief of the general staff of the PLA, commissar of the navy, and a member of the Central Military Commission Administrative Group. At the **Ninth National Congress of the Chinese Communist Party** (CCP) (1969), Li was elected to the Central Committee (CC) and to the Politburo. At the **Lushan Conference** of 1970, the conflict between the **Jiang Qing** faction and the Lin Biao faction within the party leadership surfaced. Li joined **Chen Boda**, Wu Faxian, Qiu Huizuo, and **Ye Qun** in attacking **Zhang Chunqiao** and supporting a proposal not to eliminate the office of the national president. Backing Zhang and the Jiang Qing group, Mao singled out Chen Boda as the main target of criticism and also told other supporters of Lin Biao, including Li, to conduct self-criticism. In April 1971, the CC held a meeting reviewing the ongoing **Criticize Chen and Conduct Rectification** campaign. Li's written self-criticism, along with those of other associates of Lin Biao, was discussed at the meeting. In his summary report representing the view of the CC, Premier **Zhou Enlai** criticized Huang, Wu, Ye, Li, and Qiu for following a wrong political line and practicing factionalism. In the meantime, Mao continued to make harsh comments on Lin Biao and his supporters.

On 6 September, Li learned from Liu Feng, commissar of the Wuhan Military Region, the critical comments Mao made in Wuhan about Lin Biao. Li went back to Beijing on the same day to pass the information on to Huang Yongsheng so that Huang might communicate it to Ye Qun in time. After the plot against Mao's life, allegedly directed by Lin Biao and executed by **Lin Liguo**, failed on 12 September 1971, Li, duty-bound to work with Zhou Enlai to resolve the crisis, twice changed Zhou's orders concerning the aircraft Trident 256 on the early morning of 13 September 1971 so that the plane carrying Lin Biao, Ye Qun, and Lin Liguo could take off from Shanhaiguan airport and flee the country.

After the **September 13 Incident**, Li Zuopeng was taken into custody, and his involvement with Lin Biao's alleged coup attempt came under investigation. On 20 August 1973, the CC issued a resolution concerning the Lin Biao

Anti-Party Clique. As a member of the Lin group, he was dismissed from all his official positions and was expelled from the CCP. On 25 January 1981, Li Zuopeng was sentenced to 17 years in prison for organizing and leading a counterrevolutionary clique, plotting to subvert the government, and bringing false charges against innocent people.

LIANG XIAO. A homophonic reference to "two schools," this was one of the pen names of—and the one used most frequently by—the **Peking University and Tsinghua University Great Criticism Group**.

LIAO MOSHA (1907–1990). A native of Changsha, Hunan Province, Liao was a writer and veteran member of the **Chinese Communist Party** (CCP) since 1930. In 1961, Liao, while a ranking official in the Beijing municipal government, joined **Wu Han** and **Deng Tuo** in coauthoring the column *Notes from a Three-Family Village* in *Frontline*, the official organ of the CCP Beijing Municipal Committee. He contributed learned but also entertaining essays that were often critical of the social evils of the day. A witty piece entitled "On the Harmlessness of Ghosts" was so popular that **Mao Zedong**, speaking at an enlarged Politburo standing committee session on 20 March 1966, mentioned it as evidence that **class struggle** was going on. As a prelude to the Cultural Revolution, a political campaign was launched in early May 1966 to denounce the so-called **Three-Family Village Anti-Party Clique**. Liao was named an anti-party, anti-socialist "old-hand" and a member of the "**black gang**" of the CCP Beijing Municipal Committee. During the Cultural Revolution, Liao was verbally attacked, publicly humiliated, and physically abused. From 1968 to 1975, he was imprisoned for the alleged crime of betraying the CCP. Upon release from prison, he was sent to a tree farm in Jiangxi to do manual work. He was allowed to return to Beijing in 1978.

Liao Mosha was rehabilitated in March 1979 when the CCP Central Committee approved the resolution of the Beijing Municipal Committee to reverse the verdict of the Three-Family Anti-Party Clique. In March 1983, Liao was elected vice-chairman of the Sixth Consultative Committee of the Beijing People's Congress. Liao died on 27 December 1990.

***LIBERATION DAILY* INCIDENT (1966).** This refers to the closing down of *Liberation Daily*, the official organ of the CCP Shanghai Municipal Committee, by the Shanghai College **Red Guard** Revolutionary Committee from 1 to 8 December 1966. In late November, the Red Guard **Revolutionary Committee** newspaper *Red Guard Combat News* came off the press carrying an article denouncing *Liberation Daily* as a "loyal instrument" of the Shanghai party committee in carrying out the **Bourgeois Reactionary Line**. The organization demanded that this issue of *Red Guard Combat News* be distributed together with *Liberation Daily* as a measure of "detoxification." On 1 December, after *Liberation Daily* refused to meet their demand, several thousand college Red Guards occupied the office building of the official newspaper and shut it down. The action met with strong opposition from a Shanghai workers organization called the Red Defenders Battalion. The members of the battalion demonstrated outside the *Liberation Daily* office building shouting, "We want to read *Liberation Daily!*" The Shanghai **Workers Command Post**, the battalion's political rival, supported the college Red Guards. Its members joined the college Red Guards and debated the members of the battalion. The heat of the debate led to a violent confrontation. The college Red Guards' occupation of the office building finally ended when the Shanghai party committee gave in to their demands on 5 December 1966.

LIN BIAO (1907–1971). Military strategist and **Mao Zedong**'s designated successor, Lin Biao was minister of defense (1959–1971) and sole vice-chairman of the **Chinese Communist Party** (CCP) during the first five years of the Cultural Revolution.

A native of Huanggang, Hubei Province, Lin entered the Huangpu (Whampoa) Military Academy in 1925 as part of the school's fourth class and joined the CCP in the same year. In 1927, Lin, a veteran of the Northern Expedition, took part in the Nanchang Uprising as a company commander and later joined Mao in the Jiangxi Soviet revolutionary base. During the anti-encirclement campaigns (1928–1934), the war of resistance against Japan (1937–1945), and the civil war of the late 1940s, Lin continuously distinguished himself as a military leader. He also served as president of the Anti-Japanese Military and Political University at Yan'an after the Long March. In 1955, Lin was named one of 10 grand marshals of the **People's Liberation Army** (PLA) and also entered the CCP Politburo. In 1958, he became one of five vice-chairmen of the CCP and a member of the Politburo's Standing Committee. In 1959, as Marshal **Peng Dehuai** was dismissed for criticizing the Great Leap Forward, Lin replaced Peng as minister of defense at Mao's insistence.

In the first half of the 1960s, as Mao retreated from the frontline of the central leadership after the disastrous experiment of the Great Leap Forward, Lin Biao moved closer to Mao. At the **Central Committee Work Sessions in January–February 1962**, Lin voiced support for Mao's radical policies in contrast to the cautiously critical views given by President **Liu Shaoqi** and others. In the meantime, embracing Mao's emphasis on ideology, Lin advocated "politics in command" in the armed forces and authorized the publication of the *Quotations from Chairman Mao*—to be known in the Cultural Revolution as a **Red Book of Treasures**—and its distribution among PLA personnel. Lin also formulated a "**peak theory**" that elevated Mao and **Mao Zedong Thought** to an unprecedented status and contributed much to Mao's **personality cult** during the Cultural Revolution.

In late 1965, in an attempt to consolidate his power in the armed forces, Lin instructed his trusted generals, including **Li Zuopeng**, deputy commander of the navy, to fabricate material against Lin's rival, General **Luo Ruiqing**, chief of general staff of the PLA. In February 1966, Lin allowed his name to be associated with **Jiang Qing** in a report on a symposium Jiang organized on the work of literature and the arts in the armed forces, which accorded Jiang, a figure largely unknown in the army and to the public, considerable prestige. While Lin's support contributed much to Jiang Qing's meteoric rise as the leader of the cultural revolutionaries in the CCP leadership, the eventual downfall of Luo Ruiqing as part of the so-called **Peng-Luo-Lu-Yang Anti-Party Clique** marked Mao's first major victory at the beginning stage of the Cultural Revolution.

On 18 May 1966, Lin took a further step in the direction of Mao's Revolution by delivering a high-powered speech at an **enlarged Politburo session**. In the speech—known today as the "**scripture of coup d'état**"—Lin, on the one hand, dramatized the imminent danger of an enemy takeover from within the party leadership and, on the other, idolized Mao in superlative terms.

Mao Zedong, Lin Biao, and Zhou Enlai in the lounge of the Tiananmen gate tower, autumn 1966.

In August 1966, at the **Eleventh Plenum of the Eighth CCP Central Committee,** as Mao launched an offensive against Liu Shaoqi, Lin Biao was elevated from the sixth to the second highest position in the central leadership and became the only vice-chairman of the CCP. From this point on, Lin was referred to in official media as "Chairman Mao's closest comrade-in-arms" to whom the masses in their daily prayer wished "everlasting health" after Mao's "boundless longevity." In the next few months, Lin accompanied Mao in his eight mass rally receptions for more than 10 million **Red Guards** from all over China. Politically, Lin consolidated his power, mainly in the armed forces, by offering protection and support for his trusted generals, especially his "four guardian warriors" **Huang Yongsheng, Wu Faxian,** Li Zuopeng, and **Qiu Huizuo,** while eliciting their aid to frame Marshal **He Long;** generals **Yang Chengwu, Yu Lijin,** and **Fu Chongbi;** and other officials of power and influence in the military. In April 1969, the **Ninth National Congress of the CCP** approved a revised CCP Constitution, which specified Lin as Mao's successor, while generals Huang, Wu, Li, and Qiu, along with Lin Biao's wife, **Ye Qun,** were elected to the Central Committee (CC) and the Politburo.

At the **Lushan Conference** of 1970, the conflict between the Lin Biao group and the cultural revolutionaries led by Jiang Qing surfaced over the revision of the Constitution of the People's Republic of China (PRC). Following Lin Biao's lead in the opening speech, **Chen Boda,** who had been alienated from the Jiang group, and Lin's other supporters launched an attack on **Zhang Chunqiao,** of the Jiang faction, without mentioning Zhang's name. Backing Zhang Chunqiao and the Jiang Qing group as a whole, Mao singled out Chen Boda as the main target of criticism and also told other supporters of Lin Biao to conduct self-criticism. After the Lushan Conference, political pressure on the Lin group continued in a campaign called **Criticize Chen and Conduct Rectification.** Mao made tactical personnel changes in the armed forces to weaken Lin's power while continuously, especially during his southern tour (14 August–12 September 1971), making harsh and provocative comments concerning the Lin group and even Lin himself.

In the meantime, **Lin Liguo,** son of Lin Biao and Ye Qun and deputy director of the general office of the air force, allegedly prepared a coup d'état with his commando group, the United Flotilla, for fear that Mao might remove Lin Biao as he had President Liu Shaoqi. On 6 September 1971, General Huang Yongsheng passed Mao's criticism of Lin to Ye Qun at Beidaihe resort where the Lins were staying for the summer. In the following few days, Lin Liguo allegedly acted upon Lin Biao's order and plotted against Mao's life. The alleged assassination attempt was foiled due to the abrupt changes Mao made to his itinerary. A few hours after Mao's unexpected return to Beijing on the evening of 12 September, Lin Biao, Ye Qun, and Lin Liguo boarded the jet plane Trident 256 allegedly to flee the country. On the early morning of 13 September, around 2:30 a.m., the plane crashed near Undurkhan within the border of the People's Republic of Mongolia, reportedly having run out of fuel. All nine passengers, including the three members of the Lin family, were killed in the crash.

On 18 September 1971, the CC issued a circular concerning Lin Biao's "renegade escape," charging him with treason. The political campaign that had started a year before against Chen Boda now continued to move forward but was renamed the **Criticize Lin and Conduct Rectification** campaign. In August 1973, the CC approved "The Investigative Report concerning the Counterrevolutionary Crimes of the Lin Biao Anti-Party Clique" and expelled Lin from the CCP.

See also CRITICIZE LIN AND CRITICIZE CONFUCIUS; LIN BIAO: MAY 18 SPEECH (1966); LIN LIHENG (1944–); MAO ZEDONG: SOUTHERN INSPECTION (14 August–12 September 1971); SECOND PLENUM OF THE NINTH CENTRAL COMMITTEE OF THE CHINESE COMMUNIST PARTY (23 August–6 September 1970); SEPTEMBER 13 INCIDENT (1971).

LIN BIAO: MAY 18 SPEECH (1966). Also known after **Lin Biao**'s downfall as the "scripture of coup d'état" (*zhengbian jing*), this is a notoriously militant speech that Lin delivered on 18 May 1966 at an **enlarged Politburo session**. The speech focused on three issues: First, Lin warns his audience of the ever-present threat of a counterrevolutionary coup. He cites statistics on coup attempts in the world in the past six years, lists numerous cases of usurpation in Chinese history, and finally accuses **Peng Zhen, Luo Ruiqing, Lu Dingyi**, and **Yang Shangkun** of conspiring to take power: "A bunch of bastards," Lin says, "they take risks, they wait for an opportunity, and they want to kill us. We shall execute them." Second, Lin talks about the danger of a restoration of capitalism in China. To prevent this from happening, he proposes a slogan, soon to be known as the most popular "**four never-forgets**": "Never forget class struggle, never forget proletarian dictatorship, never forget stressing politics, and never forget holding high the great red banner of **Mao Zedong Thought**." Third, Lin praises Chairman **Mao Zedong** in superlative terms. He calls Mao a "genius," "the greatest man living," and Mao Zedong Thought the "beacon light of humanity," the "universal truth." "As long as he lives," Lin says, "—ninety, one hundred years old—Chairman Mao will be our Party's supreme leader. His words are the codes of our conduct. The entire Party and the entire nation will crusade against whoever opposes him. . . . Of Chairman Mao's sayings, every sentence is truth, and each sentence surpasses ten thousand sentences of ours."

In his letter to Jiang Qing dated 8 July 1966, Mao expressed reservations about Lin's flattery. Yet, he interpreted it as a political necessity of the left: in their battle against the demons, they need a fearsome god. With Mao's approval, the CCP Central Committee issued Lin Biao's May 18 speech as an official document.

This speech had a strong impact on the Cultural Revolution in at least two aspects: First, Lin successfully created an image of hateful enemies in the mind of the masses and made people believe that the danger of a counterrevolutionary coup by the "revisionists" was imminent. Hence one of the most popular slogans during the Cultural Revolution: "Be ready to die in defense of the Party Central and Chairman Mao!" Second, the speech as an expression of Lin's "**peak theory**" contributed much to the **personality cult** of Mao Zedong and promoted the supremacy of Maoism in the ensuing years of Chinese political life.

LIN JIE (1929–). One of Mao's radical theorists, Lin was head of the Cultural Revolution group at the official organ of the **Chinese Communist Party** (CCP), the *Red Flag*. Accused of being a behind-the-scenes backer of the **May 16 Counterrevolutionary Clique**, Lin was dismissed from office in summer 1967.

A native of Wenzhou, Zhejiang Province, Lin graduated from Beijing Normal University in the 1950s. While an editor at *Red Flag*, especially during the political campaign to criticize **Wu Han, Jian Bozan**, and other "academic authorities" in early 1966, Lin became a close associate of his *Red Flag* colleagues **Qi Benyu**, head of the history group, and **Guan Feng**, one of the deputy chief editors. Lin coauthored several militant articles with them, including "Comrade Jian Bozan's View of History Should Be Criticized" (with Qi, on 25 March 1966) and "*Hai Rui Criticizing the Emperor* and *Hai Rui Dismissed from Office* Are Anti-Party and Anti-Socialist **Poisonous Weeds**" (with Guan, on 5 April 1966), both published in *Red Flag*. These articles were instrumental in setting the stage for the Cultural Revolution.

In the early phase of the Cultural Revolution, Lin was in the forefront attacking the so-called bourgeois headquarters of **Liu Shaoqi** and **Deng Xiaoping**. He was the first among central leaders to support **Tan Houlan** against the **work group** at Beijing Normal University in summer 1966. As head of the Cultural Revolution leading group at *Red Flag*, he published a number of editorials criticizing the Liu-Deng **Bourgeois Reactionary Line** and providing guidelines for the **rebel** movement. A close follower of the **Central Cultural Revolution Small Group** (CCRSG), Lin was deeply involved in the conflict between CCRSG members and veteran officials of the State Council led by Premier **Zhou Enlai**. Lin remarked on several occasions that the conflict between the CCRSG and Zhou's team was one between "a new CCRSG and an old bureaucratic apparatus." His remark was cited by the May 16 Regiment, an ultra-leftist student group, in its attack on Zhou in summer 1967. To assist **Wang Li** and Qi Benyu in their efforts to spread the fire of the Cultural Revolution into the army, Lin published editorials in *Red Flag* calling on the masses to "ferret out that small handful [of **capitalist-roaders**] within the armed forces." Soon after Mao decided to remove Wang Li, Guan Feng, and Qi Benyu from the CCRSG in August 1967, Lin was detained on the charge of being a backstage supporter of the May 16 Counterrevolutionary Clique.

After the downfall of the **Gang of Four**, Lin was named a trusted aide of the **Jiang Qing** group. He was expelled from the CCP in 1984.

LIN LIGUO (1945–1971). Son of **Lin Biao** and **Ye Qun**, Lin Liguo was deputy director of both the air force command's general office and its combat division (1969–1971). He was the chief designer of a coup plan and allegedly tried to execute a plot against **Mao Zedong**'s life.

Lin Liguo was a freshman student in physics at Peking University when the Cultural Revolution broke out in mid-1966. He joined the **People's Liberation Army** in 1967 and served as a secretary in the air force party committee office before he became a party member. On 17 October 1969, **Wu Faxian**, the air force commander and Lin Biao's close associate, appointed Lin Liguo deputy director of both the air force command's general office and its combat division. By a careful arrangement of the supporters of Lin Biao to promote the image of his son, Lin Liguo was given an opportunity—and perhaps a script, too—to speak for an entire day at a cadre meeting of the air force command, discussing his readings of Mao Zedong's works.

After the **Lushan Conference** of 1970, during which Mao launched a campaign against Lin Biao's ally **Chen Boda** and criticized Lin's associates in the armed forces, Lin Liguo committed himself to a secret mission of planning and executing an armed coup. Lin Liguo formed within the air force a special intelligence and operation team called the United Flotilla, and under Lin's command, core members of this team, including Zhou Yuchi and Yu Xinye, drafted an operation plan called the *"571 Project" Summary* in March 1971. Lin Liguo also established a secret communication network coordinating the gathering of intelligence and the training of special "combat detachments" in Beijing, Shanghai, Guangzhou, and Beidaihe. Between 8 and 12 September 1971, Lin Liguo, allegedly acting on orders penned by Lin Biao himself, carried out a plan to assassinate Mao during his southern inspection. The plan was foiled since Mao made several unexpected changes to his itinerary and suddenly returned to Beijing on the evening of 12 September.

On the same evening, Lin Liguo boarded the aircraft Trident 256 to fly to Beidaihe where his parents had been staying. In the early morning of 13 September, Lin Liguo, along with Lin Biao and Ye Qun, fled on Trident 256 and were killed when the plane crashed, supposedly because it ran out of fuel, at Undurkhan within the borders of the People's Republic of Mongolia.

See also MAO ZEDONG: SOUTHERN INSPECTION (14 August–12 September 1971).

LIN LIHENG (1944–). Also known by her familiar name Doudou, Lin Liheng, daughter of **Lin Biao** and **Ye Qun**, provided crucial intelligence to the leaders in Beijing the night before her parents fled the country in the early morning of 13 September 1971. Lin joined the **People's Liberation Army** and served as a correspondent for *Air Force News* in 1967. She later became deputy editor-in-chief of the newspaper. Staying at the Beidaihe summer resort with her parents during the few days before the **September 13 Incident**, Lin Liheng alerted the central leadership on the evening of 12 September to unusual developments surrounding Lin Biao: with the help of the security force 8341 troop unit at Beidaihe and in Beijing, Lin Liheng managed to communicate the message through several levels of command to Premier **Zhou Enlai** that Ye Qun and **Lin Liguo** (Liheng's brother) might force Lin Biao to move somewhere and that the central leadership should forbid such a move for Lin Biao's protection. She also mobilized part of Lin Biao's office staff to keep watch on Lin's actions.

After the fatal crash of Trident 256, which killed Lin Biao, Ye Qun, and Lin Liguo, Lin Liheng came under investigation. She was released in July 1974 and assigned work first on a farm and then in a factory in Henan Province. She was still under surveillance then. The Organization Department of the **Chinese Communist Party** Central Committee finally cleared her in 1981.

LIN ZHAO (1932–1968). A native of Suzhou, Jiangsu Province, Lin Zhao, born Peng Lingzhao, was enthusiastic about Communist revolution in her early years and then transformed herself into a fearless advocate for individual freedom and a fierce critic of the tyranny of the **Chinese Communist Party** (CCP). Four decades after her execution by the Communist regime on charges of counterrevolutionary activities, she became widely known thanks to a heart-wrenching independent documentary film and a number of books about her life and was greatly admired for her unflinching resolve and bravery.

The early 1950s were the years of Lin's radicalization when she was a student in journalism school and a member of a Land Reform work team. Ashamed of her father's Nationalist affiliation, she decided to **make a clean**

break with her family, adopting "Lin Zhao" as her new name, and even bringing false charges against her mother, an act that she later deeply regretted. In 1954, Lin entered Peking University and became active in poetry writing and student publication editing. A more liberal atmosphere of college life seemed to have changed her political views. During the "free airing of views" (*damingdafang*) movement in 1957 when a group of fellow students were attacked because of a **big-character poster** they wrote criticizing CCP policies, Lin came to their defense. As a result, she was named a rightist in the subsequent Anti-Rightist Campaign; her student status was suspended, and she was ordered to do service work under supervision at a reference room on the campus of Beijing's Renmin University. By the time—probably late 1959 or early 1960—she was allowed to join her parents in Shanghai due to her deteriorating health, she had already given up Communism for Christian faith. While in Shanghai, she joined a group of young intellectuals, most of them student rightists in Gansu Province, in publishing an underground magazine called *Spark* (*Xinghuo*) that carried, among other things, investigative reports on the rural-area famine caused by the CCP's Great Leap Forward policies. To this magazine Lin contributed two long poems: "The Passion of Prometheus: A Day in His Life" and "The Seagull: Give Me Freedom or Give Me Death." The government soon cracked down on the group, and Lin was arrested in October 1960. Her father committed suicide a month later. In 1965, Lin was tried and sentenced to 20 years in prison.

During her imprisonment, Lin wrote articles, letters, poems, and diaries. According to her own account, she first used a hairpin with her own blood as ink and copied the pages after prison authorities gave her pen and paper. Her prison writings were passionate condemnations of the tyranny and brutality of CCP rule. They are now part of the Hoover Institution archives at Stanford University and also exist recopied in 469 pages at the institution. Lin was so brutally abused in prison that she went on a hunger strike and made several attempts to end her own life. Eventually, her original sentence was converted to a death sentence, and she was executed on 29 April 1968. Two days later, on the morning of 1 May, Shanghai security personnel visited Lin's mother demanding that she pay five cents for the bullet used in her daughter's execution. This notorious episode was confirmed in a long report published in the 27 January 1981 issue of the CCP official organ *People's Daily*. According to Lin Zhao's younger sister Peng Lingfan, on a spring day in 1982 when an anonymous official at the Shanghai Public Security Bureau handed her Lin's manuscripts, the man said that the decision to execute Lin Zhao was approved by the CCP Politburo in Beijing.

The authorities cleared Lin Zhao's name twice after the Cultural Revolution. First, in 1980, the Shanghai People's Court issued a decision that all previous verdicts on Lin be revoked because the grievances Lin expressed in her poems and articles after she suffered a mental breakdown in August 1959 did not constitute a crime. Then, in 1981, the same court issued another judgment pronouncing Lin innocent and revoking all previous decisions, including the 1980 decision, which was now considered "legally inadequate" in dismissing Lin's guilt on the grounds of mental illness.

LITTLE RED BOOK. *See QUOTATIONS FROM CHAIRMAN MAO.*

LITTLE RED GUARDS. (*Hongxiaobing.*) This term was used during the Cultural Revolution in two different contexts: First, the term was a humbler name that **Red Guards** used for themselves in the early period of the Cultural Revolution, as in the popular slogan, "Chairman Mao is our red Commander-in-Chief (*hongsiling*), we are his loyal Little Red Guards." This usage came with the rise of the Red Guard movement in summer 1966 and was abandoned after the Red Guard movement ended in late 1968. Second, the term was used as the name of a children's organization in the country's primary schools to replace the Chinese Young Pioneers, a pro-Communism children's organization led by the Chinese Communist Youth League since the founding of the People's Republic of China.

As the Cultural Revolution intensified in summer 1966, all schools stopped regular operation. As many students in colleges and middle and high schools became Red Guards and actively participated in various campaigns on and off school campuses, children in primary schools followed their example and set up their own Red Guard organizations, attacked their teachers and school authorities, and even joined middle-schoolers in the campaign **Destroy the Four Olds**; some of these children called themselves Little Red Guards. In early 1967, it became clear to the central authority that students must return to schools. By the time primary and secondary schools gradually resumed classes following the order from a 7 March 1967 *People's Daily* editorial, the Chinese Communist Youth League—the official youth organization under the **Chinese Communist Party**—was totally dismantled in the face of numerous grassroots Red Guard organizations, while the Chinese Young Pioneers, a primary school children's organization, accused of helping carry out a "revisionist line in education," was still in the process of phasing out. Though an earlier party document, the "Notice regarding the Proletarian Cultural Revolution in Primary Schools" issued on 4 February 1967, already suggested that students in primary schools may set up Little Red Guards organizations, it was not until after the 22 December issuance of another party document specifically endorsing such an organization at Beijing's Xiangchanglu Primary School that the Little Red Guards became officially the replacement for the Chinese Young Pioneers. It remained the country's organization for primary school children until two years after the Cultural Revolution: on 27 October 1978, the central committee of the Chinese Communist Youth League passed a resolution reinstating the Chinese Young Pioneers.

LIU BING (1921–). A member of the **Chinese Communist Party** (CCP) since 1938 and for many years first deputy party secretary of Tsinghua University, Liu Bing was denounced as a member of the "**black gang**" in association with **Peng Zhen**'s CCP Beijing Municipal Committee at the beginning of the Cultural Revolution but reinstated as deputy secretary of Tsinghua in January 1970. On 13 August and 13 October 1975, Liu, along with three other veteran cadres of Tsinghua, wrote two letters to **Mao Zedong** criticizing **Chi Qun**, party secretary of Tsinghua and head of the **army propaganda team**, for his overt political ambition and overbearing work style. **Xie Jingyi**, Chi Qun's close ally at Tsinghua, was also implicated in Chi's alleged errors. The letters were passed on to Mao by **Deng Xiaoping**. Considering the letters attacking Chi and Xie to have represented a widely shared anti–Cultural Revolution sentiment, Mao's reaction was highly critical. In the harsh comments he wrote on the letters, Mao pointed out that the Tsinghua case was not isolated and that it reflected the current struggle between the two political lines—that is, the "correct" line of the Cultural Revolution and the one that betrayed it—"revisionist" and "right-wing."

After Mao's response to Liu's letters was communicated to members of the CCP Tsinghua committee on 3 November 1975, **big-character posters** appeared on the Tsinghua campus accusing Liu Bing, education minister **Zhou Rongxin**, and some other school and government officials of "negating the revolution in education and reversing the verdicts of the Cultural Revolution." This wave of criticism was known as the "great debate on the revolution in education" though dissent was not allowed. Liu Bing and his colleagues were soon dismissed from the Tsinghua party committee. Liu's downfall turned out to be the beginning of a nationwide **Counterattack the Right-Deviationist Reversal-of-Verdicts Trend** campaign against Deng Xiaoping and his overall rectification program. After the death of Mao and the fall of the **Gang of Four** in 1976, Liu Bing's verdict was reversed. In 1978, he was reassigned as party secretary of Lanzhou University in Gansu Province.

LIU GEPING (1903–1992). One of the few provincial party leaders who supported the **rebels** in the early stages of the Cultural Revolution, Liu became head of the Shanxi Provincial **Revolutionary Committee** in 1967 and a member of the **Chinese Communist Party** (CCP) Central Committee (CC) in 1969 but was eventually dismissed from office for his involvement in armed factional conflict in Shanxi.

Born of an ethnic minority Hui family in Mengchun, Hebei Province, Liu joined the CCP in 1926 and worked underground in both rural and urban areas. The Kuomintang government arrested Liu several times. In the 1930s, Liu was imprisoned at the Beiping Branch of the Military Men's Introspection House with 61 leading CCP officials, including **Bo Yibo**, An Ziwen, and Liu Lantao. Liu was one of the few who rejected the CC's proposal that they sign an Announcement Renouncing Communism so that they would be released. Liu served his full sentence and was released in 1947. After 1949, he was appointed to a series of minority-related official positions including president of the Central Institute of Nationalities, deputy head of the United Front Work Department, and governor and party secretary of Ningxia Hui Autonomous Region. Because of his moderate approach to CCP ethnic minority policies, Liu was criticized for being an "ethnic splittist" in the early 1960s.

When the Cultural Revolution began, Liu was deputy governor of Shanxi. On 10 January 1967, Liu and four other provincial leaders put out a **big-character poster** to support local rebel organizations' **power seizure** efforts. On 23 February 1967, the CC appointed Liu head of an *ad hoc* executive group to lead Shanxi's Cultural Revolution movement. In the following month, he became head of the Shanxi Provincial Revolutionary Committee. In the meantime, as some **Red Guard** organizations were working to uncover the case of the 61 party officials, **Kang Sheng, Jiang Qing,** and other members of the **Central Cultural Revolution Small Group** began to label these party cadres as members of a **Sixty-One Traitors Clique**. Liu's refusal to sign the anti-Communist announcement, then, became a much-praised heroic deed for which he was invited as a public speaker nationwide. In April 1969, Liu became a member of the CC at the **Ninth National Congress of the CCP**. However, because of Liu's deep involvement in the massive factional violence in Shanxi and because of his serious conflict with local military leaders, the CC dismissed him from office in July 1969. After the downfall of the **Gang of Four**, Liu was given an essentially ceremonial title as a member of the National Committee of the Sixth Chinese People's Political Consultative Conference.

LIU JIETING (1920–1993). A rebelling official during the Cultural Revolution, Liu became deputy head of the Sichuan Provincial **Revolutionary Committee** in 1968 and a member of the Central Committee (CC) at the **Ninth National Congress of the Chinese Communist Party** (CCP) in 1969 but was eventually dismissed from office for his involvement in a factional war in Sichuan and was imprisoned after **Mao Zedong**'s death.

A native of Pingyi, Shandong Province, Liu joined the CCP in 1938. In 1963, when he was party secretary of Yibin Prefecture, Sichuan Province, he and his wife **Zhang Xiting**—party secretary of Yibin City—along with a few other prefectural and local officials, were arrested on a charge of violating social legality and framing innocent people. With the support of **Deng Xiaoping**, **Peng Zhen**, and **Yang Shangkun** in Beijing, Li Jingquan—first secretary of both the CCP Southwest China Bureau and the CCP Sichuan Provincial Committee—had them expelled from the CCP in 1965. Liu and Zhang began to appeal their case directly to Mao Zedong. In June and August 1966, Liu and Zhang went to Beijing to lodge complaints with the CC and the **Central Cultural Revolution Small Group** (CCRSG) against Li Jingquan and his supporters in the central government. **Wang Li**, of the CCRSG, received them on 30 December 1966 and showed support for what he considered to be their **rebel** activities. Upon returning to Sichuan in early 1967, Liu and Zhang organized a group and began to attack Li Jingquan, the Southwest China Bureau, and the Sichuan party committee. Consisting of rebelling party veterans and supported by Mao and the CCRSG, the Liu group became well known nationwide.

On 4 April 1967, the CC issued a circular (*zhongfa* [67] 154) to redress the Liu Jieting case. Naming Li Jingquan a **capitalist-roader** and affirming the righteousness of Liu and his comrades in opposing Li all these years, the circular also acknowledged their right to participate in the Cultural Revolution and called on the **People's Liberation Army** officers in the area to support their revolutionary activities. In May 1968, the CC appointed Liu and Zhang deputy heads of the Sichuan Provincial Revolutionary Committee. In 1969, at the Ninth National Congress of the CCP, Liu became a member of the CC, and Zhang an alternate member. As top-level provincial officials, however, Liu and Zhang abused their power and put in prison many of the officials who had prosecuted them in 1963 and 1965. They were also deeply involved in the massive factional violence in the province, supporting one faction of mass organizations in heavily **armed conflicts** against the other. In December 1969, the CC dismissed Liu and Zhang from office. On 24 June 1978, Liu and Zhang were arrested on a charge of counterrevolution. On 24 March 1982, Liu was sentenced to 20 years in prison and Zhang to 17 years.

LIU QINGTANG (1932–2010). A native of Gai County, Liaoning Province, and a member of the **Chinese Communist Party** from 1959, Liu was an actor in the ballet troupe of the Central Song and Dance Academy. His role as the party representative in *The Red Detachment of Women*, a modern ballet first produced in 1964 and later listed as one of the **eight model dramas**, made him well known and caught **Jiang Qing**'s attention. During the early days of the Cultural Revolution, Liu was known for his loyalty to Jiang and for his denunciations of his colleagues. Despite his unpopularity, he was given a top leadership position in the ballet troupe in 1968, thanks to Jiang's backing. In both 1968 and 1969, Liu followed Jiang's instructions and attacked and persecuted hundreds of people in literature and art circles. In the early 1970s, he became a member of the State Council Cultural Group, and in January 1975, he was appointed deputy minister of culture.

Liu, along with **Yu Huiyong** and **Qian Haoliang**, was the closest ally of Jiang Qing and her group in cultural circles. The three were instrumental in politicizing art in the later stages of the Cultural Revolution. Liu was actively involved in the making of such propaganda pieces as the dance drama *The Battle Song of Youth* (*Qingchun zhan'ge*) and the film *Counterattack* (*Fanji*), both politically motivated and aimed at **Deng Xiaoping**. Liu was detained on 22 October 1976 as a loyal follower of the **Gang of Four**. He was officially arrested on 8 September 1982. On 2 November 1983, he was sentenced to 17 years in prison on the charges of being an active member of a counterrevolutionary clique, instigating counterrevolutionary activities, and bringing false charges against innocent people.

LIU REN (1909–1973). A native of Youyang, Sichuan Province, Liu joined the **Chinese Communist Party** (CCP) in 1927. He worked underground to lead the labor movement in various cities during the early 1930s. After two years of study in the Soviet Union, Liu came back to Yan'an in 1937 and served briefly as secretary-general of the Central Party School. From 1938 to 1949, he was a Communist leader in the Jin-Cha-Ji area. After the founding of the People's Republic of China, Liu was named head of the Organization Department of the CCP Beijing Municipal Committee. Later, he was appointed second party secretary of Beijing.

As the second highest official in Beijing's municipal government, Liu's downfall was inevitable when Mao decided to purge **Peng Zhen**, mayor and first party secretary of Beijing, because of Peng's resistance to the campaigns against **Wu Han** and the so-called **Three-Family Village Anti-Party Clique** in late 1965 and early 1966. In spring 1966, Mao named the CCP Beijing Municipal Committee an "impenetrable and watertight independent kingdom" ruled by Peng, of which Liu Ren was part. Liu lost his official positions after the CCP central leadership made a decision in May 1966 at the **enlarged Politburo sessions** that the entire Beijing Municipal Committee be reorganized. Liu was denounced as a die-hard follower of Peng Zhen, a revisionist, and a traitor and lost his freedom. During the high tide of the Cultural Revolution in late 1966 and 1967, Liu was frequently forced to attend **struggle meetings** and suffered not only public humiliation but also brutal physical abuse. In early 1968, Liu was imprisoned without a trial. For his refusal to acknowledge false allegations, Liu was handcuffed and fettered for several years. His health deteriorated quickly. Denied adequate and timely treatment for illness, Liu died of tuberculosis on 26 October 1973. His case was rehabilitated in 1978.

LIU SHAOQI (1898–1969). President of the People's Republic of China (PRC) (1959–1968) and vice-chairman of the **Chinese Communist Party** (CCP) (1956–1968), Liu Shaoqi was the first party theoretician to formulate **Mao Zedong Thought** as the guiding principle of the CCP in 1945 at the Seventh National Congress of the CCP and was widely acknowledged as **Mao Zedong**'s successor from the late 1950s on. In 1966, he became the chief target of the Cultural Revolution and was denounced as the "**biggest capitalist-roader within the party**" and "**China's Khrushchev.**"

A native of Ningxiang, Hunan Province, Liu enrolled in the Communist University for Laborers of the East in Moscow in 1921 and joined the newly formed CCP in the same year. After returning to China in 1922, he became involved in the Chinese labor movement and soon was one of its most influential leaders. He was elected to the Fifth Central Committee (CC) of the CCP in 1927 and became full member of the Politburo of the Sixth Central Committee in 1935. After the Long March, Liu went to Beijing to work underground as secretary of the CCP North China Bureau. In 1939 in Yan'an, at the CCP revolutionary base, he delivered a series of lectures under the title *Cultivation of a Communist*, which established his position as a major theoretician for the CCP. In 1941, he became secretary of the CCP's Central China Bureau and political commissar of the New Fourth Army. At the Seventh National Congress of the CCP held in Yan'an in April–June 1945, Liu delivered a major speech on the revision of the CCP Constitution, which was known for its original and systematic formulation of Mao Zedong Thought. In the same year, when Mao was negotiating with the Kuomintang in Chongqing, Liu Shaoqi served as acting chairman of the CCP.

When the PRC was founded in 1949, Liu became vice-chairman of the central government. In 1954, at the PRC's First People's Congress, Liu was elected head of the Congress's Standing Committee. In 1956, at the Eighth National Congress of the CCP, Liu delivered the political report highlighting the economy as the new focus of the work of the party. In May 1959, when the disaster of the CCP's radical economic policies known as "Three Red Banners" (the CCP General Line for Socialist Construction, the Great Leap Forward, and the People's Commune) had become clear, Mao relinquished his position as head of the state and retreated to the "second line of leadership," retaining his party chairmanship. Liu, then, was elected president of the PRC and chairman of the National Defense Commission and became Mao's heir apparent. He, with **Zhou Enlai** and **Deng Xiaoping**, was put in charge of the daily affairs of the central leadership. At the **Central Committee Work Sessions, 11 January–7 February 1962** (also known as **Seven Thousand Cadres Conference**), Liu, representing the CC, delivered a report concerning mainly the lessons from the experience of the CCP leadership since 1958. In his speech, Liu supplemented the written report with his own more candid views, including the well-known assessment of the officially

Mao Zedong and Liu Shaoqi prior to the Cultural Revolution. Liu was to become the primary target of the revolution.

named "three years of natural disaster" (1959–1961) in which 20 to 30 million people died of hunger: "three-part natural disaster, seven-part man-made calamity in some areas," as Liu put it in the words of peasants in Hunan Province. To revitalize the nation's economy, especially its agriculture, Liu endorsed policies that permitted farmers to cultivate private plots and sell their products on the market. These policies also allowed contracting output quotas to each farm household.

In response to the pragmatism of Liu and others, Mao decided to launch in the nation's countryside a radical **Socialist Education Movement**. In late 1964 and early 1965, Mao criticized Liu for failing to acknowledge the "contradiction between socialism and capitalism" as the essence of class struggle in the ongoing Socialist Education Movement. Mao insisted that the target of the campaign be "those **capitalist-roaders** within the party," which would soon become the main target of the Cultural Revolution as well.

In the preliminary stages of the Cultural Revolution in late 1965 and early 1966, Liu, not knowing Mao's real intentions, opted again for moderation. He and his close associates, such as **Peng Zhen**, mayor of Beijing, attempted to keep the criticism of **Wu Han**, **Jian Bozan**, and other well-known intellectuals within the spheres of academic discussion. After Peng's downfall at the **enlarged Politburo sessions, 4–26 May 1966**, Liu consulted Zhou Enlai and Deng Xiaoping on how to lead the Cultural Revolution that was officially launched at the Politburo meeting. With the acknowledgment of Mao, who had been away from Beijing, they decided to dispatch **work groups** to schools—especially the most chaotic ones—to provide leadership and guidance there, as they did during the Socialist Education Movement. After he came back from the south in July, however, Mao talked with the cultural revolutionaries in the central leadership and ordered the withdrawal of all work groups. At the **Eleventh Plenum of the Eighth CCP Central Committee** (1–12 August 1966), Mao criticized the work group policy as being repressive, and he wrote "**Bombarding the Headquarters**—My Own **Big-Character Poster**," attacking Liu without mentioning Liu's name. Liu was forced to criticize himself; he came out of the plenum demoted from number two to the number eight position within the CCP central leadership.

In October 1966, Mao launched a mass campaign against Liu Shaoqi and Deng Xiaoping, condemning their work group policy as a **Bourgeois Reactionary Line**. Toward the end of the year, Liu was denounced at mass meetings as the "biggest capitalist-roader within the party." In March 1967, the CC established a special case investigation group on Liu Shaoqi. The group submitted "An Investigative Report on the Crimes of the Traitor, Spy, and Renegade Liu Shaoqi" at the **Twelfth Plenum of the Eighth CCP Central Committee** (13–31 October 1968). Though composed of forced confessions, fabricated evidence, and deliberate contrivances of accusatory material, the report was approved by the CC. Also passed at the plenum was the motion that Liu be stripped of all official positions and permanently expelled from the CCP. In the meantime, Liu was brutally treated by the mass organizations. In October 1969, he was escorted out of Beijing. After suffering from grave illnesses and abuse for over two years, Liu died on 12 November 1969, in Kaifeng, Henan Province.

In February 1980, at the Fifth Plenum of the Eleventh CCP Central Committee, Liu Shaoqi was rehabilitated. The CC dismissed all its earlier decisions on Liu and recognized him as a "great Marxist and proletarian revolutionary."

See also COLLAR LIU BATTLEFRONT; SIXTY-ONE TRAITORS CLIQUE.

LIU TAO (1944–). A daughter of President **Liu Shaoqi** and a student at Tsinghua University, Liu Tao was a leader of the early conservative **Red Guards** at Tsinghua and director of Tsinghua's short-lived Temporary **Cultural Revolution Committee**. At the beginning of the Cultural Revolution when conflicts between students and the government-authorized **work group** occurred on the Tsinghua campus, Liu Shaoqi sent his wife, **Wang Guangmei**, as an advisor to the work group to help resolve the conflicts and guide the mass movement at Tsinghua. Under the influence of Liu Shaoqi and

Wang Guangmei, Liu Tao played a significant role in mobilizing students, especially a group of ranking officials' children at Tsinghua, to support the work group in such activities as **struggling against** the so-called **black gang** elements (those allegedly associated with the **Peng Zhen**–led Beijing party committee) and "reactionary academic authorities," attacking **Kuai Dafu** and other rebelling students, and defending Liu Shaoqi and other senior party leaders. Some of these activities continued after the work group withdrew in late July 1966.

In December 1966, when a nationwide campaign against Liu Shaoqi moved forward with full force and when the Temporary Cultural Revolution Committee at Tsinghua University was dismissed, Liu Tao, under great pressure from the **Central Cultural Revolution Small Group** and student **rebels** at Tsinghua, began to criticize herself and denounce Liu Shaoqi and Wang Guangmei with a story of how they had tried to influence the mass movement at Tsinghua through her. Liu Tao's **big-character posters** "Rebel against Liu Shaoqi, Follow Chairman Mao, and Carry out Revolution All My Life: My Preliminary Self-criticism" (28 December 1966) and "Look, the Ugly Soul of Liu Shaoqi" (2 January 1967) became well-known examples of the widespread phenomenon that children, either under pressure or swayed by the dominant ideology or both, would "**make a clean break**" with their persecuted parents to declare their own revolutionary identity during the Cultural Revolution. In 1968, Liu Tao, along with millions of Chinese youths, was sent to the countryside for **reeducation**.

"LONG LIVE THE REVOLUTIONARY REBEL SPIRIT OF THE PROLETARIAT". This is the title of a series of **big-character posters** written by the Tsinghua University Middle School **Red Guards**, which is generally regarded as classic writing of the **Old Red Guards** in the beginning stages of the Cultural Revolution. The series includes four posters that came out on 24 June, 4 July, 27 July, and 1 September 1966. The title was inspired by **Mao Zedong**'s words, "The manifold theories of Marxism in the end come down to one sentence: '**to rebel is justified**.' . . . Following this theory, we revolt, we struggle, and we build socialism" (1939; reprinted in the 5 June 1966 issue of *People's Daily*). In turn, Mao's support for these posters, along with his reception for students at the **mass rally of 18 August 1966**, made the emerging Red Guard organizations an army of crusaders nationwide against the so-called **capitalist-roaders**, supposedly a following of President **Liu Shaoqi**.

Rather than a series of arguments for the spirit of rebellion, the first three posters are made of clusters of bold assertions and spirited battle cries against "revisionists" (those believed to have "revised," or deviated from, Mao's political line, particularly in education), the "black line and **black gang**" (those associated with the fallen Beijing municipal party committee), "bourgeois rightists," "counterrevolutionaries," and the "**Four Olds**." The role of the Red Guards is that of the legendary Monkey King turning the old world upside down. Employing such metaphors as gunpowder and hand grenades in response to the criticism that they were "too rude" and "too extreme," the authors of the poster call for more thoroughgoing revolutionary violence and vow to drive out "human sympathy" (*renqing*): "We shall knock you down on the ground," they write, "and put a foot on your body." The second exposition begins with Mao's words justifying rebellion. But the authors make it clear that they are not challenging China's ultimate power; rather, as successors of revolution, they *are* the proletarian power: "We shall allow only leftists to rebel, but not you rightists. If you dare to, we shall put you down immediately. This is our logic. The state apparatus is in our hands after all." Thus ends the second poster. The fourth and last exposition came out on 1 September 1966 with the subtitle "Vow to Be International Red Guards." In this poster, the authors consider Chinese Red Guards to be sparks starting a prairie fire of revolutionary rebellion across the globe. The enemies now are U.S. imperialism, Soviet revisionism, and the reactionaries of other countries that follow them, while international red guards are to be their "executioners."

After receiving the first two posters of the series and a letter from the authors, Mao expressed strong support in a reply dated 1 August 1966, which was distributed to all attendees at the **Eleventh Plenum of the Eighth CCP Central Committee** (1–12 August 1966). On 21 August, the party organ *Red Flag* published the first three posters with a long note that characterizes the poster series as "magnificent poetry of the Great Proletarian Cultural Revolution, a crystallization of the genius and wisdom of the revolutionary youth, and an achievement nurtured by **Mao Zedong Thought**." With this enthusiastic endorsement from the central leadership, "carry out the revolutionary rebel spirit of the proletariat" became the most popular slogan in summer 1966. The militant rebel spirit represented by these posters spread across the nation and led not only to the shake-up of the party leadership at all levels as Mao had hoped but also to brutal violence against people of non-proletarian background, especially those of the so-called **seven black categories** and their children.

See also MAO ZEDONG: LETTER TO TSINGHUA UNIVERSITY MIDDLE SCHOOL RED GUARDS; RED AUGUST.

LONG MARCH TEAMS. Also known as **Red Guard** Long March Teams, these were self-organized groups of students participating in the nationwide **Great Networking** activities by traveling on foot to Beijing and to some historical sites of the Communist revolution. The first Long March Team was formed by a group of 15 student Red Guards at the Dalian Merchant Marine Institute in late August 1966. At the **mass rally of 18 August 1966**, Chairman **Mao Zedong** received and inspected an army of a million Red Guards and revolutionary masses in Tiananmen Square to show his support for the Red Guard movement and his determination to push the Cultural Revolution forward across China. In order to have a glimpse of the Chairman in person, the 15 students decided that rather than continue to struggle with the country's jammed transportation system and wait for the train tickets to be assigned to them, they would travel together on foot to Beijing. They named their group the "Dalian to Beijing Long March Red Guard Team" to show their determination to finish the course in the spirit of the Red Army that marched 25,000 *li* (12,500 kilometers) from Jiangxi to Shaanxi in the 1930s. With each member carrying a bedroll on his back, the team left Dalian, Liaoning Province, on 25 August 1966 and walked for a month, covering the distance of more than 600 miles between Dalian and Beijing. By the time they arrived in the nation's capital, China's train system had been jammed every day by hundreds of thousands of networking travelers for over a month.

Considering traveling on foot to be a way to relieve the nation's transportation system of this unprecedented overload, leaders in Beijing spoke highly of the Long March Team from Dalian. On 22 October, *People's Daily* ran an editorial entitled "Red Guards Unafraid of the Hardship of the Long March," urging students and teachers to follow the example of the Dalian team. Soon a great number of Red Guard Long March Teams were formed across China. Some were so ambitious as to vow to retrace the steps of the Red Army all the way. After the **Chinese Communist Party** Central Committee and the State Council issued a series of directives in late 1966 and early 1967, first to halt and then to end the Great Networking movement, some of the marchers, as well as the train riders, continued to travel around the country for a while and eventually went home in mid-1967.

LOYALTY DANCE. (*Zhongziwu.*) This was a ritual of worship widely practiced by people of all ages at the height of the **personality cult** of **Mao Zedong** in the early stages of the Cultural Revolution. To perform this ritual, each participant would hold in hand a copy of the ***Quotations from Chairman Mao***, and they would dance around a circle while waving the little red book and singing songs in praise of the Chairman. Eager participants would reproach those who were unwilling to dance with a popular saying: "Whether one dances well is a question of skill; whether one dances at all is a question of loyalty."

LU DINGYI (1906–1996). Propaganda chief of the **Chinese Communist Party** (CCP) since 1945 and deputy premier since 1959, Lu became one of the first victims of the Cultural Revolution among ranking leaders when he was denounced as a member of the **Peng-Luo-Lu-Yang Anti-Party Clique** at the **enlarged Politburo sessions, 4–26 May 1966**.

A native of Wuxi, Jiangsu Province, Lu joined the CCP in 1925 when he was a college student in Shanghai. He devoted the rest of his life to promoting and publicizing the political culture and ideology of the CCP. In 1945, Lu was elected to the CCP Central Committee (CC) and appointed head of the CCP Propaganda Department. In 1964, a **Five-Person Cultural Revolution Small Group** was formed at **Mao Zedong**'s suggestion to lead the rectification in cultural circles criticizing what was considered "bourgeois" or "revisionist" works. **Peng Zhen**, mayor of Beijing, was named director, and Lu deputy director. Reacting to **Yao Wenyuan**'s militant critique of **Wu Han**'s historical drama *Hai Rui Dismissed from Office*, published in Shanghai's *Wenhui Daily* in November 1965, the Five-Person Group met and put out a not-so-militant **February Outline** as a guideline for the ongoing political campaign.

Lu's involvement in the creation of this document made him a prominent target at the enlarged Politburo sessions in May 1966. Mao named his propaganda department a "palace of the King of Hell" and called for the "downfall of the King" and the "liberation of the little ghosts." Lu was under attack also due to his critical comments on **Lin Biao**'s way of promoting **Mao Zedong Thought**—"simplifying" and "vulgarizing" Mao's ideas, in Lu's view—and due to his wife Yan Weibing's attack on **Ye Qun** in a series of anonymous letters to the CC. Lu was **struggled against** and physically abused at mass rallies. He was dismissed from his major official posts in late May 1966 and arrested in May 1968. In late 1975, the CC issued a resolution concerning Lu Dingyi, in which Lu was named an "alien-class element," an "anti-party element," and a "traitor" and expelled from the CCP.

On 8 June 1979, the CC issued a document dismissing its earlier resolution and clearing Lu's name. In January 1980, Lu made his first public appearance since his arrest. Later, he was given high ceremonial positions such as vice-chairman of the Political Consultative Conference and membership in the Standing Committee of the CC Advisory Committee. Lu died on 9 May 1996.

LU PING (1914–2002). President and party secretary of Peking University and a major target of what **Mao Zedong** called the **first Marxist-Leninist big-character poster** by **Nie Yuanzi** and others, Lu Ping was one of the first victims of the Cultural Revolution. A native of Changchun, Jilin Province, Lu joined the **Chinese Communist Party** (CCP) in 1933. He was a student leader of the 1935 December Ninth Protest Movement against Japan in Beijing. After 1949, he held several important party and government positions before becoming party secretary and vice-president of Peking University in 1957, and later president of the university.

In 1964, during the **Socialist Education Movement**, Lu and his university party committee were criticized by Zhang Panshi, head of the socialist education work team from the CCP Propaganda Department, and by a group of faculty from the Department of Philosophy, including Nie Yuanzi, for allegedly carrying on a bourgeois and revisionist line. Some party leaders were denounced as **capitalist-roaders**. The Beijing municipal party committee stepped in to support Lu and the party establishment by sending **Song Shuo**, deputy director of the municipal committee's university department, to the work team as a new leading member and by appointing **Peng Peiyun**, also of the university department, as deputy party secretary of Peking University. With the assistance of the municipal committee, and especially with Mayor **Peng Zhen**'s criticism of the Zhang-led work team in January 1965, the early verdict on Lu Ping and the university party leadership was eventually reversed, and the activism of Nie and her colleagues was put down.

But the launching of the Cultural Revolution by the CCP Politburo in May 1966 provided an opportunity for the comeback of Nie and her colleagues. On 25 May 1966, Nie Yuanzi and six other faculty members of the Philosophy Department put out the **big-character poster** "What Are Song Shuo, Lu Ping, and Peng Peiyun Really Doing during the Cultural Revolution?" accusing the three of conspiring with the Beijing Municipal Committee to suppress the revolutionary ideas of the masses and mislead the ongoing Cultural Revolution. This poster soon reached Mao Zedong via **Kang Sheng**, and Mao's decision to broadcast the poster nationwide marked the beginning of Lu's rapid downfall. When *People's Daily* carried the poster on 2 June 1966, the commentator's reference to Lu was as an element of the **Three-Family Village Anti-Party Clique**. On 3 June, the reorganized CCP Beijing Municipal Committee announced the decision to remove Lu from office. Lu was then incarcerated and frequently **struggled against** at mass rallies until 1969 when the Peking University **workers propaganda team** sent him to a farm in Jiangxi Province for reeducation.

In 1975, Lu was appointed deputy head of the Ministry of the Seventh Machine Industry. After the downfall of the **Gang of Four**, Lu was completely exonerated and rehabilitated. He became a standing committee member and deputy general-secretary of the Chinese People's Political Consultative Congress in 1983. Lu Ping died on 28 November 2002.

LUO RUIQING (1906–1978). Chief of general staff of the **People's Liberation Army** (PLA) and deputy minister of defense since 1959, Luo was one of the earliest victims of the Cultural Revolution among ranking **Chinese**

Communist Party (CCP) leaders: he was removed from power in December 1965 and was denounced as a member of the **Peng-Luo-Lu-Yang Anti-Party Clique** in May 1966.

A native of Nanchong, Sichuan Province, Luo joined the Chinese Communist Youth League in 1926, and became a member of the CCP in 1928. A veteran of the Long March, Luo was appointed provost and vice-president of the Anti-Japanese Military and Political University in Yan'an in 1937 and became head of the political department of the Communist-led Eighth Route Army in 1940. After the founding of the People's Republic of China, Luo was named minister of public security. In 1959, he became a vice-premier of the State Council and a most powerful military official as chief of general staff of the PLA, secretary-general of the Central Military Commission (CMC), and deputy minister of defense.

Luo's downfall in 1965 is generally considered to be a political trade-off between Defense Minister **Lin Biao** and Chairman **Mao Zedong** at the dawn of the Cultural Revolution. In 1962, due to Lin's poor health, Mao asked **He Long**, a senior marshal, to be in charge of the daily work of the CMC. In 1964, Luo, together with He Long and Marshal **Ye Jianying**, led a successful army-wide training campaign to enhance the PLA's combat power, which was complimented by top CCP leaders including Mao. To undermine Luo's influence in the armed forces, however, Lin Biao, with the assistance of his wife, **Ye Qun**, began to gather fabricated materials against Luo. At the same time, Lin continued with his own political program in the army, promoting the **personality cult** of Mao and calling on soldiers to study Mao's published works. In November 1965, Lin sent Ye Qun to Hangzhou for a secret meeting with Mao. Ye brought with her a letter from Lin and fabricated materials against Luo Ruiqing. Frustrated with the resistance within the central leadership to the early steps of the Cultural Revolution and badly in need of Lin and the army's support, Mao agreed to purge Luo after six hours of lobbying by Ye. From 8 to 15 December, Lin chaired an enlarged session of the Standing Committee of the Politburo in Shanghai, at which, much to the surprise of a number of ranking leaders, Lin Biao's letter to Mao and the 11 pieces of fabricated material against Luo Ruiqing were circulated, and Luo was accused of opposing the principle of "politics-in-command" in the army and making moves to take over Lin Biao's power. Luo lost all his positions and his freedom, too, after the meeting. An even more serious charge was brought against Luo in a series of high-level meetings held in March 1966: Luo was accused of opposing Mao and **Mao Zedong Thought**.

On the night of 18 March 1966, Luo, in a suicide attempt, jumped from the third floor balcony of his residence and broke his left leg. The act was condemned by Lin Biao as a betrayal of the party and the country. Luo was imprisoned afterward. At the **enlarged Politburo sessions, 4–26 May 1966**, Luo was denounced as a member of the Peng-Luo-Lu-Yang Anti-Party

Clique. In late 1966 and 1967, Luo was frequently **struggled against** at mass rallies and was subjected to unbearable public humiliation and physical abuse. Unable to walk because of his broken leg, he was once thrown into a basket and dragged to the meeting by the **Red Guards**. Because he was deprived of timely medical treatment, Luo's infected leg was amputated in 1969.

In late 1973, two years after Lin Biao's downfall, Luo was finally released from prison. In December of the same year, Mao acknowledged his mistake of allowing Lin to purge Luo Ruiqing. Luo was appointed advisor of the CMC in 1975 and secretary-general of the CMC in 1977. He died of a heart attack on 3 August 1978.

LUO SIDING. Luo Siding was a pen name used by the **Shanghai Municipal Party Committee Writing Group**, a writing team headed by **Xu Jingxian** and remotely controlled by **Zhang Chunqiao** and **Yao Wenyuan**. The pen name is an oblique homonym of the Chinese term for "screw," echoing the much publicized phrase "a rust-free screw on the revolutionary machine" by Lei Feng, an army soldier and the most admired Communist hero in the early 1960s. During the Cultural Revolution, the writing group produced numerous articles—many under this pen name—to promote the interests of the ultra-leftist faction of the central leadership of the **Chinese Communist Party** and to attack its opponents.

LUSHAN CONFERENCE (23 August–6 September 1970). *See* SECOND PLENUM OF THE NINTH CENTRAL COMMITTEE OF THE CHINESE COMMUNIST PARTY (23 August–6 September 1970).

M

MA SICONG (1912–1987). A native of Haifeng, Guangdong Province, and a precocious music prodigy, Ma went to France twice—from 1924 to 1929 and again from 1930 to 1931—to study violin and composition. Upon returning, he became an accomplished performing artist and professor of music. After the People's Republic of China was founded, Ma became the first president of the Central Conservatory of Music and vice-chairman of the China Federation of Literary and Art Circles. In the early months of the Cultural Revolution, Ma was humiliated and tortured. He was threatened at knife point by the **Red Guards**, and he was called a horse (his surname also means "horse") and forced to eat grass. In November 1966, with the help of his family and close friends, Ma, still holding on to his violin, successfully escaped from Beijing to Hong Kong via Guangzhou. In January 1967, Ma, his wife, and two of their children arrived in the United States where he lived for the rest of his life. In Beijing, he was pronounced a "traitor." While in the United States, Ma remained active both as a composer and as a performing artist. His music compositions are almost exclusively variations on themes of Chinese classics and Chinese minority cultures. Ma was rehabilitated in Beijing in March 1985 by the party committee of the Central Conservatory of Music. Ma died in the United States in May 1987.

MA TIANSHUI (1912–1994). A close associate of **Zhang Chunqiao** and one of the few veteran cadres who sided with ultra-leftists during the Cultural Revolution, Ma came to be known as a "remnant of the **Gang of Four** in Shanghai" at the end of the revolution. He was an alternate member of the Ninth Central Committee (CC) of the **Chinese Communist Party** (CCP) and a full member of the Tenth CC. He was removed as a secretary of the CCP Shanghai Municipal Committee in late 1976.

Born in 1921 in Tang County, Hebei Province, Ma joined the CCP in the late 1930s. He was appointed a regional deputy party secretary in Anhui Province in 1949 and transferred to Shanghai in 1953, where, with initial responsibilities in the area of industry, he was to become head of the CCP North China Bureau's department of industry and a deputy secretary, and then a secretary of the CCP Shanghai Municipal Committee. In 1966, Ma did not show himself to be a supporter of the Cultural Revolution at first: he even complained about the **Great Networking** of **Red Guards** in a speech he gave in Beijing in November at a symposium of industrial and transportation fronts on the Cultural Revolution. But after **Lin Biao**'s criticism of this speech, Ma changed his position and offered his services to Zhang Chunqiao and the **Central Cultural Revolution Small Group**. Upon returning to Shanghai, he began to support **rebels** in their battles against the CCP Shanghai Municipal Committee headed by First Secretary Chen Pixian and Mayor Cao Diqiu.

Ma was regarded as a model cadre for the three-in-one presence of cadre, military, and masses in the new power structure after the **January Storm power seizure** movement of 1967. Accordingly, he was made a deputy head of the Shanghai **Revolutionary Committee**. Ma then turned himself into Zhang Chunqiao's right-hand man in Shanghai and persecuted Zhang's critics, including those who participated in the two mass protests known as "twice **bombarding Zhang Chunqiao**." He persecuted Cao Diqiu and other Shanghai officials on false charges. Ma was also involved in the power conflict in Beijing: in 1975, he provided materials for the **Jiang Qing** group to use in their attack on **Deng Xiaoping**.

In October 1976 when Jiang Qing and her allies were arrested in Beijing, Ma's political career was over. He was soon dismissed from office and was expelled from the CCP. Ma suffered a mental breakdown in 1978 while in prison and was thus spared a 1982 court indictment.

MAKE A CLEAN BREAK. (*Huaqing jiexian.*) This was an official imperative forcing individuals to turn against their family members, relatives, and friends who were denounced or being interrogated as class enemies. Redefining human relationship by class identity against traditional notions of kinship, love, filial duties, and personal loyalty, the **Chinese Communist Party** (CCP) issued this commandment during all political campaigns and imposed it more forcefully during the Cultural Revolution. Due to years of political education and indoctrination, some individuals, especially young people, felt ashamed of their "bad" family backgrounds or their disgraced spouses, so much so that they willingly made public statements denouncing their loved ones, severing relationships with them, and swearing their loyalty to Chairman **Mao Zedong** and his radical revolutionary line. Some exposed "crimes" allegedly committed by their kin or friends, and some even turned violent against them at **struggle meetings**. Many others in similar situations, however, acted in a similar way presumably against their own will; they renounced relationships with those close to them under pressure and often for fear of their own persecution. It was also a common practice for those in power—especially **Red Guards** or **rebels** in the numerous special case investigation groups under **revolutionary committees** during the **Rectify the Class Ranks** campaign—to force children to denounce their parents under interrogation and pressure them to confess to alleged crimes. The CCP's forceful injection of **class struggle** into private and personal relationships resulted in an unprecedented deterioration of social morality in China. It broke up many families and turned out to be one of the leading causes of suicide during the Cultural Revolution.

MAO YUANXIN (1941–). Mao Zedong's trusted aide and kinsman, Mao Yuanxin served as the Chairman's liaison at the Politburo in the last few months of Mao's life. With what he claimed to be Mao's directives, he dictated the moves of the **Chinese Communist Party** (CCP) leadership, including its decision to dismiss **Deng Xiaoping** from office in April 1976.

A native of Xiangtan, Hunan Province, Mao Yuanxin was the son of Mao Zemin, Mao Zedong's younger brother. Mao Yuanxin lost his father at the age of two and grew up under the care of his uncle. He entered the Harbin Institute of Military Engineering in 1960. Transcripts of Mao Zedong's talks with him during his college years (mostly in 1964) on such topics as **class struggle**, political training, and education reforms were widely circulated in the mid-1960s. In September 1966, after a few months of training with a unit of the **People's Liberation Army**, Mao Yuanxin returned to his former school to participate in the Cultural Revolution there. Soon he became a **rebel** organization leader. He was transferred to Liaoning Province in 1968 and became vice-chairman of the newly formed Liaoning **Revolutionary Committee** and political commissioner of the Shenyang Military Region.

While a young official in Liaoning, Mao Yuanxin launched a number of radical initiatives. In 1973, to challenge the directive from the State Council concerning the importance of college entrance examinations, he made a hero, or what he called a "sharp rock," of the college applicant **Zhang Tiesheng**, who wrote a letter of protest and plea instead of answering exam questions. In 1974, he advocated a new college admission and placement program called "from commune and to commune," modeled on the experiment of the Chaoyang Institute of Agriculture that had defined itself as an institution of higher education in the service of the local economy. Mao Yuanxin's ultraleftist politics also made Liaoning one of the most politically repressive provinces in the nation. He was instrumental in the execution of **Zhang Zhixin** in April 1975 for her political dissent.

In autumn 1975, Mao Zedong called Mao Yuanxin to Beijing to serve as his liaison with the Politburo. Already closely associated with the **Jiang Qing** group, Mao Yuanxin identified himself with the ultra-leftist faction of the CCP leadership and spoke ill of Deng Xiaoping in his conversations with Mao, especially in regard to Deng's critical view of the Cultural Revolution. Mao Yuanxin's repeated negative report on Deng apparently influenced the political judgment of Mao Zedong, who eventually decided to launch the nationwide campaign **Counterattack the Right-Deviationist Reversal-of-Verdicts Trend**. In spring 1976, especially in early April during the time of the **April 5 Movement**, Mao Yuanxin's role at the Politburo became even more crucial: Mao was bedridden and completely isolated from the outside world, so much so that Mao Yuanxin became his informer as well as his spokesman. The Politburo, on the other hand, often met just to learn Mao's directives from Mao Yuanxin. Following Mao's directives of 7 April as reported by Mao Yuanxin, the Politburo replaced Deng with **Hua Guofeng** as the person in charge. After Mao's death in September 1976, Jiang Qing proposed that Mao Yuanxin's position at the central leadership be retained. The proposal was rejected by Hua Guofeng.

In October 1976, Mao Yuanxin was arrested with the members of the **Gang of Four**. In official media, Mao Yuanxin was referred to as a "die-hard follower" (*sidang*) of the Gang of Four. He was expelled from the CCP in 1979 and sentenced to 17 years in prison in 1986 for persecution and slander, among other crimes.

MAO ZEDONG (1893–1976). Chairman of the **Chinese Communist Party** (CCP) from 1945 to 1976 and president of the People's Republic of China (PRC) from 1949 to 1959, Mao was the CCP's foremost revolutionary thinker, political leader, and military strategist. Putting in practice his theory of **continuing revolution under the dictatorship of the proletariat**, Mao designed and directed the Cultural Revolution as a nationwide campaign to uncover and denounce what he considered to be "**capitalist-roaders** within the party" and to instill revolutionary ideology and political consciousness in the mind of the masses so as to prevent China from repeating the Soviet path of "revisionism" or "capitalist restoration." Mao's legacy of ultra-leftism, however, came to an end when the cultural revolutionary faction of the CCP leadership known as the **Gang of Four** was purged shortly after his death.

Born in Xiangtan, Hunan Province, Mao was trained as a teacher at a provincial normal school. At the time of the May Fourth Movement, Mao was a radical writer and activist in his home province. He attended the first CCP National Congress in Shanghai in July 1921, which marked the founding of the CCP. In the mid-1920s, when the CCP and the Kuomintang were united against the warlords in the north, Mao, while holding important positions in both political parties, began to be involved in the peasant movement in Hunan and Guangdong. In 1927, when the CCP and the Kuomintang split, he led the Autumn Harvest Uprising and took the guerrilla army to Jinggangshan on the borders of Jiangxi and Hunan, where he started a land reform and established the CCP's first rural revolutionary base. In 1928, Mao and Zhu

De, who had led his own troops to Jinggangshan, founded the Red Army. In 1931, when the Chinese Soviet Republic was proclaimed in Jiangxi, Mao became chairman of its Central Executive Committee.

During this period, Mao articulated his vision of revolution in an essentially agrarian country and formed the strategy of building rural bases to encircle, and eventually take over, the cities. His writings on this subject as well as his more philosophical writings of the late 1930s were celebrated as successful efforts to sinicize Marxism. In late 1932, however, Mao, resistant to the instructions of the Comintern, was criticized for being too passive in his military strategies and lost his authority in military affairs. He began to come back as both a political and a military leader after the Zunyi Conference (1935) during the Long March. During the Yan'an period, Mao's authority was gradually consolidated. In 1943, during the CCP's Rectification Movement, Mao became chairman of both the Politburo and the Central Committee Secretariat. From this point on, he remained at the top of the party leadership. In 1945, at the Seventh National Congress of the CCP and the First Plenum of the Seventh CCP Central Committee, **Mao Zedong Thought** was designated as the party's guiding principle, and Mao was elected chairman of

Mao Zedong lying in state, September 1976.

the CCP Central Committee (CC) and the Central Military Commission (CMC). In 1949, Mao proclaimed the founding of the PRC and became president of the new Central People's Government.

In 1956, as Nikita Khrushchev criticized the late Soviet leader Joseph Stalin for violating social legality and promoting a cult of personality, the Eighth National Congress of the CCP removed the reference to Mao Zedong Thought from the CCP Constitution and, at the same time, declared that the principal contradiction in China's society had become the contradiction between the "advanced socialist system" and the "backward productive forces." Mao, on the other hand, was alarmed by de-Stalinization in the Soviet Union, the democratic revolution in Hungary, and the shift in focus in the CCP leadership from politics to economic development. As criticism of the CCP leadership rose in 1957, especially from intellectual circles, in response to Mao's proposal to "let a hundred flowers bloom and let a hundred schools of thought contend," Mao decided to crack down on the party's critics with an Anti-Rightist Campaign. In 1958, he endorsed the radical economic experiment the Great Leap Forward, which led to a nationwide famine and the death of 20 to 30 million farmers. In 1959, Mao resigned as state president, retreating from the "first front" of leadership.

However, when Marshal **Peng Dehuai** criticized the Great Leap policies in the same year, Mao had him dismissed as minister of defense and launched a movement against rightist elements within the party. In the meantime, efforts made by leaders on the "first front"—President **Liu Shaoqi** and others—to restore the nation's economy appeared to Mao as measures of "**economism**" lacking revolutionary commitment. By 1962, when the **Tenth Plenum of the Eighth CCP Central Committee** was held in Beijing, Mao seemed to have come to a conclusion about the emerging revisionism in socialist countries, including China. "Never forget **class struggle**," he admonished the party officials at the plenum. In the years that followed, Mao directed a theoretical debate with Soviet "revisionists"; he designed and led a **Socialist Education Movement** in China, mostly in the countryside; and he endorsed a movement led by his wife **Jiang Qing** to reform literature and the arts. Out of all these movements, Mao's idea of the Cultural Revolution gradually took shape.

In the preliminary stages of the revolution, Mao stayed away from Beijing while planning and directing the CC's every move in the capital, including the denunciation of the so-called **Peng-Luo-Lu-Yang Anti-Party Clique** at the **enlarged Politburo sessions** in May 1966. He came back to Beijing in July 1966 and made a decisive move in August at the **Eleventh Plenum of the Eighth CCP Central Committee**: on the one hand, he wrote a **big-character poster** entitled "**Bombarding the Headquarters**," implicitly criticizing Liu Shaoqi and those under his leadership for exercising "bourgeois dictatorship" and suppressing the mass movement; on the other hand, he promoted Marshal **Lin Biao** to the second highest place in the party hierarchy, replacing Liu Shaoqi—who was soon to be dismissed as **China's Khrushchev** and **the biggest capitalist-roader within the party**—as his heir apparent.

By now China's unchallenged supreme leader, Mao mobilized the **Red Guards** to attack presumed capitalist-roaders within the party and the so-called **cow-demons and snake-spirits** without. He also encouraged mass organizations to take over party and government offices in the provinces and ordered the army to support such efforts. In February 1967, Mao denounced a group of veteran leaders' anti–Cultural Revolution outbursts, known as the **February Adverse Current**, and gave much greater power to the ultra-leftist **Central Cultural Revolution Small Group**. In 1968, Mao managed to have President Liu Shaoqi officially expelled from the party. And in April 1969, the **Ninth National Congress of the CCP** passed a new constitution that designated Lin Biao as Mao's successor.

Mao had hoped to conclude his Cultural Revolution program at the Ninth Congress. But, as serious political as well as ideological conflicts developed between the Lin Biao faction and the Jiang Qing group, Mao sided with the latter and launched a campaign in 1970 to criticize **Chen Boda**, who had become an ally of Lin's. At the same time, Mao made several personnel decisions to undermine Lin's influence in the military. Eventually, Lin died in a plane crash on 13 September 1971 while allegedly fleeing the country after an aborted assassination plot against Mao.

After Lin's downfall, Premier **Zhou Enlai**, Mao's loyal assistant who had kept the country running throughout the Cultural Revolution and had helped Mao during the Lin Biao crisis, became the second-highest-ranking leader. But, fearing that Zhou as a moderate leader would be a decisive anti–Cultural Revolution force after his death, Mao never considered him as his successor; rather, he made Zhou the unnamed target of criticism in a series of political campaigns including the **Criticize Lin and Criticize Confucius** campaign (1974) and *Water Margin* **Appraisal** movement (1975–1976).

In choosing his successor, Mao wavered between **Wang Hongwen**, a member of the Jiang Qing group soon to be known as the Gang of Four, and **Deng Xiaoping**, the pragmatist former head of the CC's Secretariat who had been denounced as the second biggest capitalist-roader. Though members of the Gang of Four were Mao's ideological faithful, their increasing unpopularity and their lack of political and administrative skills tilted Mao toward Deng. But the drastic measures that Deng took in 1975 in his **overall rectification** program convinced Mao that Deng was already abandoning his legacy of the Cultural Revolution. Eventually, just a few months before his death on 9 September 1976, Mao had Deng dismissed from office and made **Hua Guofeng** his successor. Within a month of Mao's death, however, Hua, in cooperation with a number of ranking leaders and with broad support from the top to the grassroots, arrested the Gang of Four, and the radical program that Mao had cultivated in the last decade of his life was soon to be replaced by Deng Xiaoping's economic reform that indeed adopted certain measures of capitalism.

In the landmark CCP document **Resolution on Certain Questions in the History of Our Party since the Founding of the People's Republic of China** passed in 1981 at the Sixth Plenum of the Eleventh Central Committee, Mao is criticized for his grave mistake of launching the Cultural Revolution, but he is still acknowledged as the founder of the CCP, the PRC, and the PLA and as China's greatest Communist leader.

MAO ZEDONG: INSPECTION TOUR OF THREE REGIONS (1967).

From July to September 1967, just as factional conflict was widespread and escalating into a civil war, **Mao Zedong** toured North, East, and Mid-South China and inspected the situation of the Cultural Revolution in Hebei, Henan, Hubei, Hunan, Jiangxi, and Zhejiang Provinces and the city of Shanghai. On 25 September, the official organ of the **Chinese Communist Party** (CCP) *People's Daily* carried a news report about Mao's inspection tour. On 17 October, the CCP Central Committee issued "The Important Directives of Chairman Mao during an Inspection Tour of North, Mid-South, and East Regions." These directives address the following issues: 1) Overall assessment of the Cultural Revolution: Mao considers the situation of the Cultural Revolution in the entire country to be "supremely good" since the masses were truly mobilized. He acknowledges the problem of much chaos in some places but also adds that the situation "simply threw the enemy into chaos while the masses were tempered." 2) Factional conflict: Mao blames the **capitalist-roaders** for "deceiving the masses and inciting them to fight against one another." He calls for "a grand revolutionary alliance" of all factions. 3) Cadres: Mao still insists on "struggling against the capitalist-roaders within the party," but he also says that they are just "a small handful," while most cadres are good and could be criticized for their mistakes and be educated by the masses. The words "broaden the range of education; narrow the range of fire" indicate that Mao was moderating his approach on the cadre issue. 4) The **Red Guards**: In contrast to his full support and encouragement of the Red Guards' spirit of rebellion in the previous year, Mao's comments concerning the Red Guards now focus on the need to educate them, reason with them, and warn them against excesses: "Now is the time when they may make mistakes." During the inspection tour, in late August, Mao also had **Wang Li** and **Guan Feng**, two frontline extremists of the **Central Cultural Revolution Small Group**, arrested to prevent further chaos in the military and in foreign affairs. Mao's apparent concern with disorder and violence, however, did not override his generally positive feeling about the Cultural Revolution.

MAO ZEDONG: INSPECTIONS OF RED GUARDS. From 18 August to 26 November 1966, Chairman **Mao Zedong** held eight inspections of **Red Guard** troops in Beijing, receiving a total of 11 million students and teachers from all over the country. At these events, Mao wore an army uniform and a Red Guard armband and waved to his audience from the Tiananmen gate tower or an open army vehicle while the feverish crowd cheered on, chanting, "Long live Chairman Mao!" This was Mao's response to the resistance to his radical Cultural Revolution program from within the party leadership. By receiving Red Guards from across China, Mao mobilized the nation's youths for the task of spreading the fire of revolution across the country and turned Red Guards into a major political force against the party establishment.

The **mass rally of 18 August**, the first and the best-known of Mao's eight inspections, was a defining moment of the Red Guard movement. At this event, Mao accepted a Red Guard armband and acknowledged his symbolic role as the commander of the Red Guard army. **Lin Biao**, standing by Mao's side, delivered a militant speech to a crowd of one million—mostly from Beijing but also with Red Guard representatives from the provinces—calling on Red Guards to wage war against "old ideas, old culture, old customs, and old habits." The news report about the event revealed to the public for the first time the demotion of President **Liu Shaoqi** from the second-ranked position in the CCP central leadership to the eighth. The 8-18 rally triggered a massive assault on the **Four Olds** as well as a nationwide travel campaign called the **Great Networking**. Red Guards and other students began to pour into Beijing on free trains, hoping to have a glimpse of Mao in person, which prompted the Chairman to hold further inspections on 31 August, 15 September, 1 October, 18 October, and 3 November.

As a ceremonial speaker at some of these inspections, Lin Biao continued to applaud the Red Guards' militant activities, assuring them that whatever they did was right. In the meantime, the Red Guards from the capital went to the provinces to instigate the masses there to rebel against the authorities. By mid-November 1966, the masses across China were well stirred up for the revolution, as Mao had expected, whereas the nation's transportation system was on the verge of breaking down because of the Great Networking campaign. Finally, Mao's reception for Red Guards came to an end after two rather hasty inspections on 10–11 November and 25–26 November (though they were the most massive of all), in which the Chairman rode in an open car and reviewed a total of 4.5 million enthusiastic youths in the chill of Beijing's early winter season.

MAO ZEDONG: LETTER TO TSINGHUA UNIVERSITY MIDDLE SCHOOL RED GUARDS. Dated 1 August 1966, this is Mao's response to the request by Tsinghua University Middle School **Red Guards** for comments on the first two pieces of their **big-character poster** series "**Long Live the Revolutionary Rebel Spirit of the Proletariat**," which they submitted to **Jiang Qing** with a letter to Mao on 28 July. In his reply, Mao expresses strong support for the work of the Red Guard organizations at both Tsinghua University Middle School and Peking University Middle School and for "people with the same revolutionary attitude nationwide." Mao also suggests that Red Guards "leave a way out for those who have committed serious mistakes so that they may start anew with life." On the day Mao wrote the letter, the **Eleventh Plenum of the Eighth Central Committee of the Chinese Communist Party** convened. Although Mao's letter was never sent out, it was distributed as an important document at the plenum. On 3 August, Tsinghua University Middle School Red Guards released the letter to the public soon after they learned its content. With Mao's personal endorsement—one of the major steps Mao took to stir up the nation for the Cultural Revolution—Red Guard organizations sprang up across China and became an army of crusaders against what Mao saw as the state apparatus controlled by President **Liu Shaoqi**'s bourgeois headquarters.

MAO ZEDONG: MEETING WITH THE FIVE RED GUARD LEADERS (28 July 1968). Chairman **Mao Zedong** called this urgent meeting on the early morning of 28 July 1968, at which he spoke with the five most influential **Red Guard** leaders in Beijing. The five leaders were **Nie Yuanzi** of the New Beida Commune at Peking University, **Kuai Dafu** of the Jinggang Mountain Regiment at Tsinghua University, **Tan Houlan** of the Jinggang Mountain Commune at Beijing Normal University, **Han Aijing** of the Red Flag Combat Team at Beijing Aeronautical Engineering Institute, and **Wang Dabin** of the East-Is-Red Commune at Beijing Geological Institute. What prompted Mao to call for the meeting was the bloody event that had occurred the previous day on the campus of Tsinghua University, where Jinggang Mountain Red Guards under Kuai's command opened fire on a joint propaganda team of workers and **People's Liberation Army** (PLA) personnel on a mission to break a prolonged **armed conflict** between two rival Red Guard organizations there. Mao's harsh reproach of the Red Guards at the meeting and his decision to send students away from cities afterward marked the beginning of the end of the Red Guard movement in China.

Despite Mao's apparently enthusiastic support for the Red Guards and their rebellion against the old party authorities in the early stages of the Cultural Revolution, which had caused the Red Guard movement to sweep across the country in summer 1966, the focus of the Cultural Revolution, as he saw it, had shifted after the 1967 **power seizure** movement from abolishing the old party apparatus to establishing new authorities and restoring order. Mao called for a grand alliance of all **rebel** forces during his **inspection tour of three regions** in summer 1967 and warned Red Guard and rebel leaders that it might be their turn to make mistakes. However, factional conflicts among mass organizations between the radical and the **conservative** factions that resulted from several campaigns in the early stages of the Cultural Revolution persisted. The determination of each side to gain dominance in the new power structure further intensified the conflict, so much so that many places in the nation had been in a state of war since 1967.

Mao's determination to end nationwide chaos became clear in July 1968 when he authorized two central party documents—**July 3 Public Notice** and **July 24 Public Notice**—targeting the armed factional fighting in Guangxi Zhuang Autonomous Region and Shaanxi Province. Mao's decision to send the workers and PLA personnel to Tsinghua campus on 27 July was another signal of Mao's move to stop factional violence. Therefore, when the news of Kuai's comrades confronting the propaganda team with rifles and spears reached him, Mao was furious and called the meeting in the small hours of 28 July. In addition to the five Red Guard leaders, almost all the top party and government leaders, including **Lin Biao**, **Zhou Enlai**, **Chen Boda**, **Kang Sheng**, **Jiang Qing**, **Yao Wenyuan**, **Xie Fuzhi**, **Huang Yongsheng**, **Ye Qun**, and Wen Yucheng, were present, which made the meeting an unprecedented event.

The meeting started at 3:30 a.m. and lasted for five hours. At the meeting, Mao harshly criticized the widespread factional fighting in the country. To the bewilderment of the Red Guard leaders, Mao told them that he himself was behind the decision to send the propaganda team to Tsinghua and that he might resolve the factional conflict on all college campuses by sending all students away. Mao called the solution "struggle, criticism, go," which differed greatly from "**struggle, criticism, reform,**" the tasks Mao had previously entrusted to the Red Guards. This solution, combined with the movement of **educated youths** going **up to the mountains and down to the countryside,** turned out to be a decisive step on Mao's part to resolve the nation's employment crisis and, at the same time, to end the Red Guard movement altogether. For student Red Guards, the meeting at which Mao met and talked with their leaders at significant length for the first time was a turning point in their lives: they had been praised as revolutionary pioneers during almost all of the campaigns since the beginning of the Cultural Revolution, but now they were beginning to realize that they would be the targets of the next campaign—that is, to be reeducated by workers and peasants. Before long, both college and middle school students left the city for remote factories and farms, and the Red Guard movement finally came to an end.

See also ONE-HUNDRED-DAY ARMED CONFLICT ON THE TSIN-GHUA CAMPUS; WORKERS PROPAGANDA TEAM.

MAO ZEDONG: SOUTHERN INSPECTION (14 August–12 September 1971). This was a strategic tour during which **Mao Zedong** communicated to party and government officials and military generals outside Beijing his view of the **Lin Biao** faction. This tour allegedly both triggered and foiled a plan to assassinate Mao. On the early morning of 13 September, within hours of Mao's unexpected early return to Beijing (on the evening of 12 September), Lin Biao, **Ye Qun**, and their son **Lin Liguo** fled in panic and died in a plane crash.

In mid-August 1971, Mao proposed that the Third Plenum of the Ninth Central Committee of the **Chinese Communist Party** (CCP) and the **Fourth National People's Congress** convene around National Day (1 October). Mao notified Lin Biao at Beidaihe of this proposal as the decision of the CCP Central Committee (CC) and then left Beijing for Wuhan by train on 14 August. During the next 30 days, Mao traveled to Wuhan, Changsha, Nanchang, Hangzhou, and Shanghai, talking to provincial party leaders and government officials and generals at five military regions about what he considered to be the ongoing tenth line struggle in the history of the CCP that began at the 1970 **Lushan Conference** at which **Chen Boda**, along with Lin Biao's close associates **Wu Faxian**, Ye Qun, **Li Zuopeng**, and **Qiu Huizuo**, allegedly planned actions in secret and launched a surprise attack to disrupt the proceedings of the plenum.

Lin Biao's name came up quite a few times during these conversations: Mao complained about Lin's flattery and "**peak theory**" and called them "inappropriate"; he suggested that Lin should bear his share of responsibility for what happened at the Lushan Conference; and he was particularly sensitive to the commanding power in the military. "Who said the founder cannot be the commander as well?" Mao asked rhetorically in response to a popular saying that the **People's Liberation Army** was founded and led by Mao and commanded directly by Lin Biao. He was apparently concerned with Lin's influence in the army (with Wu Faxian as commander of the air force, Li Zuopeng commander of the navy, and **Huang Yongsheng** chief of general staff) when he said, "The army must be united and rectified. I just can't believe our armed forces would rebel; I just don't believe that Huang Yongsheng would be able to direct the forces to rebel." Mao also made some critical comments on Lin Biao's wife, Ye Qun, regarding her position as director of Lin's office. The focus of all these talks was the Lushan Conference, the pivotal event since the downfall of **Liu Shaoqi** during what Mao saw as the ninth line struggle within the CCP. Liu's case, however, had a conclusion, while Lin's, that of the tenth line struggle between the two head-quarters, did not: "The business of Lushan had not come to an end; it was not settled."

Despite Mao's declared intention to "protect Vice-Chairman Lin," the words about the unfinished business of Lushan and the pending Third Plenum and the People's Congress (in both of which leadership might be restructured) particularly alarmed Lin Biao and his close associates. On 5 and 6 September, their sources were finally able to provide them with reliable intelligence concerning Mao's comments during his southern tour. Then, they were said to have begun carrying out an assassination plot. Mao had been staying in Hangzhou, Zhejiang Province, since 3 September. On the night of 9 September, Mao ordered that his special train be moved out of Hangzhou to Shaoxing. On the afternoon of 10 September, Mao suddenly changed the original itinerary, called the special train back to Hangzhou, and took the train to Shanghai. When he arrived in Shanghai in the evening, Mao decided to work, meet people, and rest on the train. On the afternoon of 11 September, Mao made another unexpected decision to leave Shanghai for Beijing immediately and not to stop along the way. On the afternoon of 12 September, Mao's train entered Fengtai station in the suburbs of Beijing. There he ordered the train to stop. At Fengtai, he conferred with the leaders of the Beijing Military Region and municipal authorities for more than two hours aboard the train, finding out about the situation in Beijing and making arrangements. The train carrying Mao arrived at Beijing station at dusk, thus concluding his 30-day southern inspection.

MAO ZEDONG THOUGHT. Designated as the party's guiding principle at the Seventh National Congress of the **Chinese Communist Party** (CCP) (1945) at **Liu Shaoqi**'s proposal and hailed by Mao's handpicked successor **Lin Biao** in the 1960s as the peak of Marxism-Leninism, Mao Zedong Thought was the dominant ideology of the Cultural Revolution. As represented by the four-volume *Selected Works of Mao Zedong*, Mao Zedong Thought was considered before the Cultural Revolution to be Mao's successful sinification of Marxism—that is, his creative adaptation of a theory coming out of industrial Europe to the conditions of the essentially agrarian Chinese society. During the Cultural Revolution, Mao's theory of **continuing revolution under the proletarian dictatorship**, which informed the ongoing political movement, became a new distinguishing feature of Mao Zedong Thought. In a sanitized version introduced in the resolution of the Sixth Plenum of the Eleventh CCP Central Committee (1981), however, Mao Zedong Thought is defined as a "scientific system" that, while originating with Mao, represents a "crystallization of the collective wisdom of the CCP"; this new definition thus omitted Mao's idea of the Cultural Revolution.

See also QUOTATIONS FROM CHAIRMAN MAO.

MAO ZEDONG THOUGHT PERFORMANCE TEAMS. (*Mao Zedong sixiang wenyi xuanchuandui* or *Mao Zedong sixiang wenyi xiaofendui*.) Under the banner "arts must serve the masses" and "arts must serve the politics," these teams were formed by both professional and amateur artists to deliver songs, dances, music, and mini-dramas of pure propaganda value to the masses. These teams were usually small in size, with members from fewer than a dozen to several dozen. At the height of the Cultural Revolution (1966–1968), a large number of such teams were active in all parts of the country. Some were dispatched by professional performing troupes, but the majority of them were amateur groups affiliated with certain schools, colleges, or school districts. Since schools were not in session at the time, there were plenty of energetic, willing, and artistically inclined young men and women available as members of such teams. They performed in schools and factories, and even on city streets. Some went on tour through small towns and villages in the countryside. Most of the teams, especially those made of college and middle school students, were dismissed when the entire **Red Guard** generation of youths was sent to the countryside and factories for **reeducation**—beginning in late 1968. Some of the performance teams, however, were institutionalized in factories, enterprises, farms, and townships and survived until the end of the Cultural Revolution.

MASS DICTATORSHIP. This is the name for the legal authority that mass organizations assumed to arrest, imprison, and torture ordinary citizens; to search their homes; and to confiscate their personal belongings. Widespread persecution during the Cultural Revolution took place mostly under mass dictatorship.

The practice of mass dictatorship started at the very beginning of the Cultural Revolution when **Red Guards** took the law into their own hands while Chairman **Mao Zedong** and other government leaders cheered them on, offering no protection for innocent people from Red Guards' verbal and physical abuse and administering no punishment for violators of the law. In many places, especially on middle school and college campuses, illegal prisons known as "**cow sheds**" were set up, where people denounced as class enemies, or "**cow-demons and snake-spirits**," were detained, interrogated, and tortured. They were forced to perform manual labor during the day and to confess their "crimes" in the morning, in the evening, and sometimes before each meal. They were told to bow their heads while walking and not to speak to one another at any time. Home visits were strictly forbidden.

This kind of persecution was even more widespread in the late 1960s during the **Rectify the Class Ranks** movement when mass dictatorship became a tool of the new power organ, the **revolutionary committee**. In this period, special case groups set up by mass organizations everywhere assumed the authority of law enforcement agencies, and a vast number of

A Red Guard Mao Zedong Thought performance team performing on the street.

people suspected of having a "problematic history" (*lishi wenti*) were detained, interrogated, and tortured in illegal prisons on the premises of their work units. Members of these special case groups traveled across China to gather information in government-held personnel dossiers. Forced confessions were widely used as evidence against the detainees and whoever was named in the confessions. It was a common practice of special case groups to try to break down the detainees by forcing their family members to speak against them. This kind of psychological pressure, in combination with isolation and torture, resulted in numerous suicides. According to official estimate, the total number of people affected by the Rectify the Class Ranks campaign, including those persecuted and their family members, amounted to one-eighth of China's population.

MASS RALLY OF 18 AUGUST 1966. Officially named the "Mass Rally Celebrating the Great Proletarian Cultural Revolution" but known simply as the "8-18," this huge gathering of roughly one million people—many of them students and **Red Guards**—was held at Tiananmen Square following **Mao Zedong**'s suggestion. The event prompted a massive response among Chinese youths to Mao's Cultural Revolution program and created for both China and the world the famous image of Mao as commander-in-chief wearing a military uniform and a Red Guard armband waving over the enthusiastic crowd to join the crusade against the old, non-proletarian world.

Mao Zedong receiving a Red Guard armband while reviewing Red Guard troops from the gate tower of Tiananmen, 18 August 1966.

At 5:00 a.m. on the day of the rally, Mao, after a sleepless night, walked out of Tiananmen (Gate of Heaven) to join the masses. He invited 1,500 Red Guards to join the party leaders on Tiananmen and review the parade from there. As the rally was in progress, Mao received a Red Guard armband from **Song Binbin**, a Red Guard from the Beijing Normal University Female Middle School. On hearing her soft-sounding name, "Binbin," Mao offered a suggestion for a new name, an overtly militant one: "Be valiant!" (*yaowu*, which literally means "be militant, soldier-like") Mao said. In the following three months, Mao was to receive more than 10 million Red Guards from all over China in seven more rallies.

During the 18 August rally, **Chen Boda**, **Lin Biao**, and **Zhou Enlai** delivered speeches. Chen, director of the **Central Cultural Revolution Small Group** presiding over the rally, granted Mao three titles: "the great leader, the great teacher, and the great helmsman." In his militant speech denouncing "**capitalist-roaders**, reactionary bourgeois authorities, bourgeois **royalists**, various activities repressing the revolution, and all '**cow-demons and snake-spirits**'" and calling for the total destruction of "old ideas, old culture, old customs, and old habits" (popularly known as the **Four Olds**), Lin spoke of Mao as the "great commander of the Cultural Revolution." From this moment on, the "**four greats**" (great teacher, great leader, great commander, and great helmsman), along with the "red sun," became Mao's most popular prefix, and 18 August 1966 became the unofficial holiday of the Red Guard movement.

MASS RALLY OF 6 OCTOBER 1966. Well known for the battle cry in its full name "The Oath-Taking Rally of Revolutionary Teachers and Students Present in Beijing to Commence Fierce Firing upon the Bourgeois Reactionary Line," this gathering of over 100,000 people representing colleges all over the country was organized by the **Third Command Post** of Beijing college **Red Guards** and held at the spacious Workers Stadium in Beijing. Attending the rally were Premier **Zhou Enlai** and key members of the **Central Cultural Revolution Small Group** (CCRSG)—**Chen Boda**, **Kang Sheng**, **Jiang Qing**, and **Zhang Chunqiao**. At the rally, Red Guard representatives from Beijing Normal University, Beijing Geological Institute, Beijing Institute of Aeronautics, and schools in Guangxi, Jiangsu, Shaanxi, and other provinces criticized the **work groups** and party organizations for carrying out a **Bourgeois Reactionary Line** and repressing the Cultural Revolution in the summer months of 1966. Jiang Qing, then Zhang Chunqiao, and finally Zhou Enlai made speeches in support of the Red Guards. The rally sent out a telegram calling on the entire country to wage war against the Bourgeois Reactionary Line.

Of particular note was a document issued by the Central Military Commission and the General Political Department of the **People's Liberation Army** that Zhang Chunqiao announced in his speech. The document is entitled the "Emergency Directive concerning the Cultural Revolution in all Military Units and Schools." According to this directive, school party committees were not to resume leadership upon the dismissal of the work groups, and the popularly elected Cultural Revolution groups, committees, and congresses should become legitimate organs of power during the Cultural Revolution. The directive also stipulates that care should be taken to protect those in the minority; that all those branded by the work groups and school party committees as "counterrevolutionaries," "anti-party elements," "rightist elements," or "false leftists and true rightists" during the early stages of the movement were to have their names publicly rehabilitated; that materials written by individuals under duress were to be returned to the persons themselves; that after approval from the masses as well as the individual concerned had been attained, materials used to fabricate evidence were to be publicly destroyed. After reading the directive aloud, Zhang suggested that this important document was suitable not only for military units and military schools, but that the directive must be carried out thoroughly in non-military institutions and at all levels of party organizations as well.

The mass rally of 6 October 1966 was a significant event for the **rebel** faction of the Red Guards who were repressed by the work groups and old party committees early on but thrived after the rally. The "Emergency Directive" read at the rally had a strong impact on the evolving mass movement. Slogans such as "kick away the party committees and carry out the revolution" would become actions in the remaining months of 1966, which drove the country further into chaos. Also under this directive, a partial redress of the wrongs committed in the summer months of 1966 was under way and would become an important part of the Criticize the Bourgeois Reactionary Line campaign.

MAY 7 CADRE SCHOOL. This was a new institution set up in the remote countryside where party and government officials and college professionals were sent to perform manual labor. Supposedly, they would be tempered by hard work, educated by local peasants, and reconnected with the real life of the laboring masses. On 7 May 1968, the **revolutionary committee** of Heilongjiang Province set up the first of such schools on a farm in Liuhe, Qing'an County, and named it after **Mao Zedong**'s **May 7 Directive** (1966). On 5 October 1968, *People's Daily* published a report entitled "Liuhe 'May 7' Cadre School Presents New Experience for Revolutionizing Government Agencies," which speaks highly of cadres' "relearning" experience at the May 7 cadre school as an effective measure to counter the bureaucratic privilege that had alienated them from the masses. In an editor's note to the report, a new directive of Mao is made public for the first time, which requires all cadres, except for the elderly, the infirm, or the disabled, to take turns going down to the grassroots to do manual labor.

Soon after the publication of Mao's directive and the report on the Liuhe cadre school, thousands of May 7 cadre schools were formed all over the country. Millions of party and government officials and college and research institution professionals were sent down to do hard labor. Some returned to their original posts or were assigned other positions after a year or two of "relearning" in these schools. Others stayed there indefinitely. After the fall of **Lin Biao** in 1971, more sent-down officials and intellectuals were called back to the cities. In the last few years of the Cultural Revolution, many of these schools were already vacant. On 17 February 1979, the State Council issued a directive to close all May 7 cadre schools in the country.
See also REEDUCATION.

MAY 7 DIRECTIVE. In this letter, dated 7 May 1966, to **Lin Biao** regarding the report of the General Logistics Department of the **People's Liberation Army** (PLA) on "Further Developments of Agricultural and Sideline Production in Armed Forces," **Mao Zedong** articulated a utopian view of labor as a certain profession participating in all other major professional experiences—like a soldier who can be at the same time a worker, a farmer, and a student. On 15 May, one day ahead of the passage of the **May 16 Circular** with which the Cultural Revolution was formally launched, the **Chinese Communist Party** Central Committee authorized a nationwide in-ner-party issuance of Mao's letter to Lin with a note that calls the letter "a document of great historical significance, a new and epoch-making develop-ment of Marxism-Leninism." In the letter, Mao projects his vision of the PLA as an institution at once self-sufficient and educational. In his view, the PLA should be a great school where military professionals not only receive political, military, and cultural training but also engage in agricultural, side-line, and small-to-medium-scale industrial production and participate in all political campaigns, including the **Socialist Education Movement** (which was still going on) and the Cultural Revolution (which was just beginning). "Thus," Mao concludes, "the army is integrated with students, peasants, workers, and civilians in general."

In a similar fashion, Mao suggests that workers, peasants, students, and people from other walks of life participate in spheres of work and learning experiences other than their own. In his comments on students, however, there is an additional radical thrust: "Years of schooling should be reduced, education needs to be revolutionized, and bourgeois intellectuals' dominance over our schools has to end." As part of the Cultural Revolution program, Mao's May 7 Directive was used to name any experiment that integrated divisions of labor, especially intellectual and manual labor, as in the case of the **May 7 cadre school**, where state officials and administrative workers from the cities went to work as laborers to reform themselves; they were called "May 7 soldiers."

MAY 16 CIRCULAR (1966). Carefully edited and revised by **Mao Zedong** and approved by the Politburo on 16 May 1966, this circular of the **Chinese Communist Party** (CCP) Central Committee revoked the **February Out-line**, disbanded the **Peng Zhen**–led **Five-Person Cultural Revolution Small Group**, and announced the establishment of the new **Central Cultu-ral Revolution Small Group** under the Politburo. The circular accuses Peng of concocting the February Outline without consulting other members of the Five-Person Group and without reporting it to the CCP central leadership and Mao despite the fact that the Outline *was* produced collectively and that Mao was indeed consulted in person. According to the circular, the February Outline adopts a bourgeois perspective on the current academic discussion and obscures its political nature; in advocating the principle of "everybody being equal in front of truth," the Outline denies the class identity of truth and protects the bourgeoisie from the rightful oppression of the proletarian dictatorship; and, at the same time, the Outline attempts to disintegrate the left ranks in the name of rectification and create obstacles to the proletarian Cultural Revolution. The circular condemns the February Outline on 10 counts and concludes with a warning: "The representatives of the bourgeois class who have infiltrated our party, our government, our armed forces, and cultural circles are a group of counterrevolutionary revisionists. When the time is right, they will try to seize power, turning the proletarian dictatorship into a bourgeois dictatorship. Some of these people have already been exposed by us, some have not, and some are still in our trust and being groomed as our successors. They are of the Khrushchev type sleeping right next to us. Party cadres at all levels must be especially aware of this fact." Such an assessment of China's political situation calls for the uncovering and massive purging of hidden enemies and serves to justify a nationwide campaign. This conclusion, along with the preceding militant attack on the "bourgeois" February Outline, highlighted Mao's ultra-leftist ideology and made the May 16 Circular the first "programmatic document" of the Great Proletarian Cultural Revolution.

See also ENLARGED POLITBURO SESSIONS, 4–26 MAY 1966.

MAY 16 COUNTERREVOLUTIONARY CLIQUE. This was the term the central leadership adopted in August 1967 to refer to a small organization of college students in Beijing called the Capital May 16 Red Guards Regiment, usually abbreviated as "May 16" or "5-16" (read "five-one-six" in Chinese). But after its brief initial stage, in which only this small organization and its associates were targeted, the investigation of the "May 16" became a nationwide political witch-hunt. Though its supposed target no longer existed, over a million innocent people were incriminated, according to official estimate. The movement had no official closure and did not end until after the Cultural Revolution.

The original May 16 Regiment was an ultra-leftist group named after the **May 16 Circular** of 1966, a document issued by the **Chinese Communist Party** (CCP) Central Committee (CC) launching the Cultural Revolution. In the summer months of 1967, members of the May 16 Regiment secretly distributed pamphlets and posted slogans calling Premier **Zhou Enlai** a "black backstage supporter of the **February Adverse Current**" and a "shameful traitor of **Mao Zedong Thought**" and accused him of betraying the spirit of the May 16 Circular.

The May 16 Regiment's attack on Zhou provoked a public outcry and a quick condemnation by the central leadership. Sometime in August 1967 when **Mao Zedong** was reading a draft of **Yao Wenyuan**'s article "On Two Books by **Tao Zhu**," he named the "May 16" as an example of the counterrevolutionaries who, in Yao's words, "shout slogans that are extreme left in form but extreme right in essence, whip up the ill wind of 'suspecting all,' and bombard the proletarian headquarters": "The organizers and manipulators of the so-called 'May 16,'" Mao wrote, "are just such a conspiratorial counterrevolutionary clique and must be thoroughly exposed." The government's crackdown on the "May 16" was swift and successful.

However, after the leaders of the "May 16" were arrested, the movement to "ferret out the 'May 16'" continued. In 1968, the CCP central leadership set up a **Chen Boda**–led special case group to investigate the "May 16." At a meeting on 24 January 1970, **Lin Biao** and **Jiang Qing** called for further investigation of the "May 16." By then, the hunt for the "May 16" had already evolved into a nationwide campaign, and the "May 16"—a convenient catch-all label for those on the extreme left—was a term used to label one's enemies. In places where factional strife was intense, each side often accused the other of being the "May 16." In some work units, over 14 percent of the people were falsely named "May 16" members.

On 27 March 1970, the CC issued a "Notification concerning the Investigation of the 'May 16' Counterrevolutionary Conspiratorial Clique" to put in check widespread persecution and confusion. Yet the Notification also states that it is wrong to deny the existence of the "May 16" and that **class struggle** is so complicated that the "May 16" is just one of the many counterrevolutionary organizations actually encouraging further political witch-hunting. The Notification also names, without any factual basis, four generals, Xiao Hua, **Yang Chengwu**, **Yu Lijin**, and **Fu Chongbi**, together with three fallen cultural revolutionaries, **Wang Li**, **Guan Feng**, and **Qi Benyu**, as behind-the-scenes manipulators of the "May 16 clique."

On 8 February 1971, with Mao's approval, the CC announced its decision to form a 13-member special case task force to lead the investigation of the "May 16." Chen Boda, head of the "May 16" special case group established in 1968, was now pronounced the backstage supporter of the "May 16." In 1972, shortly after Lin Biao's downfall, Lin and Chen were named together as chief backstage manipulators of the "May 16." In the meantime, the CC special case task force continued to operate until its dissolution in late 1978 when the investigation of the "May 16" finally came to an inconclusive end.

MORNING REQUEST, EVENING REPORT. (*Zaoqingshi wanhuibao.*) This phrase refers to the ritual of the masses during the Cultural Revolution to request instructions from Chairman **Mao Zedong** in the morning and report to him in the evening about what one thought and did during the day. The ritual was invented in the early stage of the Cultural Revolution when the **personality cult** of Mao was at its height. It soon became a common practice across China. Usually performed in groups with participants standing in front of Mao's portrait at home or in public, the ritual would begin with a prayer for Mao's longevity and Vice-Chairman **Lin Biao**'s long-lasting health while everyone in the group waved the pocket-size *Quotations from Chairman Mao*. The prayer was followed by the reading of Mao's quotations. The ritual usually ended with an oath that Mao's just-chanted instructions would be carried out in action during the day. The beginning prayer was the same for the evening ritual just before bedtime. Then each participant would examine closely his or her deeds of the day against Mao's instructions and express his or her determination to follow Mao's instructions more closely and overcome any shortcomings the next day. Similar to this ritual was a slightly less common practice of reading Mao's quotations before each meal.

When gigantic Mao statues were erected on many school campuses and on the premises of state institutions in 1968, the morning ritual in the public square in front of Mao's statue became a spectacle: hundreds, and even thousands, of people (depending on the size of the institution) would come in groups and speak to the statue of the Chairman in a loud voice. The so-called class enemies—those being denounced, illegally detained, and usually forced to perform manual labor—were not allowed to participate in the ritual the way other people did; they were often herded by **Red Guards** to line up in front of the statue, bow their heads, and perform a "morning confession," in which they were forced to name their "crimes" against the Chairman and ask for punishment. In summer 1969, the central leadership attempted to stop the practice of "morning request, evening report" by dismissing it as "formalistic" in a party central document (dated 12 June 1969). But the ritual continued to be performed in many places until after the downfall of Lin Biao in 1971.

N

NANJING INCIDENT (1976). The Nanjing Incident, a spontaneous political movement in the form of a public mourning for the late Premier **Zhou Enlai** as well as a mass protest against the **Jiang Qing** group, took place in Nanjing, Jiangsu Province, in late March and early April 1976. The immediate cause of the protest was a series of slanders in the media against Zhou Enlai, especially an implicit reference to Zhou as a **capitalist-roader** supporting **Deng Xiaoping** in an article published in the 25 March issue of the Jiang Qing–controlled Shanghai newspaper *Wenhui Daily*. While careful readers across China were enraged by such insinuations and writing and calling the newspaper to protest, people in Nanjing were the first to organize and take to the street. With the approach of the traditional Qingming Festival (4 April in 1976)—a day to visit cemeteries and remember the dead—numerous wreaths honoring the late premier were made and placed in the Yuhuatai Cemetery of Revolutionary Martyrs at Meiyuan near the city of Nanjing.

On 28 March, more than 400 students and teachers from Nanjing University held Zhou's portrait, carried flower wreaths, and marched through Nanjing's busiest streets to Meiyuan. The traffic police gave them green lights, while all vehicles made way for them. More and more people joined the march while a huge number of pedestrians stood silently along the streets. The next day, college students posted or painted slogans on walls in the city and on trains passing through Nanjing—slogans commemorating Zhou, protesting against *Wenhui Daily*, and denouncing the Jiang Qing group although without mentioning names. On 1 April, an official notice came from Beijing via telephone charging the authors of posters and slogans with the crime of "splitting the central leadership." The notice further irritated the masses, so much so that not only did protest activities intensify in Nanjing, but they spread quickly to other cities, including Beijing. In the few days in late March and early April, about 667,000 people visited the Yuhuatai cemetery, and over 6,000 wreaths were laid there in honor of the late premier. Nanjing provided the first instance of public mourning as a form of protest, the signature of the nationwide **April 5 Movement**.

NANJING 12 FEBRUARY COUNTERREVOLUTIONARY CASE. The Nanjing 12 February Counterrevolutionary Case was a wrongful case against a group of students in Nanjing for their protest against the **One Strike and Three Antis** campaign and their opposition to **Lin Biao** and **Jiang Qing**. This case was related to another unjust verdict in Nanjing: on 12 February 1970, when the One Strike and Three Antis campaign was just beginning, a young man named Jin Chahua became the first victim of the campaign and was executed in Nanjing because of his critical views of the Cultural Revolution and his efforts as an organizer of a Marxism-Leninism study group. Sympathizing with Jin's views and outraged by his execution, Chen Zhuoran, a student at Nanjing No. 8 Middle School, and some of his friends and fellow students went out on the night of Jin's execution and posted on the streets six slogans, including "Immortal is the martyr Jin Chahua," "We need true Marxism," "Down with Lin Biao," and "Down with Jiang Qing." In April 1970, Chen and his friends were arrested for their involvement in the "12 February counterrevolutionary case." On 28 April 1970, a public trial was held, during which Chen's death sentence was pronounced; Su Xiaobin, one of Chen's friends, was sentenced to 15 years in prison. Wang Maoya, another student involved, was driven insane by the harsh measures and eventually committed suicide. On 13 May 1981, the Nanjing Intermediate People's Court redressed the case and pronounced all of the verdicts unjust.

NATIONAL RED WORKERS REBEL CORPS. (*Quanguo hongse zaofanzhe zongtuan.*) An organization of contract and temporary workers formed on 8 November 1966 and one of China's first national mass organizations, the Rebel Corps was known for its practical orientation in fighting for its members' job security and economic benefits. The organization initially won support from the **Central Cultural Revolution Small Group** (CCRSG), particularly **Jiang Qing** who, in a speech given on 26 December 1966, blamed President **Liu Shaoqi** for the unfair treatment of contract and temporary workers and called upon the Rebel Corps to criticize Liu's revisionist line. Yet, as the organization continued to work for its members' economic interests and as **Mao Zedong** expressed dissatisfaction with such an economic distraction in a political movement and supported some mass organizations in Shanghai in their critique of **economism**, the CCRSG eventually turned its back on the Rebel Corps. On 12 February 1967, the **Chinese Communist Party** Central Committee and the State Council issued a public announcement (*zhongfa* [67] 47) to disband all national mass organizations, including the Rebel Corps. On 15 February, the Military Control Commission of the Beijing Public Security Bureau pronounced the Rebel Corps a "reactionary organization" and ordered the arrest of its leaders.

NEW PEKING UNIVERSITY. (*Xinbeida.*) A major mass organization newspaper during the Cultural Revolution, *New Peking University* was the publication of the Peking University **Cultural Revolution Committee** from 22 August 1966 to 17 August 1968, totaling approximately 200 issues. Publication began on the day **Mao Zedong**, upon request from Peking University cultural revolutionaries led by **Nie Yuanzi**, inscribed the title "New Peking University" to replace that of the old official news bulletin. In the issues published in the early stage of the Cultural Revolution, *New Peking University* devoted much space to attacking school authorities, especially **Lu Ping** and **Peng Peiyun**, for their close association with the so-called **black gang** of the former Beijing municipal party committee led by Mayor **Peng Zhen**. During the campaign to criticize the **Bourgeois Reactionary Line**, the paper shifted its focus to criticizing the **work group** of Peking University. From late 1966 on, the New Peking University Commune, the dominant mass organization that virtually controlled the school's cultural revolution committee, sent its members to many parts of the country, first to stir up the masses for revolution in the provinces and then to engage in provincial factional fighting. Its provincial liaison offices sometimes published joint issues with local mass organizations.

When sectional battles turned into a civil war in 1967, the Peking University Cultural Revolution Committee was split into two factions: the original New Peking University Commune and a new group including the Revolutionary Rebels Headquarters, Jinggang Mountain Regiment, and Fluttering Red Flag, all of which joined hands later on to form the New Peking University Jinggang Mountain Regiment. The latter began to publish its own newspaper, *New Peking University News* (*Xinbeida bao*), on 12 July 1967. At this stage, both newspapers of Peking University mainly focused on factional battles. On 28 July 1968, at his meeting with the five **Red Guard** leaders, including Nie Yuanzi of Peking University, Mao was sharply critical of the widespread Red Guard factionalism. Within a month, *New Peking University* ceased publication; its last issue came out two days before the **workers propaganda team** and the **army propaganda team** entered the Peking University campus and took control of the school.

NEW TREND OF IDEAS. (*Xinsichao.*) This phrase denoted a strain of radical ideas embraced by some student thinkers and writers during the Cultural Revolution. The phrase first appeared as the title of a journal that a group of students at Beijing Normal University established in late 1966 and early 1967. The leader of the group was Li Wenbo who argues in "A Commune Is No Longer a State" (17 October 1966) and some other **big-character posters** that China's socialist government structure, having derived from a bourgeois system, is still a hotbed for the growth of a capitalist class, revisionism, and bureaucracy. Therefore, Li believes, the old state and party apparatus must be completely dismantled, and a new form of government must be created following the principles of the Paris Commune of 1871 by which people have the right to elect as well as replace government officials. This transformation, according to Li, is the goal of the Cultural Revolution. Pursuing a similar line of argument, the collective author of "On the New Trend of Ideas: The Declaration of the 4-3 Faction" (11 June 1967) advocates that since in socialist China some government officials had become members of a privileged class, cultural revolutions were needed to purge **capitalist-roaders** within the party, to strip them of their newly acquired privileges, and to redistribute property and political power.

Yang Xiguang, a middle school student in Hunan Province, further radicalized this line of thinking in his article "Where Is China Going?" (6 January 1968). A self-labeled ultra-leftist, Yang denounces a new class of red capitalists that consists of 90 percent of ranking officials with Premier **Zhou Enlai** as their current general representative. In his view, Chairman **Mao Zedong**'s ultimate political vision, the real goal of his Cultural Revolution program, is to do away with the old state and party apparatus completely and to establish a new form of government called "Chinese people's commune," a mass dictatorship that had already existed briefly in the Paris Commune of 1871, the Shanghai **January Storm** of 1967, and what Yang calls China's "partial revolutionary civil war" of August 1967. Mao's decision to establish the **revolutionary committee** (which included military leaders and officials from the pre–Cultural Revolution government) instead of the commune as the organ of power is to Yang a necessary concession to the bourgeoisie at the moment, a great strategic move; when the masses are mature enough, Yang predicts, they will understand Mao's vision, abandon the revolutionary committee, and turn China into a completely new society governed by the masses. Though some of these radical ideas may indeed underlie Mao's cultural revolution theory, they were invariably suppressed by the government. Yang Xiguang, the most prominent voice of the "new trend" was imprisoned for 10 years from 1968 to 1978.

NIE RONGZHEN (1899–1992). A senior leader of the **Chinese Communist Party** (CCP) and the **People's Liberation Army** (PLA), Nie played a significant role in the CCP's political and military affairs before 1949 and in the modernization of the Chinese military after the founding of the People's Republic of China (PRC). In the Cultural Revolution, Nie was one of the veteran officials involved in the 1967 **February Adverse Current**.

Born in Jiangjin, Sichuan Province, Nie took part in the Communist movement in the early 1920s while a student in France. He joined the CCP in 1923 after his return to China and was trained in the Soviet Union from 1924 to 1925. A veteran of the Northern Expedition and a leader of both the Nanchang Uprising and the Guangzhou Uprising, Nie served on prominent military posts in the Red Army in the 1930s, in the Communist-led Eighth Route Army during the Sino-Japanese War, and in the PLA's Western-China Field Army in the civil war in the second half of the 1940s. After the founding of the PRC, Nie was appointed to various high-level positions in the party, the state, and the army, including mayor of Beijing, deputy chief of general staff of the PLA, vice-premier of the State Council (1958–1975), vice-chairman of the CCP Central Military Commission (CMC) (1959–1987), and chairman of the National Defense Science and Technology Commission. He was one of 10 marshals of the PRC and a member of the Seventh and Eighth CCP Central Committee (CC). In August 1966, Nie became a member of the Politburo—an indication of his support for **Mao Zedong** at the outset of the Cultural Revolution.

In early 1967, Nie was, however, involved in the first of the "two great disturbances" of what was soon to be known as the February Adverse Current, in which a group of senior party and military leaders confronted the ultra-leftists of the **Central Cultural Revolution Small Group** (CCRSG) and accused them of persecuting veteran cadres and interfering with military affairs. Mao sided with the CCRSG and criticized Nie and his comrades. The veterans were under attack again in 1969 at the **Ninth National Congress of the CCP**; though Nie retained his membership in the CC, his power and influence in state and military affairs were much reduced. After **Lin Biao**'s demise in 1971, Mao began to seek support from the "old government" faction of the central leadership and sent friendly signals to Nie and other senior party and military leaders. Nie reappeared at the CMC Standing Committee and was named a vice-chairman of the National People's Congress in 1975. In the post-Mao era, Nie became a member of the Politburo of both the Tenth and the Eleventh CC and vice-chairman of the State Central Military Committee of the Sixth National People's Congress. Nie Rongzhen retired in 1987 and died in 1992.

NIE YUANZI (1921–). One of the well-known "five **Red Guard** leaders" in Beijing and an alternate member of the Ninth Central Committee (CC) of the **Chinese Communist Party** (CCP), Nie was chair of the Peking University **Revolutionary Committee** and head of the Capital College **Red Guards' Representative Assembly** during the Cultural Revolution.

A native of Hua County, Henan Province, Nie joined the CCP in 1938. Unlike the other four student members of the "five Red Guard leaders," Nie was a faculty member and party secretary of the Department of Philosophy at Peking University when the Cultural Revolution began. What **Mao Zedong** called the **first Marxist-Leninist big-character poster**, which Nie co-signed with six other authors on 25 May 1966, made her nationally famous. After 1 June 1966, when Mao ordered the nationwide broadcast of this poster for the purpose of mobilizing the masses to shake up the party leadership,

Nie herself became one of the henchmen upon whom Mao and the **Central Cultural Revolution Small Group** (CCRSG) relied heavily in implementing their radical policies at the grassroots. Nie, along with a few other prominent rebel Red Guard leaders, organized the **mass rally of 6 October 1966**, at which more than 100,000 people representing colleges across China gathered to launch the campaign against the **Bourgeois Reactionary Line** of **Liu Shaoqi**. During and after this campaign, Nie and her supporters participated in the nationwide bombarding of party and state leaders who did not side with Mao and the CCRSG. In 1967, Nie was appointed deputy head of the Beijing Municipal Revolutionary Committee.

During her brief career of two years as the most powerful person at Peking University, Nie became popularly known as *laofoye*, an appellation of the old Dowager Cixi of the Qing Dynasty, and was responsible for the persecution of many people. She was very involved in violent factional conflicts on the university campus as well. By summer 1968, mass organizations led by Nie and other Red Guard leaders had become so intractable that Mao finally decided to end the Red Guard movement altogether. On the early morning of 28 July 1968, Mao held a meeting with the five Red Guard leaders, including Nie. At the meeting, Mao sent a strong signal to Nie and others that they should exit China's political stage. Shortly after the meeting, a **workers propaganda team** and an **army propaganda team** were sent to Peking University to take over power from Nie and her supporters. The propaganda teams soon took her into custody and forced her to do penal labor under surveillance.

Shortly after the downfall of the **Gang of Four**, Nie was formally arrested on a counterrevolutionary charge. On 10 March 1983, the Beijing Intermediate People's Court sentenced her to 17 years in prison. She was accused of a variety of crimes including instigating attacks on party and state officials and framing and persecuting innocent people.

NINGXIA COMMUNIST SELF-STUDY UNIVERSITY. (*Ningxia gongchanzhuyi zixiu daxue.*) This reading group was formed by 13 college and middle school students in Yinchuan, Ningxia Province, in November 1969 for the purpose of studying and discussing classic texts of Marxism-Leninism. The group had a mimeographed publication called *Journal of Learning*. A total of two issues were published, carrying six articles and three reports on the condition of the Chinese countryside. In these writings, as well as in their correspondences to one another, some members of the group are critical of the **personality cult** of **Mao Zedong** and obscurantist policies of the **Chinese Communist Party**. One member, for instance, draws an analogy between the Cultural Revolution and the Republican Revolution of 1911 in which **Lin Biao** is compared to Yuan Shikai as a hidden usurper of state power. In March 1970, during the **One Strike and Three Antis** campaign, the authorities named this group an "active counterrevolutionary clique." Three members of the group were executed, one committed suicide, four received prison sentences varying from three years to life, and the rest were put under surveillance by the state. On 5 August 1978, the Ningxia Provincial Supreme Court pronounced the case of the Communist Self-Study University misjudged.

NINTH NATIONAL CONGRESS OF THE CHINESE COMMUNIST PARTY (1–24 April 1969). After years of anticipation and preparation during which grave events, especially the economic crisis and the Great Famine caused by the Great Leap Forward campaign and the turmoil across the country during the Cultural Revolution, had interrupted the regular meeting schedule of the **Chinese Communist Party** (CCP), the Ninth National Congress finally opened in the beginning of April 1969, 13 years—instead of five years as specified in the CCP Constitution—after the Eighth Congress. The entire meeting was held in secret under heavy security due to war concerns over the Sino-Soviet border dispute. Some 1,512 delegates attended the meeting representing 22 million CCP members. Chairman **Mao Zedong** called for unity in his opening speech, but the ceremonial seating on the rostrum was highly suggestive of the division within the CCP: Mao was seated in the center; on his left were **Lin Biao, Kang Sheng, Jiang Qing**, and other new stars of the Cultural Revolution; on his right were **Zhou Enlai** and prominent pre-1966 "old government" leaders.

Lin Biao, representing the Central Committee (CC), delivered the Ninth Congress Political Report. Lin spoke of the Cultural Revolution as a great political movement guided by Mao's theory of **continuing revolution under the dictatorship of the proletariat**. He surveyed the CCP history, especially its post-1949 socialist period, as merely a preparation for the Cultural Revolution and denounced **Liu Shaoqi** as the general representative of **capitalist-roaders** within the party. Liu's "counterrevolutionary conspiracy" to restore capitalism in China, according to Lin, was detected by Mao long ago and finally defeated during the Cultural Revolution. Mao's idea that **class struggle** exists in the entire historical period of socialism gained official status in Lin's report as the basic line of the CCP, while **Mao Zedong Thought** as a whole, Lin said, must command everything.

The Ninth Congress adopted a new party constitution. Mao's theory of class struggle and continuous revolution became part of the constitution's general program. Also in the general program was a specific goal to overthrow the imperialism led by the United States, the modern revisionism of the Soviet Union and its allies, and the reactionaries of all countries. According to the new constitution, party members had only compulsory duties; the rights defined in the original constitution were eliminated. In a move unprecedented in the history of the CCP, the new constitution specified Mao Zedong as the leader of the CCP and Lin Biao as Mao's "close comrade-in-arms and successor."

The election of the Ninth Central Committee was the last item on the agenda. The candidate nomination and selection proceeded with strict regulations in favor of the new establishment: Mao and Lin were designated as "natural candidates"; 12 participants of the **extended Central Cultural Revolution Small Group routine meetings** and three members of the **Central Military Commission Administrative Group** were "unanimously approved candidates"; and the number of candidates from the Eighth Central Committee was not to exceed 53. Before the election, there was much backstage maneuvering by Lin Biao, Jiang Qing, and their supporters who tried to embarrass the old leaders by reducing their votes. Behind-the-scenes activities also included those of Lin's close allies undermining the power of Jiang's group. The election results were predictable: 170 members for the CC were elected from exactly 170 candidates; 109 alternates were elected from the same number of candidates as well; Mao was elected chairman of the CC; and Lin Biao was the only vice-chairman.

The **personality cult** of Mao Zedong was at its peak at the Ninth Congress. Delegates often talked about their two greatest desires: first, to see Chairman Mao as much as possible and to hear his "great voice" as much as possible; second, to have a picture taken with Mao. Mao's brief opening speech was interrupted dozens of times by the audience shouting the slogan "Long live Chairman Mao" and singing the song "Chairman Mao, the Red Sun in Our Heart." Delegates even gathered in the Great Hall of People, the congress site, and danced the **"loyalty dance"** to demonstrate their love for the Chairman. The elevation of Lin Biao's status was no less phenomenal. As delegates were electing the all-powerful presidium at the opening session, Mao proposed that Lin be elected chairman. Lin protested, and Mao's proposal was naturally turned down. Yet, with Mao giving the opening speech and Lin announcing the adjournment of the congress at the end, and with the downfall of Liu Shaoqi and the entry of Lin Biao's name together with Mao's into the party constitution, the question of a successor to Mao that had much to do with Mao's desire for a cultural revolution seemed resolved—at least for the moment.

NIXON VISIT (1972). *See* UNITED STATES–CHINA RELATIONS.

NOTES FROM A THREE-FAMILY VILLAGE. (Sanjiacun zhaji.) See THREE-FAMILY VILLAGE ANTI-PARTY CLIQUE.

O

OLD RED GUARDS. (*Lao hongweibing.*) Also known as "Old Guards" (*lao bing*), Old Red Guards were members of **Red Guard** organizations established in the early stages of the Cultural Revolution, mostly in Beijing's middle and high schools. These organizations adopted a politically discriminating membership policy and only admitted those from families of the so-called **five red categories**. Some Old Red Guards also promoted a notorious **blood lineage theory**. Old Red Guards labeled themselves "old" when a new school of Red Guards, the **rebels** (*zaofanpai*), began to form organizations and allowed those from non-proletarian families to join. In summer 1966, when the Cultural Revolution had just been launched, Old Red Guards were the major force in denouncing the "revisionist line in education" and in attacking teachers, school authorities, "**black gang**" members, and people of the "**five black categories**." They were the ones who first embraced the words "**to rebel is justified**" and made this lesser-known 1939 quotation of Mao *the* slogan of Red Guards. They were also the most enthusiastic in the **Destroy the Four Olds** campaign and considered themselves to be the heroes of the violent and bloody **Red August**.

However, when **Mao Zedong** moved to take on the old party establishment and attack **Liu Shaoqi** and **Deng Xiaoping** in the Criticize the **Bourgeois Reactionary Line** campaign in autumn 1966, Old Red Guards—especially children of the party officials under attack—became much less enthusiastic, while the newly emerging rebel faction began to take their place as Mao's crusading army. While continuing to assail alleged traditional class enemies mostly outside the party, some Old Red Guards began to denounce the radical **Central Cultural Revolution Small Group** (CCRSG) for hijacking Mao's Cultural Revolution program with its own agenda to overthrow old party officials. In December, a group of hardcore Old Red Guards formed a Capital Red Guard **United Action Committee** in Beijing and attempted to launch a campaign against the CCRSG's "new Bourgeois Reactionary Line." But this time, unlike what the central leadership had done in the early stage of the revolution, it did not support their rebellion; rather, the United Action Committee was named a "counterrevolutionary organization" by the authorities, and many of its members were arrested. Despite their attempt to reassert themselves as revolutionaries, Old Red Guards were never able to come back again as an effective political force.

OLD THREE CLASSES. (*Laosanjie.*) This term refers to both middle school and high school classes graduating in 1966, 1967, and 1968. Students of these three classes were a major force of the **Red Guard** and **rebel** movements during the early stages of the Cultural Revolution. In 1968 and 1969, most of these students were assigned work in the countryside, at the frontier, as well as in mines and factories, thus ending their turbulent revolutionary years.

See also EDUCATED YOUTHS; UP TO THE MOUNTAINS AND DOWN TO THE COUNTRYSIDE.

"ON FAMILY BACKGROUND". (*Chushenlun.*) A celebrated essay by **Yu Luoke** criticizing the **blood lineage theory**, "On Family Background" first appeared in 100 mimeographed copies pasted on wire poles along the streets of Beijing in December 1966. Yu denoted the "Family Background Study Group" as the author. Its revised version of about 15,000 words was published on 18 January 1967 in the ***Journal of Middle School Cultural Revolution***, a mass organization newspaper to which Yu Luoke was the main contributor and of which Yu Luowen, Luoke's younger brother, was a co-founder. About 90,000 copies of this issue and a later special edition were sold in Beijing within a short period of time, and more than a million copies were printed in various forms by other mass organizations nationwide. The editors received numerous letters of support from across China.

"On Family Background" argues for the "emphasis on performance" (*zhongzai biaoxian*), a phrase in the **Chinese Communist Party** (CCP) **class line** statement: Yu writes, "On the grounds of performance, all youths are equal." But the essence of Yu's argument is equality and human rights, especially equal political and education rights for millions of youths who had been discriminated against in Chinese society because of their non-proletarian family backgrounds. "We don't recognize any right that is not achieved through one's personal efforts," Yu writes. Although Yu's point of departure is a critique of the blood lineage theory crystallized in a notorious **Red Guard** couplet, "If the father is a hero, the son is a real man; if the father is a reactionary, the son is a bastard," the real target of his criticism is a government-sanctioned system of discrimination that underlies the CCP class policy. Under this system, "those from the families of the so-called '**seven black categories**'—the 'sons-of-dogs,' that is—have already become secondary targets of the proletarian dictatorship; they are born 'sinners' . . . and treated beneath human dignity." "How do they differ, then," Yu asks, "from those living in other caste systems like blacks in America, Sudras in India, and untouchables in Japan?" Yu denounces as "serious violations of human rights" such government-sanctioned actions as verbal and physical abuse, body searches, and illegal detention that Red Guards carried out to appear "super-Maoist." Yu is also the first to note that "a new privileged class has emerged" in China and that the blood lineage theory serves to protect the vested interests of this group. Yu's embrace of equality and human rights, and his use of these very terms—a taboo during the Cultural Revolution—makes the article "On Family Background" a "'declaration of human rights' in the east," as a contemporary reader called it, and a precursor of the post–Cultural Revolution democracy movement in China.

ONE-HUNDRED-DAY ARMED CONFLICT ON THE TSINGHUA CAMPUS. (*Qinghuayuan bairi da wudou.*) This armed confrontation between two rival **Red Guard** organizations on the campus of Tsinghua University lasted for about 100 days from late April to late July 1968. This prolonged military-style factional conflict was the bloodiest incident of its kind in Beijing, causing 18 deaths and more than 1,100 injuries. The incident triggered **Mao Zedong**'s decision to dissolve all Red Guard organizations and end the Red Guard movement altogether.

The origin of the factional conflict at Tsinghua can be traced to an event in April 1967 when several columns of Red Guards under the Jinggang Mountain Regiment, one of the most influential Red Guard organizations in the country, formed a "4-14 Revolutionary Networking Group" to distinguish themselves from the rest of the regiment on the basis of their dissenting views, especially regarding how former party officials should be treated. The 4-14 group considered it necessary and right to rehabilitate most cadres and include them in the yet-to-be-formed power organ, the **revolutionary committee**, at both a departmental and university level, whereas the leaders of the regiment, including **Kuai Dafu**, who was known as the "commander," believed that former party officials were basically not worthy of rehabilitation except those who had confessed their "crimes" and were willing to "turn their spears around and strike." The issue was pressing, though, since the Cultural Revolution had already entered a new phase marked by the establishment of the new power structure in many other places. Kuai, who viewed himself as the leader of the country's Red Guard movement, pushed hard for an agenda of establishing Tsinghua's revolutionary committee by the end of May, but he was unable to settle differences with his dissenters. On 29 May 1967, the 4-14 group formally broke with the Jinggang Mountain Regiment and established its own organization called the 4-14 Regiment, which made Kuai's goal impossible to accomplish.

In spring 1968, after a series of small-scale clashes between the two competing organizations at Tsinghua, including the kidnapping and the torturing of each other's members, Kuai Dafu gave orders to launch a full-scale offensive, perhaps hoping either to subdue his rivals or force the radical faction of the **Chinese Communist Party** (CCP) leadership, which had supported him and his organization before, to intervene in his favor. On 23 April, the Jinggang Mountain Red Guards began to attack a 4-14-occupied building on campus. About 50 people were injured in the first day of fighting. In the next few days, both sides occupied more buildings and turned them into fortifications, while each side tried to seize the other's territory. During the continuous battle, rocks, bricks, and spears were used as weapons, and then rifles, incendiary bottles, homemade bombs, hand grenades, and even homemade cannons. Casualties increased on both sides, including several deaths and hundreds of injuries. On 3 July 1968, the CCP Central Committee issued nationwide a public notice concerning the armed conflict in Guangxi Province, sending a clear signal to the country that armed fighting would no longer be tolerated. In Beijing, the municipal revolutionary committee made several attempts, in the name of publicizing and implementing the **July 3 Public Notice**, to end the conflict at Tsinghua: it urged both parties to stop fighting, but nothing was accomplished.

On 27 July, a **propaganda team** of more than 30,000 workers from 61 factories in Beijing led by **People's Liberation Army** officers of central leaders' guards regiment unit 8341 was sent to Tsinghua campus to stop the factional battle. When unarmed team members started to dismantle fortifications and remove roadblocks and barbed-wire entanglements, the 4-14 members gave in to the team's demand and disarmed themselves, whereas the Jinggang Mountain Regiment, following orders from Kuai Dafu, opened fire on the workers and also attacked them with rocks, spears, and hand grenades, leaving five team members dead and more than 700 injured. Under pressure from the Beijing Municipal Revolutionary Committee, which had conducted intense negotiations with Red Guard leaders at Tsinghua, members of the Jinggang Mountain Regiment eventually began to withdraw from the campus at 2:30 a.m. on 28 July. The hundred-day armed conflict on the Tsinghua campus was finally over.

At the moment when the Jinggang Mountain Red Guards started to withdraw, Mao was calling for an emergency meeting with the five most influential leaders of the Beijing Red Guards, including Kuai Dafu. The meeting lasted for five hours from 3:30 to 8:30 a.m. on 28 July. This meeting turned out to be the beginning of the end of the Red Guard movement that Mao had once so enthusiastically supported.

See also MAO ZEDONG: MEETING WITH THE FIVE RED GUARD LEADERS (28 July 1968).

ONE STRIKE AND THREE ANTIS. (*Yida sanfan.*) This was a nationwide movement guided by three central party documents: "Directive concerning the Strike against Destructive Counterrevolutionary Activities," issued on 31 January 1970, and "Directive concerning Anti-Graft and Embezzlement and Anti-Speculation and Profiteering" and "Notice on Anti-Extravagance and Waste," issued on 5 February 1970. While the effort of these "Three Antis" mainly focused on economic affairs, the "One Strike" supposedly aimed at those inside China who coordinated with a Soviet-U.S. conspiracy to invade China; such "destructive counterrevolutionary activities" were named a "noteworthy new direction of the current class struggle." Although neither the foreign conspiracy nor the domestic echo was substantiated, according to official assessment, 1.87 million people were persecuted as traitors, spies, and counterrevolutionaries, over 284,800 were arrested, and thousands were executed during the 10-month period from February to November 1970. Prominent among the persecuted "counterrevolutionaries" were those who openly criticized the Cultural Revolution. The best known cases include those of **Yu Luoke** and **Zhang Zhixin**: Yu, author of "**On Family Background**" criticizing the **blood lineage theory**, was executed on 5 March 1970; Zhang, a most outspoken and loyal Communist, was sentenced to life in prison on 20 August 1970. Later Zhang was sentenced to death and was executed.

OVERALL RECTIFICATION (1975). (*Quanmian zhengdun.*) A major effort led by **Deng Xiaoping** to counter the ultra-leftist policies of the Cultural Revolution with pragmatic ones, to energize the national economy, and to restore normality to the country, the nationwide rectification in all major economic and sociopolitical spheres began in February 1975. It was forced to end in November of the same year when Chairman **Mao Zedong**, concerned with the criticism of the Cultural Revolution implicit in Deng's tactics, proposed to the Central Committee (CC) of the **Chinese Communist Party** (CCP) that a **Counterattack the Right-Deviationist Reversal-of-Verdicts Trend** campaign be launched.

In January 1975, Deng was appointed to a number of key leadership positions including vice-chairman of the CC, a member of the Politburo Standing Committee, vice-chairman of the Central Military Commission (CMC), chief of general staff of the **People's Liberation Army** (PLA), and first vice-premier of the State Council. With strong support from Premier **Zhou Enlai**, who was hospitalized for cancer treatment, and with blessings from Mao, Deng was formally entrusted with power to preside over the daily affairs of the party leadership, the administration, and the military.

In late February, Deng began his overall rectification program by taking the first step in a railway transportation reform to make sure that both freight and passenger trains ran full, fast, and on time. Following Deng's instruction closely, Wan Li, minister of railways, was instrumental in overhauling the nation's inefficient transportation system and setting up a rectification model for other departments. In step with the railway transportation reform was the rectification in different areas of industry and later, and to a lesser extent, in agriculture.

In the summer, the rectification program was carried out further in various fields. On 14 July, at an enlarged session of the CMC, Deng called for reform and restructuring in the PLA to resolve five problems: overstaffing, disorganization, arrogance, extravagance, and indolence. Also in July, **Hu Yaobang** was sent to the Academy of Sciences to lead the rectification work there. Both Hu and Deng emphasized science and technology as leading forces in China's quest for modernization, and they both called for respect and reward for intellectual and professional work, which had been denied since the beginning of the Cultural Revolution. With Deng's support, **Zhou Rongxin**, minister of education, spoke out about the serious problems in education caused by the Cultural Revolution. In the sensitive area of culture, literature, and the arts, Deng used Mao's slogan "let a hundred flowers bloom" and pushed for the release of certain new and classic works that had been condemned by the **Jiang Qing** group. Finally, on the party organization and personnel front, the major tasks of the rectification included the enforcement of tough measures against the lingering factionalism (*paixing*) and the demotion or dismissal of incompetent officials who had enjoyed a meteoric rise on political capital during the Cultural Revolution. Largely due to the overall rectification program, China's economy succeeded in 1975: gross national output increased by 11.9 percent in 1975, compared to 1.4 percent in 1974. And with this program, Deng won broad support across the country.

Much resistance and opposition to Deng's program came from the ultra-leftist faction of the central leadership. In spring 1975, Jiang Qing, **Zhang Chunqiao**, and **Yao Wenyuan** insisted that empiricism was the main danger at present, referring to Zhou and Deng's pragmatic approach to economy. But Mao dismissed the idea and allowed the rectification to continue. However, Deng's aggressive measures made Mao question his stance concerning the Cultural Revolution. When **Mao Yuanxin**, Mao Zedong's nephew and Jiang Qing's close associate, became the Chairman's liaison at the Politburo in October 1975, the increasingly isolated Mao became more skeptical of Deng's rectification program. Knowing the discontent within the party leadership about the Cultural Revolution, Mao hoped that the Politburo members could reach a consensus, and he proposed that Deng be in charge of drafting a resolution concerning the Cultural Revolution. Mao wanted the overall appraisal to be "30 percent error and 70 percent achievement." Deng refused, citing his absence from much of the scene of revolution. At a Politburo meeting, Deng also refuted Mao Yuanxin's alleged words to Mao Zedong that a revisionist line had emerged in the central leadership of the party. In late November, Mao Zedong finally issued instructions that a campaign to fight the trend of the "right-deviationist reversal of verdicts" begin across the country. Deng Xiaoping thus became a representative of the right deviation, and his overall rectification came to a halt.

P

PAN FUSHENG (1908–1980). One of the few provincial party leaders who supported **rebels** in the early stages of the Cultural Revolution, Pan became head of the Heilongjiang Provincial **Revolutionary Committee** in 1967 and a member of the Central Committee (CC) at the **Ninth National Congress of the Chinese Communist Party** (CCP) in 1969 but was eventually dismissed from office for his involvement in factional violence and the persecution of his political rivals in Heilongjiang.

A native of Wendeng, Shandong Province, Pan joined the CCP in 1931. In the 1950s, Pan was labeled a **conservative** in a number of political campaigns, including the agricultural collectivization movement and the Anti-Rightist Campaign. Because of his sympathy for **Peng Dehuai**'s view on the disasters of the Great Leap Forward, Pan was branded a Right-opportunist and dismissed from office in the late 1950s. But he was exonerated and rehabilitated by the central leadership in 1963. When the Cultural Revolution began, Pan was first party secretary of Heilongjiang Province. After the **Eleventh Plenum of the Eighth CCP Central Committee**, which he attended as an alternate member of the CC, Pan supported rebel **Red Guards** in their attack on the Heilongjiang party committee. In January 1967, he and army leaders of the Heilongjiang Provincial Military District supported the rebels in their **power seizure** movement, and together, they established a temporary institution, which was regarded by **Mao Zedong** as a model of the "three-in-one presence of cadre, military, and masses" in a new power structure. In March 1967, Pan was named head of the Heilongjiang Provincial Revolutionary Committee. He was granted full membership of the CC at the **Twelfth Plenum of the Eighth CCP Central Committee** (13–31 October 1968).

Shortly after the establishment of the provincial revolutionary committee, however, mass organizations in Heilongjiang were divided into two factions, and one faction opposed Pan and attempted to bring him down from power. Pan, then, became involved in factional violence, supporting those loyal to him against his opponents in massive armed confrontations. He imprisoned a number of party officials and ordinary citizens of the rival camp. He also had serious conflicts with local army leaders. So great was his involvement in factional conflicts that, in June 1971, the central leadership in Beijing decided to remove him from power and subject him to an investigation. In 1980, Pan died of illness. In 1982, the CC issued a document criticizing Pan Fusheng for the serious mistakes he made during the Cultural Revolution.

PEAK THEORY. (*Dingfenglun.*) This term was a reference to the much publicized assertion of **Lin Biao** that **Mao Zedong Thought** was the peak of Marxism-Leninism.

See also CONTINUING REVOLUTION UNDER THE DICTATORSHIP OF THE PROLETARIAT; LIN BIAO: MAY 18 SPEECH (1966); PERSONALITY CULT.

PEKING UNIVERSITY AND TSINGHUA UNIVERSITY GREAT CRITICISM GROUP. Formed in March 1974, the Peking University and Tsinghua University Great Criticism Group was a writing team in the service of the Cultural Revolution faction of the central leadership. The team was controlled by **Chi Qun** and **Xie Jingyi**, who were sent by **Mao Zedong** to Tsinghua University as members of the **army propaganda team** and the **workers propaganda team** in 1968 and later became party secretary and deputy party secretary of Tsinghua University. By the time the writing team was organized, Chi and Xie were already known as the "two soldiers" of Mao and had become such close associates of **Jiang Qing** that Jiang was able to direct every move of the writing team through Chi and Xie.

Along with the **Shanghai Municipal Party Committee Writing Group**, its counterpart in China's most populous city, the writing team of Peking University and Tsinghua University produced many articles to promote the interests of the Jiang Qing group and to attack—mostly by innuendo and by allusion—the leaders of the moderate faction, especially **Zhou Enlai** and **Deng Xiaoping**. Published mostly in top official organs such as *People's Daily* and *Red Flag* under the pen name **Liang Xiao** and reprinted immediately by many provincial and local newspapers across China, these articles were often viewed as indicating the new moves of the **Chinese Communist Party** central leadership. The team was disbanded soon after the downfall of the **Gang of Four**.

See also ALLUSORY HISTORIOGRAPHY; CONFUCIANISM VERSUS LEGALISM; CRITICIZE LIN AND CRITICIZE CONFUCIUS.

PEKING UNIVERSITY CULTURAL REVOLUTION BULLETIN NO. 9. This was a brief report by the Peking University **work group** on an eruption of violence and brutality on the university campus on the morning of 18 June

1966. On 20 June, the **Chinese Communist Party** (CCP) Central Committee (CC) distributed the bulletin to party organizations at all levels nationwide in the hopes of preventing similar violence elsewhere.

As **Mao Zedong**'s radical policies of **class struggle** on a massive scale were being articulated and advocated in such militant pieces as the *People's Daily* editorial "**Sweep Away All Cow-Demons and Snake-Spirits**" (1 June 1966), several hundred Peking University students deliberately ignored the authority of the work group and held physically abusive **struggle meetings** against more than 40 so-called **black gang** members (officials associated with the Beijing party committee under **Peng Zhen**), "bourgeois academic authorities" (professors), and "reactionary students." According to the bulletin report, some "bad people," including students, workers, and a number of people off campus, conspired in tormenting people on a "platform for fighting demons," and similar incidents happened across campus in which the so-called class enemies were smeared in the face with black ink and paraded through the streets wearing tall paper hats; some female "targets of struggle" were sexually harassed. The Peking University work group called this incident one of "disordered struggle" and was highly critical of it in its bulletin report. President **Liu Shaoqi**, who was in charge of the daily affairs of the CC at the time during Mao's absence, concurred with the work group's view upon reading the report and decided to distribute the report and a brief supporting comment together in the form of a CC circular.

In early August, however, Mao commented harshly on the bulletin and on Liu's view of it and labeled Liu's move as repression and bourgeois dictatorship. Following Mao's instructions, the CC issued a notice on 9 August 1966 to withdraw the 20 June circular. This conflict between Mao and Liu concerning the Peking University incident anticipated the movement against the **Bourgeois Reactionary Line**, which would lead to the downfall of Liu Shaoqi.

PENG DEHUAI (1898–1974). An outspoken senior leader of the **Chinese Communist Party** (CCP) and the **People's Liberation Army** (PLA), Peng was dismissed from office in 1959 for his criticism of **Mao Zedong**'s radical Great Leap Forward policies. To launch and justify the Cultural Revolution, Mao brought up the Peng Dehuai case again in late 1965 in connection with **Wu Han**'s historical play *Hai Rui Dismissed from Office*.

A native of Xiangtan, Hunan Province, Peng was a veteran of the Northern Expedition. He joined the CCP in 1928. In the same year, he led the Pingjiang Uprising and became one of the founders of the Red Army. He served as commander of the Fifth Corps of the Red Army in the 1930s, deputy commander of the Eighth Route Army in the Sino-Japanese War, and deputy commander of the PLA during the civil war of the second half of the 1940s. In 1950, after some initial reluctance, Peng accepted the appointment as commander of the Chinese army during the Korean War. A strong advocate for building a professional army, Peng was made China's first minister of defense in 1954 and one of 10 marshals in 1955—he ranked second next to Marshal Zhu De. As a senior party and government leader, Peng was a member of the Politburo from 1935 and a vice-premier from 1954.

On 14 July 1959, at the CCP Central Committee's Lushan Conference, Peng wrote Mao a candid personal letter to call his attention to the serious problems in the CCP's Great Leap Forward and People's Commune policies. Mao considered the letter to be an offense against the CCP leadership and passed it to those attending the conference as a target for criticism. On 16 August, the Central Committee (CC) passed a resolution denouncing Peng and a few other officials as a "Right-opportunist anti-party clique." Peng was soon dismissed as minister of defense and moved out of Zhongnanhai. In 1962, after the disaster caused by the Great Leap policies became clear—with 20 to 30 million peasants having died of famine—President **Liu Shaoqi** suggested that the verdict on Marshal Peng Dehuai be reconsidered, but the suggestion was dismissed by Mao. Peng wrote Mao another letter, of 80,000 words, to clarify himself, only to find himself in a more difficult situation: he was stripped of all official titles, and a special case committee was formed to investigate him further.

In September 1965, however, Mao made a surprise decision to send Peng to Sichuan Province as deputy director of the "third front" construction project as part of war preparations. But just before his departure from Beijing, **Yao Wenyuan**'s article "On the Historical Drama *Hai Rui Dismissed from Office*" was published in Shanghai with Mao's approval. The article, with implicit references to the Peng case, was to become known as the "blasting fuse" of the Cultural Revolution. On 21 December 1965, soon after Peng's arrival in Sichuan, Mao made a devastating remark concerning Peng. Yao Wenyuan's article was good, Mao said, but it did not quite hit the vital part: "The vital point is dismissal. Emperor Jiajing dismissed Hai Rui. We, in 1959, dismissed Peng Dehuai. Peng Dehuai is also Hai Rui."

As soon as the Cultural Revolution broke out, the **Central Cultural Revolution Small Group** began to seek a way to get Peng back to Beijing as a target of public criticism. Following **Jiang Qing** and **Qi Benyu**'s instructions, two Red Guard organizations—the Red Flag Combat Team of the Beijing Institute of Aeronautics and the East-Is-Red Commune of the Beijing Institute of Geology—sent their members to Sichuan to kidnap Peng. They brought Peng back to Beijing on 28 December 1966. Peng lost his freedom, but the Beijing Garrison Command acted upon instructions from Premier **Zhou Enlai** and put Peng in confinement, which sheltered him temporarily from the Red Guards' abuse.

In July 1967, however, **Kang Sheng**, **Chen Boda**, and Qi Benyu called upon the Peng special case investigation group and college **rebels** to get Peng out of the Garrison Command and **struggle against** him at mass rallies. Several **struggle meetings**, then, were held by **Red Guards**, at which Peng was so brutally beaten by the crowd that, with ribs broken, he had to be carried back to the Garrison quarters after these meetings. Peng was also placed on a truck, bareheaded and with a heavy placard hanging from his neck, and paraded through the streets of Beijing. Struggle meetings against Peng were held much more frequently in August and September by various schools and work units—more than 100 times within the two-month period.

In the meantime, major CCP organs *People's Daily*, *Red Flag*, and *Liberation Army Daily* carried five editorials in July and August 1967 denouncing Peng as the military representative of the **biggest capitalist-roader within the party** and turning him into a main target of the CCP firepower. On 17 September 1970, **Huang Yongsheng**, chief of the general staff of the PLA and **Lin Biao**'s close associate, approved a report by the Peng special case group that charged Peng with the crimes of opposing the party and having illicit relations with foreign powers and called for his expulsion from the CCP and a sentence of life imprisonment. In April 1974, Peng was diagnosed with advanced colon cancer. On 29 November 1974, he died in a small, heavily guarded, jail-like ward with newspaper-covered windows. His body was secretly transported to Sichuan and cremated under the false name Wang Chuan.

The Eleventh CC of the CCP rehabilitated Marshal Peng Dehuai at its third plenum in December 1978 and held a memorial service for him on 24 December 1978.

PENG PEIYUN (1929–). Deputy party secretary of Peking University and one of the three people under attack in what **Mao Zedong** called the **first Marxist-Leninist big-character poster** by **Nie Yuanzi** and her colleagues, Peng was an early victim of the Cultural Revolution. Born in Liuyang, Hunan Province, Peng was one of the many left-leaning students drawn to the **Chinese Communist Party** (CCP) during the war of resistance against Japan and the civil war that followed. Peng joined the CCP in 1946 while she was a student at Southwest Union University carrying out underground activities on college campuses against the Kuomintang government. After 1949, she held office related to higher education at both Tsinghua University and the CCP Beijing Municipal Committee. In 1964, during the **Socialist Education Movement**, when Peking University's president, **Lu Ping**, and his school party committee were under attack by the socialist education work team and by a number of philosophy department faculty including Nie Yuanzi, the CCP Beijing Municipal Committee led by **Peng Zhen** stepped in to support

Lu Ping and to put down Nie and her colleagues. To reinforce Lu's power, the municipal committee appointed Peng Peiyun deputy party secretary of Peking University as Lu's main assistant.

Largely because of Peng Peiyun's involvement in this political conflict on the campus of Peking University, Nie and her six colleagues made her one of the targets of criticism in the big-character poster "What Are **Song Shuo**, Lu Ping, and Peng Peiyun Really Doing in the Cultural Revolution?" which was posted on 25 May 1966. This poster accuses Peng, Song, and Lu of conspiring with the Beijing Municipal Committee to suppress the revolutionary masses and mislead the ongoing Cultural Revolution. On 2 June 1966, a *People's Daily* commentary further accuses her of being a member of the **Three-Family Village Anti-Party Clique**. On 3 June, the newly organized CCP Beijing Municipal Committee announced a decision to remove Peng Peiyun from office. Peng, then, became a main target of endless **struggle meetings**. She was also forced to do manual labor to reform herself.

Peng was reassigned work at Peking University in 1975. After the Cultural Revolution, she was rehabilitated and assumed various important positions in education institutions and agencies, including deputy minister of education in 1982. As a prominent female politician in her later years, Peng became a member of the CCP's Fourteenth and Fifteenth Central Committee and was elected vice-chairman of the Ninth National People's Congress.

PENG ZHEN (1902–1997). Mayor and first party secretary of Beijing, a member of the Politburo, and head of the **Five-Person Cultural Revolution Small Group**, Peng was among the first few ranking leaders of the **Chinese Communist Party** (CCP) to fall at the beginning of the Cultural Revolution. He was criticized for misleading the Cultural Revolution (in its developing early stage) with a revisionist **February Outline**. **Mao Zedong** particularly accused him of turning Beijing municipal government into an "impenetrable and watertight independent kingdom" and attempting to keep out the Cultural Revolution in the city he ruled.

A native of Quwo, Shanxi Province, Peng joined the CCP in 1923 and soon became a CCP underground leader in north China. In 1929, Peng was arrested in Tianjin by the Nationalist government. After his release in 1935, Peng was appointed party secretary of Tianjin and director of the CCP North China Bureau's organization department, working under **Liu Shaoqi**, the head of the bureau. He was one of the first CCP leaders to call for the "sinicizing" of Marxism. In the 1940s, Peng was assigned positions in the central leadership in Yan'an. He was named director of the CCP Department of City Work in 1944 and head of the CCP Department of Organization in 1945. He became a member of the Politburo in 1945. After the Communists took over Beijing, Peng led the municipal government of the nation's capital as both first party secretary (1948–1966) and mayor (1951–1966).

In July 1964, a Five-Person Group (to be known later as the Five-Person Cultural Revolution Small Group) was established at Mao Zedong's suggestion to lead a rectification movement in art and literature circles. As a ranking leader with a certain theoretical edge, Peng was named head of the group. But due to Peng's resistance to the emerging ultra-leftist forces in cultural circles, they, especially **Jiang Qing**, had to plan what would come to be known as the "blasting fuse" of the Cultural Revolution outside Beijing.

After much planning and work by Jiang Qing, **Zhang Chunqiao**, and **Yao Wenyuan**, *Wenhui Daily*, a Shanghai newspaper, finally published Yao Wenyuan's article "On the New Historical Drama *Hai Rui Dismissed from Office*" on 10 November 1965 with Mao's approval. **Wu Han**, the author of the historical play, was a renowned historian and also a deputy mayor of Beijing with whom Peng Zhen sympathized. Peng also did not approve of Yao's politicizing what he believed to be an academic issue. Without knowing Mao's support for Yao, Peng ordered Beijing's newspapers not to reprint Yao's article and did not change his mind until 29 November after **Zhou Enlai**'s intervention. In February 1966, as the criticism of Wu Han and a few other "academic authorities" continued, the Five-Person Group produced a policy guide to keep the criticism of Wu and others from getting too political. This document, soon to be known as the February Outline, was disseminated nationwide. Peng's action was perceived by Mao as a direct challenge to his developing Cultural Revolution program. In late March, Mao criticized the February Outline, the Beijing party committee, and the Five-Person Group on several occasions.

This led directly to Peng's downfall; even his effort to conduct a campaign in the municipal media against **Deng Tuo**, culture and education secretary of the Beijing party committee and a victim of the Cultural Revolution at its preparation stage, could not save him. From 16 to 26 April, Mao chaired an enlarged meeting of the Standing Committee of the Politburo in Shanghai. At the meeting, Peng was charged with anti-party crimes, and decisions were made to abrogate the February Outline and replace the Five-Person Group with a new group, which would soon be named the **Central Cultural Revolution Small Group**. On 1 May, Peng Zhen made no public appearance at the International Labor Day celebration. He was denounced as a member of the **Peng-Luo-Lu-Yang Anti-Party Clique** and was removed from all his positions at the **enlarged Politburo sessions, 4–26 May 1966**. Soon Peng lost his freedom. During the high tide of the Cultural Revolution in late 1966 and 1967, Peng was forced to attend **struggle meetings** and was subjected to much humiliation and physical abuse at the hands of **Red Guards**.

In February 1979, the post-Mao CCP central leadership rehabilitated Peng Zhen. In June of the same year, he was added to the Standing Committee of the Fifth National People's Congress as a vice-chairman, and in September he became a member of the Politburo. In 1983, he was elected chairman of the Standing Committee of the Sixth National People's Congress. Peng died on 26 April 1997.

PENG-LUO-LU-YANG ANTI-PARTY CLIQUE. This was the charge brought against **Peng Zhen, Luo Ruiqing, Lu Dingyi,** and **Yang Shangkun** at the **enlarged Politburo sessions, 4–26 May 1966.** The denunciation of the four ranking party leaders was celebrated at the time as the first major victory of **Mao Zedong**'s proletarian revolutionary line over a bourgeois revisionist one in the course of the Cultural Revolution.

There was, however, no evidence of the four conspiring against the **Chinese Communist Party** (CCP). Peng Zhen, mayor of Beijing and director of the **Five-Person Cultural Revolution Small Group**, was denounced because of his resistance to the campaign against **Wu Han** in late 1965 and because of his involvement in the making of the 1966 **February Outline** that defined the campaign as an "academic discussion." His apparent reservations about what would soon be known as the "blasting fuse" of the Cultural Revolution prompted Mao's remark that the Beijing party committee led by Peng was an "impenetrable and watertight independent kingdom." At an enlarged meeting of the Politburo Standing Committee held in Shanghai in April 1966, Peng was suspended from his duties as mayor of Beijing. At the Politburo's May meeting, the February Outline was delegitimized, the Five-Person Cultural Revolution Small Group dismissed, and Peng branded as the leader of the Peng-Luo-Lu-Yang Anti-Party Clique.

The downfall of General Luo Ruiqing, chief of general staff of the **People's Liberation Army** (PLA), had mainly to do with power conflicts and political differences between Luo and Marshal **Lin Biao**, minister of defense. Due to Lin's poor health, Luo conducted many PLA affairs independent of Lin. In 1964, with the authorization of Mao and the Central Military Commission, Luo led an army-wide "*dabiwu*," a mass exercise-competition that focused on combat skills. Lin made Mao believe that this exercise was meant to counter Lin's principle of "politics in command" and challenge Mao's ideological line. Luo was also known for contradicting Lin's "**peak theory**" that claimed **Mao Zedong Thought** to be "the highest and the most flexible Marxism-Leninism." Luo's view of the "peak theory," in itself a negation of Mao Zedong Thought, was interpreted in a party document as evidence of Luo's extreme hostility to Mao Zedong Thought. Luo was already dismissed from office and criticized at two high-level party meetings before he was named as part of the Peng-Luo-Lu-Yang Clique in May 1966.

Lu Dingyi, head of the Propaganda Department of the CCP Central Committee (CC), showed little interest in the Lin Biao–style promotion of political and ideological work and opposed "simplifying, vulgarizing, and making pragmatic" Mao Zedong Thought. He was also resistant to the first wave of political criticism in academic fields beginning in late 1965. He did not consent to the publication of some militant articles. Mao was critical. He called the propaganda department the "palace of the King of Hell" (*yanwang-dian*), and Lu was condemned by analogy as the King himself. Lu was also suspected of conspiring with his wife, Yan Weibing, against Lin Biao and his wife, **Ye Qun**, since Yan had been sending letters under pseudonyms to the CC exposing Ye mostly on personal matters and character issues. Yan was arrested in April 1966. Lu Dingyi was condemned as a member of the Peng-Luo-Lu-Yang Clique a month later.

Yang Shangkun was dismissed as director of the General Office of the CC in November 1965 on a charge of breaching security protocols in such activities as taping Mao's conversations.

There was no evidence that these ranking leaders were against the party. Their "cases" were not related to one another, either. But, with Mao's support, **Kang Sheng**, **Zhang Chunqiao**, and **Chen Boda** delivered tone-setting speeches at the Politburo's enlarged meeting in May 1966 incriminating the four, while the **Lin Biao May 18 speech** (also known as the "scripture of coup d'état") targeted the four as a group conspiring to stage a coup and to restore capitalism. The Peng-Luo-Lu-Yang case was used as evidence to support Mao's view that there was a bourgeois revisionist line within the party represented by **capitalist-roaders**; therefore, a cultural revolution was necessary. The dismissal of Peng, Luo, Lu, Yang, and the Peng-led Five-Person Cultural Revolution Small Group prepared the way for the rapid ascent of Lin Biao to the second highest leadership position and of Kang Sheng, **Jiang Qing**, Chen Boda, and Zhang Chunqiao as part of the newly formed powerful **Central Cultural Revolution Small Group**.

PEOPLE'S LIBERATION ARMY (PLA) DURING THE CULTURAL REVOLUTION. As **Mao Zedong**'s famous aphorism states, "Power grows from the barrel of a gun." The People's Liberation Army (PLA) has always been the army of the **Chinese Communist Party** (CCP) since its formation in 1927 (initially as the Red Army, 1927–1936; then the Eighth Route Army and the New Fourth Army during the Sino-Japanese War, 1937–1945; and finally the People's Liberation Army as of 1945). Since the founding of the People's Republic of China (PRC) upon the PLA's victory over Nationalist forces, the mandates of the PLA have not merely been to safeguard national security but also to maintain domestic order and, most important, to keep the CCP in power. In the 1960s and 1970s, it was a chief instrument that Mao, in the capacity of chairman of both the CCP and the Central Military Commission (CMC), used in preparing, launching, and further developing the Cultural Revolution. Nevertheless, the role the PLA played during this period of political upheaval was fairly complex.

In the first half of the 1960s, the PLA came to Mao's assistance in laying the groundwork for the Cultural Revolution. Shortly after the 1959 Lushan Plenum of the CCP Central Committee (CC) at which **Lin Biao** replaced **Peng Dehuai** as minister of defense, the PLA started to advocate the study of Mao's sayings as a shortcut to studying Marxism and initiated the biggest wave of Mao cult that would eventually establish Mao's position as the nation's supreme spiritual leader. In 1961, the PLA organ *Liberation Army Daily* began to carry a Mao quotation on the front page of every issue, and these quotations were reissued in 1964 in a collection that would become the **little red book** everyone waved during the Cultural Revolution. Following Lin Biao's instructions, the PLA emphasized indoctrination and thought control under the slogan "Put politics in command" and became a "great school" for producing "socialist new men" and a model for civilian institutions and organizations. The 1964 nationwide campaign to "learn from the PLA" effectively institutionalized the PLA political system in many civilian units and militarized civilian populations in the sense that civilians were ready to be mobilized as soldiers for political battles. And they were, indeed, at Mao's command in the early stages of the Cultural Revolution, and the leading forces among them, the student **Red Guards**, called themselves Mao's loyal soldiers or guards. In late 1965, General **Luo Ruiqing**, chief of general staff of the PLA and Lin Biao's rival in the armed forces, was among the first ranking officials to fall, and the purge of the so-called **Peng-Luo-Lu-Yang Anti-Party Clique** marked Mao's first major victory in launching the Cultural Revolution. On the very eve of the Cultural Revolution, it was also with the PLA as his first audience that Mao issued his utopian blueprint for the future of Chinese society known as the **May 7 Directive**.

At the **Eleventh Plenum of the Eighth CCP Central Committee** in August 1966, army chief Lin Biao, who had engineered the Mao cult and paved the way for the total hegemony of Maoism in the nation, was promoted to the second highest position in the CCP leadership. From this point on, Lin became "Chairman Mao's closest comrade-in-arms." Mao and Lin together were often referred to as the supreme commander-in-chief and the deputy commander-in-chief. They wore PLA uniforms—the rest of the central leadership followed suit almost invariably—as they inspected Red Guards from all over the country, and retired PLA uniforms also became the Red Guards' favorite attire. The Mao-Lin alliance continued as they attacked and purged not only central party leaders but also top-ranking officials of different factions in the PLA, including Marshals **He Long**, **Chen Yi**, **Xu Xiangqian**, and **Ye Jianying**. When these marshals lost their positions and influence in the CMC during the campaign against the so-called **February Adverse Current** (1967), Lin Biao, with Mao's approval, filled the vacancies with his own close associates in the PLA.

Although the two fronts of the Cultural Revolution—civilian and military—initially developed separately, the PLA, under the leadership of its ultra-leftist leaders Mao and Lin, soon became deeply involved in civilian affairs in the name of "supporting the left." When chaos became widespread with increasingly heated battles among different factions of mass organizations in early 1967 following Shanghai's **January Storm**, the PLA appeared to be the only functioning organization left, and Mao resorted to the PLA for restoring minimum public order. However, since Mao did not indicate which mass faction or factions the PLA should support in each province, his vague order became a cause for robust conflicts between the PLA's provincial district forces and field armies. Having been close to local party apparatuses, the district or regional forces tended to support **conservative** factions that typically sided with local authorities. But, since field armies received commands from the CCP Central Committee via the CMC, they generally supported **rebel** factions. As a result, widespread **armed conflicts** occurred in all parts of China because these two distinct parts of the military provided weapons and ammunitions to dueling mass factions in their bloody **power seizure** battles against each other. In a number of cases, PLA troops committed massacres by directly organizing, or getting directly involved in, the killings of members of the mass faction they opposed, as in the case of the **February 23 Incident** in Qinghai (1967) and the long-drawn armed conflict in Guangxi under **Wei Guoqing** (1967–1968).

During this period of factional battles, the PLA committed about two million troops to civilian political activities (and reportedly suffered hundreds of thousands of casualties). Military officers emerged from the chaos with greatly increased position and power, and many senior army officers headed newly formed **revolutionary committees** in charge of local government in all parts of China. At the **Ninth National Congress** of the CCP in 1969, almost one-half of the CC members elected were military officers. In 1971, about 50 percent of State Council (SC) members (including heads of military control groups at various ministries and other SC agencies) were PLA personnel.

In 1970, especially at the **Second Plenum of the Ninth CCP Central Committee** (23 August–6 September), the conflict between the predominantly military faction of the central leadership led by Lin Biao and the civilian ultra-leftists of the **Central Cultural Revolution Small Group** (CCRSG) led by **Jiang Qing** surfaced. Siding with the Jiang group, Mao reproached Lin's generals and also insinuated his displeasure with his handpicked successor himself: "Can the founder of the army also command it?" Mao asked rhetorically (in response to the popular saying of the day, "The PLA is a great army founded and led by Chairman Mao and commanded by Vice-Chairman Lin"). Shortly after Lin's death in a plane crash known as the **September 13 Incident** (1971), the military began to disengage from politics, and many PLA officers were reassigned from their provincial-level revolutionary committee posts in 1973–1974. Meanwhile, at Mao's suggestion, a policy of **rotating military region commanders** and troop units was implemented to prevent the PLA from military factionalism. After Lin Biao's downfall, generals of the Lin faction were dismissed from office, while ranking members of other factions that had been denounced and purged earlier were rehabilitated and returned to power. Ye Jianying, for instance, was reinstated as vice-chairman of the CMC in charge of daily affairs of the CMC, and **Deng Xiaoping** was appointed chief of general staff of the PLA in 1974.

In the last years of the Cultural Revolution, the PLA, though still Mao's gun as well as the party's, maintained more and more distance from Mao's ultra-leftist politics and radical policies. After Mao's death on 9 September 1976, the PLA aligned with the moderate faction of the CCP leadership, and Marshal Ye Jianying and security chief **Wang Dongxing** assisted **Hua Guofeng** in playing a crucial role in the arrest of die-hard Maoists the **Gang of Four** on 6 October, marking the end of the Cultural Revolution.

See also ALL FORCES CULTURAL REVOLUTION SMALL GROUP; ARMED CONFLICT; ARMED CONFLICT IN GUANGXI (1967–1968); ARMY PROPAGANDA TEAM; CENTRAL MILITARY COMMISSION ADMINISTRATIVE CONFERENCE OFFICE; CENTRAL MILITARY COMMISSION ADMINISTRATIVE GROUP; CHEN ZAIDAO (1909–1993); CHI QUN (1932–2001); CULTURAL REVOLUTION COMMITTEE; FEBRUARY ADVERSE CURRENT (1967); FEBRUARY SUPPRESSION OF COUNTERREVOLUTIONARIES (1967); FEBRUARY 23 INCIDENT (1967); QINGTONGXIA INCIDENT (28 August 1967); *QUOTATIONS FROM CHAIRMAN MAO*; ROTATION OF MILITARY REGION COMMANDERS (December 1973); SEPTEMBER 13 INCIDENT (1971); SIX FACTORIES AND TWO UNIVERSITIES; SUMMARY OF THE SYMPOSIUM CONVENED BY COMRADE JIANG QING AT THE BEHEST OF COMRADE LIN BIAO ON THE WORK OF LITERATURE AND THE ARTS IN THE ARMED FORCES; TWO NEWSPAPERS AND ONE JOURNAL; WEI GUOQING (1913–1989); YANG-YU-FU AFFAIR (1968).

PERSONALITY CULT. Promoted by **Lin Biao** with Mao's acquiescence, a personality cult of Chairman **Mao Zedong** became widespread in the early years of the Cultural Revolution. On the eve of the Cultural Revolution, Lin spoke of Mao as such a rare genius that it took the world hundreds of years, and China thousands of years, to produce one, and that every sentence he spoke was truth and worth 10,000 sentences in an ordinary discourse. **Mao Zedong Thought**, in Lin's view, was the peak of Marxism-Leninism. Lin's praise of Mao became all the more influential after he was elevated to the second highest position in the **Chinese Communist Party** leadership as "Chairman Mao's dearest comrade-in-arm[s]."

The Mao cult during the Cultural Revolution bore much resemblance to the imperial worship of the past: the Chinese prayer "*wansui*" (literally, "May someone live ten thousand years") that used to be reserved for emperors was now the most popular prayer for Mao, and the masses hailed Mao as the "great savior of the Chinese people" and the "reddest sun in our heart." Mao's statues were erected in public squares all over China, Mao's portraits were enshrined in private homes, and Mao's quotations were written on walls everywhere, often in gold against a red background. Such religious rituals as the "**morning request, evening report**" and the **daily reading** [of Mao's works] were widely practiced. Many quotations of Mao were set to music and chanted at public meetings. In summer and autumn 1966, tens of millions of **Red Guards** went on a pilgrimage to see the supreme leader in Beijing, and Mao granted their wishes by holding eight **inspections of Red Guard troops** between August and November 1966. In 1970, Mao himself began to voice reservations about the cult of personality. But, at the same time, he defended the practice as a strategy necessary in his battle against President **Liu Shaoqi** and the party establishment. The fervor of the Mao cult gradually receded after the downfall of Lin Biao in 1971.

See also BADGES OF CHAIRMAN MAO; FOUR GREATS; LIN BIAO: MAY 18 SPEECH (1966); LOYALTY DANCE; *QUOTATIONS FROM CHAIRMAN MAO*; THREE LOYALTIES AND FOUR LIMITLESS-NESSES.

PING-PONG DIPLOMACY (1971). The decision **Mao Zedong** made upon careful deliberation to invite the United States ping-pong team to visit China was the major diplomatic move of the People's Republic of China (PRC) toward normalizing **United States–China relations**. In late March and early April 1971, the 31st Table Tennis World Championship Game was held in Nagoya, Japan—the first international sports event in which a Chinese team participated since the beginning of the Cultural Revolution. Considering the game to be an occasion for promoting China's relations with the outside world and thinking of the strategy of "people diplomacy" that he had been exercising in China's contact with Japan, Premier **Zhou Enlai** set up a principle called "friendship first, competition second" for the Chinese ping-pong team. On 11 March, at a meeting with officials from the Ministry of Foreign Affairs and the National Sports Commission, Zhou anticipated the Chinese team's contact with the U.S. team and contemplated the possibility of mutual visits. "If the U.S. team is progressive," Zhou said, "we may invite them to come here and compete. If we can compete with the U.S. team, then the non-contact no longer makes sense."

During the game, the Chinese ping-pong team invited teams from a number of countries to visit China after the competition but had to report to Beijing and request instructions when the U.S. team expressed its wish to receive such an invitation. On 3 April, a decision was made in Beijing by the National Sports Commission and the Ministry of Foreign Affairs not to invite the U.S. team, and the draft of the decision was presented to Zhou Enlai for approval. Zhou wrote, "Considering approval," but also penned in the margin, "(You) may take their address but should indicate clearly to their principal representative that the Chinese people are opposed to the conspiracy of 'two Chinas' or 'one China and one Taiwan.'" On 5 April, Mao approved the decision. On 6 April, an internal Chinese publication carried reports of foreign news agencies about the friendship between Chinese and American ping-pong players. Late in the evening, Zhou informed Mao that in mid-March, the U.S. government lifted all restrictions on travel to the PRC and that there were differing views at the National Sports Commission and the Ministry of Foreign Affairs on whether to invite the U.S. ping-pong team. On the early morning of 7 April, Mao reversed the earlier decision and decided to issue an invitation to the U.S. delegation right away.

The U.S. ping-pong team's eight-day visit started on 10 April. Zhou Enlai gave much personal attention to the delegation's itinerary. He received all of its members in the Great Hall of the People and gave a warm speech on 14 April. With his authorization, the Forbidden City, which had been closed since the beginning of the Cultural Revolution, was open for visitors on 14 April. Also on 14 April, the Richard Nixon administration lifted trade sanctions against China. The visit of the U.S. ping-pong team, the first U.S. delegation to come to China since the founding of the PRC in 1949, marked the beginning of the end of decades of hostility between the two countries.

PIONEERS. (*Chuangye.*) Based on a script by Zhang Tianmin and produced by Changchun Film Studio in early 1975, this film celebrates the hard work and self-reliance of Chinese workers in their effort to tap the nation's oil resources. The protagonist Zhou Tingshan is modeled on Wang Jinxi, the best-known hero in China's oil industry. Because of its attention to work and production—more than just words and revolutionary rhetoric characteristic of the literary and artistic models of the time—the film was perceived as a challenge to the Cultural Revolution faction of the central leadership. **Jiang Qing** placed the film under restrictions soon after its official release on the day of the Spring Festival (11 February) in 1975, which coincided with the beginning of the **overall rectification** movement set in motion by **Deng Xiaoping**. She and her supporters at the Ministry of Culture listed 10 counts of the film's "serious political and artistic problems" and held a struggle session against Zhang Tianmin. Refusing to accept Jiang's judgment as final, Zhang wrote **Mao Zedong** on 18 July 1975, asking for a reevaluation. Via

Deng, Zhang's letter reached Mao. In a brief comment he wrote on 25 July, Mao defends the film as "having no great errors." The re-release of the film that immediately followed Mao's recommendation was celebrated nation-wide. *Pioneers* became one of the few genuinely popular films produced during the Cultural Revolution.

POISONOUS WEED. (*Ducao.*) This is the label for any writing or art deemed anti-party, anti-socialist, and non-proletarian. During the Cultural Revolution, almost all artistic and scholarly works of the past, Chinese or foreign, were dismissed as "poisonous weeds." Numerous campaigns, large and small, were launched to criticize these works. It was an important part of **Mao Zedong**'s Cultural Revolution program to involve the masses in such campaigns so that they might become sensitive to anything that might have deviated from Mao's radical ideology.

POLITBURO SESSIONS, 4–7 APRIL 1976. The Politburo held emergen-cy sessions daily between 4 April and 7 April in the face of a sudden explo-sion of public rage against the ultra-leftist faction of the party led by **Jiang Qing**—a spontaneous mass demonstration that took the form of public mourning during the traditional Qingming Festival season in Beijing's Tia-nanmen Square in memory of the late Premier **Zhou Enlai**. **Hua Guofeng** chaired these sessions, while **Mao Zedong**, sick and bedridden, controlled the sessions by communicating his instructions to the Politburo via his liai-son, **Mao Yuanxin**. A number of Politburo members, including **Deng Xiaoping**, **Ye Jianying**, **Li Xiannian**, and Su Zhenhua, were absent from some of the sessions. Deng attended the 5 April session but remained silent while **Zhang Chunqiao** was attacking him as China's Imre Nagy (leader of Hungary's democracy movement of 1956). At the session on 7 April, the Politburo passed two resolutions proposed by Mao Zedong: that Deng be dismissed from office in both the party and the government, although he could keep his party membership, and that Hua Guofeng be appointed first vice-chairman of the Central Committee of the **Chinese Communist Party** and premier of the State Council. In the resolution dismissing Deng, the protest movement at Tiananmen Square was labeled a "counterrevolutionary incident."

POOR PEASANTS MANAGEMENT COMMITTEE. (*Pinguanhui.*) This was a short form for the Poor and Lower-Middle Peasants School Man-agement Committee (*pinxiazhongnong guanli xuexiao weiyuanhui*). Compar-able to the **workers propaganda teams** sent to educational institutions in the cities, poor peasant management committees were established to lead ele-mentary and middle schools in the countryside. Their establishment was based on **Mao Zedong**'s judgment that the country's education system had been controlled by bourgeois intellectuals. School management committees were formed across China after Mao's directive concerning school leadership was publicized in **Yao Wenyuan**'s article "On the Supreme Leadership of the Working Class," which appeared in the **Chinese Communist Party** official journal *Red Flag* on 25 August 1968.

In Mao's view, education reform must be led by the working class; in the cities, this leadership was represented by workers propaganda teams in all educational institutions, while in the countryside, "poor and lower-middle peasants, the most reliable ally of the working class, shall manage schools." School management committees were made of local farmers in poor and lower-middle peasant families. Some committees also included a few teacher representatives. Most peasant members had little education. Many were illiterate. Although the committee was supposed to replace the school principal and serve as the ultimate decision-making body for all school affairs, it seldom assumed this charge effectively. In the later years of the Cultural Revolution, many committees existed merely in name. After the Cultural Revolution ended, all school management committees in the countryside were dissolved.

PORTRAIT OF AN UGLY BUNCH. (*Qunchou tu.*) A popular **Red Guard** political cartoon from the early stages of the Cultural Revolution, the drawing depicts a total of 39 caricatures of the so-called **black gang** members and **capitalist-roaders** in a group setting. The group appears to be marching in an S-shaped parade toward a cliff labeled "Capitalism." In the middle of the S-shaped squad, **Liu Shaoqi** and **Deng Xiaoping**, the number one and number two capitalist-roaders, sit in sedan chairs carried by their alleged followers. Among the recognizable figures are Beijing municipal officials named by the central authorities as "black gang" members, such as **Wu Han**, **Deng Tuo**, and **Liao Mosha**—the **Three-Family Village Anti-Party Clique**— and higher-ranking central government and military leaders denounced as capitalist-roaders, including those who had already been openly criticized, such as **Peng Zhen** and **Lu Dingyi**, and those who had yet to be officially named, like Liu Shaoqi, Deng Xiaoping, **Tao Zhu**, and **He Long**. At the lower-right corner of the drawing is a vertical line of three big Chinese characters: *qun chou tu* (literally, ugly bunch portrait). Above the cartoon are two banner slogans: "Never Forget Class Struggle!" and "Sweep Away All Cow-Demons and Snake-Spirits!"

The cartoon was first published in the 22 February 1967 issue of *East Is Red* (*Dongfang hong*), a tabloid of the Revolutionary Rebel Liaison Station of the Headquarters of Capital College Red Guards (also known as the Second Command Post). The author of the cartoon was listed as "The Provision Office for Struggling against the **Peng-Lu-Luo-Yang** Counterrevolutionary

Popular political cartoon *Portrait of an Ugly Bunch* depicting 39 ranking party officials purged or under attack, February 1967.

Revisionist Clique." The individual who actually drew the cartoon was later identified as Weng Rulan, then a student Red Guard at the China Central Academy of Fine Arts affiliated with the Second Command Post. With its instant popularity upon publication, the cartoon was reprinted many times by other Red Guard organizations and distributed nationwide. Although the same tabloid had already published several articles and two other pages of political cartoons in earlier issues condemning the falling but yet-to-be-officially named Liu, Deng, and Tao as the top capitalist-roaders, lumping them in this sweeping and populistic demonizing effort with officials already known to have fallen was nevertheless a bold stroke that helped communicate **Mao Zedong**'s battle plan in a way that was appealing to the masses.

POWER SEIZURE. (*Duoquan.*) This term refers to the activity of mass organizations in taking control of the state and party apparatus at various levels, including those of provincial government and ministries of the central government. The power seizure movement started in a few provinces in early 1967 and quickly spread out to other parts of the country.

See also JANUARY STORM (1967).

PROFESSOR EXAMINATION INCIDENT (1973–1974). (*Kaojiaoshou shijian.*) In the midst of controversy over the legitimacy of college entrance examinations, the testing of college professors on such general subjects as mathematics and science took place first in Liaoning and then in Beijing, Shanghai, Tianjin, and some other places in late 1973 and early 1974. Similar to the **Zhang Tiesheng** Incident, in which an applicant who wrote an essay pleading his case rather than answering questions at a college entrance examination was hailed as a hero daring to "go against the tide," the testing of professors for the purpose of humiliation was a reaction of cultural revolutionaries to the proposal made by the State Council's Science and Education Group in April 1973 that college applicants' examination scores be taken seriously in the admission process. The proposal, along with the positive response from educational circles, was seen by **Jiang Qing** and her supporters as a clear indication of a "resurgence of the revisionist line in education." At a reception for Politburo members and military leaders on 12 December 1973, **Mao Zedong** also spoke of Zhang Tiesheng with approval and went on to suggest that professors at "eight colleges" in Beijing be gathered and administered a test.

On the evening of 30 December 1973, 631 college professors in Beijing were told that they were invited to symposiums, only to find themselves at 17 different examination sites. They were forced to solve problems in areas that had nothing to do with their expertise. Some professors protested by refusing to take the test or by writing critical comments on the prevailing anti-intellectual trend. This event, as well as similar examinations held in other places, was publicized in symposiums, bulletins, and publications in education circles, in which the predictably low scores of the unexpected tests were used both to humiliate the professors and to trivialize testing in general.

PROVINCIAL PROLETARIAN ALLIANCE. (*Shengwulian.*) This is the abbreviated name for the Committee for the Great Alliance of the Proletarian Revolutionaries of Hunan Province. The Provincial Proletarian Alliance was formed by some 20 mass groups on 11 October 1967 against the competing Preparation Group of the Hunan **Revolutionary Committee** appointed by the leadership in Beijing. Although it was a "hodgepodge" of diverse groups, as **Mao Zedong** and other party leaders called it, the organization became well known across China due to the publicity of some radical ideas articulated by one group. This was a group of middle school students led by **Yang Xiguang**, a self-labeled ultra-leftist, who, in a long article entitled "Where Is China Going," further radicalizes what he believed to be Mao's original conception of the Cultural Revolution and calls for the total destruction of the party and state apparatus and the complete eradication of what he saw as a new "red capitalist class" made of 90 percent senior party officials. Yang also saw as the goal of the Cultural Revolution the establishment of a "Chinese people's commune" under Mao, a **mass dictatorship** modeled on the Paris Commune of 1871. On 24 January 1968, **Zhou Enlai** and members of the **Central Cultural Revolution Small Group** received the representatives of mass organizations from Hunan and denounced the Provincial Proletarian Alliance as a reactionary organization. At the reception, **Kang Sheng** gave a point-by-point critique of Yang's article, which Kang considered to be the political program of the organization.

See also NEW TREND OF IDEAS.

Q

QI BENYU (1931–). One of **Mao Zedong**'s radical theorists, head of the history group at the **Chinese Communist Party** (CCP) official organ *Red Flag*, deputy director of the Secretarial Bureau of the CCP General Office, and a member of the **Central Cultural Revolution Small Group** (CCRSG), Qi was removed from power in January 1968 as a member of the Wang-Guan-Qi Anti-Party Clique.

A native of Weihai, Shandong Province, Qi joined the CCP in the early 1950s while a student at the Central School of the Chinese Communist Youth League. Upon graduation, Qi was assigned work at the CCP General Office as an assistant to Tian Jiaying, Mao Zedong's secretary and deputy director of the General Office. In 1963, his article on Li Xiucheng, a leader of the Taiping Heavenly Kingdom peasant uprising, challenging the historian Luo Ergang's authority on the subject, won the applause of Mao, which led to his appointment on the editorial board of *Red Flag*; he later became head of the journal's history group.

Following the publication of **Yao Wenyuan**'s critique of **Wu Han**'s historical play *Hai Rui Dismissed from Office*, Qi put out "Study History for the Revolution" in a December 1965 issue of *Red Flag* in which he attacks a number of historians including Wu Han and **Jian Bozan**. Mao responded positively to the article but thought that it would have been even better had Qi named these scholars. With Mao's encouragement, Qi coauthored an essay criticizing Jian Bozan and wrote a piece by himself attacking Wu Han, both published in *People's Daily* (on 25 March 1966 and 2 April 1966, respectively). These articles established him as a radical theorist and critic. In May 1966, Qi was appointed a member of the CCRSG and began to play a significant role in bringing down the **Liu Shaoqi** and **Deng Xiaoping** faction of the central leadership. During the campaign to criticize the **Bourgeois Reactionary Line** in late 1966 and early 1967, Qi and other CCRSG members pushed the **rebel** movement forward against the old party establishment.

Of particular importance in his many speeches and writings of this period was the article "Patriotism or Betrayal? A Critique of the Reactionary Film *Inside Story of the Qing Court*," published in *People's Daily* on 30 March

1967. Approved and highly praised by Mao, this article is a classic example of the Cultural Revolution–style political insinuation and slander; it aims beyond the film at President Liu Shaoqi and refers to him for the first time in official media as the "**biggest capitalist-roader within the party**" and as "**China's Khrushchev**" without ever mentioning his name. The article stirred up a new wave in the nationwide campaign against Liu. Qi also engaged in a number of manipulative actions against Liu and other senior party leaders: he directed Red Guards to kidnap Marshal **Peng Dehuai** and instructed rebels to **struggle against** Liu Shaoqi, Deng Xiaoping, and **Tao Zhu** inside and outside the Zhongnanhai compound.

Following Mao's strategic plans and supported by **Lin Biao** and **Jiang Qing**, Qi Benyu, **Wang Li**, **Guan Feng**, and some other members of the CCRSG began to press the military to adopt Mao's Cultural Revolution policies in 1967: in their public speeches and in several articles they wrote for official media, they called on the masses to "ferret out a small handful [of **capitalist-roaders**] inside the army," which met strong resistance from the rank and file of the **People's Liberation Army** (PLA). They also began to make similar radical moves in the area of foreign affairs. Weighing revolutionary chaos against stability, Mao decided to remove Qi and his close comrades in the Cultural Revolution faction of the central leadership to maintain order and to pacify the protesting PLA officials and senior party leaders. On 13 January 1968, about four and a half months after the dismissal of Wang Li and Guan Feng, Qi was detained. On 26 January 1968, Qi's long imprisonment began.

On 14 July 1980, the post-Mao authorities officially arrested him on a counterrevolutionary charge. On 2 November 1983, the Beijing Intermediate People's Court named Qi an accomplice of the Lin Biao and the Jiang Qing counterrevolutionary cliques and sentenced him to 18 years in prison for engaging in counterrevolutionary propaganda and instigation, bringing false charges against innocent people, and inciting the masses to violence and destruction (*da-za-qiang*). After he served his prison sentence, Qi was assigned work at the Shanghai City Library.

See also WANG-GUAN-QI AFFAIR (1967–1968).

QIAN HAOLIANG (1934–). Also known as Hao Liang, a name given by **Jiang Qing** and adopted by Qian during the Cultural Revolution, Qian was born in Shaoxing, Zhejiang Province, and became a member of the **Chinese Communist Party** (CCP) in 1959. He was trained as a Peking opera singer from childhood. In 1963, Qian distinguished himself playing Li Yuhe, the hero of the revolutionary model opera *The Red Lantern*, and began to associate himself with Jiang Qing. His portrait as Li Yuhe soon became a Cultural Revolution icon. In the early stages of the Cultural Revolution, Qian led a **rebel** organization and attacked his superiors and his colleagues. He was made vice-chairman of the **revolutionary committee** of the China Peking Opera Troupe in 1967, a member of the State Council Cultural Group in 1971, and deputy minister of culture in 1975. In all of these positions, Qian carried out Jiang Qing's orders dutifully. He, **Yu Huiyong**, and **Liu Qingtang** became the closest followers and allies of Jiang Qing in cultural and art circles.

In October 1976, when the **Gang of Four** was purged, Qian was also detained. For the next five years, he was under investigation as a close associate of the Gang of Four. Expelled from the CCP but spared criminal prosecution, Qian was released from detention in 1981. He taught Peking opera at the Hebei Academy of Arts and performed both classical and modern Peking operas in various cities until retirement.

QINGTONGXIA INCIDENT (28 August 1967). In this deadly incident, **People's Liberation Army** troops attacked civilians during a factional conflict in Qingtongxia County, Ningxia Hui Autonomous Region. During the **power seizure** movement in 1967, mass organizations in Ningxia were sharply divided into two camps. There was the Preparation Committee that sided with Zhu Shengda, commander of the Ningxia Provincial Military District and a close associate of Marshal **He Long**, and there was the General Headquarters, which a field army unit on a left-supporting mission endorsed because **Kang Sheng**, who was at the time entrusted with the responsibility of resolving the factional conflict in Ningxia, had dismissed the Preparation Committee faction as "**conservatives**."

In August 1967, the civilians and peasant militia supporting the Preparation Committee launched offensives, blocking railways and highways in the province; armed fighting in Qingtongxia County was especially heavy. In a speech given on 26 August, Kang denounced Zhu Shengda as the leader of a "reactionary line" and voiced support for an "armed suppression" of the mass organizations supporting Zhu. With Kang's consent, the field army unit launched an attack on 28 August on the Preparation Committee faction in Qingtongxia County, killing 101 civilians and wounding 133. On 30 August 1967, the Central Committee (CC) of the **Chinese Communist Party** issued a directive in support of the massacre, denouncing the Preparation Committee offensive in Qingtongxia as a "counterrevolutionary rebellion." On 21 January 1979, the CC redressed the case of the Qingtongxia Incident and pronounced the verdict of "counterrevolutionary rebellion" unjust.

QIU HUIZUO (1914–2002). A close associate of **Lin Biao** and popularly known as one of Lin's "four guardian warriors," Qiu Huizuo was director of the General Logistics Department (GLD) of the **People's Liberation Army** (PLA) (1959–1971), deputy chief of general staff of the PLA, and a member of the **Central Military Commission Administrative Group** (1968–1971).

Born in Xingguo, Jiangxi Province, Qiu joined the Red Army in 1929, became a member of the **Chinese Communist Party** (CCP) in 1932, and participated in the Long March in 1934–1935. In the late 1940s, Qiu was a ranking political officer in Lin Biao's Fourth Field Army. Qiu was made lieutenant general in 1955 and director of the GLD in 1959.

In the early stages of the Cultural Revolution, Qiu, known for his "wayward" lifestyle, was a popular target of the **rebels** in the GLD. In response to his request for help, Lin Biao arranged a dramatic rescue, moving Qiu from the GLD's compound to a safe place in Beijing's Western Hills in the early hours of 25 January 1967—a moment of "rebirth" in Qiu's own words. In May 1967, Lin named him, along with **Li Zuopeng** and **Wu Faxian**, a leader of the "proletarian revolutionaries of the armed forces." Qiu, in return, helped Lin fight his political enemies and consolidate power for Lin in the armed forces. In particular, he lashed out at General Xiao Hua, director of the General Political Department of the PLA, and created chaos in that department. In his own GLD, Qiu authorized the torture and persecution of 462 people, causing eight deaths. In 1968, Qiu was appointed deputy chief of general staff of the PLA and member of the Central Military Commission Administrative Group. At the **Ninth National Congress of the CCP** (1969), Qiu was elected to the Central Committee (CC) and the Politburo.

At the **Lushan Conference** of 1970, the conflict between the **Jiang Qing** faction and the Lin Biao faction surfaced. Qiu joined **Chen Boda**, Wu Faxian, Li Zuopeng, and **Ye Qun** in attacking **Zhang Chunqiao** and supporting a proposal not to eliminate the position of the president of state. Backing Zhang and the Jiang Qing group, **Mao Zedong** singled out Chen Boda as the main target of criticism and also told other supporters of Lin Biao, including Qiu, to conduct self-criticism.

After the **September 13 Incident** of 1971, Qiu's involvement in Lin Biao's alleged power-takeover scheme was under investigation. On 20 August 1973, the CC issued a resolution concerning the Lin Biao Anti-Party Clique. As a member of the Lin group, Qiu Huizuo was dismissed from all his official positions and was permanently expelled from the party. On 25 January 1981, Qiu was sentenced to 16 years in prison for organizing and leading a counterrevolutionary clique, plotting to subvert the government, and bringing false charges against innocent people.

QUEEN OF THE RED CAPITAL. (*Hongdu nühuang.*) A biography of **Jiang Qing** published in Hong Kong in the mid-1970s, this book was for quite some time mistaken for a Chinese translation of Roxane Witke's *Comrade Chiang Ch'ing*.

QUOTATIONS FROM CHAIRMAN MAO. Also known as the little red book (mostly outside China), this collection of 427 quotations of Chairman **Mao Zedong** in 33 categories, produced in pocket size with a red plastic cover, was the most printed and the most widely distributed book during the Cultural Revolution. The *Quotations* was originally a product of the political education program **Lin Biao** initiated in the early 1960s after he became minister of defense and was put in charge of the daily work of the Central Military Commission. Advocating the study of Mao's works as a shortcut to studying Marxism-Leninism, Lin recommended that soldiers in the **People's Liberation Army** (PLA) learn by heart short passages from Mao's works. Following Lin's instruction, *Liberation Army Daily* began in May 1961 to carry a quotation from Mao on the front page of each issue. In January 1964, the PLA General Political Department put out a collection based on the *Liberation Army Daily* selections. A fuller version of 433 entries came out later in the year and was distributed widely in the PLA. By the time the second edition—consisting of 427 definitive entries with Lin Biao's inscription—was issued on 1 August 1965, the *Quotations* had already been distributed far beyond the PLA.

The image of Lin Biao standing next to Mao and waving a copy of the *Quotations*—a picture taken at Mao's reception for the **Red Guards**—fueled the explosive popularity of this book in the early stages of the Cultural Revolution and contributed much to the hegemony of Maoism and the **personality cult** of the Chairman. The book was further popularized by its late 1966 reprint that carries a "Foreword to the Second Edition," which, written in the name of Lin Biao, hails Mao as "the greatest Marxist-Leninist of our times who, with genius and creativity, has inherited, defended, and developed Marxism-Leninism in all areas and brought Marxism-Leninism up to a brand new stage." The foreword also recommends a method of studying Mao's words with questions in mind for quick results, like "raising a pole to see the shadow." This edition is the most widely distributed official version—about 740,000,000 copies were printed between 1966 and 1968, almost one copy per person in the People's Republic of China.

The *Quotations*, then, became a scripture everyone carried. People read and recited passages from it during the daily ritual of "**morning request, evening report**" and political study hours and waved the booklet as they cheered or shouted slogans at mass rallies. Popular quotations were all set to music. They were sung at public events, broadcast on the radio, and used as accompanying music for the **loyalty dance** and keep-fit exercises. By 1966, the *Quotations* was also being translated into all major languages and distributed outside China. It became a bestseller worldwide.

R

REBELS. (*Zaofanpai.*) This term refers to the radical mass faction during the Cultural Revolution. The early rebels, later known as **Old Red Guards**, were mostly children of ranking officials in Beijing middle schools. When the first organization of **Red Guards** was established at Tsinghua University Middle School, the founders were inspired by the words of Chairman **Mao Zedong**, "**To rebel is justified**," and put out three expositions of a **big-character poster** entitled **"Long Live the Revolutionary Rebel Spirit of the Proletariat"** in June and July 1966. The authors of the poster claim that rebellion is the soul of **Mao Zedong Thought** and that, by following Mao's command, they would turn the old world upside down, smash it to pieces, and create a proletarian new world. In August 1966, the **Chinese Communist Party** (CCP) theoretical organ *Red Flag* carried the three-part poster in support of the rebelling of the Red Guards. "Rebels," then, became a popular revolutionary term for enthusiastic youths.

In the name of rebellion, this first group of rebels, the Old Red Guards, attacked the traditional enemies labeled "**seven black categories**" and launched a culturally devastating battle against the so-called **Four Olds**. As the Cultural Revolution continued to unfold, however, the early rebels soon became **conservatives** (though they never called themselves as such) in line with the old power establishment represented by many of their parents, who were now denounced as **capitalist-roaders**. The notorious **blood lineage theory** that some of them had embraced in the early stages of the Cultural Revolution also became a target of criticism during the campaign to criticize the **Bourgeois Reactionary Line**.

In the meantime, a new mass faction emerged during this campaign. Many people—especially many students—in this group had been politically discriminated against due to their non-proletarian family background. There were also temporary and contract workers without job security and some CCP members unfairly treated in the political movements before the Cultural Revolution. In the early stages of the Cultural Revolution, some members of this group were persecuted by party officials, the **work groups**, and Old Red Guards. Eventually, it was this group, rather than the early Red Guards, that the term "rebels" came to identify. Supported by Mao and the **Central Cultural Revolution Small Group** and joined by a great number of people with working-class backgrounds, this faction of mass organizations became the major force against the old party and state apparatus in the campaign to criticize the Bourgeois Reactionary Line and during the **power seizure** movement initiated by the **January Storm** of 1967.

During the nationwide violent factional battles in 1967 and 1968, all competing factions, radical or moderate, invariably called themselves "rebels" and often dismissed their rivals as "conservatives." By 1969, when Mao decided to put the mass movement to an end, some rebels had already become part of the newly established power structure and served on **revolutionary committees** at local and provincial levels, and a number of them, such as **Wang Hongwen**, were even elected to the Central Committee at the **Ninth National Congress of the CCP**. Yet, some others became targets of the "Ferret Out the 'May 16'" campaign, the **Rectify the Class Ranks** campaign, and the **One Strike and Three Antis** movement largely due to their involvement in prolonged factional violence and in activities that the central leadership deemed politically extreme and destructive.

RECTIFY THE CLASS RANKS. Commonly known as "Rectify Ranks" (*qingdui*), this was a campaign conducted by **revolutionary committees** at various levels to investigate and uncover class enemies—traitors, spies, capitalists, "Kuomintang dregs," **capitalist-roaders** within the **Chinese Communist Party** (CCP), and those of the "**five black categories**"—who had supposedly infiltrated the revolutionary camp and messed up class ranks. As an important step toward accomplishing the tasks of the Cultural Revolution, "**struggle, criticism, and reform**," as **Mao Zedong** conceived them, the Rectify Ranks campaign began in late 1967; it lasted longer and claimed more lives than any other movement during the Cultural Revolution.

The term "rectify the class ranks" was first introduced by **Jiang Qing** in her talk with the representative of Beijing workers on 27 November 1967. On 21 February 1968, a team made up of the personnel of the **People's Liberation Army**'s unit 8341, Mao's guards regiment at Zhongnanhai, moved into the Beijing Xinhua Printing Factory to establish military control. They soon produced the "Experience of the Military Control Commission at the Beijing Xinhua Printing Factory in Mobilizing the Masses to Struggle against the Enemies." Following Mao's directive, the CCP Central Committee (CC) and the **Central Cultural Revolution Small Group** distributed the "Experience" nationwide on 25 May 1968 as a model for conducting the Rectify the Class Ranks campaign. Later, both the editorial that *People's Daily*, *Red Flag*, and *Liberation Army Daily* jointly carried on 1 January 1969 and the political report of the CC for the **Ninth National Congress of the CCP** (April 1969) publicized Mao's directive on the Rectify Ranks campaign: the campaign should be "firmly grasped," said Mao, yet at the same time "give a way out" for those being investigated; "no one is to be executed; most are not to be arrested."

However, despite Mao's warning against massive and relentless persecution (which already implied the existence of the problem), illegal imprisonment, systematic torture, trial by suspicion, and conviction by forced confessions were common during the campaign. The almost routine use of isolation, torture, and, particularly, the so-called ideological work that special case personnel under the leadership of the revolutionary committee, the current power organ, often forced family members and relatives to perform on victims, made this campaign psychologically the cruelest. It had the highest suicide rate of all political campaigns and persecuted the largest number of people. For instance, at Tsinghua University, one of the exemplary **Six Factories and Two Universities** where Mao's 8341 security unit sent **army propaganda teams**, 1,228 of its 6,000 staff members were investigated; in the first two months of the Rectify Ranks campaign, more than 10 people were harassed to death on the Tsinghua campus. According to official estimate, in the 10 months from February to November 1970, 1.87 million alleged "traitors," "spies," and "counterrevolutionaries" were uncovered in the nation, and more than 284,800 people were arrested. All together, the number of people affected by the campaign either as victims or as family members of victims reached an unprecedented 100 million, one-eighth of China's population. Since its later stages merged with the **One Strike and Three Antis** campaign and with the investigation of the so-called **May 16 Counterrevolutionary Clique**, the campaign to rectify the class ranks had no closure until the end of the Cultural Revolution itself.

RED AUGUST. (*Hongbayue.*) This term refers to a time in late summer 1966 when a series of landmark events in the **Red Guard** movement took place while brutal violence against innocent citizens surged, especially in Beijing. To Red Guards of the time who proudly named August 1966 as such, it was a month of excitement, empowerment, and glory—a month of Red Guards—while to many ordinary citizens, especially the surviving victims of Red Guard violence, "Red August" was synonymous for lawlessness, bloodiness, and terror.

On 1 August 1966, **Mao Zedong** wrote to Tsinghua Middle School Red Guards in response to their letter to him and their **big-character poster** series entitled "**Long Live the Revolutionary Rebel Spirit of the Proletariat.**" Mao reiterated his own words "**To rebel is justified**" and expressed strong support for the Red Guard movement. In the eye of Red Guards, Mao's writing marked the beginning of a "red" August. The distribution of Mao's letter as a party document on 3 August led to an explosive development of Red Guard organizations nationwide. The second, and greater, wave of such development came after Mao inspected over a million Red Guards and "revolutionary masses" (mostly students) at a mass rally in Tiananmen Square on 18 August. His inspection set off a Red Guard traveling campaign called the **Great Networking**, in which tens of millions of Red Guards from the provinces rode on free trains to Beijing to see Mao and to acquire revolutionary experience while Red Guards in Beijing traveled to other parts of the country to spread the fire of the Cultural Revolution.

Mao's support also inspired Red Guards to expand revolution from schools to society as a whole. Beginning on 19 August, Beijing's Red Guards launched a campaign on city streets called **Destroy the Four Olds**. In a few days, they changed the names of hundreds of streets, shops, restaurants, hotels, shopping plazas, schools, and hospitals, dismissing traditional names as feudalist, capitalist, imperialist, or revisionist and replacing them with proletarian labels. They issued orders to barbershops, tailor shops, shoe shops, and photo studios to ban any product or style deemed non-proletarian. Standing on the corners of busy streets, they would stop any passerby with what they considered an unacceptable look and punish the person on the spot. Red Guards even changed the traffic rules (for a short period) so that red—signifying revolution—meant "go" and green "stop." They stood with traffic police officers at intersections to redirect the traffic, making sure that the color red should prevail. The government endorsed all these activities.

The war against the "old world" led to the destruction of countless churches, temples, theaters, libraries, used-book stores, and historical sites. With the government's acquiescence, and even support and assistance, Red Guards ransacked private homes and confiscated personal belongings of the alleged "class enemies," especially people of the so-called **five black categories**. Brutality against teachers, school officials, people of the "five black categories," and so-called **black gang** members became widespread. On 25 August, the **Capital Red Guard Pickets** was formed in Beijing's Xicheng District—and soon in several other districts as well—to exercise control over the lawless activities and violence committed by the city's many independent Red Guard organizations. But, contrary to this intention, some members of the Pickets themselves set up private courts in their schools to torture, and even kill, innocent people. According to statistics from the Beijing Public Security Bureau, in a period of 40 days in late August and September in the city of Beijing alone, 1,772 people were killed or committed suicide, 33,695 homes were ransacked, and 85,000 people of the "five black categories" were expelled from Beijing to their hometowns, mostly in poverty-stricken rural areas. This kind of lawlessness and violence was committed by Red Guards in other parts of the country as well.

RED BOOK OF TREASURES. (*Hongbaoshu.*) This was a popular term during the Cultural Revolution for the four-volume set of the *Selected Works of Mao Zedong*. It was also a popular name for the much shorter ***Quotations from Chairman Mao***. Published in 1951, 1952, 1953, and 1960, the four volumes were massively produced in the initial years of the Cultural Revolution. Over 86.4 million copies were printed in the year 1967 alone, some with red covers. In the late 1960s, the one-volume edition of the *Selected Works* came out, wrapped in a red plastic jacket and available in portable size as well. A bible for the population, the *Selected Works* became a common gift item and an object of worship, which contributed much to the hegemony of **Mao Zedong Thought** and the **personality cult** of the Chairman.

RED GUARDS. (*Hongweibing.*) This is a generic name for the youth organizations that were formed at the beginning of the Cultural Revolution and served as a major political force for Chairman **Mao Zedong** in the battle against traditional culture and the old party establishment from summer 1966 to summer 1968. The term also refers to the members of these organizations. Red Guards shocked the world with their radical Communist idealism, their rebel spirit in defiance of authorities, and their extreme—often violent—social behavior.

The first Red Guard organization was formed on 29 May 1966 by a dozen students at Tsinghua University Middle School. They chose the name "Red Guards" to express their vow to be Mao's guards fighting against those who, in Mao's words, conspired to change the color of Communist China. In June and July, the Tsinghua Middle School Red Guards put out a series of **big-character posters** entitled "**Long Live the Revolutionary Rebel Spirit of the Proletariat,**" which helped popularize Mao's words "**To rebel is justified**" as a catchphrase of the Red Guard movement. During the same period, students from other middle and high schools in Beijing also formed Red Guard organizations, adopting such fashionable names as "Red Flag," "East Wind," or "East Is Red." On 1 August, Mao, after reading a copy of the posters on rebel spirit, wrote the Tsinghua Middle School Red Guards a letter demonstrating his "enthusiastic support" for their "rebellion against the reactionaries." Mao's letter was never posted, but after it was circulated as a party document and made its way to the public in early August 1966, Red Guard organizations mushroomed in the country. The early Red Guard organizations carried a politically discriminating membership policy in accordance with the notorious **blood lineage theory**, admitting only students from families of the "**five red categories.**"

On 18 August, Mao, wearing a Red Guard armband on his left arm, inspected a million Red Guards and revolutionary masses from the Tiananmen rostrum while **Lin Biao**, the vice-chairman of the **Chinese Communist Party**, standing next to Mao, called for a thoroughgoing attack on "old ideas, old culture, old customs, and old habits." As Mao's inspection hastened the birth of tens of thousands more new Red Guard organizations in the country, Lin's call inspired Red Guards to launch a **Destroy the Four Olds** campaign against traditional culture, first in the city of Beijing and then all over the country. The campaign led not only to severe damage to countless temples, churches, and cultural and historic relics but also to the youthful rejection of many traditional values and virtues of Chinese society such as respect for teachers and older people, loyalty to friends, and humaneness based on empathy. During this campaign, Red Guard brutality became widespread against teachers, school officials, and other alleged "class enemies" old and new.

In the meantime, Mao's inspections of Red Guards continued. A nationwide traveling campaign called the **Great Networking** brought tens of thousands of Red Guards from all over the country to Beijing each day, whereas Red Guards from Beijing went to the provinces to stir up revolution there. The Great Networking campaign effectively energized millions of Chinese youths with fearless rebel spirit to serve as Mao's crusaders against his opponents and their alleged followers in the central, provincial, and local party leadership. As Mao directed the revolution's focus from criticizing liberal intellectuals and a small number of "**black gang**" members to toppling party and government officials in October 1966, Red Guard organizations began to divide into two factions: the **Old Red Guards** who played a major role in earlier campaigns now became less enthusiastic since many of their parents were party officials and had become targets of the new round of attacks, while the newly emerging **rebel** Red Guards, a faction that included many members from non-proletarian families, were now supported by the **Central Cultural Revolution Small Group** and replaced the Old Red Guards as Mao's crusading army against the old party establishment in the campaign to criticize the **Bourgeois Reactionary Line**, which eventually led to the downfall of **Liu Shaoqi** and **Deng Xiaoping**.

As the Cultural Revolution developed into its **power seizure** phase in 1967, beginning with Shanghai's **January Storm**, factional conflict among Red Guard organizations (and among other mass organizations as well) intensified in the country. The fight for a greater share of power in the **revolutionary committee**, now the new organ of power, often led to both verbal disputes and physical violence. To restore order, Mao ordered army troops to intervene in the name of "supporting the left" and called upon all mass factions to form a "grand alliance." And yet, the factional conflict continued to escalate and became increasingly violent. By late 1967 and early 1968, large-scale armed confrontations occurred in many places, and the country was in chaos.

Finally, in July 1968, Mao made a few decisive moves to end factional violence: after approving nationwide issuance of two public notices concerning the armed conflict in two provinces, Mao, on 27 July, dispatched a **workers propaganda team** of 30,000 led by **People's Liberation Army** officers to break up a prolonged factional confrontation known as the **One-Hundred-Day Armed Conflict on the Tsinghua Campus**. After Red Guards at Tsinghua University opened fire and killed five and injured hundreds of the propaganda team members, Mao called an emergency meeting with the leaders of the five most influential Red Guard organizations in Beijing. At the meeting, the Chairman showed his determination to end the country's chaos and informed the Red Guard leaders of his plan to send all students away from the country's college campuses. Mao's decision, along with the movement of **educated youths** going **up to the mountains and down to the countryside**, effectively put an end to the Red Guard movement.

After the exit of this generation of Red Guards from China's political scene, the name "Red Guards" was retained for a youth organization at middle and high schools under the control of the school authorities—an *ad hoc* substitute, in many cases, for the official Communist Youth League. In August 1978, the Chinese Communist Youth League announced its decision to abolish the Red Guard organization.

See also MASS RALLY OF 18 AUGUST 1966; MAO ZEDONG: MEETING WITH THE FIVE RED GUARD LEADERS (28 July 1968).

RED GUARDS' REPRESENTATIVE ASSEMBLY. (*Hongdaihui.*) Born of a need for coordinating activities among **Red Guard** organizations, this assembly generally functioned as the headquarters of participating Red Guard organizations. On 22 February 1967, the Representative Assembly of the Capital College Red Guards was established in Beijing with the support as well as the advice of central leaders. On 25 March of the same year, middle school Red Guards in Beijing established their assembly as well. Before long, such assemblies were formed in many other places in the country at county, city, regional, and provincial levels. The purpose of establishing an assembly was to place a certain collective authority over self-governed, largely independent, poorly disciplined, and often factionally inclined Red Guard groups so that coordination and a certain degree of control could be exercised to shape the direction and priorities of the Red Guard movement.

However, factionalism continued to hold the upper hand and undermined severely the authority of many assemblies; some of them ceased functioning before long because of the conflicts between rival Red Guard organizations. A national representative assembly of Red Guards was never formed. When the new power organ, the **revolutionary committee**, was established after the **power seizure** movement of 1967, a few positions on the committee were usually given to the leaders of the local assembly as representatives of the Red Guards. In 1968 and 1969, when the Red Guard movement came to an end, Red Guard assemblies were gradually phased out.

RED PERIPHERIES. (*Hongwaiwei.*) This was a humiliating name for those students who willingly and actively participated in the campaigns launched by **Red Guards** but who were not allowed to join Red Guard organizations because their family backgrounds were not of the hardcore **"five red categories"** though not of the so-called **five black categories**, either. These included children of ordinary teachers, civil servants, freelancers, street vendors, poor urban residents, middle peasants, and so forth. The term "Red Peripheries" was used only for a short period in the early phase of the Cultural Revolution when some Red Guards were actively promoting a **blood lineage theory**. This was also the time when **Mao Zedong** was voicing his warm support for the Red Guard movement and receiving Red Guards in Tiananmen Square, which accorded a Red Guard high revolutionary status with which tens of millions of Chinese youths wanted to identify themselves.

Enthusiastic about the revolution and afraid of being viewed as less revolutionary than Red Guards, some students from non-proletarian families followed the actions of Red Guards as much as they could and even formed their own organizations under the category that Red Guards referred to as "Red Peripheries" or "Red Exteriors." When the campaign to criticize the **Bourgeois Reactionary Line** started in October 1966, many new Red Guard or rebel organizations were formed. With admission policies much less rigid than those of the **Old Red Guards**, these organizations opened doors to students with less favorable family backgrounds, though admissions for those from families of the "five black categories" remained difficult. By now the term "Red Peripheries" had become obsolete.

REEDUCATION. (*Zaijiaoyu.*) This is a term **Mao Zedong** used several times during the Cultural Revolution to refer to what he considered to be a necessary ideological reform for intellectuals, professionals, and middle school, high school, and college graduates. In Mao's view, they had been book educated and school trained, but their ideas were often non-revolutionary, with marks of bourgeois and revisionist ideology. Therefore, they needed to live with workers, peasants, and soldiers, be identified with them, and be reeducated by them, so as to become proletarian.

See also EDUCATED YOUTHS; MAY 7 CADRE SCHOOL; UP TO THE MOUNTAINS AND DOWN TO THE COUNTRYSIDE.

REGULATIONS ON STRENGTHENING PUBLIC SECURITY DUR-ING THE GREAT PROLETARIAN CULTURAL REVOLUTION (1967). Popularly known as the Six Regulations of Public Security, this document, coded *zhongfa* [67] 19, was issued nationwide by the Central Committee (CC) of the **Chinese Communist Party** and the State Council on 13 January 1967. It not only reiterated legal action against common criminals but also legitimized harsh measures of political repression and social discrimination in the name of public security. Aside from forbidding various kinds of violent crime and illicit contact with foreign governments, the regulations defined as punishable counterrevolutionary crimes any "slandering on the great leader Chairman **Mao [Zedong]** and his dear comrade-in-arms **Lin Biao**" in the form of sending anonymous letters, posting pamphlets, or writing and shouting slogans.

The regulations also prescribed restrictions for citizens belonging to a long list of categories of political outcasts. These categories included landlords, rich peasants, counterrevolutionaries, bad elements, and rightists, those who are or used to be reformed through labor, the former backbone members of the Kuomintang and its affiliated youth league, the former leaders of cults or religious groups, those who used to serve in the Nationalist army or government at or above certain levels (which the regulations specify meticulously), former but "not yet reformed" convicts, profiteering vendors, and family members of those punished by law. People in these categories were not allowed to travel to participate in **Great Networking** activities, to join mass organizations by changing their names or falsifying their personal history, to play any backstage role in any organization, or to establish their own organizations; violation of any of these regulations was severely punishable. The regulations led to the persecutions of a large number of innocent people by both mass organizations and security agencies at various levels. Soon after the Cultural Revolution, the CC annulled this document and then charged the **Gang of Four** and Minister of Public Security **Xie Fuzhi** with the crime of formulating such repressive measures.

REN YI. *See* "SONG OF THE EDUCATED YOUTHS OF NANJING".

RESOLUTION ON CERTAIN QUESTIONS IN THE HISTORY OF OUR PARTY SINCE THE FOUNDING OF THE PEOPLE'S REPUB-LIC OF CHINA. (*Guanyu jianguo yilai dang de ruogan lishi wenti de jueyi*.) Adopted on 27 June 1981 at the Sixth Plenum of the Eleventh Central Committee (CC) of the **Chinese Communist Party** (CCP) and covering the 32 years of CCP rule since 1949, especially the 10 years of the Cultural Revolution (May 1966–October 1976), this document represents by far the most comprehensive assessment of the Cultural Revolution made by the post-Mao CCP leadership. It is also the first official central document that takes a critical stand, both politically and theoretically, toward the Cultural Revolution.

The CC considered the resolution to be both necessary and important, so much so that the CC waited more than two years after the Cultural Revolution to begin the drafting of the document, and it took more than a year and a half for a writing team led by Hu Qiaomu, a chief CCP historian and theorist, to finish the project. The stated purpose of the resolution is to review **Mao Zedong**'s legacy and conclude a highly problematic chapter in the CCP history—"preferably in broad strokes rather than in detail," as **Deng Xiaoping** suggested—so that both the party and the nation might be united, leave the past behind, and look ahead. Of the fairly detailed instructions that he offered on nine occasions between March 1980 and June 1981, Deng considered the appropriate assessment of Chairman Mao to be the most important. On the one hand, Deng said, the resolution should be critical of Mao's mistakes, truthfully and unequivocally. On the other hand, the legitimacy of the **Twelfth Plenum of the Eighth CCP Central Committee** (at which President **Liu Shaoqi** was officially expelled from the CCP) and the **Ninth National Congress of the CCP** (at which a new CCP Constitution was adopted that designates **Lin Biao** as Mao's successor) must be acknowledged, and the banner of **Mao Zedong Thought** should not be abandoned; for to abandon this banner means to deny the "glorious history of our party."

Embracing Deng's concern for both the truth of the Cultural Revolution and the legitimacy of the party leadership under Mao as the principal guideline, the resolution deals with two conflicting issues. On the one hand, it names the Cultural Revolution as the cause for "the most severe setback and the heaviest losses the party, the state, and the people had suffered since the founding of the People's Republic of China," criticizes Mao's ultra-leftism as an erroneous ideology informing the Cultural Revolution, and recognizes the partial responsibility of the CCP central leadership for the revolution. On the other hand, the resolution blames Lin Biao, **Jiang Qing**, and their two counterrevolutionary cliques for taking advantage of Mao's errors, committing crimes behind his back, attempting to seize power, and so on, and charges them as chief culprits responsible for causing the national disaster. The resolution upholds Mao Zedong Thought as the guiding principle of the CCP while excluding Mao's theory of **continuing revolution under the dictatorship of the proletariat** from Mao Zedong Thought proper in spite of Mao's own judgment.

Apparently, the resolution reflects a dilemma the post-Mao CCP leadership faced: the leadership gained its legitimacy by following the will of the people and abandoning Mao's Cultural Revolution program, but a thoroughgoing critique of the Cultural Revolution might again put the legitimacy of the CCP leadership itself in question. As a landmark central document intended to bring closure to the most troubling period of the CCP history, the resolution clarifies a number of historical issues to some extent and serves a strategic purpose, but its value is nevertheless reduced because of its inherent contradictions.

REVOLUTION IN EDUCATION. (*Jiaoyu geming.*) Also known as "educational reform" (*jiaoyu gaige*), the project was proposed by **Mao Zedong** in the late 1950s to make education serve the interest of proletarian politics and to integrate education with labor and production. In a letter to **Lin Biao**, dated 7 May 1966, Mao demanded that years of schooling be shortened and that education be revolutionized, and he called for an end to the "reign of bourgeois intellectuals in our schools." These words made the "revolution in education" one of the most important tasks of the Cultural Revolution. The revolution in education took such radical steps as abolishing the college entrance examination system, politicizing educational material for schools at all levels, recruiting college students only from workplaces and army units, and reducing college education uniformly to three years. There was also an invention called "open-door schooling" in which college students went off campus and took factories and fields as classrooms where workers and peasants assumed the role of professors. A nationwide enforcement of radical measures like these, along with the official propaganda debasing learning in general, resulted in a drastic degradation of knowledge at all levels of education and a decline in educational quality during the Cultural Revolution.

In the early 1970s, **Zhou Enlai** and **Deng Xiaoping**, with broad support from educational circles, made some efforts to restore normality to the nation's chaotic education system, such as reintroducing entrance exams as a part of the selection process for college admissions and allowing high school graduates to be directly enrolled in college, but these efforts were denounced by the ultra-leftist faction of the central leadership as signs of a massive **"right-deviationist reversal of verdicts"** and eventually failed. The real reversal of the cultural revolutionary educational reform did not take place until late 1977, a year after the end of the Cultural Revolution, when the national college entrance examination system was reinstalled.

See also MAY 7 DIRECTIVE; WORKER-PEASANT-SOLDIER STUDENTS.

REVOLUTION IN PEKING OPERA. This term refers to the reform efforts to modernize the traditional Chinese music theater Peking opera (*jingju*), which started in the early 1960s but later became politicized and radicalized by **Jiang Qing**. At a work session of the **Chinese Communist Party** (CCP) Central Committee in September 1963, **Mao Zedong** called upon artists in the traditional Chinese theater to "weed through the old to bring forth the new" (*tuichen chuxin*) so that characters on stage would not be just "kings and princes, generals and ministers, talented scholars and lovely beauties" (*diwangjiangxiang caizijiaren*). In fact, before 1963, quite a few theatrical companies, not only of Peking opera but also some other regional operas, had already begun to experiment with traditional forms and to produce contemporary musical dramas with revolutionary themes. Following Mao's 1963 directive, several troupes created a number of new revolutionary Peking operas including *Shajia Creek* (*Shajiabang*), *Taking Tiger Mountain by Stratagem* (*Zhiqu weihushan*), *Raid on the White Tiger Regiment* (*Qixi baihutuan*), and *The Red Lantern* (*Hongdeng ji*).

From 5 June to 31 July 1964, a festival of Peking opera on contemporary themes was held in Beijing. Twenty-nine opera troupes and about 2,000 people participated in the festival and produced 37 theatrical works. Jiang Qing attended this festival and delivered the speech "On the Revolution in Peking Opera," in which she dismissed all historical plays as feudalist and bourgeois works and advocated such propaganda principles as "giving prominence to politics" and "giving prominence to positive revolutionary figures." In her effort to further radicalize the Peking opera reform, Jiang virtually drove all historical plays and most artists off the stage. When Jiang Qing's speech was published in the CCP theoretical organ *Red Flag* in May 1967, it became a guideline that all artists and writers had to follow.

Under the direction of Jiang, the original Peking opera reform soon turned into a political movement and became the "revolution in Peking opera." Jiang also took advantage of the reform, tempered with a few of its early accomplishments, such as *Shajia Creek*, *Taking Tiger Mountain by Stratagem*, and *The Red Lantern*, and claimed credit for their creation. During the Cultural Revolution, these plays, along with a few others, were officially named the **eight model dramas**, and Jiang became "the great standard-bearer" of revolution in art and literature.

REVOLUTIONARY COMMITTEE. This was the name of the new power organ established after traditional government and party apparatuses were abolished in 1967. The 1967 **January Storm** in Shanghai marked the beginning of a nationwide **power seizure** movement in which mass organizations overthrew party and government authorities and took the governing power in their hands. Encouraged by **Mao Zedong**, this movement was carried out systematically at all levels, including local and provincial government and the leadership of all the nation's schools, state institutions and organizations, factories, and collectively owned communes in the countryside in 1967 and 1968. The new power organ that was established to replace the old governing authorities was first named in Shanghai as a "people's commune," but Mao Zedong eventually favored the example of Heilongjiang and Shandong Provinces with the three-in-one presence of party cadres, military officers, and representatives of mass organizations in a "revolutionary committee," which made the new power organ in Shanghai change its name on 24 February. This name became official when the party organ *Red Flag* published an editorial on 10 March 1967 citing Mao's directive. The Constitution of the People's Republic of China revised in 1975 and again in 1978 designated the revolutionary committee as the official organ of power. A decision was made in July 1979 at the Second Session of the Fifth National People's Congress that the use of "revolutionary committee" as the name of any governing body be discontinued.

See also SHANGHAI PEOPLE'S COMMUNE.

RITTENBERG, SIDNEY (1921–). More popularly known in China by his Chinese name Li Dunbai, Rittenberg is an American who lived in China from 1944 to 1980. Once a member of the U.S. Communist Party, he was the first American citizen to join the **Chinese Communist Party** (CCP). Though a sympathizer of Chinese revolution during his early years in China and a leader of radicalized foreign nationals as well as a staunch supporter of Chairman **Mao Zedong** during the Cultural Revolution, Rittenberg was imprisoned twice for a total of 16 years, first as an alleged spy (1949–1955) and second as an alleged member of the **May 16 Counterrevolutionary Clique** (1967–1977).

A native of Charleston, South Carolina, Rittenberg became a labor organizer as a young man. He joined the U.S. Communist Party while attending the University of North Carolina at Chapel Hill. During World War II, he was enlisted in the army and was sent to China in 1944. At the end of the war, he decided to stay in China to work for the United Nations' famine relief program. This led to his meeting with Mao Zedong, Zhu De, **Zhou Enlai**, and other leaders of the CCP in Yan'an in 1946. Rittenberg claims to have assisted CCP leaders, including Mao, in translating their messages into English. He also worked for the Xinhua News Agency and Radio Peking (the official foreign language news station renamed China Radio International in 1993) after he was released from prison in 1955.

Rittenberg was a presence of considerable influence during the early stages of the Cultural Revolution: as head of a 70-member mass organization called "Dr. Norman Bethune Yan'an Rebel Group," he led political campaigns at Radio Peking. On 8 April 1967, the CCP official organ the *People's Daily* published a long article written by him, with the author identified as a noted "international revolutionary." On 10 April, he represented a **rebel** faction of foreign nationals at a **struggle session** denouncing **Wang Guangmei**, the wife of President **Liu Shaoqi**, at Tsinghua University. He also attacked some foreign citizens who were living in Beijing at the time. In the heat of these frantic activities, Rittenberg became involved in Chinese political affairs at an upper level and came to be associated with ultra-leftist members of the **Central Cultural Revolution Small Group**, including **Wang Li** and **Qi Benyu**. Consequently, as Wang and Qi were purged in 1967 and 1968, Rittenberg was implicated. He was criticized and denounced as a member of the May 16 Counterrevolutionary Clique and was arrested in February 1968 with several other members of the "Dr. Norman Bethune Yan'an Rebel Group." He was imprisoned for nearly 10 years.

In November 1977, Rittenberg was finally released and rehabilitated. In March 1980, he moved back to the United States. In 1993, he published *The Man Who Stayed Behind*, a book about his experiences in China. Currently, Rittenberg and his wife provide consulting services for large American corporations with interests in China.

RONG GUOTUAN (1937–1968). Born in Hong Kong, Rong came to mainland China in 1957 as an outstanding ping-pong player. In 1959, when he won the men's singles championship at the 25th Table Tennis World Championship Game, he instantly became a national hero, since this was the very first world championship won by a Chinese in any international sports event. In 1961, at the 26th World Championship Game, he led his team to the team title. He was appointed head coach of the Chinese women's ping-pong team in 1963 and turned it into a world champion team at the 28th World Championship Game. Suspected of being a foreign agent, Rong was persecuted during the Cultural Revolution. Rong hanged himself on 20 June 1968, with a note in his pocket that read, "I am not a spy." Rong's name was cleared by the National Sports Commission in June 1978.

ROTATION OF MILITARY REGION COMMANDERS (December 1973). Following **Mao Zedong**'s suggestion that commanders of military regions should rotate because it was not good for anyone to stay in one place for too long, the Central Military Commission issued an order on 22 December 1973 to reassign eight military region commanders by having the current commanders exchange places with one another.

ROYALISTS. (*Baohuangpai.*) Also known as "bourgeois royalists." *See* CONSERVATIVES.

S

SCRIPTURE OF COUP D'ÉTAT. (*Zhengbian jing.*) *See* LIN BIAO: MAY 18 SPEECH (1966).

SECOND PLENUM OF THE NINTH CENTRAL COMMITTEE OF THE CHINESE COMMUNIST PARTY (23 August–6 September 1970). Also known as the Lushan Conference, the Second Plenum of the Ninth Central Committee (CC) of the **Chinese Communist Party** (CCP) marked a significant turning point in the course of the Cultural Revolution. The plenum was held at the state resort at Lushan, Jiangxi Province, and presided over by Chairman **Mao Zedong**. At the meeting, a fissure appeared within the "proletarian headquarters" newly consolidated at the **Ninth National Congress of the CCP**. A power struggle between two groups of leaders— **Lin Biao** and his associates, on the one hand, and **Jiang Qing** and her supporters, on the other—took the form of a noisy dispute over two questions: whether Mao Zedong was a genius and whether the Chinese leadership should eliminate the position of the president of state. As Mao voiced support for the Jiang group and denounced **Chen Boda** (who had been gradually alienated from Jiang and had become more closely associated with Lin), making Chen the first victim of his strategic move against Lin Biao, the downfall of Mao's handpicked successor began.

There were three discussion topics on the original plenum agenda: a revision of the Constitution of the People's Republic of China (PRC); the nation's economic planning; and China's war-readiness (regarding mainly the potential threat from the Soviet Union). But these issues were overshadowed at the meeting by a bizarre drama of power intrigue. At the opening ceremony, Lin Biao delivered a long speech that he had supposedly cleared with Mao. In the speech, Lin said that Mao was a genius and that it should be ordained by the constitution that Mao be the "head of the proletarian dictatorship," referring to the position of the president of state that Mao, in the eye of others, either declined to take due to modesty or simply wished to abolish. On 24 August, a pamphlet entitled "Engels, Lenin, and Chairman Mao on Genius," compiled by Chen Boda and approved by Lin, was distributed among delegates. Knowing that Jiang Qing's close ally **Zhang Chunqiao** had opposed the inclusion of "genius" along with two other modifiers praising Mao in the revised PRC Constitution, Chen Boda, **Ye Qun**, **Wu Faxian**, **Li Zuopeng**, and **Qiu Huizuo**—all Lin Biao's associates—stirred up a storm in discussion groups, denouncing those who denied Mao's genius and vowing to "uncover" the counterrevolutionaries. Most delegates enthusiastically embraced the "genius" theory and supported the request that Mao be president of state, although perhaps only a few veteran leaders, who also voiced support, acted with the understanding that the radical faction of the central leadership was under attack.

The situation took a dramatic turn after Jiang Qing, Zhang Chunqiao, and **Yao Wenyuan** went to see Mao on the morning of 25 August and lodged a complaint against Chen Boda and his comrades. Mao personally convened an enlarged session of the Politburo to stop discussion of Lin Biao's speech and to order Chen to go through self-examination. Mao also ruled that the issue of installing the national president not be raised again. On 31 August, Mao wrote "Some Views of Mine," in which he dismissed Chen's theory of genius as "fabrication," "sophistry," and the "tricks of those who claim to but do not really understand Marx." During the remainder of the plenum, the denunciation of Chen continued. Lin Biao's cohorts disassociated themselves from Chen and criticized themselves.

The plenum concluded with Mao's call for ranking cadres to study Marxism and with the decision of the CC to investigate Chen Boda's case. A year later, just before Lin Biao's fatal plane crash (known as the **September 13 Incident**), Mao was to define the conflict at the Lushan Conference as a "struggle between two headquarters," and the "tenth [inner-party] line struggle." He also spoke of the activities of the Lin group at the meeting as premeditated, organized, and guided by a program that consisted of a theory on "genius" and a call to install the national president, despite the fact that Mao himself had allowed the association of his name with "genius" to enter previous party documents and that the proposal to install the national president was supported by almost all the delegates at Lushan, including **Kang Sheng**, the advisor to the **Central Cultural Revolution Small Group**.

See also ELIMINATING THE OFFICE OF THE NATIONAL PRESIDENT.

SEPTEMBER 13 INCIDENT (1971). Also known simply as "9-13," the September 13 Incident refers to the plane crash on the morning of 13 September 1971 in Mongolia that killed **Lin Biao**, **Ye Qun**, their son **Lin Liguo**, and six others as they were fleeing China allegedly after an aborted coup d'état. The incident became a turning point in the Cultural Revolution: the downfall of **Mao Zedong**'s "closest comrade-in-arms," who promoted the **personality cult** of Mao in the early stages of the Cultural Revolution, whose ascent in the central leadership of the **Chinese Communist Party** (CCP) had been celebrated as a major achievement of the Cultural Revolution, and whose future as Mao's successor had been written into the CCP Constitution, shocked the nation to such an extent that many were disillusioned by politics and began to think critically of the Cultural Revolution. However, it took 10 more years for the CCP Central Committee (CC) to formulate its own judgment on the Cultural Revolution in connection with Lin Biao's case: the historic **Resolution on Certain Questions in the History of Our Party since the Founding of the People's Republic of China** states that the downfall of the Lin Biao clique "virtually pronounced the failure in both theory and practice of the Cultural Revolution."

According to the official version of the September 13 Incident and of the events leading up to it, Lin aimed to take power by schemes and intrigues as early as August and September 1970 at the **Second Plenum of the Ninth CCP Central Committee**, also known as the Lushan Conference. Speaking against Mao's wish to **eliminate the office of the national president**, Lin insisted in his opening speech at the plenum that Mao was a genius and that it should be ordained by the constitution that Mao be the "head of the proletarian dictatorship." Taking Lin's speech as a signal for action, **Chen Boda** and Lin's close associates **Wu Faxian**, Ye Qun, **Li Zuopeng**, and **Qiu Huizuo** stirred up a storm in group sessions denouncing those who dared to deny Mao's genius, particularly **Zhang Chunqiao** who had followed Mao's wish (largely unknown to others) and insisted on excluding from the new constitution the word "genius" and two other modifiers in praise of Mao. Later, Mao interpreted Lin's support for restoring the office of the national president and his insistence on calling Mao a genius as a political program and theoretical program for **power seizure**. Although not attacking Lin directly while condemning Chen and chiding Lin's cohorts during the **Criticize Chen and Conduct Rectification** campaign after the Lushan Conference, Mao considered Lin to be behind the power intrigue: "Someone couldn't wait to become president," he said.

In October 1970, the Investigation and Research Group under the CCP Office of the Air Force Command, a secret intelligence team for Lin Biao, was renamed the United Flotilla with Lin Liguo as the leader or *kang-man-de*, a self-styled code name simulating the English "commander." On 21 March 1971, the core of this group of air force officers met in Shanghai to assess the political situation regarding Lin Biao's position in the CCP leadership and to plot a power seizure for him. Those attending the meeting, including Lin Liguo, decided to proceed with their plan by peaceful means for the moment, considering Mao's authority and popularity, but at the same time to be prepared for an armed coup. The blueprint for the latter, at Lin Liguo's suggestion, was to be called the "571 Project," as the pronunciation of the numbers *wu-qi-yi* homophonically rhymes with the Chinese characters for "armed uprising." Yu Xinye, a key member of the United Flotilla, was entrusted with the drafting of the *"571 Project" Summary*, which he finished on 23 March. Lin Biao was named in the official history of the CCP as the commanding force behind both the formation of the United Flotilla and the creation of the 571 Project.

During his **southern inspection** from 14 August to 12 September 1971, Mao Zedong repeatedly talked about the tenth line struggle in the CCP's history and the struggle between two headquarters, both referring to the power intrigue at the 1970 Lushan Conference. He voiced strong criticism of Chen Boda and Lin Biao's close associates but, at the same time, warned his audience not to pass on his words to Beijing. On 5 and 6 September, when Mao's criticism finally reached Beidaihe resort (where Lin Biao and Ye Qun had been staying for the summer), Lin and Ye came to the conclusion that at the Third Plenum of the CCP's Ninth Central Committee and the **Fourth National People's Congress**, supposedly to be held soon around 1 October 1971, their political career would come to an end. So they, according to the official version of the event, decided to assassinate Mao in Shanghai and stage a coup in Beijing. On 7 September, Lin Liguo told the members of the United Flotilla to be first-degree war-ready. On 8 September, Lin Biao was said to have given his handwritten command for an armed coup: "Act according to the order carried by Comrades Liguo and Yuchi." ("Yuchi" refers to Zhou Yuchi, Lin Liguo's close associate.) Lin Liguo then consulted with the key members of the United Flotilla and came up with five ways of assassinating Mao in and near Shanghai. In the meantime, Mao, while in Hangzhou, must have noticed something suspicious. He made a series of abrupt changes to his travel schedule and came back to Beijing on the evening of 12 September.

After the assassination plan failed, Lin Biao allegedly decided to proceed with the second plan: on 13 September, he and his family were to fly south to Guangzhou, where he and Ye Qun were to meet his generals **Huang Yongsheng**, Wu Faxian, Li Zuopeng, Qiu Huizuo, and others to form another central government for a divided country of north and south. On the evening of 12 September, Lin Liguo boarded the aircraft Trident 256 and flew from Beijing to Shanhaiguan, the city nearest Beidaihe with an airfield. He intended for his father to use this special plane on his flight the next day to Guangzhou. At 10:30 p.m., Premier **Zhou Enlai** received a telephone call from the office of the security troop unit 8341 communicating a report from **Lin Liheng**, Lin Biao's daughter, concerning the unusual developments at Beidaihe. A series of decisive moves made by Zhou upon hearing the report, including a telephone conversation with Ye Qun, made Lin Biao and Ye Qun believe that they were being watched. Lin Biao, then, decided to abandon the second plan (of flying south to Guangzhou) and adopt the third: flying northwest out of the country to Irkutsk in the Soviet Union. Lin and his followers rushed through Beidaihe security to Shanhaiguan airfield in Lin's bulletproof sedan, and Trident 256, with nine people aboard, took off at 12:32 a.m. on 13 September.

After Lin Biao left Beidaihe, Lin Liheng notified Beijing. Zhou Enlai issued orders to turn on the radar system in north China to track the path of Trident 256 and to communicate a message to those on board the plane that they should return, that he would meet them in person at any airport. Zhou also reported to Mao Zedong, who reportedly replied, "Rain will fall, widows will marry. Can't help it." In the meantime, Trident 256 reached China's border and crossed into the air space of the People's Republic of Mongolia at 1:50 a.m. Forty minutes later, the plane crashed to the ground near Undurkhan, reportedly due to a lack of fuel. The crash killed all of the passengers, eight men and one woman. On 18 September 1971, the CC issued a circular concerning Lin Biao's "renegade escape," charging him with treason.

More than any other major event in the Cultural Revolution, the 9-13 Incident, along with the events leading up to it, lacks a definitive account. Various versions and interpretations conflict in significant ways with the official one summarized above. Some historians argue that there was no solid and convincing evidence that Lin Biao was ever interested in the position of president of state, while others, not necessarily disagreeing with the former on the issue of the president of state, consider Lin's promotion of the cult of Mao to be sufficient evidence of his political ambition and opportunism. Still some others argue that Lin, suffering from serious ill health and reluctant to engage in politics, was forced into a high position by Mao and then became a victim of Mao's obsession with power. More specifically relevant to the 9-13 Incident were the forming of the United Flotilla, the drafting of the *"571 Project" Summary*, and the plan to assassinate Mao Zedong. But in some personal as well as scholarly accounts, evidence of Lin Biao directing all these actions, and even of his knowledge of them, was at best circumstantial. And finally, as Lin Liheng reported to Beijing on the night of 12 September, she saw the trouble at Beidaihe as a problem of kidnapping: that of Ye Qun and Lin Liguo plotting together without Lin Biao's knowledge and eventually forcing Lin Biao to flee the country.

SEVEN BLACK CATEGORIES. (*Heiqilei.*) A commonly used pejorative, the "seven black categories" refers to those who were labeled as landlords, rich peasants, counterrevolutionaries, bad elements, rightists, capitalists, and "**black gang**" members. The last two categories were an addition to the "**five black categories**" during earlier stages of the Cultural Revolution.

SEVEN THOUSAND CADRES CONFERENCE. *See* CENTRAL COMMITTEE WORK SESSIONS, 11 JANUARY–7 FEBRUARY 1962.

SHAKING HANDS THE SECOND TIME. (*Di'erci woshou.*) Widely circulated and hand copied during the Cultural Revolution, *Shaking Hands the Second Time* is a novel about love and patriotism among Chinese intellectuals for which its author, Zhang Yang, was arrested and imprisoned. Due to the popularity of the novel, the persecution of Zhang became one of the best-known wrongs in the later stage of the Cultural Revolution. Inspired by real-life stories of some foreign-trained scientists coming home to serve their beloved motherland, Zhang began to work on a long story about patriotism in 1964. His writing was interrupted when the authorities arrested him during the **One Strike and Three Antis** campaign in 1970 because he had made critical remarks about **Lin Biao** with friends in a reading group in the Hunan countryside. After his release in December 1972, Zhang resumed writing and named a 200,000-word manuscript version of his novel *Return*. While still in the revision stage, the manuscript was shared by friends and soon copied by many hands and circulated among **educated youths** in many parts of China. The final version of the novel incorporates numerous stylistic improvements and some additional subplots from the hands of anonymous readers. The title of the novel was also changed to *Shaking Hands the Second Time*.

While the second handshake refers to the reunion of two lovers after years of separation, the story focuses on the woman, a distinguished nuclear physicist trained in the United States, who extricates herself from various obstructions set up by the U.S. government and comes back to China, only to find her beloved already married. As she is about to leave Beijing for the United States, brokenhearted, Premier **Zhou Enlai** comes to the airport and persuades her to stay and work for her motherland. In five years, with her contributions, China successfully detonates its first nuclear bomb. As patriotic as the story was, the authorities still found its high regard for intellectuals unacceptable and labeled the novel reactionary. Following **Yao Wenyuan**'s instruction, the Hunan Provincial Bureau of Public Security arrested Zhang on 7 January 1975 and attempted to impose a death sentence upon him. After the downfall of the **Gang of Four**, Zhang began to appeal his case but was not successful until 1979. In July that year, a few months after Zhang's release, *Shaking Hands the Second Time* was published and, with 4.3 million copies sold, became one of the best-selling works in the history of the People's Republic of China.

SHANGHAI MUNICIPAL PARTY COMMITTEE WRITING GROUP. This was a team of writers in the service of the Cultural Revolution faction of the central leadership. It was controlled by **Xu Jingxian**, deputy head of the Shanghai **Revolutionary Committee**, who also served as party secretary of the writing group. **Zhang Chunqiao** and **Yao Wenyuan**, both originally based in Shanghai and both having played major roles in turning Shanghai into a cultural revolutionary base, directed every move of the writing group through Xu. Along with the **Peking University and Tsinghua University Great Criticism Group**, its counterpart in Beijing, the Shanghai writing team produced numerous articles publicizing **Mao Zedong**'s political programs, promoting the interest of the **Jiang Qing** group, and attacking—mostly by innuendo and by allusion—the leaders of the moderate faction, especially **Zhou Enlai** and **Deng Xiaoping**. These articles were often carried in major newspapers in Beijing and Shanghai under such pen names as **Ding Xuelei** and **Luo Siding** and reprinted immediately by provincial and local papers across China. The team was disbanded soon after the downfall of the **Gang of Four**.

See also ALLUSORY HISTORIOGRAPHY; CONFUCIANISM VERSUS LEGALISM; CRITICIZE LIN AND CRITICIZE CONFUCIUS.

SHANGHAI PEOPLE'S COMMUNE. This was the name initially adopted by the new power organ in Shanghai at the suggestion of **Zhang Chunqiao** following the **January Storm** of 1967. Zhang called the Shanghai **power seizure** movement the "January revolution" and apparently based his naming of the new power organ on two sources. First, in his "**Bombarding the Headquarters**" (5 August 1966), **Mao Zedong** spoke highly of a **bigcharacter poster** by **Nie Yuanzi** and others at Peking University as the "declaration of the Paris Commune of the 1960s—Beijing Commune." Second, the **Sixteen Articles**, adopted at the **Eleventh Plenum of the Eighth Central Committee of the Chinese Communist Party** on 8 August 1966, designates that power organs established during the Cultural Revolution should be modeled on the Paris Commune of 1871. Mao, however, never conceived the goal of the Cultural Revolution as abolishing the supreme leadership of the Communist party. In a conversation with Zhang Chunqiao and **Yao Wenyuan** in mid-February 1967, he questioned the place of the party in a commune and indicated his preference for "**revolutionary committee**" as the name for the new power organ. Following Mao's directive, Shanghai People's Commune changed its name to Shanghai Revolutionary Committee on 24 February 1967.

SHI CHUANXIANG (1915–1975). A nightman (someone whose job was to clean out neighborhood excrement) and a well-known national model worker, Shi was a deputy to the National People's Congress before the Cultural Revolution. Born in 1915 to a poor peasant's family in Shandong Province, Shi became a nightman in Beijing at a young age. After 1949, his hard work and loyalty to the party earned him the title of national model worker. Chairman **Mao Zedong**, President **Liu Shaoqi**, and some other leaders of the **Chinese Communist Party** (CCP) received him several times. The picture of Liu Shaoqi's handshake with Shi at the 1959 National Labor Heroes

Conference was carried in the CCP official organ *People's Daily*, making Shi instantly famous. In the early months of the Cultural Revolution, Shi, knowing little about the power struggle in the central leadership, led a **conservative** mass organization called the Capital Workers Defense Regiment in Beijing and took a clear stance of defending Liu Shaoqi, whom Mao was trying hard to overthrow.

When members of the **Central Cultural Revolution Small Group** (CCRSG) began to push the **rebel** movement forward following Mao's battle plan, **Chen Boda** accused Shi of having been "bought over by the bourgeoisie," and **Jiang Qing** called him a "blackleg." In December 1966, during the Criticize the **Bourgeois Reactionary Line** campaign, Shi's organization was crushed by the rebels with strong support from the CCRSG. Shi himself was subject to public humiliation and brutal physical abuse at many **struggle meetings**. Many times he was also paraded through the streets of Beijing on a truck—tied up, bareheaded, with a placard hanging from his neck that read "blackleg" or some other denunciatory and insulting title. His handshake with Liu Shaoqi became criminal evidence against him. In 1971, Shi was expelled from Beijing to his hometown in a rural area in Shandong. The ruthless abuse had physically destroyed Shi: he was paralyzed and unable to speak. Upon the intervention of Premier **Zhou Enlai**, Shi was brought back to Beijing for medical treatment in 1973. He died in May 1975. Shi Chuanxiang was officially rehabilitated in 1978.

SHI YUNFENG (1948–1976). A worker at the First Optical Instrument Factory in Changchun, Jilin Province, Shi was executed for his critical judgment of the Cultural Revolution and his sympathy for President **Liu Shaoqi**. During the Cultural Revolution, Shi read a number of Marxist books and also learned much about Chinese politics from his uncle and other party veterans. On 26 October 1974, he mailed to 14 party organizations at the provincial, city, and district levels about two dozen leaflets in which he names the Cultural Revolution an anachronistic and reactionary turmoil. The revolution, from his perspective, is a serious "anti-party incident" since it started with a coup illegally ousting President Liu Shaoqi and violates party principles in promoting the **personality cult** of **Mao Zedong**. Shi also posted a slogan on a main street of Changchun denouncing the ultra-leftists for causing the disaster of the Cultural Revolution and calling for the rehabilitation of Liu Shaoqi.

Shi's protest caught the attention of the leadership in Beijing. **Wang Hongwen** and some other central leaders soon sent public security agents to Changchun to oversee an investigation of the Shi Yunfeng case. On 24 December 1974, Shi was arrested on a counterrevolutionary charge. Due to his direct criticism of Mao, Shi was sentenced to death by the city intermediate court even after the downfall of the **Gang of Four**. On 19 December

1976, Shi was executed after a public trial in the form of a mass rally. In March 1980, the Jilin provincial party committee pronounced Shi's conviction unjust.

SINGLE SPARK COMBAT TEAM. (*Xingxingzhihuo zhandoudui.*) Active only for a brief period of time in late August and early September 1967, this small student organization was known for its unequivocal opposition to the **Central Cultural Revolution Small Group** (CCRSG). The combat team was made up of a number of **Old Red Guards** and "moderate" **rebels** at Beijing No. 26 Middle School and adopted the approach of distributing leaflets at midnight to publicize their political views, which were in some ways similar to those of the Capital Red Guard **United Action** Committee. They considered the current state of the Cultural Revolution to be one of political hijacking in which key members of the CCRSG, especially **Jiang Qing**, carried out ultra-leftist policies for their own political gains in the name of Chairman **Mao Zedong**. Regarding college campuses as the CCRSG's only base, the combat team accused the radical faction of the party leadership of alienating the great majority of "**conservative**" workers, peasants, and soldiers who were, in their view, actually resistant to the Cultural Revolution. They also detected the conflict between the CCRSG and Premier **Zhou Enlai** and supported Zhou. On 6 September 1967, **Kang Sheng** denounced the Single Spark Combat Team as a counterrevolutionary organization. Its key members were arrested on 12 September. The case against this organization was redressed after the Cultural Revolution.

SIX FACTORIES AND TWO UNIVERSITIES. (*Liuchang erxiao.*) This is a common reference to the institutions to which Chairman **Mao Zedong** dispatched **army propaganda teams** made up of the personnel of the **People's Liberation Army** (PLA) unit 8341, the central leaders' guards regiment, to conduct "**struggle, criticism, reform**" experiments of the Cultural Revolution so that models might be set up for the whole country. The six factories were the Beijing Knitting and Weaving General Plant, Beijing Xinhua Printing Factory, Beijing No. 3 Chemical Factory, Beijing Beijiao Timber Mill, Beijing February 7 Locomotive Factory, and Beijing Nankou Locomotive and Machinery Plant. The two universities were Peking University and Tsinghua University.

The experiments began in early 1968 when the PLA teams were beginning to be dispatched to the factories. From mid-1968 to the early 1970s, a series of reports were written about the ways Mao's policies were carried out in these institutions, which came to be known as the "experiences of the six factories and two universities." As accounts of activities to be emulated, some of the reports were distributed nationwide as documents of the **Chinese**

Communist Party Central Committee, often with Mao's comments, including his admonition against torture and his advice to "offer a way out" for intellectuals. And some others were published with striking headlines in the party organs *People's Daily* and *Red Flag*.

While in some ways having served the purpose of regulating the otherwise completely haphazard and violent actions of mass organizations across the country, these reported models themselves were highly problematic. Most of them still emphasized **class struggle**, and many examples of implementing moderate policies turned out to be fake. For instance, the well-known report of Tsinghua University (dated 20 January 1969) that focused on gentler approaches to intellectuals demonstrated ways of "**reeducating**" (as compared to "denouncing") intellectuals and "offering them a way out." However, in reality, more than one-fifth of the staff members at Tsinghua were investigated as special cases, 178 of them were named class enemies, and more than 10 people died of persecution during the first two months of the **Rectify the Class Ranks** movement. After the Cultural Revolution, the Tsinghua party committee declared all the persecution cases wrongful and, at the same time, concluded that the report of 20 January 1969 was falsified. The post–Cultural Revolution Chinese government came to similar conclusions about most of the so-called experiences of the six factories and two universities.

SIX REGULATIONS OF PUBLIC SECURITY. (*Gongan liutiao.*) *See* REGULATIONS ON STRENGTHENING PUBLIC SECURITY DURING THE GREAT PROLETARIAN CULTURAL REVOLUTION (1967).

SIXTEEN ARTICLES. (*Shiliu tiao.*) This was a common reference to the 16-part "Resolutions of the Central Committee of the **Chinese Communist Party** (CCP) concerning the Great Proletarian Cultural Revolution." Adopted at the **Eleventh Plenum of the Eighth Central Committee of the CCP** on 8 August 1966, the Sixteen Articles, along with the **May 16 Circular**, was named a "programmatic document" providing guidelines for the Cultural Revolution. The document defines the tasks of the revolution as "**struggle, criticism, reform**"—that is, to **struggle against** the **capitalist-roaders** ("those in power within the party who are taking the capitalist road"), to criticize bourgeois academic authorities and bourgeois ideology, and to conduct reform in education, literary and art production, and other social institutions. The document calls on party leadership at all levels to mobilize the masses, encouraging them to express their views freely by writing **big-character posters** and participating in great debates and exposing all "**cow-demons and snake-spirits**" (i.e., class enemies). This, according to the document, is the way to the masses' self-liberation and self-education.

The Sixteen Articles also names cultural revolution groups, **cultural revolution committees**, and cultural revolution congresses as temporary organs of power during the revolution. They should be modeled on the Paris Commune of 1871 and established through general elections under the leadership of the CCP. The document laments the failure of a great number of leaders to understand the Cultural Revolution and calls for the removal of capitalist-roaders and the seizure of power by leftist forces. On 9 August, the day after its passage at the plenum, the Sixteen Articles appeared on the front page of all major newspapers in the country with the banner headline in bold red characters. Since the May 16 Circular was distributed internally at certain levels of party leadership and was yet to be made public, the Sixteen Articles became the first official published document laying out **Mao Zedong**'s radical policies as guidelines for the Cultural Revolution.

SIXTY-ONE TRAITORS CLIQUE. The case of the so-called Sixty-One Traitors Clique was framed by **Kang Sheng** and the **Central Cultural Revolution Small Group** (CCRSG) not only to bring down ranking officials including **Bo Yibo**, An Ziwen, and Liu Lantao but also to incriminate President **Liu Shaoqi**.

In 1936, Ke Qingshi, head of the Organization Department of the North China Bureau of the **Chinese Communist Party** (CCP), suggested to Liu Shaoqi, representative of the CCP Central Committee (CC) at the bureau, that the CCP members captured by the Kuomintang and currently imprisoned at the Beiping Branch of the Military Men's Introspection House be asked to sign the Announcement Renouncing Communism so that they could be released and work for the party. Liu Shaoqi and the North China Bureau approved Ke's proposal and reported to the CC accordingly. Zhang Wentian, general secretary of the CCP, and the CC approved it as well. After Bo Yibo and his fellow prisoners acted upon the instructions from the CC and obtained their release, they received work assignments from the CC in due course. In 1945, at the Seventh National Congress of the CCP, the Credentials Committee ruled in the cases of 12 delegates and two alternates among the 61 that they were not to be affected by this experience and that they met the qualifications for delegates.

In August 1966, Kang Sheng, who was actually on the Credentials Committee at the Seventh Congress and therefore knew firsthand the truth of the case, ordered the Task Force on the Special Case of **Peng Zhen** to investigate this clear and long-settled matter. In the meantime, with Kang's support, some **Red Guards** at Nankai University "uncovered" a "clique of sixty-one traitors" as they searched through pre-1949 newspapers of Beiping (as Beijing was called at the time). On 16 September 1966, Kang sent **Mao Zedong** photocopies of the newspapers that carried the anti-Communist announcements. Kang wrote that he had long been suspicious of the decision Liu

Shaoqi had made 30 years before, and that now evidence showed that the decision was indeed anti-Communist. Members of the CCRSG, **Jiang Qing**, **Guan Feng**, and **Qi Benyu**, soon joined Kang Sheng in inciting the Red Guards to probe further the case of the 61.

Zhou Enlai, on the other hand, tried to persuade both Mao and the Red Guards to do otherwise. Regarding the CCP Northwest Bureau's request for a ruling on a Red Guard inquiry about the release of Liu Lantao, first secretary of the Northwest Bureau, from the Kuomintang prison, Zhou wrote Mao on 24 November 1966, suggesting that the CC admit that it knew this case and that the case was already resolved. Mao then wrote, "Handle the case accordingly," and Zhou acted immediately upon Mao's ruling by wiring the Northwest Bureau on behalf of the CC. Two days later, a similar request came from the Jilin provincial party committee concerning Zhao Lin, acting first secretary of Jilin Province and one of the 61. To protect Zhao, Zhou Enlai responded personally by wire to the Jilin Normal University Red Guards on 30 November, stressing the CC's full knowledge of Zhao Lin's release from prison and advising them not to make announcements or do interrogation at mass meetings and not to distribute pamphlets or to paste up slogans.

Despite Zhou's effort, Mao changed his original stand on this matter and sided with Kang Sheng, Jiang Qing, and their supporters. On 16 March 1967, with Mao's approval, the CC issued the "Instructions on Materials concerning Such Self-Confessing Traitors as Bo Yibo, Liu Lantao, An Ziwen, and Yang Xianzhen." The instructions ruled that "Liu Shaoqi, with consent of Zhang Wentian and behind Chairman Mao's back, planned and decided upon the action of self-confessing and betrayal taken by Bo Yibo and others." Further attempts were made to incriminate Liu. With specific instructions from Kang Sheng, the Nankai Red Guards tried to force Zhang Wentian to make false confessions and place all the responsibility on Liu. Zhang's refusal led to a 523-day virtual house arrest. An Ziwen was asked three times to provide evidence that Liu Shaoqi was a traitor. After his third refusal, An, who was already in jail then, was put in shackles. The instigation of Kang Sheng and company along with the ruling of the CC on the case of the Sixty-One Traitors Clique led to a nationwide witch-hunt to "ferret out traitors," which resulted in widespread persecution.

On 26 December 1978, with the CC's approval of an investigative report filed by its organization department, the case of the 61 was finally redressed, and its victims were rehabilitated.

SNAIL INCIDENT (1973–1974). (*Woniu shijian.*) As **United States–China relations** were becoming normalized thanks to the mutual efforts of both governments, the Fourth Machine Ministry proposed to the Central Committee (CC) of the **Chinese Communist Party** in 1973 that

China import a color kinescope production line from the United States. Upon the approval of the CC, the Fourth Machine Ministry contacted the Corning Corporation and dispatched a 12-member fact-finding team to the United States at the end of the year. During their visit, each member of the delegation received a fine glass snail, a Corning product, as a souvenir. In February 1974, more than a month after the delegation's return, a young cadre at the Fourth Machine Ministry wrote **Jiang Qing** about the glass snails. Jiang personally came to the Fourth Machine Ministry on 10 February and talked about the "snail incident" as an insult to China because the choice of the gift implied that China was moving forward at a snail's pace. Jiang also suggested that a protest be lodged at the newly established U.S. Liaison Office in Beijing, that the glass snails be returned, and that the projected acquisition of a color kinescope production line be canceled.

In the week that followed, mass rallies denouncing the United States were held at the Fourth Machine Ministry and two other ministries, and tremendous pressure was put on Premier **Zhou Enlai**. Zhou instructed the Ministry of Foreign Affairs to investigate and clarify the matter and then consented to the conclusion of the investigative report, which was to be approved by **Mao Zedong** as well, that the snail is a fond image in the eye of Americans and that the Corning Corporation's reception of the Chinese delegation was warm and friendly. With Zhou's instruction, the Politburo also met and decided to stop issuing the script of Jiang Qing's 10 February speech at the Fourth Machine Ministry and to recall those that had already been issued. With these concrete steps taken by Zhou, the disturbance caused by the so-called snail incident was soon quieted.

SOCIALIST EDUCATION MOVEMENT (1962–1966). Also known as the "Four Cleans" (*siqing*) movement, the Socialist Education Movement was a nationwide campaign following a radical line of **class struggle** and political education initiated by **Mao Zedong** at the trend-setting **Tenth Plenum of the Eighth Central Committee of the Chinese Communist Party** (CCP) in September 1962, in response to some CCP leaders' remedial approach to the disastrous consequences of the Great Leap Forward of the late 1950s. The movement started in late 1962. Its middle stage—the fourth year of the projected seven years—merged with the beginning of the Great Proletarian Cultural Revolution (which was once called the *Socialist* Cultural Revolution). Its focus on the struggle against **capitalist-roaders** became the focus of the Cultural Revolution, though the main site of the struggle shifted in 1966 from rural areas and local governments to cities and higher levels of the CCP leadership.

The Socialist Education Movement had its local beginnings as a campaign against family farming and official corruption in the provinces of Hebei and Hunan and then was launched as a nationwide campaign to "clean up accounts, warehouses, assets, and work-points" (hence the "Four Cleans") in communes and county-level government, along with the urban "Five Antis" (against corruption, profiteering, waste, decentralism, and bureaucracy) as a sideline. In 1963, the CCP issued two documents commonly known as the "Early Ten Articles" (May 1963) and the "Later Ten Articles" (September 1963) to guide the movement. The Early Ten Articles includes Mao's warning that in the absence of class struggle "landlords, rich peasants, counterrevolutionaries, bad elements, **cow-demons and snake-spirits**" would all come out, and corrupted officials would collaborate with enemies, which would inevitably lead to a "counterrevolutionary restoration" on a national scale in the near future. In November 1963, government workers as well as college professors and students were organized into work teams and sent to the countryside to help carry out the campaign. Leaders of these work teams included ranking officials such as **Chen Boda** and **Wang Guangmei**, wife of President **Liu Shaoqi**. Wang Guangmei's work report, the "Taoyuan Experience," induced Liu Shaoqi's remark that the party branch at the Taoyuan production brigade of the Luwangzhuang Commune in Hebei Province was "basically not Communist." Liu passed the report to Mao. It was later distributed among party members as a work model for the Socialist Education Movement.

From 15 December 1964 to 14 January 1965, the CCP Politburo held a work meeting to assess the ongoing Socialist Education Movement. At one of the few sessions he attended, Mao criticized Liu Shaoqi for complicating and therefore obscuring the main issue of the campaign with the so-called overlapping contradictions while failing to acknowledge the contradiction between socialism and capitalism as the essence of class struggle in the Socialist Education Movement. At Mao's suggestion, the Politburo adopted a document entitled "Some Current Problems Raised in the Socialist Education Movement," also known as the "Twenty-Three Articles," to override all the previous documents. The "Four Cleans" is redefined in this document as the "purification of politics, economics, organization, and ideology." The key differences between Mao and Liu are reflected in Article Two, "The Nature of the Campaign," which includes the statement that the "focus of this movement is to punish those in power within the party who take the capitalist road." Article Two also states, "Of capitalist-roaders some are in the foreground; some in the background. . . . Even in the central government there are those who are against socialism." For the first time since the Socialist Education Movement began, capitalist-roaders were named as the main target. The same point was to be emphasized in the party guideline for the Cultural Revolution, the **Sixteen Articles**.

By the end of 1965, the Socialist Education Movement had been carried out in about one-third of the counties and communes in the nation. During the first half of 1966, members of Four Cleans work teams were called back to the cities to participate in the Cultural Revolution. The Socialist Education Movement ended without an official closure.

SONG BINBIN (1947–). Both existentially and coincidentally, Song Binbin became the most prominent **Red Guard** icon when, on 18 August 1966, a brief exchange took place between her and Chairman **Mao Zedong** at Tiananmen gate tower: for the Chairman, a Red Guard armband and for Song, an admonishment for dropping her genteel-sounding name ("Binbin") for the militant "Yaowu."

A daughter of Song Renqiong, first secretary of the Northeast Bureau of the **Chinese Communist Party** (CCP) Central Committee, Song Binbin was admitted to the CCP as a probationary member in April 1966 while a student at Beijing Normal University Female Middle School. On 2 June 1966, she joined two other students in posting the school's first **big-character poster** promoting the Cultural Revolution and soon became a deputy head of the newly formed "assembly of revolutionary teachers and students" and, later, a leading member of one of the school's two Red Guard organizations. Acting as an *ad hoc* school authority, the assembly named a number of teachers and school officials to be denounced and publicly humiliated at **struggle meetings**. Among those named was Deputy Principal **Bian Zhongyun**, who was beaten to death by a group of students on 5 August.

At the **mass rally of 18 August 1966**, the first of Mao's eight inspections of Red Guard troops in Beijing, Song put a Red Guard armband on Mao's arm. Upon hearing her genteel-sounding name, "Binbin," Mao said, "Be valiant" ("*yaowu ma*," literally, "Be militant")! An article entitled "I Put a Red Armband on Chairman Mao's Arm" by "Song Yaowu (Song Binbin)" was published in *Guangming Daily* on 20 August 1966 and reprinted in the CCP organ *People's Daily* the following day. The brief drama at Tiananmen tower gate captured by a photo of an enthusiastic Song facing a smiling Mao, along with subsequent massive official propaganda, made Song Binbin— now transformed into Song Yaowu in the popular eye—instantly famous nationwide as a symbol of the Red Guards' unconditional loyalty to Chairman Mao and militant stance against Mao's enemies; Song Binbin herself, however, years later, was to say that she had neither adopted the name Song Yaowu nor written the 20 August 1966 *Guangming Daily* article. In 1972, after three years in the countryside as an **educated youth** receiving **reeducation** from local peasants in Inner Mongolia, Song entered the Changchun Geology Institute as a **worker-peasant-soldier student**. She went to the

United States for graduate studies in 1980 and worked for the Massachusetts Department of Environmental Protection after completing a doctorate at the Massachusetts Institute of Technology in 1989.

In 2007, when Beijing Normal University Female Middle School (now a co-ed institution named Beijing Normal University Experimental Middle School) was celebrating its 90th anniversary at the Great Hall of the People on Tiananmen Square, Song Binbin entered her name into a competition for the 90 most distinguished alumni and was named as one of the 90. The extravagant school photo album made for this occasion displayed her portrait with Mao juxtaposed to the portrait of Bian Zhongyun on the opposite page, which provoked much public rage, especially the indignation of Bian's widower, Wang Jingyao, who wrote in an open letter to the current school principal that the Red Guard armband Song Binbin gave Mao was "stained with Comrade Bian Zhongyun's blood." On 12 January 2014, Song joined some 20 former schoolmates at a gathering to make formal apologies to teachers and students persecuted during the Cultural Revolution. She bowed to Bian Zhongyun's bust and read a prepared statement expressing her regret for "not being able to protect" Bian and other victims. The substitution of an incompetent protector for the commonly perceived Red Guard role as a willing executioner in her self-description, however, provoked another protest from Wang Jingyao who, not invited to the gathering, dismissed Song Binbin's apology as sham.

"SONG OF THE EDUCATED YOUTHS OF NANJING". (*Nanjing zhiqingzhige.*) This is a song about the pensive mood of the **educated youths** in the countryside for which its author/composer, Ren Yi, was persecuted. A student of Nanjing No. 5 High School, Ren went to work in a rural area of Jiangsu Province at the end of 1968. In May 1969, at the request of his friends in the village, Ren, a guitar player, composed a song dedicated to educated youths, based on an earlier melody, and put down Nanjing No. 5 High School students as the collective author. Originally consisting of three verses and entitled "My Hometown," the song soon spread across China and became so popular among educated youths in the countryside that the title was changed by its singers in different places to "Song of the Educated Youths" with their own place-name. The song also began to have dozens of different versions developed and modified by its singers; the longest one having seven verses. Present in most of these versions were the themes of parting sorrows and homesickness, of love and friendship, and of the harshness and uncertainty of life.

In just a few months after its original creation, the song had become so well known that Radio Moscow broadcast a choral version of it in August 1969 with the title "Song of the Educated Youths of China." The attention of a "revisionist" country soon brought misfortune to the original author of the song. On 19 February 1970, largely due to the pressure from **Jiang Qing**, **Zhang Chunqiao**, and **Yao Wenyuan**, Ren was arrested by local authorities. Charged with the crime of "composing a reactionary song and sabotaging the movement of educated youths going **up to the mountains and down to the countryside**," Ren was sentenced to 10 years in prison on 3 August 1970. In August 1978, the district court that had sentenced him finally pronounced him not guilty but still judged his song as "representing a strong petty bourgeois sentiment."

SONG SHUO (1921–1969). Deputy head of the university department of the Beijing Municipal Committee of the **Chinese Communist Party** (CCP) and a major target of what **Mao Zedong** called the **first Marxist-Leninist big-character poster** by **Nie Yuanzi** and others, Song Shuo was an early victim of the Cultural Revolution. A native of Zhejiang Province, Song joined the CCP in 1945 while an organizer of the underground student movement in Beijing. After 1949, he served as deputy head of the university department of the CCP Beijing Municipal Committee and party secretary of Beijing Industrial University. In 1964, during the **Socialist Education Movement**, when Peking University president **Lu Ping** and his school party committee were under attack by the socialist education work team and by a number of philosophy department faculty including Nie Yuanzi, the CCP Beijing Municipal Committee led by **Peng Zhen** stepped in to support Lu Ping and to put down Nie and her colleagues. To assist Lu, the municipal committee sent Song Shuo to Peking University and made him a leading member of the socialist education work team.

Largely because of Song's involvement in this political conflict on the campus of Peking University, Nie and her six philosophy department colleagues attacked him in the **big-character poster** "What Are Song Shuo, Lu Ping, and **Peng Peiyun** Really Doing in the Cultural Revolution?" which was posted on 25 May 1966. This poster accuses Song, Lu, and Peng of conspiring with the Beijing Municipal Committee to suppress the revolutionary ideas and activities of the masses and mislead the ongoing Cultural Revolution on campus. On 2 June 1966, a *People's Daily* commentary names Song a member of the **Three-Family Village Anti-Party Clique**. On 3 June, the newly organized CCP Beijing Municipal Committee announced a decision to remove Song Shuo from office. Song, then, became a main target of endless **struggle meetings** and incarceration. He died of lung cancer on 29 October 1969. His name was cleared in 1979 by the CCP Beijing Municipal Committee.

SPRING SEEDLING. (*Chunmiao*). Directed by Xie Jin and others and produced by the Shanghai Film Studio in 1975, *Spring Seedling* was the first feature film set in the Cultural Revolution. Its release was celebrated by the ultra-leftist-controlled official media but criticized by **Deng Xiaoping**, whose judgment of the film became his liability during the **Counterattack the Right-Deviationist Reversal-of-Verdicts Trend** campaign. The film was adapted from a play about a **barefoot doctor** fighting against a revisionist line in health care and seizing power in a commune hospital. To make insinuations against Deng Xiaoping, however, **Xu Jingxian**, a member of the Shanghai municipal party committee and a close ally of the **Jiang Qing** group, instructed the film crew to change the character of the old hospital director from a problematic, error-making, and yet ultimately savable cadre into an "unrepentant" **capitalist-roader**. When the film was being previewed by party leaders before its public release, Deng was said to have pronounced it "ultra-leftist" and left in the middle of the preview session. After Deng was dismissed from office for the second time in January 1976, the writing groups of the **Gang of Four** criticized his view on the film in several articles. But, eventually, the post–Cultural Revolution Chinese leadership concurred with Deng's view and dismissed *Spring Seedling* as the first conspiratorial film made under the influence of the Gang of Four.

SS *FENGQING* INCIDENT (1974). The maiden voyage of the SS *Fengqing*, a Chinese-made (*Fengqinglun shijian*), 10,000-ton oceangoing freighter, was taken by **Jiang Qing** and her supporters as an opportunity for making insinuations against **Zhou Enlai** and **Deng Xiaoping** for promoting a "worship of foreign things" and adopting a "slavish comprador philosophy." The aggressiveness of the attack led to a direct confrontation between Deng and Jiang at a Politburo meeting on 17 October 1974 and eventually to **Mao Zedong**'s admonition to **Wang Hongwen** not to follow Jiang Qing.

In early 1974, as the Shanghai branch of the China Oceangoing Transportation Company, a state agency under the Ministry of Transportation, was checking the SS *Fengqing* upon delivery, their questions were interpreted as "worshipping things foreign." After the freighter departed from the port of Shanghai on 4 May, and especially as it sailed past the turbulent waters of the Cape of Good Hope, Jiang Qing and **Zhang Chunqiao** complained about what they considered to be less-than-adequate news coverage and decided to make the SS *Fengqing*'s homecoming a huge political event—an occasion for both celebration and attack. The ship arrived on 30 September, but concerned that the coverage of the 1 October National Day celebrations might overshadow that of the SS *Fengqing*, **Yao Wenyuan** made arrangements so that there would be no news report about the ship's homecoming until 9 October. On 12 October, the Shanghai *Liberation Daily* and *Wenhui Daily* carried long articles celebrating the successful completion of the SS *Feng-*

qing's first voyage. These articles characterize the development of shipbuilding in modern Chinese history as a series of struggles between those who worship Confucianism and foreign things and patriots who oppose Confucianism. Aiming to implicate Zhou Enlai by way of **allusory historiography**, the authors of these articles name a number of historical personages from Qing officials Zeng Guofan and Li Hongzhang to denounced Communist leaders **Liu Shaoqi** and **Lin Biao** as pursuers of "a slavish comprador philosophy." "As to shipbuilding," the authors write, "they held that building ships was not as good as purchasing them and that purchasing was not as good as chartering. They all carried out a policy of national betrayal."

On 14 October, Jiang Qing and her followers received a long report on Li Guotang and Gu Wenguang, two cadres from Beijing with assignments onboard the SS *Fengqing* during its first voyage. According to the report, during the voyage Li and Gu expressed reservations about the ultra-leftists' criticism of the State Council and Ministry of Transportation policy of shipbuilding and purchasing; they considered the combination of building and purchasing as both practical and necessary and refused to characterize it as a policy of "national betrayal." Jiang singled out Li Guotang, deputy political commissioner of the SS *Fengqing* crew, along with the Ministry of Transportation and the State Council, as targets of her "proletarian indignation" and wrote furious comments, with which Zhang Chunqiao, Yao Wenyuan, and Wang Hongwen invariably concurred. Due to the comments from the **Gang of Four**, Li and Gu were **struggled against** at mass rallies, and the "Li-Gu incident" was termed a "reactionary political incident."

In the meantime, Jiang Qing brought the issue to the Politburo. At a Politburo meeting on the evening of 17 October, Jiang and her supporters pressed Deng Xiaoping for an opinion on the SS *Fengqing* incident. Deng said the issue required further investigation that was actually being undertaken. In response to Jiang's further question of whether he was for or against criticizing a "slavish comprador philosophy," Deng retorted: "How could the Politburo members cooperate, since you impose your views on others? Should everyone write down an opinion in agreement with yours?" The Jiang group met after the Politburo meeting and decided that Wang Hongwen would fly to Changsha, Hunan, to relate to Mao their version of the Politburo meeting before Deng could give his. The purpose of the trip, according to Wang's later confession, was to prevent Deng from becoming the first deputy premier, since such had long been Zhou Enlai's wish and since Mao had just made a proposal earlier in October that Deng be given that important position in charge of the central government's daily affairs while Premier Zhou was in the hospital for cancer treatment. In his conversation with Mao the following day, Wang Hongwen described the 17 October Politburo meeting as another **Lushan Conference** of 1970 (in which the Jiang Qing group was under attack). Wang also informed Mao of Zhou Enlai's frequent meetings with Deng Xiaoping, **Ye Jianying**, **Li Xiannian**, and others and offered his suspicion that these meetings might concern personnel issues to be finalized in the forthcoming **Fourth National People's Congress**. Much to Wang's disappointment, Mao did not side with the Jiang Qing group this time as he did at the Lushan Conference; instead, he advised Wang to talk more with Premier Zhou and Marshal Ye, to be careful about Jiang Qing, and not to follow her. These words from Mao sufficiently put the SS *Fengqing* Incident to an end.

STRUGGLE AGAINST. (*Dou* or *pidou*.) A commonly used term during the Cultural Revolution, especially in its early stages, to "struggle against" someone means to denounce and criticize the person publicly in a group meeting or at a mass rally. **Struggle meeting**, the name of such a gathering, derives from the verbal phrase "struggle against." In addition to verbal harassment, a struggle meeting often involved physical abuse of the victims.
    See also SIXTEEN ARTICLES; VIOLENT STRUGGLE.

STRUGGLE, CRITICISM, REFORM. (*Dou pi gai*.) This is a brief reference to the tasks of the Cultural Revolution proposed by the Central Committee of the **Chinese Communist Party** in August 1966.
    See also SIXTEEN ARTICLES.

STRUGGLE MEETING. (*Duozheng hui* or *pidou hui*.) This is the name for any group meeting or mass rally at which people labeled "class enemies" were **struggled against**—that is, criticized and denounced. The victims at such a meeting were usually forced to stand with heads hung or to kneel down on the edge of a raised platform facing the crowd. They were often forced to hang a big sign board from their neck with a denunciatory label written on it and with the victim's name crossed out in red ink. On some occasions, there were guards standing behind them and holding their arms in a humiliating and painful position called the "**jet plane style**." Sometimes the victims were forced to wear humiliating attire, as in the case of **Wang Guangmei**, wife of President **Liu Shaoqi**, who was among 300 alleged class enemies and "**cow-demons and snake-spirits**" at a rally of 300,000 people. Accusatory speeches were read aloud at struggle meetings, with intermittent slogan-shouting. The victims were often subjected to brutal physical abuse at such meetings. In the early stages of the Cultural Revolution, the army belt with a bronze buckle was the **Red Guards**' favorite instrument of torture for such occasions. There were numerous cases, especially in summer and autumn 1966, in which victims committed suicide after a struggle meeting; some were even beaten to death at the meeting.

SUMMARY OF THE SYMPOSIUM CONVENED BY COMRADE JI-ANG QING AT THE BEHEST OF COMRADE LIN BIAO ON THE WORK OF LITERATURE AND THE ARTS IN THE ARMED FORCES. (*Lin Biao tongzhi weituo Jiang Qing tongzhi zhaokai de budui wenyi gongzuo zuotanhui jiyao.*) This is one of the key documents with which **Mao Zedong** made a foray into the field of literature and the arts so as to launch the Cultural Revolution. At the request of **Jiang Qing** in Mao's name, **Lin Biao** endorsed her proposal to hold a symposium on 2–20 February 1966 with four ranking officers in charge of the work of literature and the arts in the armed forces. During the 19 days of the symposium, Jiang watched films with the participants, took them to dramatic performances, led

Former Defense Minister Peng Dehuai and former CCP General Secretary Zhang Wentian at a struggle meeting of a hundred thousand, 26 July 1967.

the study sessions of Mao's works concerning literature and the arts, and conducted discussions and interviews. The summary report of the symposium, which was twice revised by **Chen Boda**, **Zhang Chunqiao**, and two other officials and thrice edited by Mao himself, reflects Jiang Qing's harsh judgment on China's literary and art productions since 1949. The final version of the Summary was issued by the Central Committee of the **Chinese Communist Party** on 10 April 1966 to provincial and ministerial party committees.

According to the Summary, almost all of the literary and artistic works created in the first 16 years of the People's Republic of China were politically problematic because they were dictated by an "anti-party and anti-socialist black line in opposition to the thought of Chairman Mao, a black line that combines bourgeois literary theory and modern revisionist literary theory with the so-called Literature and Arts of the 1930s." This was the first time that such a completely negative assessment of the state of literature and the arts appeared in an official document. More specifically, the Summary enumerates the **"eight black theories"** dominating the field of literature and the arts, which were to become guidelines in the ensuing militant attacks upon writers and artists during the Cultural Revolution. In contrast to such slandering of the majority of writers and artists, the Summary celebrates the rise of "modern revolutionary Peking operas," products of Jiang Qing's "experimental fields." The flattery of Jiang Qing by the Summary as an inspiring reader of **Mao Zedong Thought** and an experienced worker in the fields of the arts and literature served to prepare her rise in China's political scene during the Cultural Revolution.

"SUSPECTING ALL". (*Huaiyi yiqie.*) Also worded as "suspecting all, overthrowing all," this slogan was embraced by many **Red Guards** in the early stages of the Cultural Revolution. The story of Karl Marx's conversations with his daughter in which the father names "Suspect all" as his favorite motto made the slogan popular among rebellious youths. In summer and fall 1966, several **big-character posters** were written by both **Old Red Guards** and **rebels** to promote thoroughgoing skepticism as a guiding principle of the mass movement. **Tao Zhu**, then number four in rank in the **Chinese Communist Party** (CCP) central leadership, voiced conditional endorsement for the slogan in step with Chairman **Mao Zedong**'s call upon the masses to dismantle old party and state apparatuses. Since **revolutionary committees** were being established as new organs of power in early 1967, however, CCP leaders began to dismiss the slogan as anarchistic and "left in form but right in essence." According to a speech **Zhang Chunqiao** gave on 1 February 1967, it was a strategic decision of the CCP central leadership not to denounce the slogan earlier because, at that time, a negative response to the slogan from the central leadership might have been used by those still in power as an excuse to suppress the ongoing mass movement. Later in the year, in an article published in the 8 September 1967 issue of *People's Daily*, **Yao Wenyuan** took Tao Zhu's earlier remark out of context and charged him with the crime of using the slogan to turn the spearhead of the mass movement against Mao. With the publication of this article, "suspecting all" as a popular slogan was officially outlawed.

"SWEEP AWAY ALL COW-DEMONS AND SNAKE-SPIRITS". (*Hengsao yiqie niuguisheshen.*) Written under the direction of **Chen Boda**, head of the **Central Cultural Revolution Small Group** (CCRSG) and leader of the **work group** for Beijing's journalistic agencies, and also revised by Chen, this notoriously titled piece was a *People's Daily* editorial published on 1 June 1966, publicly inaugurating the Cultural Revolution. While attempting to explain the ideological and cultural spheres as the main battleground of class struggle after the proletariat power takeover and to define the Cultural Revolution as such a battle, the article specifies "bourgeois experts, scholars, and academic authorities" as major enemies (referred to as "cow-demons and snake-spirits") to be swept away. The editorial also calls on the masses to crusade against "old ideas, old cultures, old customs, and old habits" of the exploiting classes. These terms were introduced for the first time and soon became known as the **Four Olds** in popular vocabulary. As one of the most influential pieces of political writing during the Cultural Revolution, this editorial made Chinese intellectuals (teachers, writers, and artists), instead of party officials (*dangquanpai*) as specified in the party central committee document **May 16 Circular**, the initial targets of violent attacks by the **Red Guards** and, with its condemnation of the Four Olds, caused unprecedented damage to traditional culture. The phrase "cow-demons and snake-spirits" dehumanized targets of the campaign and contributed much to the widespread persecution of innocent people.

T

TAN HOULAN (1937–1982). One of the well-known "five **Red Guard** leaders" in Beijing, Tan was head of the mass organization Jinggang Mountain Commune at Beijing Normal University and a prominent leader of the Capital College **Red Guards' Representative Assembly**.

A native of Wangcheng, Hunan Province, Tan joined the **Chinese Communist Party** in 1958. When the Cultural Revolution broke out, she was a student of political education at Beijing Normal University. Because of her opposition to the **work group** at Beijing Normal University, she was named a reactionary student during the **Anti-Interference Campaign** initiated by the **Liu Shaoqi** and **Deng Xiaoping** leadership in late June and early July 1966. With support from the **Central Cultural Revolution Small Group** (CCRSG), her name was eventually cleared. Then Tan founded a nationally influential rebel student organization, the Jinggang Mountain Regiment (which later changed its name to Jinggang Mountain Commune) at her university. The organization, with Tan as its leader, soon became a major mass force at the service of **Mao Zedong** and the CCRSG in their offensive against the so-called **capitalist-roaders** during and after the Criticize the **Bourgeois Reactionary Line** campaign in late 1966 and early 1967.

Following instructions from **Qi Benyu**, of the CCRSG, Tan led more than 200 Red Guards to Qufu, the hometown of Confucius in Shandong Province, in November 1966 to sweep away the **Four Olds** there. They held anti-Confucian mass rallies of 100,000 people on 28 and 29 November. Together with local student rebels, they destroyed thousands of tombs, stone tablets, ancient books, and valuable calligraphies and paintings. The historic Confucian Homestead, Confucian Temple, and Confucian Cemetery were all vandalized. In the chaotic years of 1967 and 1968, Tan and her organization were closely associated with such ultra-leftist party officials as **Wang Li**, **Guan Feng**, Qi Benyu, and **Lin Jie** and deeply involved in nationwide factional violence and in the campaign to "ferret out the small handful [of capitalist-roaders] in the army." They also closely followed the orders of the radical officials to attack such ranking party and state leaders as **Tan Zhenlin** and **Luo Ruiqing**. For her achievements as a student leader, Tan was named head of the **revolutionary committee** of Beijing Normal University and appointed a member of the Standing Committee of the Beijing Municipal Revolutionary Committee in 1967.

However, Tan's downfall began in summer 1968 when Mao decided to put an end to the Red Guard movement. On the early morning of 28 July 1968, Mao met with the five Red Guard leaders, including Tan Houlan. At the meeting, Mao sent a strong signal to Tan and others that they should exit China's political stage. Shortly after Mao's reception, a **workers propaganda team** and an **army propaganda team** were sent to Beijing Normal University to take over power from Tan and rebel students. Tan was taken into custody by the propaganda teams from 1970 to 1975. In 1978, after the downfall of the **Gang of Four**, the Beijing Public Security Bureau ordered the arrest of Tan on a counterrevolutionary charge. Tan was released on bail for medical treatment of cancer in summer 1981. In June 1982, five months before her death, the Beijing People's Prosecutor's Office announced that, on the grounds of Tan's sincere confessions of her crimes, it would not bring a suit against her.

See also MAO ZEDONG: MEETING WITH THE FIVE RED GUARD LEADERS (28 July 1968).

TAN LIFU (1945–). Son of a ranking official, Tan was a leader of the **Red Guards** at Beijing Industrial University and a strong supporter of the **work group** policy adopted by the central leadership under **Liu Shaoqi** in summer 1966. Tan was also the most notorious advocate of the **blood lineage theory** in the early stages of the Cultural Revolution. Shortly after the couplet "If the father is a hero, the son is a real man; if the father is a reactionary, the son is a bastard" appeared at Beijing middle schools, Tan enthusiastically embraced the couplet as a manifestation of truth as well as a revolutionary slogan.

In the **big-character poster** "Words Prompted by the Antithetical Couplet" (12 August 1966), which Tan coauthored with Liu Jing, also a son of a ranking official, Tan suggested that the couplet—as a creation of the masses based on experience—be adopted as the party's **class line**. On 20 August 1966, Tan gave a long speech at a debate about the fate of the work group at Beijing Industrial University. In the speech, Tan called on Red Guards and students with a proletarian family background to **struggle against** those from "bad" families, whom he referred to as "sons-of-dogs," "reactionary students," and "rightists." Tan's naming of his fellow students as targets of the revolution served well to divert the focus of the political movement and protect the work group and party officials, which went contrary to the battle call **Mao Zedong** made earlier in the month for "**bombarding the headquarters**" within the party.

Already a key member of the Preparation Group of the **cultural revolution committee** of Beijing Industrial University, largely due to his earlier support for the work group and to his political activism, Tan now became a political star: his 20 August speech was printed and distributed in cities and towns across China by work groups and party establishments at various levels and was used as a tool by work groups and party officials to refocus the main targets of the movement from **capitalist-roaders** within the party to traditional class enemies of the so-called **seven black categories** and their children. Consequently, political persecution and physical abuse of those with a "bad" family background, especially teachers and students, surged nationwide, and "Tan Lifu" became a terrifying and infamous name. In October 1966, Mao launched a campaign to criticize the **Bourgeois Reactionary Line**, in which the blood lineage theory became one of the main targets of criticism; Tan himself was named a reactionary student.

TAN ZHENLIN (1902–1983). Vice-premier in charge of agriculture and a close associate of Premier **Zhou Enlai**, Tan was known for his volcanic rage against members of the **Central Cultural Revolution Small Group** (CCRSG) during the **February Adverse Current** of 1967. A native of Youxian, Hunan Province, Tan Zhenlin joined the **Chinese Communist Party** (CCP) in 1926 and served in various ranking positions in the Red Army in the late 1920s and early 1930s. He conducted guerrilla warfare against the Nationalist forces in the south after the Red Army marched north. Later he became a division commander in the New Fourth Army during the war of resistance against Japan and deputy political commissioner of the Third Field Army during the civil war of the late 1940s. After 1949, Tan became governor of Zhejiang and then of Jiangsu. He also became third secretary of the CCP East China Bureau. Tan was transferred to Beijing in 1954, elected to the CCP Politburo in 1958, and appointed deputy premier in 1959.

The most outspoken and the most quick-tempered of all Zhou Enlai's cabinet members, Tan was annoyed by the politically ambitious **Jiang Qing** in the early days of the Cultural Revolution and called her the "[Empress] Wu Zetian of today's China." On 16 February 1967, at a top-level briefing session in Huairen Hall at the CCP headquarters in the Zhongnanhai compound, Tan—furious with **Zhang Chunqiao** and other members of the CCRSG—accused them of persecuting veteran cadres. Calling the Cultural Revolution "the cruelest struggle in party history," he vowed to fight the ultra-leftists through to the end even if the cost was imprisonment and death. The next day, Tan wrote **Lin Biao** a letter reiterating his stand against the cultural revolutionaries and venting his rage. On the night of 18 February, **Mao Zedong** convened part of the Politburo to a meeting, during which he sharply criticized the veteran officials who had protested against the Cultural

Revolution at the Huairen Hall briefing. In the subsequent political campaign against the February Adverse Current, Tan was singled out as the leader of the rebellious veteran cadres and **struggled against** by the masses. At mass rallies, Jiang Qing often called for Tan's downfall. Of the marshals and deputy premiers who spoke out on 16 February, Tan was the only one to be put on a **capitalist-roader** list with **Liu Shaoqi, Deng Xiaoping, Peng Zhen**, and others in a number of 1968 CCP official documents. Also in 1968, Tan was sent to Guangxi to do manual labor.

At the end of 1972, Zhou Enlai, taking a hint from Mao, arranged to move Tan back to Beijing. Tan was officially "liberated" (*jiefang*) in May 1973. But any titles and positions given to him from this point on were mostly ceremonial, including vice-chairman of the standing committee of both the fourth (1974) and fifth (1978) National People's Congress and vice-chairman of the CCP Advisory Committee (1982). Tan was formally rehabilitated by the CCP Central Committee in January 1980. He died on 30 September 1983.

TANG WENSHENG (1943–). A young diplomat and English interpreter, Tang was one of **Mao Zedong**'s liaisons at the Politburo in the early 1970s and deputy head of the North America and Oceania Department of the Ministry of Foreign Affairs in the later years of the Cultural Revolution.

Born in New York City in 1943 and known by her English name Nancy Tang, Tang was a daughter of the overseas **Chinese Communist Party** (CCP) veteran Tang Mingzhao. When her parents returned to China in 1950, they brought the seven-year-old Tang Wensheng with them. Upon graduation from the Beijing Institute of Foreign Languages in 1965, Tang became an English interpreter at the Ministry of Foreign Affairs. In the early years of the Cultural Revolution, Tang was a staunch **conservative**, supporting Minister **Chen Yi** and Premier **Zhou Enlai** and opposing the **rebels** and the so-called **May 16 Counterrevolutionary Clique**. Tang was soon chosen by the premier as his chief English interpreter. At the end of 1970, when Chairman Mao Zedong received the American journalist Edgar Snow, Tang began serving as Mao's main English interpreter, while her colleague and friend **Wang Hairong** was note taker. Assisting Mao in his diplomatic activities, Tang was involved in some of the most important events in the foreign affairs of the People's Republic of China during the Cultural Revolution, including much of the work that eventually led to the normalization of **United States–China relations**.

Due to her convenient access to Mao, Tang also became deeply involved in top-level CCP politics. Leaders of all factions within the central leadership often had to depend on her, as well as on her friend and ally Wang Hairong, for communications with Mao. At the **Tenth National Congress of the CCP** (24–28 August 1973)—just two years after she joined the CCP—Tang entered the Central Committee (CC) as an alternate member. In 1974, she was appointed deputy head of the North America and Oceania Department of the Ministry of Foreign Affairs. As one of the new power-holders at the ministry, she was also involved in the persecution of a number of innocent cadres and government workers during a series of political campaigns.

After Mao's death in 1976, Tang remained in office; she retained her seat in the CC as an alternate member in August 1977 at the Eleventh National Congress of the CCP. However, not long after the Eleventh Congress, she was taken into custody and put under investigation. Tang was reassigned as deputy editor-in-chief of the English *China Daily* in 1984 and then became director of the Foreign Affairs Bureau of the Ministry of Railways. In 1999, she was appointed deputy chair of the All-China Federation of the Returned Overseas Chinese.

TAO ZHU (1908–1969). Promoted to the Standing Committee of the **Chinese Communist Party** (CCP) Politburo at **Mao Zedong**'s suggestion, Tao ranked fourth in the party central leadership at the **Eleventh Plenum of the Eighth Central Committee of the CCP** (1–12 August 1966). He assisted Premier **Zhou Enlai** in tending to daily affairs of the state and carried out certain moderate measures during the early stages of the Cultural Revolution before he was pronounced the nation's number three **capitalist-roader** after **Liu Shaoqi** and **Deng Xiaoping**.

A native of Qiyang, Hunan Province, and a member of the fifth graduating class of the Huangpu (Whampoa) Military Academy, Tao Zhu joined the CCP in 1926. In 1927, he participated in the Nanchang Uprising as a company commander. In 1930, he led a well-known operation in Xiamen, Fujian Province, to rescue Communists from a Kuomintang prison. Tao was arrested by the Kuomintang in 1933 and was imprisoned until the beginning of the war of resistance against Japan in 1937. Tao went to Yan'an in 1940 and held various ranking positions in charge of political and ideological work in the army. In 1948, Tao represented the CCP and the **People's Liberation Army** (PLA) in negotiations with Kuomintang general Fu Zuoyi for the PLA's peaceful takeover of power in Beijing. From 1949 to 1965, Tao was a top CCP official in southeastern China whose positions included governor of Guangdong Province, first secretary of the CCP South China Bureau, and political commissar of the Guangzhou Military Region. A man of letters, Tao also published in this period two collections of essays on self-cultivation in the spirit of Communist ideals.

Tao was appointed deputy premier of the State Council in 1965. At the **enlarged Politburo sessions** in May 1966, he was made executive secretary of the CCP Central Committee (CC) Secretariat and director of the CCP Propaganda Department (replacing **Lu Dingyi**). He also became advisor of the **Central Cultural Revolution Small Group** (CCRSG). With these positions, and as a member of the Politburo Standing Committee after August,

Tao worked more closely with Zhou Enlai than with the ultra-leftists in the CCRSG: on the one hand, he talked frequently with representatives of mass organizations and offered instructions on the Cultural Revolution as Mao had intended; on the other hand, he helped design and enact policies to minimize the disruptive impact of the Cultural Revolution on the national economy. Tao also made attempts to protect a number of people, including the well-known historian Professor Chen Yinque and Wang Renzhong, a member of the CCRSG, against attacks from the masses; he was sometimes confrontational in his meetings with **Red Guards** and **rebels**.

Eventually, Tao Zhu alienated himself from the CCRSG. On 4 January 1967, **Jiang Qing** attacked him in a public speech. On 8 January, Mao spoke against Tao at a meeting of central leaders, accusing him of being dishonest, of carrying out the Liu-Deng political line, and of promoting Liu's and Deng's public image. Tao was then dismissed from office and brought down as "China's biggest bourgeois royalist," "counterrevolutionary two-face," "traitor," along with a host of other pejorative labels. In September 1967, Mao approved publication of **Yao Wenyuan**'s article "On Two Books by Tao Zhu," which made Tao the highest CCP leader officially denounced at the time—before Liu Shaoqi and Deng Xiaoping, who were denounced but yet to be named by official media. Tao was both physically and mentally abused at **struggle meetings**. He was sent to Anhui in October 1968 when he became gravely ill. He died on 30 November 1969.

On 24 December 1978, the CC held a memorial service for Tao Zhu to redress the case and to clear Tao's name.

TENTH NATIONAL CONGRESS OF THE CHINESE COMMUNIST PARTY (24–28 August 1973). Held in Beijing about two years after the downfall of **Mao Zedong**'s handpicked successor **Lin Biao**, the Tenth National Congress was a meeting of 1,249 delegates representing 2.8 million members of the **Chinese Communist Party** (CCP). A few days before the meeting, on 20 August 1973, the Central Committee (CC) approved "An Investigative Report on the Counterrevolutionary Crimes of the Lin Biao Anti-Party Clique" and expelled from the party Lin Biao, **Chen Boda**, **Ye Qun**, **Huang Yongsheng**, **Wu Faxian**, **Li Zuopeng**, and **Qiu Huizuo**, all of whom except Lin and Chen were newly elected into the Politburo at the First Plenum of the **Ninth National Congress of the CCP**. However, the Tenth Congress refused to reflect on grave errors of the Ninth Congress and of the party's Cultural Revolution policies in general; on the contrary, it affirmed the "correctness of both the political and the organizational lines of the Ninth Congress."

At the meeting, **Zhou Enlai**, on behalf of the CC, delivered the political report, which was drafted mostly by **Zhang Chunqiao** and **Yao Wenyuan** and approved by Mao. The report denounced Lin Biao and his cohorts for carrying out anti-party activities behind the façade of Mao worship. It also acknowledged that China was still a poor, developing country and needed to build a stronger socialist economy. Yet the report also criticized a draft version of the Ninth Congress political report, allegedly written by Chen Boda following Lin Biao's instructions but dismissed by Mao, which embraced **Liu Shaoqi's economism**. The report thus contradicted Zhou's recent effort against ultra-leftist policies and reaffirmed Mao's notion of **class struggle** and intra-party struggle, which, according to the report, "will last for a long period of time and will occur again ten times, twenty times, thirty times."

The second item on the Congress agenda was **Wang Hongwen's** report on the revision of the CCP Constitution. In the draft version of the constitution he submitted, and later adopted by the Congress, the words in the Ninth Congress–approved constitution identifying Lin Biao as Mao's "close comrade-in-arms and successor" were deleted. Additions included Mao's recent call upon party members to "go against the tide," a clear indication of Mao's concern that the trend had increasingly favored ending and negating the Cultural Revolution.

With **Deng Xiaoping**, Chen Yun, **Tan Zhenlin, Zhao Ziyang**, and a few other "old government" officials elected into the CC, moderate and pragmatic elements in the party leadership gained some ground at the Tenth Congress. At the opening of the Congress, Deng Xiaoping was also elected member of the presidium. On the other hand, the Tenth Congress saw further consolidation of power of the cultural revolutionaries closely associated with **Jiang Qing**: Zhang Chunqiao was elected general secretary of the Congress and became member of the powerful Politburo Standing Committee. **Kang Sheng** was promoted to vice-chairman of the CC. And months before the Congress, Mao recommended Wang Hongwen to take charge of the CCP Constitution revision group and later to chair the Congress Election/Preparation Committee (both Zhou Enlai and **Ye Jianying** were under Wang's leadership in this committee). At the First Plenum held immediately after the Congress, Wang was elected a member of the Politburo Standing Committee and one of the five vice-chairmen of the CC. The meteoric rise of Wang, who was on his way to becoming a member of the **Gang of Four**, was a major part of Mao's plan to select, test, and train another successor after the fall of Lin Biao.

TENTH PLENUM OF THE EIGHTH CENTRAL COMMITTEE OF THE CHINESE COMMUNIST PARTY (24–27 September 1962). The first plenum of the **Chinese Communist Party** Central Committee after the Great Famine of the late 1950s and early 1960s (commonly known by the euphemism of "three years of natural disasters" or "three difficult years") that claimed 20 to 30 million lives, this meeting marked a crucial transition in party policies from pragmatic approaches rectifying the mistakes of the late 1950s Great Leap Forward to a radical ultra-leftist line emphasizing **class struggle**. At the meeting, those who supported remedial measures, such as allowing contract production and private plots in the countryside in the early 1960s, were criticized for "taking the capitalist road." Two committees were formed to investigate the "verdict-reversing attempts" of the **Peng Dehuai** and **Xi Zhongxun** "anti-party cliques." The Plenum Bulletin contains a statement that Chairman **Mao Zedong** carefully edited and revised concerning the long-lasting struggle between proletarian and bourgeois classes and between socialist and capitalist courses in a post-revolution period.

The statement specifies the capitalist tendencies of a small portion of the Chinese population and the pressures from imperialist countries as evidence of class struggle and of the danger of the restoration of capitalism. Inevitably, it warns, both domestic and foreign bourgeois influences will find their way into the ruling Communist party and foster revisionism (an implicit reference to the post-Stalin Soviet liberalization) within the party. Although the economic guideline of "readjustment, consolidation, substantiation, and upgrading," formulated by **Li Fuchun** and **Zhou Enlai** and adopted at the previous plenum, was upheld, and although the proposal from **Liu Shaoqi** and others about the "priority of economy" was accepted, Mao's "reaffirmation of class struggle" at the Tenth Plenum set the tone for Chinese political life in the years leading up to the Cultural Revolution. The statement concerning class struggle anticipated the late 1960s formulation of Mao's theory of **continuing revolution under the dictatorship of the proletariat**. And the slogan "Never forget class struggle" as a summary of the bulletin was to become a rallying cry during the Cultural Revolution.

THIRD COMMAND POST. (*Sansi.*) This was an abbreviated name for the Capital College Red Guards Revolutionary Rebel Headquarters (*shoudu dazhuan yuanxiao hongweibing zaofan zong silingbu*). Perhaps the most influential **Red Guard** alliance in Beijing's Red Guard movement, this city-wide conglomerate was formed on 6 September 1966. In order to differentiate itself from two existing college Red Guard headquarters in Beijing, the coalition referred to itself as the "Red Third Command Post (*hong sansi*)," or "Third Command Post." Organizations in this alliance were generally of the school of Red Guards known as "**rebels**." Their members, especially the early members, had resisted the **work groups** and their policies in the early phase of the Cultural Revolution and had therefore been repressed by those in power, including school party committees and work groups. Another distinctive characteristic of these organizations was their critical stand toward the **blood lineage theory** promoted by some **Old Red Guards** who accepted only students from families in the "**five red categories**" as members of their organizations. The leaders of the Third Command Post included **Kuai Dafu**, of Tsinghua University, and **Wang Dabin**, of Beijing Geological Institute.

After a slow beginning due to pressure from rival Red Guard organizations, the alliance and its member organizations grew quickly in October 1966 when the campaign to criticize the **Bourgeois Reactionary Line** started, and, with the support of the **Central Cultural Revolution Small Group** (CCRSG), the Third Command Post became a major battling force in the campaign. It also became well known as the first mass coalition openly denouncing President **Liu Shaoqi** on the streets of Beijing in October 1966 when Liu was still in power in the public eye. With the endorsement from the CCRSG and with their own relatively inclusive policy toward students from politically less-privileged families, many member organizations of the alliance turned their minority status quickly into a dominant one among competing organizations in their institutions, which made the Third Command Post the largest Red Guard force in Beijing and the most influential one in the country until the end of the Red Guard movement in late 1968.

THREE LOYALTIES AND FOUR LIMITLESSNESSES. (*Sanzhongyu siwuxian.*) This was a common reference to two slogans popular at the height of the **personality cult** of Chairman **Mao Zedong** in the early stages of the Cultural Revolution: "Be loyal to Chairman Mao, to **Mao Zedong Thought**, and to Chairman Mao's proletarian revolutionary line"; and "Love, believe, worship, and be loyal to Chairman Mao, Mao Zedong Thought, and Chairman Mao's proletarian revolutionary line without limit."

THREE OLD PIECES. (*Laosanpian.*) This was a popular reference to the three essays of **Mao Zedong** that **Lin Biao** promoted in the 1960s as the main course for a "revolution of consciousness" and a shortcut to studying Marxism-Leninism. The pieces are "In Memory of Norman Bethune" (1939, a tribute to the Canadian Communist Dr. Bethune who died helping the Chinese fight the Japanese invaders); "Serve the People" (1944, a funeral speech in memory of Zhang Side, an altruistic Communist soldier); and "The Foolish Old Man Who Removes the Mountains" (1945, an essay on perseverance). In his talk to ranking military officers on 18 September 1966 about "bringing the study of Chairman Mao's works to a new stage," Lin Biao spoke of the "three old pieces" as works not only suitable for soldiers but also necessary for officers to read as well; they are "easy to understand but difficult to apply" and need to be taken as "mottoes." Lin's words were widely publicized by official media, especially in "Take the 'three old pieces' as a Required Course for Nurturing the New Humanity of Communism" by the editorial department of *People's Daily* (28 October 1966) and

"The 'three old pieces' as Mottoes for a Revolutionary" by the editorial department of *Liberation Army Daily* (3 December 1966). The three essays, then, became part of the core material for the **daily reading** (*tiantiandu*) of the masses. As a result of repeated study, many, especially elementary and middle school students, learned the "three old pieces" by heart. The popularity of these pieces also helped promote the **personality cult** of Mao during the Cultural Revolution.

THREE PROMINENCES. (*Santuchu.*) This is a reference to the formula coined by **Jiang Qing** for artists to follow in their creative work: give prominence to positive characters among all characters; give prominence to main heroes among positive characters; and give prominence to the central character among main heroes.

See also EIGHT MODEL DRAMAS.

THREE TRIPS TO TAOFENG. A production of the Jin opera (the local opera of Shanxi Province), *Three Trips to Taofeng* was named a "big **poisonous weed**" and became a target of criticism nationwide in early 1974 for its alleged attempt to overturn the **Liu Shaoqi** verdict and negate the Cultural Revolution. Coauthored by artists at the provincial Cultural Bureau of Shanxi and based on a true story told in the report "A Horse" in the 25 July 1965 issue of *People's Daily*, the opera portrayed good peasants: farmers of one production brigade offered apologies, abundant compensation, and further production assistance to another brigade after the former cheated the latter on a horse deal. When the opera was staged in Beijing in late January and early February 1974, **Yu Huiyong**, a close associate of **Jiang Qing** in the Ministry of Culture, attacked the opera on two accounts: First, "Taofeng" replaced yet suggested "Taoyuan," the place where not only the original true story was said to have taken place, but also where **Wang Guangmei**, wife of Liu Shaoqi, led a work team conducting the **Socialist Education Movement** in the mid-1960s; therefore, according to Yu, the authors must have intended to reverse the verdict against Liu Shaoqi. Second, with no depiction of class conflict, the opera advocated Liu Shaoqi's theory on the extinction of **class struggle**.

On 28 February, a long critique of the opera by a writing team, with **Yao Wenyuan**'s editorial touches and Jiang Qing's and **Zhang Chunqiao**'s approval, appeared in *People's Daily*. The article was carried in 32 major newspapers across the nation. Its views were echoed in more than 500 pieces of criticism. More than 30 pieces of fiction and drama were labeled "copies of *Three Trips to Taofeng*" and criticized. Titles with "*tao*" (peach) or "*ma*" (horse) in them became suspect. Xie Zhenhua, first party secretary of Shanxi Province, was verbally abused by Jiang Qing and **Wang Hongwen** and denounced by the masses in his provincial capital. The main author Jia Ke was dismissed from his official post at the provincial Cultural Bureau. And the young critic Zhao Yunlong from Shanxi was persecuted to death because of his unpublished article that was mildly critical of Jiang Qing's ideas of literature and the arts. The literary inquisition and the political persecution related to *Three Trips to Taofeng* were part of a movement that the Jiang Qing group had attempted to mount against an alleged "return of the black line" in literature and the arts. The case of *Three Trips to Taofeng* was, in fact, fabricated: Taoyuan was not the place where the real story took place, as Yu Huiyong had suggested; therefore, the Wang Guangmei connection was completely false.

THREE-FAMILY VILLAGE ANTI-PARTY CLIQUE. (*Sanjiacun fandang jituan.*) This was the charge brought against **Deng Tuo**, culture and education secretary of the **Chinese Communist Party** (CCP) Beijing Municipal Committee and editor-in-chief of the Beijing party committee's official journal *Frontline*; **Wu Han**, historian and deputy mayor of Beijing; and **Liao Mosha**, director of the Department of the United Front of the Beijing party committee, in spring 1966 for the alleged conspiracy of these three in making insinuations in their writings against socialism and party leadership.

From 1961 to July 1964, Deng, Wu, and Liao coauthored the column *Notes from a Three-Family Village (Sanjiacun zhaji)* in *Frontline*. During this period, each of them contributed about 20 essays to the column. These pieces, often short, were wide-ranging in topic and sometimes addressed the ills of the times either directly or by embedding criticism in their discussion of history, philosophy, culture, and literature. The column was well received by readers.

On 10 November 1965, **Yao Wenyuan**'s article "On the New Historical Drama *Hai Rui Dismissed from Office*" appeared in Shanghai's *Wenhui Daily*. The article, approved by **Mao Zedong** and soon to become the "blasting fuse" of the Cultural Revolution, accused Wu Han, the author of the historical play, of using a story of the past to criticize the present. Without knowing Mao's firm support for Yao, **Peng Zhen**, first secretary of the Beijing municipal party committee, refused to reprint the article in the city's newspapers. He, as head of the **Five-Person Cultural Revolution Small Group**, also led the group in preparing a policy guide—later known as the **February Outline**—to keep the criticism of Wu and others within the realm of academia. With the approval of the CCP Central Committee, the document was disseminated to the entire nation in February 1966. Considering Peng's actions to be attempts to stop the progress of the Cultural Revolution, Mao launched a major offensive against Peng Zhen and his Beijing party committee. On several occasions in March 1966, Mao harshly criticized the

Beijing party committee, the Five-Person Group, and *Notes from a Three-Family Village*, prompting the cultural revolutionaries in the CCP leadership to take action.

On 8 May 1966, *Liberation Army Daily* and *Guangming Daily* carried articles attacking *Notes from a Three-Family Village*. Two days later, Shanghai newspapers *Wenhui Daily* and *Liberation Daily* published Yao Wenyuan's article "On Reactionary Nature of the Three-Family Village's *Evening Chats at Yanshan* and *Notes from a Three-Family Village*." A massive nationwide campaign against the three immediately followed. On 18 May, shortly after the campaign started, Deng Tuo committed suicide. And, with their freedom lost, Wu and Liao were subject to brutal physical abuse by the masses at numerous **struggle meetings**. Wu died in prison in October 1969. Liao, also imprisoned, was the only survivor of the three. In 1979, the post-Mao Beijing party committee pronounced the case of the Three-Family Village Anti-Party Clique unjust.

TIAN HAN (1898–1968). Playwright, president of the China Association of Dramatists, and vice-president of the China Federation of Literary and Art Circles, Tian Han was attacked during the Cultural Revolution both for his playwriting and for his being one of the **"Four Fellows"** allegedly antagonistic to, and ridiculed by, the revered modern Chinese writer Lu Xun in the 1930s.

Born in Changsha, Hunan Province, Tian Han was educated in normal schools in both Changsha and Tokyo and established himself as a playwright in Shanghai in the 1920s. He joined the League of Leftist Writers in 1930 and became a member of the **Chinese Communist Party** in 1932. The song "March of the Volunteers" (*Yiyongjun jinxingqu*), which Tian Han wrote in 1934 for a film, was so popular and spiritually uplifting as to become the national anthem of the People's Republic of China (PRC) in 1949.

After the founding of the PRC, Tian was given a number of ranking administrative and honorary positions. In the meantime, Tian continued to write plays and operas, mostly based on historical or legendary material. One of these works finally caused problems for him: the historical drama *Xie Yaohuan* was named a "big **poisonous weed**" in a long article published in *People's Daily* on 1 February 1966. Tian Han was considered reactionary because, along with **Wu Han**, Tian was said to be "pleading in the name of the people" (*weimin qingming*) against the Communists' mistakes and misrule. During the Cultural Revolution, Tian's association with **Zhou Yang**, Xia Yan, and Yang Hansheng in the 1930s, dismissed by the sharp-tongued Lu Xun as the "Four Fellows," became a crime. Tian was **struggled against** by the masses and abused both verbally and physically. He was imprisoned without due process of law. Tian died in prison on 10 December 1968. A memorial service was held by the China Federation of Literary and Art Circles in April 1979 to clear Tian Han's name.

TIANANMEN INCIDENT (1976). Also known as the Tiananmen Square Incident, the gathering of millions of people at Tiananmen Square during the traditional Qingming Festival season in early April 1976 was at once an outpouring of grief over the death of Premier **Zhou Enlai** and a mass protest against the cultural revolutionaries among the top leaders of the **Chinese Communist Party** (CCP)—namely, the **Jiang Qing** group supported by Chairman **Mao Zedong**. Branded "counterrevolutionary" by the CCP central leadership at the time but formally redressed two years after the Cultural Revolution, the Tiananmen Incident, as part of a broader **April 5 Movement** in urban China, not only pronounced the bankruptcy of the Cultural Revolution but also marked the first time that ordinary citizens came together and challenged the regime.

The death of Zhou Enlai on 8 January 1976 caused profound sorrow in the nation. Most people sympathized with the premier as he pushed for China's modernization program but was constantly abused by the cultural revolutionaries within the central leadership. Sorrow turned into indignation when orders came from the party leadership restricting mourning activities. In late February, citizens of Beijing, Shanghai, and other major cities were beginning to conduct mourning activities in defiance. People were further enraged when *Wenhui Daily*, a newspaper controlled by Jiang Qing and her supporters in Shanghai, attempted twice in March to defame the late premier by insinuation.

On 28 March, college students and teachers at Nanjing University first turned a mourning ritual into an openly political act challenging the ultra-leftists in Beijing. The spirit and the strategy of what was to be known as the **Nanjing Incident** soon spread to other cities, including Beijing. In late March and early April, despite orders from the central leadership forbidding mourning, people in Beijing streamed into Tiananmen Square and gathered around the Monument of People's Heroes. By official estimate, more than two million people visited the square on Qingming Festival Day (4 April 1976) alone. Scrolls with highly charged elegies commemorating Zhou and denouncing Jiang and her supporters were hanging on wreaths and from trees. Political statements were composed as poems and were posted on the base of the monument and on lamp posts and tree trunks. Some people were giving political speeches or chanting poems, while others were listening and applauding. Such a broad sharing of sorrow and spontaneous political engagement was unprecedented in China's recent history.

Mourning for Zhou Enlai and protesting against the Jiang Qing group in Tianan-men Square, April 1976.

In the meantime, the central leaders were preparing for a crackdown. Plainclothes police were sent to the square to take pictures, copy poems, and record speeches. The Politburo, led by **Hua Guofeng**, met on the evening of 4 April and came to the conclusion that what was taking place at the center of Beijing was a premeditated and well-organized counterrevolutionary act. With Mao's approval, 8,000 police and militia men and 200 vehicles were deployed in the early morning of 5 April to clear the square of all wreaths, scrolls, and flowers, and 57 citizens guarding the wreaths at the square were arrested.

During the day on 5 April, some citizens came back to the square and demanded the return of the wreaths and the release of their comrades. Clashes occurred between civilians and the police. Some police vehicles were turned over and burned. The Workers Militia Headquarters near the square was also set on fire by the angry crowd. In the evening, chairman of the Beijing **Revolutionary Committee** Wu De's speech was repeatedly broadcast at Tiananmen Square labeling the event at the square as reactionary and urging people to leave. Late that evening, more than 200 citizens remaining in the square were severely beaten and were taken away by the combined force of police, militiamen, and **People's Liberation Army** soldiers. On the evening of 7 April, the Politburo met and, at Mao's proposal, passed two resolutions: that Hua Guofeng be appointed first deputy chairman of the CCP Central Committee (CC) and premier of the State Council and that **Deng Xiaoping**, whose name was mentioned in association with the "counterrevolutionary event" at Tiananmen Square, be dismissed from his posts in both the party and the state. In the weeks that followed, extensive investigations and arrests took place in Beijing and other cities.

At the Third Plenum of the Eleventh Central Committee of the CCP held in December 1978, the official reassessment was made that the "Tiananmen Incident of 1976 was entirely a revolutionary event," and the decision was reached that the earlier erroneous resolutions of the CC be withdrawn.

TIANANMEN POEMS. Tiananmen Poems is an anthology of poems that was posted or chanted at Tiananmen Square during the **April 5 Movement** (1976); the anthology was edited by Tong Huaizhou and published in 1978 by People's Literature Press. Tong Huaizhou, the pen name adopted by the 16 faculty members at Beijing Second Foreign Language Institute who collected the poems, puns on "sharing memories [of Premier] Zhou" and strikes the major theme of the poems. The 1978 edition was based on a widely distributed and enormously popular two-volume *Revolutionary Poems* edited by the same group and unofficially published in 1977. The collection includes literary pieces in a variety of poetic forms, such as classical and modern poems, songs, elegiac couplets, and memorial speeches.

In addition to paying homage to the late Premier **Zhou Enlai**, many of these works are an outlet of rage of the authors against the ultra-leftist faction of the **Chinese Communist Party** leadership, especially **Mao Zedong**'s closest followers and Zhou's political enemies **Jiang Qing**, **Zhang Chunqiao**, and **Yao Wenyuan**, who are referred to in these poems as "careerists," "conspirators," "monsters," and "demons." The officially repressed and privately censored resentment of the populace toward the Cultural Revolution found its expression for the first time, which also marked a turning point for Chinese literature and art during the turbulent decade. Despite the government's repressive measures, including orders to search for and confiscate the Tiananmen poems, these highly political and emotional pieces were treasured by readers and were secretly preserved and circulated throughout China. Eventually, the post-Mao leadership rehabilitated the **Tiananmen Incident** in December 1978—soon after the publication of the *Tiananmen Poems*.

"TO REBEL IS JUSTIFIED". (*Zaofan youli.*) A popular slogan of the **Red Guards** and **rebels** during the Cultural Revolution, these words were first pronounced by **Mao Zedong** in a speech he delivered in Yan'an on 20 December 1939 to mark the 60th birthday of Joseph Stalin: "The manifold theories of Marxism in the end come down to one sentence: 'to rebel is justified.' . . . Following this theory, we revolt, we struggle, and we build socialism." The **Chinese Communist Party** organ *People's Daily* first published this quotation on 5 June 1966, which inspired considerable enthusiasm and violence of the Red Guards in their attacks upon the "**seven black categories**" and **Four Olds** in the first wave of the Cultural Revolution. In autumn and winter 1966, during the campaign to criticize the **Bourgeois Reactionary Line**, the four-character slogan developed into an eight-character couplet: "Revolution is no crime (*geming wuzui*); to rebel is justified," and became even more popular. It was chanted everywhere in China by rebels at **struggle meetings** against **capitalist-roaders**.

TSINGHUA UNIVERSITY 4-14 FACTION. *See* ZHOU QUANYING (1943–).

TWELFTH PLENUM OF THE EIGHTH CENTRAL COMMITTEE OF THE CHINESE COMMUNIST PARTY (13–31 October 1968). Also known as the Enlarged Twelfth Plenum, the meeting was held in Beijing to expel **Liu Shaoqi** from the **Chinese Communist Party** (CCP) and to make preparations for the **Ninth National Congress of the CCP**. The legitimacy of the plenum organization was highly questionable under the existing CCP Constitution: A majority of the Central Committee (CC) members and alternate members having been denounced and criticized by this time, only 40 of the 87 living CC members and 19 of the 86 living alternate members were allowed to attend the plenum. Ten of the 19 attending alternate members had to be selected to fill the vacancies as full members so that the total number of delegates from the Eighth Central Committee would be more than 50 percent. The plenum was enlarged to include non-CC members that made up over 57 percent of the delegates; they were granted the right to vote as well.

In his opening speech, Chairman **Mao Zedong** called upon the delegates to assess the Cultural Revolution, while his own words made any critical judgment virtually impossible: "This Great Cultural Revolution is entirely necessary and extraordinarily timely in strengthening the proletarian dictatorship, preventing the restoration of capitalism, and building socialism." As the question of assessment became the focus of small group discussions, **Lin Biao, Jiang Qing**, and their close associates seized the opportunity to attack the top-ranking leaders **Chen Yi, Ye Jianying, Li Fuchun, Li Xiannian, Xu Xiangqian**, and **Nie Rongzhen** as major forces in the anti–Cultural Revolution **February Adverse Current** of 1967. Zhu De, Chen Yun, and Deng Zihui were also attacked for their "consistent right deviation." The Plenum Communiqué celebrated the defeat of the February Adverse Current and of the "evil wind" of spring 1968—allegedly stirred up by military generals

Yang Chengwu, Yu Lijin, and **Fu Chongbi** to reverse the verdict on the February Adverse Current—as a great victory of Mao's proletarian revolutionary line over the **bourgeois reactionary** one.

The CC Special Cases Investigation Group led by **Zhou Enlai** and controlled by Jiang Qing, **Kang Sheng**, and **Xie Fuzhi** submitted "An Investigative Report on the Crimes of the Traitor, Spy, and Renegade Liu Shaoqi." The report consisted of forced confessions, fabricated evidence, and deliberate contrivances of accusatory material. This document and the motion that Liu Shaoqi be permanently expelled from the CCP were passed at the plenum. All delegates supported the motion but **Chen Shaomin**, the only CC member who refused to raise her hand when votes were taken. A proposal was made that Liu be put on public trial and that **Deng Xiaoping**, the "number two **capitalist-roader**," be expelled from the party as well. But the proposal was not adopted due to Mao's disapproval.

Since all major newspapers carried the Plenum Communiqué after the meeting adjourned, Liu Shaoqi was identified officially for the first time as "**China's Khrushchev**" and as the "**biggest capitalist-roader within the party**," two charges that official organs had so far frequently cited without mentioning the name of the accused. The downfall of Liu Shaoqi was a decisive victory for Mao over what he called "bourgeois headquarters." The CCP, in Mao's judgment and in the words of the Plenum Communiqué, was "finally ready, ideologically, politically, and organizationally, for the Ninth Congress" and for a drastic overhaul of the party leadership and the party constitution.

TWO NEWSPAPERS AND ONE JOURNAL. (*Liangbao yikan.*) This was a common reference to the newspapers *People's Daily* (*Renmin ribao*) and *Liberation Army Daily* (*Jiefangjun bao*) and the journal *Red Flag* (*Hongqi*), three periodicals that frequently carried joint editorials articulating instructions of the central leadership as guidelines for the ongoing Cultural Revolution. *People's Daily* is the official newspaper of the **Chinese Communist Party** (CCP) and has been the party's most effective propaganda tool since its initial publication on 15 May 1946. During all political campaigns, including the Cultural Revolution, its editorials were often published with the approval of Chairman **Mao Zedong**, and sometimes even written by Mao himself. *Liberation Army Daily* is the official publication of the Central Military Commission—initially a weekly (1956–1958) and then a daily paper. The paper began as early as 1961 to carry on its front page quotations of Mao, which were to be assembled into the *Quotations from Chairman Mao*. A harbinger of the hegemony of **Mao Zedong Thought** even before the Cultural Revolution, the paper continued to play an important role throughout. *Red Flag* has been the official theoretical journal of the CCP Central Committee since June 1958. It usually publishes articles of considerable length articulating the party's political programs and policies. During the Cultural Revolution, all three publications were under the tight control of the radical faction of the CCP leadership.

U

ULANFU (1906–1988). The top Mongolian official of the **Chinese Communist Party** (CCP), Ulanfu was first party secretary of the Inner Mongolian Autonomous Region, a member of the Politburo, vice-premier of the State Council, and chairman of the Nationalities Affairs Committee. He was brought down and imprisoned in the early stages of the Cultural Revolution for his alleged "regional nationalism." He was also accused of leading an "anti-party, anti-state clique of the new **Inner Mongolia People's Revolutionary Party**."

Born in the Tumet Banner of the Bayan Tala League in Inner Mongolia, Ulanfu distinguished himself as a revolutionary student leader in the early 1920s. After he joined the CCP in 1925, Ulanfu went to Moscow to study Marxism at Sun Yat-sen University. Upon returning to China in 1929, he worked underground in western Inner Mongolia for some time and then was appointed to a number of leading positions in the CCP ethnic minorities front, including political commissar of the Independent Mongol Brigade of the National Army, provost of the Yan'an Nationalities Institute, chairman of the Nationalities Affairs Committee of the Shaanxi-Gansu-Ningxia Broader Region Government, chairman of the People's Government of the Inner Mongolia Autonomous Region, and commander and political commissar of the Inner Mongolia Self-Defense Army. He was elected an alternate member of the Central Committee (CC) at the Seventh National Congress of the CCP in 1945. After the founding of the People's Republic of China (PRC), Ulanfu was appointed first party secretary of the Inner Mongolia Autonomous Region and second secretary of the CCP North China Bureau. He entered the Politburo as an alternate member at the Eighth National Congress of the CCP in 1956.

Ulanfu was one of the first victims among CCP provincial leaders at the outset of the Cultural Revolution. Since he strongly opposed Han chauvinism and insisted on the uniqueness, and hence the real autonomy, of the Inner Mongolia Autonomous Region before 1966, the Beijing leadership accused him of promoting "regional nationalism" and called him a "revisionist" and "ethnic splittist." Based on this judgment and under the guidance of **Liu**

Shaoqi and **Deng Xiaoping**, the CCP North China Bureau held a special meeting from 22 May to 25 July 1966 to denounce Ulanfu. At the meeting, Liu and Deng criticized Ulanfu in harsh terms for his refusal to carry out the party's **class struggle** policies in Inner Mongolia and accused him of creating an "independent kingdom." On 27 July, two days after the meeting, the bureau adopted a resolution to dismiss Ulanfu from office, pending approval of the CC. On 27 January 1967, the CC issued a document (coded *zhongfa* [67] 31) transmitting the North China Bureau's July 1966 report concerning Ulanfu's mistakes. Ulanfu was now named the biggest **capitalist-roader** in Inner Mongolia, and his long imprisonment began. In 1968, during the **Rectify the Class Ranks** movement, the cultural revolutionaries in the central leadership fabricated evidence of a "new Inner Mongolia People's Revolutionary Party." Ulanfu was named the leader of this organization and accused of opposing the CCP and betraying the state. Widespread violence and brutality in the campaign to uncover the "new Inner Mongolia People's Revolutionary Party" was the cause of over 16,000 deaths.

Ulanfu returned to China's political scene in 1973 when he regained his CC membership at the **Tenth National Congress of the CCP**. In 1975, he was elected vice-chairman of the National People's Congress. After his formal rehabilitation in 1979, Ulanfu was appointed to several prominent positions in the central leadership, including membership in the Politburo, vice-president of the PRC, and vice-chairman of Chinese People's Political Consultative Conference. Ulanfu died on 8 December 1988.

UNDERGROUND READING MOVEMENT. (*Dixia dushu yundong.*) This refers to the widespread phenomenon of youths reading banned books during the Cultural Revolution, especially after 1967 when students' initial enthusiasm about the revolution was receding and when the movement of **educated youths** going **up to the mountains and down to the countryside** began. Since almost all books—except works of **Mao Zedong** and officially sanctioned Marxist and revolutionary authors—were branded "feudalist, bourgeois, and revisionist" at the time and therefore were restricted in all library collections and inaccessible to the public, private collections that survived the **Destroy the Four Olds** campaign in the early days of the Cultural Revolution became the only source of books outside the official canon. These books came to be circulated among friends and sometimes even copied by hand to reach more readers. Urban youths from the same school but sent to different rural areas often managed to stay in touch and exchange books by getting together while on furlough visiting their parents in the cities and by paying one another visits in the countryside.

Prominent among the books they shared were the popularly named "**grey books and yellow books**," two series of recent foreign works in translation, including books on Nazi Germany and Stalinist and post-Stalin "revisionist"

Russia, which were internally published for restricted circulation among ranking officials before the Cultural Revolution. Readers of the Cultural Revolution generation were particularly drawn to them because they found in these books revealing parallels with the current Chinese situation.

In the late 1960s and early 1970s, quite a number of reading and correspondence groups were formed in Beijing, Shanghai, and other provinces. Members of these groups exchanged books and engaged in discussion and debate over political issues of shared interest. Well known among these groups were the **Baiyangdian poetry group** and two groups censored by the government during the **One Strike and Three Antis** campaign: the **Hu Shoujun Clique** (at Shanghai's Fudan University) and the **Fourth International Counterrevolutionary Clique** (a network of readers and correspondents based in Beijing with pen pals in Shanghai and Shanxi Province). Despite government suppression, however, the readership of the so-called feudalist, bourgeois, and revisionist books continued to grow as the poverty of culture deepened over the years and became more keenly felt. And books of this kind, especially those about Germany and Russia in the 1930s, stimulated readers as they struggled to free themselves from the shackles of official ideology and groped for a critical perspective on the Cultural Revolution.

UNINTERRUPTED REVOLUTION. (*Buduan geming.*) This was Mao's theory guiding the Cultural Revolution. *See also* CONTINUING REVOLUTION UNDER THE DICTATORSHIP OF THE PROLETARIAT.

UNITED ACTION COMMITTEE. (*Liandong.*) This was an abbreviated name for the Capital Red Guard United Action Committee, whose members were mostly children of ranking **Chinese Communist Party** (CCP) officials. Composed of society's elites, the United Action Committee was known for its members' conceited, arrogant, and sometimes violent behavior, as well as their bold actions in challenging the authority of the **Central Cultural Revolution Small Group** (CCRSG). This organization was formed on 5 December 1966 by a group of **Old Red Guards** from a number of middle and high schools in Beijing. Many of these Old Red Guards came from families of CCP officials and were founding members of the earliest **Red Guard** organizations in the country's capital. They believed that a Red Guard organization should only admit students from politically privileged families of the "**five red categories**," that the primary task of the Cultural Revolution was to ensure the country's power stayed in the hands of "red descendants," and that they themselves, as red descendants, were to be tempered by experience during the Cultural Revolution so as to be prepared to succeed to power in the future.

In the early phase of the Cultural Revolution, these Old Red Guards were enthusiastic in waging battles against the "revisionist line" in education and in attacking allegedly anti-socialist intellectuals, "**black gang**" members in the old Beijing municipal government, and traditional "class enemies" of the "**five black categories**." However, when **Mao Zedong** directed the revolution to aim at those in power as the main targets, the Old Red Guards lost their passion for the revolution and hence lost support from the CCRSG. At this point, a new school of Red Guards known as "**rebels**" took their place as fearless warriors. In this new political development, their parents were under attack, and their status as red descendants was lost. Feeling betrayed by the revolution, especially by the radical faction of the central leadership of the CCRSG, the leaders from a dozen Old Red Guard organizations in Beijing met on 27 November to analyze current political trends and discuss strategies in response to these trends. A proposal was made at this meeting that a committee be formed to coordinate actions for Beijing's Old Red Guards.

Soon after the United Action Committee was formally established on 5 December, its members put out **big-character posters** on the walls around Tiananmen Square and in several busy intersections in Beijing protesting the purge of high-ranking officials and attacking the radical CCRSG. In these posters, they criticized the CCRSG for carrying out a "new Bourgeois Reactionary Line" and called for the restoration of **Mao Zedong Thought** as it was before the Cultural Revolution. They also clashed with the CCRSG-supported rebels on several occasions. These actions led to the detention of several members of the United Action Committee, which in turn triggered the move of the organization to storm the offices of the Ministry of Public Security several times in December 1966 and January 1967. Their open challenge to the cultural revolution faction of the central leadership both in word and in deed provoked further reactions from the authorities. On 17 January 1967, the United Action Committee was named a reactionary organization. Most of its members were soon put in prison. On 22 April, Mao Zedong, having met considerable protest from veteran leaders, ordered the release of all United Action Committee members.

UNITED STATES–CHINA RELATIONS. Relations between the United States and China underwent a dramatic change during the Cultural Revolution as both governments' perceptions of international geopolitics changed, especially in regard to the commonly felt threat from the Soviet Union. U.S. president Richard Nixon's historic visit to China in February 1972 and the signing of a joint communiqué (known as the "Shanghai Communiqué") officially ended an era of hostility and conflict between the two nations that had existed since 1949.

Hostility between the two countries since the founding of the People's Republic of China (PRC) and the Korean War continued into the mid-1960s: the United States was denounced by China as the world's number one imperialist power, although a "paper tiger," as **Mao Zedong** put it, while China was considered by the United States as part of the East Bloc sharing a Communist ideology with the Soviet Union. As the **China-Soviet Debate**, a theoretical prelude to the Cultural Revolution, intensified, and as the relations between the two countries drastically deteriorated, China began to call the USSR a superpower of "social imperialism" and its leadership a "new tsar." In Mao's theory of three worlds, the Soviet Union, along with the United States, was part of the First World. In the beginning years of the Cultural Revolution, Beijing considered both the United States and the Soviet Union its enemies. Toward the end of the 1960s, however, Moscow's increasingly heavy military buildup on the China-Soviet border, on the one hand, and friendly signals from Washington, on the other, made the Chinese leaders reconsider their geopolitical strategies.

Subtle diplomatic gestures indicating willingness to normalize relations between China and the United States were made by the United States in 1969 soon after President Nixon took office: While armed conflicts were taking place on the border between China and the Soviet Union, President Nixon was requesting assistance from President Yahya Khan of Pakistan and President Nicolae Ceaușescu of Romania to mediate contact between the United States and China. In early 1970, ambassador-level talks between the United

Mao Zedong and Richard Nixon, 21 February 1972.

States and China resumed in Warsaw, and in late 1970, as Nixon was beginning to refer to China as the People's Republic, Chairman Mao Zedong, already acquainted with Nixon's intention coming through both the Romanian and Pakistani channels, received the American author and journalist Edgar Snow both in public and in private and told him that Nixon was welcome to visit Beijing in any capacity he chose. In March 1971, the Nixon administration lifted restrictions on travel to China by U.S. citizens. In April of the same year, improvising what was soon to be known as **ping-pong diplomacy**, Mao approved the issuing of an invitation to the U.S. ping-pong team to visit China after the World Championship Game in Japan, and Premier **Zhou Enlai** gave an exceptionally warm reception to all members of the team.

With the help of President Yahya Khan, Nixon's national security advisor, Henry Kissinger, made two secret visits to Beijing in July and October 1971. These two trips prepared for President Nixon's state visit to China on 21–28 February 1972. Nixon met Mao and talked with Zhou Enlai. On 27 February, the two countries issued a joint communiqué, with both sides embracing the prospects of normalizing relations. The most crucial statement in the communiqué was the U.S. acknowledgment that there was only one China and that Taiwan was part of China. In 1973, liaison offices were set up in both Beijing and Washington. Scientific and trade ties were soon established. In 1979, three years after the Cultural Revolution, the PRC and the United States finally established formal diplomatic relations.

UNNATURAL DEATHS. The Cultural Revolution claimed millions of lives and inflicted excruciating pain, physical and mental, on hundreds of millions. Due to information control by the government for the sake of its legitimacy, however, nearly a half century after the Cultural Revolution ended, the total number of unnatural deaths—including those of prisoners of conscience executed by authorities at various levels, of innocent people who were tortured to death or killed by **Red Guard** organizations and military troops, and those who committed suicide in response to humiliation and physical and psychological abuse—remains unclear. Relevant reports and statistical information exist, but they are classified and unavailable to independent researchers.

There is reliable information, though, regarding unnatural deaths resulting from some events and in some localities. For instance, 1,772 people died abnormal deaths in Beijing during a brutal 40-day period known as **Red August** in 1966. The investigation of the "**Inner Mongolia People's Revolutionary Party**" case in 1968 during the **Rectify the Class Ranks** campaign led to 16,222 deaths and 87,188 cases of severe injury. From mid-August to late October 1967, 9,093 people were killed or committed suicide in **Dao County** and its surrounding areas in Hunan Province. And government sources show that about 89,000 people died of unnatural causes in Guangxi Zhuang Autonomous Region during the Cultural Revolution.

Various scholarly studies have also made it clear that a majority of unnatural deaths resulted from political persecutions by the so-called **mass dictatorship** under **revolutionary committees**, including local authorities- and military-sponsored mass killings, especially during the Rectify the Class Ranks campaign that began in late 1967. The percentage of deaths from **armed conflicts** between factions of mass organizations was comparatively small, and so was the percentage of victims—about 135,000 total—charged with "counterrevolutionary" crimes and sentenced to death by the courts during the Cultural Revolution.

Many independent researchers have made efforts to assess the nationwide death toll. Their assessments range from one to eight million, averaging around two to three million. In 2003, two U.S.-based scholars performed a detailed study of statistics drawn from 1,500 officially published Chinese county annals and estimated that the number of unnatural deaths was between 750,000 and 1.5 million, with roughly an equal number of people permanently injured. This figure, however, does not cover unnatural deaths in China's major cities during the same period. Meanwhile, according to classified statistics by the Central Committee of the **Chinese Communist Party** released by political journals in Hong Kong, the unnatural death toll is between 1.73 and 3.18 million. Among these, 1.25 million deaths resulted from political persecutions involving party and government organizations at various levels.

UP TO THE MOUNTAINS AND DOWN TO THE COUNTRYSIDE. (*Shangshan xiaxiang.*) Officially known as "the movement of the **educated youths** going up to the mountains and down to the countryside," this descriptive phrase refers to the nation's unprecedented massive relocation of urban and suburban middle school and high school graduates during the Cultural Revolution, especially between 1967 and 1969 when the **Red Guard** generation—the middle school and high school **old three classes** (*laosanjie*) of 1966, 1967, and 1968—along with the middle school class of 1969, left the city for the countryside. Ideologically, the movement was supposedly part of **Mao Zedong**'s Cultural Revolution project to temper book-educated youths against the corrupting influence of the city-dwelling bourgeoisie and to bridge the gap between the city and the country, between mental and manual labor. Economically, though without official acknowledgment at the time, this program might have been the government's response to the enormous nationwide employment crisis caused by the ongoing revolution.

Beginning spontaneously from the grassroots and supported by Mao and the central and local governments in the mid-1950s, urban and suburban youths' moving to and settling down in the countryside actually preceded the Cultural Revolution. But it did not become a nationwide exodus until late 1967 when the turbulent initial stage of the revolution, of which urban youths had been the major force, was coming to an end while there was still no college or employment available for them in the cities. The movement gained momentum after *People's Daily* published, on 22 December 1968, Mao's directive calling on "educated youths to go to the countryside to receive **reeducation** from the poor and lower-middle peasants." The year 1969 saw more urban youths move to the countryside than any other year, while 1980, four years after the official termination of the Cultural Revolution, marked the end of the movement. By then, the number of youths who had gone to the countryside had reached 17 million.

There were two very different kinds of relocation for youths from cities. One kind was working on a state-owned farm: on the gigantic quasi-military farms called "production-construction corps" (*shengchan jianshe bingtuan*) in such frontier provinces and minority autonomous regions as Heilongjiang, Yunnan, and Inner Mongolia, new farm workers from cities earned a low but guaranteed monthly salary and were entitled, theoretically at least, to free health care and family leave. The other kind was "joining a production team" (*chadui*): in a usually poverty-stricken area of the country, youths from cities joined local peasants in a collectively owned production unit and had to manage to survive on their own, as local peasants did, without help from the state. The second kind of settlement was much harder for middle school and high school graduates.

Out of desperation for his son's hardship as he joined a production team in the countryside, a schoolteacher named **Li Qinglin**, of Fujian Province, wrote Mao Zedong on 20 December 1972, detailing his son's hard life in the countryside, on the one hand, and exposing the corruption of officials (whose children were able to leave the countryside and return to the city because of their parents' connections), on the other. A brief but sympathetic response that Mao wrote on 25 April 1973 led to a special State Council work meeting in June 1973 and the passage of new state policies that, among other things, allowed one child in the family to stay with the parents in the city and instituted state financial support for urban youths in the countryside. In August 1973, the Central Committee of the **Chinese Communist Party** authorized a nationwide issuance of the State Council work meeting report, and a *People's Daily* editorial called for the protection of the educated youths in the countryside and the punishment of those who abused them. To a certain extent, the new policies and propaganda helped improve the living conditions and the political environment of the urban youths in the countryside. But the improvement could not reverse the "going-back-to-the-city trend" (*fancheng* *feng*) that was in the forming. By 1980, when the nation's urban youth relocation program was abandoned, most of those who went to the countryside earlier had already returned to their home cities.

See also WOMEN DURING THE CULTURAL REVOLUTION.

URGENT ANNOUNCEMENT (9 January 1967). This was a public notice signed by 32 mass organizations in Shanghai to denounce **economism**—a series of materialistically motivated activities prompted by the demands that contract and temporary workers made in late 1966 for pay raises, job security, and other benefits that regular state employees enjoyed. The announcement assumed the authority of the law and government and prescribed 10 measures against the escalating chaos caused by the economic malpractices of both the rebelling workers and the managing government officials. These measures included upholding **Mao Zedong**'s dictum to "grasp revolution and promote production," forbidding workers' networking (*chuanlian*) activities, postponing solutions to the problems of wages and benefits until the end of the Cultural Revolution, and punishing those who dared to oppose the revolution and sabotage production. The last measure was an authorization for the Shanghai municipal party committee and bureau of public security to carry out the measures prescribed in the announcement itself and charge whoever violated these measures with the crime of sabotaging the Cultural Revolution.

Following Mao's instruction, the Central Committee of the **Chinese Communist Party**, the State Council, the Central Military Commission, and the **Central Cultural Revolution Small Group** sent the collective author of the announcement a congratulatory telegram on 11 January 1967, in which these mass organizations are praised for "taking the destiny of the proletarian dictatorship and the destiny of the socialist economy firmly in [their] own hands." The joint authorship of a congratulatory note, or of any document, by the four top agencies of Beijing was unprecedented. Given such prestige, Shanghai, already both the vanguard and the stronghold of ultra-leftism, was on its way to becoming a model for **power seizure** that Mao was establishing for the whole nation.

V

VIOLENT STRUGGLE. (*Wudou.*) The term refers to a common practice, conducted mostly by **Red Guards**, of physically abusing citizens denounced as class enemies in the early stages of the Cultural Revolution. Victims were usually beaten at **struggle meetings**, in their own homes when the residence was being searched and ransacked by Red Guards, and on the streets through which they were forced to parade with tall hats on their heads and huge placards hanging from their necks identifying them as criminals. The army belt with a bronze buckle, used as a whip, was the Red Guards' favorite instrument of torture at the time. Physical abuse and public humiliation led to numerous deaths nationwide. During a period of 40 days from late August through September 1966, 1,772 innocent people died of torture or suicide in the city of Beijing alone.

Wudou, the Chinese original for "violent struggle," also means "violent conflict" in another context.

See also ARMED CONFLICT.

W

WANG DABIN (1944–). One of the well-known "five **Red Guard** leaders" in Beijing, Wang was head of the mass organization East-Is-Red Commune at the Beijing Geological Institute and a prominent leader of the Capital College **Red Guards' Representative Assembly** during the Cultural Revolution.

In the early stage of the Cultural Revolution, Wang followed his schoolmate **Zhu Chengzhao** to oppose the **work group** sent by the Ministry of Geology. In August 1966, Zhu, Wang, and a few other students formed a rebel organization called the "East-Is-Red Commune" at the Beijing Geological Institute. At this time and during the campaign to criticize the **Bourgeois Reactionary Line**, **Mao Zedong** and the **Central Cultural Revolution Small Group** (CCRSG) supported the East-Is-Red Commune and used the organization as an effective force in their offensive against the so-called **capitalist-roaders** within the party. In December 1966, Wang Dabin and Zhu Chengzhao followed the instructions from **Qi Benyu**, of the CCRSG, and led a team to Chengdu, Sichuan Province, to kidnap Marshal **Peng Dehuai**. However, after talking with Peng and reading much classified material about the Lushan Conference of 1959, Zhu began to see problems in party politics and the CCRSG. Since Zhu and his inner circle were planning an offensive against the CCRSG, Wang leaked the information to the central leaders. Zhu was soon taken into custody, and Wang was named head of the East-Is-Red Commune and later became head of the **revolutionary committee** of the Beijing Geological Institute. He was also appointed a member of the Standing Committee of the Beijing Municipal Revolutionary Committee. In 1967 and 1968, Wang and his organization were deeply involved in nationwide factional violence and in the campaign to "ferret out the small handful [of capitalist-roaders] in the army."

Wang's downfall began in summer 1968 when Mao decided to put an end to the Red Guard movement. In the early morning of 28 July 1968, Mao held a meeting with the five Red Guard leaders, including Wang Dabin. At the meeting, Mao sent a strong signal to Wang and others that they should exit China's political stage. Shortly after Mao's reception, a **workers propagan-**

da team and an **army propaganda team** were sent to the Beijing Geological Institute to take over power from Wang and rebel students. In 1978, Wang was arrested and sentenced by the Wuhan Intermediate People's Court to nine years in prison for instigating counterrevolutionary activities and framing and persecuting innocent people.

See also MAO ZEDONG: MEETING WITH THE FIVE RED GUARD LEADERS (28 July 1968).

WANG DONGXING (1916–). Mao Zedong's trusted top-level security chief, Wang Dongxing was promoted to the Politburo during the Cultural Revolution. He played a key role in bringing down the **Gang of Four** shortly after Mao's death but was forced to give up his active political duties in 1980 due to his literal adherence to Mao's legacy.

A native of Yiyang, Jiangxi Province, a member of the **Chinese Communist Party** (CCP) from 1932, and a veteran Red Army officer in the Long March, Wang was made a major general in 1955. On 11 November 1965, Wang, while bearing the chief responsibility for the security of the central leadership, especially that of the Zhongnanhai compound, replaced **Yang Shangkun** as director of the general office of the CCP Central Committee (CC). During the Cultural Revolution, Wang, along with **Xie Fuzhi**, minister of public security, had control over the release of personal files of the central leaders. From 1968 on, Wang served as chief of both the CC Security Bureau and the **People's Liberation Army** General Staff Security Bureau.

At the **Second Plenum of the Ninth CCP Central Committee** held in Lushan, Jiangxi Province, in August and September 1970, Wang misread Mao's intention in proposing to **eliminate the office of the national president** and offered support for **Lin Biao** and **Chen Boda** when both spoke against the proposal, implicitly attacking **Zhang Chunqiao**. After Mao denounced Chen and criticized Lin's associates, Wang began to criticize himself at the general office of the CC and also at the gatherings of the 8341 central security troop unit, of which Wang himself was in charge. From 14 August to 12 September 1971, Wang accompanied Mao on his **southern inspection**, during which Mao spoke well of Wang's self-criticism and trustworthiness while making insinuations against Lin Biao. An alternate member of the Politburo since 1969, Wang became a regular member in 1973 at the First Plenum of the Tenth Central Committee of the CCP.

After Mao's death in September 1976, Wang worked closely with **Hua Guofeng** and **Ye Jianying** to purge the Gang of Four. His role as security chief in this episode was acknowledged when he was elected vice-chairman of the CCP and a member of the Politburo Standing Committee at the First Plenum of the Eleventh Central Committee of the CCP in August 1977. However, Wang did not consider the purge of the **Jiang Qing** group as the first step the CCP leadership took in reversing Mao's Cultural Revolution policies in general, and he insisted on being literally faithful to Mao's legacy. In 1977, he supported Hua Guofeng in promoting a slogan called "two whatever's" (adhere to whatever directives Mao had given and whatever decisions Mao had made), and in 1978, he challenged **Deng Xiaoping**'s reformist dictum, "Practice is the only test for truth." Wang also objected to the CC's reversal of verdict on the **Tiananmen Incident** and opposed the reinstatement of those veteran leaders who had been dismissed or denounced by Mao, such as Chen Yun, **Peng Zhen**, and **Bo Yibo**.

Wang's opposition to rehabilitation and reform met with so much critical reaction from ranking cadres in the central leadership that he had to conduct self-criticism at the Politburo sessions in late 1978 and resign from his position as vice-chairman of the CCP in early 1980. At the Twelfth National Congress of the CCP (September 1982), Wang was elected an alternate member of the CC. In 1985, and again in 1987, he was elected to the CC's Advisory Committee. His 1997 memoir on Mao's conflict with Lin Biao, recording and interpreting past events from a strictly Maoist perspective, provoked considerable criticism from historians.

WANG GUANGMEI (1921–2006). Wang suffered severely from public humiliation, physical abuse, and 12 years of imprisonment during the Cultural Revolution, largely because she was the wife of President **Liu Shaoqi**, the so-called number one **capitalist-roader** in the country.

A native of Tianjin, Wang graduated from Furen University in Beijing in 1943 as a student of physics. In January 1946, she was hired as an interpreter for the **Chinese Communist Party** (CCP) delegation to the Beiping Military Coordinating Bureau, an organization consisting of representatives of the Kuomintang (the Nationalists), the CCP, and the United States to oversee the implementation of the truce agreement between the Nationalist and the Communist armies. Wang went to Yan'an in October of the same year and became an interpreter for the CCP Central Military Commission. In 1948, she joined the CCP and married Liu Shaoqi in August. After the founding of the PRC, Wang worked for the General Office of the CCP Central Committee (CC) as a personal secretary to Liu.

In November 1963, Wang joined the work team dispatched by the CCP Hebei Provincial Committee to the Taoyuan Production Brigade in Funing County to lead the **Socialist Education Movement** there. At a meeting held by the CCP Hebei Provincial Committee in July 1964, Wang, as deputy team leader, presented a report on the team's work experience at Taoyuan. Upon recommendation by Liu Shaoqi and approval by **Mao Zedong**, the report was disseminated nationwide in September 1964 as a party-sanctioned exemplar for the ongoing political movement. In the early stages of the Cultural Revolution, Wang, again, became a member of the central leadership's task force, the **work group**. On 19 June 1966, Liu sent Wang as an advisor to the work group at Tsinghua University, where clashes between students and the work group had occurred. Before long, **Kuai Dafu** and a few others at Tsinghua who had tried to drive the work group off campus were denounced as "anti-party students" until Mao pronounced the work group policy repressive upon his return to Beijing and ordered the withdrawal of all work groups on 29 July.

Wang's activities as an advisor to the work group at Tsinghua and her earlier involvement in the Socialist Education Movement at Taoyuan soon became the targets of criticism by **Red Guards**; they were used to implicate Liu Shaoqi as well in the Criticize the **Bourgeois Reactionary Line** campaign. The Tsinghua Red Guards, led by Kuai Dafu and encouraged by the **Central Cultural Revolution Small Group** (CCRSG), spearheaded a national campaign to demonize Liu Shaoqi. As a part of the campaign, the Red Guards denounced Wang's work group activities at Tsinghua and condemned her Taoyuan report as an anti-party and anti-Socialist "**poisonous weed.**" On 10 April 1967, the Tsinghua Red Guards, with full support of the CCRSG, forced Wang, along with 300 "**black gang**" members, including **Peng Zhen**, **Lu Dingyi**, **Bo Yibo**, and Jiang Nanxiang, to attend a mass rally on the university campus and subjected all of them to public humiliation and physical abuse. Wang was forced to stand in front of a crowd of 300,000 people, wearing a necklace of ping-pong balls, a pair of high-heeled shoes, and an embarrassingly small old silk dress. The sensational Red Guard tabloids with giant photographs and cartoons of Wang were freely distributed on the streets of Beijing the day after the rally and quickly circulated nationwide.

In September 1967, Wang was formally arrested though she had been detained separately from her husband since 18 July after a violent **struggle meeting** in Zhongnanhai compound, the residential quarters of top CCP officials. Wang spent the next 12 years in prison. The last time she saw her husband was 5 August 1967 at a struggle meeting held in their own home by the rebels in Zhongnanhai. At the **Twelfth Plenum of the Eighth Central Committee of the CCP** (13–31 October 1968), Liu was named a "traitor, spy, and renegade" and expelled permanently from the CCP. He died on 12 November 1969. Wang did not learn about the death of her husband until several years later. In 1969, **Kang Sheng** and **Jiang Qing** attempted to bring a death sentence against Wang, but their effort was deterred by Mao.

Wang was released from prison and rehabilitated in 1979. She was appointed head of the Foreign Affairs Office of the Chinese Academy of Social Sciences in the same year. In February 1980, the CC formally rehabilitated her husband Liu Shaoqi. In 1983, Wang was elected a member of the Standing Committee of the Sixth Chinese People's Political Consultative Conference.

WANG HAIRONG (1938–). A young diplomat, Wang was a rising star on China's political scene as **Mao Zedong**'s liaison at the Politburo in the early 1970s. Wang was also appointed head of the Protocol Department of the Ministry of Foreign Affairs and deputy foreign minister during the Cultural Revolution.

A native of Changsha, Hunan Province, and a granddaughter of Mao Zedong's cousin Wang Jifan, Wang was a student of foreign languages at the Beijing Teachers' College in the early 1960s. On the eve of the Cultural Revolution, Wang became known for her conversations with Mao concerning school education, which were to inspire **Red Guards** in rebellion against their teachers and the so-called revisionist line in education at the beginning of the Cultural Revolution. Upon completion of her short-term training in English at the Beijing Institute of Foreign Languages in 1965, Wang was assigned work at the General Office of the Ministry of Foreign Affairs. In the early stages of the Cultural Revolution, Wang was a staunch **conservative** supporting Foreign Minister **Chen Yi** and Premier **Zhou Enlai** and opposing the **rebels** and the so-called **May 16 Counterrevolutionary Clique**. Because of her special relationship to Mao, Wang had the privilege of entering Zhongnanhai and conversing with Mao, which lent much authority to her voice in the mass movement.

At the end of 1970 when Mao received the American journalist Edgar Snow, Wang Hairong started to serve as note taker for Mao, while her close friend and political ally **Tang Wensheng** was Mao's chief English interpreter. Wang was appointed head of the Protocol Department of the Ministry of Foreign Affairs in 1971 and later was promoted to the position of deputy minister. Assisting Mao in his diplomatic activities, Wang and Tang were involved in China's most significant events in foreign affairs during the Cultural Revolution, including major steps toward normalization of **United States–China relations**.

The convenient access to Mao also led to Wang's and Tang's deep involvement in top-level politics of the **Chinese Communist Party** (CCP). On the one hand, leaders of all factions within the central leadership, including Zhou Enlai, **Deng Xiaoping**, **Kang Sheng**, and the **Jiang Qing** group later to be known as the **Gang of Four**, often had to depend on them for communications with Mao. On the other hand, Mao used them as liaisons between himself and the Politburo. With the great privilege of attending a number of CCP Politburo meetings, Wang and Tang earned the nickname "probationary Politburo members." Assuming positions as Mao's spokespersons and closely following Mao's shifting attitudes toward different factions of the central leadership, Wang and Tang were known to have insulted not only the cultural revolutionaries of the Jiang Qing group but also the moderate leaders such as Zhou Enlai (at the **enlarged Politburo sessions, 25 November–5 December 1973**), and Deng Xiaoping (in 1975 during the **Counterattack the Right-**

Deviationist Reversal-of-Verdicts Trend campaign). On their way to positions of power at the Ministry of Foreign Affairs, they were also involved in the persecution of a number of innocent cadres and government workers in a series of political campaigns.

After Mao's death in 1976, Wang was dismissed from office and put under investigation. Then, after a few years of training at the Central Party School, Wang was reassigned as deputy head of the Consultant Section of the State Council in 1984.

WANG HONGWEN (1935–1992). A **rebel** leader turned vice-chairman of the **Chinese Communist Party** (CCP) and a member of the **Gang of Four**, Wang enjoyed a meteoric rise to power unprecedented in the history of the CCP and became the third-highest-ranking leader and a candidate for **Mao Zedong**'s successor after the downfall of **Lin Biao**.

A native of Changchun, Jilin Province, Wang was a Korean War veteran and joined the CCP in 1953. When the Cultural Revolution broke out in 1966, Wang was a security officer at a cotton textile factory in Shanghai. In late 1966, Wang, as a leader of the Shanghai mass organization **Workers Command Post**, was involved in both the **Anting Incident** (a transportation crisis on 20 November) and the **Kangping Avenue Incident** (factional violence on 30 December). Wang followed **Zhang Chunqiao** and **Yao Wenyuan** closely in Shanghai's **January Storm** of 1967 to take power from the municipal government. In February 1967, Wang became vice-chairman of the newly formed Shanghai **Revolutionary Committee**. Later that year, Wang orchestrated a bloody factional battle known as the **August 4 Incident** in the Shanghai Diesel Engine Factory. In 1969, he was elected to the Ninth Central Committee of the CCP.

In September 1972, Wang Hongwen was transferred to Beijing at Mao's suggestion. He was given the privilege of attending the meetings of the Politburo, the State Council, and the Central Military Commission. Also at Mao's suggestion, Wang was put in charge of revising the CCP Constitution. At the **Tenth National Congress of the CCP** (August 1973), Wang was made vice-chairman of the CCP and a member of the Politburo. He ranked number three in the CCP leadership, after Mao and **Zhou Enlai**. In 1974, while Premier Zhou was hospitalized for cancer treatment, Wang was entrusted for a short period of time with the responsibility of managing the daily affairs of the central government.

Already closely associated with Zhang Chunqiao and Yao Wenyuan in Shanghai, Wang Hongwen soon became part of the inner circle of the **Jiang Qing** group after he came to Beijing. In October 1974, Wang flew to Changsha, Hunan Province, to brief Mao on the **SS _Fengqing_ Incident** and the subsequent confrontation between Jiang Qing and **Deng Xiaoping** at a Politburo meeting. Wang's mission for the Jiang group was to attack Zhou Enlai and Deng Xiaoping so as to prevent Deng from becoming first deputy premier at the forthcoming **Fourth National People's Congress**, but Mao responded with an admonition that he stay closer to Zhou Enlai than to Jiang Qing. Mao was apparently disappointed in Wang; eventually he chose **Hua Guofeng** as his successor instead of Wang Hongwen. In the meantime, Wang stayed close to the Jiang group and became a member of the Gang of Four. He continued to pay close attention to the cultural revolutionary base of Shanghai, and in 1975, the year of success for Deng Xiaoping's **overall rectification** program, Wang told his supporters there that the Shanghai militia should be prepared for a guerrilla war.

On 6 October 1976, within a month of Mao's death, Wang was arrested in Beijing as a member of the Gang of Four. Due to his formal ranking in the central leadership (as vice-chairman of the CCP), he was listed as the first of the four in the 14 October news release about their arrest. In July 1977, Wang was formally dismissed from all his official posts and expelled from the party. On 23 January 1981, Wang was sentenced by a special court of the Supreme People's Court of the People's Republic of China to life imprisonment on a number of charges including plotting to subvert the government and instigating a military rebellion. Wang Hongwen died on 3 August 1992.

WANG LI (1921–1996). Mao Zedong's radical theorist, deputy editor-in-chief of the **Chinese Communist Party** (CCP) official organ *Red Flag*, deputy head of the CCP Foreign Liaison Department, and a member of the **Central Cultural Revolution Small Group** (CCRSG), Wang was dismissed from office in August 1967 as a member of the Wang-Guan-Qi Anti-Party Clique.

A native of Huai'an, Jiangsu Province, Wang Li joined the CCP in 1939 while working for the CCP in the Nationalist Northeast Army. In the 1940s, Wang held various regional posts responsible for propaganda work in Shandong Province under the CCP East China Bureau. Between 1953 and 1955, he served as an advisor to the Vietnamese Communists in the area of propaganda and education. In 1958, Wang was appointed to the editorial board of *Red Flag*. He soon became one of the CCP's leading writers on the theoretical and political issues of the international Communist movement. In the first half of the 1960s, Wang actively engaged in theoretical writing in the **China-Soviet Debate**. Under the leadership of **Kang Sheng**, Wang took part in drafting the "Nine Commentaries" criticizing Soviet revisionism and also participated in negotiations with Soviet leaders as a member of the CCP delegation to Moscow in 1962. During this period, Wang was promoted to deputy editor-in-chief of *Red Flag* and deputy head of the CCP Foreign Liaison Department. In 1964, Wang began to attend meetings of the Politburo Standing Committee as a non-voting delegate.

In the early stages of the Cultural Revolution, Wang actively engaged in the drafting of a number of significant political documents, including the **May 16 Circular**, its appendix "Chronology of the Two-Line Struggle at the Cultural Front from September 1965 to May 1966," and the 2 June 1966 *People's Daily* commentary "Hail the First Big-Character Poster from Peking University." On 28 May 1966, when the CCRSG was formed, Wang became a member of the group. During the campaign to criticize the **Bourgeois Reactionary Line** in late 1966 and early 1967, Wang and other CCRSG members pushed the **rebel** movement forward against the old party establishment. In 1967, it was partly through Wang's formulation, which Mao Zedong appreciated and approved, that Mao's cultural revolution theory became a theory of **continuing revolution under the dictatorship of the proletariat**: on 18 May 1967, to mark the anniversary of the passage of the May 16 Circular, *People's Daily* and *Red Flag* carried a joint editorial entitled "A Great Historical Document" written by Wang Li and revised by Mao, which published the phrase "revolution under the dictatorship of the proletariat" for the first time and called Mao's theory represented by this phrase "the third great landmark in the development of Marxism."

In July 1967, the central leadership sent a delegation, of which Wang was a member, to Wuhan to resolve factional conflicts. Because Wang expressed support for the local rebel faction, members of the **conservative** mass organization Million-Strong Mighty Army and soldiers of the Wuhan Military Region took him by force and interrogated him at a mass rally on 20 July 1967, which came to be known as the **July 20 Incident**. Upon his return to Beijing, Wang received a hero's welcome from **Lin Biao** and other central leaders. In the meantime, following Mao's instructions, Wang, along with **Guan Feng** and **Qi Benyu**, attacked Foreign Minister **Chen Yi** and began to interfere with foreign affairs: in a speech he gave on 7 August 1967, Wang supported the rebels' effort to seize power at the Ministry of Foreign Affairs—a radical move about which Premier **Zhou Enlai** soon lodged a complaint to Mao. With the support of Lin Biao and **Jiang Qing**—and with the approval of Mao—Wang, Guan, Qi, and some other members of the CCRSG also began to press the military to adopt Mao's Cultural Revolution policies: in their public speeches and in several articles they wrote for official media, they called on the masses to "ferret out a small handful [of **capitalist-roaders**] inside the army," which met strong resistance from the rank and file of the **People's Liberation Army**.

To maintain order in foreign and military affairs, to reassure Zhou Enlai, and to pacify military leaders, Mao soon decided to remove Wang and his colleagues from power and named them the Wang-Guan-Qi Anti-Party Clique. At the end of August 1967, Wang Li and Guan Feng were detained. On 26 January 1968, the two, along with Qi Benyu, were imprisoned.

In 1980, a court in Beijing named Wang an accomplice of the Lin Biao and Jiang Qing counterrevolutionary cliques. He was officially expelled from the CCP at the same time. Wang remained imprisoned until January 1982. After his release, Wang wrote about the early stages of the Cultural Revolution in a number of memoirs, including *Witnessing History: The Memories of the Cultural Revolution* (Hong Kong, 1993) and *Wang Li's Reflections* (Hong Kong, 2001), both of considerable value as an insider's accounts of China's recent history. Wang died of cancer on 21 October 1996.

See also WANG-GUAN-QI AFFAIR (1967–1968).

WANG PEIYING (1915–1970). Born in Kaifeng, Henan Province, and educated at a well-known Catholic female secondary school in Kaifeng, Wang assisted her husband in underground work for the **Chinese Communist Party** (CCP) in the 1940s. She joined the CCP in 1950 and served as a nurse and a custodian at the Railway Ministry's Institute of Professional Design after she was transferred to Beijing in 1955. Between 1963 and 1965, the authorities of her work unit sent Wang to a mental hospital a number of times for diagnosis and treatment because Wang had been openly calling for Chairman **Mao Zedong** to step down while praising President **Liu Shaoqi** and the Soviet leader Nikita Khrushchev (who was being denounced by the CCP as a revisionist during the **China-Soviet Debate**). Wang also submitted a written application for permission to withdraw from the CCP. Between mid-1965 and June 1968, Wang was hospitalized as a mental patient. Then she was transferred from the hospital to an illegal detention facility commonly known as a "**cow shed**" on the premises of the Institute of Professional Design. There she was condemned to forced labor under **mass dictatorship** and subject to physical abuse. This was a time when Liu Shaoqi was denounced nationwide as the nation's **biggest capitalist-roader** and **China's Khrushchev**, and eventually as a "traitor, spy, and renegade" named in a CCP resolution passed at the **Twentieth Plenum of the Eighth CCP Central Committee** in October 1968. Yet Wang continued to voice her support for Liu, writing down rather incoherent lines of what was considered a vicious attack on Mao and the CCP and even shouting "Long live Liu Shaoqi" in public places. On 21 October 1968, the military control commission of the Beijing Public Security Bureau arrested Wang on the charge of counterrevolutionary crimes. During her imprisonment, she was tortured and paraded through the streets with a bridle over her mouth to prevent her from speaking. On 27 January 1970, she was put on public trial, sentenced to death, and executed. She was reportedly strangled to stop her from shouting slogans on her way to the execution ground.

After the Cultural Revolution, Wang's case was reexamined. In March 1980, Beijing Intermediate People's Court issued a corrected verdict concluding that because of her mental illness since 1963, Wang should be exempt from legal responsibilities for the "nonsense" she pronounced. The party authorities of the Institute of Professional Design, on the other hand, issued a much more positive-sounding resolution in April to clear Wang's name and held a memorial service for her in May. It was not until June 2011, however, that legal authorities, under much pressure from Wang's children, issued a complete verdict reversal on the Wang case without any mention of mental illness.

WANG RENZHONG (1917–1992). A native of Jingxian, Hebei Province, and a member of the **Chinese Communist Party** (CCP) from 1933, Wang served after the founding of the People's Republic of China as first party secretary of Hubei Province, first secretary of the CCP Mid-South Bureau, and political commissioner of the Wuhan Military Region. On 28 May 1966, when the **Central Cultural Revolution Small Group** (CCRSG) was formed, Wang was named deputy director of the group. On 16 July 1966, he escorted **Mao Zedong** in the latter's much publicized swim in the Yangtze River. Wang's lack of enthusiasm for the ultra-leftist cause of Mao, however, eventually led to his downfall: in autumn 1966, as he stayed in the southern city of Guangzhou recuperating from an illness, **Jiang Qing** and some other members of the CCRSG, especially **Guan Feng** and **Qi Benyu**, offered support to some mass organizations in Wuhan in their attack on Wang. On 8 September 1967, when *People's Daily* carried an article by **Yao Wenyuan** criticizing **Tao Zhu**, Wang Renzhong was implicated; he was referred to as Tao's man and a counterrevolutionary revisionist. In 1978, a year after the purge of the **Gang of Four**, Wang began to assume important leadership positions again. He was appointed first party secretary of Shaanxi Province. Later he served as head of the CCP's propaganda department and vice-premier of the State Council. He was a member of the CCP's Eleventh, Twelfth, and Thirteenth Central Committee. Wang Renzhong died in Beijing on 16 March 1992.

WANG SHENYOU (1946–1977). An outspoken critic of the radical policies **Mao Zedong** had engineered since the 1950s, Wang was persecuted during the Cultural Revolution and was executed by the post-Mao government in 1977.

A student of East-China Normal University, he was branded a reactionary and was imprisoned for two years in the early stages of the Cultural Revolution because he sympathized with the early targets of the revolution, such as **Wu Han** and **Deng Tuo**, and because he wrote his dissenting views into his diary and named the Cultural Revolution a movement doomed to bring China backward. After his release, Wang was forced to do manual labor on campus and at a **May 7 cadre school**. During a period of eight years under surveillance, Wang read widely and studied Marxist works and economics and wrote friends and family members about what he learned and thought. In September 1976, after he resisted the attempt of his supervisor from the **workers propaganda team** to take away a long letter he was writing to his girlfriend, Wang was arrested again. While in prison, he was ordered to write out the same letter as his "confession." The result was an article of 60,000 words in several chapters, in which Wang, from what he believes to be an authentic Marxist perspective, offers a comprehensive critical assessment of China's economic and foreign policies and political programs since the collectivization movement of the mid-1950s. While acknowledging Mao's achievements as a leader of Chinese revolution before 1949, Wang criticizes Mao for ignoring China's historical and economic conditions and deviating from Marxism in his Great Leap Forward and People's Commune policies that resulted in a human disaster in the late 1950s and the early 1960s. He was also sharply critical of Mao's political campaigns, including the Anti-Rightist Campaign of 1957, the Anti-Right-Deviationist Campaign of 1959, the **Socialist Education Movement** of the mid-1960s, and the 10 years of the Cultural Revolution, and his criticism engages Mao on a theoretical front as well. For instance, citing Engels on the importance of productivity and a strong economic base, Wang, on the one hand, considers Mao's blueprint of social transformation—the establishment of a commune and elimination of division of labor for contemporary China, as laid out in Mao's **May 7 Directive**—to be a utopian dream divorced from historical reality and deviating from socialism. On the other hand, Wang speaks highly of Marshal **Peng Dehuai**, who had been dismissed from office in 1959 for writing Mao about the problems of the Great Leap Forward policies. Much of Wang's view is echoed, though with much euphemism, in the **Resolution on Certain Questions in the History of Our Party since the Founding of the People's Republic of China**, which the Central Committee of the **Chinese Communist Party** (CCP) adopted in 1981.

Wang's private letter, however, was judged by the post-Mao government to be a reactionary piece against Mao. On 27 April 1977, six months after the downfall of the **Gang of Four**, Wang was executed after a public trial at which he learned the sentence for the first time but was not allowed to defend himself. For the reversal of the Wang verdict, the leaders of the CCP Shanghai Municipal Committee met 19 times and debated among themselves. In the 1980s, they eventually approved a low-key statement to redress the Wang Shenyou case.

WANG XIAOYU (1914–1995). One of the few provincial party leaders who supported the **rebels** in the early stages of the Cultural Revolution, Wang became head of the Shandong Provincial **Revolutionary Committee**

in 1967 and a member of the **Chinese Communist Party** (CCP) Central Committee (CC) in 1969 but was eventually dismissed from office for his involvement in armed factional conflict in Shandong.

A native of Yidu, Shandong Province, Wang joined the CCP in 1938 and worked in rural areas of northern Shandong for many years. Wang was appointed deputy chief-prosecutor of Shandong Province in 1954. He was named a rightist during the Anti-Rightist Campaign and demoted until 1964 when his case was redressed. When the Cultural Revolution broke out, Wang reported to the **Central Cultural Revolution Small Group** that some party officials in Qingdao were planning to mobilize workers and peasants against the rebel students who were attacking the city leadership. For this report, Wang was praised by **Mao Zedong** in his 7 September directive. After that, Wang emerged as a rising star on China's political scene. During the **January Storm** of 1967, Wang, following secret instructions from **Kang Sheng**, organized rebels to seize power in Qingdao.

On 3 February 1967, Wang became head of the newly established Shandong Provincial Revolutionary Committee. He gathered more power later on as head of the CCP core group of the Shandong Revolutionary Committee and first political commissioner of the Jinan Military Region. Shortly after he took these leading positions, however, Wang became deeply involved in widespread factional violence in the province. He also persecuted a large number of innocent cadres and ordinary citizens who did not side with him. Of particular importance was Wang's conflict with local military leaders, which was the main reason for his downfall: in May 1969, barely a month after he became a member of the CC at the **Ninth National Congress of the CCP** (1–24 April 1969), the central leadership named him a bourgeois careerist. Two years later, Wang was dismissed from office and was taken into custody. Wang was formally expelled from the CCP in 1979.

WANG XIUZHEN (1935–). A leader of **rebel** workers in Shanghai and a close associate of **Zhang Chunqiao**, Wang was a member of both the Ninth and the Tenth Central Committees of the **Chinese Communist Party** (CCP), a deputy head of the Shanghai **Revolutionary Committee**, and a secretary of the CCP Shanghai Municipal Committee. In late 1976, she was removed from power as a "remnant of the **Gang of Four** in Shanghai."

A native of Liaoyang, Liaoning Province, and a provincial model worker, Wang joined the CCP in 1952. In 1956, she was enrolled in the Shanghai School of Textile Industry. Upon graduation, she began to serve as a technician at the Shanghai Thirtieth Textile Factory. At the beginning of the Cultural Revolution, Wang was the first worker at the factory to write **big-character posters** criticizing the factory party leadership and the **work group**. In the early stages of her career as an activist and rebel leader, she met **Wang Hongwen**, a security officer at the Shanghai Seventeenth Textile Factory.

They worked together to found the Shanghai Workers Revolutionary Rebel Headquarters, commonly known as the **Workers Command Post**, and to organize campaigns against the municipal authorities headed by First Secretary Chen Pixian and Mayor Cao Diqiu. Wang was involved in the **Anting Incident** of November 1966, during which she met Zhang Chunqiao. After the incident was resolved with the official acknowledgment of the Workers Command Post by Zhang and the central leadership, Wang became a loyal follower of Zhang and the **Central Cultural Revolution Small Group**.

During Shanghai's **power seizure** movement known as the **January Storm**, Zhang Chunqiao named Wang Xiuzhen a deputy head of the Shanghai Revolutionary Committee. Later, Wang and other leaders of the committee, including **Ma Tianshui** and **Xu Jingxian**, helped Zhang persecute his critics, especially those involved in the two incidents of the **Bombarding Zhang Chunqiao** campaign. Wang and her associates also brought false charges against Cao Diqiu, Wei Wenbo, and other senior officials in Shanghai. Later, Wang and other followers of the Gang of Four in Shanghai became deeply involved in the power conflict in Beijing and attacked **Deng Xiaoping** and other party veterans.

In October 1976, when the Gang of Four was detained in Beijing, Wang and other Gang "remnants" plotted an armed rebellion in Shanghai, but the plan was aborted. As soon as **Hua Guofeng** and the central leadership took full control of Shanghai, Wang was arrested. She was dismissed from office and expelled from the CCP. On 21 August 1982, the Shanghai Supreme Court convicted Wang of several counts of counterrevolutionary crimes and sentenced her to 17 years in prison.

WANG-GUAN-QI AFFAIR (1967–1968). The detention and investigation of the cultural revolutionaries **Wang Li** and **Guan Feng** in August 1967 and of **Qi Benyu** in January 1968 was a strategic move **Mao Zedong** made to pacify the protesting senior party officials and military leaders and hence a major setback for Mao's own ultra-leftist policies during the Cultural Revolution.

Known as the "Three Littles" of the **Central Cultural Revolution Small Group** (CCRSG) in charge of propaganda, broadcasting, and newspapers/periodicals, Wang Li, Guan Feng, and Qi Benyu were among the most active members of the group. In the early stages of the Cultural Revolution, their writing and speeches contributed much to the prevalence of leftist extremism, including **Red Guard** violence. In 1967, encouraged by **Lin Biao** and **Jiang Qing** (and with the approval of Mao), Wang, Guan, Qi, and some other members of the CCRSG began to press the military to adopt Mao's Cultural Revolution policies: they called on the masses to "ferret out a small handful [of **capitalist-roaders**] inside the army," which met with strong resistance from the rank and file of the **People's Liberation Army** (PLA).

They also began to make similar radical moves in the area of foreign affairs, including Wang Li's notorious 7 August speech in which he supported the rebels' demand to "collar" Foreign Minister **Chen Yi** (here Wang was actually rephrasing Mao's instructions) and backed their effort to seize power at the ministry. As a result, the party committee office of the Foreign Ministry was soon shut down by the rebels. Chaos in foreign affairs further intensified when Red Guards stormed the office of the **British Chargé** in Beijing on 22 August. Weighing revolutionary chaos against stability and order, Mao decided to sacrifice Wang and his two close comrades to maintain order and to pacify protesting PLA officials and senior party leaders soon after he received an accusatory report from Premier **Zhou Enlai**. Following Mao's specific instructions, Zhou called a meeting on 30 August 1967 to announce Mao's order that Wang and Guan "take a leave and criticize themselves." Qi Benyu was detained later on 13 January 1968. On 26 January, all three were sent to the prison at Qincheng.

Their downfall was made known to the public for the first time on 24 March 1968 by Lin Biao and Jiang Qing as they addressed an audience of some 10,000 military officers. Both spoke vehemently against their three former followers. According to Jiang, the three had been working for **Liu Shaoqi**, **Deng Xiaoping**, and **Tao Zhu** ever since the beginning of the Cultural Revolution. Wang, Guan, and Qi became "chameleons" and "crawling insects" in public propaganda. Officially, they were known as the Wang-Guan-Qi Anti-Party Clique. In 1980, a court in Beijing named Wang Li and Guan Feng accomplices of the Lin Biao and the Jiang Qing counterrevolutionary cliques. They were officially expelled from the CCP at the same time. In November 1983, Qi Benyu was tried and convicted of specific instances of slandering and persecuting innocent people and inciting the masses to violence and destruction, including the destruction of the Confucian Temple in the hometown of Confucius. Qi was sentenced to 18 years in prison.

WATER MARGIN APPRAISAL (1975–1976). (*Ping Shuihu.*) A political movement at the final stage of the Cultural Revolution, the reading and critiquing of the classical Chinese novel *Water Margin* was defined by official media as a political education for the masses against revisionism and capitulationism; however, the real, yet unnamed, purpose of the campaign was to make insinuations against **Zhou Enlai** and **Deng Xiaoping** as "capitulators within the party" betraying **Mao Zedong**'s Cultural Revolution program.

The campaign was initiated by some comments Mao made on *Water Margin* on the evening of 14 August 1975 to Lu Di, a reading companion from Peking University. Mao considered *Water Margin* to be a good negative example for teaching the masses about capitulators. In the novel, Song Jiang, chief of the outlaws at Liangshan, renamed Chao Gai's Hall of Brotherhood the Hall of Righteous Loyalty and encouraged the outlaws to accept amnesty and serve the emperor. In just three hours after he read Mao's comments on *Water Margin* the next day, **Yao Wenyuan** wrote Mao a letter with a campaign plan, which Mao soon approved. Then, variant editions of the novel were published, major newspapers and periodicals were crowded with articles on *Water Margin*, and the masses were required to study and discuss the subject. To clarify the unsaid, **Jiang Qing** told her supporters at the Ministry of Culture in late August 1975 about the "practical significance" of Mao's comments: "The crucial point in reviewing this novel is that Chao Gai was made a mere figurehead. Now in our party, some people attempt to make Chairman Mao a figurehead." Jiang made further insinuations so aggressively in a speech she gave in September that Mao ordered that her speech script not be distributed.

Deng Xiaoping and Zhou Enlai were known for their different responses to the movement of the *Water Margin* Appraisal. Deng said at a meeting of provincial leaders: "What is the *Water Margin* Appraisal? The Chairman read the 71-chapter version in three months. After that, the Chairman made these comments. But some people are making a big deal out of this and playing intrigues." Zhou, who was dying of cancer, took the issue much more seriously. Just before a surgical procedure on 20 September 1975, Zhou carefully reviewed and signed the transcriptions of the report on the Kuomintang-fabricated **Wu Hao affair** that he presented at Mao's suggestion at a high-level meeting in June 1972. And just as the nurse wheeled him into the operating room, Zhou said loudly, "I am loyal to the party and loyal to the people. I am not a capitulator." In the meantime, the *Water Margin* Appraisal movement continued until the death of Mao Zedong in fall 1976.

WEI GUOQING (1913–1989). A member of the Zhuang ethnic minority, Wei joined the **Chinese Communist Party** (CCP) in 1931 and served as a senior leader of Guangxi Province (the name changed to Guangxi Zhuang Autonomous Region in 1958) since 1955. When the Cultural Revolution broke out in 1966, Wei was chairman (governor) of Guangxi, first secretary of the CCP Guangxi Autonomous Region Committee, and first political commissar of the Guangxi Military District.

Born in 1913 to a poor peasant family of Donglan County, Guangxi Province, Wei joined the CCP-led local peasant militia at the age of 15. The peasant force was soon incorporated into the Red Army where Wei began a long military career. He participated in the Long March (1934–1935) and was gradually promoted to higher ranks in the Communist-led forces during the Sino-Japanese War (1937–1945) and the civil war between the Communist and Nationalist armies (1946–1949). By the end of the civil war, Wei became political commissar of the Tenth Corps of the **People's Liberation Army** (PLA) Third Field Army. After the founding of the People's Republic of China (PRC), Wei served as mayor and party secretary of Fuzhou City, Fujian Province, for a short period before he was appointed to head a Chinese military advisory group to Vietnam in 1950. In Vietnam, Wei's group helped the Viet Minh, a Communist-led independence coalition, in regularizing its army and strategizing a number of important military campaigns, including the Battle of Dien Bien Phu (1954), against French colonial forces. The decisive victory of the Viet Minh army in the Dien Bien Phu campaign led to the signing of the *1954 Geneva Accords* in which France agreed to withdraw its forces from all of its colonies in French Indochina. Wei won respect from, and developed a close relationship with, top Vietnamese Communist leaders during his stay in Vietnam, which may have helped save him in the Cultural Revolution.

In the early days of the Cultural Revolution, Wei, like many of his peers in the country, was denounced by rebelling **Red Guards** as a **capitalist-roader** and struggled to hang on to power. However, unlike his peers in other provinces, Wei was never really removed from office. This was largely due to the location of Guangxi: bordering Vietnam and hence at the forefront of the "Support Vietnamese against the American Aggression" campaign. It was also due to the key position Wei held in the campaign. When the Cultural Revolution approached its "heyday" in early 1967 with the **power seizure** movement sweeping the nation, the Vietnam War also escalated with an increasing presence of U.S. troops and intensified U.S. bombing. Since the beginning of the Vietnam War, China had openly supported the Viet Cong and sent large amounts of military supplies, food, goods, and equipment to Vietnam. Starting in June 1965, upon the request of Vietnamese Communist leaders, China had also been secretly sending its own troops to Vietnam, including forces specializing in anti-aircraft artillery and railway engineering—all much needed by the Viet Cong. Guangxi held a strategic and the most critical location for transporting supplies and troops to Vietnam by land, especially via railway. Wei, as head of the party, government, and military apparatuses of Guangxi Autonomous Region, was in a crucial position for the operation. Thus, despite the fact that he was as unenthusiastic, and even obstructive, toward Red Guard rebellions as many of his counterparts in other provinces, Wei escaped ouster as a capitalist-roader. On 6 November 1967, he submitted a piece of self-criticism to the CCP Central Committee (CC), the **Central Cultural Revolution Small Group** (CCRSG), and rival factions of Guangxi mass organizations—that is, the Joint Headquarters of Proletarian Revolutionaries (which was backed by Wei and the Guangxi Military District) and the 4-22 Revolutionary Action Command Post (which pursued Wei's ouster and initially enjoyed support from the CCRSG). Wei's self-criticism, well received by the CC and by Chairman **Mao Zedong** himself, was disseminated nationwide as part of a CC document on 12 November and forwarded to all mass organizations in Guangxi. A follow-up CC decision, dated 18 November, put Wei in charge of preparation for establishing the Guangxi **Revolutionary Committee**.

Against the pattern of provincial power shift at the time, the Guangxi case is rather unique, and Wei's comparatively secure position in power actually made the fight between **rebels** and **conservatives** in Guangxi fiercer. In 1968, violence escalated into **armed conflict**. Without backing from the military, 4-22 rebels began to stop cargo trains to Vietnam and break into military warehouses for weapons and military supplies. This led to the CC's issuance of the **July 3 Public Notice** condemning these and similar activities as "counterrevolutionary crimes" committed by "a small handful of class enemies." Although the July 3 Public Notice helped end armed conflict, it bore a heavy toll. In the name of fighting counterrevolutionaries and punishing class enemies, slaughters—even **cannibalism**—occurred in both urban and rural areas; some were large in scale. The victims included not only the intransigent 4-22 rebels but also a very large number of people of the so-called **five black categories** of class enemies and their family members, including women and children. Government sources show that about 89,000 people died of unnatural causes in Guangxi during the Cultural Revolution.

On 26 August 1968, when the revolutionary committee of the Guangxi Autonomous Region was finally formed, Wei was named head of the committee. He remained in this position until late 1975 when the central leadership reassigned him to lead the revolutionary committee of Guangdong Province. After the fall of the **Gang of Four**, Wei was promoted to the central leadership: In August 1977, he was appointed director of the PLA's General Political Department, replacing **Zhang Chunqiao** who had been in prison since October 1976 as a key member of the Gang of Four. Wei retired from this position in 1982 but remained a vice-chairman of the National People's Congress Standing Committee until his death.

WOMEN DURING THE CULTURAL REVOLUTION. The **Chinese Communist Party** (CCP) continued during the Cultural Revolution to advocate women's liberation and gender equality known by such popular slogans as "Time has changed; men and women are the same," and "Women hold up half the sky." This was a policy the CCP instituted since it took power in 1949, and patriarchal bias was criticized as a vestige of the feudal and capitalist societies of Old China. With forceful policy execution and effective propaganda, China achieved considerable success under Communist rule in transforming the consciousness of the population, especially among urban residents, regarding sex and gender and in liberating women from household confinements, turning them into a significant labor force, and promoting their education and social status.

The notion of women's status being equal to that of men's under CCP rule, however, was conceived not on the basis of equal humanity, as it had been by enlightened intellectuals during the late Qing Dynasty and the May Fourth era; it was based on arbitrarily defined class status for the purpose of advancing Communism, and everyone was equal before the law of proletarian revolution, while humanism was denounced as bourgeois ideology. Therefore, heroes and heroines in the **eight model dramas** dominating the literature and art scene of the Cultural Revolution were invariably de-sexed revolutionaries, and romantic love, especially feelings, authentic or stereotypical, that were traditionally associated with the "gentler" sex, were dismissed as bourgeois or petit-bourgeois sentiments and must be abolished to be genuinely revolutionary. The popular line from Chairman **Mao Zedong**'s poem "Militia Women," "They love their battle array, not silks and satins" (*bu ai hongzhuang ai wuzhuang*); the ballet much praised by **Jiang Qing** entitled *Red Detachment of Women*; and officially endorsed real-life models such as the "'Iron Girls' Team" (*tieguniang dui*) at the Dazhai Production Brigade in rural Shanxi inspired women to redefine their roles. Skirts were considered remnants of the **Four Olds** to be swept away during the Cultural Revolution; women wore similar clothes as men, and the retired army uniform became the favorite attire of **Red Guards**, men and women alike. They were encouraged to play equal roles in political campaigns and strike out vehemently, even violently, against class enemies of all sorts at **struggle meetings** and on the streets in answer to Mao's call to rebel and "be valiant" (literally, "be militant": *yaowu*, as Mao said to female Red Guard **Song Binbin** at a mass rally). As a result, women, especially students in urban areas, and men were equally Spartanized, militarized, and brutalized, so much so that it was in the hands of a group of young female students at the elite Beijing Normal University Female Middle School that Principal **Bian Zhongyun** was beaten to death in public on 5 August 1966. Bian was the first educational professional to be killed during the Cultural Revolution.

Gender equality based on revolutionary status, which often took the form of **blood lineage** determination, testified quite accurately in Chinese reality to an Orwellian absurdity that everyone is equal, but some are more equal than others. Take marriage, for instance, even though the government advocated freedom to fall in love and to marry (therefore against the tradition of arranged marriages), local authorities replaced parental authorities of the past in the sense that they had the power to disapprove, or at least discourage, the marriage of a party member to a person labeled a class enemy or a person from a politically inferior family background to maintain the class purity of party ranks. Following the party's **class line**, they also discriminated against those with such a family background in educational opportunities and job assignments. Consequently, at the end of the Cultural Revolution, there was a sizeable population of unmarried adults, especially in rural areas, of unfavorable political status; women suffered more humiliation because of society's stronger bias against single women than against single men. The divorce rate was at a record high during the Cultural Revolution because women, and at times their husbands, were under pressure to **make a clean break** (*huaqing jiexian*) with their spouses when the latter were targeted as class enemies. Though women's social status did improve, at least theoretically and as a matter of political correctness, gender inequality persisted as an economic reality. In rural communes, for instance, men earned more "work points" (*gongfen*) and hence were paid more than women for doing the same kind of work for the same work hours. Due to the worsening economic situation nationwide during the Cultural Revolution and to the differences between comparatively rich and comparatively poor areas, the situation of women being traded as commodities in marriage was worsening as well. As urban youths were sent to rural areas in the campaign to go **up to the mountains and down to the countryside** for **reeducation** by the peasants, young women suffered more injustice than young men, not just because they had to perform the same physically challenging manual labor but also because many young women were taken advantage of and sexually abused by local cadres. The abuse became more common when bargains could be made over such opportunities as returning to the city or being recommended for college admissions as **worker-peasant-soldier students**. In prison, sexual violation added to torture also made female inmates' lives much more unbearable than their male counterparts, as in the case of **Zhang Zhixin**, a well-known prisoner of conscience.

The popularity of the notion of women "holding half the sky" did not translate into a reality for women's proportional participation in leadership. In fact, women's representation in party and government leadership remained extremely small, and elected or appointed female officials were treated as the second sex in official listings with the label "female" in parentheses inserted following their names. Though the Cultural Revolution did lead to the appointment of two women to the powerful Politburo for the first time in CCP history, they both were spouses of highest-ranking leaders—CCP Chairman Mao Zedong's wife, Jiang Qing, and Vice-Chairman **Lin Biao**'s wife, **Ye Qun**—and the rise and fall of these two women closely followed those of their husbands: Ye was killed with Lin in a plane crash known as the **September 13 Incident**, while Jiang was arrested as head of the **Gang of Four** shortly after the death of Mao in 1976.

See also CHEN SHAOMIN (1902–1977); DING ZUXIAO (1946–1970) AND LI QISHUN (1947–1970); LI JIULIAN (1946–1977); LIN LIHENG (1944–); LIN ZHAO (1932–1968); LIU TAO (1944–); NIE YUANZI (1921–); PENG PEIYUN (1929–); TAN HOULAN (1937–1982); TANG WENSHENG (1943–); WANG GUANGMEI (1921–2006); WANG HAIRONG (1938–); WANG PEIYING (1915–1970); WANG XIUZHEN

(1935–); WU GUIXIAN (1938–); XIE JINGYI (1937–); YAN FENGY-ING (1930–1968); ZHANG XITING (1928–1993); ZHANG YUFENG (1944–).

WORK GROUPS. (*Gongzuozu.*) Also known as the Cultural Revolution work groups, these were teams of party officials and government workers dispatched to colleges, middle schools, and some government institutions in early June 1966 to direct the Cultural Revolution movement. After the Cultural Revolution was publicly launched on 1 June 1966 with the publication of the *People's Daily* editorial "**Sweeping Away All Cow-Demons and Snake-Spirits**" and the nationwide broadcasting of a **big-character poster** by **Nie Yuanzi** and others at Peking University, the masses, especially students in Beijing who had already been engaged in the criticism of municipal party officials and the so-called reactionary academic authorities, were quickly mobilized and began to challenge the authorities in their own institutions. In the face of the fast-developing mass movement, **Liu Shaoqi** and **Deng Xiaoping**, who were in charge of party and state affairs while Chairman **Mao Zedong** was away from Beijing, called an enlarged meeting of the Politburo Standing Committee and made a decision at the meeting to dispatch work groups on a mission to guide the movement, and contain fires, at schools and some government institutions in Beijing. (The work group policy had been adopted by the party before for the purpose of directing political campaigns.)

With Mao's approval, the newly restructured **Chinese Communist Party** (CCP) Beijing Municipal Committee first sent out a work group to Peking University on 4 June. Soon many more work groups were dispatched to other places in Beijing. Party leadership in other cities also began to deploy work groups, following Beijing's example. With minimum instructions from the central leadership, these teams tended to support, if not totally side with, the CCP authorities of a given institution and attempted to keep the mass movement under the control of the party. They also made an effort to contain violence. In some institutions, conflicts developed between work groups and the students who considered the operation of the work groups as repressive. Some students who challenged the work groups' authority in their institutions were condemned as "anti-party die-hards" and subject to mass criticism at **struggle meetings**. Conflicts also developed in the central leadership between the radical members of the **Central Cultural Revolution Small Group** (CCRSG), who wanted to have work groups withdrawn, and the Liu-Deng leadership, which chose to hold on to the decision made by the Politburo.

Upon returning to Beijing on 18 July 1966, Mao sided with the CCRSG and dismissed Beijing's political scene as cold and desolate. Speaking at a party meeting on 21 July, Mao criticized the work group policy as repressive and obstructing the ongoing political movement. Following Mao's instruction, thc Beijing party committee held a meeting of 10,000 people on 29 July and announced its decision to withdraw all work groups. Liu Shaoqi, Deng Xiaoping, and **Zhou Enlai** made self-criticisms at the meeting for their roles in dispatching work groups. Later Mao denounced the work groups for carrying out a **Bourgeois Reactionary Line**, which became the main target of criticism in a nationwide campaign in October 1966.

See also *PEKING UNIVERSITY CULTURAL REVOLUTION BULLETIN NO. 9.*

WORKER-PEASANT-SOLDIER STUDENTS. (*Gong-nong-bing xueyuan.*) This term refers to college students admitted between 1970 and 1976 when colleges required of their applicants at least two years of work experience or military service and recruited students from factories, farms and communes, and military units, basing admission decisions on "recommendations by the masses, approval by the leadership of the applicant's work unit, and review by the college." The official propaganda in the first half of the 1970s named this non-traditional way of selecting college students as an important achievement of the "**revolution in education**." The practice was delegitimized in late 1977 when the traditional system of entrance examinations was restored for testing college applicants.

The idea of "revolution in education" came from a series of remarks Mao Zedong made at the dawn of the Cultural Revolution, including his letter to **Lin Biao**, dated 7 May 1966 and later known as the **May 7 Directive**, in which Mao called for radical reforms to end "the bourgeois intellectuals' reign in our schools." He thought that students should learn to be workers, peasants, and soldiers while engaging in criticizing the bourgeoisie. Following Mao's directive, the Ministry of Education issued a document on 13 June 1966, proposing that the current bourgeois college admissions system relying on test scores be abolished and that a new enrollment system based on recommendations and selections be adopted. The central leadership approved the document and decided that the college recruitment work be postponed for half a year. In fact, there were no college admissions for the next four years. When colleges finally began to admit students again in 1970, they had already had Mao's new directive to follow: "There still should be colleges," Mao wrote in what was to be known as the **July 21 Directive** in 1968. "I am referring mainly to schools of science and technology. But . . . students should be selected from the workers and peasants with practical experience, study for a few years in college, and then go back to the work of production." The recruitment began at selected schools in October 1970 and expanded nationwide in 1972. There was no entrance examination. To be admitted, the applicants only needed popular support and leadership approval from their work units as well as the approval of the college recruiting team.

According to government instructions concerning college admissions issued in the early 1970s, the main task of worker-peasant-soldier students was "attending the college, running the college, and reforming the college with **Mao Zedong Thought**." Professors, on the other hand, had a very limited role to play in their students' education, since the professors were to be reformed. One of the "newly emerging things" in education was called "open-door schooling": students and teachers would go to factories or to the countryside with a project and learn from workers and peasants there. Qualifications for entering students were supposed to include a middle school education (the first nine years of education) or the equivalent, but, without standard entrance examinations to test students, their levels of education varied greatly and were mostly quite low.

In the face of these problems, **Zhou Enlai** suggested in 1972 that some high school students should be allowed to enter college without two years of labor, and the State Council issued a document in April 1973 suggesting that college applicants' examination scores be considered in addition to the recommendations from their work units. These attempts to restore order and quality in education invariably failed due to the much stronger countermeasures and political campaigns launched by the radical faction of the party leadership against the "reversal of trend in education." The real reversal did not take place until August 1977 when **Deng Xiaoping**, who had just been reinstated and had offered to take charge of the affairs of education and scientific research, called for a work meeting on college admissions. Late 1977 saw the first nationwide college entrance examination, officially ending the non-testing of worker-peasant-soldier students for college admissions.

See also ZHANG TIESHENG (1950–).

WORKERS COMMAND POST. (*Gongzongsi.*) This is the shortened name for the Shanghai Workers' Revolutionary Rebel Command Post (*Shanghai gongren geming zaofan zongsilingbu*). Being the first cross-industry **rebel** organization of factory workers in the country and having close connections with the cultural revolution faction of the central leadership, this organization was the stronghold of ultra-leftism in Shanghai and became well known for its decisive role in the **January Storm**, Shanghai's **power seizure** movement.

In late 1966, when a proposal to establish a cross-industry mass organization in Shanghai was rejected by both the Shanghai municipal party committee and Beijing's central government, rebel leaders, including **Wang Hongwen**, then a security officer at a cotton textile factory in Shanghai and later a member of the **Gang of Four**, mobilized 2,000 workers on a train ride to Beijing to appeal their case, and their protest at Anting Station near Shanghai led to a transportation crisis. With the support of **Zhang Chunqiao**, deputy head of the **Central Cultural Revolution Small Group**, and the approval of

Chairman **Mao Zedong**, however, the Workers Command Post eventually gained legitimacy as a cross-industry mass organization and became loyal to Zhang and his radical comrades in Beijing. Again with the support of Zhang, the Workers Command Post crushed the Red Defenders Battalion, a mass organization and the political rival of the Workers Command Post in Shanghai, in a bloody confrontation known as the **Kangping Avenue Incident**, at the end of 1966.

In January 1967, Zhang Chunqiao and **Yao Wenyuan** went to Shanghai and directed the Workers Command Post, now the dominant mass organization in Shanghai, in a power seizure effort to topple the municipal party committee and gain control of the city government, an effort applauded by Mao. When the new power organ **Shanghai People's Commune** (later changed to Shanghai **Revolutionary Committee**) was established, Zhang and Yao became the top two officials, and a number of Workers Command Post leaders, including Wang Hongwen, were given important positions as well. Wang was eventually transferred to Beijing and became vice-chairman of the **Chinese Communist Party** in August 1973.

See also ANTING INCIDENT (1966).

WORKERS INSURRECTION JOURNAL. (*Gongren zaofan bao.*) A newspaper published by the **Workers Command Post** (*gongzongsi*) of Shanghai and one of the longest-lasting mass organization publications in the country, the *Insurrection Journal* started on 28 December 1966 and ended on 15 April 1971, with a total publication of 445 issues. Founded at the high tide of the campaign to criticize the **Bourgeois Reactionary Line**, the paper declared in its first issue a critical stance against the power establishment of the **Chinese Communist Party** (CCP) Shanghai Municipal Committee and the CCP East China Bureau. It became one of the three major newspapers in eastern China after rebels seized power in Shanghai during the **January Storm**, the other two being the official *Liberation Daily* and *Wenhui Daily*. In its quasi-official status after the Shanghai **power seizure**, the *Journal* operated in step with the CCP's political moves and was distributed via post offices and bookstores across China. Soon after its restoration, however, the CCP Shanghai Municipal Committee issued a document on 9 April 1971 concerning the ways of improving journalistic publications. In compliance with the requirements of this document, the publication of the *Workers Insurrection Journal* came to an end.

WORKERS PROPAGANDA TEAM. (*Gongxuandui.*) This is the abbreviated name for the Workers **Mao Zedong Thought** Propaganda Team (*gongren Mao Zedong sixiang xuanchuan dui*). Formed initially for the purpose of leading the Cultural Revolution in its "**struggle, criticism, reform**" phase in educational institutions, the first such team was dispatched by **Mao Zedong** on a much more urgent mission and was therefore unusually large: On 27 July 1968, a "Capital Workers Mao Zedong Thought Propaganda Team" consisting of 30,000 factory workers led by **People's Liberation Army** (PLA) officers entered the campus of Tsinghua University to stop a factional battle known as the **One-Hundred-Day Armed Conflict** between two rival **Red Guard** organizations. After the team took over the campus, it became the new authority there. On 25 August, the **Chinese Communist Party** (CCP) official organ *Red Flag* published **Yao Wenyuan**'s article "On the Supreme Leadership of the Working Class," publicizing for the first time Mao's directive concerning the workers propaganda team: "The proletarian education reform must be led by the working class. . . . Workers propaganda teams will stay in schools, participate in the 'struggle, criticism, reform' movement, and lead schools forever." While previewing the draft version of Yao's article, Mao also added: "Workers and PLA soldiers should be dispatched to all places where there is a concentration of intellectuals, whether they be schools or other institutions, so that the monopoly by intellectuals in these institutions shall be broken." On the same day, the CCP Central Committee (CC), the State Council, the Central Military Commission, and the **Central Cultural Revolution Small Group** issued a circular announcing the decision of the central leadership to dispatch workers propaganda teams to all schools in urban areas. As this decision was being implemented in the cities, **Poor Peasants Management Committees** were established in the countryside for the same purpose. Workers and PLA propaganda teams were also dispatched to research institutions and some government agencies.

These teams were instrumental in stopping factional fighting, restoring order, and establishing authorities to end chaos. As schools began to function more or less normally, however, the propaganda teams became much less effective, and oftentimes obstructive and misleading, in managing these institutions not just because of their characteristic adherence to a line of political propaganda but also because of team members' general lack of education and expertise. In the later years of the Cultural Revolution, many teams diminished greatly in size and played no significant role in running the institutions they were assigned to. In November 1977, the CC approved a proposal by the Ministry of Education to withdraw workers propaganda teams from all schools in the country.

See also ARMY PROPAGANDA TEAM.

WORKERS' REPRESENTATIVE ASSEMBLY. (*Gongdaihui.*) This was an organization established in the early phase of the Cultural Revolution to replace the official labor union when the union was accused of following a capitalist and revisionist line and forced out of power. Under the influence of the **Red Guard** movement, so many workers' **rebel** organizations were established that the leaders of these organizations considered it necessary to have an overarching organization—an assembly—to coordinate their activities. Again, with the **Red Guards' Representative Assembly** as a model, the workers' representative assembly was established in many cities and provinces as headquarters for rebel organizations. A national representative assembly, however, was never formed. Some assemblies ceased functioning when factional battles broke out among their constituencies. After the **power seizure** movement swept across the country in 1967, a few positions representing workers in the newly established **revolutionary committee** were often given to the leaders of the local assembly. The assembly continued to represent workers until the official labor union resumed its function after the **Ninth National Congress of the Chinese Communist Party** in 1969.

WU DE (1913–1995). Born in Fengrun, Hebei Province, Wu joined the **Chinese Communist Party** (CCP) in 1933 and became a leader in the labor movement and also in the CCP underground organization in North China. After the founding of the People's Republic of China, Wu was appointed deputy minister of fuels and industry. In 1952, he became mayor and deputy party secretary of Tianjin. From 1955 to 1966, he was the top CCP official in Jilin Province. After the downfall of **Peng Zhen** and his Beijing party committee at the **enlarged Politburo sessions, 4–26 May 1966**, Wu was transferred to Beijing and appointed second secretary of the reorganized CCP Beijing Municipal Committee. He was made deputy head of the newly established Beijing **Revolutionary Committee** in 1967 and filled the vacancies left by the death of **Xie Fuzhi** in 1972 as head of the Beijing Revolutionary Committee and first party secretary. In 1973, Wu became a member of the Politburo.

In 1976, Wu actively supported the cultural revolutionaries within the central leadership in cracking down on the **April 5 Movement**. At the Politburo meeting held on the evening of 4 April, he spoke of **Deng Xiaoping** as an inspiration for the protesting masses at **Tiananmen** Square. On the evening of 5 April, a statement by Wu denouncing what was happening at the Square was repeatedly broadcast to the crowd there. The mass protest was suppressed by force later in the evening and was condemned as a counterrevolutionary act by the central leadership in the following days. Wu's role in the notorious Tiananmen crackdown made him so unpopular, especially among citizens in Beijing, that he was referred to by many as "No Virtue," which is pronounced in Chinese as *wu de*, exactly like his name.

After the fall of the **Gang of Four** in 1976, Wu remained in high positions until December 1978 when the post-Mao leadership formally rehabilitated the Tiananmen Incident at the **Third Plenum of the Eleventh CCP Central Committee**. In the same month, Wu was dismissed as first party secretary of Beijing. In February 1980, he was removed from the Politburo. In April of the same year, Wu resigned as vice-chairman of the Standing Committee of the National People's Congress. In 1982, however, he was given a membership in the Advisory Committee of the CCP Central Committee. Wu died on 29 November 1995.

WU FAXIAN (1915–2004). A close associate of **Lin Biao** and popularly known as one of Lin's "four guardian warriors," Wu Faxian was commander of the air force of the **People's Liberation Army** (PLA) (1965–1971), deputy chief of the general staff of the PLA, and deputy head of the **Central Military Commission Administrative Group** (1967–1971).

Born in Yongfeng, Jiangxi Province, Wu joined the Red Army in 1930 and became a member of the **Chinese Communist Party** (CCP) in 1932. He participated in the Long March as a regimental political commissar and remained in the armed forces for the rest of his political career. During both the war of resistance against Japan and the civil war of the late 1940s, Wu was a ranking political officer under Lin Biao. In 1955, Wu was made lieutenant general. Nominated by Lin Biao in the capacity of defense minister, Wu succeeded General Liu Yalou as commander of the air force in 1965 after Liu's death.

In the early stages of the Cultural Revolution, Wu was attacked by the **rebels** within the armed forces. Lin Biao intervened and protected him. Lin named him, along with **Li Zuopeng** and **Qiu Huizuo**, a leader of the "proletarian revolutionaries of the armed forces." Wu, in the meantime, helped Lin fight his political enemies: fabricating evidence and offering false testimonies, Wu was instrumental in bringing down Marshal **He Long** and General **Luo Ruiqing**, both attacked by Lin Biao. In 1967, Wu was appointed deputy chief of general staff of the PLA and deputy head of the Central Military Commission Administrative Group. At the **Ninth National Congress of the CCP** (1969), Wu was elected to the Central Committee (CC) and the Politburo. On 17 October 1969, Wu promoted **Lin Liguo**, son of Lin Biao, from the position of an office secretary to deputy director of both the air force command's general office and its combat division. He also told his subordinates that all matters of the air force must be reported to Lin Liguo. The authority and the privilege thus accorded allowed Lin Liguo to form his United Flotilla, a special intelligence and operation team made up of die-hard Lin Biao loyalists, and carry out within the air force such subversive activities as the drafting of the *"571 Project" Summary*.

At the **Lushan Conference** of 1970, the conflict between the **Jiang Qing** faction and the Lin Biao faction surfaced. Wu joined **Chen Boda**, Li Zuopeng, Qiu Huizuo, and **Ye Qun** in attacking **Zhang Chunqiao** and supporting a proposal not to eliminate the position of the president of state. Backing Zhang Chunqiao and the Jiang Qing group, Mao singled out Chen Boda as the main target of criticism and also told other supporters of Lin Biao, including Wu, to conduct self-criticism. In April 1971, the CC held a meeting reviewing the ongoing **Criticize Chen and Conduct Rectification** campaign. Wu's written self-criticism, along with those of Huang, Ye, Li, and Qiu, was discussed at the meeting. In his summary report representing the view of the CC, Premier **Zhou Enlai** criticized Huang, Wu, Ye, Li, and Qiu for following a wrong political line and practicing factionalism. After the alleged plot against Mao's life failed in September 1971, Wu was at first cooperative with Lin Biao in his further moves. But on the night of 12 September and the early morning of 13 September, as Lin Biao was known to be fleeing the country, Wu turned against Lin and cooperated with Zhou Enlai. He reportedly suggested shooting down the Trident 256 that carried Lin Biao, Ye Qun, and Lin Liguo, a proposal rejected by Zhou.

After the **September 13 Incident**, Wu Faxian was detained, and his involvement with Lin Biao's alleged coup attempt was placed under investigation. On 30 August 1973, the CC issued a resolution concerning the Lin Biao Anti-Party Clique. As a member of the Lin group, Wu Faxian was dismissed from all his official positions and was permanently expelled from the CCP. On 25 January 1981, Wu Faxian was sentenced to 17 years in prison for organizing and leading a counterrevolutionary clique, plotting to subvert the government, and bringing false charges against innocent people.

WU GUIXIAN (1938–). A native of Henan Province and a National Model Worker at the Northwest No. 1 Textile Factory in Xianyang, Shaanxi Province, before the Cultural Revolution, Wu was one of the few ranking leaders in the central government promoted from the grassroots during the Cultural Revolution. She became an alternate member of the Politburo in August 1973 after serving as deputy director of the **revolutionary committee** of Shaanxi Province for five years. In January 1975, she was appointed vice-premier of the State Council. In late 1977, a year after the downfall of the **Gang of Four**, Wu was dismissed from Beijing. She later became deputy party secretary of the Northwest No. 1 Textile Factory.

WU HAN (1909–1969). Historian, writer, and deputy mayor of Beijing, Wu Han was the author of the historical play *Hai Rui Dismissed from Office* and the coauthor of the journal column *Notes from a Three-Family Village*, the two most prominent targets of criticism in the preparation stage of the Cultural Revolution.

Born in Yiwu, Zhejiang Province, Wu joined the faculty of Tsinghua University in 1934, specializing in the history of the Ming Dynasty (1368–1644). As a ranking member of the China Democratic League, Wu was also known for his active engagement in contemporary politics. After 1949, Wu was elected to the Standing Committee of the Chinese People's

Political Consultative Conference and took a number of culture- and education-related administrative positions, including director of the Beijing Cultural and Educational Commission and member of the Scientific Research Planning Committee of the State Council. He joined the **Chinese Communist Party** (CCP) in 1957. While carrying out his administrative duties, Wu continued to write both as a scholar and as an educator promoting cultural literacy. He was popular as editor-in-chief of a number of history series for a general audience.

In late 1959 and 1960, against the background of the CCP's disastrous Great Leap Forward policies, Wu wrote several articles in praise of Hai Rui (1514–1587), a legendary upright official of the Ming Dynasty, to support **Mao Zedong**'s call for the kind of outspokenness and truthfulness exemplified by Hai Rui. Upon invitation from the Peking Opera Company of Beijing, Wu also wrote *Hai Rui Dismissed from Office* for the stage, highlighting a spirit of "pleading in the name of the people" represented by the protagonist. In 1961, at the request of the journal *Frontline*, the official organ of the CCP Beijing Municipal Committee, Wu joined **Deng Tuo** and **Liao Mosha** in coauthoring the column *Notes from a Three-Family Village*. In his contributions, Wu showed himself to be an acute and critical observer of manners and morals, and his criticism did not spare officials.

On 10 November 1965, the Shanghai newspaper *Wenhui Daily* carried **Yao Wenyuan**'s article "On the New Historical Drama *Hai Rui Dismissed from Office*," which accused Wu Han of disparaging the present with a story of the past. In late December, Mao spoke favorably of Yao's article and talked about what he perceived as the "vital part" of Wu's play: a parallel between Hai Rui's dismissal and Marshal **Peng Dehuai**'s (for Peng's criticism of the Great Leap Forward policies). On 20 March 1966, speaking at an enlarged Politburo session, Mao named Wu and **Jian Bozan**, another historian, "Communist Party members opposing the Communist Party." With these devastating remarks from Mao and the political campaign launched in May 1966 against the so-called **Three-Family Village Anti-Party Clique**, Wu Han's fate was sealed. After the Cultural Revolution broke out, Wu was repeatedly **struggled against** and physically abused by the masses. In 1968, Wu was arrested for allegedly betraying the party. On 11 November 1969, he died in prison. Because of Wu's alleged crimes, his wife, Yuan Zhen, was subject to "reform through labor" and died on 18 March 1969. Their daughter, Wu Xiaoyan, suffered a mental breakdown. She was arrested in 1975 and committed suicide on 23 September 1976.

In March 1979, the CCP Central Committee approved the resolution of the Beijing Municipal Committee to reverse the verdict of the Three-Family Anti-Party Clique. Wu Han's name was cleared.

WU HAO AFFAIR. "Wu Hao" was an alias **Zhou Enlai** once used. The so-called Wu Hao Affair originally referred to the fabrication of a story by the Kuomintang in the 1930s about Zhou Enlai's breaking away from the **Chinese Communist Party**. During the Cultural Revolution, **Jiang Qing** and her supporters made several attempts to reopen this case to defame Zhou, and **Mao Zedong**'s apparent reluctance to close the case altogether deeply troubled Zhou Enlai.

Between 16 and 21 February 1932, several Shanghai newspapers carried the "Announcement of Wu Hao and Others Quitting the Communist Party," a notice fabricated by a Kuomintang intelligence unit. The Communists in Shanghai, Chen Yun and **Kang Sheng** among them, resorted to various means to refute the rumor, while the Provisional Central Government of the Chinese Soviet in Jiangxi issued an official notice in the name of Mao Zedong, head of the Soviet, rebuking the Shanghai newspapers for running the fabricated notice. In the meantime, Zhou Enlai left Shanghai for the Central Soviet in Jiangxi in December 1931, two months before the fabricated notice appeared. In 1943, during the rectification campaign in Yan'an, Zhou Enlai spoke of the Wu Hao Affair in detail, and the case was clarified and closed.

During the campaign to "ferret out traitors" in early summer 1967, some **Red Guards** at Nankai University looked through pre-1949 Chinese newspapers and discovered the fabricated notice. As soon as they identified Wu Hao as Zhou Enlai, they sent a copy of the newspaper story to Jiang Qing. On 17 May 1967, Jiang wrote Zhou Enlai, **Lin Biao**, and Kang Sheng that some Red Guards "found an anti-Communist announcement, at the head of which was a Zhou so-and-so, and they wanted to talk to me in person." Zhou noted on Jiang's letter that the announcement was "a fabrication of the enemy." To clarify the matter, Zhou searched the old Shanghai newspapers and wrote Mao on 19 May, enclosing the related materials. Upon reading the letter and the attached materials, Mao offered no opinion; instead, he instructed that these materials be sent to Lin Biao and the **Central Cultural Revolution Small Group** for review before they were filed. To protect himself, Zhou had his letter to Mao and the accompanying materials photographed and archived in October and November 1967. He wrote Jiang Qing on 10 January 1968 and notified her of the filing of the photographs.

In response to a Beijing student's written inquiry, Mao wrote on 16 January 1968: "This matter is already all cleared up as rumor trumped up by the Kuomintang." But four years later, Mao suggested that Zhou speak to party leaders about the Wu Hao Affair. Zhou presented the case at a meeting on 23 June 1972. Based on the opinions of Mao and the Politburo, Zhou also announced that the tape recordings of the meeting and the transcripts were to be filed in the Central Archives and that every provincial-level party committee was to preserve a copy so that no further speculation on the so-called Wu Hao Affair would occur. After the meeting, however, the filing of Zhou's recordings was indefinitely delayed.

Three years later, Zhou, suffering from cancer, knew that he did not have long to live. The "Wu Hao Affair" was heavy on his mind. Just before surgery, he asked to have the June 1972 records brought to him. In shaky hand, he signed his name to the records with the notation, "Before entering the operating room, 20 September 1975."

X

XI JINPING (1953–). General secretary of the **Chinese Communist Party** (CCP) and chairman of the Central Military Commission since November 2012, Xi Jinping is the first of the **Red Guard** generation, and a "princeling," too, to hold China's highest office.

A native of Beijing and son of veteran Communist **Xi Zhongxun**, Xi Jinping was a student at Beijing's August 1 Academy (*bayi xuexiao*, an elite boarding school that children of many ranking officials attended) when the Cultural Revolution broke out. Because his father was dismissed from office in 1962 for alleged involvements in an "anti-party novel" case, Xi Jinping did not qualify for membership of the politically privileged "**five red categories**" and was, therefore, not allowed to join the Red Guard organizations that embraced a **blood lineage theory**. He largely shared the political views of the **Old Red Guards** (whose parents had yet to be purged like his father), though, and was said to have participated in their activities as a "**Red Periphery.**" In 1969, Xi went to the countryside of Shaanxi's Yanchuan County as an **educated youth** to receive **reeducation** from local peasants. After a number of unsuccessful attempts to use family connections to remove himself from the countryside, Xi decided to stay and work hard to prove his own worth. He submitted a number of applications for CCP membership and was eventually admitted to the party in 1974 and soon became party secretary of his production brigade. In fall 1975, he came back to Beijing as a **worker-peasant-soldier student** of chemical engineering at Tsinghua University.

Xi opted for officialdom upon graduation in 1979, gradually rising from posts at grassroots levels. He received a Ph.D. in law from Tsinghua University in 2002, but the dissertation that earned him the terminal degree was widely suspected to have been written *for* him rather than by him while he was serving at various top-level positions in Fujian Province. As China's highest-ranking leader since 2012, Xi is known for continuing the country's economic reform, promoting a nationalist agenda called the Chinese Dream, launching a wide-range offensive against graft (though the targets among officials remain selective), and enforcing harsher measures against freedom of speech. Though **Bo Xilai**, mayor of Chongqing and member of the Politburo who challenged the CCP central leadership with certain populist Cultural Revolution rhetoric and policy measures, was officially convicted and sentenced under Xi Jinping's reign, Xi's own vision, and vocabulary, too, often bears the marks of Maoism as well, as in his promotion of a populist "mass line," his determination both to "hunt tigers and swat flies" in the anti-graft campaign mainly through party security and intelligence agencies, and his push for tighter ideological control with "seven no-talking's" (*qi bu jiang*, seven topics forbidden because they undermine the party's absolute authority).

XI ZHONGXUN (1913–2002). Native of Fuping County, Shaanxi Province, and a member of the **Chinese Communist Party** (CCP) since 1928, Xi was one of the founders of the Communist base in the Shaan-Gan-Ning border region where the Long March ended. This experience exposed him to the danger of persecution almost three decades later: in 1962, while a vice-premier of the State Council, he was implicated in a literary inquisition concerning a novel entitled *Liu Zhidan*, and this "anti-party novel" case turned out to be one of the preludes to the Cultural Revolution.

Liu Zhidan, a Communist leader who died in battle in 1936, was Xi Zhongxun's comrade-in-arms in the Shaan-Gan-Ning revolutionary base in the early 1930s. In the mid-1950s, instructions came down from the CCP Propaganda Department commissioning a novel based on the life of Liu Zhidan. Upon request from the designated author Li Jiantong, Xi made suggestions for revisions on the work in progress. When the novel began to appear in installments in a number of newspapers in 1962, however, Yan Hongyan, party chief of Yunnan Province who had also been involved in Communist activities in Shaanxi in the 1930s, challenged the author on the historical truthfulness of the novel and informed **Kang Sheng** of the dispute. A veteran of both Joseph Stalin's Purge of the 1930s and Mao's attack on his political rivals in the name of rectification during the Yan'an period, Kang, without even reading the novel, came to the conclusion that everything related to this writing project was part of a conspiracy to reverse the verdict on Gao Gang, a ranking official purged by Mao in 1954, who happened to have been with Liu Zhidan and Xi Zhongxun as Communist leaders in the Shaan-Gan-Ning border region in the early 1930s. The year 1962, especially later in the year when the **Tenth Plenum of the Eighth CCP Central Committee** was convened, was a turning point in Chinese politics because this was the time when Mao reiterated the significance of **class struggle**, anticipating the Cultural Revolution in less than four years. Kang's judgment of the novel *Liu Zhidan* was then timely support for Mao's political move and prompted Mao to say in his opening speech at the Tenth Plenum, "Using a novel to carry out anti-party activities is a great invention" in preparation for a power takeover.

A few months later, a special case committee led by Kang identified more "evidence" of the novel's anti-party nature, including its depiction of the Shaan-Gan-Ning border region leadership as the savior of the Red Army, implicitly slighting Mao's Jinggang Mountain model, and its portrayal of too perfect a character based on Xi Zhongxun's life story that served as political capital for Xi's ambitions. Xi was then dismissed from office as a member of an anti-party clique.

It was not until 1978 that Xi's name was cleared. In the same year, he was appointed party secretary of Guangdong Province. He supported the initiative of building free-market-oriented special economic zones, which made Guangdong's Shenzhen area a model for the country's reform and opening program. In January 1987, when paramount leader **Deng Xiaoping** gathered a number of senior officials at a private meeting with **Hu Yaobang** to reprimand Hu for his liberal sympathies and force him to resign as general secretary of the CCP, Xi was the only one there opposing the party elders' illegal move, calling it a "drama of forced abdication."

Xi Zhongxun was known as one of the few CCP officials without deep involvements in intra-party politics and persecutions. His son **Xi Jinping**, China's top leader since 2012, is often seen as a disappointing comparison to his father who had a decent reputation for moderation and fairness.

XIE FUZHI (1909–1972). Minister of public security and head of the Beijing municipal government, Xie was an ally of both the **Lin Biao** group and the **Jiang Qing** group and a close follower of **Mao Zedong**'s radical policies during the Cultural Revolution. Born in Huang'an, Hubei Province, Xie Fuzhi joined the **Chinese Communist Party** (CCP) in 1931 and participated in the Long March. He was named a general in 1955 and, upon Mao's recommendation, became minister of public security in 1959. In 1965, Xie was appointed vice-premier of the State Council. He was elected an alternate member of the Politburo in August 1966 and a regular member in April 1969. In 1967, he became chairman of the Beijing **Revolutionary Committee** and political commissioner of the Beijing Military Region. He was also a member of the Central Special Cases Investigation Group and, along with **Wang Dongxing**, had control over the release of personal files of the central leaders.

In the capacity of public security chief, special case investigator, and the top municipal official of Beijing, Xie did much to protect the past secrets of Jiang Qing and, at the same time, to frame cases against such veteran leaders as **Liu Shaoqi**, **Deng Xiaoping**, and Zhu De. He was instrumental in producing the notorious **Six Regulations of Public Security**, which was issued nationwide on 13 January 1967 as a CCP Central Committee (CC) document. The repressive measures prescribed in this document caused widespread persecution of innocent people, especially those of the blacklisted classes and categories. His instructions to investigators and law enforcement officers that they may "break rules and regulations (*qinggui jielü*) and choose the best methods" in their investigations and that they "should not apply the policy of benevolence (*renzheng*)" to counterrevolutionaries resulted in much abuse and torture in prisons and other agencies under the Ministry of Public Security. In July 1967, Xie, as a member of the CC delegation, got involved in a sectional conflict in Wuhan, Hebei Province, which led to a four-day mass rally and protest known as the **July 20 Incident**. Xie was at the peak of his political career when he died of illness in March 1972.

On 6 October 1980, the CC issued an investigative report concerning Xie's crimes and announced a decision to expel Xie Fuzhi from the CCP. On 23 January 1981, a special court of the Supreme People's Court named Xie Fuzhi a prime culprit of both the Lin Biao and the Jiang Qing counterrevolutionary cliques.

XIE JINGYI (1937–). A native of Shangqiu, Henan Province, Xie was trained as a cryptographer and served as one at the general office of the **Chinese Communist Party** (CCP) Central Committee in the Zhongnanhai compound, where she came to know **Mao Zedong** personally. Xie's political career began in July 1968 when she was sent to Tsinghua University as a member of the **workers propaganda team**. Later she became deputy head of the Tsinghua **Revolutionary Committee** and a close ally of **Chi Qun**, a member of the **army propaganda team** and head of the Tsinghua Revolutionary Committee. Known as the "two soldiers" of Mao and close followers of **Jiang Qing**, Xie and Chi virtually ruled Tsinghua until the downfall of the **Gang of Four** in October 1976.

During this period, Xie and Chi worked fairly closely, taking orders from Jiang and enacting radical policies on the Tsinghua campus—policies that affected the entire educational establishment from the **Rectify the Class Ranks** movement of the late 1960s and early 1970s to the **Counterattack the Right-Deviationist Reversal-of-Verdicts Trend** campaign in 1976. Xie rose rapidly in the CCP leadership: she became a member of the CCP's Tenth Central Committee and a party secretary of the Beijing municipal government in 1973 and a member of the Standing Committee of the **Fourth National People's Congress**. She was arrested with the Gang of Four within a month of Mao's death. She was expelled from the party. But, unlike Chi Qun who was sentenced to 18 years in prison, Xie was spared of criminal charges reportedly due to her acknowledgment of guilt and her confession.

XU JINGXIAN (1933–2007). A leader of rebelling Shanghai government functionaries and a close associate of **Zhang Chunqiao**, Xu was a member of both the Ninth and the Tenth Central Committee (CC) of the **Chinese**

Communist Party (CCP), a deputy head of the Shanghai **Revolutionary Committee**, and a secretary of the CCP Shanghai Municipal Committee. In late 1976, he was removed from power as a "remnant of the **Gang of Four** in Shanghai."

A native of Shanghai, Xu was an activist in the CCP-led student underground movement against the Kuomintang in Shanghai before 1949. He joined the CCP in the early 1950s, became a productive writer, and made his name as the author of the revolutionary drama *The Young Generation* in 1964. In the first half of the 1960s, Xu rose steadily in the municipal party hierarchy of Shanghai and eventually became party secretary of the **Shanghai Municipal Party Committee Writing Group** and established close working relationships with Zhang Chunqiao and **Yao Wenyuan**, who were then in charge of party propaganda work in Shanghai before the Cultural Revolution.

When the Cultural Revolution broke out, Xu, at the encouragement of Zhang Chunqiao, led the writing group to rebel against the CCP Shanghai Municipal Committee and formed a radical "Rebel Station of Shanghai Party Organs." On 18 December 1966, Xu's organization and the **Workers Command Post** took the lead at a mass rally in "bombarding" the Shanghai party committee. Xu attacked the municipal leadership in a long speech at the rally, and because he and members of his organization were all party functionaries, their role turned out to be critical in bringing down the CCP Shanghai Municipal Committee headed by First Secretary Chen Pixian and Mayor Cao Diqiu. In the **January Storm** of 1967, Zhang Chunqiao named Xu a deputy head of the Shanghai Revolutionary Committee. Later, Xu and other leading members on the committee, including **Ma Tianshui** and **Wang Xiuzhen**, helped Zhang persecute his critics, especially those involved in the two incidents of the **Bombarding Zhang Chunqiao** campaign. Xu and his associates also brought false charges against Cao Diqiu, Wei Wenbo, and other senior officials in Shanghai.

In the meantime, Xu began to involve himself in the power conflict in Beijing and became a lieutenant of the Gang of Four in various nationwide political campaigns. He and his associates in Shanghai were particularly active in attacking **Chen Yi** during the movement against the **February Adverse Current** in the late 1960s and criticizing **Deng Xiaoping** during the **Counterattack the Right-Deviationist Reversal-of-Verdicts Trend** campaign in 1975 and 1976. As a reward for his loyalty to top-level cultural revolutionaries, Xu was admitted into the CC as a full member and appointed a party secretary of Shanghai when the CCP power structure was reestablished. Ranking third next to Zhang Chunqiao and Yao Wenyuan in the CCP Shanghai Municipal Committee, he earned the popular nickname "Xu Number Three" in Shanghai.

In October 1976, when members of the Gang of Four were detained in Beijing, Xu and other Gang "remnants" plotted a **Counterrevolutionary Armed Rebellion in Shanghai**, but the plan was aborted. As soon as **Hua Guofeng** and the central leadership took full control of Shanghai, Xu was arrested. He was dismissed from office and expelled from the CCP. On 21 August 1982, the Shanghai Supreme Court convicted Xu of several counts of counterrevolutionary crimes and sentenced him to 18 years in prison.

XU SHIYOU (1905–1985). Born in Xin County, Henan Province, on 28 February 1905, Xu started his long military career at age 15 as a soldier in the troops of the warlord Wu Peifu. He joined the **Chinese Communist Party** (CCP) in 1927 and participated in the CCP-led Huangma Uprising in Hubei Province. A veteran of the Long March (1934–1935), the Sino-Japanese War (1937–1945), the civil war of the second half of the 1940s, and the Korean War (1950–1953), Xu rose steadily in the ranks of the CCP-led military forces as a distinguished commanding officer. In 1955, Xu was appointed commander of the Nanjing Military Region, a position he continued to hold until the end of 1973.

In the **power seizure** phase of the Cultural Revolution initiated by Shanghai's 1967 **January Storm**, some **rebel** organizations in Nanjing, the capital of Jiangsu Province, formed an alliance and took over the Jiangsu provincial government on 26 January. The mass organizations that did not participate, however, cried foul and formed a "Foul!" faction (*pi pai*, "*pi*" in Chinese, meaning "fart") in opposition to the "Hail!" faction (*hao pai*, "*hao*" in Chinese, meaning "good") consisting of mass organizations that benefited from the power takeover. Intense factional fighting then ensued. After painstaking efforts to broker a deal between the two sides failed, leaders in Beijing decided to ignore the newly formed *ad hoc* provincial government and directed that military control be imposed on the entire Jiangsu Province. Xu, as commander of the Nanjing Military Region involved in the military control mission backstage, became entangled with Jiangsu's civilian affairs. Facing resistance from some mass organizations, mostly of the "Hail!" faction, the Military Control Commission detained some rebels. But the factional conflict continued and even spread into the military establishment. Each side sought and won some support from Beijing, and the conflicting opinions among central leaders consequently affected the local situation so much that not only did the factional battle escalate, some mass organizations even called for Xu's ouster. When **Chen Zaidao**, commander of the Wuhan Military Region, was purged as one of "the handful of **capitalist-roaders** in the military" after the **July 20 Incident** (1967) in Wuhan, rebels in Nanjing launched a new campaign to bring Xu down, calling him "the Chen Zaidao of Nanjing."

Eventually, Chairman **Mao Zedong** came to Xu's rescue when he realized that the move instigated by members of the **Central Cultural Revolution Small Group** against alleged capitalist-roaders in the military establishment had gone so far as to threaten the stability of the military, and of the country at large. Mao made gestures of support by receiving Xu in Shanghai on 18 August 1967, and inviting Xu to Beijing to join him and other leaders on 1 October to inspect the National Day celebration parade from the top of Tiananmen Rostrum. When the **revolutionary committee** of Jiangsu Province was established in March 1968, Xu was named to lead the new power establishment. In 1969, he was elected a member of the Politburo.

Though Xu was not brought down, he received much criticism locally and from the central leadership, especially after the Cultural Revolution, for taking advantage of the nationwide campaign against the so-called **May 16 Counterrevolutionary Clique** to retaliate against the rebels and the military personnel who had opposed him; many people in Jiangsu were falsely charged and persecuted in a four-year period until Xu was reassigned commander of the Guangzhou Military Region in December 1973. He continued to hold this military post until 1980 and his membership in the Politburo until 1982. Xu was elected a vice-chairman of the CCP Central Advisory Committee in 1982 and remained in this position until his death.

XU XIANGQIAN (1901–1990). A senior official of the **Chinese Communist Party** (CCP) and the **People's Liberation Army** (PLA), Xu played an important role in China's political and military affairs before 1949 and held prominent positions in the party, the state, and the army after the founding of the People's Republic of China (PRC). In the Cultural Revolution, Xu was one of the veteran officials involved in the 1967 **February Adverse Current**.

Born in Wutai, Shanxi Province, Xu was a member of the first graduating class of the Huangpu (Whampoa) Military Academy and a veteran of the Northern Expedition. He joined the CCP in 1927 and participated in the Guangzhou Uprising in the same year. Xu was general commander of the Fourth Front Red Army in the Long March, deputy commander of the 129th Division of the Eighth Route Army in the Sino-Japanese War, and commander of the First Corps of the PLA's East Field Army during the civil war in the second half of the 1940s. Xu was the first chief of the general staff of the PLA (1949–1954) after the founding of the PRC. In 1955, Xu was appointed one of 10 marshals of the PRC. Xu served as a vice-chairman of the CCP Central Military Commission (CMC) from 1959 to 1987 and as a member of the Politburo from 1966 to 1969 and again from 1977 to 1987.

In January 1967, upon recommendation by **Jiang Qing** and approval by **Mao Zedong**, Xu was appointed head of the All-Army Cultural Revolution Group. This appointment, along with Xu's entry into the Politburo in August

1966, was evidence that he initially supported Mao's Cultural Revolution program. In February 1967, however, Xu, along with **Tan Zhenlin, Chen Yi**, and several other senior party and military leaders, sharply criticized the radicals of the **Central Cultural Revolution Small Group** at a top-level meeting at the Zhongnanhai compound. The outburst of their anti–Cultural Revolution sentiment was denounced by Mao as a February Adverse Current. In March 1967, Xu was removed as head of the All-Army Cultural Revolution Group. In April, he was criticized at an enlarged meeting of the CMC. Later, **rebels** searched his house, confiscated his personal belongings, and posted the slogan "Down with Xu Xiangqian" on the streets of Beijing. The veterans of the February Adverse Current came under attack again in 1969 at the **Ninth National Congress of the CCP**; though Xu retained his membership in the CC, his power and influence in military affairs were much reduced.

After **Lin Biao**'s demise in 1971, Mao began to seek support from the "old government" faction of the central leadership and sent friendly signals to Xu and other senior party and military leaders. Xu reappeared at the CMC Standing Committee and was named a vice-chairman of the National People's Congress in 1975. In the post-Mao era, Xu was reelected a member of the Politburo of both the Tenth and the Eleventh CC. He served as defense minister and vice-premier of the State Council from 1978 to 1980 and vice-chairman of the CMC from 1983 to 1988. He died on 21 September 1990.

Y

YAN FENGYING (1930–1968). Born in Tongcheng, Anhui Province, Yan was China's best-known singer of the regional musical theater called the *huangmei* opera. She started her performing career at the age of 15. In the 1950s and the first half of the 1960s, Yan devoted all her efforts to popularizing and perfecting the *huangmei* opera form. She joined the **Chinese Communist Party** (CCP) in 1960 and became a member of the executive council of the China Federation of Literary and Art Circles in the same year. During the Cultural Revolution, Yan was accused of attacking the revolutionary **model operas**. She was denounced as a representative of the "black line in literature and arts," a counterrevolutionary, and a Kuomintang spy. She was humiliated and tortured.

On the night of 7 April 1968, Yan tried to kill herself by overdosing on sleeping pills. Instead of rushing her to a hospital, however, her persecutors from her work unit held a **struggle meeting** at her bedside. When she was eventually taken to a hospital, no medical worker would give her emergency treatment without permission from her work unit. Yan died on 8 April 1968. Upon her death, doctors dissected her body under the supervision of a **People's Liberation Army** representative from Yan's work unit supposedly in search of a micro-transmitter for sending intelligence to the Kuomintang. Yan's name was cleared by the CCP Anhui provincial committee in May 1978. A memorial service was held for her in August 1978 by the Cultural Bureau of Anhui Province.

YANG CHENGWU (1914–2004). An alternate member of the **Chinese Communist Party** (CCP) Central Committee (CC) from 1956 and acting chief of general staff of the **People's Liberation Army** (PLA) since 1966, General Yang was persecuted by **Lin Biao** and **Jiang Qing** in 1968 as a member of the so-called Yang-Yu-Fu Anti-Party Clique.

Born in a poor peasant family in Fujian Province, Yang began his military career as a young Red Army soldier in 1929 when he was 15. In the following year, he joined the CCP. Rising quickly in army ranks due to his military prowess, Yang served as commander of the Red Army First Corps under Lin

Biao during the Long March, commander of the independent division of the Eighth Route Army in the war of resistance against Japan, and commander of the Central-Hebei Military District and of the PLA Third Corps in the civil war of the second half of the 1940s. After 1949, he was appointed commander of the Beijing Military Region and deputy chief of general staff.

Yang's initial prominence in the Cultural Revolution was largely a result of his activities at a high-level CCP meeting held in Shanghai at the end of 1965 and the **enlarged Politburo sessions** in May 1966: at both meetings, he was at the forefront attacking General **Luo Ruiqing**, chief of general staff of the PLA. After the fall of Luo, Lin Biao, with Chairman **Mao Zedong**'s approval, appointed Yang acting chief of general staff. However, Lin and his wife, **Ye Qun**, soon began to question Yang's loyalty. First, since Yang would accompany Mao on trips out of Beijing, Lin and Ye were eager to find out from Yang what Mao said on these trips concerning Lin and were frustrated with Yang's evasiveness about any statements Mao made. Second, after the **February Adverse Current** of 1967, Yang not only disobeyed Lin's order not to pass party documents to Marshal **Ye Jianying** but also followed the instructions of **Zhou Enlai** to put in place certain measures for the protection of other old marshals. Third, Yang declined Lin's request that he disregard facts and help establish Ye Qun's early party membership. And fourth, Yang supported **Yu Lijin**, political commissioner of the air force, after **Lin Liguo**, Lin Biao's son, joined the air force and led a faction against Yu. In March 1968, when Lin Biao sought support from the Jiang Qing group for the removal of Yang Chengwu and Yu Lijin, Jiang asked Lin to dismiss **Fu Chongbi**, commanding officer of the Beijing Garrison Command, as well. As a result of this political bargain, the three generals were named by Lin, with the approval of Mao, as a Yang-Yu-Fu Anti-Party Clique. Yang was arrested on 22 March 1968 and imprisoned for six years.

After the downfall of Lin Biao and his associates in September 1971, Mao began to seek support from other factions in the army. In December 1973, Mao acknowledged some of the mistakes he made concerning the **Yang-Yu-Fu Affair**. The names of the three generals were cleared in July 1974. Yang was reappointed deputy chief of general staff of the PLA and commander of the Fuzhou Military Region in 1975. In March 1979, the CC officially rehabilitated the case of the Yang-Yu-Fu Affair by publicizing its 1974 decision for the first time. Yang became a member of both the Eleventh and Twelfth CC. He was also elected vice-chairman of the Chinese People's Political Consultative Conference in 1983.

YANG SHANGKUN (1907–1998). Director of the General Office of the **Chinese Communist Party** (CCP) Central Committee (CC) and an alternate member of the CCP Secretariat, Yang was named a member of the **Peng-**

Luo-Lu-Yang Anti-Party Clique at the enlarged Politburo sessions, 4–26 May 1966, and became one of the earliest victims of the Cultural Revolution among ranking CCP leaders.

A native of Tongnan, Sichuan Province, Yang joined the Chinese Communist Youth League in 1925 and became a member of the CCP in 1926. After a five-year training stint at Zhongshan University in Moscow, Yang came back to China in 1931 to lead the labor movement in Shanghai and an anti-Japanese propaganda campaign in Jiangsu Province. Yang joined the CCP Central Soviet Government in Jiangxi in 1933, became an alternate member of the CC in 1934, and served as political commissioner of the Red Army's Third Infantry during the Long March. He began to work directly under **Liu Shaoqi** at the CCP North China Bureau in 1937 and became secretary of the bureau in 1938 upon Liu's departure. Yang went to Yan'an in 1941 and became secretary-general of the CCP Central Military Commission (CMC) in 1945. In 1948, Yang was appointed, and was to remain until 1965, director of the General Office of the CC, an important office that coordinates the daily affairs of the CC and offers services to help top CCP leaders in their daily lives. In 1956, he became an alternate secretary of the CCP Central Secretariat at the First Plenum of the Eighth CCP Central Committee while continuing to hold other important positions as the general secretary of both the CC General Office and the CMC.

On 11 November 1965, Yang was suddenly removed from the General Office. On a charge of stealing top party secrets, he was accused of tapping **Mao Zedong**'s, as well as other Politburo members', conversations and providing documents and archives to others for copying without proper authorization, while the fact was, according to the post-Mao leadership's defense of Yang, that Yang simply performed his duty in recording Mao's conversations with foreign visitors. According to **Wang Li**'s recollection, Mao also condemned Yang for having persecuted leftists as rightists, including those with connections to Mao. For punishment, Yang was demoted and exiled to the provinces. In May 1966, Yang was named a member of the Peng-Luo-Lu-Yang Anti-Party Clique at the enlarged Politburo sessions. In July, he was detained for investigation and lost his freedom.

Yang's name was cleared in 1978. He was then appointed to several important positions in Guangdong Province. In 1980, Yang became a member of the core leadership in Beijing. The high positions he served in the next 13 years included secretary-general of the CMC, member of the Politburo, first vice-chairman of the CMC, and above all, president of the People's Republic of China (1988–1993). Yang retired from all his positions at the end of 1993. He died on 14 September 1998.

YANG XIANZHEN (1896–1992). Born in Yunxian, Hubei Province, Yang was a veteran member of the **Chinese Communist Party** (CCP) and one of the party's leading Marxist theorists. He served as provost and vice-president of the Institute of Marxism-Leninism and became president and party secretary when the institute was renamed the Higher Party School of the CCP Central Committee (CC) in 1955. Yang was demoted to vice-president in 1961 because of his critical remarks about the Great Leap Forward. In 1964, he was criticized for formulating the idea of "two combine into one" as the complement or antithesis of "one divides into two" (a phrase **Mao Zedong** often used) in the dialectic. Named "bourgeois spokesman within the party" and accused of opposing **Mao Zedong Thought** and advocating revisionism, Yang was dismissed from office in 1965.

During the Cultural Revolution, Yang was named by **Kang Sheng** as a political target to bring down. He was **struggled against** at the Higher Party School. He was also imprisoned for eight years (1967–1975) as a member of the so-called **Sixty-One Traitors Clique**. After he was released from prison in 1975, Yang was sent to Shaanxi, where he remained doing manual labor until 1978. On 16 December 1978, the CC dismissed the Sixty-One Traitors Clique as a case of injustice. On 4 August 1980, the CC approved the Party School's review of Yang's case, and Yang Xianzhen was finally rehabilitated. In his last years, Yang served as a member on the Advisory Committee of the CC. Yang died on 25 August 1992.

YANG XIGUANG (1948–2004). A self-labeled ultra-leftist and the leading theorist of the mass organization the **Provincial Proletarian Alliance** of Hunan Province, Yang Xiguang was persecuted by the government for his insistence on articulating and further theorizing what he believed to be **Mao Zedong**'s original conception of the Cultural Revolution. Yang was the son of a ranking **Chinese Communist Party** official who was implicated in the case of the **Peng Dehuai** Anti-Party Clique in 1959.

When the Cultural Revolution began in 1966, Yang was a student at Changsha No. 1 Middle School in the capital city of Hunan. Inspired by Mao's critique of an emerging bureaucratic bourgeois class within the ruling party and his ideas of continuous revolution based on such a critique, Yang began to observe the development of the Cultural Revolution from a perspective that he considered to be Mao's original intention of the revolution. As an intellectually inclined political rebel, Yang wrote a series of essays in which he judges the new establishment of the **revolutionary committee** as falling far short of Mao's political ideal and denounces the current "red" capitalist class in the new power structure with Premier **Zhou Enlai** as its general representative. A takeover by the militia would be necessary in his view to usher in a genuine proletarian dictatorship under Mao through general elections with the Paris Commune of 1871 as a model. Prominent among these essays is a long article entitled "Where Is China Going?" which **Kang Sheng** named the reactionary political program of the Provincial Proletarian Alliance of Hunan.

Yang was arrested in 1968 and sentenced to 10 years in prison. The post-Mao government released him in 1978 but refused to redress his case. He then changed his name to "Yang Xiaokai" because, with a still "problematic" personal record, he could not find a job. In 1983, Yang went to Princeton University as a doctoral student in economics and received his Ph.D. in 1988. He died on 7 July 2004, at which time he was a chair professor in economics at Monash University, Australia.

See also NEW TREND OF IDEAS.

YANG-YU-FU AFFAIR (1968). Also known as the March 24 Incident, this was a case in which **Lin Biao** and **Jiang Qing** framed three ranking military leaders: the acting chief of general staff of the **People's Liberation Army** (PLA) and director of the **Central Military Commission Administrative Group**, **Yang Chengwu**; the air force political commissar, **Yu Lijin**; and the commanding officer of the Beijing Garrison Command, **Fu Chongbi**. The replacement of these three by Lin's close associates further strengthened Lin's power in the military and gave Lin full control of the Central Military Commission Administrative Group. The downfall of Yang, Yu, and Fu also set off a nationwide campaign against a "right-deviationist reversal-of-verdicts trend."

On 22 March 1968, the **Chinese Communist Party** (CCP) Central Committee (CC), the State Council, the Central Military Commission (CMC), and the **Central Cultural Revolution Small Group** (CCRSG) jointly issued two orders removing Yang Chengwu, Yu Lijin, and Fu Chongbi from power in the military and appointing **Huang Yongsheng** chief of general staff of the PLA and Wen Yucheng commanding officer of the Beijing Garrison Command. On the evening of 24 March, the decision was announced at a meeting of 10,000 middle- and high-ranking military cadres at the Great Hall of the People. In his long speech at the meeting, Lin Biao made several charges against the three generals, including a conspiracy of Yang and Yu to take control of the air force and an armed storming of the CCRSG ordered by Yang and led by Fu.

On the early morning of 25 March, **Mao Zedong** came out to greet the assembled and show his support for Lin's handling of the Yang-Yu-Fu Affair. The two orders were read for the first time on the afternoon of 27 March at a mass rally of 100,000 civilians and military personnel in Beijing. In her speech at the rally, Jiang Qing identified Yang, Yu, and Fu as representatives of a "right-deviationist reversal-of-verdicts trend." In the CC's political report delivered by Lin Biao at the **Ninth National Congress of the CCP**, the Yang-Yu-Fu Affair was referred to as an "evil trend to reverse the verdict on the **February Adverse Current**." None of the charges was substantiated, though Yang, Yu, and Fu were indeed sympathetic with the old marshals involved in the so-called February Adverse Current of 1967.

At a CMC meeting on 21 December 1973, more than two years after Lin Biao's downfall, Mao Zedong said: "The case of Yang-Yu-Fu should be reversed. It was all Lin Biao's doing. I made a mistake in listening only to his side of the story." In July 1974, Yang, Yu, and Fu were rehabilitated. On 28 March 1979, the CC officially cleared the case of the Yang-Yu-Fu Affair by publicizing its 1974 decision for the first time.

YAO WENYUAN (1931–2005). A key member of the **Central Cultural Revolution Small Group** (CCRSG), second secretary of the Shanghai Municipal Committee of the **Chinese Communist Party** (CCP), and a member of the CCP Politburo from 1969 to 1976, Yao was one of **Mao Zedong**'s trusted cultural revolutionaries and the author of the article "On the New Historical Drama *Hai Rui Dismissed from Office*," which came to be known as the "blasting fuse" of the Cultural Revolution. He was generally considered *de facto* head of the CCP Propaganda Department after 1971. Yao was arrested in 1976 as a member of the **Gang of Four**.

A native of Zhuji, Zhejiang Province, Yao was a son of Yao Pengzi, a left-wing writer in the 1930s. Yao joined the CCP in 1948 while a high school student in Shanghai. After the **People's Liberation Army** took over Shanghai from the Nationalists, Yao started to work as a correspondent for the CCP-controlled media. By 1957, his militant criticism of allegedly bourgeois, revisionist, and reactionary writers had already caught the attention of Chairman Mao Zedong. On 10 June 1957, Mao applauded one of Yao's essays attacking rightists and recommended it for nationwide distribution.

In the first half of the 1960s, Yao was involved in Mao's backstage strategic planning of the Cultural Revolution and became a close ally of **Jiang Qing**. Around 1963, he followed **Zhang Chunqiao**, director of the Propaganda Department of the CCP Shanghai Municipal Committee, to work for Jiang in her **revolution in Peking opera** program. Yao rose to prominence in 1965 when he, following instructions from Zhang and Jiang, wrote "On the New Historical Drama *Hai Rui Dismissed from Office*" attacking **Wu Han**. In 1966, Yao published a series of articles attacking **Deng Tuo**, **Peng Zhen**, and the CCP Beijing Municipal Committee, which earned him the nickname "proletarian golden stick." A rising star on China's political scene, Yao was named a member of the newly established CCRSG in May 1966 and began to play a significant role in bringing down the **Liu Shaoqi** and **Deng Xiaoping** faction of the central leadership in the ensuing months. During the Criticize the **Bourgeois Reactionary Line** campaign, Yao and other CCRSG members pushed the **rebel** movement forward against the old party establishment. He also actively engaged in Shanghai's **January Storm**, instigating rebels to take power from the senior leaders of the Shanghai government, Chen Pixian and Cao Diqiu. After the fall of Chen and Cao, Yao became vice-chairman of the Shanghai **Revolutionary Committee** and, later, second secretary of the CCP Shanghai Municipal Committee.

As a theorist, Yao helped Mao formulate the theory of **continuing revolution under the dictatorship of the proletariat**: On 7 November 1967, *People's Daily*, *Red Flag*, and *Liberation Army Daily* carried a joint editorial entitled "March Forward along the Road of the October Socialist Revolution: Commemorating the 50th Anniversary of the Great October Socialist Revolution." Drafted by Yao and **Chen Boda**, the editorial sums up in six points the theory of the Cultural Revolution and names it Mao's most significant contribution to Marxism. In 1969, Yao was elected to the Politburo at the **Ninth National Congress of the CCP**.

After the downfall of **Wang Li**, **Guan Feng**, and **Qi Benyu** in late 1967 and Chen Boda in 1970—all of them radical writers and theorists in the service of Mao's cultural revolution politics—Yao became Mao's most trusted writer, propaganda chief, and ideological watchdog. In the ensuing years until October 1976, Yao was the person in charge of *People's Daily*, *Red Flag*, and virtually all other newspapers and periodicals in China. During this period, Yao was further involved in the top-level power struggle of the CCP and became a member of the Jiang Qing–led Gang of Four. With the nation's propaganda apparatus under his control, Yao, with Mao's support, advocated the political interests and ideology of his faction and helped edge out several political rivals, including **Lin Biao** and his associates in 1971 and Deng Xiaoping and his supporters in 1975 and 1976.

On 6 October 1976, within a month of Mao's death, **Hua Guofeng** and **Ye Jianying** ordered the arrest of Yao and other members of the Gang of Four. On 23 January 1981, a special court of the Supreme People's Court of the People's Republic of China convicted Yao of a series of crimes, including organizing and leading a counterrevolutionary clique and participating in Jiang Qing's activities to usurp state power, and sentenced him to 20 years in prison.

YE JIANYING (1897–1986). A senior leader of the **Chinese Communist Party** (CCP) and the **People's Liberation Army** (PLA), Ye played a significant role in China's political and military affairs before, during, and after the Cultural Revolution. Of particular importance was his involvement in the **February Adverse Current** of 1967 and in the ousting of the **Gang of Four** in October 1976. The latter put to an end the decade-long turmoil of the Cultural Revolution.

A native of Mei County, Guangdong Province, and a graduate of the Yunnan Military Academy, Ye became deputy director of the Department of Instruction at the Huangpu (Whampoa) Military Academy in 1924 when the academy was founded. He participated in the Northern Expedition in 1926, joined the CCP in 1927, and became one of the leaders of the Guangzhou Uprising. After two years of study in Moscow, Ye returned to China in 1930 and became chief of staff of the Red Army and later assumed the presidency of the Red Army School. A leading officer during the Long March, Ye was credited with reporting to **Mao Zedong** about Zhang Guotao's dubious moves and saving the troops led by Mao and Zhu De. In the war of resistance against Japan and the civil war afterward, Ye, as chief of staff of the Eighth Route Army and then of the PLA, continued to distinguish himself as a top military analyst of the CCP.

After the founding of the People's Republic of China (PRC), Ye was appointed to a number of prominent government and military positions, including mayor of Beijing, governor of Guangdong, commander of the South-China Military Region, president and political commissar of the PLA Military Academy, and vice-chairman of the CCP Central Military Commission (CMC). In 1955, Ye was made one of 10 marshals of the PRC. He became a member of the CCP Central Committee (CC) in 1945 and a member of the Politburo in August 1966 at the **Eleventh Plenum of the Eighth Central Committee of the CCP**.

In the early stages of the Cultural Revolution, Ye rose steadily in the CCP central leadership. He supported Mao's move to purge **Luo Ruiqing**, chief of general staff of the PLA and general secretary of the CMC, and led the CC **work group** on the Luo case in May 1966. He also took Luo's place as general secretary of the CMC. As the revolution continued to unfold, however, Ye was taken aback by the moves of the ultra-leftist forces against the military establishment. In February 1967, Ye, along with **Tan Zhenlin**, **Chen Yi, Xu Xiangqian**, and a few other senior party and military leaders, sharply criticized the radicals of the **Central Cultural Revolution Small Group** at a top-level meeting in Zhongnanhai. The outburst of their anti–Cultural Revolution sentiment was denounced by Mao as a February Adverse Current. Ye was soon removed as general secretary of the CMC. The veterans were under attack again in April 1969 at the **Ninth National Congress of the CCP**. Although Ye, alone of all the veterans involved in the February Adverse Current, was allowed to retain his seat in the Politburo, he was nevertheless exiled from Beijing in October 1969.

Mao began to enlist Ye's support in his strategic move against the **Lin Biao** faction after the **Lushan Conference** of 1970. In July 1971, Ye was entrusted with the responsibility of receiving U.S. secretary of state Henry Kissinger during the latter's secret visit to Beijing. After Lin Biao's demise in 1971, Ye took charge of the daily affairs of the military in the capacity of vice-chairman of the CMC. Ye became a vice-chairman of the CCP in 1973 and minister of defense in 1975. In between these two appointments, however, Ye and Premier **Zhou Enlai** were harshly criticized at the **enlarged**

Politburo sessions, **25 November–5 December 1973**, for carrying out a "right-wing capitulationist line" or **Zhou-Ye revisionist line** in their negotiations with the United States. Eventually, in 1976, during the **Counterattack the Right-Deviationist Reversal-of-Verdicts Trend** campaign, Mao removed Ye from power because he followed both **Deng Xiaoping** and Zhou Enlai closely to carry out a rectification program.

Within a month of Mao's death, Ye worked closely with **Hua Guofeng** and **Wang Dongxing** in making the decision to arrest the Gang of Four on 6 October 1976. In March 1977, Ye resumed his responsibility for the daily affairs of the CMC. In March 1978, he was elected chairman of the Standing Committee of the National People's Congress. Ye retired in 1985 and died on 22 October 1986.

YE QUN (1917–1971). Wife of **Lin Biao** and liaison between Lin and his supporters in the armed forces during the Cultural Revolution, Ye was director of the office of Lin Biao, a member of the **All Forces Cultural Revolution Small Group**, and a member of the **Central Military Commission Administrative Group** (1967–1971).

Born in Minhou (Fuzhou), Fujian Province, Ye Qun took part in the 9 December anti-Japanese, patriotic movement in Beijing in 1935 as a middle school student. In the early stages of the war of resistance against Japan, Ye was briefly associated with a Kuomintang-controlled youth organization before she went to Yan'an to join the Communists in 1938. She married Lin Biao in 1942. After the Communists took power in 1949, she began to serve as Lin Biao's secretary and, officially belonging in the military, eventually attained the rank of full colonel.

Ye Qun became actively involved in politics in the central leadership in late 1965 when she assisted Lin Biao in bringing down **Luo Ruiqing**, chief of general staff of the **People's Liberation Army**. Ye telephoned **Li Zuopeng**, deputy commander of the navy, and advised him on how to frame Luo in a report Lin Biao had asked him to write. At the end of November, Ye carried Lin's personal letter to Hangzhou to see **Mao Zedong** on the alleged problems of Luo, and her six-hour verbal report to Mao was mainly based on Li Zuopeng's fabrications. Following Mao's instruction, the Standing Committee of the Politburo held an enlarged session in Shanghai in December 1965 to criticize Luo. Ye, who was not even a Central Committee (CC) member at the time, not only attended the meeting but also spoke three times for almost 10 hours altogether, enumerating Luo's "crimes" of opposing **Mao Zedong Thought** and attempting to take over Lin Biao's power at the Ministry of Defense.

Ye's political engagement went further after the Cultural Revolution began in mid-1966. In August 1966, Lei Yingfu, a ranking officer in the Department of General Staff, fabricated material against President **Liu Shaoqi** at Ye's suggestion. Following Ye's instruction, Song Zhiguo, of the general office of the Central Military Commission (CMC), wrote in September to frame Lin and Ye's personal enemy, Marshal **He Long**. In October, at **Jiang Qing**'s request, Ye instructed Jiang Tengjiao, a ranking officer of the air force, to conduct a dramatic "ransacking household" (*chaojia*) by **Red Guards** at the homes of some notable personages in Shanghai in search of material that might reveal what Jiang Qing thought to be her embarrassing past as a film actress. On 11 January 1967, Ye was named a member of the All Forces Cultural Revolution Small Group, her first official title of political significance. After the **February Adverse Current** of 1967, Ye was involved in activities to frame marshals **Xu Xiangqian** and **Ye Jianying**. In August 1967, when the Central Military Commission Administrative Group was formed to take over the daily affairs of the CMC, Ye was appointed one of its four founding members. In 1969, at the **Ninth National Congress of the Chinese Communist Party**, Ye was elected to the CC and the Politburo.

At the **Lushan Conference** of 1970, the conflict between the Jiang Qing faction and the Lin Biao faction surfaced. Ye joined **Chen Boda**, **Wu Faxian**, Li Zuopeng, and **Qiu Huizuo** in attacking **Zhang Chunqiao** and supporting a proposal not to **eliminate the office of the national president**. She, along with other supporters of Lin, was reproached by Mao. On 6 September 1971, when General **Huang Yongsheng** informed Ye of the critical remarks on Lin Biao that Mao made during his **southern inspection**, Ye was said to have passed the intelligence to Lin right away, and the two allegedly made a decision to let their son, **Lin Liguo**, execute a plot against Mao's life. The alleged assassination plan was foiled due to changes Mao made on his itinerary. On the evening of 12 September, Mao's sudden and unexpected return to Beijing and **Zhou Enlai**'s telephone conversation with Ye Qun made Ye believe that their scheme was detected. She boarded the jet plane Trident 256 with Lin Biao and Lin Liguo and fled the country on the early morning of 13 September. About two hours after taking off, Trident 256 crashed near Undurkhan in Mongolia, killing all passengers onboard.

Ye Qun's role in the **September 13 Incident** and the events leading up to it still lacks a definitive account today. Apparently, after she stepped into the political arena of the **Chinese Communist Party** (CCP) central leadership in late 1965, Ye took an increasingly active role mediating between the frail, increasingly reclusive Lin Biao and his cohorts in the armed forces. Yet it remains a question whether, as the official version of history has it, Ye was simply Lin Biao's loyal agent or, according to her daughter **Lin Liheng**'s eyewitness account, Ye was a much more manipulative and domineering figure who plotted with Lin Liguo in the last few days of their lives without Lin Biao's knowledge.

See also WOMEN DURING THE CULTURAL REVOLUTION.

YILIN DIXI. Made up of the Chinese transliteration of pen names that Vladimir Ilyich Lenin once used, this was the pseudonym that Liu Wozhong and Zhang Licai, two students at Beijing Agricultural University High School, adopted in their "Open Letter to Comrade **Lin Biao**" criticizing Lin's **"peak theory"** concerning **Mao Zedong** and **Mao Zedong Thought**. The specific target of criticism in this letter is a speech Lin gave at the Military Academy on 18 September 1966, in which Lin spoke of Mao as a rare genius that could emerge once in several hundred years, an unmatched thinker looking far beyond capitalism and therefore standing much higher than Marx, Engels, Lenin, and Stalin.

In their critique of Lin's speech, Liu and Zhang embrace Joseph Stalin's assessment of Leninism in the context of monopoly capitalism and judged Lin Biao's comparison of Mao with his revolutionary predecessors to be ahistorical and therefore wrong. While acknowledging Mao Zedong Thought as the most applicable theory of Marxism in current times, they disagree with Lin's view that **People's Liberation Army** personnel should devote 99 percent of their political study to reading Mao's works; the percentage is inappropriate, they argue, because it is necessary to study the classic texts of earlier Marxist thinkers in order to understand the development of Mao's ideas. They also criticize Lin for being out of touch with the masses and out of touch with theory, too, which includes Mao's speculation on replacing the old state apparatus with a "commune of the east" as the ultimate goal of the Cultural Revolution.

Liu and Zhang posted their open letter as a **big-character poster** on the campus of Tsinghua University on 15 November 1966, and then distributed it as handbills. Their critique of Lin Biao soon became known across China. They were **struggled against** as counterrevolutionaries on school campuses in Beijing. The authorities arrested them on 20 December 1966 on a charge of attacking the proletarian revolutionary headquarters. The post-Mao government rehabilitated Liu and Zhang and, on 18 June 1979, officially pronounced the original verdict unjust.

YIN-YANG HAIRCUT. (*Yinyang tou.*) A head half shaved, this was a hideous haircut **Red Guards** forced on their victims as a sign of humiliation, especially during the early days of the Cultural Revolution. The brutal act was often carried out with scissors in public at **struggle meetings**. To minimize humiliation, some victims went to barbershops afterward to have their whole heads shaved but were denied service. Some others tried to cover their heads with hats but were often ordered by Red Guards to take them off. Compared to the tall dunce caps forced on victims, the big placards hanging from their necks, and other ingenious inventions of the revolutionary masses for humiliating people, the yin-yang haircut stood out as a non-removable label of class enemies and a symbol of shame.

Red Guards giving Li Fanwu, governor of Heilongjiang Province, a humiliating yin-yang haircut at a struggle meeting.

YU HUIYONG (1925–1977). Born in Shandong Province, Yu joined the **People's Liberation Army** in 1946 and the **Chinese Communist Party** (CCP) in 1949. He caught the attention of **Jiang Qing** in 1965 when he, as a composer, was involved in the making of the Peking operas *Taking Tiger Mountain by Stratagem* (*Zhiqu weihushan*) and *On the Dock* (*Haigang*). Produced by the Shanghai Peking Opera Troupe, both operas were to be on the list of the **eight model dramas** promoted by Jiang Qing. Yu was a lecturer at the Shanghai Conservatory of Music at the time. Due to his contribution to the production of the two operas, Jiang, accompanied by **Zhang Chunqiao**, then director of the CCP Shanghai propaganda department, received him in person.

Jiang's high regard for him proved to be a political fortune to Yu during the Cultural Revolution. In October 1966, Zhang rescued Yu from the "**cow shed**" (where people labeled class enemies, or "**cow-demons and snake-spirits**," were detained) at the Shanghai Conservatory of Music and made him a member of a performance team that Jiang had asked to form in Shanghai for the purpose of producing the two model operas in Beijing. Shortly after Shanghai's **January Storm** of 1967, Yu was made chairman of the **revolutionary committee** of the Shanghai Conservatory of Music and, later, party secretary of the Shanghai Cultural Bureau. In July 1971, Yu, an enthusiastic supporter and advocate of Jiang Qing's radical propagandist art theory and experiment, was named deputy director of the newly formed State Council Cultural Group. He became a member of the Tenth Central Committee of the CCP in August 1973 and minister of culture in January 1975.

During these years, Yu, along with **Liu Qingtang** and **Qian Haoliang**, represented Jiang Qing and her group in cultural and art circles. Taking orders from Jiang, he launched attacks on a number of well-known literary and artistic productions and events, including the Jin opera *Three Trips to Taofeng*, a painting exhibition in Beijing (which Yu labeled "black"), and the film *Pioneers* (*Chuangye*). These attacks provided ammunition for the ultra-leftist faction of the CCP leadership against their political rivals such as **Zhou Enlai** and **Deng Xiaoping** and drastically deepened political repression in cultural and artistic circles. On 22 October 1976, Yu was detained as a die-hard follower of the **Gang of Four**. He committed suicide on 28 August 1977 while in detention. In September 1977, Yu was expelled from the CCP. In October 1983, more than six years after his death, the party committee of the Ministry of Culture issued a document officially dismissing Yu from his posts both within and outside the party.

YU LIJIN (1913–1978). Political commissar of the air force, General Yu was persecuted by **Lin Biao** and **Jiang Qing** in 1968 as a member of the so-called Yang-Yu-Fu Anti-Party Clique. Born in Dayan, Hubei Province, Yu joined the Red Army in 1928 and became a member of the **Chinese Communist Party** (CCP) in 1930. A veteran of the Long March and a long-time political officer in the army, Yu was appointed political commissar of the air force in the Nanjing Military Region after 1949 and later political commissar of the air force of the **People's Liberation Army**.

In the early stages of the Cultural Revolution, Yu came under attack by **rebels** in the military until he was appointed a member of the **All Forces Cultural Revolution Small Group** in January 1967. But Yu soon had conflicts with **Wu Faxian**, commander of the air force and Lin Biao's close associate, especially after **Lin Liguo**, son of Lin Biao, joined the air force and received special treatment from Wu. Lin Liguo's entry led to a split of the Air Force Command personnel into two factions: his own supporters and those of Yu Lijin's. The Lin supporters fabricated the story of a romantic and slightly salacious affair between one of Yu's secretaries and the daughter of **Yang Chengwu**, acting chief of general staff, and had the secretary arrested. Yang suggested to Wu that the arrest was not appropriate and that Yu's secretary should be released. This suggestion was soon used by Lin Biao as evidence of a Yang-Yu conspiracy to take over power at the Air Force Command.

In March 1968, when Lin Biao sought support from Jiang Qing's group for removing Yang Chengwu and Yu Lijin from power, Jiang asked Lin to dismiss **Fu Chongbi**, the commanding officer of the Beijing Garrison Command, as well. As a result of this political bargain, the three generals were named by Lin, with the approval of **Mao Zedong**, as anti-party elements in the army. Yu was arrested on 23 March 1968 and imprisoned for six years.

In December 1973, more than two years after the downfall of Lin Biao, Mao acknowledged his mistakes concerning the **Yang-Yu-Fu Affair**. The names of the three generals were cleared in July 1974. Yu was reappointed first political commissar of the Civil Aviation Administration of China and second political commissar of the air force. Yu died in 1978. In March 1979, the CCP Central Committee officially cleared the case of the Yang-Yu-Fu Affair by publicizing its 1974 decision for the first time.

YU LUOKE (1942–1970). An outspoken critic of the **blood lineage theory** and the discriminatory **class line** of the **Chinese Communist Party**, Yu sacrificed his life advocating equal rights for the underprivileged and the oppressed. He was China's pioneer of democratic consciousness during the Cultural Revolution.

A native of Beijing, Yu was born into a family that was considered politically untrustworthy in post-1949 China. His grandfather's class status was that of a capitalist. His father, an engineer, was branded "rightist" in 1957. Despite his academic excellence, Yu Luoke was denied a college education due to his family background. After high school, first as a farmer at Red Star People's Commune in the Beijing suburbs and then an apprentice at the Beijing People's Machine Factory, Yu taught himself Chinese classics and Western philosophy. The influence of his readings, Jean-Jacques Rousseau's *Discourse on the Origin and Foundations of Inequality among Men* among them, was noticeable in his article **"On Family Background"** for which he was best known during the Cultural Revolution.

Yu was remarkably independent in his political thinking when almost the whole nation was carried away by the fever of the Cultural Revolution. Upon reading **Yao Wenyuan**'s article "On the New Historical Play *Hai Rui Dismissed from Office*," which is known as the prologue to the Cultural Revolution, Yu presented his counterargument in several articles defending the playwright **Wu Han**'s high regard for Hai Rui. One of the articles was published in Shanghai's *Wenhui Daily* on 13 February 1966 as an example of bad criticism; it was shortened by the editor and retitled "It Is Time to Fight Mechanistic Materialism." Some of his journal entries of this period show his critical views about the **personality cult** of **Mao Zedong** and the **model operas** promoted by **Jiang Qing** and his skepticism toward the Cultural Revolution in general, all of which were to be counted as evidence of his "counterrevolutionary crimes" later on.

The brutality of the **Red August** of 1966 and the notoriety of the blood lineage theory represented by a **Red Guard** couplet ("If the father is a hero, the son is a real man; if the father is a reactionary, the son is a bastard") eventually prompted Yu to write "On Family Background," a critique of government-sanctioned, Red Guard–promoted "class" discrimination against tens of millions of youths from non-proletarian families. The mimeographed version of this article came out in December 1966. The revised version was published on 18 January 1967 in the *Journal of Middle School Cultural Revolution* and soon became one of the most widely circulated articles during the Cultural Revolution. Letters of support poured in from all parts of China. In the three months that followed, Yu wrote a number of articles on the same issue and published them in the *Journal of Middle School Cultural Revolution* as well as two other mass organization newspapers. He also participated in public debates over the theory of family lineage.

Yu's outlets were blocked on 13 April 1967 when **Qi Benyu**, a member of the **Central Cultural Revolution Small Group**, spoke of "On Family Background" as a "reactionary" piece attacking socialism as a caste system. The authorities arrested Yu on 5 January 1968 and executed him on 5 March 1970. His "crimes," as listed in his court verdict, included "writing reactionary letters, poems, and diaries calumniating the proletarian headquarters," "planning to organize a counterrevolutionary clique," "threatening to plot assassinations," and "intending to sabotage the proletarian dictatorship." On 21 November 1979, Beijing Intermediate People's Court redressed Yu's case and pronounced the earlier court decision unjust.

Z

ZHANG CHUNQIAO (1917–2005). Deputy head of the **Central Cultural Revolution Small Group** (CCRSG), head of the Shanghai **Revolution Committee** (1967–1976), first secretary of the Shanghai Municipal Committee of the **Chinese Communist Party** (CCP) (1971–1976), a member of the CCP Politburo (1969–1976) and its standing committee (1973–1976), vice-premier of the State Council (SC) (1975–1976), and director of the General Political Department of the **People's Liberation Army** (PLA) (1975–1976), Zhang was a leading ultra-leftist intellectual and government official who was deeply involved in Chairman **Mao Zedong**'s backstage strategic planning of the Cultural Revolution and played a significant role in the politics of the central leadership during the revolution. Zhang was arrested in 1976 as a member of the **Gang of Four** and remained unrepentant after the Cultural Revolution.

A native of Juye, Shandong Province, Zhang was a leftist writer in Shanghai who, assuming the pen name Di Ke, had debated with Lu Xun in the 1930s. Zhang joined the CCP in 1936. At the outbreak of the war of resistance against Japan, Zhang went to the Communist base Yan'an and worked as a leading editor in several local newspapers. After the founding of the People's Republic of China (PRC), Zhang returned to Shanghai and assumed several important posts in the area of journalism and political propaganda under the CCP Shanghai Municipal Committee, including editor-in-chief of the committee's official organ *Liberation Daily*, director of the committee's department of cultural work and department of propaganda, and an alternate secretary of the municipal committee. In 1958, when the radical Great Leap Forward policies were beginning to be implemented, Zhang published an article entitled "Eradicate the Ideology of the Bourgeois Right," advocating the abolition of material incentives in all production units. Mao applauded the article and recommended its reprint in the CCP official organ *People's Daily*.

In the first half of the 1960s, Zhang became involved in Mao's strategic moves for the launching of the Cultural Revolution and became a close ally of **Jiang Qing**. Together with **Yao Wenyuan**, Zhang actively supported

Jiang's **revolution in Peking opera** program. He also worked with Jiang in 1965 in planning an attack on **Wu Han** and helped Yao Wenyuan in writing and publishing a critique of Wu's historical play *Hai Rui Dismissed from Office*—an article to be known as the "blasting fuse" of the Cultural Revolution. In February 1966, Zhang was involved in the symposium organized by Jiang on literature and arts in the armed forces. After the symposium, Zhang, along with **Chen Boda**, edited and revised the **Summary of the Symposium** before it was handed to Mao for further revision. Containing a harsh judgment on China's literary and art productions since 1949, this summary report was issued by the CCP Central Committee (CC) in April 1966 in preparation for the Cultural Revolution.

Zhang was named deputy head of the CCRSG in May 1966 and began to play a significant role in bringing down the **Liu Shaoqi** and **Deng Xiaoping** faction of the central leadership in the ensuing months. During the Criticize the **Bourgeois Reactionary Line** campaign, Zhang and other CCRSG members pushed the **rebel** movement forward against the old party establishment. In December 1966, Zhang instigated rebels at Tsinghua University and other schools to denounce President Liu Shaoqi at a mass rally in Tiananmen Square. He also supported the Shanghai **Workers Command Post** during the **Anting Incident** and led the Shanghai rebels' **power seizure** movement in January 1967. After Chen Pixian and Cao Diqiu, the senior leaders of the Shanghai government, were overthrown, Zhang became chairman of the newly established Shanghai Revolutionary Committee and, later, first secretary of the CCP Shanghai Municipal Committee. In 1969, Zhang was elected to the Politburo at the **Ninth National Congress of the CCP**.

After the downfall of **Wang Li**, **Guan Feng**, and **Qi Benyu** in late 1967 and Chen Boda in 1970—all of them radical writers and theorists in the service of Mao's cultural revolution politics—Zhang became China's foremost Maoist theoretician. In an article entitled "On Complete Dictatorship over the Bourgeoisie," published in April 1975, Zhang presented an authoritative Maoist theoretical justification for the Cultural Revolution. Considering Zhang Chunqiao to be a faithful student of his Cultural Revolution ideology and a possible successor, Mao made him a member of the Standing Committee of the Politburo in August 1973 and second vice-premier of the SC and director of the General Political Department of the PLA in January 1975.

In the 1970s, Zhang was deeply involved in the power conflict in the central leadership. At the **Lushan Conference** of 1970, he was the unnamed target of attack by the **Lin Biao** faction. After the downfall of Lin, in the evolving conflict between cultural revolutionaries and the politically moderate **Zhou Enlai** and Deng Xiaoping, Zhang became a member of the Jiang Qing–led Gang of Four. In late 1975, Zhang and his colleagues convinced

Mao of Deng Xiaoping's anti–Cultural Revolution stand and finally defeated Deng during the **Counterattack the Right-Deviationist Reversal-of-Verdicts Trend** campaign.

On 6 October 1976, within a month of the death of Mao, **Hua Guofeng** and **Ye Jianying** ordered the arrest of Zhang and the other members of the Gang of Four. On 23 January 1981, a special court of the Supreme People's Court of the People's Republic of China convicted Zhang of a series of crimes, including organizing and leading a counterrevolutionary clique and initiating and continuing to plot power takeovers from the state government, and sentenced him to death with a two-year reprieve. Zhang protested all accusations by maintaining his silence throughout the trial. Before the trial, he had stated that he was still a firm Maoist and supported all the radical policies of the Cultural Revolution.

ZHANG TIESHENG (1950–). Also known as the "hero of the blank examination paper," Zhang Tiesheng wrote a note of protest and plea after a series of poor performances at the college entrance examination in 1973. His note was used effectively by the ultra-leftist faction of the **Chinese Communist Party** leadership as a political weapon against what they considered to be an attempt to restore the old education system supported by **Zhou Enlai**. Zhang, the 23-year-old applicant, was elevated by **Jiang Qing** and her supporters to the status of a hero with the courage to "go against the tide." The incident contributed much to the debasement of knowledge and learning in general and the worsening of the nation's higher education in particular in the last three years of the Cultural Revolution.

As of 1970 when colleges began to admit students, admission decisions had been based on recommendations from applicants' work units. In April 1973, however, the State Council approved a document submitted by its Science and Education Group cautiously suggesting that college applicants' examination scores be considered in addition to recommendations. Zhang Tiesheng, an **educated youth** working in the countryside in Liaoning Province, was recommended by his commune to take part in the regional examination. Overwhelmed by the language and math tests and frustrated further by chemistry and physics, Zhang Tiesheng wrote a letter to the "respected leaders" on the back of the examination sheets. In the letter, Zhang explained how his total devotion to the work in the countryside cost him study time. He also attacked other candidates who did better in the tests as bookworms craving college for their own benefit and ignoring their proper occupation.

Zhang's letter caught the attention of **Mao Yuanxin**, **Mao Zedong**'s nephew and a ranking official in Liaoning, who had already become Jiang Qing's close associate. Mao Yuanxin made the decision to publish the letter with an editor's note, and he edited both. On 19 July 1973, Zhang's letter, along with the editor's note, appeared in *Liaoning Daily* under the title "A

Thought-Provoking Examination Paper." Three weeks later, all major newspapers, including *People's Daily*, reprinted the letter and the note. Mao Yuanxin talked about Zhang Tiesheng as a "sharp rock" that he could use to attack others. Jiang Qing called Zhang a hero who dared to go against the tide. Mao Zedong also noticed Zhang, mentioning him with approval while suggesting that professors at Beijing's eight institutes be gathered and given a test. Following the publication of Zhang's letter, an anti-intellectual propaganda campaign began nationwide, in which the newly revived attention to examination scores was denounced as the bourgeois counteroffensive against the **revolution in education**. As a result of such propaganda, the trashing of culture and knowledge went further in schools at all levels.

Zhang Tiesheng himself, on the other hand, was admitted as a **worker-peasant-soldier student**, as college students were then called, at the Tieling Institute of Agriculture in Liaoning in autumn 1973. He soon became a party member and was given a responsible position in the school's leadership. In 1975, he was made a member of the Standing Committee of the **Fourth National People's Congress**. Zhang became more politically active in 1976 as a follower of the Jiang Qing group: in Liaoning, Beijing, and Shanxi, he talked about himself as a sword and a gun, attacked veteran cadres as "restoration maniacs," and called for an organizational "surgery" with an "iron hand." In March 1977, five months after the downfall of the **Gang of Four**, Zhang Tiesheng was arrested on a charge of counterrevolutionary crimes. He was sentenced to 15 years in prison.

ZHANG XITING (1928–1993). A rebelling official during the Cultural Revolution, Zhang became deputy head of the Sichuan Provincial **Revolutionary Committee** in 1967 and an alternate member of the Central Committee at the **Ninth National Congress of the Chinese Communist Party** in 1969. She was dismissed from office for her involvement in a factional war in Sichuan. On 24 June 1978, Zhang and her husband, **Liu Jieting**, also an official in Sichuan, were arrested on a counterrevolutionary charge. On 24 March 1982, Zhang was sentenced to 17 years in prison.

ZHANG YUFENG (1944–). Born in Mudanjiang, Heilongjiang Province, Zhang served as an attendant on the special train for central leaders in the 1960s and caught the attention of Chairman **Mao Zedong**. In 1970, she was transferred to Zhongnanhai to work as an attendant at Mao's residence. Her relationship with Mao was said to be intimate. In late 1974, she was appointed Mao's confidential secretary. As Mao's health was worsening, Zhang, as one of the few who could still make out Mao's increasingly unclear vocal expressions, became indispensable as an intermediary between Mao and other leaders. After Mao's death, Zhang was transferred out of

Zhongnanhai to work at Bureau No. 1 of Historical Archives. She eventually went back to her first employer, the Ministry of Railways. In the meantime, she led an editorial effort on Mao's private library, which resulted in the publication of the 24-volume *Mao Zedong Book Collection* in 2001.

ZHANG ZHIXIN (1930–1975). A loyal Communist who made known her critical view of the ultra-leftist policies of the **Chinese Communist Party** (CCP), especially those of the Cultural Revolution, through regular channels within CCP organizations, Zhang was imprisoned for more than five years and eventually executed as an "active counterrevolutionary."

A native of Tianjin and a graduate of People's University, Zhang joined the CCP in 1955 and became a secretary (*ganshi*) of arts and literature at the Propaganda Department of the CCP Liaoning Provincial Committee in 1957. In the early stages of the Cultural Revolution, Zhang criticized **Lin Biao**'s promotion of Mao's **personality cult** and Lin's "**peak theory**" and questioned Lin's motives. When the **Ninth National Congress of the CCP** was held in 1969, Zhang, while working at a **May 7 cadre school** and under surveillance, spoke out against the inclusion in the newly revised CCP Constitution of Lin Biao as Chairman **Mao Zedong**'s successor. She also criticized **Jiang Qing**, the so-called standard-bearer of the proletarian arts and literature, for virtually destroying arts and literature.

Zhang saw the persecution of President **Liu Shaoqi** as unjust and the ultra-leftist policies of the CCP as the direct cause of nationwide factional violence and chaos during the Cultural Revolution. Zhang's criticism also went beyond the Cultural Revolution: she expressed sympathy for Marshal **Peng Dehuai**, who was dismissed from office in 1959 for his criticism of Mao's Great Leap Forward policies. Peng's letter to Mao, in Zhang's view, was not anti-party; rather, writing a letter to the party chairman was a legitimate move endorsed by the party constitution. Zhang also pointed out that Mao had made mistakes in the late 1950s and that the leftist policies of the CCP, which began in 1958, continued and went much further during the Cultural Revolution.

Because of her sharply critical views, the provincial authorities of Liaoning ordered Zhang's arrest on 26 September 1969 on a counterrevolutionary charge. While in prison, she refused to acknowledge her "crimes" and insisted on her right to speak out, for which she was so brutally abused that she eventually suffered a mental breakdown. On 26 February 1975, the standing committee of the Liaoning provincial party committee, led by **Mao Yuanxin**, resolved to have Zhang Zhixin executed. Two hours before her execution on 4 April, the executioners cut Zhang's vocal cords to prevent her from speaking.

On 31 March 1979, the CCP Liaoning Provincial Committee redressed her case and named her a revolutionary martyr. On 11 August 1979, Beijing's *Guangming Daily* published a long report about Zhang Zhixin's life; the details of her persecution shocked the whole nation. Since then, Zhang has become a national symbol of integrity, courage, conviction, and opposition to tyranny.

ZHAO YONGFU. *See* FEBRUARY 23 INCIDENT (1967).

ZHAO ZIYANG (1919–2005). Out of power as a provincial-level official for most of the Cultural Revolution, Zhao rose to prominence as an economic reformer upon appointment as first party secretary of Sichuan Province in October 1975 and, along with **Hu Yaobang**, was the major force of liberalization in the capacity of premier of the State Council (1980–1987) and general secretary of the **Chinese Communist Party** (CCP) (1987–1989) until his ouster in 1989 because of his sympathies for the protesting students during the Tiananmen democracy movement (April–June 1989).

Born Zhao Xiuye from a landlord family in Hua County, Henan Province, Zhao joined the Communist Youth League in 1932 and the CCP in 1938. In 1951, Zhao was transferred from a prefectural party secretary position in Henan to Guangdong Province, assisting **Tao Zhu** in leading the CCP South China Bureau and Guangdong provincial government. He eventually became first secretary of the CCP Guangdong Provincial Committee (1965–1967). During the Great Leap Forward campaign, Zhao led a work team to Guangdong's Leinan County to inquire into the difficulties of state grain requisition. Based on a wrong conclusion that peasants had been hiding extra grain for their own consumption, he led a campaign against grain-hoarding and reported this experience to the provincial party committee. On 22 February 1959, the CCP Central Committee (CC) issued Zhao's report with Chairman **Mao Zedong**'s lengthy comments and launched a nationwide campaign against grain-hoarding. Though both Zhao Ziyang and Tao Zhu were soon to notice and acknowledge their mistakes and institute remedial measures, the campaign against grain-hoarding had a grave impact on the already severe Great Famine (1958–1962) that resulted in over 600,000 starvation deaths in Guangdong and 20 to 30 million nationwide.

During the Cultural Revolution's **power seizure** movement in early 1967, Zhao, as the highest-ranking official in Guangdong, was caught in a double bind. Under much pressure from the mass organization Guangdong Provincial Revolutionary Rebel Alliance, Zhao opted to concede the power of the provincial party committee and provincial government on 22 January without consulting top leaders in Beijing. Mao, who had been encouraging **rebels** to attack old party apparatuses, was nevertheless displeased; he ordered Premier

Zhou Enlai to investigate the case and reproach Zhao. Meanwhile, power struggles, and even armed conflicts, occurred between the Rebel Alliance and a rival **Red Guard** organization supported by Guangzhou Military Region troops until order was restored in mid-March by the newly formed military control commission under the military region commander, General **Huang Yongsheng**. Zhao then became the major target of attack by the masses in the province and later exiled to a factory in Hunan Province as a laborer. Zhao's rehabilitation began in 1971 when he was recalled from Hunan and appointed a deputy party chief in Inner Mongolia. After the downfall of **Lin Biao**, which implicated Huang Yongsheng, Zhao was reinstated as first secretary of the CCP Guangdong Provincial Committee and also served as the head of the Guangdong Revolutionary Committee and the political commissar of the Guangzhou Military Region.

In 1975, as **Deng Xiaoping** launched his **overall rectification** program, Zhao was put in charge of China's most populous province, Sichuan. As a maturing realist leaving Cultural Revolution dogma behind, Zhao introduced a series of market-oriented, liberalizing economic policies, including loosening restrictions on the size and use of family plots, contracting output quotas to each farm household, and substituting townships for people's communes. These reform measures led to an increase in industrial production by 81 percent and agricultural output by 25 percent within three years. Zhao's experiments were so successful that a popular line of praise spread from Sichuan to other parts of the country: "If you want food, look for Ziyang" (*yao chi liang, zhao Ziyang*).

As Deng Xiaoping came back to power again in the late 1970s and, as China's paramount leader, began to promote his Reform and Opening policies against Mao's Cultural Revolution legacy, Deng used Zhao's "Sichuan experience" as a model for the nationwide economic reform. Seeing in Zhao the potential of becoming his successor, Deng pushed for his speedy ascent to various central party and government positions. In 1979, Zhao entered the CCP Politburo. In 1980, Zhao became one of the Politburo's standing committee members and premier of the State Council. He was put in charge of the country's economic matters and also played a leading role in foreign affairs and scientific developments. In 1987, he was elected general secretary of the CCP after his colleague Hu Yaobang was forced to resign from this highest position in the party. In the 1980s, mainly due to the efforts of Zhao and Hu, China's economy underwent profound structural changes and gradually abandoned static central planning and oriented toward the free market, achieving an enormous success. Culturally and politically, too, the decade was widely considered an age of renaissance after the repressive Cultural Revolution era; Chinese society was more open and freer despite periodic setbacks caused by the conservative faction of the central leadership.

In late June 1989, however, Zhao was dismissed from all his official positions because of his unyielding position against imposing martial law in the city of Beijing against the demonstrating students and other citizens during the Tiananmen democracy movement (also known as "June Fourth" because of the brutal military crackdown during the early morning hours of 4 June). On the early morning of 19 May, Zhao went to Tiananmen Square to see the students on a hunger strike. With tears in his eyes, he made a moving speech, begging the students to end their hunger strike and promising that the door of dialogue with the government would remain open. This act was seen by the old guards in the party leadership as evidence of Zhao's attempt to "split the party" and "support the riot." For the remainder of his life, Zhao was under virtual house arrest. He could have been reinstated, as Deng Xiaoping repeatedly said, if he were willing to acknowledge his mistake. But, believing that he was on the right side of history, Zhao refused to give in; instead, he insisted that the June Fourth crackdown was a "brutal violation of socialist legality." Zhao Ziyang died on 17 January 2005.

ZHOU ENLAI (1898–1976). Vice-chairman of the **Chinese Communist Party** (CCP) (1956–1976) and premier of the People's Republic of China (PRC) (1949–1976), Zhou was China's chief administrator, negotiator, and diplomat. A supporter of **Mao Zedong**'s Cultural Revolution, Zhou was entrusted with the responsibility of managing the daily affairs of the party and the state from August 1966 until his death in January 1976. Moderate and pragmatic in his approach to both state affairs and party politics, he was the single most important stabilizing factor in the CCP leadership during this turbulent period. Despite his painstaking and tactical efforts to deradicalize Mao's ultra-leftist policies, however, he never openly opposed Mao's decisions. In later stages of the Cultural Revolution, as he became the unnamed target of political campaigns launched by the ultra-leftists of the **Jiang Qing** group with Mao's consent, his reputation as a sane, humane, and upright leader soared among the populace. Eventually, not long after his death, he became the inspiration for the **April 5 Movement** of 1976—an unprecedented spontaneous mass protest against the ultra-leftist faction of the CCP leadership, anticipating a swift end to the Cultural Revolution.

A native of Shaoxing, Zhejiang Province, Zhou was a student leader in Tianjin during the May Fourth Movement. He studied in both Japan (1917–1919) and France (1920–1924). He joined the CCP in 1921 and became a leader of the CCP's European branch. Upon returning from France, he was appointed, among other ranking political and military positions in both the CCP and the Nationalist Kuomintang, director of the political department of the Huangpu (Whampoa) Military Academy where Chiang Kaishek was commandant. In July 1927, Zhou played a major role in organizing the Nanchang Uprising, the first military insurrection of the Communists against the Kuomintang. In late 1931, as he joined Mao Zedong and Zhu De in the Communist rural base in Jiangxi, he was appointed secretary of the CCP's Jiangxi Soviet Central Bureau and replaced Mao as political commissar of the Red Army. During the Long March (1934–1935) and during the Yan'an years that followed, however, Zhou supported Mao's political and military strategies and helped establish Mao's central leadership in both the party and the army. In late 1936, he negotiated with Chiang Kai-shek to form a Nationalist-Communist alliance against the invading Japanese army.

During the war of resistance against Japan, while working with non-Communists and promoting the United Front in the Kuomintang-occupied areas, Zhou successfully cultivated the image of the CCP and won broad sympathy and support for the CCP among liberal politicians and intellectuals. As he returned to Yan'an in 1943 to participate in the Rectification Movement under Mao's leadership, however, he was attacked as the representative of the "empiricist faction" within the party. Zhou survived by pleading guilty and harshly criticizing himself.

When the PRC was founded in 1949, Zhou served as premier (1949–1976) and foreign minister (1949–1958). He was in charge of designing and implementing the country's economic policies in the form of a series of five-year plans. His rather cautious and pragmatic approach to economic matters was often criticized by Mao in the late 1950s. On the diplomatic front, Zhou's success was enormous: he went to Moscow in 1950 to negotiate a 30-year China-Soviet treaty of alliance; he represented the PRC at the 1954 Geneva Conference and at the 1955 Afro-Asian conference in Bandung, Indonesia; and he traveled broadly throughout Asia, Africa, and Europe in the late 1950s and early 1960s to promote China's relations with Third World countries. The historic meeting between Mao Zedong and U.S. president Richard Nixon in February 1972 was, to a great extent, arranged and implemented by Zhou in cooperation with his U.S. counterpart, Henry Kissinger.

In April 1966, when Mao was stirring up revolution by making angry and harshly critical comments about **Peng Zhen** and **Lu Dingyi**, Zhou, who was in charge of the daily activities of the central government at the time during President **Liu Shaoqi**'s absence from Beijing, indicated his support for the revolution for the first time in a formal work report, which virtually legitimized Mao's otherwise personal views. But Zhou's support was nevertheless riddled with ambiguity throughout. In the heat of the violent **Red Guard** movement, Zhou made arrangements within the limits of his power to protect veteran cadres and notable personages from the Red Guards' attack. When the first mass campaign against Liu Shaoqi and **Deng Xiaoping** was about to begin, he tried in vain to persuade Mao to soften the harsh political sentence that their policies were a **Bourgeois Reactionary Line**. As the revolution was spreading rapidly across the country, he tried to stabilize the nation's economy by tactically publicizing Mao's words "grasp revolution and promote production." During the **February Adverse Current** of 1967, he tried to remain neutral as a number of military marshals and vice-premiers vented their anti–Cultural Revolution rage at the ultra-leftists of the **Central Cultural Revolution Small Group**, only to betray his stand by identifying himself and the veteran leaders together as "us." In the early 1970s, Zhou began to talk about the importance of knowledge and the possibility of enrolling high school graduates directly in college—propositions that were in conflict with the current practice of the "**revolution in education**."

Zhou Enlai's position in the CCP leadership was on the rise during the Cultural Revolution. At the **Eleventh Plenum of the Eighth Central Committee of the CCP** (1–12 August 1966), he became the third-highest-ranking leader of the CCP. After the downfall of **Lin Biao** in September 1971, he became second, next to Mao. As his status and power increased, however, Zhou was facing greater challenges and provocations from the ultra-leftist faction of the CCP leadership who, along with Mao, envisioned Zhou as a formidable anti–Cultural Revolution force after Mao's death. And, as indispensable as Zhou was, Mao never considered him as his successor; rather, Mao often equated Zhou's meticulous attention to details and superb skills as an administrator with the neglect of more important matters and the lack of firm ideological and political conviction.

From 25 November to 5 December 1973, **enlarged Politburo sessions** were convened at Mao's suggestion to criticize Zhou for his "right revisionist line" and "capitulationism" in foreign policy because of his negotiations with the United States on the sensitive issue of military exchange. Jiang Qing called the conflict between Zhou and Mao the "eleventh line struggle within the party." A month later, in January 1974, another general offensive against Zhou was launched in the name of an anti–Lin Biao campaign known as **Criticize Lin and Criticize Confucius**, which was followed by yet another implicitly anti-Zhou movement: that of the *Water Margin* **Appraisal** (1975–1976). The attack on Zhou in both of these campaigns took the form of **allusory historiography** in which Confucius and Song Jiang—a capitulator in the historical romance *Water Margin*, in Mao's view—were depicted with considerable resemblance to China's current premier.

Zhou was instrumental in Deng Xiaoping's reinstatement as vice-premier in 1973. In December 1974, Zhou, gravely ill with cancer and escorted by hospital nurses, flew to Changsha to discuss personnel matters with Mao in preparation for the forthcoming **Fourth National People's Congress**. Zhou recommended Deng for the position of first vice-premier against **Zhang Chunqiao**, the candidate of the Jiang Qing group. In the opening session of the Fourth Congress on 13 January 1975, Zhou delivered the government work report, confirming the "four modernizations" (modernization in industry, agriculture, national defense, and science and technology) as the long-range goal of the PRC.

Zhou Enlai's painstaking efforts to deflate the influence of ultra-leftism and to restore normality to China won sympathy nationwide. By the time of his death on 8 January 1976, he had become the most respected Communist leader in China. As Zhou's body was transported to the Beijing Babaoshan Cemetery for cremation via Chang'an Avenue on the afternoon of 11 January, an estimated one million citizens lined the street waiting in bitter cold to pay their respects to the late premier. Mao Zedong, absent from Zhou's funeral, commented harshly on a briefing report with the words "Restoration [of capitalism] in the name of mourning." In the meantime, the traditional custom of paying homage to the dead during the Qingming Festival season (in late March and early April) provided an occasion for another, and more powerful, outpouring of public grief at the loss of Zhou in major cities of China, which turned into a venting of public rage against ultra-leftism as well. The memory of the late premier had thus become a rallying point for the masses against the Cultural Revolution.

See also CONFUCIANISM VERSUS LEGALISM; NANJING INCIDENT (1976); PING-PONG DIPLOMACY (1971); TIANANMEN INCIDENT (1976); UNITED STATES–CHINA RELATIONS; WU HAO AFFAIR; ZHOU-YE REVISIONIST LINE.

ZHOU QUANYING (1943–). A student at Tsinghua University, Zhou was a leader and theorist of the 4-14 Headquarters, a moderately inclined **rebel** organization. As an antithesis of the ultra-leftist **new trend of ideas**, Zhou articulated his rather conservative assessment of the political state of the nation in a much-publicized article entitled "The 4-14 Trend Shall Prevail" (3 August 1967). Rejecting the notion that a privileged bourgeois bureaucratic class had formed within the **Chinese Communist Party** (CCP) since it became the ruling party in China in 1949, Zhou regards the 17 years of Communist rule before the Cultural Revolution a proletarian dictatorship under the leadership of Chairman **Mao Zedong**. The number of so-called **capitalist-roaders** within the party is extremely small. He therefore opposes the drastic overhaul of the political system and the violent struggle through which power is to be redistributed. Zhou was highly critical of the nationwide mass movement following the directions of the **Central Cultural Revolution Small Group** (CCRSG) because it was drawing the entire country further and further into chaos.

Many moderate rebels sympathized with these ideas, and Zhou's article became quite popular among them. Later, in other writings, Zhou singled out **Chen Boda**, head of the CCRSG, as a target of criticism and also made known his observations of the conflicts among members of the CCRSG, **Zhou Enlai, Lin Biao**, and other top leaders, which led to his detention by the authorities. He was released after Mao mentioned his name at a **meeting with the five Red Guard leaders** and said that a theorist should be freed.

But Zhou was officially arrested on 19 May 1978 because of a **big-character poster** he wrote in 1977 in which he reversed his earlier views and exposed the privileges the CCP officials enjoy. He was finally released in December 1979 after the government pronounced his case misjudged.

ZHOU RONGXIN (1917–1976). As minister of education when Vice-Premier **Deng Xiaoping** was conducting an **overall rectification** program in 1975, Zhou followed Deng closely and criticized various forms of anti-intellectualism promoted in the Cultural Revolution. In the subsequent anti-Deng **Counterattack the Right-Deviationist Reversal-of-Verdicts Trend** campaign, Zhou was denounced as Deng's right-hand man and an enemy of the **revolution in education**.

Born in Penglai, Shandong Province, Zhou Rongxin joined the **Chinese Communist Party** (CCP) in 1937. He was appointed deputy minister of education in 1959 and secretary-general of the State Council in 1965. In late 1966 and early 1967, **Jiang Qing** and her supporters accused Zhou of carrying out a **Bourgeois Reactionary Line** (that of **Liu Shaoqi**) and supporting the repressive **Red Guard** organizations, such as the **Pickets** of the Xicheng District in Beijing, in the early stages of the Cultural Revolution. Zhou was publicly denounced and humiliated. In January 1975, when Deng Xiaoping assumed various top leadership positions and took charge of the daily affairs of the CCP Central Committee (CC) and the State Council, Zhou was appointed minister of education. Urged by Deng to speak out, Zhou became one of the few vocal advocates of Deng's policies and worked diligently to control the damage caused by the Cultural Revolution in education and to restore normality to the nation's schools.

In late 1975, when Chairman **Mao Zedong** began to criticize Deng and prepare for an anti-Deng campaign, the field of education was Mao's breakthrough point, and Zhou Rongxin became a prominent target in the so-called great debate on the revolution in education. Zhou was accused of negating the revolution in education and opposing Mao's education policies. He was repeatedly **struggled against** despite his ill health. At a struggle meeting held at the Ministry of Education on 12 April 1976, Zhou suffered a heart-attack. He died the next day. Zhou's name was cleared by the CC in 1977.

ZHOU YANG (1908–1989). A man of letters and a veteran Communist in cultural work, Zhou Yang was denounced during the Cultural Revolution as a representative of the "revisionist black line in arts and literature." Born in Yiyang, Hunan Province, Zhou Yang joined the **Chinese Communist Party** (CCP) in 1927. In the first half of the 1930s, Zhou was deeply involved in the activities of the League of Leftist Writers in Shanghai, editing its official organ, *Literature Monthly*, and providing the CCP leadership for the League.

He went to the revolutionary base Yan'an in 1937. In the next 30 years—up to the beginning of the Cultural Revolution—Zhou Yang assumed a number of culture-related official positions including president of the Lu Xun Institute of Arts and Literature, deputy head of the Propaganda Department of the CCP Central Committee, deputy minister of culture of the People's Republic of China, and vice-president of the China Federation of Literary and Art Circles. He was also appointed a member of the **Five-Person Cultural Revolution Small Group** in July 1964. Zhou Yang was attacked during the Cultural Revolution for leading a "revisionist black line" in cultural spheres and for being one of the "**Four Fellows**" allegedly antagonistic to, and ridiculed by, the revered modern Chinese writer Lu Xun in the 1930s. He was imprisoned for nine years until July 1975 when **Mao Zedong** said that Lu Xun would not agree to shut up the likes of Zhou Yang.

After his full rehabilitation in 1979, Zhou was appointed to numerous ranking positions including president of the China Federation of Literary and Art Circles, vice-president of the Chinese Academy of Social Sciences, and deputy head of the CCP Propaganda Department. As one of the few ranking cadres of the CCP capable of serious critical reflection upon the grave mistakes committed by themselves and by the CCP leadership as a whole, Zhou played an important role in the post–Cultural Revolution "Liberation of Thinking" movement and began to reassess the ideology of the CCP from a humanist perspective in the 1980s. Zhou Yang died on 28 July 1989.

ZHOU-YE REVISIONIST LINE. This was the charge against **Zhou Enlai** and **Ye Jianying** for their allegedly "right-wing capitulationism" in dealing with the United States in late 1973 in the face of threat from the Soviet Union.

See also ENLARGED POLITBURO SESSIONS, 25 NOVEMBER–5 DECEMBER 1973.

ZHU CHENGZHAO (1943–1998). A well-known **rebel** student leader, Zhu was a founder of the mass organization East-Is-Red Commune at the Beijing Geological Institute and the Capital College Red Guards Revolutionary Rebel Headquarters (commonly known as the **Third Command Post**). In August 1966, Zhu, a senior student of hydrology at the Beijing Geological Institute, criticized the **work group** sent by the Ministry of Geology and, together with his schoolmate **Wang Dabin**, formed the mass organization East-Is-Red Commune. This organization won the full support of the **Central Cultural Revolution Small Group** (CCRSG) during the campaign to criticize the **Bourgeois Reactionary Line**. Following instructions from **Qi Benyu**, of the CCRSG, Zhu and Wang led a team to Sichuan Province in December 1966 to kidnap Marshal **Peng Dehuai** to Beijing to be **struggled**

against by the masses. This mission gave Zhu an opportunity to talk with Peng and read classified information about the Lushan Conference of 1959. In the meantime, he came to know Marshal **Ye Jianying** through his friend Ye Xiangzhen, daughter of Marshal Ye.

The unexpected exposure to internal information, the influence of Peng and Ye, and the misfortune of his own father—a veteran Communist denounced as a member of the "**black gang**" of the Beijing party committee at the outset of the Cultural Revolution—apparently enabled him to see the serious problems of party politics and of the CCRSG, so much so that in January 1967, Zhu and some of his close friends began to plan a campaign to challenge the CCRSG. However, Wang Dabin leaked the information to the central leaders. **Chen Boda** and some other members of the CCRSG soon took preemptive measures to persecute Zhu and Ye Xiangzhen as a "counterrevolutionary clique" and called upon their fellow students to struggle against them. Zhu, then, was held incommunicado for a number of years. His case was eventually cleared by the post-Mao leadership in the late 1970s.

Glossary

Andongni'aoni de *Zhongguo* (Antonioni's *China*) 安东尼奥尼的 (中国)

Anting shijian (Anting Incident) 安亭事件

Baimaonü (*White-Haired Girl*) (白毛女)

baiwan xiongshi (Million-Strong Mighty Army) 百万雄师

Baiyangdian shige qunluo (Baiyangdian poet group) 白洋淀诗歌群落

bajie shi'erzhong quanhui (Twelfth Plenum of the Eighth Central Committee of the Chinese Communist Party) 八届十二中全会

bajie shiyizhong quanhui (Eleventh Plenum of the Eighth Central Committee of the Chinese Communist Party) 八届十一中全会

bajie shizhong quanhui (Tenth Plenum of the Eighth Central Committee of the Chinese Communist Party) 八届十中全会

baohuangpai (royalists) 保皇派

baoshoupai (conservatives) 保守派

bayiba (mass rally of 18 August 1966, also 8-18) 八一八

Beijing daxue Qinghua daxue dapipanzu (Great Criticism Group of Peking University and Tsinghua University) 北京大学清华大学大批判组

Bian Zhongyun 卞仲耘

bianselong (chameleon) 变色龙

Bo Xilai 薄熙来

Bo Yibo 薄一波

buduan geming (uninterrupted revolution) 不断革命

Changping can'an (Changping County massacre) 昌平惨案

changzheng dui (long march team) 长征队

chanshazi (add sand to the mix) 掺沙子

Chen Boda 陈伯达

Chen Erjin 陈尔晋

Chen Lining 陈里宁

Chen Pixian 陈丕显

Chen Shaomin 陈少敏

Chen Xilian 陈锡联

Chen Yi 陈毅

Chen Yonggui 陈永贵

Chen Zaidao 陈再道

Chi Qun 迟群

chijiao yisheng (barefoot doctor) 赤脚医生

chou laojiu (the stinking old ninth) 臭老九

Chuangye (*Pioneers*) (创业)

Chunmiao (*Spring Seedling*) (春苗)

chushen (family background) 出身

Chushenlun ("On Family Background") (出身论)

da chuanlian (great networking) 大串连

da lianhe (grand alliance) 大联合

da minzhu (great democracy) 大民主

da pipan (great criticism) 大批判

da, za, qiang (strike, smash, snatch) 打, 砸, 抢

dangnei zuidade zouzipai (the biggest capitalist-roader within the party) 党内最大的走资派

Daoxian can'an (Dao County massacre) 道县惨案

Daxing can'an (Daxing County massacre) 大兴惨案

dazibao (big-character poster) 大字报

Deng Tuo 邓拓

Deng Xiaoping 邓小平

Di'erci woshou (*Shaking Hands the Second Time*) (第二次握手)

Ding Xuelei (pen name) 丁学雷

Ding Zuxiao 丁祖晓

dingfenglun (peak theory) 顶峰论

dou, pi, gai (struggle, criticism, reform) 斗, 批, 改

dousi pixiu (fight selfishness, repudiate revisionism) 斗私批修

douzheng hui (struggle meeting) 斗争会

Dujuanshan (*Azalea Mountain*) (杜鹃山)

eryue bingbian (February Mutiny) 二月兵变

eryue niliu (February Adverse Current) 二月逆流

eryue tigang (February Outline, short for "Five-Person Cultural Revolution Small Group's Outline Report concerning the Current Academic Discussion") 二月提纲

eryue zhenfan (February Suppression of Counterrevolutionaries) 二月镇反

fan chaoliu (going against the tide) 反潮流

fan ganrao (Anti-Interference campaign) 反干扰

fandong xueshu quanwei (reactionary academic authority) 反动学术权威

fan'geming liangmian pai (counterrevolutionary two-faces) 反革命两面派

Fanji (*Counterattack*) (反击)

fanji youqing fan'an feng (Counterattack the Right-Deviationist Reversal-of-Verdicts Trend campaign) 反击右倾翻案风

feizhengchang siwang (unnatural deaths) 非正常死亡

feng, zi, xiu (feudalism, capitalism, revisionism) 封, 资, 修

fengqinglun shijian (SS *Fengqing* incident) 风庆轮事件

Fu Chongbi 傅崇碧

Fu Lei 傅雷

gao, da, quan (high, large, perfect) 高, 大, 全

geming weiyuanhui (revolutionary committee) 革命委员会

geren chongbai (personality cult) 个人崇拜

gongan liutiao (Six Regulations of Public Security, short for "Regulations on Strengthening Public Security during the Great Proletarian Cultural Revolution") 公安六条

gongdaihui (workers' representative assembly) 工代会

gongnongbing xueyuan (worker-peasant-soldier students) 工农兵学员

gongxuandui (workers propaganda team) 工宣队

gongzongsi (Workers Command Post, short for the Shanghai Workers Revolutionary Rebel Command Post) 工总司

gongzuozu (work group) 工作组

gouzaizi (son of a bitch) 狗崽子

Gu Zhun 顾准

Guan Feng 关锋

Guanyu jianguo yilai dang de ruogan lishi wenti de jueyi (*Resolution on Certain Questions in the History of Our Party since the Founding of the People's Republic of China*) (关于建国以来党的若干历史问题的决议)

Guanyu pantu, neijian, gongzei Liu Shaoqi zuixing de shencha baogao (*Investigative Report on the Crimes of the Traitor, Spy, and Renegade Liu Shaoqi*) (关于叛徒, 内奸, 工贼刘少奇罪行的审查报告)

Hai Rui baguan (*Hai Rui Dismissed from Office*) (海瑞罢官)

Haigang (*On the Dock*) (海港)

Han Aijing 韩爱晶

He Long 贺龙

heibalun (eight black theories) 黑八论

heibang (black gang) 黑帮

heicailiao (black material) 黑材料

heihua (black words) 黑话

heiqilei (seven black categories) 黑七类

heishou (black hands) 黑手

heiwulei (five black categories) 黑五类

hongbaoshu (red book of treasures) 红宝书

hongbayue (Red August) 红八月

hongdaihui (Red Guards' representative assembly) 红代会

Hongdengji (*Red Lantern*) (红灯记)

Hongdu nühuang (*Queen of the Red Capital*) (红都女皇)

honghaiyang (red sea) 红海洋

hongse kongbu (red terror) 红色恐怖

Hongse niangzijun (*Red Detachment of Women*) (红色娘子军)

hongwaiwei (Red Peripheries) 红外围

hongweibing (Red Guards) 红卫兵

hongwulei (five red categories) 红五类

hongxiaobing (Little Red Guards) 红小兵

Hu Shoujun 胡守钧

Hu Yaobang 胡耀邦

Hua Guofeng 华国锋

huaiyi yiqie (doubt all) 怀疑一切

Huang Shuai 黄帅

Huang Yongsheng 黄永胜

huaqing jiexian (make a clean break) 划清界限

huipishu he huangpishu (grey books and yellow books) 灰皮书和黄皮书

huoshao yingguo zhuhua daibanchu (British Chargé Incident) 火烧英国驻华代办处

Ji Dengkui 纪登奎

Jian Bozan 翦伯赞

Jiang Qing 江青

Jiang Tengjiao 江腾蛟

Jiefang ribao shijian (*Liberation Daily* Incident) 解放日报事件

jieji luxian (class line) 阶级路线

jieji zhengce (class policy) 阶级政策

jingji zhuyi (economism) 经济主义

jingju geming (revolution in Peking Opera) 京剧革命

Jinguang dadao (*Golden Road*) (金光大道)

jiu Liu huoxian (Collar Liu Shaoqi Battlefront) 揪刘火线

jiuda (Ninth National Congress of the Chinese Communist Party) 九大

jiujie erzhong quanhui (Second Plenum of the Ninth Central Committee of the Chinese Communist Party) 九届二中全会

jiuping (Nine Commentaries) 九评

jiuyisan shijian (September 13 [1971] Incident) 九一三事件

Juelie (*Breaking*) (决裂)

junwei bangong huiyi (Central Military Commission Administrative Conference Office) 军委办公会议

junwei banshizu (Central Military Commission Administrative Group) 军委办事组

junxuandui (army propaganda team) 军宣队

kaimen banxue (open-door schooling) 开门办学

Kang Sheng 康生

Kangpinglu shijian (Kangping Avenue Incident) 康平路事件

keyi jiaoyuhao de zinü (educable children) 可以教育好的子女

Kuai Dafu 蒯大富

lao hongweibing (Old Red Guards) 老红卫兵

Lao She 老舍

laosanpian (three old pieces) 老三篇

laowupian (five old pieces) 老五篇

Li Desheng 李德生

Li Dunbai (Sidney Rittenberg) 李敦白

Li Fuchun 李富春

Li Jiulian 李九莲

Li Qinglin 李庆霖

Li Qishun 李启顺

Li Wenbo 李文波

Li Xiannian 李先念

Li Xuefeng 李雪峰

Li Yizhe (pen name) 李一哲

Li Zaihan 李再含

Li Zuopeng 李作鹏

liandong (United Action Committee, short for the Capital Red Guard United Action Committee) 联动

Liang Xiao (pen name) 梁效

liangbao yikan (two newspapers and one journal) 两报一刊

lianhe jiandui (United Flotilla) 联合舰队

Liao Mosha 廖沫沙

Lin Biao 林彪

Lin Liguo 林立果

Lin Liheng 林立衡

Lin Zhao 林昭

Liu Bing 刘冰

Liu Geping 刘格平

Liu Jieting 刘结挺

Liu Qingtang 刘庆棠

Liu Ren 刘仁

Liu Shaoqi 刘少奇

Liu Tao 刘涛

liuchang erxiao (six factories and two universities) 六厂二校

liuliu tongling (June 6 [1967] Circular Order) 六六通令

liushiyiren pantu jituan (Sixty-One Traitors Clique) 六十一人叛徒集团

Longjiang song (*Ode to Longjiang River*) (龙江颂)

Lu Dingyi 陆定一

Lu Ping 陆平

Lun gongchandangyuan de xiuyang (*Cultivation of a Communist*) (论共产党员的修养)

Luo Ruiqing 罗瑞卿

Luo Siding (pen name) 罗思鼎

luxian douzheng (line struggle) 路线斗争

Ma Sicong 马思聪

Ma Tianshui 马天水

Mao Yuanxin 毛远新

Mao Zedong 毛泽东

Mao Zedong sixiang (Mao Zedong Thought) 毛泽东思想

Mao Zedong sixiang wenyi xiaofendui (Mao Zedong Thought performance team) 毛泽东思想文艺小分队

Mao Zedong sixiang wenyi xuanchuandui (Mao Zedong Thought performance team) 毛泽东思想文艺宣传队

Mao Zedong sixiang xuanchuandui (Mao Zedong Thought performance team) 毛泽东思想宣传队

Maozhuxi yulu (*Quotations from Chairman Mao*) (毛主席语录)

Nanjing shijian (Nanjing Incident) 南京事件

Nanjing zhiqingzhige ("Song of the Educated Youths of Nanjing") (南京知青之歌)

Nei ren dang (Inner Mongolia People's Revolutionary Party) 内人党

ni banshi, wo fangxin ("I feel at ease with you in charge") "你办事, 我放心"

Nie Rongzhen 聂荣臻

Nie Yuanzi 聂元梓

niuguisheshen (cow-demons and snake-spirits) 牛鬼蛇神

niupeng (cow shed) 牛棚

Pan Fusheng 潘复生

Paoda silingbu ("Bombarding the Headquarters") (炮打司令部)

Peng Dehuai 彭德怀

Peng Peiyun 彭佩云

Peng Zhen 彭真

Peng-Luo-Lu-Yang fandang jituan (Peng-Luo-Lu-Yang Anti-Party Clique) 彭罗陆杨反党集团

penqishi (jet plane style) 喷气式

pi Chen zhengfeng (Criticize Chen [Boda] and Conduct Rectification campaign) 批陈整风

pi Deng, fanji youqing fan'an feng (Criticize Deng [Xiaoping] and Counterattack the Right-Deviationist Reversal-of-Verdicts Trend campaign) 批邓, 反击右倾翻案风

pi Lin pi Kong (Criticize Lin [Biao] and Criticize Confucius campaign) 批林批孔

pi Lin zhengfeng (Criticize Lin [Biao] and Conduct Rectification campaign) 批林整风

pidou hui (struggle meeting) 批斗会

ping *Shuihu* (*Water Margin* Appraisal campaign) 评(水浒)

pingpang waijiao (ping-pong diplomacy) 乒乓外交

pinguanhui (poor peasants management committee) 贫管会

pinxuandui (poor peasants propaganda team) 贫宣队

pipan zichanjieji fandong luxian (Criticize the Bourgeois Reactionary Line campaign) 批判资产阶级反动路线

po sijiu (Destroy the Four Olds campaign) 破四旧

Qi Benyu 戚本禹

Qian Haoliang (Hao Liang) 钱浩梁（浩亮）

qiersi bugao (July 24 [1968] Public Notice) 七二四布告

qieryi daxue (July 21 university) 七二一大学

qingdui (Rectify Ranks, short for Rectify the Class Ranks campaign) 清队

Qinggong mishi (*Inside Story of the Qing Court*) (清宫秘史)

qinghuayuan bairi da wudou (one-hundred-day armed conflict on the Tsinghua campus) 清华园百日大武斗

qingli jieji duiwu (Rectify the Class Ranks campaign) 清理阶级队伍

Qingtongxia shijian (Qingtongxia Incident) 青铜峡事件

qiqianren dahui (Seven Thousand Cadres Conference, a common reference to the Chinese Communist Party Central Committee Work Sessions in January–February 1962) 七千人大会

qisan bugao (July 3 [1968] Public Notice) 七三布告

Qiu Huizuo 邱会作

Qixi baihutuan (*Raid on White Tiger Regiment*) (奇袭白虎团)

quanguo hongse laodongzhe zaofan zongtuan (National Red Workers Rebel Corps) 全国红色劳动者造反总团

quanjun wenhua geming xiaozu (All Forces Cultural Revolution Small Group) 全军文化革命小组

quanmian zhengdun (overall rectification) 全面整顿

Qunchou tu (*Portrait of an Ugly Bunch*) 群丑图

qunzhong zhuanzheng (mass dictatorship) 群众专政

Ren Yi 任毅

renmin jiefang jun (People's Liberation Army) 人民解放军

Rong Guotuan 容国团

ru fa douzheng (Confucianism vs. Legalism) 儒法斗争

Sanjiacun zhaji (*Notes from a Three-Family Village*) (三家村札记)

sanjiehe (three-in-one presence of cadre, military, and masses) 三结合

Sanshang Taofeng (*Three Trips to Taofeng*) (三上桃峰)

sansi (Third Command Post, also known as the Revolutionary Rebel Headquarters of Capital College Red Guards) 三司

santuchu (three prominences) 三突出

sanzhongyu siwuxian (three loyalties and four limitlessnesses) 三忠于四无限

Shajiabang (*Shajia Creek*) (沙家浜)

shanggang shangxian (elevate minor faults to the level of principle violation) 上纲上线

Shanghai renmin gongshe (Shanghai People's Commune) 上海人民公社

shangshan xiaxiang (up to the mountains and down to the countryside) 上山下乡

shehuizhuyi jiaoyu yundong (Socialist Education campaign) 社会主义教育运动

Shengda de jieri (*Grand Festival*) (盛大的节日)

shengwulian (Provincial Proletarian Alliance, short for the Committee for the Grand Alliance of the Proletarian Revolutionaries of Hunan Province) 省无联

Shi Chuanxiang 时传祥

Shi Yunfeng 史云峰

shida (Tenth National Congress of the Chinese Communist Party) 十大

shiliutiao (Sixteen Articles, short for "Resolution of the Chinese Communist Party Central Committee concerning the Great Proletarian Cultural Revolution") 十六条

shiyiyue heifeng (black wind in November) 十一月黑风

shoudu hongweibing jiuchadui (Capital Red Guard Pickets) 首都红卫兵纠察队

shuai shitou (throw rocks) 甩石头

sida (four bigs) 四大

sige weida (four greats) 四个伟大

sijie renda (Fourth National People's Congress of the People's Republic of China) 四届人大

sijiu (Four Olds) 四旧

siqing yundong (Four Cleans campaign) 四清运动

sirenbang (Gang of Four) 四人帮

sitiao hanzi (Four Fellows) 四条汉子

siwu yundong (April 5 [1976] movement) 四五运动

sixin (Four New's) 四新

Song Binbin 宋彬彬

Song Shuo 宋硕

Tan Houlan 谭厚兰

Tan Lifu 谭力夫

Tan Zhenlin 谭震林

Tao Zhu 陶铸

Tian Han 田汉

Tiananmen shichao (*Tiananmen Poems*) (天安门诗抄)

Tiananmen shijian (Tiananmen Incident) 天安门事件

tiancailun (genius theory) 天才论

tiantiandu (daily reading) 天天读

tugu naxin (get rid of the old and take in the new) 吐故纳新

wa qiangjiao (dig up cornerstones) 挖墙角

Wang Dabing 王大宾

Wang Dongxing 汪东兴

Wang Guan Qi shijian (Wang-Guan-Qi Affair) 王关戚事件

Wang Guangmei 王光美

Wang Hongwen 王洪文

Wang Li 王力

Wang Peiying 王佩英

Wang Renzhong 王任重

Wang Shenyou 王申酉

Wang Xiaoyu 王效禹

Wang Xiuzhen 王秀珍

Wei Guoqing 韦国清

wengong wuwei (verbal attack and armed defense) 文攻武卫

wenhua geming weiyuanhui (cultural revolution committee) 文化革命委员会

wenhua geming wuren xiaozu (Five-Person Cultural Revolution Small Group) 文化革命五人小组

wenyi heixian (black line in literature and arts) 文艺黑线

woniu shijian (Snail Incident) 蜗牛事件

Wu De 吴德

Wu Faxian 吴法宪

Wu Guixian 吴桂贤

Wu Han 吴晗

Wu Hao shijian (Wu Hao Affair) 伍豪事件

wuchanjieji zhuanzheng xia jixu geming (continuing revolution under the dictatorship of the proletariat) 无产阶级专政下继续革命

Wulanfu (Ulanfu) 乌兰夫

wuqi ganxiao (May 7 cadre school) 五七干校

wuqi zhishi (May 7 directive) 五七指示

wuqiyi gongcheng jiyao (*"571 Project" Summary*) "571工程"纪要

wushi zi jiandang fangzhen (fifty-word party-building principle) 五十字建党方针

wuyiliu fan'geming jituan (May 16 Counterrevolutionary Clique) 五一六反革命集团

wuyiliu tongzhi (May 16 Circular) 五一六通知

Xi Jinping 习近平

Xi Zhongxun 习仲勋

xianghua ducao (fragrant flowers and poisonous weeds) 香花毒草

xiaopachong (crawling insects) 小爬虫

xiaoyaopai (bystanders) 逍遥派

Xie Fuzhi 谢富治

Xie Jingyi 谢静宜

Xu Jingxian 徐景贤

Xu Shiyou 许世友

Xu Xiangqian 徐向前

xuetonglun (blood lineage theory) 血统论

Yan Fengying 严凤英

Yang Chengwu 杨成武

Yang Shangkun 杨尚昆

Yang Xianzhen 杨献珍

Yang Xiguang 杨曦光

Yang Yu Fu shijian (Yang-Yu-Fu affair) 杨余傅事件

yangbanxi (model dramas) 样板戏

Yanshan yehua (*Evening Chats at Yanshan*) (燕山夜话)

Yao Wenyuan 姚文元

Ye Jianying叶剑英

Ye Qun 叶群

yida sanfan (One Strike and Three Antis campaign) 一打三反

Yilin Dixi (pen name) 伊林·涤西

yingshe shixue (allusory historiography) 影射史学

Yinyangtou (yin-yang haircut) 阴阳头

yiyue fengbao (January Storm) 一月风暴

yiyue geming (January Revolution) 一月革命

youqing fan'an feng (right-deviationist reversal-of-verdicts trend) 右倾翻案风

Yu Huiyong 于会泳

Yu Lijin 余立金

Yu Luoke 遇罗克

zaijiaoyu (reeducation) 再教育

zaofan youli ("To rebel is justified") "造反有理"

zaofanpai (rebels) 造反派

zaoqingshi wanhuibao (morning request, evening report) 早请示，晚汇报

Zhang Chunqiao 张春桥

Zhang Tiesheng 张铁生

Zhang Xiting 张西挺

Zhang Yang 张扬

Zhang Yufeng 张玉凤

Zhang Zhixin 张志新

Zhao Yongfu 赵永夫

Zhao Ziyang 赵紫阳

zhengbian jing (scripture of coup d'état) 政变经

zhengzhiju huiyi (Politburo sessions) 政治局会议

zhengzhiju kuoda huiyi (enlarged sessions of the Politburo) 政治局扩大会议

Zhiqu weihushan (*Taking Tiger Mountain by Stratagem*) (智取威虎山)

zhishi qingnian (educated youth) 知识青年

zhongguo de Heluxiaofu (China's Khrushchev) 中国的赫鲁晓夫

zhongguo gongchandang (Chinese Communist Party) 中国共产党

zhonggong Shanghai shiwei xiezuozu (Chinese Communist Party Shanghai Municipal Committee Writing Group) 中共上海市委写作组

zhonggong zhongyang (Chinese Communist Party Central Committee) 中共中央

zhongsu lunzhan (China-Soviet debate) 中苏论战

zhongyang gongzuo huiyi (Chinese Communist Party Central Committee work session) 中央工作会议

zhongyang junwei (Central Military Commission) 中央军委

zhongyang wenge pengtouhui (extended Central Cultural Revolution Small Group routine meeting) 中央文革碰头会

zhongyang wenge xiaozu (Central Cultural Revolution Small Group) 中央文革小组

zhongyang zhuan'an shencha xiaozu (Central Special Case Examination Group) 中央专案审查小组

zhongyang zuzhizu xuanchuanzu (Central Organization and Propaganda Group) 中央组织组宣传组

zhongziwu (loyalty dance) 忠字舞

Zhou Enlai 周恩来

Zhou Quanying 周泉缨

Zhou Rongxin 周荣鑫

Zhou Yang 周扬

Zhu Chengzhao 朱成昭

zhua geming, cu shengchan (grasp revolution, promote production) 抓革命, 促生产

zichanjieji fandong luxian (Bourgeois Reactionary Line) 资产阶级反动路线

zilaihong (born-red) 自来红

zouzibenzhuyidaolu de dangquanpai (power-holder taking the capitalist road) 走资本主义道路的当权派

zouzipai (capitalist-roader) 走资派

zuigao zhishi (highest directive) 最高指示

Bibliography

CONTENTS

INTRODUCTION

This bibliography is a selection of English- and Chinese-language material on the Cultural Revolution published from 1966 to the present. The sources are arranged topically in 14 sections.

The first section, on general works, includes major historical documents, general analyses, and period histories, as well as such reference tools as bibliographies, dictionaries, chronicles, and yearbooks. The sources listed under the next two sections, "Mao Zedong and the Cultural Revolution" and "CCP Leaders and the Cultural Revolution," concern the role of the central leadership of the Chinese Communist Party (CCP) during the Cultural Revolution and cover a wide range of topics from Mao's conception of the Cultural Revolution to the factional conflicts and subsequent purge at the top level of the party.

By contrast, the following two sections, "Red Guards and Urban Youth Reeducation" and "Rebels, Masses, and Violence," focus on various stages of the Cultural Revolution at the grassroots level. Highlighting the phenomenon of the Red Guards and other forms of mass participation in the Cultural Revolution, titles in these sections explore the dynamics of these mass movements, and some of them attempt to explain why and how the mass movements led to a state of nationwide anarchy and violence. The section on "Heterodox Thoughts," also focusing on the grassroots movement, contains both documents and the analyses of ideas that deviate from official Maoism. These documents and studies reveal, to some extent, the painstaking efforts of China's younger generation in search of identity and a more democratic society during the years of tight ideological control.

The People's Liberation Army (PLA) played a complex role during the Cultural Revolution. The titles listed in the section on the army's participation cover topics such as the functions of the PLA in regional or local government, its control over the mass movements, its conflicts with the party's ultra-leftists, and its vital role in the power struggles of the central government. In addition, some titles here also relate the personal experiences of high-ranking army officers.

For overviews of Chinese society in many other aspects, the reader may consult publications included in the sections "Society and Social Life," "Education and Intellectuals," "Arts and Science," "Foreign Policy and Foreign Relations," and "Cultural Revolution in the Provinces." Such peculiar phenomena as the administration of workers propaganda teams, the May 7 cadre school, the eight model dramas, and the politics of a reevaluation of Confucianism and Legalism are examined by the works in these sections. So are the strategic changes in China's foreign policy exemplified by the normalization of diplomatic relations with the United States and Japan in the 1970s.

The next section, "Fiction and Memoirs," includes mostly what has become known as the "literature of the wounded" and "literature of reflection"—works that came out after 1976 portraying private lives against the broad background of the Cultural Revolution. Some of them, in the form of novels, short stories, films, poems, biographies, and autobiographies, depict simultaneously a disillusioning journey of the individual and that of the nation.

The titles under "Aftermath," the final section of the bibliography, examine the impact of the Cultural Revolution on contemporary China and on the world at large. Some of them focus on a critical assessment of the Cultural Revolution, and some explore the relationship between the Cultural Revolution and China's subsequent economic reform in the 1980s and the pro-democracy movement in 1989. One repeated theme found in many works in this section is the disillusionment of most Chinese citizens toward their government and toward the ideology of communism.

This bibliography does not include any Internet sources because the value of the existing English sites about the Cultural Revolution is quite limited, and some of them are not stable, either. However, there are a number of reliable and resourceful Chinese-language sites on the Internet; the most useful are the Virtual Museum of the Cultural Revolution at http://museums.cnd.org/cr/, which is a rich database of Cultural Revolution documents, studies, and memoirs; the Memorial for Victims of the Chinese Cultural Revolution at http://www.chinese-memorial.org/, which includes more than 600 biographies of individuals who were killed or harassed to death during the Cultural Revolution; and the Forum on Local History of the Cultural Revolution at http://www.difangwenge.org/, which focuses on materials and studies of the Cultural Revolution in the provinces.

GENERAL WORKS: REFERENCES, DOCUMENTS, AND ANALYSES

English Language

Adhikari, G. *What Do They Want to Achieve by This "Cultural Revolution."* New Delhi: D. P. Sinha, 1966.

Ahn, Byung-joon. "The Cultural Revolution and China's Search for Political Order." *China Quarterly* 58 (1974): 249–285.

———. *Ideology, Policy and Power in Chinese Politics and the Evolution of the Cultural Revolution, 1959–1965.* Dissertation. Columbia University, 1972. Ann Arbor, Mich.: University Microfilms, 1977.

An, Pyong-jun. *Chinese Politics and the Cultural Revolution: Dynamics of Policy Processes.* Seattle: University of Washington Press, 1976.

Armbruster, Frank E., John W. Lewis, David Mozingo, and Tang Tsou. *China Briefing.* Chicago: University of Chicago Press, 1968.

Asian Research Centre, ed. *The Great Cultural Revolution in China.* Hong Kong: Asia Research Centre, 1967; Rutland: Charles E. Tuttle, 1968; Melbourne: Fleshch, 1968.

———, ed. *The Great Power Struggle in China.* Hong Kong: Asian Research Centre, 1969.

Austin, Paul Britten. *China: The Revolution Continued.* Trans. Jan Myrdal and Gun Kessle. New York: Vintage, 1972.

Barnouin, Barbara, and Changgen Yu. *Ten Years of Turbulence: The Chinese Cultural Revolution.* New York: Kegan Paul International, 1993.

Baum, Richard. "Ideology Redivivus." *Problem of Communism* 16.3 (1967): 1–11.

Baum, Richard, and Louise B. Bennett, eds. *China in Ferment: Perspectives on the Cultural Revolution.* Englewood Cliffs, N.J.: Prentice Hall, 1971.

Bennett, Gordon A. "China's Continuing Revolution: Will It Be Permanent?" *Asian Survey* 10.1 (1970): 2–17.

Benton, Gregor, and Alan Hunter, eds. *Wild Lily, Prairie Fire: China's Road to Democracy, Yan'an to Tian'anmen, 1942–1989.* Princeton, N.J.: Princeton University Press, 1995.

Brugger, William. *China: Radicalism to Revisionism, 1962–1979.* London: Croom Helm, 1981.

———. "The Ninth National Congress of the Chinese Communist Party." *World Today* 25.7 (1969): 297–305.

Buchanan, John Hayward. *The Cultural Revolution in China.* Thesis. University of Mississippi, 1968.

Carry the Great Proletarian Cultural Revolution through to the End. Peking: Foreign Languages Press, 1966.

Chang, Hsin-cheng. *The Great Proletarian Cultural Revolution: A Terminological Study*. Berkeley: University of California Press, 1967.

Chang, Parris H. *Radicals and Radical Ideology in China's Cultural Revolution*. New York: Research Institute on Communist Affairs, Columbia University, 1973.

Chang, Teh-kuang. *The Cultural Revolution and the Political Modernization of Communist China: Prepared for Delivery at the 8th World Congress of the International Political Association, Munich, Federal German Republic, August 31–September 5, 1970*. N.p.: International Political Science Association, 1970.

Chang, Tony H. *China during the Cultural Revolution, 1966–1976: A Selected Bibliography of English Language Works*. Westport, Conn.: Greenwood, 1999.

Chen, Lin. *The Image of the Cultural Revolution of China*. Dissertation. University of Wisconsin, 1995.

Chen, Shaoyu (Wang Ming). *China: Cultural Revolution or Counterrevolutionary Coup?* Moscow: Novosti Press Agency Publishing House, 1969.

Chen, Theodore Hsi-en. "A Nation in Agony." *Problems of Communism* 15.6 (1966): 14–20.

Chi, Wen-shun. "The Great Proletarian Cultural Revolution in Ideological Perspective." *Asian Survey* 9 (1969): 563–579.

———. *The Great Proletarian Cultural Revolution in Ideological Perspective*. China Series Reprint. C-12. Berkeley: Center for Chinese Studies, 1974.

———, comp. and ed. *Readings in the Chinese Communist Cultural Revolution: A Manual for Students of the Chinese Language*. Berkeley: University of California Press, 1971.

China after the Cultural Revolution. Brussels: Universite libre de Bruxelles, 1972. 2 vols.

China after the Cultural Revolution: A Selection from the Bulletin of the Atomic Scientists. New York: Random House, 1970.

"China in Transition." *Political Quarterly* 45.1 (1974): 1–114.

Ching, Shui-hsien. *Rifle Rectifies Rifle in Mao's Cultural Revolution*. Taipei: Asian Peoples' Anti-Communist League, 1969.

Chiou, Chwei Liang. *Ideology and Political Power in Mao Tse-tung's Cultural Revolution, 1965–1968*. Dissertation. University of California, Riverside, 1977.

Chong, Woei Lien. *China's Great Proletarian Cultural Revolution: Master Narratives and Post-Mao Counternarratives*. Lanham, Md.: Rowman & Littlefield, 2002.

Christiansen, Wilbur Norman. *The Cultural Revolution in China*. Auckland: New Zealand–China Society, 1967.

Chu, Djang. "A Psychological Interpretation of the Chinese Cultural Revolution." *World Affairs* 130 (1967): 26–33.

Chu, Godwin C., Philip H. Cheng, and Leonard Chu. *The Roles of Tatzepao in the Cultural Revolution: A Structural-Functional Analysis.* Carbondale: Southern Illinois University, 1972.

Chu, Wenlin. "An Analysis of the Peiping Regime's Important Personnel." *Issues & Studies* 6.8 (1970): 69–80.

Chui, Chui-liang. *Maoism in Action: The Cultural Revolution.* St. Lucia: University of Queensland Press; New York: Crane, Russak, 1974.

Chung, Hua-min. *Cultural Revolution in 1969.* Hong Kong: Union Research Institute, 1970.

Circular of the Central Committee of the Chinese Communist Party, May 16, 1966: A Great Historical Document. Peking: Foreign Languages Press, 1967.

Clark, Paul. *The Chinese Cultural Revolution: A History.* New York: Cambridge University Press, 2008.

Clements, K. P. "A Symbolic Interpretation of the Great Proletarian Cultural Revolution 1965–1968." *Political Science* 24 (1972): 14–21.

Colleen, Diane Adele. *The Genesis and Development of the Great Proletarian Cultural Revolution in China from 1953 to 1968.* Thesis. Northeastern Illinois State College, 1969.

Committee of Concerned Asian Scholars. *China: Inside the People's Republic.* New York: Bantam, 1972.

Communiqué of the Enlarged 12th Plenary Session of the Eighth Central Committee of the Communist Party of China (Adopted on October 31, 1968). Peking: Foreign Languages Press, 1968.

Communiqué of the Second Plenary Session of the Ninth Central Committee of the Communist Party of China, September 6, 1970. Peking: Foreign Languages Press, 1970.

Constitution of the Communist Party of China (Adopted by the Ninth National Congress of the Communist Party of China on April 14, 1969). Peking: Foreign Languages Press, 1969.

Constitution of the People's Republic of China. Peking: Foreign Languages Press, 1975.

The Cultural Revolution in China: Its Origins and Course. Dehra Dun: EBD, 1968.

D'Avray, Anthony. *Red China through Mao's Long March to the Cultural Revolution: A Phased Historical Case Study in Problem Solving and Decision Making.* London: AEM, 1978.

Dai, Shen-Yu. "Peking's 'Cultural Revolution.'" *Current History* 51 (1966): 134–139.

Damien, G. D. "The Dialectical Structure of the Chinese Great Proletarian Cultural Revolution." *Orbis* 14 (1970): 192–217.

Daubier, Jean. *A History of the Chinese Cultural Revolution.* Trans. Richard Seaver. New York: Vintage, 1974.

Davis, Raymond M. *China's Cultural Revolution.* Albion: Albion College, 1984.

Decision of the Central Committee of the Chinese Communist Party concerning the Great Proletarian Cultural Revolution (Adopted on August 8, 1966). Peking: Foreign Languages Press, 1966.

Deliusin, Lev Petrovich. *The "Cultural Revolution" in China.* Moscow: Novosti Press Agency Publishing House, 1967.

Deshingkar, Giri D. "Causes of the Cultural Revolution." *China Report* 3.1 (1966): 9–12.

Deutscher, Isaac. *The Cultural Revolution in China.* London: Bertrand Russell Peace Foundation, 1967.

Dittmer, Lowell. *China's Continuous Revolution: The Post-Liberation Epoch, 1949–1981.* Berkeley: University of California Press, 1987.

———. "Chinese Communist Revisionism in Comparative Perspective." *Studies in Comparative Communism* 13.1 (1980): 3–40.

———. "'Line Struggle' in Theory and Practice: The Origins of the Cultural Revolution Reconsidered." *China Quarterly* 72 (1977): 675–712.

Documents of the First Session of the Fourth National People's Congress of the People's Republic of China. Peking: Foreign Languages Press, 1975.

Documents of the Ninth National Congress of the Communist Party of China. Hong Kong: Hsinghua News Agency, 1969.

Documents of the Tenth National Congress of the Communist Party of China. Hong Kong: Foreign Languages Press, 1973.

Domes, Jurgen. "Some Results of the Cultural Revolution in China." *Asian Survey* 11 (1971): 932–940.

———. *Cultural Revolution in China: Documents and Analysis.* Courrier de l'Extreme-Orient 6. Brussels: Centre d'étude, du sud-est asiatique et de l'Extreme-Orient, 1974.

Dorrill, William F. *Power, Policy and Ideology in the Making of China's "Cultural Revolution."* Santa Monica, Calif.: RAND Corp., 1968.

———, et al. *China in the Wake of the Cultural Revolution.* McLean, Md.: Research Analysis Corporation, 1969.

Doyle, Jean Louise. *Conflict Management in the Chinese Cultural Revolution: A Case Study in Political Change.* Dissertation. Boston University, 1973. Ann Arbor, Mich.: University Microfilms, 1973.

Dutt, Gargi, and Vidya P. Dutt. *China's Cultural Revolution.* New York: Asian Publishing House, 1970.

Esmein, Jean. *The Chinese Cultural Revolution.* New York: Anchor Books, 1973; London: Deutsch, 1975.

Esherick, Joseph, and Paul Pickowicz. *The Chinese Cultural Revolution as History.* Stanford, Calif.: Stanford University Press, 2006.

Fairbank, John King. *Mao and the Cultural Revolution: China Scholar John King Fairbank Examines Mao's Cultural Revolution.* Audio cassette. Center for Cassette Studies, 1972. 1 cassette.

Fan, Kuang Huan. *The Chinese Cultural Revolution: Selected Documents.* New York: Grove Press, 1968.

Feng, Hai. "The Cultural Revolution and the Reconstruction of the Chinese Communist Party." *Asia Quarterly* 4 (1972): 303–320.

Friedman, Edward. "Cultural Limits of the Cultural Revolution." *Asian Survey* 9.3 (1969): 188–201.

Frolic, B. Michael. "What the Cultural Revolution Was All About." *New York Times Magazine,* 24 October 1971.

Fu, Zhengyuan. *Autocratic Tradition and Chinese Politics.* Cambridge: Cambridge University Press, 1993.

Gamberg, Ruth. *Marxism and the Cultural Revolution in China: A New Kind of Revolution.* New York: Far East Reporter, 1975.

Garver, John W. *The Great Proletarian Cultural Revolution: Two Roads to Different Colors.* Thesis. Boulder: University of Colorado, 1973.

Germain, Ernest. "The Cultural Revolution: An Attempt at Interpretation." *International Socialist Review* 29 (1968): 38–64.

Gittings, John. "The Prospects of the Cultural Revolution in 1969." *Bulletin of the Atomic Scientists* 25 (1969): 23–28.

———. "What Was It All About." *Far Eastern Economic Review,* 20 October 1969, 36–37.

Goehlert, Robert, ed. *The Chinese Cultural Revolution: A Selected Bibliography.* Monticello: Vance Bibliographies, 1988.

Goldman, Merle D. "In the Wake of the Cultural Revolution." *Current History* 65 (1973): 129–131, 136.

Gray, Jack, and Patrick Cavendish. *Chinese Communism in Crisis: Maoism and the Cultural Revolution.* New York: Praeger, 1968.

Great Proletarian Cultural Revolution in China. Peking: Foreign Language Press, 1966–1969. 10 vols.

Gunawardhana, Theja. *China's Cultural Revolution.* Colombo: Colombo Apothecaries' Company, 1967.

Gupte, R. S. "Mao's Great Proletarian Cultural Revolution." *International Review of History and Political Science* 6 (1969): 80–90.

Hah, Chong-do. "The Dynamics of the Chinese Cultural Revolution: An Interpretation Based on an Analytical Framework of Political Coalition." *World Politics* 24 (1972): 182–220.

Harding, Harry, Jr. "China: Toward Revolutionary Pragmatism." *Asian Survey* 11.1 (1971): 51–67.

He, Henry Yuhuai. *Dictionary of the Political Thought of the People's Republic of China.* Armonk, N.Y.: Sharpe, 2000.

Heaslet, Juliana Pennington. *The Cultural Revolution, 1966–1969: The Failure of Mao's Revolution in China*. Dissertation. University of Colorado, 1971.

Hinton, Harold C., ed. *The People's Republic of China, 1949–1979: A Documentary Survey*. Wilmington: Scholarly Resources, 1980. 5 vols.

Hinton, William H. *The Cultural Revolution in China*. Rec. 3 December 1970. Audiocassette. Pacific Tape Library, 1970. 1 cassette.

———. *"Fanshen" Re-examined in the Light of the Cultural Revolution*. Boston: New England Free Press, 1969.

———. *Turning Point in China: An Essay on Cultural Revolution*. New York: Monthly Review, 1972.

Ho, Ping-ti, and Tang Tsou, eds. *China's Heritage and the Communist Political System*. Vol. 1 of *China in Crisis*. Chicago: University of Chicago Press, 1968.

Hoagland, Amanda Blanchard. *The Cultural Revolution in China*. Thesis. Bowdoin College, 1977.

Hook, Brian. "China's Cultural Revolution: The Preconditions in Historical Perspective." *World Today*, November 1967, 454–464.

———. "The Post-Plenum Development of China's Proletarian Cultural Revolution." *World Today*, November 1966, 467–475.

Hsia, Adrian. *The Chinese Cultural Revolution*. Trans. Gerald Onn. New York: McGraw-Hill; Seabury Press, 1972.

Hsiao, Gnen T. "The Background and Development for the Proletarian Cultural Revolution." *Asian Survey* 7.6 (1967): 383–404.

Hsieh, Chen-Ping. "Another Great Proletarian Cultural Revolution." *Asian Affairs* 1 (1974): 390–401.

Hsiung, James Chieh. *Ideology and Practice: The Evolution of Chinese Communism*. New York: Praeger, 1970.

Hsiung, Yin Tso. *Red China's Cultural Revolution*. New York: Vantage Press, 1968.

Huberman, Leo, and Paul Sweezy. "The Cultural Revolution in China." *Monthly Review* 18.8 (1967): 1–17.

———. *The Cultural Revolution in China: A Socialist Analysis*. Boston: New England Free Press, 1967.

Hunter, Iris. *They Made Revolution within the Revolution: The Story of Great Proletarian Cultural Revolution*. Chicago: RCP Publications, 1986.

Hwang, Tien-chien. *Analysis of the "Cultural Revolution" of CCP in 1966*. Taipei: Asian Peoples' Anti-Communist League, Republic of China, 1966. 2 vols.

———. *1967, a Year of Precariousness for Chinese Communists*. Taipei: Asian Peoples' Anti-Communist League, Republic of China, 1968.

Important Documents on the Great Proletarian Cultural Revolution in China. Peking: Foreign Languages Press, 1970.

Joffe, Ellis. "China in Mid-1966: 'Cultural Revolution' or Struggle for Power?" *China Quarterly* 26 (1966): 123–131.

Johnson, Chalmers A. "China: The Cultural Revolution in Structural Perspective." *Asian Survey* 8 (1968): 1–15.

———. *China: The Cultural Revolution in Structural Perspectives.* Berkeley: Center for Chinese Studies, 1974.

———. "The Two Chinese Revolutions." *China Quarterly* 39 (1969): 12–29.

———, ed. *Ideology and Politics in Contemporary China.* Seattle: University of Washington Press, 1973.

Jordan, James D. "Political Orientation of the PLA." *Current Scene* 11.1 (1973): 1–14.

Joseph, William A. *The Critique of Ultra-Leftism in China, 1958–1981.* Stanford, Calif.: Stanford University Press, 1984.

Joseph William A., Christine P. W. Wong, and David Zweig, eds. *New Perspectives on the Cultural Revolution.* Cambridge, Mass.: Council on East Asian Studies, Harvard University, 1991.

Karol, K. S. *The Second Chinese Revolution.* Trans. Mervyn Jones. New York: Hill and Wang, 1974.

———. "Why the Cultural Revolution?" *Monthly Review* 19 (1967): 22–34.

Kay, Gary Winn. *An Analysis of China's Great Proletarian Cultural Revolution.* Thesis. University of Georgia, 1969.

Kirby, E. Stuart. "The Framework of the Crisis in Communist China." *Current Scene* 6.2 (1968): 1–10.

Kraljic, John R. *An Evaluation of the Cultural Revolution in China.* Thesis. Texas A&M University, 1974.

Kwan, Yum K. *Estimating Economic Effects of the Great Leap Forward and the Cultural Revolution in China.* Tilburg, Netherlands: Center for Economic Research, Tilburg University, 1995.

Lau, Chi-Shing. *The Great Proletarian Cultural Revolution: China 1965–1976.* Las Vegas, N.Mex.: New Mexico Highlands University, 1980.

Lau, Yee-fui, Hong Wan-yee, and Yeung Saicheung, eds. *Glossary of Chinese Political Phrases.* Hong Kong: Union Research Institute, 1977.

Lee, Hong Yung. *The Politics of the Chinese Cultural Revolution: A Case Study.* Berkeley: University of California Press, 1978.

Lee, Tsong-Tyan. *The Republic of China and "Cultural Revolution": A Study in the Politics of Culture.* Thesis. University of San Francisco, 1983.

Leung, Edwin Pak-wah, ed. *Historical Dictionary of Revolutionary China, 1839–1976.* Westport, Conn.: Greenwood, 1992.

Levenson, Joseph Richmond. "Communist China in Time and Space: Roots and Rootlessness." *China Quarterly* 39 (1969): 1–11.

———. *Revolution and Cosmopolitanism: The Western Stage and the Chinese Stages*. Berkeley: University of California Press, 1971.

Li, Kwok-sing. *A Glossary of Political Terms of the People's Republic of China*. Trans. Mary Lok. Hong Kong: Chinese University Press, 1995.

Liao, Gailong. "Historical Experiences and Our Road of Development." Trans. Oi-va Kwan. *Issues & Studies* 17.10 (1981): 65–94; 17.11 (1981): 81–110; 17.12 (1981): 79–104.

Liao, Kuang-sheng. *Internal Mobilization and External Hostility in Communist China, 1949–1962 and 1967–1969*. Dissertation. University of Michigan, 1974.

———. "Linkage Politics in China: Internal Mobilization and Articulated External Hostility in the Cultural Revolution 1967–1969." *World Politics* 28 (1976): 590–610.

Lieberthal, Kenneth, with James Tong and Sai-cheung Yeung. *Central Documents and Politburo Politics in China*. Ann Arbor: Center for Chinese Studies, University of Michigan, 1978.

Lindbeck, John M. H., ed. *China: Management of a Revolutionary Society*. Seattle: University of Washington, 1971.

Liu, Guokai. *A Brief Analysis of the Cultural Revolution*. Ed. Anita Chan. Armonk, N.Y.: Sharpe, 1987.

Liu, Judith. *Life out of Balance: The Chinese Cultural Revolution and Modernization*. Dissertation. University of California, San Diego, 1985.

London, I. D., and T. L. Lee. "Socio/Psycholinguistics of the Cultural Revolution: An Empirical Study." *Psychological Reports* 40 (1977): 343–356.

Lowy, George, ed. *Documents on Contemporary China, 1949–1975: A Selected Research Collection in Microfiche*. Greenwich, Conn.: JAI Press, 1976. 2 vols.

MacFarquhar, Emily. "China: Mao's Last Leap." *Economist Brief Booklets* (London) 6 (1968): 1–24.

MacFarquhar, Roderick. *The Coming of the Cataclysm, 1961–1966*. Vol. 3 of *The Origins of the Cultural Revolution*. New York: Columbia University Press, 1997.

———. *Contradictions among the People 1956–1957*. Vol. 1 of *The Origins of the Cultural Revolution*. New York: Columbia University Press, 1974.

———. *The Great Leap Forward, 1958–1960*. Vol. 2 of *The Origins of the Cultural Revolution*. New York: Columbia University Press, 1983.

MacFarquhar, Roderick, and John King Fairbank, eds. *Revolutions within the Chinese Revolution, 1966–1982*. Part 2 of *The People's Republic*. New York: Cambridge University Press, 1991.

MacFarquhar, Roderick, and Michael Schoenhals. *Mao's Last Revolution*. Cambridge, Mass.: Harvard University Press, 2006.

Mackerras, Colin, and Neale Hunter. *China Observed: 1964–1967*. London: Pall Mall, 1968.

Malone, Rupert A. *The Great Proletarian Cultural Revolution, 1966–1968.* Thesis. Northeastern Illinois University, 1975.

Man, Chang. *The Great Proletarian Cultural Revolution in 1968.* Hong Kong: Union Research Institute, 1969.

Marchant, Leslie Ronald. *The Turbulent Giant: Communist Theory and Practice in China.* Sydney, N.S.W.: Australia and New Zealand Book Co., 1975.

Matsushita, Teruo. "The Great Cultural Revolution and Principle of Law of the Proletarian Dictatorship." *Monthly Review* (New York), December 1967, 1–48.

Michael, Franz. "China after the Cultural Revolution: The Unresolved Succession Crisis." *Orbis* 17.2 (1973): 315–333.

Milton, Chris. *Cultural Revolution in China.* Chicago: Students for a Democratic Society, 1969.

Milton, David, et al. *People's China: Social Experimentation, Politics Entry into the World Scene 1966 through 1972.* New York: Random House, 1974.

Mittler, Barbara. *A Continuous Revolution: Making Sense of Cultural Revolution Culture.* Cambridge, Mass.: Harvard University Asia Center, 2012.

Moses, John Shuster. *An Analysis of the Great Proletarian Cultural Revolution.* Thesis. College of William and Mary, 1970.

Myers, James T., Jurgen Domes, and Erik von Groeling, eds. *Chinese Politics: Documents and Analysis.* Columbia: University of South Carolina Press, 1986–1995. 4 vols.

National Committee on United States–China Relations. *China after the Cultural Revolution.* Conversations from Wingspread. R-46. Audiocassette. Johnson Foundation, 1973. 1 cassette.

Nee, Victor, and James Peck, eds. *Essays on the Chinese Cultural Revolution.* New York: Pantheon Books, 1974.

Noumoff, S. J. "China's Cultural Revolution as a Rectification Movement." *Pacific Affairs* 40.3–4 (1967–1968): 221–234.

Oksenberg, Michel, et al. "China: Forcing the Revolution to a New Stage." *Asian Survey* 7.1 (1967): 1–15.

———. "Communist China: A Quiet Crisis in Revolution." *Asian Survey* 6.1 (1966): 1–12.

———. *The Cultural Revolution: 1967 in Review.* Ann Arbor, Mich.: Center for Chinese Studies, University of Michigan, 1968.

———. "The Institutionalization of the Chinese Communist Revolution: The Ladder of Success on the Eve of the Cultural Revolution." *China Quarterly* 36 (1968): 61–92.

———. "Political Changes and Their Causes in China, 1949 to 1972." *Political Quarterly* 45.1 (1974): 95–114.

Party History Research Centre. *History of the Chinese Communist Party: A Chronology of Events, 1919–1990.* Beijing: Foreign Languages Press, 1991.

Peng, Shu-tse. *Behind China's Great Cultural Revolution.* New York: Merit Publishers, 1967.

Pfeffer, Richard M. "Serving the People and Continuing the Revolution." *China Quarterly* 52 (1972): 620–653.

Pietrusza, David. *The Chinese Cultural Revolution.* San Diego, Calif.: Lucent Books, 1997.

Possony, Stefan Thomas. *The Revolution of Madness.* Taipei: Institute of International Relations, 1971.

"Reconstruction of the Communist Party." *China News Analysis* 6 (1970): 1–7.

Red Guard Newspapers. Japanese. Selections. Tokyo: Rikuetsu, 1980.

Red Guard Publication. Washington, D.C.: Center for Chinese Research Materials, Association of Research Libraries, 1975–1979. 20 vols. (vol. 6).

Red Guard Publication. Supplement 1. Washington, D.C.: Center for Chinese Research Materials, Association of Research Libraries, 1978. 8 vols. (vol. 4).

Red Guard Publication. Supplement 2. Washington, D.C.: Center for Chinese Research Materials, Association of Research Libraries, 1978. 8 vols.

Resolution on CPC History (1949–1981). Beijing: Foreign Languages Press, 1981.

Robertson, Frank. "China since the Cultural Revolution." *World Survey* 44 (1972): 1–16.

Robinson, Joan. "The Cultural Revolution in China." *International Affairs* (London) 44.2 (1968): 214–227.

———. *The Cultural Revolution in China.* Baltimore, Md.: Penguin, 1969.

Robinson, Thomas W., ed. *The Cultural Revolution in China.* Berkeley: University of California Press, 1971.

Russell, Maud. *The Ongoing Cultural Revolution in China.* New York: Far Eastern Reporter, 1968.

———. *Some Background on China's Great Proletarian Cultural Revolution.* Far East Reporter. New York: Maud Russell Publisher, n.d.

Schoenhals, Michael. *CCP Central Documents from the Cultural Revolution: Index to an Incomplete Data Base.* Stockholm: Center for Pacific Asia Studies at Stockholm University, 1993.

———, ed. *China's Cultural Revolution, 1966–1969: Not a Dinner Party.* Armonk, N.Y.: Sharpe, 1996.

Schwarz, Henry G. "The Great Proletarian Cultural Revolution." *Orbis* 10 (1966): 803–822.

Selden, Mark, with Patti Eggleston, eds. *People's Republic of China: A Documentary History of Revolutionary Changes.* New York: Monthly Review Press, 1979.

Seybolt, Peter J., ed. *Through Chinese Eyes.* New York: Praeger, 1974. 2 vols.

Snow, Edgar. *The Long Revolution.* New York: Vintage, 1973.

Song, Yongyi, et al., eds. *The Chinese Cultural Revolution Database (CD-ROM & Index).* Hong Kong: Universities Service Center for China Studies, Chinese University of Hong Kong, 2002.

Song, Yongyi, and Sun Dajin, comps. *The Cultural Revolution: A Bibliography, 1966–1996.* Cambridge, Mass.: Harvard-Yenching Library, Harvard University, 1998.

Sorich, Richard, ed. *Cultural Revolution: Red Guard Translations: Bibliography, Index.* Vol. 1 of *Document on Contemporary China, 1949–1975: A Selected Research Collection in Microfiche.* Greenwich, Conn.: JAI Press, 1976.

Starr, John Bryan. *Ideology and Culture: An Introduction to the Dialectic of Contemporary Chinese Politics.* New York: Harper and Row, 1973.

Sullivan, Lawrence R. *Historical Dictionary of the People's Republic of China, 1949–1997.* Lanham, Md.: Scarecrow Press, 1997.

Teiwes, Frederick C. "Before and After the Cultural Revolution." *China Quarterly* 58 (1974): 332–348.

Teng, Chen. *Historical Materialism and China's Great Cultural Revolution.* New York: Vantage Press, 2003.

Tenth National Congress of the Communist Party of China: Documents. Peking: Foreign Thurston, Anne F., and Alan Bickley. *China's Cultural Revolution.* Conversations from Wingspread. R-1285. Audiocassette. Johnson Foundation, 1987. 1 cassette.

Tong, Te-kong. *The Uncultured Cultural Revolution in China: A Background Survey.* New York: Columbia University, 1966.

Trager, Frank N., and William Henderson, eds. *Communist China, 1949–1969: A Twenty-Year Appraisal.* New York: New York University Press, 1970.

Tsao, James Jhy-yuan. *Chinese Communist Cultural Revolution: An Analytical Reappraisal from the Historical Point of View.* Dissertation. American University, 1974. Ann Arbor, Mich.: University Microfilms, 1974.

Tsou, Tang. "The Cultural Revolution, Then and Now." *New York Times*, 1 September 1974.

Union Research Institute, ed. *CCP Documents of the Great Proletarian Cultural Revolution.* Hong Kong: Union Research Institute, 1969.

———, ed. *Documents of Chinese Communist Party Central Committee, Sept. 1956–Apr. 1969.* Hong Kong: Union Research Institute, 1971. 2 vols.

Van Voorhis, Richard, ed. *China and the Great Cultural Revolution*. Tokyo: World Student Christian Federation, 1969.

Varma, S. P. "China's Cultural Revolution." *Political Science Review* 6 (1967): 58–78.

Vermont Academy of Arts and Sciences. Delegation to the People's Republic of China. *Considering the Cultural Revolution*. Montpelier, Vt.: The Academy, 1977.

Walder, Andrew George, and Xiaoxia Gong, eds. and trans. *China's Great Terror: New Documentation on the Cultural Revolution*. Armonk, N.Y.: Sharpe, 1993.

Wang, Hsueh-wen. "The Nature and Development of the Great Cultural Revolution." *Issues & Studies* 4 (1968): 11–21.

Wang, James C. F. *The Cultural Revolution in China: An Annotated Bibliography*. New York: Garland, 1976.

Wang, Li. *An Insider's Account of the Cultural Revolution: Wang Li's Memoirs*. Trans. Michael Schoenhals. Armonk, N.Y.: Sharpe, 1994.

Wang, Li, Yi-Hsueh Chia, and Li Hsin. *The Dictatorship of the Proletariat and the Great Proletarian Cultural Revolution*. Peking: Foreign Languages Press, 1967.

Weakland, John H. *Cultural Aspects of China's "Cultural Revolution."* Palo Alto, Calif.: Mental Research Institute, 1969.

Wheelwright, Edward Lawrence. *Cultural Revolution in China*. San Francisco: Bay Area Radical Education Project, 1967.

Wich, Richard. "The Tenth Party Congress: The Power Structure and the Succession Question." *China Quarterly* 58 (1974): 231–248.

Wylie, Ray. "Revolution within a Revolution?" *China after the Cultural Revolution*. A Selection from *Bulletin of the Atomic Scientists*, 29–32. New York: Vintage, 1970.

Yan, Jiaqi, and Gao Gao. *The Ten-Year History of the Chinese Cultural Revolution*. Taipei: Institute of Current China Studies, 1988.

———. *Turbulent Decade: A History of the Cultural Revolution*. Trans. D. W. Y. Kwok. Honolulu: University of Hawaii Press, 1996.

Yeh, Hsiang-chih. *The Cause and Effect of the "Cultural Revolution."* Taipei: World Anti-Communist League, China Chapter, 1970.

Yu, Hen Mao. *Fishy Winds and Bloody Rains*. Taipei: World Anti-Communist League, 1970.

Zanegin, B., et al. *China and Its Cultural Revolution: A Soviet Analysis*. Washington, D.C.: Joint Publications Research Service, 1969.

Zhelokhovtsev, Aleksei Nikolaevich. *The "Cultural Revolution": A Close-up: An Eyewitness Account*. Moscow: Progress Publishers, 1975.

Zhong, Xinyuan. *"Red, the Color of the People": A Choreographic Piece of the Chinese Cultural Revolution*. Thesis. University of California, Los Angeles, 1993.

Zhou, Yuan, ed. *The New Collection of the Red Guard Publications: Part I, Newspapers*. Oakton, Md.: Center for Chinese Research Materials (in English and Chinese), 1999. 20 vols.

Zuo Jiping. "Political Religion: The Case of the Cultural Revolution in China." *Sociological Analysis* 52.1 (1991): 99–110.

Chinese Language

Chao, Feng, ed. 巢峰编. *"Wen hua da ge ming" ci dian* "文化大革命"词典. Hong Kong: 港龙出版社, 1993.

Chen, Donglin 陈东林; and Du, Pu, eds. 杜蒲编. *Nei luan yu kang zheng: wen hua da ge ming de shi nian* 内乱与抗争: 文化大革命的十年. Changchun: 吉林人民出版社, 1994. 2 vols.

Fairbank, John King, ed. 费正清 编. *Jian qiao Zhong hua ren min gong he guo shi: Zhongguo ge ming nei bu de ge ming 1966–1982* 剑桥中华人民共和国史: 中国革命内部的革命 1966–1982. Beijing: 中国社科院出版社, 1994.

Gao, Gao 高皋; and Yan, Jiaqi 严家其. *"Wen hua da ge ming" shi nian shi 1966–1976* "文化大革命"十年史 1966–1976. Tianjin: 天津人民出版社, 1986.

Hao, Jian, ed. 郝建 编. *Wen ge si shi nian ji: 2006 Beijing Wen hua da ge ming yan tao hui quan ji lu*文革四十年祭: 2006 北京文化大革命研讨会全记录. Fort Worth, Tex.: 溪流出版社, 2006.

Hei, Yannan 黑雁南. *Shi nian dong luan* 十年动乱. Hong Kong: 星辰出版社, 1988.

Hong wei bin zi liao (Red Guard Publications) 红卫兵资料. Washington, D.C.: Center for Chinese Research Materials 中国研究资料中心, 1975–1979. 20 vols.

Hong wei bin zi liao: xu bian 1 (Red Guard Publications Supplement 1) 红卫兵资料: 续编 (一). Washington, D.C.: Center for Chinese Research Materials 中国研究资料中心, 1980. 8 vols.

Hong wei bin zi liao: xu bian 2 (Red Guard Publications Supplement 2) 红卫兵资料: 续编 (二). Oakton, Va.: Center for Chinese Research Materials 中国研究资料中心, 1980. 8 vols.

Ji, Xichen 纪希晨. *Shi wu qian li de nian dai: yi wei Ren min ri bao lao ji zhe de bi ji* 史无前例的年代: 一位人民日报老记者的笔记. Beijing: 人民日报出版社, 2006.

Jin, Chunming 金春明. *Wen hua da ge ming shi gao* 文化大革命史稿. Chengdu: 四川人民出版 社, 1995.

Liu, Guokai 劉國凱. *Ren min wen ge lun* 人民文革論. Hong Kong: 博大出版社, 2006.

———. *Wen hua ge ming jian xi* 文化革命簡析. Hong Kong: 博大出版社, 2006.

Liu, Qingfeng, ed. 刘青峰 编. *Wen hua da ge ming: shi shi yu yan jiu* 文化大革命: 史实与研究. Hong Kong: 香港中文大学出版社, 1996.

Liu, Xiao 劉曉. *Yi shi xing tai yu wen hua da ge ming* 意識形態與文化大革命. Taipei: 洪葉文化事業有限公司, 2000.

MacFarquhar, Roderick 麦克法夸尔, and Michael Schoenhals 沈迈克. *Mao Zedong zui hou de ge ming* 毛泽东最后的革命. Hong Kong: 星克尔出版公司, 2009.

Song, Rushan 宋如山. *Zhongguo wen hua da ge ming shi dian: (1966–1976 nian)* 中國文化大革命事典: (1966–1976年). Hong Kong: 星輝圖書有限公司, 2009.

Song, Yongyi, ed. 宋永毅 编. *A New Collection of Red Guard Publications.* Part 2, *A Special Compilation of Newspapers in Beijing Area* 新编红卫兵资料 II. Oakton, Va.: Center for Chinese Research Materials, 2001. 36 vols.

———, ed. *A New Collection of Red Guard Publications.* Part 3, *A Comprehensive Compilation of Tabloids in the Provinces* 新编红卫兵资料 III. Oakton, Va.: Center for Chinese Research Materials, 2005. 52 vols.

———, ed. *Wen hua da ge ming: li shi zhen xiang he ji ti ji yi* 文化大革命: 歷史真相和集體記憶. Hong Kong: 田園書屋, 2007. 2 vols.

Song, Yongyi, et al., eds. 宋永毅 等编. *Zhongguo wen hua da ge ming wen ku* 中国文化大革命文库 (网络数据库). Hong Kong: 香港中文大学中国研究服務中心, 2002–2013.

Tan, Fang 谭放; and Zhao, Wumian 赵无眠. *Wen ge da zi bao jing xuan* 文革大字报精选. Vancouver: 明镜出版社, 1996.

Tan, Tianrong 谭天荣. "Xin Zhongguo yu 'wen hua da ge ming'" 新中国与"文化大革命." 当代中国研究 (2006.1): 26–42.

Tang, Shaojie 唐少杰. "'Wen hua de ge ming' zai Zhongguo xian dais hi zhong de di wei" "文化大革命"在中国现代史中的地位. 当代中国研究 (2005.4): 73–76.

Wang, Nianyi 王年一. *Da dong luan de nian dai* 大动乱的年代. Zhengzhou: 河南人民出版社, 1988.

———. "Wen ge man tan" 文革漫谈. 二十一世纪 (2006.10): 36–54.

"Wen hua da ge ming" yan jiu zi liao "文化大革命" 研究资料. Beijing: 中国人民解放军国 防大学党史党建政工教研室, 1988. 3 vols.

Xi, Xuan 席宣; and Jin, Chunming 金春明. *"Wen hua da ge ming" jian shi* "文化大革命" 简史. Beijing: 中共党史出版社, 1996.

Xing, Xiaoqun 邢小群. "Kou shu shi yu 'wen ge' yan jiu" 口述史与"文革"研究. 当代中国研究 (2006.2): 82–93.

Yan, Changgui 阎长贵; and Wang, Guangyu 王广宇. *Wen shi qiu xin ji* 问史求信集. Beijing: Yang, Jianli, et al. 楊建利 等. *Hong se ge ming yu hei se zao fan: "wen ge" san shi zhou nian ji nian yan jiu wen ji* 红色革命與黑色造反: "文革" 三十周年纪念研究文集. Pleasant Hill, Calif.: 二十一世紀中國基金會, 1997.

Yang, Kelin 楊克林. *Wen hua da ge ming bo wu guan* 文化大革命博物館. Hong Kong: 天地圖書有限公司: 新大陸出版社有限公司, 2002. 2 vols.

Zhang, Hua, et al. 张化 等. *Hui shou "wen ge"* 回首 "文革." Beijing: 中共党史出版社, 2000. 2 vols.

Zhao, Wumian 赵无眠. *Wen ge da nian biao* 文革大年表. Vancouver: 明镜出版社, 1996.

Zhou, Liangxiao 周良霄; and Gu, Juying 顾菊英, eds. *Shi nian wen ge qian qi (1965.11–1969.4) xi nian lu Shi nian wen ge zhong shou chang jiang hua zhuan xin lu* 十年文革前期 (1965.11–1969.4) 系年录 十年文革中首长讲话传信录. Hong Kong: 新大陆出版社有限公司, 2008.

Zhou, Yuan, ed. 周原 编. *A New Collection of Red Guard Publications.* Part 1, *Newspapers* 新编红卫兵资料. Oakton, Va.: Center for Chinese Research Materials, 1999. 20 vols.

MAO ZEDONG AND THE CULTURAL REVOLUTION

English Language

An, Tai Sung. *Mao Tse-tung's Cultural Revolution.* Indianapolis, Ind.: Pegasus, 1972.

An, Thomas S. *Mao and the Cultural Revolution.* Merrut, India: Sadhna Prakashan, 1971.

Bachman, David. "Li Zhisui, Mao Zedong, and Chinese Elite Politics." *China Journal* 35 (1996): 113–120.

Benewick, Robert, and Stephanie Donald. "The Personality Cult of Mao Zedong." *China Review* 2 (1995): 33–34.

Bridgham, Philip. "Mao's 'Cultural Revolution': Origin and Development." *China Quarterly* 29 (1967): 1–35.

———. "Mao's Cultural Revolution in 1967: The Struggle to Seize Power." *China Quarterly* 34 (1968): 6–36.

———. "Mao's Cultural Revolution: The Struggle to Consolidate Power." *China Quarterly* 41 (1970): 1–34.

Chang, Jung, and Jon Halliday. *Mao: The Unknown Story.* New York: Knopf, 2005.

Chang, Parris H. "Mao's Great Purge: A Political Balance Sheet." *Problems of Communism* 18.2 (1969): 1–10.

———. "Mao Tse-tung and His Generals." *Military Review* 53.9 (1973): 19–27.

Cheek, Timothy. *Mao Zedong and China's Revolutions: A Brief History with Documents*. New York: Palgrave Macmillan, 2002.

Cheng, Yinghong. "Ideology and Cosmology: Maoist Discussion on Physics and the Cultural Revolution." *Modern Asian Studies* (February 2006): 109–149.

Chiou, Chwei Liang. *Maoism in Action: The Cultural Revolution*. New York: Crane, Russak & Co., 1974.

Chong, Woei Lien, and Tak-wing Ngo. *Perspectives on Mao and the Cultural Revolution: Special Theme Issue on the 30th Anniversary of China's "Great Proletarian Cultural Revolution."* Leiden: Leiden University, 1996.

Delaurier, F. Gregory. *Mao Zedong and the Paradox of Power*. Dissertation. Cornell University, 1990.

Dittmer, Lowell. "Mao Zedong: Ten Years After." *Australian Journal of Chinese Affairs* 16 (1986): 113–118.

Dunayevskaya, Raya. *Mao's China and the "Proletarian Cultural Revolution."* Detroit, Mich.: News & Letters, 1968.

Elegant, Robert S. *Mao's Great Revolution*. New York: World Publishing Co., 1971.

Fan, K. H., ed. *Mao Tse-tung and Lin Piao: Post Revolutionary Writings*. New York: Anchor Books, 1972.

Fitzgerald, C. P. "Mao and the Chinese Cultural Tradition." *Politico* 42.3 (1977): 483–493.

Garcia, Jaime Humberto. *Mao Tse-tung and the Great Proletarian Cultural Revolution*. Thesis. Northern Arizona University, 1981.

Gelman, Harry. "Mao and the Permanent Purge." *Problems of Communism* 9.6 (1966): 2–14.

Gordner, John. *Chinese Politics and Succession to Mao*. New York: Holmes and Meier Publishers, 1984.

Gray, Jack. *Chinese Communism in Crisis: Maoism and the Cultural Revolution*. London: Pall Mall, 1968.

———. "Mao's Economic Thoughts." *Far Eastern Economic Review*, 15 January 1970, 16–18.

Halpern, Nina. "Mao Zedong Thought and the Cultural Revolution." *Spring-Autumn Papers* (Ann Arbor) (1984): 37–46.

Han, Suyin. *Wind in the Tower: Mao Tse-tung and the Chinese Revolution, 1949–1975*. London: Cape, 1976.

Harding, Harry. *Maoist Theories of Policy-making and Organization: Lessons from the Cultural Revolution in China.* Santa Monica, Calif.: RAND Corp., 1969.

———. *Modernization and Mao: The Logic of the Cultural Revolution and the 1970s.* Santa Monica, Calif.: RAND Corp., 1970.

Hollingworth, Clare. *Mao and the Men against Him.* London: Jonathan Cape Ltd., 1985.

Hsueh, Chun-Tu. "The Cultural Revolution and Leadership Crisis in Communist China." *Political Science Quarterly* 82 (1967): 169–190.

Ito, Kikazo, and Minoru Shibata. "The Dilemma of Mao Tse-tung." *China Quarterly* 38 (1968): 58–77.

Kane, Steven Daniel. *The Proletarian Cultural Revolution of Mao Tse-tung: A Western Analysis.* Thesis. Hardin-Simmons University, 1968.

Karnow, Stanley. *Mao and China: A Legacy of Turmoil.* New York: Penguin, 1990.

———. *Mao and China: Inside China's Cultural Revolution.* New York: Penguin, 1984.

Kuo, Esther Tai-Chun. *Mao Tse-tung as a Political Leader: Political Skills, Transformative Thinking and the Chinese Communist Political System.* Dissertation. University of Oregon, 1991.

La Dany, L. "Mao's China: The Decline of a Dynasty." *Foreign Affairs* 14.4 (1967): 610–623.

Lee, Feigon. *Mao: A Reinterpretation.* Chicago: Ivan R. Dee, International, 2002.

Lee, Hong Yung. "Mao's Strategy for Revolutionary Change: A Case Study of the Cultural Revolution." *China Quarterly* 77 (1979): 50–73.

Leese, Daniel. *Mao Cult: Rhetoric and Ritual in China's Cultural Revolution.* New York: Cambridge University Press, 2011.

Lemon, Sumner Pike. *The Loyal Parent: An Analysis of the Role Played by Zhou Enlai in China's Cultural Revolution, 1966–1969.* Waterville, Maine: Colby College, 1993.

Leys, Simon. *The Chairman's New Clothes: Mao and the Cultural Revolution.* Trans. Carol Appleyard and Patrick Goode. Rev. ed. London: Allison & Busby, 1981.

Li, Zhisui. *The Private Life of Chairman Mao.* New York: Random House, 1994.

Lifton, Robert Jay. *Revolutionary Immortality: Mao Tse-tung and the Chinese Cultural* Lotta, Raymond, ed. *And Mao Makes 5: Mao Tse-tung's Last Great Battle.* Chicago: Banner Press, 1978.

Mamo, David. "Mao's Model for Socialist Transition Reconsidered." *Modern China* 7.1 (1981): 55–81.

"Mao Fails to Build His Utopia: A Political Assessment of Communist China." *Current Scene* 6.15 (1968): 1–9.

Mits, F. T. "Mao's Revolutionary Successors: Part I—The Wanderers." *Current Scene* 5.13 (1967): 1–7.

Morrison, Joe, and Jonathan Unger, eds. *Mao Zedong and the Cultural Revolution*. Armonk, N.Y.: Sharpe, 1985.

Myers, James T. "The Fall of Chairman Mao." *Current Scene* 6.10 (1968): 1–18.

Powell, David E. "Mao in Stalin's Mantle." *Problems of Communism* 17.2 (1968): 21–30.

Powell, Patricia, and Shitao Huo. *Mao's Graphic Voice: Political Posters from the Cultural Revolution*. Madison, Wis.: Elvehjem Museum of Art, 1996.

Rittenberg, Sidney, and Amanda Bennett. *The Man Who Stayed Behind.* New York: Simon & Schuster, 1993.

Schoenhals, Michael, ed. *Mao's Great Inquisition: The Central Case Examination Group, 1966–1979*. Chinese Law and Government. 29.3. Armonk, N.Y.: Sharpe, 1996.

Schram, Staurt, ed. *Chairman Mao Talks to the People: Talks and Letters, 1956–1971*. New York: Pantheon Books, 1974.

———. "Mao Tse-tung and Liu Shao-chi, 1939–1969." *Asian Survey* 12.4 (1972): 275–293.

Schrift, Melissa, and Keith Pilkey. "Revolution Remembered: Chairman Mao Badges and Chinese Nationalist Ideology." *Journal of Popular Culture* 30.2 (1996): 169–198.

Sen, Narayan. "The Setting of the 'Red Sun.'" *China Report* 29.2 (1993): 197–211.

Snow, Edgar. "Mao and the New Mandate." *World Today* 25.7 (1969): 289–297.

Solomon, Richard H. *Mao's Revolution and the Chinese Political Culture.* Berkeley: University of California Press, 1971.

———. "On Activism and Activists: Maoist Conception of Motivation and Political Role Linking State to Society." *China Quarterly* 39 (1969): 76–114.

Solomon, Richard H., with Talbott W. Huey. *A Revolution Is Not a Dinner Party: A Feast of Images of the Maoist Transformation of China.* Garden City, N.Y.: Anchor Press, 1975.

Spitz, Allan. "Mao's Permanent Revolution." *Review of Politics* 30 (1968): 440–454.

Starr, John Bryan. *Continuing the Revolution: The Political Thought of Mao.* Princeton, N.J.: Princeton University Press, 1979.

Terrill, Ross. *Mao: A Biography.* Sydney, N.S.W: Hale & Iremonger, 1995.

Topper, Henry C. *From the Commune to the Cultural Revolution: A Discussion of Party Leadership and Democracy in Lenin and Mao.* Dissertation. Johns Hopkins University, 1991.

Wagemann, Mildres Lina Ellen. *The Changing Image of Mao Tse-tung: Leadership Image and Social Structure.* Dissertation. Cornell University, 1974.

Wang, Ruoshui. "The Maid of Chinese Politics: Mao Zedong and His Philosophy of Struggle." *Journal of Contemporary China* 10 (1995): 66–80.

Wang, Xizhe. *Mao Zedong and the Cultural Revolution.* Hong Kong: Plough Publications, 1981.

White, Thomas N., ed. *A Definitive Translation of Mao Tse-tung on Literature and Art: The Cultural Revolution in Context.* Washington, D.C.: Alwhite Publications, 1967.

Whyte, Martin King. "Bureaucracy and Modernization in China: The Maoist Critique." *American Sociological Review* 38.2 (1973): 149–163.

Wilson, Dick, ed. *Mao Tse-tung in the Scales of History: A Preliminary Assessment.* New York: Cambridge University Press, 1977.

Chinese Language

Chang, Jung 張戎. *Mao Zedong: xian wei ren zhi de gu shi* 毛澤東: 鮮為人知的故事. Hong Kong: 開放出版社, 2006.

Chen, Kuide 陈奎德. "Mao Zedong 'zao fan' Mao ti zhi" 毛泽东"造反"毛体制. 北京之春, (1996.7): 55–58.

Chen, Xiaoya 陳小雅. *Zhongguo "fei pian": Mao Zedong de ming an* 中國"廢片": 毛澤東的命案. Carle Place, N.Y.: 明鏡出版社, 2006.

———. *Zhongguo "Niu zai": Mao Zedong de "gong an" ji xing wei, xin li fen xi* 中國"牛仔": 毛澤東的"公案"及行為, 心理分析. Carle Place, N.Y.: 明鏡出版社, 2005.

———. *Zhongguo "zhang fu": Mao Zedong de qing shi* 中國"丈夫": 毛澤東的情事. Hong Kong: 共和出版社, 2005.

Gong, Xiaoxia 龔小夏. "Mao Zedong de wei ji jin zhu yi yi shi xing tai" 毛泽东的伪激进主义 意识形态. 北京之春 (1996.11): 35–42.

Guo, Jinrong 郭金榮. *Mao Zedong di huang hun sui yue* 毛澤東的黃昏歲月. Hong Kong: 天地圖書有限公司, 1996.

Han, Zuo 韩作. *Mao Zedong qing shi: fu lu Mao Zedong 10 ge zi nu de zao yu* 毛泽东情史: 附录毛泽东10个子女的遭遇. Hong Kong: 东西文化事业公司, 1993.

Hu, Angang 胡鞍鋼. *Mao Zedong yu wen ge* 毛澤東與文革. Hong Kong: 大風出版社, 2009.

Hu, Sheng 胡绳. "Mao Zedong yi sheng suo zuo de er jian da shi" 毛泽东一生所做的二件大事. 中共党史研究 (1994.1): 1–8.

Jin, Dalu 金大陆. "Shanghai wen ge shi qi Mao Zedong xiang zhang de liu tong yu sheng chan" 上海文革时期毛泽东像章的流通与生产. 二十一世纪 (2006.6): 57–66.

Jin, Zhong 金鐘. *Fan pan de yu yi: Mao Zedong si ren yi sheng Li Zhisui he ta wei wan cheng de hui yi lu* 反叛的御醫: 毛澤東私人醫生李志綏和他未完成的回憶錄. Hong Kong: 開放雜誌社, 1997.

Li, Rui 李銳. *Li Rui tan Mao Zedong* 李銳談毛澤東. Hong Kong: 時代國際出版有限公司, 2005.

Li, Zehou 李泽厚; and Liu, Zaifu 刘再覆. "Mi xin yi si xing tai: Mao Zedong bei ju ping shuo zhi yi" 迷信意识形态: 毛泽东悲剧评说之一. 明报月刊 (1995.2): 92–96.

———. "Mi xin zhan zheng jing yan: Mao Zedong bei ju ping shuo zhi er" 迷信战争经验: 毛泽东悲剧评说之二. 明报月刊 (1995.3): 106–112.

Li, Zhisui 李志绥. *Mao Zedong si ren yi sheng hui yi lu* 毛泽东私人医生回忆录. Taipei: 时报文化出版企业有限公司, 1994.

Lu, Di 蘆笛. *Mao Zedong de jin chen he nu ren: ling xiu men liu xia de mi tuan* 毛澤東的近臣和女人: 領袖們留下的謎團. Carle Place, N.Y.: 明鏡出版社, 2010.

Pang, Xianzhi 逄先知; and Feng, Hui 冯蕙. *Mao Zedong nian pu 1893–1949* 毛泽东年谱 1893–1949. Beijing: 中央文献出版社, 2002.

Pang, Xianzhi 逄先知; and Jin, Chongji 金冲及. *Mao Zedong zhuan, 1949–1976* 毛泽东传, 1949–1976. Beijing: 中央文献出版社, 2003.

Qian, Liqun 錢理群. *Mao Zedong shi dai he hou Mao Zedong shi dai, 1949–2009: ling yi zhong li shi shu xie* 毛澤東時代和後毛澤東時代, 1949–2009: 另一種歷史書寫. Taipei: 联经出版公司, 2012.

Quan, Yanchi 权延赤. *Zou xia shen tan di Mao Zedong* 走下神坛的毛泽东. Huhehaote: 內蒙古人民出版社, 1998.

Shan, Shaojie 單少傑. *Mao Zedong zhi zheng chun qiu (1949–1976)* 毛澤東執政春秋 (1949–1976). Hong Kong: 明鏡出版社, 2001.

Shen, Yuan 申淵. *Wo ta zhi ce: Mao Zedong gong wei yi wen* 臥榻之側: 毛澤東宮闈軼聞. Hong Kong: 五七學社出版公司, 2011.

Song, Yongyi 宋永毅. "'Wen hua da ge ming' he fei li xing de Mao Zedong" "文化大革命"和非理性的毛泽东. 当代中国研究 (2008.4): 52–81.

Tong, Te-kong 唐德剛. *Mao Zedong zhuan zheng shi mo, 1949–1976* 毛澤東專政始末, 1949–1976. Taipei: 遠流出版事業股份有限公司, 2005.

Wang, Ruoshui 王若水. "Mao Zedong wei shen me yao fa dong wen ge: wo de yi xie kan fa" 毛泽东为什麼要发动文革: 我的一些看法. 明报月刊 (1996.10): 20–30.

———. *Xin fa xian de Mao Zedong: pu ren yan zhong de wei ren* 新發現的毛澤東: 僕人眼中的偉人. Hong Kong: 明報出版社, 2003. 2 vols.

Wang, Xizhe 王希哲. "Mao Zedong yu wen hua da ge ming" 毛泽东与文化大革命. 七十年代 (1981.2): 26–49.

Wang, Yi 王毅. "'Wan wu sheng zhang kao tai yang' yu yuan shi chong bai" "万物生长靠太阳"与原始崇拜. 二十一世纪 (1995.10): 125–132.

Wei, Zhengtong 韋政通. *Mao Zedong yu wen hua da ge ming* 毛澤東與文化大革命. Taipei: 立緒文化事業有限公司, 2009.

Xiao, Yanzhong, ed. 萧延中 编. *Wan nian Mao Zedong: guan yu li lun yu shi jian de yan jiu* 晚年毛泽东: 关于理论与实践的研究. Beijing: 春秋出版社, 1989.

Xin, Ziling 辛子陵. *Hong tai yang de yun luo: qian qiu gong zui Mao Zedong* 紅太陽的隕落: 千秋功罪毛澤東. Hong Kong: 書作坊, 2007.

Yang, Kuisong 楊奎松. *Zou xiang po lie: Mao Zedong yu Mosike de en en yuan yuan* 走向破裂: 毛澤東與莫斯科的恩恩怨怨. Hong Kong: 三聯書店(香港)有限公司, 1999.

Yang, Zhong Mei 楊中美. *Hong chao yan shi: Mao Zedong de nu ren* 紅朝艷史: 毛澤東的女人. Taipei: 時報文化出版企業股份有限公司, 2007.

Zhao, Feng 赵丰. *"'Zhong zi' xia de yin ying*"忠字"下的阴影. Beijing: 朝华出版社, 1993.

Zhao, Wumian 赵无眠. *Zhen jia Mao Zedong* 真假毛泽东. Vancouver: 明镜出版社, 1996.

Zheng, Qian 郑谦. *Mao Zedong shi dai de Zhongguo, 1949–1976* 毛泽东时代的中国, 1949–1976. Beijing: 中共党史出版社, 2003.

Zheng, Qian 郑谦; and Han, Gang 韩钢. *Wan nian sui yue: 1956 nian hou de Mao Zedong* 晚年岁月: 1956年后的毛泽东. Beijing: 中国青年出版社, 1993.

Zheng, Xuejia 郑学稼. *Cong wen ge dao Shi yi da: Mao Zedong ban yan de zui hou bei ju* 从文革到十一大: 毛泽东扮演的最后悲剧. Taipei: 黎明文化事业公司, 1978.

Zhu, Zhongli 朱仲丽. *Wo zhi dao de Mao zhu xi* 我知道的毛主席. Beijing: 中国青年出版社, 1998.

CCP LEADERS AND THE CULTURAL REVOLUTION

English Language

An, Tai Sung. *The Lin Piao Affair*. Philadelphia: Foreign Policy Research Institute in Anderson, Dennis J. *Kang Sheng: A Political Biography, 1924–1970*. Dissertation. St. John's University, 1973.

Andors, S. "The Dynamics of Mass Campaigns in Chinese Industry: Initiators, Leaders, and Participants in the Great Leap Forward, the Cultural Revolution, and the Campaign to Criticize Lin Biao and Confucius." *Bulletin of Concerned Asian Scholars* 8.4 (1976): 37–46.

Andreas, Joel. "Battling over Political and Cultural Power during the Chinese Cultural Revolution." *Theory and Society* 31.4 (2002): 463–519.

Ansley, Clive Malcolm. *The Heresy of Wu Han: His Play "Hai Jui's Dismissal" and Its Role in China's Cultural Revolution.* Toronto: University of Toronto Press, 1971.

Baum, Richard, and Frederick C. Teiwes. "Liu Shao-Chi and the Cadres Question." *Asian Survey* 13.4 (1968): 323–345.

Brosh, Charles L. *The End of the Chinese Cultural Revolution and the Fall of Lin Piao: A Study of the Relationship of Changing Chinese Policies and the Decline of Lin Piao, 1966–71.* Thesis. Georgetown University, 1978.

Brown, Cheryl Luvenia. *Restoring a One-Party Regime in China: A Study of Party Branches, 1964–1978.* Dissertation. University of Michigan, 1983. Ann Arbor, Mich.: University Microfilms, 1990.

Byron, John, and Robert Pack. *The Claws of the Dragon: Kang Sheng: The Evil Genius behind Mao and His Legacy of Terror in the People's China.* New York: Simon & Schuster, 1992.

The Case of Wu Han in the Cultural Revolution. White Plains, N.Y.: International Arts and Sciences Press, 1969–1970. 5 parts.

Chai, Winberg. "The Reorganization of the Chinese Communist Party, 1966–1968." *Asian Survey* 8.11 (1968): 901–910.

Chang, Chen-pang. "The Present and Future Situation of the Chinese Communist Party and Administration." *Chinese Communist Affairs* 5.5 (1968): 15–28.

Chang, David W. *Zhou Enlai and Deng Xiaoping in the Chinese Leadership Succession Crisis.* Lanham, Md.: University Press of America, 1984.

Chang, Hsin-cheng. *Evening Chats at Yenshan: Or, the Case of Teng To.* Berkeley: Center for Chinese Studies, University of California, 1970.

Cheek, Timothy. "Deng Tuo: Culture, Leninism and Alternative Marxism in the Chinese Communist Party." *China Quarterly* 87 (1981): 470–492.

———. "Studying Deng Tuo: The Academic Politician." *Republican China* 15.2 (1990): 1–15.

Cheng, Chu-yuan. "The Power Struggle in Red China." *Asian Survey* 6.9 (1966): 469–483.

Cheng, Peter. "Liu Shao-chi and the Cultural Revolution." *Asian Survey* 11.10 (1971): 943–957.

———. "The Root of China's Cultural Revolution: The Feud between Mao Tse-tung and Liu Shao-chi." *Orbis* 11.4 (1968): 1160–1178.

Chung, Hua-min, and Arthur C. Miller. *Madame Mao: A Profile of Chiang Ch'ing.* Hong Kong: Union Research Institute, 1968.

"The Conflict between Mao Tse-tung and Liu Shao-chi over Agricultural Mechanization in Communist China." *Current Scene* 6.17 (1968): 1–20.

"The Cultural Revolution: Act III—The Maoists against Liu Shao-chi." *Current Scene* 5.6 (1967): 1–10.

Deng, Rong. *Deng Xiaoping and the Cultural Revolution: A Daughter Recalls the Critical Years.* New York: Doubleday, 2005.

Dittmer, Lowell. "The Cultural Revolution and the Fall of Liu Shao-chi." *Current Scene* 11 (1973): 1–13.

———. "Death and Transfiguration: Liu Shaoqi's Rehabilitation and Contemporary Chinese Politics." *Journal of Asian Studies* 40.3 (1981): 455–479.

———. *Liu Shao-ch'i and the Chinese Cultural Revolution: The Politics of Mass Criticism.* Berkeley: University of California Press, 1975.

———. *Liu Shaoqi and the Chinese Cultural Revolution.* Armonk, N.Y.: Sharpe, 1998.

———. "Revolution and Reconstruction in Contemporary Chinese Bureaucracy." *Journal of Comparative Administration* 5.4 (1974): 443–486.

Dorrill, William F. "Leadership and Succession in Communist China." *Current History* 49.289 (1965): 129–135, 179–180.

Ebon, Martin. *Lin Piao: The Life and Writings of China's New Ruler.* New York: Stein and Day, 1970.

Fenwick, Ann Elizabeth. *The Gang of Four and the Politics of Opposition: China, 1971–1976.* Dissertation. Stanford University, 1983.

Forster, Keith. "The Politics of Destabilization and Confrontation: The Campaign against Lin Biao and Confucius in Zhejiang Province, 1974." *China Quarterly* 107 (1986): 433–462.

Fox, Galen. *Campaigning for Power in China during the Cultural Revolution Era, 1967–1976.* Dissertation. Princeton University, 1978. Ann Arbor, Mich.: University Microfilms, 1979.

Funnell, Victor. "Bureaucracy and the Chinese Communist Party." *Current Scene* 9.5 (1971): 1–14.

Galenovich, Yu. "The 'Special Case' of Liu Shaoqi." *Far Eastern Affairs* 1 (1989): 99–104.

Gao, Wenqian, Peter Rand, and Lawrence R. Sullivan. *Zhou Enlai: The Last Perfect Revolutionary.* New York: Public Affairs, 2007.

Ginneken, Jaap van. *The Rise and Fall of Lin Piao.* New York: Avon Books, 1977.

Gittings, John. "The Chinese Puzzle: Cultural Revolution and the Dismissal of P'eng Chen." *World Today,* 22 July 1966, 275–284.

Gong, Xiaoxia. *Repressive Movements and the Politics of Victimization: Patronage and Persecution during the Cultural Revolution.* Dissertation. Harvard University, 1995.

Hai, Feng. "Cultural Revolution and the Reconstruction of the Chinese Communist Party." *Asia Quarterly* 4 (1972): 303–320.

Harding, Harry, and Melvin Gurtov. *The Purge of Lo Jui-ching: The Politics of Chinese Strategic Planning.* Santa Monica, Calif.: RAND Corp., 1971.

Harman, Richard Snyder. *The Maoist Case against Liu Shaochi (1967): A Leadership Crisis in the Chinese People's Republic.* Dissertation. University of Virginia, 1969.

Heinzig, D. "Chinese Cultural Revolution as a Struggle for Power." *Political Studies* 199 (1971): 475–482.

Hinton, Harold C. *An Introduction to Chinese Politics.* New York: Praeger, 1973.

———. *Policymaking and the Power Struggle in Communist China during the Cultural Revolution.* Arlington, Va.: Institute for Defense Analyses, 1968.

Howard, Patricia Michael. *The Impact of the Cultural Revolution on the Changing Nature of Authority in the People's Republic of China.* Thesis. University of Saskatchewan, Regina, 1973.

Hsu, Kai-yu. "The Chinese Communist Leadership." *Current History* 57.337 (1969): 129–136.

Hwang, Tien-chien. *Transformation of Mao-Lin Faction's Tactical Line for Power Seize.* Taipei: Asian Peoples' Anti-Communist League, 1968.

Jin, Qiu. *The Culture of Power: The Lin Biao Incident in the Cultural Revolution.* Stanford, Calif.: Stanford University Press, 1999.

Kampen, Thomas. "The CCP's Central Committee Departments (1921–1991): A Study of Their Evolution." *China Report* 29.3 (1993): 299–317.

Kau, Michael Y. M., ed. *Lin Piao Affair: Power Politics and Military Coup.* White Plains, N.Y.: International Art and Science Press, 1975.

Kent, A. E. *Indictment without Trial: The Case of Liu Shao-Ch'i.* Canberra: Department of International Relations, Research School of Pacific Studies, Institute of Advanced Studies, Australian National University, 1969.

Klein, Donald W. "A Question of Leadership: Problems of Mobility Control and Policy-Making in China." *Current Scene* 5.7 (1967): 1–8.

———. "The State Council and the Cultural Revolution." *China Quarterly* 35 (1968): 78–95.

Klein, Donald, and Lois B. Hager. "The Ninth Central Committee." *China Quarterly* 45 (1971): 37–56.

Ko, Wei-shin. *Organizational Change of the Chinese Communist Party during the Cultural Revolution, 1966–1969.* Thesis. Western Illinois University, 1974.

Kruze, Uldis. *The Political Reconstitution of Peking Municipality: Politics and Polemics of the Cultural Revolution.* Thesis. Indiana University, 1976.

Lewis, John W., ed. *Party Leadership and Revolutionary Power in China.* Cambridge: Cambridge University Press, 1970.

Li, Tien-min. "Lin Piao's Situation." *Issues & Studies* 8.2 (1971): 66–74.

———. *The Mao-Lin Relationship and Lin Piao's Future.* Taipei: Institute of International Relations, 1971.

Liang, Hubert S. *China's Cultural Revolution and the Impact of the Gang of Four*. Audiocassette. University of Maine, Formington, 1981. 1 cassette.

Lieberthal, Kenneth. *Mao vs Liu? The Cultural Evolution on the Revolution of Urban Policy, 1946–1949*. Hong Kong: Center of Asian Studies, University of Hong Kong, 1970.

Lin Biao. *Quotation from Lin Piao*. Hong Kong: Chih Luen Press, 1971.

"Lin Piao and the Cultural Revolution." *Current Scene* 8.14 (1970): 1–14.

"Lin Piao: A Political Profile." *Current Scene* 7.5 (1969): 1–16.

Liu, Shin. *The Relationships among Ideology, Policy and Economic Performance: Mao Tsetung, Liu Shaochi and the Economy in China*. Dissertation. University of Nebraska–Lincoln, 1991.

Liu, Xuemin. *Poetry as Modernization: "Misty Poetry" of the Cultural Revolution*. Dissertation. University of California, Berkeley, 1992.

Liu, Yueh-sun. *Current and the Past of Lin Piao*. Santa Monica, Calif.: RAND Corp., 1967.

Longley, Linda. *Jiang Qing and Cultural Revolution*. Dissertation. University of Nevada, Las Vegas, 1996.

Louie, Kam. *Critiques of Confucius in Contemporary China*. New York: St. Martin's, 1980.

Lubell, Pamela. *The Chinese Communist Party and the Cultural Revolution: The Case of the Sixty-One Renegades*. New York: Palgrave Macmillan, 2002.

Ly, Singko. *The Fall of Madam Mao*. New York: Vantage Press, 1979.

Maloney, Joan M. "Chinese Women and Party Leadership: Impact of the Cultural Revolution." *Current Scene* 0.4 (1972): 10–15.

Maomao. *Deng Xiaoping and the Cultural Revolution: A Daughter Recalls the Critical Years*. New York: C. Bertelsmann, 2005.

Mehnert, Klaus. *Peking and the New Left: At Home and Abroad*. Berkeley: Center for Chinese Studies, University of California, 1969.

Michael, Franz. "The Struggle for Power." *Problems of Communism* 16.3 (1967): 12–21.

Morgan, Maria Chan. *Leadership Strategy at the Intermediate Level: Tao Zhu's Political Strategies in Guangdong Province, the People's Republic of China: 1959–1967*. Dissertation. Stanford University, 1987.

Nathan, Andrew J. "A Factionalism Model for CCP Politics." *China Quarterly* 53 (1973): 34–66.

Neuhauser, Charles. "The Chinese Communist Party in the 1960s: Prelude to the Cultural Revolution." *China Quarterly* 32 (1967): 3–36.

———. "The Impact of the Cultural Revolution on the Chinese Communist Party Machine." *Asian Survey* 8.6 (1968): 465–488.

Pfeffer, Richard M. "The Pursuit of Purity: Mao's Cultural Revolution." *Problems of Communism* 18 (1969): 12–25.

Possony, Stephan T. "The Chinese Communist Cauldron." *Orbis* 13.3 (1969): 783–821.

Potter, Pitman B. *From Leninist Discipline to Socialist Legalism: Peng Zhen on Law and Political Authority in the PRC.* Stanford, Calif.: Stanford University Press, 2003.

Pusey, James R. *Wu Han: Attacking the Present through the Past.* Harvard East Asian Monographs 33. Cambridge, Mass.: East Asian Research Center, Harvard University, 1969.

Pye, Lucian W. *The Authority Crisis in Chinese Politics.* Chicago: Center for Public Policy, University of Chicago, 1967.

Ragvald, Lars. *Yao Wenyuan as a Literary Critic and Theorist: The Emergency of Chinese Zhdanovism.* Dissertation. University of Stockholm, 1978.

Robinson, Thomas W. "Chou En-lai's Political Style: Comparisons with Mao Tse-tung and Lin Piao." *Asian Survey* 10.12 (1970): 1101–1116.

———. *Lin Piao as an Elite Type.* Santa Monica, Calif.: RAND Corp., 1971.

———. *A Political-Military Biography of Lin Biao.* Santa Monica, Calif.: RAND Corp., 1971. 2 vols.

Ross, Robert S. "From Lin Biao to Deng Xiaoping: Elite Instability and China's U.S. Policy." *China Quarterly* 118 (1989): 265–299.

Russo, Alessandro. "How Did the Cultural Revolution End? The Last Dispute between Mao Zedong and Deng Xiaoping, 1975." *Modern China*, April 2013, 239–279.

Schram, Stuart R. "The Limits of Cataclysmic Change: Reflections on the Place of the 'Great Proletarian Cultural Revolution' in the Political Development of the People's Republic of China." *China Quarterly* 108 (1986): 613–624.

———, ed. *Authority Participation and Cultural Change in China.* Cambridge: Cambridge University Press, 1973.

Schwartz, Benjamin I. "The Reign of Virtue: Some Broad Perspectives on Leader and Party in the Cultural Revolution." *China Quarterly* 35 (1968): 1–17.

"Selected Documents concerning Criticism of Li Hsien-nien during the Cultural Revolution." *Issues & Studies* 17.2 (1981): 64–74.

Shih, Victor, Wei Shan, and Mingxing Liu. "Gauging the Elite Political Equilibrium in the CCP: A Quantitative Approach Using Biographical Data." *China Quarterly*, March 2010, 79–103.

Song, Yongyi. "The Role of Zhou Enlai in the Cultural Revolution: A Contradictory Image from Diverse Sources." *Issues & Studies* 37.2 (2001): 1–28.

Sullivan, Lawrence Robert. *Ideology and the Politics of Cultural Revolution: The Development of Chinese Communist Doctrine, 1915–1934.* Thesis. University of Michigan, 1976.

Tai, Dwan. *Chiang Ching: The Emergence of a Revolutionary Political Leader*. New York: Exposition Press, 1974.

Teiwes, Frederick C. "A Review Article: The Evolution of Leadership Purges in Communist China." *China Quarterly* 41 (1970): 123–135.

Teiwes, Frederick C., and Warren Sun. *The Tragedy of Lin Biao: Riding the Tiger during the Cultural Revolution, 1966–1971*. Honolulu: University of Hawaii Press, 1996.

Terrill, Ross. *Madame Mao: A White-Boned Demon: A Biography of Madame Mao Zedong*. New York: Simon & Schuster, 1992.

Ting, Wang. *Chairman Hua: Leader of the Chinese Communists*. St. Lucia: University of Queensland Press, 1980.

Tsou, Tang. "The Cultural Revolution and the Chinese Political System." *China Quarterly* 38 (1969): 63–91.

Tupman, Bill. *Purges and Government Expansion: A Comparative Study of the American Loyalty Security Programme, the Soviet Great Purge and the Chinese Cultural Revolution*. Exeter: University of Exeter, 1978.

Uhalley, Stephen, Jr. "The Cultural Revolution and the Attack on the 'Three Family Village.'" *China Quarterly* 27 (1966): 149–161.

Vogel, Ezra F. "From Revolutionary to Semi-Bureaucrat: The 'Regularization' of Cadres." *China Quarterly* 29 (1967): 36–60.

Wei, Yung. "Elite Conflicts in Chinese Politics: A Comparative Note." *Studies in Comparative Communism* 7.1–2 (1974): 64–73.

Weng, Feng. *Lin Piao and His Armed Rebellion Thinking*. Taipei: Asian Peoples' Anti-Communist League, 1967.

Wikte, Roxane. *Comrade Chiang Ch'ing*. Boston: Little, Brown, 1977.

Wong-Sandor, Helen Ka-shing. *Paths to Political Leadership in the People's Republic of China, 1966–1976: Thirteen Cases*. Dissertation. University of Melbourne, 1984.

Wu, Tien-wei. *Lin Biao and the Gang of Four: Counter-Confucianism in Historical and Intellectual Perspective*. Carbondale: Southern Illinois University Press, 1983.

Yahuda, Michael. "Deng Xiaoping: The Statesman." *China Quarterly* 135 (1993): 551–572.

Yao, Mingle. *The Conspiracy and Death of Lin Biao*. New York: Knopf, 1983.

Yao, Wenyuan. *On the Social Basis of the Lin Piao Anti-Party Clique*. Peking: Foreign Languages Press, 1975.

Zhang, Chunqiao. *On Exercise All-round Dictatorship over the Bourgeoisie*. Peking: Foreign Languages Press, 1975.

Zhang, Yunsheng. *True Account of Maojiawan: Reminiscences of Lin Biao's Secretary by Zhang Yunsheng*. Trans. Nancy Liu. Armonk, N.Y.: Sharpe, 1993.

Chinese Language

Chen, Boda 陈伯达; and Chen, Xiaonong 陈晓农. *Chen Boda Yi gao: yu zhong zi shu ji qi ta* 陈伯达遗稿: 狱中自述及其他. Hong Kong: 天地图书有限公司, 1998.

Chen, Donglin 陈东林. "Zhang Chunqiao de 'pan tu' yu dang yuan shen fen zhi mi" 张春桥的"叛徒"与党员身份之谜. 二十一世纪 (2011.4): 62–73.

Chen, Pixian 陈丕显. *Chen Pixian hui yi lu: zai "yi yue feng bao" de zhong xin* 陈丕显回忆录: 在"一月风暴"的中心. Hong Kong: 三聯書店, 2005.

Chen, Xiaonong, ed. 陈晓农 编. *Chen Boda zui hou kou shu hui yi* 陈伯达最后口述回忆. Hong Kong: 阳光环球出版香港有限公司, 2005.

Dai, Jiafang 戴嘉枋. *Zou xiang hui mie: "wen ge" wen hua bu zhang Yu Huiyong chen fu lu* 走向毁灭: "文革"文化部长于会泳沉浮录. Beijing: 光明日报出版社, 1994.

Ding, Kaiwen 丁凯文. "'Jiu yi san Lin Biao chu zou shi jian' yan jiu shu ping" "九一三林彪出走事件"研究述评. 当代中国研究 (2007.2): 141–159.

———, ed. *Chong shen Lin Biao zui an* 重审林彪罪案. Carle Place, N.Y.: 明镜出版社, 2004.

Ding, Longjia 丁龙嘉; and Tingyu 听雨. *Kang Sheng yu "Zhao Jianmin yuan an"* 康生与"赵健民冤案." Beijing: 人民出版社, 2006.

Fan, Shuo 范硕. *Ye Jianying zai fei chang shi qi, 1966–1976* 叶剑英在非常时期, 1966–1976. Beijing: 华文出版社, 2006.

Gao, Hua 高华. "Ge ming zheng zhi de bian yi he tui hua: 'Lin Biao shi jian' de zai kao cha" 革命政治的变异和退化: "林彪事件"的再考察. 二十一世纪 (2006.10): 69–87.

Gao, Wenqian 高文謙. *Wan nian Zhou Enlai* 晚年周恩來. Carle Place, N.Y.: 明鏡出版社, 2003.

Gu, Baozi 顾保孜 · *Zhong Nan Hai ren wu chun qiu* 中南海人物春秋. Beijing: 中国青年出版社, 2000.

Huang, Wenhua, et al. 黄文华 等. *Deng Xiaoping Jiangxi meng nan ji* 邓小平江西蒙难记. Hong Kong: 明星出版社, 1990.

Huang, Zheng 黄峥. *Liu Shaoqi yuan an shi mo* 刘少奇冤案始末. Beijing: 九州出版社, 2012.

Li, Zuopeng 李作鹏. *Li Zuopeng hui yi lu* 李作鹏回憶錄. Hong Kong: 北星出版社, 2011. 2 vols.

Li shi de shen pan bian ji zu, ed. "历史的审判"编辑组 编. *Li shi de shen pan* 历史的审判. Beijing: 群众出版社, 1981.

Li shi de shen pan (xu ji) bian ji zu, ed. "历史的审判 (续集)" 编辑组 编. *Li shi de shen pan: xu ji* 历史的审判: 续集. Beijing: 群众出版社, 1986.

Lin, Qingshan 林青山. *Kang Sheng wai zhuan* 康生外传. Changchun: 吉林人民出版社, 1988.

Maomao 毛毛. *Wo de fu qin Deng Xiaoping: "wen ge" sui yue* 我的父亲邓小平: "文革"岁月. Beijing: 中央文献出版社, 2000.

Mingxiao 明晓; and Chinan 赤南. *Mou sha Mao Zedong di hei se "tai zi"* 謀殺毛澤東的黑色 "太子." Hong Kong: 香港中華兒女出版社, 2000.

Mu, Xin 穆欣. *Jie hou chang yi: shi nian dong luan ji shi* 劫後長憶: 十年動亂紀事. Hong Kong: 新天出版社, 1997.

Peng, Dehuai 彭德怀. *Peng Dehuai zi shu* 彭德怀自述. Beijing: 人民出版社, 1981.

Qiu, Chengguang 邱承光. *Xin ling de dui hua—Qiu Huizuo yu er zi tan wen hua da ge ming* 心灵的对话—邱会作与儿子谈文化大革命. Hong Kong: 北星出版社, 2010. 2 vols.

Qiu, Huizuo 邱会作. *Qiu Huizuo hui yi lu* 邱会作回忆录. Hong Kong: 新世纪出版社, 2011. 2 vols.

Quan, Yanchi 权延赤. *Tao Zhu zai "wen hua da ge ming" zhong* 陶铸在"文化大革命"中. Beijing: 中共中央党校出版社, 1991.

———. *Long hu dou: He Long yu Lin Biao di shu si zhi zheng* 龍虎鬥: 賀龍與林彪的殊死之爭. Hong Kong: 天地圖書有限公司, 1997.

Shi, Yun 史雲; and Li, Danhui 李丹慧. *Nan yi ji xu de "ji xu ge ming": cong pi Lin dao pi Deng, 1972–1976* 難以繼續的 "繼續革命": 從批林到批鄧, 1972–1976. Hong Kong: 香港中文大學當代中國文化研究中心, 2008.

Song, Yongyi 宋永毅. "Bei yan cang de li shi: Liu Shaoqi dui 'wen ge' de du te gong xian" 被掩藏的历史: 刘少奇对"文革"的独特贡献. 当代中国研究 (2006.3): 32–55.

Tao, Siliang 陶斯亮. *Yi feng zhong yu fa chu de xin: wo he wo de fu qin Tao Zhu mu qin Zeng Zhi* 一封终于发出的信: 我和我的父亲陶铸母亲曾志. Beijing: 當代中國出版社, 2013.

Tumen 图们; and Xiao, Sike 肖思科. *Te bie shen pan: Lin Biao, Jiang Qing fan ge ming ji tuan shou shen shi lu* 特别审判: 林彪, 江青反革命集团受审实录. Beijing: 中央文献出版社, 2003.

Wang, Dongxing 汪东兴. *Wang Dongxing hui yi: Mao Zedong yu Lin Biao fan ge ming ji tuan de dou zheng* 汪东兴回忆: 毛泽东与林彪反革命集团的斗争. Beijing: 当代中国出版社, 1997.

Wang, Li 王力. *Wang Li fan si lu* 王力反思录. Hong Kong: 香港北星出版社, 2001. 2 vols.

———. *Xian chang li shi: wen hua da ge ming zhong ji shi* 现场历史: 文化大革命中纪事. Hong Kong: 牛津大学出版社, 1994.

Wang, Nianyi 王年一; and He, Shu 何蜀. "1970 nian de Lushan hui yi ji Mao Zedong, Li Biao chong tu zhi ti yuan—zai 'she guo jia zhu xi' zhi zheng de bei hou" 1970年的庐山会议及毛泽东, 林彪冲突之起源—在"设国家主席"之争的背后. 当代中国研究 (2001.1): 137–152.

Wang, Nianyi 王年一; He, Shu 何蜀; and Chen, Zhao 陈昭. "Mao Zedong bi chu lai de 'Jiu yi san Lin Biao chu tao shi jian'" 毛泽东逼出来的"九·一三林彪出逃事件." 当代中国研究 (2004.2): 137–154.

Wang, Yi 王毅. "'Zhong yang wen ge xiao zu' ji qi wen hua ji yin" "中央文革小组"及其文化基因. Hong Kong: 二十一世纪 (1998.12): 55–60.

Wen, Xiang 温相. *Wan nian Lin Biao* 晚年林彪. Hong Kong: 东西文化事业有限公司, 2007.

Wu, De 吴德; and Zhu, Yuanshi 朱元石. *Wu De kou shu: shi nian feng yu ji shi: wo zai Beijing gong zuo de yi xie jing li* 吴德口述: 十年风雨纪事: 我在北京工作的一些经历. Beijing: 当代中国出版社, 2013.

Wu, Faxian 吴法宪. *Sui yue jian nan: Wu Faxian hui yi lu* 岁月艰难: 吴法宪回忆录. Hong Kong: 香港北星出版社, 2006. 2 vols.

Wu, Guang 武光. *Bu shi meng: dui "wen ge" nian dai de hui yi* 不是梦: 对"文革"年代的回忆. Beijing: 中共党史出版社, 2000.

Wu, Runsheng 吴润生. *Lin Biao yu wen hua da ge ming* 林彪與文化大革命. Carle Place, N.Y.: 明鏡出版社, 2006.

Wu, Si 吴思. *Chen Yonggui chen fu Zhongnanhai: gai zao Zhongguo de shi yan* 陈永贵沉浮 中南海: 改造中国的试验. Guangzhou: 花城出版社, 1993.

Xin, Ziling 辛子陵. *Lin Biao zheng zhuan* 林彪正傳. Hong Kong: 利文出版社, 2002.

Yang, Xiaokai 杨小凯. "Zhou Enlai yu wo de ming yun: jian ping Zhou de fu za xing" 周恩来 与我的命运: 兼评周的复杂性. 开放 (1994.5): 44–47.

Ye, Yonglie 叶永烈. *"Si ren bang" xing wang. Shang zhong xia juan* "四人帮"兴亡. 上中下卷. Beijing: 人民日报出版社, 2009.

Yu, Ruxin, ed. 余汝信 编. *"Jiu yisan" hui wang—Lin Biao shi jian shi shi yu bian xi* "九一三"回望—林彪事件史实与辨析. Hong Kong: 新世纪出版社, 2013.

Zhang, Min 张民. *Zhou Enlai yu "Shou du gong zuo zu": yi ge gong zuo zu cheng yuan de qin shen jing li* 周恩来与"首都工作组":一个工作组成员的亲身经历. Beijing: 中央文献出版社, 2009.

Zhang, Yunsheng 张云生. *"Lin Biao mi shu hui yi lu"* 林彪秘书回忆录. Hong Kong: 存真社, 1988.

Zhang, Zhanbin 張湛彬. *Wen ge di yi wen zi yu: "san jia cun" an shi mo* 文革第一文字狱: "三家村"案始末. Hong Kong: 太平洋世纪出版社, 1998.

RED GUARDS AND URBAN YOUTH REEDUCATION

English Language

Baum, Richard. "China: Year of the Mangoe." *Asian Survey* 9.1 (1969): 1–17.

Bennett, Gordon A., and Ronald N. Montaperto. *Red Guard: The Political Biography of Dai Hsiao-Ai*. Garden City, N.Y.: Doubleday, 1971.

Bernstein, Thomas P. *Up to the Mountains and Down to the Villages: The Transfer of Youth from Urban to Rural China*. New Haven, Conn.: Yale University Press, 1977.

Bonnin, Michel. *The Lost Generation: The Rustication of China's Educated Youth (1968–1980)*. Hong Kong: The Chinese University Press, 2013.

Britton, Dale Gregory. *Chairman Mao and the Red Guards: A "Top and Bottom" Alliance against the CCP Bureaucracy, June to December 1966*. Thesis. University of Virginia, 1992.

Chan, Anita. *Children of Mao: Personality Development and Political Activism in the Red Guard Generation*. Seattle: University of Washington Press, 1985.

———. "Dispelling Misconceptions about the Red Guard Movement: The Necessity to Re-examine Cultural Revolution Factionalism and Periodization." *Journal of Contemporary China* 1.1 (1992): 61–85.

Chan, Che Po. *From Idealism to Pragmatism: The Change of Political Thinking among the Red Guard Generation in China*. Dissertation. University of California, Santa Barbara, 1991.

Chan, Ching-yee Aris. *From Docile Students to Ferocious Red Guards: A Study of the Mentality and Behavior of Politicized Youths in Guangzhou, 1963–1968*. Hong Kong: University of Hong Kong, 1997.

Chen, Yixin. "Lost in Revolution and Reform: The Socio-economic Pains of China's Red Guards Generation, 1966–1996." *Journal of Contemporary China* 8.21(1999): 219–240.

Dorman, David. "The Red Guards: A Planned Phase in China's Revolution." *Social Studies* 62.6 (1971): 265–268.

Fang, Xiaoli. "Special Student Movement in Modern China: Re-identification and Re-evaluation of the Red Guard Movement." *Chinese Culture* 37.3 (1996): 111–130.

Funnell, Victor C. "The Chinese Communist Youth Movement 1949–1966." *China Quarterly* 42 (1970): 105–130.

Gittings, John. "A Red Guard Repents." *Far Eastern Economic Review*, 10 July 1969, 123–126.

Gold, Thomas B. "Back to the City: The Return of Shanghai's Educated Youth." *China Quarterly* 84 (1980): 755–770.

Granqvist, Hans. *The Red Guard: A Report on Mao's Revolution.* Trans. Erik J. Friis. London: Pall Mall; New York: Praeger, 1967.

Harris, Leon Scott. *The Origins of the Cultural Revolution and the Rise of the Red Guard Movement: September 1965–July 1967.* Thesis. Brandeis University, 1972.

Heaslet, Juliana P. "The Red Guards: Instruments of Destruction in the Cultural Revolution." *Asian Survey* 12 (1972): 1032–1047.

Heaton, Bill. "Why the Red Guard?" *Journal of the Society for Asian Studies* 1.1 (1968): 53–61.

Hilton, Carma, et al. *Morning Sun.* Videocassette. London: [Distributed by] Jane Balfour Services, 2003.

Hsiang, Nai-kuang. "The Chinese Young Communist League after the Great Culture Revolution." *Chinese Communist Affairs* 6 (1969): 29–41.

Huang, Alice Aizhen. *Psychology of the Red Guard: A Psychosocial Study of the Cultural Revolution in China.* Dissertation. University of Alberta, 1991.

Hunt, Carroll Ferguson. *From Claws of the Dragon.* Grand Rapids, Mich.: Frances Asbury Press, 1988.

Israel, John. "The Red Guards in Historical Perspective: Continuity and Change in the Chinese Youth Movement." *China Quarterly* 30 (1967): 1–32.

Jiang, Yarong, and David Ashley. *Mao's Children in the New China: Voices from the Red Guard Generation.* London: Routledge Kegan Paul, 2000.

Kang, Xue Pei. *In the Countryside.* Huntsville: Texas Review Press, 1992.

Kato, Hiroki. *The Red Guard Movement, May, 1966–January, 1967: A Case of a Student Movement in China.* Dissertation. University of Chicago, 1974.

———. "The Red Guard Movement: Its Origin." *Asian Forum* 5.2 (1973): 79–110.

Kaya, Okinori. *The Turmoil in Communist China over the "Cultural Revolution" and Red Guards.* Tokyo: Japan National Foreign Affairs Foundation, 1969.

Klinghoffer, Herbert Shelby. *The Student Movement in the Chinese Cultural Revolution.* Thesis. George Washington University, 1971.

Kong, Shuyu. "Swan and Spider Eater in Problematic Memoirs of the Cultural Revolution." *Position* 7.1 (1999): 239–252.

Kuriyama, Yoshihiro. *Political Leadership and Students in China (1966–1968) and France (1968).* Dissertation. University of California, Berkeley, 1973.

Lau, Joseph S. M. "The Wounded and the Fatigued: Reflections on Post-1976 Chinese Fiction." *Journal of Oriental Studies* 20 (1982): 128–142.

Lawrence, Susan V. "The Legacy of the Red Guards." *US News & World Report,* 20 May 1996: 40–43.

Leader, Shelah Gilbert. "The Communist Youth League and the Cultural Revolution." *Asian Survey* 14.8 (1974): 700–715.

Lee, Hong Yung. *The Politics Mobilization of the Red Guards and Revolutionary Rebels in the Cultural Revolution.* Chicago: n.p., 1973. 2 vols.

———. "The Radical Students in Kwangtung during the Cultural Revolution." *China Quarterly* 64 (1975): 645–683.

———. *A Research Guide to Red Guard Publications, 1966–1969.* Armonk, N.Y.: Sharpe, 1989.

———. "Utility and Limitations of the Red Guard Publications as Source Publications: A Bibliographical Survey." *Journal of Asian Studies* 34.3 (1975): 779–793.

Lin, Jing. *Factors Underlying the Red Guards' Participation in "Class Struggle" and Their Compliant Aggressiveness during the Cultural Revolution, and Implications for Chinese Education.* Dissertation. University of Michigan, 1990.

———. *The Red Guards' Path to Violence: Political, Educational, and Psychological Factors.* New York: Praeger, 1991.

Ling, Ken. *Red Guard: From Schoolboy to "Little General" in Mao's China.* Trans. Miriam London and Ta-ling Lee. London: MacDonald and Co., 1972.

London, Miriam, and Ivan D. Long. "China's Lost Generation: The Fate of the Red Guards since 1968." *Saturday Review World*, 30 November 1974, 12–15, 18–19.

Luo, Zi-ping. *A Generation Lost: China under the Cultural Revolution.* New York: H. Holt, 1990.

McLaren, Anne. "The Educated Youth Return: The Poster Campaign in Shanghai from November 1978 to March 1979." *Australian Journal of Chinese Affairs* 2 (1979): 1–20.

Pan, Chaoying, and Raymond J. De Jaegher. *Peking's Red Guards: The Great Proletarian Cultural Revolution.* New York: Twin Circle Pub. Co., 1968.

Peiping's "Red Guards." Taipei: Institute of Political Research, 1966.

Perry, Elizabeth J., and Hsun Li. *Revolutionary Rudeness: The Language of Red Guards and Rebel Workers in China's Cultural Revolution.* Bloomington: East Asian Studies Center, Indiana University, 1993.

Prahye, Prabhakar. "Why Red Guards?" *China Report* 3.1 (December 1966–January 1967): 4–8.

Raddock, David M. "Between Generations: Activist Chinese Youths in Pursuit of a Political Role in the San-fan and in the Cultural Revolution." *China Quarterly* 79 (1979): 511–529.

———. "The 'Revolutionary Successor': Some Psychological Perspectives on Youth in Cultural Revolution." *China Report* 11.3 (1975): 21–32.

"The Revival of the Communist Youth League." *Current Scene* 8.5 (1970): 1–7.

Roberts, William Taft. *Student Unrest in Communist China: The 100 Flowers and the Cultural Revolution.* Thesis. University of California, Berkeley, 1968.

Rosen, Stanley. *Red Guard Factionalism and the Cultural Revolution in Guangzhou (Canton).* Boulder, Colo.: Westview, 1982.

———. *Red Guard Factionalism in China's Cultural Revolution: A Social Analysis.* Boulder, Colo.: Westview, 1981.

———. *The Role of Sent-Down Youth in the Chinese Cultural Revolution: The Case of Guangzhou.* Berkeley: Center for Chinese Studies, University of California, 1981.

Seybolt, Peter J. *The Rustication of Urban Youth in China: A Social Experiment.* White Plains, N.Y.: Sharpe, 1977.

Singer, Martin. *Educated Youth and the Cultural Revolution in China.* Ann Arbor, Mich.: Center for Chinese Studies, University of Michigan, 1971.

Walder, Andrew G. "Beijing Red Guard Factionalism: Social Interpretations Reconsidered." *Journal of Asian Studies* 61.2 (2002): 437–471.

———. *Fractured Rebellion: The Beijing Red Guard Movement.* Cambridge, Mass.: Harvard University Press, 2009.

Wang, Hsueh-wen. "Ten Years of the Red Guard Movement." *Issues & Studies* 12.10 (1976): 39–53.

Weiss, Ruth. "Lost Generation—Saved from the Brink?" *Eastern Horizon* 19.12 (1980): 8–12.

Wen, Chung-kuo. "The Rustication Policy and Youth Movements in Mainland China." *Issues & Studies* 17.1 (1981): 53–71.

Whitehead, Raymond L. "China's Youth and the Cultural Revolution." *China Notes* 7.1 (1968–1969): 5–10.

Wilson, Richard W., and Amy A. Wilson. "The Red Guards and the World Student Movement." *China Quarterly* 42 (1970): 88–104.

Yang, Guobin. *China's Red Guard Generation: The Ritual Process of Identity Transformation, 1966–1999.* Dissertation. New York University, 2000.

———. "China's Zhiqing Generation." *Modern China* 29.3 (2003): 267–296.

———. "The Limited Effects of Social Movements: Red Guards and the Transformation of Identity." *Sociological Forum* 15.2 (2000): 379–406.

———. *Red Guards on the Road: "The Great Linkup" and Its Horizon-Broadening Effects on China's Red Guard Generation.* Thesis. University of North Carolina at Chapel Hill, 1997.

Yin, Hongbiao. "Ideological and Political Tendencies of Factions in the Red Guard Movement." *Journal of Contemporary China* 5.13 (1996): 269–281.

Zhang, Xiaowei. *Children of the Cultural Revolution: Class and Caste in Mao's China*. Dissertation. University of California, Berkeley, 1992. Ann Arbor, Mich.: University Microfilms, 1993. 9305131.

Zhang, Zhongwen. "A Self-Taught Youth." *Eastern Horizon* 20.5 (1981): 13–16.

Zhou, Xueguang, and Liren Hou. "Children of the Cultural Revolution: The State and the Life Course in the People's Republic of China." *American Sociological Review* 64.1 (1999): 12–37.

Chinese Language

Ai, Xiaoming 艾晓明. *Xue tong: yi ge hei wu lei zi nu de wen ge ji yi* 血统：一个黑五类子女 的文革记忆. Guangzhou: 花城出版社, 1994.

An, Zhi 安知. *Zhi qing chen fu lu* 知青沉浮录. Chengdu: 四川人民出版社, 1989.

Bai, Miao 白描. *Shanbei: Beijing zhi qing qing ai lu* 陕北：北京知青情爱录. Xi'an: 陕西旅游 出版社, 1993.

Beidao 北島; and Cao, Yifan 曹一凡. *Bao feng yu de ji yi: 1965–1970 nian de Beijing si zhong* 暴風雨的記憶：1965–1970年的北京四中. Hong Kong: Oxford University Press, 2011.

Bu, Weihua 卜偉華. *"Za lan jiu shi jie": wen hua da ge ming de dong luan yu hao jie, 1966–1968* "砸爛舊世界"：文化大革命的動亂與浩劫, 1966–1968. Hong Kong: 香港中文大學當代中國文化研究中心, 2008.

Chen, Xiaojin 陈小津. *Wo de "wen ge" sui yue* 我的"文革"岁月. Beijing: 中央文献出版社, 2009.

Deng, Peng 邓鹏. *Wu sheng de qun luo: "wen ge" qian shang shan xia xiang lao zhi qing hui yi lu (xu)* 無聲的群落："文革" 前上山下乡老知青回忆录 (续). Chongqing: 重庆出版社, 2009.

Deng, Xian 邓贤. *Zhongguo zhi qing meng* 中国知青梦. Beijing: 人民文学出版社, 1993.

Dong, Guoqiang 董国强. *Qin li "wen ge": 14 wei Nanjing da xue shi sheng de kou shu li shi* 亲历"文革"：14位南京大学师生的口述历史. New York: 柯捷出版社, 2010.

Du, Honglin 杜鸿林. *Feng chao dang luo 1955–1979: Zhongguo zhi shi qing nian shang shan xia xiang yun dong shi* 风潮荡落 1955–1979: 中国知识青年上山下乡运动史. Shenzhen: 海天出版社, 1993.

Huang, Yanmin 黄延敏. "'Po si jiu' yun dong de fa zhan mai luo" "破四旧"运动的发展脉络. 二十一世纪 (2013.6): 71–82.

Jiang, Pei 江沛. *Hong wei bing kuang biao* 红卫兵狂飙. Zhengzhou: 河南人民出版社, 1994.

Jin, Dalu, ed. 金大陆 编. *Ku nan yu feng liu: "lao san jie"ren de dao lu* 苦难与风流："老三届"人的道路. Shanghai: 上海人民出版社, 1994.

Jin, Yucheng 金宇澄. *Piao bo zai hong hai yang: wo de da chuan lian* 飘泊在红海洋: 我的大串聯. Taipei: 時報文化出版企業有限公司, 1996.

Kuai, Dafu 蒯大富. *Qinghua wen ge wu shi tian* 清华文革五十天. Hong Kong: 中国文化传播出版社, 2013.

Li, Yinhe 李银河. "'Lao san jie' nü xing de qing chun qi" "老三届"女性的青春期. 二十一世纪 (1997.2): 65–69.

Liang, Heng 梁恒; and Xia, Zhuli 夏竹丽 (Judith Shapiro). *Ge ming zhi zi* 革命之子. Hong Kong: 远东评论出版社, 1983.

Lin, Xianzhi 林贤治. *Lao yin: "ke yi jiao yu hao de zi nü" de ji ti ji yi* 烙印: "可以教育好的子女"的集体记忆. Guangzhou: 花城出版社, 2010.

Liu, Xiaobo 刘晓波. "Wo cong shi yi sui kai shi xi yan: wei 'wen ge' san shi nian er zuo" 我从十一岁开始吸烟: 为"文革"三十年而作. 争鸣 (1996.5): 87–89.

Liu, Xiaomeng 刘小萌. "Xia xiang nü zhi shi qing nian hun yin pou xi" 下乡女知识青年婚姻剖析. 二十一世纪 (1995.8): 57–65.

Liu, Xiaomeng 刘小萌; and Ding, Yizhuang, et al. 定宜庄 等. *Zhong guo zhi qing shi dian* 中国知青事典. Chengdu: 四川人民出版社, 1995.

Mi, Hedu 米鹤都. *Hui yi yu fan si: hong wei bing shi dai feng yun ren wu: kou shu li shi zhi yi* 回憶與反思: 紅衛兵時代風雲人物: 口述歷史之一. Hong Kong: 中國書局有限公司, 2011.

———. *Hui yi yu fan si: hong wei bing shi dai feng yun ren wu—kou shu li shi zhi 2* 回憶與反思: 紅衛兵時代風雲人物—口述歷史之二. Hong Kong: 中國書局有限公司, 2011.

———. *Xin lu: tou shi Gongheguo tong ling ren* 心路: 透视共和国同龄人. Beijing: 中央文献出版社, 2011.

Nie, Shuren 聂树人. *Beijing tian di liang pai de dou zheng* 北京天地两派的斗争. Hong Kong: 中国文化传播出版社, 2013.

Qiu, Xinmu 邱新睦. "'Zhi shi qing nian shang shan xia xiang' yan jiu zong shu" "知识青年上山下乡"研究综述. 当代中国研究 (2003.4): 113–140.

Ren, Guoqing 任国庆. "Chen tong de 'shi ming'—Hui gu 'Zhi shi qing nian shang shan xia xiang yun dong'" 沉痛的"使命"—回顾"知识青年上山下乡运动." 当代中国研究 (2003.4): 104–112.

Ren, Zhichu 任知初. *"Hong wei bing" yu "xi pi shi"* "红卫兵"与"嬉皮士." Vancouver: 明镜 出版社, 1996.

Song, Bolin 宋柏林; and Yu, Ruxin 余汝信. *Hong wei bing xin shuai lu: Qinghua fu zhong lao hong wei bing shou ji* 红卫兵兴衰录: 清华附中老红卫兵手记. Hong Kong: 德赛出版有限公司, 2006.

Sun, Nutao 孙怒涛. *Liang zhi de kao wen: yi ge Qing hua wen ge tou tou de xin lu li cheng* 良知的拷问: 一个清华文革头头的心路历程. Hong Kong: 中国文化传播出版社, 2013.

Tang, Jinhe 唐金鹤. *Dao xia de ying cai* 倒下的英才. Hong Kong: 科華圖書出版公司, 2009.

Tang, Shaojie 唐少杰. "Qinhua da xue wen ge zhong de 'fei zheng chang si wang'" 清华大学文革中的"非正常死亡" 二十一世纪 (2006.2): 56–64.

———. "Wen hua da ge ming de yi shou duan hun qu—Mao Zedong zhao jian hong wei bing wu da ling xiu de tan hua" 文化大革命的一首断魂曲—毛泽东召见北京红衞兵五大领袖的谈话. 二十一世纪 (2006.10): 55–68.

———. *Yi ye zhi qiu: Qinghua da xue 1968 nian "bai ri da wu dou"* 一葉知秋: 清華大學1968年"百日大武鬥." Hong Kong: 中文大學出版社, 2003.

Wang, Shenghui 王盛辉. "1992 nian yi lai 'Hong wei bing' yan jiu shu ping" 1992年以来"红卫兵"研究述评. 当代中国研究 (2004.3): 127–145.

Wang, Youqin 王友琴. "1966: Xue sheng da lao shi de ge ming" 1966: 学生打老师的革命. 二十一世纪 (1995.8): 33–46.

Wu, Wenguang 吴文光. *Ge ming xian chang: yi bu ji lu pian de pai she shou ji* 革命现场: 一部纪录片的拍摄手记. Taipei: 时报出版公司, 1994.

Xiao, Fuxing 肖复兴. *Jue chang lao san jie* 绝唱老三届. Beijing: 新华出版社, 2012.

Yin, Hongbiao 印红标. "Hong wei bing yun dong de liang da chao liu" 红卫兵运动的两大潮流. 二十一世纪 (1992.10): 26–38.

Xu, Aijing 許愛晶. *Qinghua Kuai Dafu* 清華蒯大富. Hong Kong: 中國文革歷史出版社, 2011.

Xu, Youyu 徐友渔. *1966, wo men na yi dai de hui yi* 1966, 我们那一代的回忆. Beijing: 中國文联出版公司, 1998.

———. *Xing xing se se de zao fan: hong wei bing jing shen su zhi de xing cheng ji yan bian* 形形色色的造反: 紅衞兵精神素質的形成及演變. Hong Kong: 香港中文大學出版社, 1999.

———. *Zhi mian li shi* 直面历史. Beijing: 中国文联出版社, 2000.

Zhang, Chenchen 张晨晨. "Wen ge chu qi de ji ti bao li" 文革初期的集体暴力. 二十一世纪 (2008.12): 52–62.

REBELS, MASSES, AND VIOLENCE

English Language

Bennett, Gordon A. *Yundong: Mass Campaign in Chinese Communist Leadership.* Berkeley: Center for Chinese Studies, University of California, 1976.

Chi, Benjamin. *In the Name of the Revolution: The Phenomenon of Violence in the Great Proletarian Cultural Revolution, 1966–1968.* Dissertation. Duke University, 1995.

Chung, Jae Ho. *The Mass Line in the Chinese Cultural Revolution: A Comparison with the Yenan Revolution.* Dissertation. Brown University, 1985.

Dittmer, Lowell. "Mass Line and Mass Criticism in China: An Analysis of the Fall of Liu Shao-chi." *Asian Survey* 13 (1973): 772–792.

It's Right to Rebel. Dir. Julia Spark. Prod. Granada Television. Audiocassette. Films for the Humanities, 1984. 1 cassette.

Lee, Ming-Hsien. *Content Analysis of the Coverage of Chinese Mass Movements by Three Newspapers: The* New York Times, *the* Wall Street Journal *and the* Kansas City Times. Dissertation. Central Missouri State University, 1988.

Lin, Weiran. *An Abortive Chinese Enlightenment: The Cultural Revolution and Class Theory.* Dissertation. University of Wisconsin-Madison, 1996.

Lipman, Jonathan N., and Stevan Harrell, eds. *Violence in China: Essays in Culture and Counterculture.* Albany: State University of New York Press, 1990.

Liu, Alan P. "Mass Campaign and Political Development in China." *Current Scene* 11.8 (1973): 1–9.

———. "Mass Communication and Media in China's Cultural Revolution." *Journalism Quarterly* 46.2 (1969): 314–319.

Lu, X. Y. "A Step toward Understanding Popular Violence in China's Cultural Revolution." *Pacific Affairs* 67.4 (1994–1995): 533–563.

Su, Yang. *Collective Killings in Rural China during the Cultural Revolution.* New York: Cambridge University Press, 2011.

Walder, Andrew G. "Collective Behavior Revisited: Ideology and Politics in the Chinese Cultural Revolution." *Rationality and Society* 6.3 (1994): 400–421.

Walder, Andrew G., and Yang Su. "The Cultural Revolution in the Countryside: Scope, Timing and Human Impact." *China Quarterly* 173 (2003): 74–99.

Wang, Hsuehwen. "A Study of Big-Character Poster." *Issues & Studies* 12.4 (1976): 1–11.

Wang, Youqin. "Student Attacks against Teachers: The Revolution of 1966." *Issues & Studies* 37.2 (2001): 29–79.

White, Lynn T. *Policies of Chaos: The Organizational Causes of Violence in China's Cultural Revolution.* Princeton, N.J.: Princeton University Press, 1989.

Yu, Hen Mao. *Fishy Winds and Bloody Rains: The Struggle between "Rebels" and "Power Holders" in the Chinese Communist Camp.* Taipei: World Anti-Communist League, China Chapter, 1970.

Chinese Language

Chen, Jide 陳冀德. *Sheng feng qi shi: "wen ge" di yi wen yi kan wu "Zhao xia" zhu bian hui yi lu* 生逢其時: "文革"第一文藝刊物"朝霞"主編回憶錄. Hong Kong: 時代國際出版有限公司, 2008.

Chen, Yinan 陈益南. *Qing chun wu hen: yi ge zao fan pai gong ren de shi nian wen ge* 青春无痕: 一个造反派工人的十年文革. Hong Kong: 中文大学出版社, 2006.

Di, Jiu 地久; and Zhiwu 致武. *Xue yu huo de jiao xun: wen ge zhong da wu dou can an ji shi* 血与火的教训: 文革重大武斗惨案纪实. Wulumuqi: 新疆大学出版社, 1993.

Gao, Shuhua 高樹華; and Cheng, Tiejun 程鐵軍. *Nei Meng wen ge feng lei: yi wei zao fan pai ling xiu de kou shu shi* 內蒙文革風雷: 一位造反派領袖的口述史. Carle Place, N.Y.: 明鏡出版社, 2007.

Gu, Xunzhong 顾训中. "'Wen ge' feng yun ren wu de zai ren shi—Xu Jingxian ge an jie du" "文革"风云人物的再认识—徐景贤个案解读. 当代中国研究 (2008.4): 82–101.

He, Shu 何蜀. *Wei Mao zhu xi er zhan: wen ge Chongqing da wu dou shi lu* 為毛主席而戰: 文革重慶大武鬥實錄. Hong Kong: 三聯書店(香港)有限公司, 2010.

Hua, Linshan 华林山. "Wen ge qi jian qun zhong xing dui li pai xi cheng yin" 文革期间群众性对立派系成因. 二十一世纪 (1995.10): 49–60.

———. "Zheng zhi po hai yu zao fan yun dong" 政治迫害与造反运动. 二十一世纪 (1996.8): 46–53.

Li, Musen 李木森; and He, Shu 何蜀. *Wo shi zen yang cheng wei zao fan pai* 我是怎样成为造反派. Chongqing: 自印本, 2006.

Li, Yuejun 李月军. "Duan zao ji qing de mu ou—lun 'Hong wei bing'de zheng zhi she hui hua" 锻造激情的木偶—论"红卫兵"的政治社会化. 当代中国研究 (2005.4): 77–88.

Lin, Qishan 林启山. "'Wen ge' shi qi Hunan sheng Shaoyang xian 'Hei sha feng' shi jian shi mo" "文革"时期湖南省邵阳县"黑杀风"事件始末. 当代中国研究 (2009.3): 55–86.

Liu, Guokai 劉國凱. *Guangzhou hong qi pai de xing wang* 廣州紅旗派的興亡. Hong Kong: 博大出版社, 2006.

Nie, Yuanzi 聂元梓. *Nie Yuanzi hui yi lu* 聂元梓回忆录. Hong Kong: 时代国际出版有限公司, 2004.

Shen, Fuxiang 沈福祥. *Zheng rong sui yue: shou bu gong ren zao fan pai hui yi lu* 崢嶸歲月: 首部工人造反派回憶錄. Hong Kong: 時代國際出版有限公司, 2010.

Song, Yongyi 宋永毅. "'Wen ge' zhong de bao li yu da tu sha" "文革"中的暴力与大屠杀. 当代中国研究 (2002.3): 143–151.

———, ed. *Wen ge da tu sha* 文革大屠殺. Hong Kong: 開放雜誌社, 2002.

Su, Yang 苏阳. "'Wen ge' zhong de ji ti tu sha: San sheng yan jiu" "文革"中的集体屠杀: 三省研究. 当代中国研究 (2006.3): 117–140.

Tan, Hecheng 譚合成. *Xue de shen hua: gong yuan 1967 nian Hunan Daoxian wen ge da tu sha ji shi* 血的神話: 公元1967年湖南道縣文革大屠殺記實. Hong Kong: 天行健出版社, 2010.

Tong, Xiaoxi 童小溪. *Ji duan nian dai de gong min zheng zhi: qun zhong de wen hua da ge ming shi* 極端年代的公民政治: 群眾的文化大革命史. Hong Kong: 中國文化傳播出版社, 2011.

Wang, Youqin 王友琴. "Liu shi san ming shou nan zhe he Beijing da xue wen ge" 六十三名受难者和北京大学文革. 二十一世纪 (2006.2): 42–55.

———. *Wen ge shou nan zhe: guan yu po hai, jian jin yu sha lu de xun fang shi lu* 文革受難者: 關於迫害, 監禁與殺戮的尋訪實錄. Hong Kong: 開放雜誌社, 2004.

———. "Wenge dou zheng hui, 1–2" 文革斗争会, 1–2. 领导者 (2013.3): 118–126; (2013.4): 118–126.

Xu, Jingxian 徐景賢. *Shi ian yi meng: qian Shanghai Shi wei shu ji Xu Jingxian wen ge hui yi lu* 十年一夢: 前上海市委書記徐景賢文革回憶錄. Hong Kong: 時代國際出版有限公司, 2004.

Xu, Youyu 徐友渔. "Zai shuo wen ge zhong de zao fan pai: yu Hua Linshan shang que" 再说文革中的造反派: 与华林山商榷. 二十一世纪 (1996.2): 122–128.

Yang, Xiaokai 杨小凯. "Ge ming shou xian si le, cai neng wan sui: bu ying wei zao fan pai fan an" 革命首先死了, 才能万岁: 不应为造反派翻案. 中国之春 (1990.11): 55–57.

———. "Wen ge de zheng zhi po hai yu fan po hai yun dong" 文革的政治迫害与反迫害运动. 中国之春 (1993.5): 48–50.

———. "Wen ge zhong de zheng zhi po hai he fan zheng zhi po hai" 文革中的政治迫害和反政治迫害. 北京之春 (1996.9): 27–29.

Yin, Hongbiao 印红标. "Pi pan zi chan jie ji fan dong lu xian: zao fan yun dong de xing qi" 批判资产阶级反动路线: 造反运动的兴起. 二十一世纪 (1995.10): 61–68.

Zheng, Guanglu 鄭光路. *Wen ge wu dou: wen hua da ge ming shi qi Zhongguo she hui zhi te shu nei zhan* 文革武斗: 文化大革命時期中國社會之特殊內戰. Paramus, N.J.: 美國海馬圖書出版公司, 2006.

Zhou, Lunzuo 周倫佐. *"Wen ge" zao fan pai zhen xiang* "文革"造反派真相. Hong Kong: 田園書屋, 2006.

Zhou, Ziren 周孜仁. *Hong wei bing xiao bao zhu bian zi shu: Zhongguo wen ge si shi nian ji* 紅衛兵小報主編自述: 中國文革四十年祭. Euless, Tex.: 溪流出版社, 2006.

HETERODOX THOUGHTS

English Language

Burton, Barry. "The Cultural Revolution's Ultra-Left Conspiracy: The 'May 16 Group.'" *Asian Survey* 11.11 (1971): 1029–1053.

Chan, Anita, Stanley Rosen, and Jonathan Unger, eds. *On Socialist Democracy and the Chinese Legal System: The Li Yizhe Debates.* Armonk, N.Y.: Sharpe, 1985.

Chen, Erjin. *China: Crossroads Socialism.* Trans. Robin Munro. London: Verso Books, 1984.

Crevel, Maghiel van. "Underground Poetry in the 1960s and 1970s." *Modern Chinese Literature* 9.2 (1996): 169–219.

Guangming, Ribao, comp. *Paragons of Chinese Courage: Ten Who Braved the Storm of the Cultural Revolution.* Gosford, N.S.W.: Lotus Publishing House, 1989.

Heilmann, S. "The Suppression of the April 5th Movement and the Persecution of Counterrevolutionaries in 1976." *Issues & Studies* 30.1 (1994): 37–64.

Lee, Leo Ou-fan. *Dissident Trends since the Cultural Revolution: A Report and an Evaluation.* N.p.: n.p., 1979.

Leijonhufvud, Göran. *Going against the Tide: On Dissent and Big Character Posters in China.* Scandinavian Institute of Asian Studies Monograph Series 58. London: Curzon Press, 1990.

Li, Lu. *Moving the Mountain: My Life in China from the Cultural Revolution to Tian'anmen Square.* London: Macmillan, 1990. London: Pan, 1990.

Rosen, Stanley. "Guangzhou's Democracy Movement in Cultural Revolution Perspective." *China Quarterly* 101 (1985): 1–31.

Song, Yongyi. "A Glance at the Underground Reading Movement during the Cultural Revolution." *Journal of Contemporary China* (May 2007): 325–333.

Song, Yongyi, and Zehao Zhou, eds. and trans. *Heterodox Thoughts during the Cultural Revolution.* Part 1. Armonk, N.Y.: Sharpe, 2001.

———, eds. and trans. *Heterodox Thoughts during the Cultural Revolution.* Part 2. Armonk, N.Y.: Sharpe, 2001.

Starr, John Bryan. "Revolution in Retrospect: The Paris Commune through Chinese Eyes." *China Quarterly* 49 (1972): 106–125.

Unger, Jonathan. "Whither China? Yang Xiguang, Red Capitalists, and the Social Turmoil of the Cultural Revolution." *Modern China* 17.1 (1991): 3–37.

Van Ginekan, Jaap. "The 1967 'Plot of the May 16 Movement.'" *Journal of Contemporary China* 2.3 (1972): 237–254.

Williams, James Harley. *Fang Lizhi's Big Bang: Science and Politics in Mao's China.* Dissertation. University of California, Berkeley, 1994.

Woody, Peter R. *Opposition and Dissent in Contemporary China.* Stanford, Calif.: Hoover Institution Press, 1977.

Wu, Yiching. *The Cultural Revolution at the Margin: Chinese Socialism in Crisis.* Cambridge, Mass.: Harvard University Press, 2014.

Yang, Xiguang. *Captive Spirits: Prisoners of the Cultural Revolution.* Hong Kong: Oxford University Press, 1997.

Chinese Language

Buping 不平. *Tiao zhan Mao Zedong* 挑战毛泽东. Middletown, N.J.: 成家出版社, 2003.

Chen, Zhihong 陳志宏. *A Study on Today's Poems and Poets* 今天詩群研究. Thesis (M.Phil.). Hong Kong: Hong Kong Baptist University, 1998.

Ding, Qun, ed.丁群. *Lu Xiulan yu zhong yi wen* 陆兰秀狱中遗文. Middletown, N.J.: 成家出版社, 2000.

Ding, Xueliang 丁学良. *Ge ming yu fan ge ming zui yi: cong wen ge dao Chongqing mo shi* 革命与反革命追忆：从文革到重庆模式. Taipei: 联经出版事业股份有限公司, 2013.

Ding, Dong 丁東. *Yue du wen ge* 閱讀文革. Hong Kong: 時代國際出版有限公司, 2011.

Ding, Dong 丁东; and Xie, Yong 谢泳. "Zhongguo 'wen ge' min jian si xiang gai guan" 中国"文革"民间思想概观. 中国研究 (1996.8): 38–42.

Gu, Zhun 顾准. *Gu Zhun ri ji* 顾准日记. Beijing: 经济日报出版社, 1997.

———. *Gu Zhun wen gao* 顾准文稿. Beijing: 中国青年出版社, 2002.

Guo, Yukuan 郭宇宽. *Wang Peiying ping zhuan* 王佩英评传. Beijing: 张可心印, 2011.

Hu, Anning 胡安宁. "Wang Shenyou yu wo" 王申酉与我. 探索 (1988.6): 75–83.

Hu, Ping 胡平. *Cang liang de mou zi* 苍凉的眸子. Beijing: 十月文艺出版社, 1989.

Hua po ye mu de yun xing 划破夜幕的陨星. Beijing: 群众出版社, 1981.

Lei, Yi 雷颐; and Shi, Yun 石云. "Kuang re, huan mie, pi pan: 'wen ge' 10 nian qing nian si chao chu tan" 狂热，幻灭，批判："文革"10年青年思潮初探. 青年研究 (1991.2): 30–35.

Li Yizhe shi jian: wen ge zhong yi chang zi xia er shang de min zhu yu fa zhi de su qiu 李一哲事件：文革中一场自下而上的民主与法制的诉求. Hong Kong: 中国焦点出版社, 2010.

Liu, Wenzhong 劉文忠. *Fan wen ge di yi ren ji qi tong an fan* 反文革第一人及其同案犯. Marco: 崇適文化出版拓展有限公司, 2008.

Lu, Lian 鲁礼安. *Yang tian chang xiao: yi ge dan jian shi yi nian de hong wei bing yu zhong yang tian chang xiao* 仰天长啸: 一个单监十一年的红卫兵狱中吁天录. Hong Kong: 中文大学出版社, 2005.

Lu, Shuning 卢叔宁. *Jie hui can bian* 劫灰残编. Beijing: 中国文联出版社, 2000.

Turner, Mia 米雅; and Hsiao-han 曉涵. *789 ji zhong ying* 789集中營. Brampton, Ont.: 明鏡出版社, 1998.

Shen, Zhanyun 沈展云. *Hui pi shu, huang pi shu* 灰皮书, 黄皮书. Guangzhou: 花城出版社, 2007.

Song, Yongyi 宋永毅. "Cong Mao Zedong de yong hu zhe dao ta de fan dui pai—'Wen ge' zhong nian qing yi dai jue xing de xin lu li cheng" 从毛泽东的拥护者到他的反对派— "文革"中年青一代觉醒的心路历程. 当代中国研究 (2005.4): 89–107.

———. "Pai bie, shi shi yu wen ge yi duan si chao" 派别, 史实与文革异端思潮. Hong Kong: 二十一世纪 (1998.12): 119–124.

———. "Wen ge zhong de huang pi shu he hui pi shu" 文革中的黄皮书和灰皮书. 二十一世纪 (1997.8): 59–64.

———. "Wen hua da ge ming zhong de yi duan si chao" 文化大革命中的异端思潮. 二十一世纪 (1996.8): 54–68.

Song, Yongyi 宋永毅; and Sun, Dajin 孙大进. *Wen hua da ge ming he ta de yi duan si chao* 文化大革命和它的异端思潮. Hong Kong: 田园书屋, 1997.

Tong, Huaizhou, ed. 童怀周 编. *Bing chen qing ming jian wen lu* 丙辰清明见闻录. Beijing: 工人出版社, 1979.

———, ed. *Tiananmen shi chao* 天安门诗抄. Beijing: 人民文学出版社, 1978.

Wang, Junsheng 王军胜. *Wen ge chen si lu: shi nian wen ge xin lu li cheng ou xin ji zai* 文革沉思录: 十年文革心路历程呕心记载. Shanghai: 自印本, 2005.

Wang, Shenyou 王申酉. *Wang Shenyou wen ji* 王申酉文集. Taipei: 高文出版社, 2002.

Xu, Xiao 徐晓. *Min jian shu xin: Zhongguo min jian si xiang shi lu* 民间书信: 中国民间思想实录. Hefei: 安徽文艺出版社, 2000.

Xu, Youyu 徐友渔. "Wen ge zhong de yi duan si chao he hong wei bing si xiang zhuan xiang" 文革中的异端思潮和红卫兵思想转向. 二十一世纪 (1996.10): 52–65.

Yang, Jian 杨健. *Wen hua da ge ming zhong de di xia wen xue* 文化大革命中的地下文学. Beijing: 朝华出版社, 1993.

Yang, Xiguang 杨曦光. *Niu gui she shen lu: wen ge qiu jin zhong de jing ling* 牛鬼蛇神录: 文革囚禁中的精灵. Hong Kong: 牛津大学出版社, 1994.

Yin, Hongbiao 印紅標. *Shi zong zhe de zu ji: wen hua da ge ming qi jian de qing nian si chao* 失蹤者的足跡: 文化大革命期間的青年思潮. Hong Kong: 中文大學出版社, 2009.

———. "Wen ge hou xu jie duan de min jian si chao" 文革后续阶段的民间思潮. Hong Kong: 二十一世纪 (2010.2): 40–48.

Yu, Luojing, ed. 遇罗锦. *Yu Luoke yu "Zhong xue wen ge bao"* 遇罗克与 "中学文革报." Hong Kong: 晨钟书局, 2013.

Yu, Luowen 遇罗文. *Wo jia* 我家. Beijing: 中国社会科学出版社, 2000.

Yu, Xiguang, ed. 余习广编. *Wei bei wei gan wang you guo: wen hua da ge ming shang shu ji* 位卑未敢亡忧国: 文化大革命上书集. Changsha: 湖南人民出版社, 1989.

Zheng, Yi 郑义. *Li shi de yi bu fen: yong yuan ji bu chu de shi yi feng xin* 历史的一部分:　永远　寄不出的十一封信.　Taipei: 万象图书股份有限公司, 1993.

Zhou, Quanying 周泉缨. *Wen hua da ge ming shi li shi de shi cuo: dui Mao Zedong zhu xi gong kai dian ming ping pan wo de hui ying* 文化大革命是历史的试错:　对毛泽东主席公开点名评判我的回应. Hong Kong: 银河出版社, 2006.

Zhu, Xueqin 朱学勤. *Si xiang shi shang de shi zhong zhe* 思想史上的失踪者. Changchun: 长春出版社, 1999.

THE ARMY'S PARTICIPATION

English Language

"Army Rule: Part I: Inner Party Relations." *China News Analysis*, 10 May 1968, 1–7.

"Army Rule: Part II: Personnel Changes." *China News Analysis*, 17 May 1968, 1–7.

"Army Rule: Part III: Soldiers in the Maze." *China News Analysis*, 31 May 1968, 1–7.

"Army Rule: Part IV: In Factories." *China News Analysis*, 7 June 1968, 1–7.

"Army Rule: Part V: In the Villages." *China News Analysis*, 14 June 1968, 1–7.

"Army Rule: Part VI: In Schools." *China News Analysis*, 5 July 1968, 1–7.

Bullard, Monte R. *China's Political Military Evolution: The Party and the Military in the People's Republic of China, 1960–1984*. Boulder, Colo.: Westview, 1985.

Chang, Parris H. "Regional Military Power: The Aftermath of the Cultural Revolution." *Asian Survey* 12.12 (1972): 999–1013.

Chien, Yu-shen. *China's Fading Revolution: Army Dissent and Military Divisions, 1967–68.* Hong Kong: Center of Contemporary Chinese Studies, 1969.

Chiu, S. M. "China's Military Posture." *Current History* 53.313 (1967): 155–160.

Chu, Wenlin. *Personnel Changes in the Military Regions and Districts before and after the Cultural Revolution.* Taipei: Institute of International Relations, 1971.

"Decline in the Prestige of the PLA." *China News Analysis,* 16 June 1967, 1–7.

Den, Hitoki. *The Role of the PLA in the Cultural Revolution, 1966–1967.* Thesis. Cornell University, 1979.

Desphande, G. P. "The PLA and the Cultural Revolution." *China Report* 3.3 (1967): 12–16.

Domes, Jurgen. "The Cultural Revolution and the Army." *Asian Survey* 8 (1968): 349–363.

———. "Generals and Red Guards: The Role of Huang Yung-sheng and the Canton Military Area Command in the Kuangtung Cultural Revolution." *Asia Quarterly* (1971): 3–31, 123–259.

———. "The Role of the Military in the Formation of Revolutionary Committees, 1967–68." *China Quarterly* 44 (1970): 112–145.

Dreyer, June. "China's Minority Nationalities in the Cultural Revolution." *China Quarterly* 35 (1968): 96–109.

Fetov, V. "The Army: A Reliable Supporter of Mao." *Reprints from the Soviet Press,* 22 August 1969, 15–25.

Fraser, Angus M. *The Changing Role of the PLA under the Impact of the Cultural Revolution.* Arlington, Va.: Institute for Defense Analyses, International and Social Studies Division, 1969.

Gittings, John. "The Chinese Army's Role in the Cultural Revolution." *Pacific Affairs* 39.3–4 (1966/67): 269–289.

———. "The Cultural Revolution and the Chinese Army: A Study in Escalation." *World Today,* 23 April 1967, 166–176.

———. "Reversing the PLA Verdicts." *Far Eastern Economic Review,* 25 July 1968, 191–193.

Jencks, Harlan W. *The Politics of Chinese Military Development, 1945–1977.* Dissertation. University of Washington at Seattle, 1978. 2 vols.

Joffe, Ellis. "The Chinese Army after the Cultural Revolution: The Effects of Intervention." *China Quarterly* 55 (1973): 450–477.

———. "The Chinese Army in the Cultural Revolution: The Politics of Intervention." *Current Scene* 8.18 (1970): 1–25.

———. *The PLA in Politics and Politics in the PLA, 1965–1966.* New York: Columbia University, 1966.

Johnson, Chalmers. "Lin Piao's Army and Its Role in Chinese Society: Part I and II." *Current Scene* 4.13–14 (1966): 1–11.

Kau, Michael Y. M. *The People's Liberation Army and China's Nation-Building.* White Plains, N.Y.: International Arts and Sciences Press, 1973.

Lee, Luke Wen-yuen. *Role of the Military in Mainland China's Power Struggle: 1966–1969.* Dissertation. University of Idaho, 1975.

Liu, Alan P. L. "The 'Gang of Four' and the Chinese People's Liberation Army." *Asian Survey* 19.9 (1979): 817–837.

Marks, Paul C. "Two Steps Forward, One Step Backward: The Place of the Cultural Revolution in the Modernization of the PLA." *Issues & Studies* 25.2 (1989): 75–94.

"Military Rule." *China News Analysis*, 14 April 1967, 1–7.

Munthe-Kaas, Harald. "Problems for the PLA." *Far Eastern Economic Review*, 5 October 1967, 39–43.

Nelson, Harvey W. *The Chinese Military System: An Organizational Study of the Chinese People's Liberation Army.* Boulder, Colo.: Westview, 1977.

———. "Military Bureaucracy in the Cultural Revolution." *Asian Survey* 14.4 (1974): 327–395.

———. "Military Forces in the Cultural Revolution." *China Quarterly* 51 (1972): 444–474.

Ockman, Howard. *Bureaucratic Dynamics of Army Intervention in the Chinese Cultural Revolution.* Dissertation. Harvard University, 1973.

Pappas, Nicholas John. *Ideology and the Chinese People's Liberation Army in the Cultural Revolution.* Thesis. University of Virginia, 1970.

Parish, William L., Jr. "Factions in Chinese Military Politics." *China Quarterly* 56 (1973): 667–699.

"PLA Soldiers in Politics." *China News Analysis*, 4 April 1969, 1–7.

Powell, Ralph L. "The Increasing Power of Lin Piao and the Party-Soldiers in 1956–1966." *China Quarterly* 34 (1968): 38–65.

———. "The Party, the Government and the Gun." *Asian Survey* 10.6 (1970): 441–471.

———. "The Power of the Chinese Military." *Current History* 59.349 (1970): 129–133, 175–178.

Powell, Ralph L., and Chong-kun Yoon. "Public Security and the PLA." *Asian Survey* 12.12 (1972): 1082–1100.

Scobell, Andrew. *China's Use of Military Force: Beyond the Great Wall and the Long March.* Cambridge: Cambridge University Press, 2003.

Sims, Stephen A. "The New Role of the Military." *Problems of Communism* 18.6 (1969): 26–32.

Tao, Lung-sheng. *Civil-military Relations in China: Lin Piao and the PLA, 1959–1966.* Dissertation. University of Hawaii, Honolulu, 1971.

Vyas, Jagdishchandra I. *The Role of People's Liberation Army in Present Cultural Revolution in China.* Thesis. Utah State University, 1968.

Wang, James C. F. *The People's Liberation Army in Communist China's Political Development: A Contingency Analysis of the Military's Perception and Verbal Symbolization during the Cultural Revolution.* Dissertation. University of Hawaii, 1971.

———. "The Political Role of the People's Liberation Army as Perceived by the Chinese Communist Press in the Cultural Revolution." *Issues & Studies* 10.8 (1974): 57–71.

Whiting, Kenneth R. "The Role of the Chinese People's Liberation Army in the Last Decade." *Air University Review* 25.6 (1974): 2–24.

Whitson, William W., and Chen-hsia Huang. *The Chinese High Command: A History of Military Politics, 1921–71.* New York: Praeger, 1973.

———. "The Concept of Military Generation: The Chinese Communist Case." *Asian Survey* 13.11 (1968): 921–947.

———. "The Field Army in Chinese Communist Military Politics." *China Quarterly* 37 (1969): 1–30.

———. *The Political Dynamics of the Chinese Communist Military Elite, Part II: The Role of the Military Elite in the Cultural Revolution (1966–1968).* Taipei: n.p., 1967.

———, ed. *The Military and Political Power in China in the 1970s.* New York: Praeger, 1972.

Wilson, D. C. "The Role of the People's Liberation Army in the Cultural Revolution." *Papers on Far Eastern History* 3 (1971): 27–59.

Yuan, Albert S. *The Role of the People's Liberation Army in Early Phases of the Great Proletarian Cultural Revolution.* Thesis. Utah State University, 1972.

Zhu, Fang. *Party-Army Relations in Maoist China, 1949–1976.* Dissertation. Columbia University, 1994.

Chinese Language

Chen, Zaidao 陈再道. *Hao jie zhong de yi mu: Wuhan qi er ling shi jian qin li ji* 浩劫中的一幕: 武汉七二零事件亲历记. Beijing: 解放军出版社, 1989.

Ding, Kaiwen 丁凯文. *Jie fang jun yu wen hua da ge ming* 解放军與文化大革命. New York: 明镜出版社, 2013.

Ding, Sheng 丁盛; Jin, Guang 金光; and Yu, Ruxin 余汝信. *Luo nan ying xiong: Ding Sheng Jiang jun hui yi lu* 落难英雄: 丁盛将军回忆录. Hong Kong: 星克尔出版有限公司, 2009.

Ding, Shu 丁抒. "Mao Zedong 'wen ge' chu qi zai jun nei de bu shu yu Ye Jianying de jue qi" 毛泽东"文革"初期在军内的部署与叶剑英的崛起. 当代中国研究 (2006.3): 56–74.

Dong, Baocun 董保存. *Yang Yu Fu shi jian zhen xiang* 杨余傅事件真相. Beijing: 解放军出版社, 1988.

He, Shu 何蜀. "'Wen ge' zhong de 'Jiu jun nei yi xiao chuo' wen ti bian xi" "文革"中的 "揪军内一小撮"问题辨析. 当代中国研究 (2004.1): 145–160.

Huang, Yao 黄瑶. *San ci da nan bu si de Luo Ruiqing da jiang* 三次大难不死的罗瑞卿大将. Beijing: 中共党史出版社, 1994.

Li, Ke 李可; and Hao, Shengzhang 郝生章. *"Wen hua da ge ming" zhong de ren min jie fang jun* "文化大革命"中的人民解放军. Beijing: 中共党史资料出版社, 1989.

Li, Zhenxiang 李振祥; and Li, Yuan 黎原. *Si shi qi jun zai Hunan "san zhi liang jun" ji shi* 四十七军在湖南"三支两军"纪实. Changsha: 自印本, 2004.

Lu, Hong 盧弘. *Jun bao nei bu xiao xi: "wen ge" qin li shi lu* 軍報內部消息: "文革"親歷實錄. Hong Kong: 時代國際出版有限公司, 2006.

Qian, Gang 钱钢. "Cong Jie fang jun bao (1956–1969) kan 'jie ji dou zheng' yi ci de chuan bo" 从解放军报(1956–1969)看"阶级斗争"一词的传播. 二十一世纪 (2003.6): 50–60.

Shen, Xiaoyun 申晓云. "Wen ge zhong qiang gan zi li mian chug e wei hui—Guangxi 'wu dou' zheng xiang" 文革中枪杆子里面出革委会—广西"武斗"真相. 当代中国研究 (2013.1): 141–182.

Tang, Shaojie 唐少杰. "Wen ge zhong jun guan de ji ti jin jian" 文革中军官的集体觐见. Hong Kong: 二十一世纪 (2013.2): 42–49.

Wu, Di 吴迪. "1967 nian Neimenggu 'zao fan pai' yu Neimenggu jun qu de chong tu—Wen ge zhong jun dui xiang xue sheng kai de di yi qiang" 1967年内蒙古"造反派"与内蒙古军区的冲突—文革中军队向学生开的第一枪. 当代中国研究 (2002.3): 152–160.

Xu, Hailiang 徐海亮. *Wuhan "qi er ling" shi jian shi lu* 武漢"七二〇"事件實錄. Hong Kong: 中國文化傳播出版社, 2010.

Yu, Ruxin, ed. 余汝信 编. *Luo Ruiqing an* 罗瑞卿案. Hong Kong: 香港新世纪出版社, 2014.

SOCIETY AND SOCIAL LIFE

English Language

Analysis of the Draft of the Revised Constitution of the Chinese Communist Regime. Taipei: World Anti-Communist League, 1971.

Andors, Phyllis. *The Unfinished Liberation of Chinese Women, 1949–1980.* Bloomington: Indiana University Press, 1983.

Andors, Stephen. *China's Industrial Revolution: Politics, Planning, and Management, 1949 to the Present.* New York: Pantheon Books, 1977.

———. *Workers and Workplaces in Revolutionary China.* White Plains, N.Y.: Sharpe, 1977.

Axilrod, Eric. *The Economic Theory of the Two Tendencies in the Cultural Revolution.* Hong Kong: Chinese University of Hong Kong, 1971.

———. *The Political Economy of the Chinese Revolution.* Hong Kong: Union Research Institute, 1972.

Baum, Richard. *Revolution and Reaction in Rural China: The Struggle between Two Roads during the Socialist Education Movement (1962–1966) and the Great Proletarian Cultural Revolution (1966–1968).* Dissertation. University of California, Berkeley, 1970.

Bettelheim, Charles. *Cultural Revolution and Industrial Organization in China: Changes in Management and the Division of Labor.* New York: Monthly Review Press, 1974.

Brosseau, Maurice. *The Cultural Revolution in Chinese Industry.* Dissertation. University of Chicago, 1982.

Bryan, Derek. "Changing Social Ethics in Contemporary China." *Political Quarterly* 45.1 (1974): 49–57.

Chan, Leslie W. *The Taching Oilfield: Maoist Model for Economic Development.* Canberra: Australian National University Press, 1974.

Chao, Jonathan. *A History of the Church in China since 1949.* Grand Rapids, Mich.: Institute of Theological Studies, 1993. 12 audio cassettes and a study guide.

Chen, Jack. *Inside the Cultural Revolution.* London: Sheldon Press, 1976.

———. *A Year in Upper Felicity: Life in a Chinese Village during the Cultural Revolution.* New York: Macmillan, 1973.

Cheng, C. K. "Two Decades of Experiment in Communization." *Journal of Asian and African Studies* 4.2 (1969): 81–105.

Cheng, Chu-yuan. *The Economy of Communist China, 1949–1969: With a Bibliography of Selected Materials on Chinese Economic Development.* Ann Arbor: University of Michigan, Center for Chinese Studies, 1971.

———. "The Effects of the Cultural Revolution on China's Machine-Building Industry." *Current Scene* 8.1 (1970): 1–15.

Chi, Wen-shun. "Sun Yeh-fang and His Revisionist Economics." *Asian Survey* 12.10 (1972): 897–900.

"China's Taching Oil Field: Eclipse of an Industrial Model." *Current Scene* 6.16 (1968): 1–10.

"Communist China Economy at Mid-year 1968: Eighteen Months of Disorder." *Current Scene* 6.12 (1968): 1–16.

Constitution of the People's Republic of China. Peking: Foreign Languages Press, 1975.

Croll, Elisabeth, ed. *Women's Movement in China: A Selection of Readings, 1949–1973.* London: Anglo-Chinese Educational Institute, 1974.

Dean, Genevieve. "China's Technological Development." *New Scientist,* 18 May 1972, 371–373.

―――. *Science and Technology in the Development of Modern China: An Annotated Bibliography.* Research Aids of the East Asian Institute. London: Mensell Information Publishing, 1974.

―――. "Science, Technology and Development: China as a Case Study." *China Quarterly* 51 (1972): 520–534.

Dernberger, Robert. "Economic Realities and China's Political Economics." *Bulletin of the Atomic Scientists* 25.2 (1969): 34–42.

―――. "Radical Ideology and Economic Development in China: The Cultural Revolution and Its Impact on the Economy." *Asian Survey* 12.12 (1972): 1048–1065.

Diamant, Neil Jeffrey. *Revolutionizing the Family: Politics, Love, and Divorce in Urban and Rural China, 1949–1968.* Berkeley: University of California Press, 2000.

Diao, Richard K. "The Impact of the Cultural Revolution on China's Economic Elite." *China Quarterly* 42 (1970): 65–87.

Dittmer, Lowell. *Ethics and Rhetoric of the Chinese Cultural Revolution.* Berkeley: Center for Chinese Studies, Institute of East Asian Studies, University of California, 1981.

Dixon, John. *Chinese Welfare System 1949–1979.* New York: Praeger, 1981.

Domes, Jurgen. *Socialism in the Chinese Countryside: Rural Social Policies in the People's Republic of China, 1949–1979.* London: C. Hurst & Co., 1980.

Donnithorne, Audrey. "China's Cellular Economy: Some Economic Trends since the Cultural Revolution." *China Quarterly* 52 (1972): 606–618.

―――. *China's Economic System.* New York: Praeger, 1967.

Fan, K. T. "The Ethics of Liberation: The Example of China." *Monthly Review* 25.11 (1974): 34–44.

―――. *The Making of the New Human Being in the People's Republic of China.* New York: Maud Russell, 1974.

Fan, Kuang Huan, and K. T. Fan, eds. *From the Other Side of the River: A Portrait of China Today.* New York: Doubleday, 1975.

"The Food and Population Balance: China's Modernization Dilemma." *Current Scene* 9.6 (1971): 1–7.

Frolic, B. Michael. *Mao's People: Sixteen Portraits of Life in Revolutionary China.* Cambridge, Mass.: Harvard University Press, 1980.

Funnell, Victor C. "Social Stratification." *Problems of Communism* 17.2 (1968): 14–20.

Goodstadt, Leo F. *China's Search for Plenty: The Economics of Mao Tse-tung*. New York: Weatherhill, 1973.

———. "Wages in Command." *Far Eastern Economic Review*, 6 August 1970, 52–54.

Gray, Jack. "The Economics of Maoism." *Bulletin for the Atomic Scientists* 25.2 (1969): 42–51.

———. "Politics in Command: The Maoist Theory of Social Change and Economic Growth." *Political Quarterly* 45.1 (1974): 26–48.

Gurley, John G. *China's Economy and the Maoist Strategy*. New York: Monthly Review Press, 1976.

Gurley, W. "Maoist Economic Development: The New Man in the New China." *Center Magazine* (Center for Study of Democratic Institutions, Santa Barbara, Calif.) 3.3 (1970): 25–33.

Han, Dongping. *Cultural Revolution in Villages*. Thesis. University of Vermont, 1992.

Hemmel, Vibeke, and Pia Sindbjerg. *Women in Rural China: Policy towards Women before and after the Cultural Revolution*. London: Curzon Press, 1984.

Hinton, William. *Shenfan: The Continuing Revolution in a Chinese Village*. London: Secker and Warburg, 1983.

Honig, Emily. "Socialist Sex: The Cultural Revolution Revisited." *Modern China* 29.2 (2003): 143–176.

Howard, Roger. *"Grasp Revolution, Promote Production": Struggles over Socialist Construction in China, 1973–1976*. Dissertation. University of British Columbia, 1981.

Howe, Christopher. "Economic Trends and Policies." *Political Quarterly* 45.1 (1974): 12–25.

Huang, Lucy Jen. "The Role of Religion in Communist Chinese Society." *Asian Survey* 11.7 (1971): 693–708.

Hughes, T. J. "China's Economy—Retrospect and Prospect." *International Affairs* (Catham House) 46.1 (1970): 63–73.

Hung, Yuchiao. *The Effect of Cultural Revolution on Chinese Communist's Economy*. Taipei: Asian Peoples' Anti-Communist League, 1969.

"Industrial Development in China: A Return to Decentralization." *Current Scene* 6.22 (1968): 1–18.

Johnson, Kay Ann. *Women, the Family, and Peasant Revolution in China*. Chicago: University of Chicago Press, 1983.

Klein, Donald W. "Victims of the Great Proletarian Cultural Revolution." *China Quarterly* 27 (1966): 162–165.

Kuo, Leslie T. C. *Agriculture in the People's Republic of China: Structural Changes and Technical Transformation*. New York: Praeger, 1976.

Kwan, Yum K., and Gregory C. Chow. *Estimating Economic Effect of the Great Leap Forward and the Cultural Revolution in China.* Hong Kong: Hong Kong University of Science and Technology, Department of Economics, 1995.

Lan, Jiang. *A Critical Study of the May 7 Cadre School of the People's Republic of China during the Cultural Revolution, 1966–1976.* Thesis. Northern Illinois University, 1989.

Larson, Wendy. "Never So Wild: Sexing the Cultural Revolution." *Modern China* 25.4 (1999): 423–450.

Leader, Shelah Gilbert. "The Emancipation of Chinese Women." *World Politics* 24.1 (1973): 55–79.

Lee, Rensselaer W., III. "Ideology and Technical Innovation in Chinese Industry, 1949–1971." *Asian Survey* 12.8 (1972): 649–661.

Liden, David LeRoy. *The Economic Aspects of the Great Proletarian Cultural Revolution.* Thesis. University of Massachusetts, 1968.

Lockett, Martin. *Cultural Revolution and Industrial Organization in a Chinese Enterprise: The Beijing General Mill, 1966–1981.* Oxford: Oxford Center for Management Studies, Templeton College, 1985.

Loescher, Gil, with Ann Dull Loescher. *The Chinese Way: Life in the People's Republic of China.* New York: Harcourt, 1974.

Lyons, Thomas P. *Economic Integration and Planning in Maoist China.* New York: Columbia University Press, 1987.

MacDougall, Colina. "The Cultural Revolution in the Communes: Back to 1958?" *Current Scene* 7.7 (1969): 1–11.

———. "Revolution on China's Railroads." *Current Scene* 6.4 (1968): 1–16.

———. *Stranger in China.* New York: Morrow, 1973.

Meaney, Constance Squires. *Stability and the Industrial Elite in China and the Soviet Union.* Berkeley: Institute of East Asian Studies, University of California–Berkeley, Center for Chinese Studies, 1988.

Meisner, Mitchell R. *In Agriculture Learn from Dazhai Theory and Practice in Chinese Rural Development.* Dissertation. University of Chicago, 1977.

Milton, David, Nancy Milton, and Franz Schurmann, eds. *People's China: Social Experimentation, Politics, Entry onto the World Scene, 1966 through 1972.* New York: Vintage, 1974.

Oksenberg, Michel, ed. *China's Developmental Experience.* Proceedings of the Academy of Political Science 31.1. New York: Academy of Political Science, 1973.

Orleans, Leo A. "China: The Population Record." *Current Scene* 10.5 (1972): 10–19.

———. *Every Fifth Child: The Population of China.* Stanford, Calif.: Stanford University Press, 1972.

"Peking's Programs to Move Human and Material Resources to the Countryside." *Current Scene* 7.18 (1969): 1–17.

Perkins, Dwight. "Economic Growth in China and the Cultural Revolution (1960–April 1967)." *China Quarterly* 30 (1967): 33–48.

———. "Mao Tse-tung's Goals and China's Economic Performance." *Current History* 9.1 (1971): 1–13.

Powell, Ralph L. "Soldiers in the Chinese Economy." *Asian Survey* 11.8 (1971): 742–760.

Prybyla, Jan. "China's Economy: Experiments in Maoism." *Current History* 59.349 (1970): 159–180.

———. "The Economic Cost." *Problems of Communism* 17.2 (1968): 1–3.

Richman, Barry. "Ideology and Management: The Chinese Oscillate." *Columbia Journal of World Business* 6.1 (1971).

Roberson, Virginia. *Chinese Women and the Cultural Revolution: Rhetoric and Reality.* Thesis. University of Virginia, 1990.

Schran, Peter. "Institutional Continuity and Motivational Change: The Chinese Industrial Wages System, 1950–1973." *Asian Survey* 14.11 (1974): 1014–1032.

Sheridan, Mary. "The Emulation of Heroes." *China Quarterly* 33 (1968): 47–72.

Sidel, Ruth. *Revolutionary China: People, Politics, and Ping-pong.* New York: Delacorte Press, 1974.

Sidel, Victor W., and Ruth Sidel. *Serve the People: Observation on Medicine in the People's Republic of China.* Boston: Beacon Press, 1974.

Snow, Edgar. "Success or Failure? China's 70,000 Communes." *New Republic*, 26 June 1971, 19–23.

Sou, Jin-young. *The Taching Campaign and China's Rural Policy, 1964–1979.* Dissertation. University of Washington, 1980.

"Sources of Labor Discontent in China: The Worker-Peasant System." *Current Scene* 6.5 (1968): 1–28.

Tien, H. Yuan. *China's Population Struggle: Demographic Decisions of the People's Republic of China, 1949–1969.* Columbus: Ohio State University Press, 1973.

Tung, Robert. *The Unfortunate Seven Million: Understanding the Cultural Revolution.* Courrier de l'Extreme-Orient 6. Bruxelles: Centre d'étude du sud-est asiatique et de l'Extreme-Orient, 1968.

Unger, Jonathan. "Cultural Revolution Conflict in the Villages." *China Quarterly*, March 1998, 82–107.

———. "Mao's Million Amateur Technicians." *Far Eastern Economic Review*, 3 April 1971, 115–118.

Van Every, David A. *Great Uproar on the Way to Heaven: Lives from Mao's Cultural Revolution.* Thesis. Florida State University, 1993.

Veilleux, Louis. *The Paper Industry in China from 1949 to the Cultural Revolution.* Pub. Series 2. Toronto: University of Toronto-York, 1978.

Walker, Richard L. "Cultural, Political and Social Impacts of the Proletarian Cultural Revolution." *Chinese Culture* 11 (1970): 63–68.

Washenko, Steve. "Agriculture in Mainland China—1968." *Current Scene* 7.6 (1969): 1–12.

Watson, Andrew. *Living in China.* Totowa: Rowman & Littlefield, 1975.

Wehnohs, John R. "Agriculture in Mainland China—1967: Cultural Revolution versus Favorable Weather." *Current Scene* 5.21 (1967): 1–12.

Welch, Holmes. "Buddhism since the Cultural Revolution." *China Quarterly* 40 (1969): 127–136.

———. *Buddhism under Mao.* Cambridge, Mass.: Harvard University Press, 1972.

Wertheim, W. F. "Polarity and Equality in the Chinese Peoples' Communes." *Journal of Contemporary Asia* 4.1 (1974): 24–35.

"What Price Revolution: China's Economy in 1967." *Current Scene* 5.18 (1967): 1–10.

Wheelwright, Edward Lawrence, and Bruce J. McFarlane. *The Chinese Road to Socialism: Economics of the Cultural Revolution.* Harmondsworth: Penguin, 1973.

White, Gordon. "Politics and Social Status in China." *Pacific Affairs* 51.4 (1978–79): 561–584.

———. *Politics of Class and Class Origin: The Case of the Cultural Revolution.* Canberra: Australian National University, 1976.

White, Sydney D. "From 'Barefoot Doctor' to 'Village Doctor' in Tiger Springs Village: A Case Study of Rural Health Care Transformations in Socialist China." *Human Organization* 57.4 (1998): 480–491.

Whyte, Martin King. "The Tachai Brigade and Incentives for the Peasant." *Current Scene* 7.16 (1969): 1–13.

Wong, John H. G. (Heet-Ghin). *Agricultural Development and Peasant Behavior in China during the Cultural Revolution.* Dissertation. Massachusetts Instituite of Technology, 1992.

Woodward, Dennis. "Rural Campaigns: Continuity and Change in the Chinese Countryside: The Early Post-Cultural Revolution Experience (1969–1972)." *Australian Journal of Chinese Affairs* 6 (1981): 97–124.

Wright, Tim. "'Grasping Revolution and Promoting Production': The Cultural Revolution in Chinese Coal Mines." *Papers on Far Eastern History* 22 (1980): 51–92.

Wu, Yuan-li. "Economics, Ideology and the Cultural Revolution." *Asian Survey* 8.3 (1968): 223–245.

Wu, Yuanli. *Economic Prospects of Communist China and the Cultural Revolution.* Rec. 16 February 1967. Audiotape. University of Hawaii, 1967. 1 audiotape.

Xin, Fang. *Buddhism before and after the Cultural Revolution.* Thesis. Northern Illinois University, 1994.

Yu, Chieh-hua. *The Effects of Communist Cultural Revolution upon the Political and Social Life of the People in the Chinese Mainland.* Thesis. University of Manila, 1970.

Zhang, Heather, X. *Progress or Retrogression for Chinese Women? The Cultural Revolution (1966–76) Revisited.* Glasgow: Department of Government, University of Strathclyde, 1995.

Zhang, Xiaowei. *Children of the Cultural Revolution: Family Life and Political Behavior in Mao's China.* Boulder, Colo.: Westview, 2000.

Zhao, Yongchang. *China's Great Cultural Revolution and Its Communication Structure.* Thesis. University of Hawaii at Manoa, 1994.

Zhong, Xueping, Zheng Wang, and Bai Di. *Some of Us: Chinese Women Growing up in the Mao Era.* New Brunswick, N.J.: Rutgers University Press, 2001.

Zweig, David. *Agrarian Radicalism in China.* Cambridge, Mass.: Harvard University Press, 1989.

Chinese Language

Bai, Ge 白戈. *1966–1976—Zhongguo bai xing sheng huo shi lu* 1966–1976—中国百姓生活实录. Beijing: 警官教育出版社, 1996.

Jin, Chunming 金春明. *"Wen ge" shi qi guai shi guai yu* "文革"时期怪事怪语. Beijing: 求实出版社, 1989.

Jin, Dalu 金大陆. *Fei chang yu zheng chang: Shanghai "wen ge" shi qi de she hui sheng huo* 非常与正常: 上海"文革"时期的社会生活. Shanghai: 上海辞书出版社, 2011. 2 vols.

Li, Chengrui 李成瑞. "Shi nian nei luan qi jian wo guo jing ji qing kuang fen xi: jian lun zhe yi qi jian tong ji shu zi de ke kao xing" 十年内乱期间我国经济情况分析: 兼论这一期间统计数字的可靠性. 经济研究 (1984.1): 4–8.

Lin, Riqing, ed. 林日清 编. *Wen ge qi jian min jian liu chuan gui shen feng shui qu shi lu* 文革期间民间流传鬼神风水趣事录. Hong Kong: 科华图书出版公司, 1982.

Liu, Suinian 柳随年; and Wu, Qungan, eds. 吴群敢编. *"Wen hua da ge ming" shi qi de guo min jing ji* "文化大革命"时期的国民经济. Haerbin: 黑龙江人民出版社, 1986.

Liu, Xinghua 刘兴华; and Hua, Zhang 华章. *Feng kuang sui yue: wen ge ku xing shi lu* 疯狂岁月: 文革酷刑实录. Beijing: 朝华出版社, 1993.

Longzi, ed. 龙子 编. *Ji zuo xiao lei lu* 极左笑泪录. Guangzhou: 花城出版社, 1993.

Ren, Ximin 任喜民. *Wen ge xiao liao da quan* 文革笑料大全. Hong Kong: 镜报文化企业有限公司, 1993.

Tao, Dan 陶丹. "Wen ge zhong de nü hai zi" 文革中的女孩子. 女性研究 7 (1993.9): 7–8.

Xiang, Zhanji 项展骥. *Zhongguo da lu ren min sheng huo chuan zhen* 中国大陆人民生活传真. Taipei: 黎明文化事业公司, 1977.

Xu, Ben 徐贲. "'Wen ge' shi qi de wu zhi wen hua he ri chang sheng huo zhi xu" "文革"时期的物质文化和日常生活秩序. 当代中国研究 (2006.3): 141–154.

Xu, Buxun 徐步洵. *Jie zhi: wen ge shi qi Shanghai shi min de gu shi ji qi ta* 劫智: 文革時期上海市民的故事及其他. Taiperi: 秀威資訊科技股份有限公司, 2003.

Zhang, Xianglin, ed. 张湘霖编. *Huang tan sui yue qi wen lu: gong he guo dang an ji lu* 荒诞岁月奇闻录: 共和国档案记录. Taiyuan: 北岳文艺出版社, 1993.

EDUCATION AND INTELLECTUALS

English Language

Adjimamudova, B. "Tian Han, the Honest Son of China." *Far Eastern Affairs* 4 (1988): 86–97.

Alley, Rewi. *Building a Socialist Educational System in China: China's Cultural Revolution in Education.* New York: Maud Russell, 1974.

———. *China's Cultural Revolution in Education.* New York: Far East Reporter, 1974.

Andreas, Joel. *Rise of the Red Engineers: The Cultural Revolution and the Origins of China's New Class.* Stanford, Calif.: Stanford University Press, 2009.

Barlow, Tani E., and Donald M. Lowe. *Teaching China's Lost Generation: Foreign Experts in the People's Republic of China.* San Francisco: China Books & Periodicals, 1987.

Bastid, Marianne. "Economic Necessity and Political Ideals in Educational Reform during the Cultural Revolution." *China Quarterly* 42 (1970): 16–45.

Baum, Richard Dennis. *Revolution and Reaction in Rural China: The Struggle between Roads during the Socialist Education Movement (1962–1966) and the Great Proletarian Cultural Revolution (1966–1968).* Dissertation. University of California, Berkeley, 1970. Ann Arbor, Mich.: University Microfilms, 1971.

Bietz, Gray Roy. *The Politics of Educational Reform in the People's Republic of China: Revolution Destruction, 1966–1968.* Dissertation. New York University, 1972.

Blumenthal, Eileen Polley. *Models in Chinese Moral Education: Perspectives from Children's Books.* Dissertation. University of Michigan, 1976.

Bratton, Dale Lester. *The Politics of Educational Reform in the People's Republic of China, 1966–1973.* Dissertation. University of California, Berkeley, 1978.

Chai, Trong R. "The Chinese Academy of Sciences in the Cultural Revolution: A Test of the 'Red and Expert' Concept." *Journal of Politics* 43.4 (1981): 1215–1229.

Chakrabarti, Sreemati. *Mao, China's Intellectuals, and the Cultural Revolution.* New Delhi: Sanchar Publishing House, 1998.

Chan, Sylvia. *Political Assessment of Intellectuals before the Cultural Revolution.* Adelaide: University of Adelaide, 1977.

Chang, Parris H. "The Cultural Revolution and Chinese Higher Education: Change and Controversy." *Journal of General Education* 26.3 (1974): 187–194.

Chen, Theodore Hsi-en. *The Moaist Educational Revolution.* New York: Praeger, 1974.

Chu, Hun-ti. "Education in Mainland China." *Current History* 59.349 (1970): 165–182.

Chu, Wenchang. *The Case of Comrade Feng Ting and the Three Main Issues in the Great Proletarian Cultural Revolution.* Pittsburgh: Research Committee of the Committee on Asian Studies, University of Pittsburgh, 1966.

Dejthamrong, Orawan. *The Impact of the Great Proletarian Cultural Revolution on the Concept of Mental versus Manual Labor in the Educational System of Communist China.* Dissertation. Roosevelt University, 1974.

"Education Reform and Rural Settlement in Communist China." *Current Scene* 8.17 (1970): 1–7.

"Educational Reform in Rural China." *Current Scene* 7.3 (1969): 1–17.

Elzinga, Aant. *Red or Expert: Working Notes on Theory of Science Seen in the Light of the Chinese Revolutionary Experience and Chinese Science Policy Debate.* Goteborg: Institute for Theory of Science, University of Gothenburg, 1977–1978. 3 vols.

Fen, Sing-Nan. "The May 7 Cadre Schools in the People's Republic of China: 1968–1976." *Administration and Society* 18.1 (1986): 29–43.

Fisher, Tom. "Wu Han, the Cultural Revolution, and the Biography of Zhu Yuanzhang: An Introduction." *Ming Studies* 11 (1980): 33–43.

Fraser, Stewart E. *China—the Cultural Revolution, Its Aftermath and Effects on Education and Society: A Select and Partially Annotated Bibliography.* London: University of London Institute of Education, 1972.

———. *Chinese Education and Society: A Bibliographic Guide.* White Plains, N.Y.: International Arts and Sciences Press, 1972.

Fraser, Stewart E., and John N. Hawkins. "Chinese Education: Revolution and Development." *Phi Delta Kappan*, April 1972, 487–500.

Friesen, Todd K. *Revolution in Education: Radical Reform in China's Universities, 1969–1976.* Thesis. University of Virginia, 1992.

Glassman, Joel. "Obstacles to Policy Implementation in Communist China: The Struggle for Educational Reform." *Asia Quarterly* 1 (1979): 3–26.

Goldman, Merle. *China's Intellectuals: Advice and Dissent.* Cambridge, Mass.: Harvard University Press, 1981.

Gregory, Peter B. *China: Education since the Cultural Revolution: A Selected, Partially Annotated Bibliography of English Translations.* San Francisco: Evaluation and Research Analysts, 1972. 1 vol.

Hamrin, Carol Lee, and Timothy Cheek, eds. *China's Establishment Intellectuals.* Armonk, N.Y.: Sharpe, 1986.

Han, Dongping. *The Unknown Cultural Revolution: Educational Reforms and Their Impact on China's Rural Development.* New York: Garland Publishing International, 2000.

———. "Impact of the Cultural Revolution on Rural Education and Economic Development: The Case of Jimo County." *Modern China* 27.1 (2001): 59–91.

Hannum, Emily, and Xie Yu. "Trends in Educational Gender Inequality in China: 1949–1985." *Research in Social Stratification and Mobility* 13 (1994): 73–98.

Hawkings, John N. *Educational Theory in the People's Republic of China: The Report of Chien Chun-jui.* Honolulu: University of Hawaii Press, 1971.

Hayhoe, Ruth, ed. *Education and Modernization: The Chinese Experience.* New York: Pergamon Press, 1992.

Holderman, James B. *The Great Proletarian Cultural Revolution and Its Effects on Education in the People's Republic of China: Education in the People's Republic of China.* Transcript January 1981, South Carolina Library, University of South Carolina.

Hsu, Kuang-liang. *Chinese Communist Education: Cultural Revolution and Aftermath.* Dissertation. George Peabody College, 1972. Ann Arbor, Mich.: University Microfilms, 1972.

Hu, Changtu. *A New Era in Chinese Higher Education: The Impact of the Great Cultural Revolution.* New York: Columbia University, 1967.

Hung, Chang-tai. "The Red Line: Creating a Museum of the Chinese Revolution." *China Quarterly* (December 2005): 914–933.

Kan, David. *The Impact of the Cultural Revolution on Chinese Higher Education.* Kowloon: Union Research Institute, 1971.

Kao, George, ed. *Two Writers and the Cultural Revolution: Lao She and Chen Jo-hsi.* Hong Kong: Chinese University Press, 1980.

Kwong, Julia. *Chinese Education in Transition: Prelude to the Cultural Revolution.* Montreal: McGill-Queen's University Press, 1979.

————. *Cultural Revolution in China's Schools, May 1966–April 1969.* Stanford, Calif.: Hoover Institution Press, 1988.

Lipelt, Roger R. *The Great Proletarian Cultural Revolution: The Use of an Educational Group in Politics.* Thesis. Winona State College, 1970.

Liu, Liping. *Gains and Losses: Five Teachers' Perspectives on Their Cultural Revolution Educational Experiences and Current Teaching Philosophy.* Dissertation. Harvard University, 1997.

Lofstedt, Jan-Ingvar. *Chinese Education Policy: Changes and Contradictions, 1949–1979.* Stockholm: Almqvist & Wiksell International, 1980.

MacDougall, Colina. "Education in China: Bringing Up Baby." *Far Eastern Economic Review,* 30 January 1969, 194–195.

Machetzki, Rudiger. "China's Education since the Cultural Revolution." *Political Quarterly* 45.1 (1974): 59–74.

Mazur, Mary G. *A Man of His Times: Wu Han, the Historian.* Chicago: University of Chicago, 1993.

————. "Studying Wu Han: The Political Academic." *Republican China* 15.2 (1990): 17–39.

Meng, Xin, and R. G. Gregory. "The Impact of Interrupted Education on Subsequent Education Attainment: A Cost of the Chinese Cultural Revolution." *Economic Development and Cultural Change* 50.4 (2002): 935–960.

Ong, Ellen K. "Education in China since the Cultural Revolution." *Studies in Comparative Communism* 3.3–4 (1970): 158–176.

Pepper, Susanne. "Education and Political Development in Communist China." *Studies in Comparative Communism* 3.3–4 (1970): 132–157.

————. *Radicalism and Education Reform in 20th-Century China: The Search for an Ideal Development Model.* Cambridge: Cambridge University Press, 1996.

Ray, Dennis M. "'Red and Expert' and China's Cultural Revolution." *Pacific Affairs* 43 (1970): 22–33.

"Recent Developments in Chinese Education." *Current Scene* 10.7 (1972): 1–6.

Reece, Bob. "Education in China: More of the Same." *Far Eastern Economic Review,* 13 June 1968, 563–565.

Rosen, Stanley. "Chinese Education in Transition." *Current History* 82.485 (1983): 254–258, 277.

Scalapino, Robert A., ed. *Elites in the People's Republic of China.* Seattle: University of Washington Press, 1972.

Seybolt, Peter J., comp. *Revolution Education in China: Documents and Commentary.* White Plains, N.Y.: International Arts and Sciences Press, 1973.

————. *The University since the Cultural Revolution.* China Conversations. Audiocassette. Social Studies Services for National Committee on U.S.-China Relations, Inc., 1970. 1 cassette.

Sherman, James C. *Mao Tse-tung's Concept of High Education*. Dissertation. University of Denver, 1972.

Shirk, Susan Lee. *The Chinese Communist Educational System in the Cultural Revolution*. Thesis. University of California, Berkeley, 1968.

Shockro, Ellen Krosney. *The Effects of the Cultural Revolutionary Experiment on Teachers and Teaching in the People's Republic of China 1966–1973*. Dissertation. Claremont Graduate School, 1980.

Singer, Ethan, and Arthur W. Galston. "Education and Science in China." *Science*, January 1972, 15–23.

Swetz, Frank J. "Chinese Education and the Great Cultural Revolution: A Search for Relevance." *Contemporary Education* 44.3 (1973): 155–160.

Teng, Ssu-yu. *Education and Intellectual Life in China after the Cultural Revolution*. Bloomington: East Asian Studies Program, Indiana University, 1972.

Terrill, Ross. "The Siege Mentality." *Problems of Communism* 15.2 (1967): 1–10.

Thurston, Anne F. *Enemies of the People: The Ordeal of the Intellectuals in China's Great Cultural Revolution*. Cambridge, Mass.: Harvard University Press, 1988.

Tong, James Wai-keung. *Reforms in Higher Education in People's Republic of China since the Great Proletarian Cultural Revolution, 1966–1971*. Thesis. University of the Philippines, 1972.

Unger, Jonathan. *Education under Mao: Class and Competition in Canton Schools, 1960–1980*. New York: Columbia University Press, 1982.

Waller, Derek J. "China: Red or Expert?" *Political Quarterly*, April–June 1967, 122–131.

———. "Revolutionary Intellectuals or Managerial Modernizers." *Political Quarterly*, January–March 1974, 5–12.

Wan, Guofang. "The Educational Reforms in the Cultural Revolution in China: A Postmodern Critique." *Education* 122.1 (2001): 21–33.

Wang, Robert S. "Educational Reforms and Cultural Revolution: The Chinese Evaluation Process." *Asian Survey* 15 (1975): 758–774.

Yagoda, Maida Weissman. *Inter-party Conflict and Its Effect on Policies Adopted towards the Intellectuals Prior to and during the Great Proletarian Cultural Revolution in the People's Republic of China*. Dissertation. New York University, 1977.

Yin, Chih-peng. *The Cultural Revolution in Chinese Higher Education: The Mass Line*. Thesis. Columbia University, 1973. Ann Arbor, Mich.: University Microfilms, 1976.

Yin, Lu-Jun. *Against Destiny: Feng Yu-Lan and a New Hermeneutics of Confucianism*. Palo Alto, Calif.: Stanford University, 1992.

Chinese Language

Bei huai ji: hui yi san shi wei wen xue jia yi shu jia 悲怀集: 回忆三十位文学家艺术家. Beijing: 人民文学出版社, 1979.

Fan, Daren 范達人. *"Wen ge" yu bi chen fu lu: "Liang Xiao" wang shi* "文革"革御笔沉浮錄: "梁效"往事. Hong Kong: 明報出版社, 1999.

Feng, Yulan 冯友兰. *San song tang zi xu* 三松堂自序. Beijing: 三联书店, 1984.

He, Li 贺黎; and Yang, Jian, eds. 杨健 编. *Wu zui liu fang: 66 wei zhi shi fen zi wu qi gan xiao gao bai* 无罪流放: 66位知识分子五·七干校告白. Beijing: 光明日报出版社, 1998.

Huang, Weijing 黄伟经. *Chou lao jiu suan lao jiu xiang lao jiu* 臭老九酸老九香老九. Guangzhou: 花城出版社, 1993.

Ji, Xianlin 季羡林. *Niu peng za yi* 牛棚杂忆. Beijing: 华艺出版社, 2008.

Li, Yong, ed. 李永 编. *"Wen hua da ge ming" zhong de ming ren zhi yu* "文化大革命"中的名人之狱. Beijing: 中央民族学院出版社, 1993.

Li, Yong, ed. 李永 编. *"Wen hua da ge ming" zhong de ming ren zhi si* "文化大革命"中的名人之死. Beijing: 中央民族学院出版社, 1993.

Lin, Daoqun 林道群; and Wu, Zanmei, eds. 吴赞梅 编. *Zhe ye shi li shi: cong si xiang gai zao dao Wen hua ge ming 1949–1979* 这也是历史: 从思想改造到文化革命1949–1979. Hong Kong: 牛津大学出版社, 1993.

Liu, Jikun 刘济昆. *Xue luo zai Zhongguo de tu di shang: niu peng jian yu wu qi gan xiao sheng huo ji shi* 雪落在中国的土地上: 牛棚监狱五七干校生活纪实. Hong Kong: 昆仑制作公司, 1990.

Liu, Qingfeng 刘青峰. "Shi lun wen ge qian Zhongguo zhi shi fen zi dao de yong qi de lun sang" 试论文革前中国知识分子道德勇气的沦丧. 知识分子冬季号 (1990): 37–44.

Pei, Yiran 裴毅然. "Wen ge kuang tao zhong de zhi shifen zi" 文革狂涛中的知识份子. 二十一世纪 (2006.2): 65–74.

Shi, Lei 时磊; and Yang, Decai 杨德才. "Wen ge shi qi de jiao yu kuo zhan" 文革时期的教育扩展. Hong Kong: 二十一世纪 (2010.2): 49–58.

Wang, Donglin 汪东林. *Shi nian feng bao zha qi shi di zheng xie zhi ming ren shi* 十年风暴乍起时的政协知名人士. Beijing: 中国文史出版社, 1996.

Wang, Youqin 王友琴. "Cong shou nan zhe kan fan you he wen ge de guan lian: yi Beijing da xue wei li" 从受难者看反右和文革的关联: 以北京大学为例. 二十一世纪 (2007.8): 76–85.

Xie, Yong 谢泳. "1949 zhi 1976 nian jian Zhongguo zhi shi fen zi ji qi ta jie ceng zi sha xian xiang zhi po xi" 1949年至1976年间中国知识分子及其它阶层自杀现象之剖析. 当代中国研究 (2001.3): 98–124.

Yu, Guangyuan 于光远. *"Wen ge" zhong de wo* "文革"中的我. Guangzhou: 广东人民出版社, 2011.

Zhang, Ming 张鸣; and Le, Qun, cds. 乐群 编. *"Wen hua da ge ming" zhong de ming ren zhi si* "文化大革命"中的名人之思. Beijing: 中央民族学院, 1994.

Zhou, Quanhua 周全华. *"Wen hua da ge ming" zhong de "jiao yu ge ming"* "文化大革命"中的"教育革命." Guangzhou: 广东教育出版社, 1999.

Zhu, Xueqin 朱学勤. "Liu shi nian dai de jiao yu wei ji yu ba shi nian dai de yu yan po yi" 六十年代的教育危机与八十年代的语言破译. 读书 (1992.1): 18–23.

Zhuofei 濯非. *Ying zu jie ming liu zai wen ge de gu shi* 英租界名流在文革的故事. Hong Kong: 明報出版社有限公司, 2005.

ARTS AND SCIENCE

English Language

Ahn, Byung-joon. "The Politics of Peking Opera, 1962–1965." *Asian Survey* 12.12 (1972): 1066–1081.

Alt, Wayne Edward. *The Dispute Prior to the Cultural Revolution over the Propositions "Two Forms into One" and "One Divides into Two."* Thesis. Ohio State University, 1984.

Arthur, Robert David. *The Cultural Revolution in Theater.* Thesis. Duke University, 1988.

Barmé, Geremie. *In the Red: On Contemporary Chinese Culture.* New York: Columbia University Press, 1999.

Bergesen, Albert James. "A Durkhemian Theory of 'Witch-Hunts' with the Chinese Cultural Revolution of 1966–1969 as an Example." *Journal for the Scientific Study of Religion* 17.1 (1978): 19–29.

Berner, Boel. *China's Science through Visitors' Eyes.* Lund: Research Policy Program, University of Lund, 1975.

Chambers, David Wade. *Red and Expert: A Case Study of Chinese Science in the Cultural Revolution.* Victoria, Australia: Deakin University, 1984.

Chang, Man. *The People's Daily and the Red Flag Magazine during the Cultural Revolution.* Hong Kong: Union Research Institute, 1969.

Chen, Ming-May Jessie, and S. M. Mazharul Haque. *Representation of the Cultural Revolution in Chinese Films by the Fifth Generation Filmmakers: Zhang Yimou, Chen Kaige, and Tian Zhuangzhuang.* Lewiston, N.Y.: Edwin Mellen Press, 2007.

Chen, Xihe. *The Major Developments and Their Ideological Implications of Chinese Film and Film Education since the Cultural Revolution.* Dissertation. Ohio State University, 1994.

Chin, Luke Kai-hsin. *The Politics of Drama Reform in China after 1949: Elite Strategy of Resocialization.* Dissertation. New York University, 1980. Ann Arbor, Mich.: University Microfilms, 1980.

Chiu, Melissa, and Zheng Sheng Tian. *Art and China's Revolution.* New York: Asia Society in Association with Yale University Press, 2008.

Clark, Paul. *Chinese Cinema: Culture and Politics since 1949.* New York: Cambridge University Press, 1987.

———. "Film-making in China: From the Cultural Revolution to 1981." *China Quarterly* 94 (1983): 304–322.

Cohen, Joan Lebold. *The New Chinese Painting, 1949–1986.* New York: H. N. Abrams, 1987.

Cushing, Lincoln. *Chinese Posters: Art from the Great Proletarian Cultural Revolution.* San Francisco: Chronicle Books, 2007.

Dittmer, Lowell, and Chen Ruoxi. *Ethics and Rhetoric of the Chinese Cultural Revolution.* Berkeley: Center for Chinese Studies, University of California, 1981.

Elzinga, Aant. *Red or Expert: Working Notes on Theory of Science Seen in the Light of the Chinese Revolutionary Experience and Chinese Science Policy Debate.* Goteborg: Institute for Theory of Science, University of Gothenburg, 1977–1978.

Esposito, Bruce John. "The Cultural Revolution and Science Policy and Development in Mainland China." *Courrier de l'Extreme Orient* 48 (1971): 114–138.

Evans, Harriet, and Stephanie Donald. *Picturing Power in the People's Republic of China: Posters of the Cultural Revolution.* Lanham, Md.: Rowman & Littlefield, 1999.

Fan-Long, Chun Grace. *A Study of Idiomatic Piano Compositions during the Cultural Revolution in the People's Republic of China.* Thesis. University of North Texas, 1991.

Fokkema, Douwe Wessel. "Maoist Ideology and Its Exemplification in the New Peking Opera." *Current Scene* 10.8 (1972): 13–20.

Galikowski, Maria. *Art and Politics in China, 1949–1984.* Hong Kong: Chinese University Press, 1998.

Goldman, Merle. *Literary Dissent in Communist China.* Cambridge, Mass.: Harvard University Press, 1967.

He, Joe. *A Historical Study on the "Eight Revolutionary Model Operas" in China's Great Cultural Revolution.* University of Nevada, Las Vegas, 1992.

King, Richard, and Ralph C. Croizier. *Art in Turmoil: The Chinese Cultural Revolution, 1966–76.* Vancouver: University of British Columbia Press, 2010.

Kraus, Richard Curt. *Piano and Politics in China: Middle-Class Ambitions and the Struggle over Western Music.* New York: Oxford University Press, 1989.

Liao, Futing. *Virtues Reflected in Children's Picture Story Books during the Chinese Cultural Revolution.* Thesis. University of Georgia, 1985.

Lubkin, Gloria B. "Physics in China." *Physics Today,* December 1972, 23–28.

Ma, Shuhui Nettie. *The Curricular Content of Elementary Music in China between 1912 and 1982.* Dissertation. University of North Texas, 1989. Ann Arbor, Mich.: University Microfilms, 1990.

Mackerras, Colin. "Chinese Opera after the Cultural Revolution (1970–1972)." *China Quarterly* 55 (1973): 478–510.

———. *Performing Arts in Contemporary China.* London: Routledge and Kegan Paul, 1981.

Mao's Graphic Voice: Pictorial Posters from the Cultural Revolution. Madison, Wis.: Elvehjem Museum of Art, 1996.

Mehnert, Klaus. *The Cultural Revolution in Chinese Theater.* Audiocassette. Pacific Tape Library, 1978. 1 cassette.

Meserve, Walter J., and Ruth I. Meserve. "China's Persecuted Playwrights: The Theater in Communist China's Current Cultural Revolution." *Journal of Asian and African Studies* 5 (1970): 209–215.

New Archaeological Finds in China: Discoveries during the Cultural Revolution. Peking: Foreign Languages Press, 1972–1978. 2 vols.

Oldham, C. H. G. "Science Travels the Mao Road." *China after the Cultural Revolution: A Selection from Bulletin of the Atomic Scientists.* New York: Vintage, 1970. 219–228.

———. "Technology in China: Science for the Masses?" *Far Eastern Economic Review,* 16 May 1968, 353–355.

Ong, Henry. *Madame Mao's Memories: A Play.* Washington, D.C.: Three Continents Press, 1992.

Reader, Wei Jia. *Chinese Cinema after the Cultural Revolution: From Revival to a New Creative Era, 1977–1986.* Thesis. Ohio State University, 1987.

Science for the People (Organization). *China: Science Walks on Two Legs.* New York: Discus Books/Avon, 1974.

Shapiro, Judith. *Mao's War against Nature: Politics and the Environment in Revolutionary China.* Cambridge: Cambridge University Press, 2001.

Sheng, Bright. *H'un: Laceration: In Memorial 1966–1976: For Orchestra.* New York: G. Schirmer, 1995. 1 score.

Shih, Joseph Anderson. "Science and Technology in China." *Asian Survey* 12.8 (1972): 662–675.

Snow, Lois Wheeler. *China on Stage: An American Actress in the People's Republic of China.* New York: Random House, 1972.

Suttmeier, Richard P. "Science Policy Shifts, Organizational Change and China's Development." *China Quarterly* 62 (1975): 207–241.

Wei, Chunjuan Nancy, and Darryl E. Brock. *Mr. Science and Chairman Mao's Cultural Revolution: Science and Technology in Modern China.* Lanham, Md.: Lexington Books, 2013.

Wilkinson, Endymion. *The People's Comic Book: Red Women's Detachment and Other Chinese Comics.* New York: Doubleday, 1973.

Wilkinson, Endymion. *Translation of the People's Comic Book.* New York: Anchor Press, 1973.

Wivell, Charles J. *The Fate of Comedy in the Cultural Revolution.* N.p.: n.p., 1979.

Wong, Cynthia P. *The East Is Red: Musicians and Politics of the Chinese Cultural Revolution, 1966–1976.* Thesis. Florida State University, 1993.

Chinese Language

Dai, Jiafang 戴嘉枋. *Yang ban xi de feng feng yu yu: Jiang Qing, yang ban xi ji nei mu* 样板戏的风风雨雨： 江青， 样板戏及内幕. Beijing: 中华工商联合出版社, 1994.

Ding, Wang 丁望. *Zhongguo da lu xin wen jie wen hua da ge ming zi liao hui bian* 中国大陆新闻界文化大革命资料汇编. Hong Kong: 香港中文大学, 1973.

Gao, Minglu 高名潞. "Lun Mao Zedong de da zhong yi shu mo shi" 论毛泽东的大众艺术模式. 二十一世纪 (1993.12): 61–73.

Liu, Bing 刘兵. "Wen ge zhong de 'Zi ran bian zheng fa za zhi'" 文革中的"自然辩证法杂志". 二十一世纪 (1997.2): 59–64.

Qu, Jingcheng 屈敬诚; and Xu, Liangying 许良英. "Guan yu wo guo 'wen hua da ge ming' shi qi pi pan Aiyinsitan he ta de xiang dui lun yun dong de chu bu kao cha" 关于我国"文化大革命"时期批判爱因斯坦和他的相对论运动的初步考察. 自然辩证法通讯 (1985.1): 16–22.

Shi, Yonggang 师永刚; Liu, Qiongxiong 刘琼雄; and Xiao, Yifei 肖伊绯. *Ge ming yang ban xi: 1960 nian dai de hong se ge ju* 革命样板戏: 1960 年代的红色歌剧. Beijing: 中国发展出版社, 2012.

Wang, Molin 王墨林. "Mei you shen ti de xi ju: man tan yang ban xi" 没有身体的戏剧: 漫谈样板戏. 二十一世纪 (1992.2): 93–98.

Wu, Di 吴迪. "Cong yang ban xi kan 'Wen yi wei zheng zhi fu wu' de zao shen gong neng" 从样板戏看"文艺为政治服务"的造神功能. 当代中国研究 (2001.3): 87–97.

Xia, Xingzhen 夏杏珍. *1975: wen tan feng bao ji shi* 1975: 文坛风暴纪实. Beijing: 中共党史出版社, 1995.

Xu, Weixin 徐唯辛. *Li shi Zhongguo zhong sheng xiang: 1966–1976* 历史中国众生相: 1966–1976. Beijing: 自印本, 2013.

FOREIGN POLICY AND FOREIGN RELATIONS

English Language

Achminow, Herman F. "Crisis in Mao's Realm and Moscow's China Policy." *Orbis* 41.4 (1968): 1179–1192.

Adie, W. A. C. "China Returns to Africa." *Current Scene* 10.8 (1972): 1–12.

Allen, Thomas Harrell. *An Examination of the Communicative Interaction between the United States and the People's Republic of China from January 1969 to February 1972.* Dissertation. Ohio State University, 1973.

Ambroz, Oton. *Realignment of World Power: The Russo-Chinese Schism under the Impact of Mao Tse-tung's Last Revolution.* New York: R. Speller, 1972. 2 vols.

An, Tai Sung. *The Sino-Soviet Territorial Dispute.* Philadelphia: Westminster Press, 1973.

Barcata, Louis. *China in the Throes of the Cultural Revolution: An Eye Witness Report.* New York: Hart Pub. Co., 1968.

Barnds, William J., ed. *China and America: The Search for a New Relationship.* New York: New York University Press, 1977.

Barnett, Doak A. "China and U.S. Policy: A Time of Transition." *Current Scene* 13.10 (1970): 1–10.

———. *A New U.S. Policy toward China.* Washington, D.C.: Brookings Institution, 1971.

Barnett, Doak A., and Edwin O. Reischauer, eds. *The United States and China: The Next Decade.* New York: Praeger, 1970.

Barnouin, Barbara, and Changgen Yu. *Chinese Foreign Policy during the Cultural Revolution.* London: Kegan Paul International, 1998.

Biberaj, Elez. *Albania and China: A Study of an Unequal Alliance.* Boulder, Colo.: Westview, 1986.

Borisov, Oleg Borisovoch, and B. T. Koloskov. *Soviet-Chinese Relations, 1945–1970.* Bloomington: Indiana University, 1975.

Bortmes, Leroy Thomas. *China's Support for Wars of National Liberation Following the Cultural Revolution, 1969–1973*. Thesis. University of Virginia, 1980.

Buss, Claude Albert. *China: The People's Republic of China and Richard Nixon*. San Francisco: Freeman & Co., 1972.

Cantoni, Robert. *The Cultural Revolution and Chinese Foreign Policy: An Interpretation*. Cambridge, Mass.: Center for International Affairs, Harvard University, 1973.

Chen, King C., ed. *China and the Three Worlds: A Foreign Policy Reader*. White Plains, N.Y.: Sharpe, 1979.

Cohen, Jerome Alan, ed. *The Dynamics of China's Foreign Relations*. Harvard East Asian Monographs 39. Cambridge, Mass.: Harvard University, 1970.

Conference on China's Cultural Revolution Heritage and Foreign Relations. *China: A Seminar on China's Cultural Heritage and Foreign Relations*. San Francisco: Institute of Sino-American Studies, 1967.

The Cultural Revolution and China's Foreign Policy, Working Session, June 26–27, 1968: Proceedings. Brussels: Centre d'étude du sud-est asiatique et de l'Extreme Orient, 1968.

Davis, Ira Mitchell. *Soviet Response to the Cultural Revolution in China*. Thesis. University of Virginia, 1972.

Deshpande, Govind P. *China's Cultural Revolution: A View from India*. Bombay: Economic and Political Weekly, 1971.

Fitzgerald, Charles P. "Reflection on the Cultural Revolution in China." *Pacific Affairs* 41 (1968): 51–59.

Fitzgerald, Stephen. "Overseas Chinese Affairs and the Cultural Revolution." *China Quarterly* 40 (1969): 103–126.

Fokkema, Douwe Wessel. *Report from Peking: Observations of a Western Diplomat on the Cultural Revolution*. Montreal: McGill-Queen's University Press, 1972.

Garver, John W. *China's Decision for Rapprochement with the United States, 1968–1971*. Boulder, Colo.: Westview, 1973.

Gurtov, Melvin. "The Foreign Ministry and Foreign Affairs during the Cultural Revolution." *China Quarterly* 40 (1969): 65–102.

———. *The Foreign Ministry and Foreign Affairs in China's "Cultural Revolution."* Santa Monica, Calif.: RAND Corp., 1969.

Hansen, Joseph. *Maoism vs. Bolshevism: The 1965 Catastrophe in Indonesia, China's "Cultural Revolution" & the Disintegration of World Stalinism*. New York: Pathfinder Press, 2000.

Hao, Xiaoming. Time Magazine *and the Chinese Cultural Revolution, 1966–1976: A Content Analysis*. Thesis. University of Missouri–Columbia, 1990.

Hefron, Peter Oslin. *Ideology and Chinese Foreign Policy during the Eighth Central Committee, 1956–1969.* Dissertation. Fletcher School of Law and Diplomacy, Tufts University, 1976.

Hinton, Harold C. *China's Turbulent Quest: An Analysis of China's Foreign Relations since 1949.* Bloomington: Indiana University Press, 1972.

———. "Sino-Soviet Relations in the Brezhnev Era." *Current History* 61.361 (1971): 135–141, 181.

Holbo, Paul Sothe. *United States Policies toward China: From the Unequal Treaties to the Cultural Revolution.* New York: Macmillan, 1969.

Holdridge, John H. *Crossing the Divide: An Insider's Account of Normalization of US-China Relations.* Lanham, Md.: Rowman & Littlefield, 1997.

Holmes, Robert A. "China-Burma Relations since the Rift." *Asian Survey* 12.8 (1972): 686–700.

Hsu, Kwang-han. *The Role of the Word during the Great Cultural Revolution.* Hong Kong: Centre of Asian Studies, University of Hong Kong, 1971.

Ivanov, Ury. *Ten Years of My Life in the Great Cultural Revolution.* Dandenong: Dandenong College of TAFE, 1985.

Jan, George P. "The Ministry of Foreign Affairs in China since the Cultural Revolution." *Asian Survey* 17.6 (1977): 513–529.

Jensen, Daniel Delano. *Nixon's Trip to China, 1972: Three Views.* Dissertation. Illinois State University, 1982.

Kau, Michael Y. M., and Christopher J. Szymanski. *The Chinese Foreign Ministry Elite and the Cultural Revolution.* Edwardsville: Southern Illinois University, 1973.

Kim, Samuel S. "The People's Republic of China in the United Nations: A Preliminary Analysis." *World Politics* 26.3 (1974): 299–330.

Kim, Young Mun. *Chinese Foreign Policy toward the Third World in the 1970s, the Theory and Practice of the Three Worlds.* Dissertation. University of California, Riverside, 1979.

Kissinger, Henry. *The White House Years.* London: Weidenfeld, 1979.

Klein, Sidney. "The Cultural Revolution and China's Foreign Trade: A First Approximation." *Current Scene* 5.19 (1967): 1–11.

Laqueur, Walter, and Leopold Labedz, eds. *The Soviet Union and the Great Proletarian Cultural Revolution in China.* London: Information Bulletin, Ltd., 1967.

Legge, Terrence H. *Ideology, Tradition and Power in China: The Foreign Ministry in the Cultural Revolution.* Thesis. University of Guelph, 1977.

Lie, Tek Tjeng. *An Indonesian View: The Great Proletarian Cultural Revolution.* Jakarta: Lembaga Ilmu Pengetahuan Indonesia, 1970.

———. *Some Indonesian Remarks on Modern China Studies: The Great Proletarian Cultural Revolution as Seen from Djakarta.* Djakarta: Lembaga Ilmu Pengetahuan Indonesia, 1971.

Low, Alfred D. *The Sino-Soviet Dispute.* Madison, N.J.: Fairleigh Dickinson University Press, 1978.

Ma, Jisen. *The Cultural Revolution in the Foreign Ministry of China: A True Story.* Hong Kong: Chinese University Press, 2004.

Macciocchi, Maria Antonietta. *Daily Life in Revolutionary China.* New York: Monthly Review Press, 1972.

Mozingo, David P. *China's Foreign Policy and the Cultural Revolution.* International Relations of East Asia Project, Interim Report 1. Ithaca, N.Y.: Cornell University, 1970.

Nixon, Richard. *The Memoirs of Richard Nixon.* London: Sidgwick and Jackson, 1978.

Ojha, Ishwer C. *Chinese Foreign Policy in an Age of Transition: The Diplomacy of Cultural Despair.* Boston: Beacon Press, 1969.

Pan, Stephen C. Y. "China and Southeast Asia." *Current History* 57.337 (1969): 164–167, 180.

Prevas, John. *The Soviet Reaction to the Cultural Revolution in China.* Thesis. University of Maryland, College Park, 1969.

Progressive Labor Party. *The Great Proletarian Cultural Revolution and the Reversal of Workers' Power in China.* Boston: New England Free Press, n.d.

Pye, Lucian W. "Coming Dilemmas for China's Leaders." *Foreign Affairs* 44.3 (1966): 387–402.

Ravenel, Earl C., ed. *Peace with China? U.S. Decisions for Asia.* New York: Liverwright, 1971.

Robinson, Thomas W. "The Sino-Soviet Border Dispute." *American Political Science Review* 64.4 (1972): 1175–1202.

Seth, S. P. "China's Foreign Policy: Post Cultural Revolution." *Asia Quarterly* 2 (1976): 137–155.

Shaw, Brian. "China and North Vietnam: Two Revolutionary Paths, Part I and Part II." *Current Scene* 9.11 (1971): 1–12; 9.12 (1971): 1–11.

Simon, Sheldon W. "Some Aspects of China's Asian Policy in the Cultural Revolution and Its Aftermath." *Pacific Affairs* 44 (1971): 18–38.

Sutter, Robert G. *Chinese Foreign Policy after the Cultural Revolution, 1966–1977.* Boulder, Colo.: Westview, 1978.

Tretiak, Daniel. "The Chinese Cultural Revolution and Foreign Policy." *Current Scene* 8.7 (1970): 1–26.

———. *The Chinese Cultural Revolution & Foreign Policy: The Process of Conflict & Current Policy.* Waltham, Mass.: Westinghouse Electric Corp., Advanced Studies Group, 1970.

———. "Is China Preparing to 'Turnout'? Changes in Chinese Levels of Attention to the International Environment." *Asian Survey* 11.3 (1971): 219–237.

Van Ness, Peter. *Revolution and Chinese Foreign Policy: Peking's Support for Wars of National Liberation.* Berkeley: University of California Press, 1970.

Warren, Susan. *China's Voice in the United Nations.* New York: World Winds Press, 1974.

Wedeman, Andrew Hall. *The East Wind Subsides: Chinese Foreign Policy and the Origins of the Cultural Revolution.* Washington, D.C.: Washington Institute Press, 1987.

Whiting, Allen Suess. *Chinese Domestic Politics and Foreign Policy in the 1970s.* Ann Arbor: Center for Chinese Studies, University of Michigan, 1977.

Wich, Richard. *Sino-Soviet Crisis Politics: A Study of Political Change and Communication.* Cambridge, Mass.: Council on East Asian Studies, 1980.

Wishnick, Elizabeth Anne. *Ideology and Soviet Policy towards China, 1969–89.* Dissertation. Columbia University, 1992.

World Student Christian Federation. *Report of an Asian Working Party on the Rise of China.* Geneva: The Federation, 1967.

Wu, Friedrich W. Y. "From Self-Reliance to Interdependence? Developmental Strategy and Foreign Economic Policy in Post-Mao China." *Modern China* 7.4 (1981): 445–482.

Wu, Yuan-li. *As Peking Sees Us.* Stanford, Calif.: Hoover Institution Press, 1969.

Yahuda, Michael B. "Chinese Foreign Policy after 1963: The Maoist Phase." *China Quarterly* 36 (1968): 93–113.

Yu, George T. "Working on the Railroad: China and the Tanzania-Zambia Railway." *Asian Survey* 11.11 (1971): 1101–1117.

Yuan, Weiping. *A Historical Study of China's Cultural Revolution and Its Coverage by the* New York Times. Thesis. Oklahoma State University, 1989.

Zagoria, Donald S. *Vietnam Triangles: Moscow, Peking, Hanoi.* New York: Pegasus, 1967.

Zanegin, B., et al. *China and Its Cultural Revolution: A Soviet Analysis.* Washington, D.C.: Joint Publications Research Service, 1969.

Zhang, Ling. *American Images of the Chinese Cultural Revolution: A Study of Selected Periodicals.* Thesis. Western Illinois University, 1989.

Chinese Language

Bo, Weihua 卜伟华. "Wen ge zhong de wai jiao ji zuo wen ti" 文革中的外交极左问题. 二十一世纪 (2006.6): 36–45.

Cadart, Claude 高达乐; Cheng, Yingxiang, trans. 程映湘译. "Faguo shi Mao zhu yi de lei bie yu xing shuai 1966–1979" 法国式毛主义的类别与兴衰 1966–1979. 二十一世纪 (1996.10): 24–34.

Chen, Dunde 陈敦德. *Mao Zedong, Nikesong zai 1972: wo shou* 毛泽东, 尼克松在1972: 握手. Beijing: 昆仑出版社, 1996.

Cheng, Xiaonong 程晓农. "Mao Zedong xiang Sidalin xue dao le shen me?—Zhong Su 'wen hua ge ming' bi jiao ji qi qi shi" 毛泽东向斯大林学到了什么？—中苏"文化革命"的比较及其启示. 当代中国研究 (2006.3): 104–116.

Cheng, Yinghong 程映虹. *Mao zhu yi ge ming: er shi shi ji de Zhongguo yu shi jie* 毛主義革命: 二十世紀的中國與世界. Hong Kong: 田園書屋, 2008.

———. "Mao zhu yi he 'wen ge' yu Xinjiapo zuo yi yun dong jian de guan xi" 毛主义和"文革"与新加坡左翼运动间的关系. 当代中国研究 (2008.1): 105–136.

———. "Xiang shi jie shu chu ge ming—'Wen ge' zai ya fei la de ying xiang chu tan" 向世界输出革命—"文革"在亚非拉的影响初探. 当代中国研究 (2006.3): 75–103.

Du, Lan 杜兰. "Wen ge shi yi chang fan she hui yun dong" 文革是一场反社会运动. 二十一世纪 (1996.8): 28–36.

Gong, Li 宫力. *Xiao qiu da kai wai jiao xin ju mian* 小球打开外交新局面. Shenyang: 辽宁人民出版社, 1997.

He, Shu 何蜀. "Bei feng kuang de nian dai yu nong de wai guo ren—zai hua wai guo zhuan jia de 'wen ge' jing li" 被疯狂的年代愚弄的外国人—在华外国专家的"文革"经历. 当代中国研究 (2002.2): 140–160.

———. "Wen ge zhong de 'wai guo zao fan pai'" 文革中的"外国造反派." 二十一世纪 (1996.10): 43–51.

Jia, Situo 加斯托. "Mao zhu yi yu Faguo zhi shi fen zi" 毛主义与法国知识分子. 二十一世纪 (1996.8): 25–27.

Jiajia, Meiguangxing 加加美光行. "Wen hua da ge ming yu xian dai Riben" 文化大革命与现代日本. 二十一世纪 (1996.8): 15–24.

Li, Danhui 李丹慧. "1969 nian Zhong Su bian jie chong tu: yuan qi yu jie guo" 1969 年中苏边界 冲突: 缘起与结果. 当代中国史研究 (1996.3): 39–50.

Ma, Jisen 馬繼森. *Wai jiao bu wen ge ji shi* 外交部文革紀實. Hong Kong: 中文大學出版社, 2003.

Niu, Dayong 牛大勇. "Leng zhan guo ji huan jing yu wen hua da ge ming de qi yuan" 冷战国际环境与文化大革命的起源. 二十一世纪 (2000.6): 57–67.

Shi, Yun 史云. "1973 nian Jixinge fang hua yu 'Bang Zhou hui yi' feng bo" 1973年基辛格访华与"帮周会议"风波. 二十一世纪 (2006.6): 46–56.

Xu, Youyu 徐友渔. "Xi fang xue zhe dui Zhongguo wen ge de yan jiu" 西方学者对中国文革的研究. 二十一世纪 (1995.10): 79–91.

Yang, Rongjia 楊榮甲. *Gongheguo wai jiao bu mi xin: yi ge wai jiao guan zai wen ge de qin shen jing li* 共和國外交部秘辛: 一個外交官在文革的親身經歷. Hong Kong: 大山文化出版社有限公司, 2011.

CULTURAL REVOLUTION IN THE PROVINCES

English Language

Bennett, Gordon. "Military Regions and Provincial Party Secretaries: One Outcome of China's Cultural Revolution." *China Quarterly* 54 (1973): 294–307.

Brown, Kerry. *The Purge of the Inner Mongolian People's Party in the Chinese Cultural Revolution, 1967–69: A Function of Language, Power and Violence.* Folkestone, Kent: Global Oriental, 2006.

Chang, Parris H. "The Revolutionary Committee in China: Two Case Studies: Heilungkiang and Honan." *Current Scene* 6.9 (1968): 1–37.

Chen, Weixing. *Ideology and Rural Development in China, 1959–1991.* Dissertation. Northern Illinois University, 1992.

"China's Revolutionary Committees." *Current Scene* 6.21 (1968): 1–18.

Conklin, William E. *The Paris Commune and the Shanghai Commune: Theory and Practice in the Chinese Cultural Revolution.* Thesis. Bowdoin College, 1987.

The Cultural Revolution in the Provinces. Cambridge, Mass.: East Asian Research Center, Harvard University, 1971.

Dong, Guoqiang. "Factions in a Bureaucratic Setting: The Origins of Cultural Revolution Conflict in Nanjing." *China Journal* 65.65 (2011): 2–25.

Dong, Guoqiang, and Andrew G. Walder. "Nanjing's Failed 'January Revolution' of 1967: The Inner Politics of a Provincial Power Seizure." *China Quarterly* (September 2010): 675–692.

———. "Nanjing's 'Second Cultural Revolution' of 1974." *China Quarterly*, December 2012, Endicott, Stephen Lyon. *Red Earth: Revolution in a Sichuan Village.* London: I. B. Tauris, 1988.

Falkenheim, Victor C. "The Cultural Revolution in Kwangsi, Yunna and Fukien." *Asian Survey* 9 (1969): 580–597.

Feurtado, Gardel. "The Formation of Provincial Revolutionary Committees, 1966–68: Heilungkiang and Hopei." *Asian Survey* 12.12 (1972): 1014–1031.

Forster, Keith. *The Hangzhou Incident of 1975: The Impact of Factionalism on a Chinese Provincial Administration.* Dissertation. University of Adelaide, 1985.

————. *Rebellion and Factionalism in a Chinese Province: Zhejiang, 1966–1976.* Armonk, N.Y.: Sharpe, 1990.

————. "Repudiation of the Cultural Revolution in China: The Case of Zhejiang." *Pacific Affairs* 59 (1986): 5–27.

Goldstein, Melvyn C., Ben Jiao, and Tanzen Lhundrup. *On the Cultural Revolution in Tibet: The Nyemo Incident of 1969.* Berkeley: University of California Press, 2009.

Gray, Sherry. *Bombard the Headquarters: Local Politics and Citizen Participation in the Great Proletarian Cultural Revolution and the 1989 Movement in Shenyang.* Dissertation. University of Denver, 1992.

Hinton, William. *Hundred Day War: The Cultural Revolution at Tsinghua University.* New York: Monthly Review Press, 1972.

Ho, Denise Y. "Revolutionizing Antiquity: The Shanghai Cultural Bureaucracy in the Cultural Revolution, 1966–1968." *China Quarterly* (September 2011): 687–705.

Hunter, Neale. *Shanghai Journal: An Eyewitness Account of the Cultural Revolution.* New York: Praeger, 1969; Boston: Beacon Press, 1971.

Hyer, Paul V., and William Heston. "The Cultural Revolution in Inner Mongolia." *China Quarterly* 36 (1968): 114–128.

Knight, Sophia. *Window on Shanghai: Letters from China, 1965–67.* London: Andre Deutsch, 1967.

Kruze, Uldis. *Political Reconstitution of Peking Municipality: Politics and Polemics of the Cultural Revolution.* Dissertation. Indiana University, 1976.

MacKerras, Colin, and Neale Hunter. *China Observed: 1964–1967.* London: Pall Mall, 1968.

Martin, Charles Michael. *Red Guards and Political Institutions: A Study of Peking and Canton.* Dissertation. Harvard University, 1975.

McMillan, Donald Hugh. *Chinese Communist Power and Policy in Xinjiang, 1945–1977.* Boulder, Colo.: Westview, 1979.

Montaperto, Ronald N. "The Origins of 'Generational Politics': Canton 1966." *Current Scene* 8.11 (1969): 1–16.

Nee, Victor, and Don Layman. *The Cultural Revolution at Peking University.* New York: Monthly Review Press, 1969.

Oksenberg, Michel, and James Tong. "The Evolution of Central-Provincial Fiscal Relations in China, 1971–1984: The Formal System." *China Quarterly* 125 (1991): 1–32.

Perry, Elizabeth J., and Xun Li. *Proletarian Power: Shanghai in the Cultural Revolution.* Boulder, Colo.: Westview, 1997.

"Provincial Party Congresses." *China News Analysis,* 28 February 1969, 1–7.

Raddock, David Miles. *Origins of the Political Behavior of Chinese Adolescents: The Case of the Beginnings of the Cultural Revolution in Canton.* Dissertation. Columbia University, 1974. Ann Arbor, Mich.: University Microfilms, 1974.

————. *Political Behavior of Adolescents in China: The Cultural Revolution in Kwangchow.* Tucson: University of Arizona Press, 1977.

"The Revolutionary Committee and the Party in the Aftermath of the Cultural Revolution." *Current Scene* 8.8 (1970): 1–10.

"Revolutionary Committee Leadership—China's Current Provincial Authorities." *Current Scene* 6.18 (1968): 1–28.

Robinson, Thomas W. "The Wuhan Incident: Local Strife and Provincial Rebellion during the Cultural Revolution." *China Quarterly* 47 (1971): 413–438.

Sneath, David. "The Impact of the Cultural Revolution in China on the Mongolians of Inner Mongolia." *Modern Asian Studies* 28.2 (1994): 409–430.

"Stalemate in Szechwan." *Current Scene* 6.11 (1968): 1–13.

Sutton, Donald S. "Consuming Counterrevolution: The Ritual and Culture of Cannibalism in Wuxuan, Guangxi, China, May to July 1968." *Comparative Studies in Society and History* 37.1 (1995): 136–172.

Sweeney, Nancy Winston. *The Hong Kong Disturbance and the Cultural Revolution, 1967.* Thesis. Miami University, 1981.

Teiwes, Frederick C. *Provincial Leadership in China: The Cultural Revolution and Its Aftermath.* Ithaca, N.Y.: China-Japan Program, Cornell University, 1974.

Terrill, Ross. *Flowers on an Iron Tree: Five Cities of China.* Boston: Little, Brown, 1975.

Wang, Shaoguang. *Failure of Charisma: The Cultural Revolution in Wuhan.* Hong Kong: Oxford University Press, 1995.

Watson, Andrew. *The Cultural Revolution in Sian.* Adelaide, Australia: Center for Asian Studies, University of Adelaide, 1967.

White, Lynn T. "Local Autonomy in China during the Cultural Revolution: The Theoretical Uses of an Atypical Case." *American Political Science Review* 70 (1976): 479–491.

Woody, W. *The Cultural Revolution in Inner Mongolia: Extracts from an Unpublished History.* Trans. Michael Schoenhals. Stockholm: Center for Pacific Asia Studies, Stockholm University, 1993.

Zheng, Yi. *Scarlet Memorial: Tales of Cannibalism in Modern China.* Trans. T. P. Sym. Boulder, Colo.: Westview, 1996.

Chinese Language

Cheng, Chao 程超; and Wei, Haoben, eds. 魏皓奔 编. *Zhejiang "wen ge" ji shi* 浙江"文革"纪事. Hangzhou: 浙江方志" 编辑部, 1989.

Ding, Wang, ed. 丁望 编. *Beijing shi wen hua da ge ming yun dong* 北京市文化大革命运动. Hong Kong: 明报月刊社, 1970.

———, ed. *Zhong nan di qu wen hua da ge ming yun dong* 中南地区文化大革命运动. Hong Kong: 明报月刊社, 1972.

Guangxi wen ge da shi nian biao bian xie xiao zu 广西文革大事年表编写小组. *Guangxi wen ge da shi nian biao* 广西文革大事年表. Nanning: 广西人民出版社, 1990.

Haifeng 海枫. *Guangzhou di qu wen ge li cheng shu lue* 广州地区文革历程述略. Hong Kong: 友联研究所, 1971.

———. *Hai feng wen hua ge ming gai shu* 海丰文化革命概述. Hong Kong: 中报周刊, 1969.

He, Shu 何蜀. "Wen ge zhong suo wei de 'Shanghai yi yue ge ming'—Mao Zedong zhi zao de yi ge 'Wen ge yang ban'" 文革中所谓的"上海一月革命"—毛泽东制造的一个"文革样板." 当代中国研究 (2001.2): 159–168.

Li, Xun 李逊. *Da beng kui: Shanghai gong ren zao fan pai xing wang shi* 大崩溃: 上海工人造反派兴亡史. Taipei: 时报文化出版企业有限公司, 1996.

———. "Gong ren jie ji ling dao yi qie?— 'Wen ge' zhong Shanghai 'gong ren zao fan pai' ji gong ren jie ji de di wei" 工人阶级领导一切？—"文革"中上海　"工人造反派"及工人阶级的地位. 当代中国研究 (2006.2): 44–56.

Qizhi 啓之. *Nei Meng wen ge shi lu: "min zu fen lie" yu "wa su" yun dong* 内蒙文革實錄： "革民族分"裂"與與挖肅"肅運動. Hong Kong: 天行健出版社, 2010.

Shanghai "wen ge" shi liao zheng li bian zhuan xiao zu 上海"文革"史料整理编撰小组. *Shanghai "wen hua da ge ming" shi hua* 上海"文化大革命"史话. Shanghai: 内部出版, 1992. 3 vols.

Tumen 图们; and Kong, Di 孔弟. *Gong he guo zui da yuan an* 共和国最大冤案. Beijing: 法律出版社, 1993.

Wang, Shaoguang 王绍光. *Chao fan ling xiu de cuo bai: wen hua da ge ming zai Wuhan* 超凡领袖的挫败： 文化大革命在武汉. Hong Kong: 中文大学出版社, 2009.

Weise 唯色; and Zerenduoji 澤仁多吉. *Sha jie: si shi nian de ji yi jin qu, jing tou xia de Xizang wen ge* 殺劫: 四十年的記憶禁區, 鏡頭下的西藏文革. Taipei: 大塊文化出版股份有限公司, 2006.

Xiaoming 曉明. *A Painful History: Cultural Revolution in Guangxi Province* 廣西文革痛史鉤沉. Hong Kong: 新世紀出版社, 2007.

Zhong gong Guangxi Zhuang zu zi zhi qu wei yuan hui zheng dang ling dao xiao zu ban gong shi, ed. 中共广西壮族自治区委员会整党领导小组办公室 编. *Wen ge ji mi dang an: Guangxi bao gao* 文革机密档案: 广西报告. Deer Park, N.Y.: 明镜出版社, 2014.

FICTION AND MEMOIRS

English Language

Berry, Chris. "Stereotypes and Ambiguities: An Examination of the Feature Films of the Chinese Cultural Revolution." *Journal of Asian Culture* 6 (1982): 37–72.

Cao, Guanlong. *The Attic: Memoir of a Chinese Landlord's Son*. Berkeley: University of California Press, 1996.

Chang, Hsien-liang. *Grass Soup*. Boston: D. R. Godine, 1995.

Chang, Hsin-cheng. *The Little Red Book and Current Chinese Language*. Berkeley: Center for Chinese Studies, University of California, 1968.

Chang, Jung. *Wild Swans: Three Daughters of China*. London: Harper Perennial, 2004.

Chen, Da. *China's Son: Growing up in the Cultural Revolution*. Donauplex: Laurel Leaf, 2004.

Chen, Jo-hsi. *The Execution of Mayor Yin, and Other Stories from the Great Proletarian Cultural Revolution*. Bloomington: Indiana University Press, 1978; London: Allen & Unwin, 1979.

Cheng, Nien. *Life and Death in Shanghai*. London: Grafton, 1986.

Compestine, Ying Chang. *Revolution Is Not a Dinner Party: A Novel*. New York: H. Holt, 2007.

Coulson, Joan M. Beck. *Daughter of the Landlord: Life History of a Chinese Immigrant*. Thesis. San Jose State University, 1989.

Dai, Sijie. *Balzac and the Little Chinese Seamstress*. New York: Knopf, 2002.

Feng, Jicai. *Ten Years of Madness: Oral Histories of China's Cultural Revolution*. San Francisco: China Books & Periodicals, 1996.

———. *Voices from the Whirlwind: An Oral History of the Chinese Cultural Revolution*. New York: Pantheon Books, 1991.

Forster, Lelia Merrell. *Nien Cheng: Courage in China*. Chicago: Childrens Press, 1992.

Galk, Marian. "Some Remarks on 'Literature of the Scars' in the People's Republic of China (1977–1979)." *Asian and African Studies* 18 (1982): 53–74.

Gao, Yuan. *Born Red: A Chronicle of the Cultural Revolution.* Stanford, Calif.: Stanford University Press, 1987.

Gordon, Eric. *Freedom Is a Word.* London: Hodder & Stoughton, 1971.

Grey, Anthony. *Hostage in Peking.* London: Michael Joseph, 1970.

Harbert, Mary Ann. *Captivity: 44 Months in Red China.* London: Delacorte Press, 1973.

Huang, Joe C. *Heroes and Villains in Communist China: The Contemporary Chinese Novel as a Reflection of Life.* London: C. Hurst, 1973.

Huang, Shaorong. *To Rebel Is Justified: A Rhetorical Study of China's Cultural Revolution Movement, 1966–1969.* Lanham, Md.: University Press of America, 1996.

Hunt, Carroll Ferguson. *From the Claws of the Dragon.* Grand Rapids, Mich.: F. Asbury Press, 1988.

Hsu, Kai-yu. *The Chinese Literary Scene: A Writer's Visit to the People's Republic of China.* New York: Vintage, 1975.

Ivanov, Ury. *Ten Years of My Life in the Great Cultural Revolution.* Dandenong, Australia: Dandenong College of TAFE, 1985.

Ji, Feng-Yuan, Koenraad Kuiper, and Shu Shaogu. "Language and Revolution: Formulae of the Cultural Revolution." *Language in Society* 19.1 (1990): 61–79.

Jiang, Ji-li. *Red Scarf Girl: A Memoir of the Cultural Revolution.* New York: HarperCollins, 1997.

King, Richard. *A Shattered Mirror: The Literature of the Cultural Revolution.* Dissertation. University of British Columbia, 1984.

———. "'Wounds' and 'Exposure': Chinese Literature after the Gang of Four." *Pacific Affairs* 54.1 (1981): 82–99.

Lam, Wai Ling. *Yuh-lan: A Translation and Commentary on a Chinese Story of the Cultural Revolution Period.* Thesis. Iowa State University, Science and Technology, 1978.

Larson, Wendy. *From Ah Q to Lei Feng: Freud and Revolutionary Spirit in 20th-Century China.* Stanford, Calif.: Stanford University Press, 2009.

Leung, Laifong. *Morning Sun: Interviews with Chinese Writers of the Lost Generation.* Armonk, N.Y.: Sharpe, 1994.

Li, Yan. *Daughters of the Red Land.* Toronto: Sister Vision, 1995.

Li, Zhengsheng. *Red-Color News Soldier.* New York: Phaidon Press, 2003.

Liang, Diane Wei. *The Eye of Jade: A Novel.* New York: Simon & Schuster, 2008.

Liang, Heng, and Judith Shapiro. *After the Nightmare: A Survivor of the Cultural Revolution Reports on China Today.* New York: Knopf, 1986.

———. *Return to China: A Survivor of the Cultural Revolution Reports on China Today.* London: Chatto & Windus, 1987.

———. *Son of the Revolution.* New York: Vintage, 1984.

Ling, Ken. *The Revenge of Heaven: Journal of a Young Chinese.* New York: Ballantine, 1972.

Link, Eugene Perry, ed. *Stubborn Weeds: Popular and Controversial Chinese Literature after the Cultural Revolution.* Bloomington: Indiana University Press, 1983; London: Blond & Briggs, 1984.

Liu, Li-p'ing. *She Smiles in Her Tears: Three Years' Experience in the Countryside during the Chinese Cultural Revolution.* MALS Thesis. 1992.

Liu, Sola. *Chaos and All That.* Trans. Richard King. Honolulu: University of Hawaii Press, 1994.

Liu, Xuemin. *Poetry as Modernization: "Misty Poetry" of the Cultural Revolution.* Dissertation. University of California, Berkeley, 1992.

Lo, Fulang. *Morning Breeze: A True Story of China's Cultural Revolution.* San Francisco: China Books & Periodicals, 1989.

Lo, Ruth Earnshaw, and Katharine S. Kinderman. *In the Eye of the Typhoon: An American Woman in China during the Cultural Revolution.* New York: Harcourt Brace Jovanovich, 1980; Da Capo, 1987.

Lu, Hsin-hua, et al. *The Wounded: New Stories of the Cultural Revolution, 77–78.* Hong Kong: Joint Pub. Co., 1979.

Ma, Bo. *Blood Red Sunset: A Memoir of the Chinese Cultural Revolution.* Trans. Howard Goldblatt. New York: Viking, 1995.

Ma, Sheng-Mei. "Contrasting Two Survival Literatures: On the Jewish Holocaust and the Chinese Cultural Revolution." *Holocaust and Genocide Studies* 2.1 (1987): 81–93.

Maxwell, Stanley M. *The Man Who Couldn't Be Killed: An Incredible Story of Faith and Courage during China's Cultural Revolution.* Boise: Pacific Press Publishing Association, 1995.

Min, Anchee. *Red Azalea.* New York: Pantheon Books, 1994.

Ming, Sung, and Min Tsu. *Never Alone: A Story of Survival under the Gang of Four.* Kansas City: Beacon Hill Press, 1983.

Mittler, Barbara. "'Eight Stage Works for 800 Million People': The Great Proletarian Cultural Revolution in Music—a View from Revolutionary Opera." *Opera Quarterly,* April 2010, 377–401.

Morin, Edward, ed. *The Red Azalea: Chinese Poetry since the Cultural Revolution.* Trans. Fang Dai and Dennis Ding. Honolulu: University of Hawaii Press, 1990.

Nanchu. *Red Sorrow: A Memoir.* New York: Arcade Publishing, 2001.

Niu-Niu. *No Tears for Mao: Growing up in the Cultural Revolution.* Trans. Enne Amman and Peter Amman. Chicago: Academy Chicago Publishers, 1995.

Peng, Jialin. *Wild Cat: Stories of the Cultural Revolution.* Dunvegan, ON: Cormorant Books, 1990.

Pollard, D. E. "The Short Story in the Cultural Revolution." *China Quarterly* 73 (1978): 99–121.

Prybyla, Jan. "Hundred Flowers of Discontent." *Current History* 80 (1981): 254–257, 274.

Ross, James R. *Caught in a Tornado: A Chinese American Woman Survives the Cultural Revolution.* Boston: Northeastern University Press, 1994.

Shen, Fan. *Gang of One: Memoirs of a Red Guard.* Lincoln: University of Nebraska Press, 2004.

Sherrard, Howard M. "The Cultural Revolution in China, as an Australian Engineer Sees It." *Eastern Horizon* 7 (1968): 41–44.

Sorokin, V. "Chinese Literature Mirrors the Changing Reality." *Far Eastern Affairs* 2 (1986): 105–122.

Sun-Childers, Jaia, and Douglas Childers. *The White-Haired Girl.* New York: Picador USA/St. Martin's Press, 1996.

Taylor, Julia C. *Female Suicide in Chinese Drama: Selected Plays from the Yuan Dynasty to the Cultural Revolution.* Thesis. University of Wisconsin, 1990.

To-to. *Looking Out from Death: From the Cultural Revolution to Tiananmen Square: The New Chinese Poetry of Duoduo.* Trans. Gregory Lee and John Cayley. London: Bloomsbury, 1989.

Wang, Lulu. *The Lily Theater: A Novel.* New York: Anchor, 2001.

Wang, Ping. *Foreign Devil: A Novel.* Minneapolis: Coffee House Press, 1996.

Wen, Chihua. *The Red Mirror: Children of China's Cultural Revolution.* Boulder, Colo.: Westview, 1995.

Wood, Frances. *Hand-Gernade Practice in Peking: My Part in the Cultural Revolution.* North Pomfret, Vt.: Trafalgar Square Publishing, 2001.

Wu, Emily Yimao, and Larry Engelmann. *Feather in the Storm: A Childhood Lost in Chaos.* New York: Pantheon Books, 2006.

Wu, Ningkun. *Single Tear: A Family's Persecution, Love, and Endurance in Communist China.* Boston: Little, Brown, 1993.

Xiao, Li Cao. *The Autumn Winds of My Youth.* Vancouver: Xiao, 1984.

Yang, Chiang. *A Cadre School Life: Six Chapters.* Trans. Geremie Barmé and Bennett Lee. Hong Kong: Joint Publishing Co., 1982.

———. *Lost in the Crowd: A Cultural Revolution Memoir.* Melbourne: McPhee Gribble, 1989.

———. *Six Chapters of Life in a Cadre School: Memoirs from China's Cultural Revolution.* Boulder, Colo.: Westview, 1986.

Yang, Rae. *Spider Eaters: A Memoir.* Berkeley: University of California Press, 1997.

Yang, Xiao-ming. *The Rhetoric of Propaganda: A Tagmemic Analysis of Selected Documents of the Cultural Revolution of China.* New York: Peter Lang, 1994.

Yee, Lee, et al. *The New Realism: Writings from China after the Cultural Revolution.* New York: Hippocrene Books, 1983.

Yu, Chun. *Little Green: Growing up during the Chinese Cultural Revolution.* New York: Simon & Schuster/Paula Wiseman Books, 2005.

Yu, Shiao-ling, ed. *Chinese Drama after the Cultural Revolution: An Anthology.* Chinese Studies 3. Lewiston, N.Y.: Edwin Mellen Press, 1997.

———. *The Cultural Revolution in Post-Mao Literature.* Dissertation. University of Wisconsin, Madison, 1983. Ann Arbor, Mich.: University Microfilms, 1983.

Zarrow, Peter. "Meanings of China's Cultural Revolution: Memoirs of Exile." *Position* 7.1 (1999): 165–191.

Zhai, Zhenhua. *Red Flower of China.* New York: SOHO; Toronto: Lester Publishing, 1992.

Zhang, Ange. *Red Land Yellow River: A Story from the Cultural Revolution.* Toronto: Groundwood Books, 2004.

Zhang, Zhimei. *Foxspirit: A Woman in Mao's China.* Montreal: Vehicule Press, 1992.

Zhu, Xiaodi. *Thirty Years in a Red House: A Memoir of Childhood and Youth in Communist China.* Amherst: University of Massachusetts Press, 1998.

Chinese Language

Acheng 阿城. *Qi wang* 棋王. Beijing: 作家出版社, 1985.

Chen, Baichen 陈白尘. *Niu peng ri ji* 牛棚日记. Beijing: 生活读书·新知三联书店, 1995.

Chen, Kaige 陈凯歌. *Shao nian Kaige* 少年凯歌. Taipei: 远流出版事业股份有限公司, 1991.

Feng, Jicai 冯骥才. *Yi bai ge ren de shi nian* 一百个人的十年. Nanjing: 江苏文艺出版社, 1991.

Gu, Hua 古华. "Fu rong zhen" 芙蓉镇. 当代 (1981.1): 157–231.

Guo, Xiaodong 郭小东. *Zhongguo dang dai zhi qing wen xue* 中国当代知青文学. Guangzhou: 广东高等教育出版社, 1988.

Laogui 老鬼. *Xue se huang hun* 血色黄昏. Beijing: 工人出版社, 1987.

Li, Ping 礼平. "Wan xia xiao shi de shi hou" 晚霞消失的时候. 十月 (1981.1): 77–134.

Liang, Xiaosheng 梁晓声. *"Zhe shi yi pian shen qi de tu di"* 这是一片神奇的土地. 北方文学 (1982.8): 2–14.

Lu, Xinhua, et al. 卢新华等. *Shang hen: Zhongguo da lu xiao shuo xuan* 伤痕: 中国大陆小说选. Taipei: 幼狮文化事业公司, 1982.

Ma, Junxiang 马军骧. "Ge ming dian ying de xiu ci ce lue" 革命电影的修辞策略. 二十一世纪 (1993.12): 52–60.

Shi, Tiesheng 史铁生. *Wo de yao yuan de Qingpingwan* 我的遥远的清平湾. Beijing: 十月文艺出版社, 1985.

Wang, Jiaping 王家平. *Wen hua da ge ming shi qi shi ge yan jiu* 文化大革命时期诗歌研究. Kaifeng: 河南大学出版社, 2004.

Wang, Kun 王坤. "Chong gao de tui bian: xin shi qi wen xue zhong de 'wen ge'" 崇高的蜕变：新时期文学中的"文革." 二十一世纪 (1995.8): 112–119.

Wang, Xiaobo 王小波. *Huang jin shi dai* 黄金时代. Taipei: 联经出版事业公司, 1992.

Wu, Shanzeng 武善增. *Wen xue hua yu de ji bian yu fu mie: "wen ge" zhu liu wen xue hua yu yan jiu* 文学话语的畸变与覆灭："文革"主流文学话语研究. Zhengzhou: 河南大学出版社, 2011.

Wu, Yimao 巫一毛. *Bao feng yu zhong yi yu mao* 暴风雨中一羽毛. Hong Kong: 明报出版社有限公司, 2007.

Xiao, Min 肖敏. *20 shi ji 70 nian dai xiao shuo yan jiu: "wen hua da ge ming" hou qi xiao shuo xing tai ji qi yan shen* 20世纪70年代小说研究："文化大革命"后期小说形态及其延伸. Beijing: 中國社会科学出版社, 2012.

Xu, Zidong 許子東. Dang dai xiao shuo yu ji ti ji yi: xu shu wen ge 當代小說與集體記憶：敘述文革. Taipei: 麥田出版, 2000.

———. "Wen ge xiao shuo zhong de zui yu fa" 文革小说中的罪与罚. 二十一世纪 (1999.12): 113–121.

Yu, Luojin 遇罗锦. Chun tian de tong hua 春天的童话. Hong Kong: 远方出版社, 1983.

———. Dong tian de tong hua 冬天的童话. Beijing: 人民文学出版社, 1985.

Zhou, Ming, ed. 周明 编. Li shi zai zhe li chen si 历史在这里沉思. Vols. 1–3. Taiyuan: 太岳出版社, 1989. 3 vols.

———, ed. Li shi zai zhe li chen si 历史在这里沉思. Vols. 4–6. Beijing: 华夏出版社, 1989. 3 vols.

AFTERMATH

English Language

Barnett, Doak A. *China after Mao*. Princeton, N.J.: Princeton University Press, 1967.

———. *Uncertain Passage: China's Transition to the Post-Mao Era*. Washington, D.C.: Brookings Institution, 1974.

Bentley, G. E., Jr. "The Ashes and the Phoenix: China's Universities since the Decade of Turmoil." *South Atlantic Quarterly* 83.4 (1984): 457–466.

Berry, Chris. *Postsocialist Cinema in Post-Mao China: The Cultural Revolution after the Cultural Revolution*. Asheville, N.C.: Frontlist Books, 2004.

Bert, Wayne. "The Maoist Model, Development & Democracy." *Polity* 13.4 (1981): 697–708.

Blecher, Marc J., and Gordon White. *Micropolitics in Contemporary China: A Technical Unit during and after the Cultural Revolution.* White Plains, N.Y.: Sharpe, 1979; London: Macmillan, 1980.

Bloodworth, Dennis, and Jingbing Bloodworth. *Heirs Apparent: What Happens When Mao Dies?* New York: Straus, 1973.

Bonavia, David. *Verdict in Peking: The Trail of the Gang of Four.* London: Burnett, 1984.

Brugger, Bill. *China: The Impact of the Cultural Revolution.* Canberra: Australian National University Press; London: Croom Helm; New York: Barnes & Noble, 1978.

———, ed. *China since the Gang of Four.* New York: St. Martin's, 1980.

Butterfield, Fox. *China, Alive in the Bitter Sea.* New York: Bantam, 1983.

Buultjens, Ralph. *China after Mao: Death or Revolution?* New York: International Book Trading, 1979.

Chan, Anita. "Looking Back on the Chinese Cultural Revolution." *Problems of Communism* 37.2 (1988): 68–75.

Chang, Parris H. "Who Gets What, When and How in Chinese Politics—a Case Study of the Strategies of Conflict of the Gang of Four." *Australian Journal of Chinese Affairs* 2 (1979): 21–42.

Chang, Y. C. (Chang, Yi-chun). *Factional and Coalition Politics in China: The Cultural Revolution and Its Aftermath.* Praeger Special Studies in International Politics and Government. New York: Praeger, 1976.

———. "The Trial of the Gang of Four." *Asian Thought and Society* 6.16 (1981): 70–72.

Chao, Yah-lee. *Communication and Cultural Change in China, 1949–1985.* Dissertation. Ohio State University, 1985.

Chen, Jie, and Peng Deng. *China since the Cultural Revolution: From Totalitarianism to Authoritarianism.* Westport, Conn.: Praeger, 1995.

Cheng, Chung-ying. "Attacks on the 'Gang of Four.'" *Chinese Studies in Philosophy* 9.2 (1977–1978): 4–82.

Cheng, Joseph Y. S. "China's Foreign Policy after the Fall of the Gang of Four." *Asia Pacific Community* 10 (1980): 51–67.

Chi Hsin (Research Group). *The Case of the Gang of Four: With First Translation of Teng Hsiao-ping's "Three Poisonous Weeds."* Hong Kong: Cosmos Books, 1978.

Chin, Steve S. K., ed. *Gang of Four: First Essays after the Fall: Selected Seminar Papers on Contemporary China, II.* Hong Kong: Centre of Asian Studies, University of Hong Kong, 1977.

China: The Revolution Is Dead, Long Live the Revolution. Montreal: Black Rose Books, 1977.

Ch'iu, K'ung-yuan. "Proceedings of the Eleventh CCP Congress: An Analysis." *Issues & Studies* 13.10 (1977): 1–12.

Chlou, C. L. "Maoism in the Purge of the 'Gang of Four.'" *World Review* 16.3 (1977): 14–27.

Collier, John. *Dynamics of Socialism*. London: Marram Books, 1986.

"The Cultural Revolution and Its Aftermath." *Asian Survey* 12.12 (1972): 999–1100.

Deane, Hugh, and William H. Hinton. "Mao's Rural Policies Revisited." *Monthly Review* (New York) 40.10 (1989): 1–9.

Deng, Zhong, and Donald J. Treiman. "The Impact of the Cultural Revolution on Trends in Educational Attainment in the People's Republic of China." *American Journal of Sociology* 103.2 (1997): 391–429.

Derbyshire, Ian. *Politics in China from Mao to Deng*. Edinburgh: W. & R. Chambers, 1987.

Dittmer, Lowell. "Bases of Power in Chinese Politics: A Theory and an Analysis of the Fall of the 'Gang of Four.'" *World Politics* 31.1 (1978): 26–60.

Domes, Jurgen. *China after the Cultural Revolution: Politics between Two Party Congresses*. Trans. Annette Berg and David Goodman. Berkeley: University of California Press, 1977.

———. "The 'Gang of Four' and Hua Kuo-feng: Analysis of Political Events in 1975–76." *China Quarterly* 71 (1977): 473–497.

Domes, Jurgen, and Marie-luise Nath. *China after the Cultural Revolution: Politics between Two Party Congresses*. London: C. Hurst, 1976.

Fen, Sing-Nan. "The Cultural Revolution: A Tragic Legacy." *Change* 17.2 (1985): 41, 46–47.

Feng, Jicai. *Let One Hundred Flowers Bloom*. Trans. Christopher Smith. London: Viking, 1995.

Field, Robert M. "The Impact of the 'Gang of Four' on Industrial Output in Kweichow." *China Quarterly* 73 (1978): 137–139.

Gao, Mobo C. F. "Maoist Discourse and a Critique of the Present Assessments of the Cultural Revolution." *Bulletin of Concerned Asian Scholars* 26.3 (1994): 13–31.

———. "Memoirs and Interpretation of the Cultural Revolution." *Bulletin of Concerned Asian Scholars* 27.1 (1995): 49–57.

Gates, Millicent Anne, and E. Bruce Geelhoed. *The Dragon and the Snake: An American Account of the Turmoil in China, 1976–1977*. Philadelphia: University of Pennsylvania Press, 1986.

Garside, Roger. *Coming Alive: China after Mao*. New York: McGraw-Hill; London: Deutsch, 1981.

Gold, Thomas B. "After Comradeship: Personal Relations in China since the Cultural Revolution." *China Quarterly* 104 (1985): 657–675.

Goldman, Merle D. "The Aftermath of China's Cultural Revolution." *Current History* 61 (1971): 165–170, 182.

———. "China's Ideological Controversies against the Background of the Cultural Revolution." *Asian Thought and Society* 2 (1977): 239–252.

———. "Chinese Ideology after the Cultural Revolution." *Current History* 69 (1975): 68–69, 100–101.

———. *New Perspectives on the Cultural Revolution: May 15–17, 1987.* Cambridge, Mass.: John King Fairbank Center for East Asian Research, Harvard University, 1987. 2 vols.

Great Trial in Chinese History: The Trial of the Lin Biao and Jiang Qing Counter-revolutionary Cliques, Nov. 1980–Jan. 1981. Beijing: New World Press, 1981.

Gudoshnikov, L. M., Rostislav Mikhailovich Neronov, and Boris Petrovic Barakhta. *China: Cultural Revolution and After.* New Delhi: Sterling, 1978.

Guo, Jian. "Politics of Othering and the Postmodernization of the Cultural Revolution." *Postcolonial Studies* 2.2 (1999): 213–229.

———. "Resisting Modernity in Contemporary China: The Cultural Revolution and Postmodernism." *Modern China* 25.3 (1999): 343–377.

Harding, Harry. "Reappraising the Cultural Revolution." *Wilson Quarterly* 4 (1980): 132–141.

Hardy, Leslie. *Chinese Higher Education in the Aftermath of the Cultural Revolution.* Thesis. McGill University, 1978.

He, Henry Yuhuai. *Cycles of Repression and Relaxation: Politicoliterary Events in China, 1976–1989.* Bochum: N. Brockmeyer, 1992.

Hiniker, Paul J. "Cultural Revolution Revisited: Dissonance Reduction or Power Maximization." *China Quarterly* 94 (1983): 282–303.

Hsu, Immanuel Chung-yueh. *The Rise of Modern China.* New York: Oxford University Press, 1995.

Jain, Jagdish. *After Mao What? Army, Party, and Group Rivalries in China.* New Delhi: Radiant Publishers, 1975; Boulder, Colo.: Westview, 1976; London: Martin Robertson, 1976.

Jameson, Fredric. "Periodizing the 60s." In *The 60s without Apology,* 178–209. Minneapolis: University of Minnesota Press, 1984.

Joyce, Karen Mecartney. *The Impact of the Cultural Revolution on Attitudes about Political Participation and Authority among Chinese Graduate Students in the United States.* Thesis. MIT, 1989.

Kitching, Beverley M. *Science Policy Making in China since the Cultural Revolution.* Queensland, Australia: Griggith University, 1982.

Laaksonen, Oiva. *Management in China during and after Mao in Enterprises, Government, and Party.* New York: Walter de Gruyter, 1988.

Law, Kam-yee, ed. *The Chinese Cultural Revolution Reconsidered: Beyond Purge and Holocaust.* New York: Palgrave Macmillan, 2003.

Lin, Shau-ling. *In Search for Political Developmental Theory: A Retrospect on the Chinese Cultural Revolution.* Thesis. Queens College, 1985.

Lu, Xing. *Rhetoric of the Chinese Cultural Revolution: The Impact on Chinese Thought, Culture, and Communication.* Columbia: University of South Carolina Press, 2004.

Lu, Zhongti, and Celia Millward. "Chinese Given Names since the Cultural Revolution." *Names* 37.3 (1989): 265–280.

Maitan, Livio. *Party, Army, and Masses in China: A Marxist Interpretation of the Cultural Revolution and Its Aftermath.* London: NLB, 1976.

Meisner, Maurice J. *Mao's China and After: A History of the People's Republic.* New York: Free Press, 1999.

Montgomery, Broaded C. "China's Lost Generation: The Status Degradation of an Educational Cohort." *Journal of Contemporary Ethnography* 20.3 (1991): 352–379.

Mulligan, William A. "Remnants of the Cultural Revolution in Chinese Journalism of the 1980s." *Journalism Quarterly* 65.1 (1988): 20–25.

Munthe-Kaas, Harald. *Aftermath of the Cultural Revolution.* China Conversations. Audiocassette. United Nations National Committee on US-China Relations, 1970. 1 cassette.

Onate, Andres D. "Hua Kuo-feng and the Arrest of the 'Gang of Four.'" *China Quarterly* 75 (1978): 540–565.

Noumoff, S. J. "Trans-Historical Values of the Reassessment of the Cultural Revolution." *China Report* 17.2 (1981): 51–70.

Payne, Robert. *A Rage for China.* New York: Holt, 1977.

Perkins, Dwight Heald. *China's Economic Policy and Performance during the Cultural Revolution and Its Aftermath.* Cambridge, Mass.: Harvard Institute for International Development, Harvard University, 1984.

Pepper, Suzanne. "An Interview on Changes in Chinese Education after the 'Gang of Four.'" *China Quarterly* 72 (1977): 815–824.

Petras, James. "The Chinese Cultural Revolution in Historical Perspective." *Journal of Contemporary Asia* 27.4 (1997): 445–460.

Pitcher, Dixon. "The Survival of the Higher Educational System of China Following the Cultural Revolution." Utah State University, 1984.

Prybyla, Jan S. "The Chinese Economy after the 'Gang of Four.'" *Current History* 73.429 (1977): 68–72, 86.

Pye, Lucian W. "Reassessing the Cultural Revolution." *China Quarterly* 108 (1986): 597–612.

Rethinking the "Cultural Revolution." Beijing: Beijing Review, 1987.

The Revolution Is Dead, Long Live the Revolution: Readings on the Great Proletarian Cultural Revolution from an Ultra-left Perspective. Hong Kong: The 70's, 1976.

Schoenhals, Michael. "Unofficial and Official Histories of the Cultural Revolution: A Review Article." *Journal of Asian Studies* 48.3 (1989): 563–572.

Sharma, K. R. *China: Revolution to Revolution*. New Delhi: Mittal Publications, 1989.

Sheng, Wen Ching. *Golden Bridge: A Study of the People's Commune in Rural China*. Dissertation. University of Rochester, 1993.

Shenkar, Oded. "The Cultural Revolution against the Chinese Bureaucracy: An Ideological Structural Analysis." *Asian Profile* 11.4 (1983): 323–338.

Shiu, Lai Hung. *Formal Organization in China's Industry after the Cultural Revolution*. San Francisco University, 1977.

Snow, Edgar. "Aftermath of the Cultural Revolution: Mao Tse-tung and the Cost of Living." *New Republic* 164.15 (1971): 18–21.

Su, Wenming, ed. *China after Mao: A Collection of 80 Topical Essays*. Beijing: Beijing Review, 1984.

Teiwes, Frederick C., and Warren Sun. *The End of the Maoist Era: Chinese Politics during the Twilight of the Cultural Revolution, 1972–1976*. Armonk, N.Y.: Sharpe, 2007.

Thurston, A. F. "Victims of China's Cultural Revolution: The Invisible Wounds." *Pacific Affairs* 57 (1984–1985): 599–620.

Ting, Lee-hsia Hsu. "Chinese Libraries during and after the Cultural Revolution." *Journal of Library History* 16.2 (1981): 417–434.

Tsou, Tang. *The Cultural Revolution and Post-Mao Reforms: A Historical Perspective*. Chicago: University of Chicago Press, 1986.

Uberoi, Patricia. "The Cultural Revolution Revisited." *China Report* 22.2 (1986): 147–150.

Usov, V. "Confessions of a Chinese Marshall." *Far Eastern Affairs* 5 (1987): 138–142.

Wakeman, Frederic, Jr. "Historiography in China after Smashing the 'Gang of Four.'" *China Quarterly* 76 (1978): 891–911.

Wang, Gungwu. "May 4th and the GPCR: The Cultural Revolution Remedy." *Pacific Affairs* 52 (1979–1980): 674–690.

Wang, Hsueh-wen. "The 'Gang of Four' Incident: Official Expose by a CCPCC Document." *Issues & Studies* 13.9 (1977): 46–58.

———. *Higher Education on China Mainland since Cultural Revolution*. Taipei: World Anti-Communist League, China Chapter, 1980.

Wang, James C. F. "Values of the Cultural Revolution." *Journal of Communication* 27 (1977): 41–46.

Wang, Miao. *Impact of the Great Proletarian Cultural Revolution on Communist China's Foreign Policy*. Thesis. University of Oklahoma, 1977. Ann Arbor, Mich.: University Microfilms, 1979.

Wang, Shao-nan. "An Analysis of 'Gang of Four' Trial." *Asian Outlook* 16.2 (1981): 21–27.

Wang, Yuan. *The Impact of the Cultural Revolution on Intellectuals in China.* Dissertation. University of Wisconsin, La Crosse, 1994.

Waste, Robert J. "Public Administration in China: Impressions of Some of the Changes since the Cultural Revolution." *Administration & Society* 17.4 (1986): 501–508.

Wu, Guang. *China 1966–1976, Cultural Revolution Revisited: Can It Happen Again?* New York: Nova Science Publishers, 2011.

Xu, Ben. "The Cultural Revolution and Modernity: The Contradictory Political Implications of Postmodernism in China." *Journal of Contemporary China* 8.21 (1999): 241–262.

Yang, Guobin, and Ming-Bao Yue. "Introduction: Gilded-Age Memories of the Cultural Revolution." *China Review* 5.2 (2005): 1–11.

Zook, Kirsten Cantrell. *Marriage Customs as a Social Barometer: The Trend toward Traditionalism in Post-Cultural Revolutionary China.* Thesis. Lake Forest College, 1993.

Chinese Language

Chen, Jiaqi 陈家琪. "Yi dai lang man zhu yi shou nan zhe de zhi qing ji yi" 一代浪漫主义受难者的知青记忆. 二十一世纪 (2013.6): 117–121.

Chen, Yixin 陈意新. "Cong xia fang dao xia gang 1968–1998" 从下放到下岗 1968–1998. 二十一世纪 (1999.12): 122–136.

Chen, Yu 陈雨; and Tao, Dongfeng 陶东风. "Ji nian xian li pian yu wen ge li shi ji yi" 纪念献礼片与文革历史记忆. 二十一世纪 (2013.2): 31–41.

Ding, Dong 丁东. "Zhi qing jing li he yi dai ren de jia zhi qu xiang" 知青经历和一代人的价值取向. 二十一世纪 (2013.4): 23–30.

———. "Zhui sui Mao Zedong de 'fan ge ming'—Chong fang yuan shou du 'hong wei bing' ling xiu" 追随毛泽东的 "反革命"—重访原首都高校"红卫兵"领袖. 当代中国研究 (2006.2): 72–81.

Ding, Wang 丁望. *Li xing de guan cha* 理性的观察. Taipei: 联经出版事业公司, 1977.

Gao, Gao 高皋. *Hou wen ge shi: Zhongguo zi you hua chao liu* 后文革史: 中国自由化潮流. Taipei: 联经出版社, 1993. 2 vols.

Gedeman 哥德曼. "Wen hua da ge ming de fei xiao ji ying xiang" 文化大革命的非消极影响. 知识分子 (1986.3): 47–49.

Guo, Jian 郭建. "Dang dai zuo pai wen hua li lun zhong de wen ge you ling" 当代左派文化理论中的文革幽灵. 二十一世纪 (2006.2): 29–41.

———. "Wen ge si chao yu hou xue" 文革思潮与后学. 二十一世纪 (1996.6): 116–122.

Guo, Tan 郭坦. *San dai ren dui hua lu: guan yu dang dai Zhongguo "dai gou" de miao shu he zheng ming* 三代人对话录: 关于当代中国"代沟"的描述和争鸣. Beijing: 中国青年出版社, 1993.

Hou, Jichun, ed. 侯吉淳 编. *Cong Wei Jingsheng dao Wuerkaixi: Zhongguo da lu min zhu yun dong zong lan 1957–1989* 从魏京生到吾尔开希: 中国大陆民主运动总览1957–1989. Taipei: 海风出版社, 1989.

Li, Yingming 李英明. *Deng Xiaoping yu wen ge hou de Zhongguo da lu* 邓小平与文革后的中国大陆. Taipei: 时报文化出版企业有限公司, 1995.

Li, Zehou 李泽厚; and Liu, Zaifu 刘再复. *Gao bie ge ming: hui wang er shi shi ji Zhongguo* 告别革命: 回望二十世纪中国. Hong Kong: 天地图书公司, 1995.

Luo, Jinyi 羅金義; and Zheng, Wenlun 鄭文龍. *Hao jie yi wai: zai lun wen hua da ge ming* 浩劫以外: 再論文化大革命. Taipei: 風雲論壇出版社有限公司, 1997.

Meisner, Maurice J. 莫里斯·迈斯纳; Du, Pu 杜蒲; and Li, Yuling, trans. 李玉玲 译. *Mao Zedong de Zhongguo ji Mao Zedong hou de Zhongguo* 毛泽东的中国及毛泽东后的中国. Chengdu: 四川人民出版社, 1992.

Pan, Mingxiao 潘鸣啸. "'Wen ge yi dai' shang tai zhi zheng: cha yi he zai ?" "文革一代"革上台执政: 差异何在？二十一世纪 (2013.4): 4–14.

Shan, Zhengping 单正平. Wen hua da ge ming: Shen quan zheng zhi xia de guo jia zui cuo 文化大革命: 神权政治下的国家罪错. 当代中国研究 (2003.3): 23–37.

Su, Shaozhi 苏绍智. *Shi nian feng yu: wen ge hou de da lu li lun jie* 十年风雨: 文革后的大陆理论界. Taipei: 时报文化出版有限公司, 1996.

Tan, Zongji 谭宗级; and Zheng, Qian, et al. 郑谦 等. *Shi nian hou de ping shuo: " wen hua da ge ming" shi lun ji* 十年后的评说: "文化大革命"史论集. Beijing: 中共党史资料出版社, 1987.

Xiao, Donglian 蕭冬連. *Li shi de zhuan gui: Cong bo luan fan zheng dao gai ge kai fang, 1979–1981* 歷史的轉軌: 從撥亂反正到改革開放, 1979–1981. Hong Kong: 香港中文大學當代中國文化研究中心, 2009.

Xiguang 习广. "Wen hua da ge ming dui she hui zhu yi zhi du de tu po" 文化大革命对社会主义制度的突破. New York: 知识分子春季号 (1986): 10–16.

Xu, Ben 徐贲. "Bian hua zhong de wen ge ji yi" 变化中的文革记忆. 二十一世纪 (2006.2): 19–28.

Xu, Youyu 徐友渔. "Shang shan xia xiang dui zhi qing yi dai si xiang xing cheng de ying xiang" 上山下乡对知青一代思想形成的影响. 二十一世纪 (2013.4): 15–22.

Zhang, Lun 张伦. "Zhi shi fen zi, quan li he min zhu—Hou Mao shi dai yi lai de min zhu hua yu he shi jian" 知识分子, 权力和民主权力后毛时代以来的民主话语和实践. 当代中国研究 (2003.3): 4–22.

Zheng, Yi 郑义. *Hong se ji nian bei* 红色纪念碑. Taipei: 华视文化公司, 1993.

About the Authors

Guo Jian is a professor of English and Chinese at the University of Wisconsin–Whitewater. He has a bachelor of arts in Chinese from Beijing Normal University and a Ph.D. in English from the University of Connecticut at Storrs. He has published internationally in both Chinese and English on Chinese literature, modern Chinese history, and Western critical theory. He is coeditor of *The Chinese Cultural Revolution Database* (2002, 2006, 2013), *The Chinese Anti-Rightist Campaign Database* (2010, 2013), *The Chinese Great Leap Forward / Great Famine Database* (2013), and *The Database of the Chinese Political Campaigns in the 1950s: From Land Reform to State-Private Partnership* (2014). He is also cotranslator (with Stacy Mosher) of Yang Jisheng's *Tombstone: The Great Chinese Famine, 1958–1962* (2012).

Yongyi Song is on the library faculty at California State University, Los Angeles. He has a master of arts in China studies from the University of Colorado and a master of library science from Indiana University at Bloomington. He is chief editor of *The Cultural Revolution Database* (2002, 2006, 2013), *The Chinese Anti-Rightist Campaign Database* (2010, 2013), and *The Chinese Great Leap Forward / Great Famine Database* (2013), coauthor (with Dajin Sun) of *The Cultural Revolution: A Bibliography, 1966–1996* (1998), and coeditor (with Zehao Zhou) of *The Cultural Revolution & Heterodox Thoughts* I and II (2001). He is also the 2004 recipient of the 21st-Century Librarian National Award (School of Information Studies, Syracuse University) and the 2005 Paul Howard Award for Courage (American Library Association).

Yuan Zhou is curator for the East Asian Library of the University of Chicago. He has a bachelor of arts from Peking University and a Ph.D. in library and information science from the University of Illinois at Urbana–Champaign. He is the compiler and editor of *A New Collection of Red Guard Publications: Part I* (1999), a 20-volume set of reprinted Red Guard newspapers published during the Cultural Revolution. He is coeditor of *The Chinese Cultural Revolution Database* (2002, 2006, 2013), *The Chinese Anti-Rightist Campaign Database* (2010, 2013), and *The Chinese Great Leap Forward / Great Famine Database* (2013). He has also published articles on various topics in library and information science, including collection development, applications of information technology, library history, and the development of East Asian libraries.